DUMBARTON OAKS STUDIES

XXIX

ARMENIAN GOSPEL ICONOGRAPHY
The Tradition of the Glajor Gospel

ARMENIAN GOSPEL ICONOGRAPHY
The Tradition of the Glajor Gospel

Thomas F. Mathews and Avedis K. Sanjian

with contributions by

Mary Virginia Orna, O.S.U. and James R. Russell

edited by Thomas F. Mathews

Dumbarton Oaks Research Library and Collection

Washington, D.C.

Publication of this book has been aided
by grants from the
Ahmanson Foundation
the Alex Manoogian Cultural Fund
of the Armenian General Benevolent Union
and the
Millard Meiss Publication Fund of the College Art Association.

MM

Library of Congress Cataloging-in-Publication Data

Mathews, Thomas F.
Armenian gospel iconography : the tradition of the Glajor Gospel / Thomas F. Mathews and Avedis K. Sanjian; with contributions by Mary Virginia Orna and James R. Russell; edited by Thomas F. Mathews.
p. cm.—(Dumbarton Oaks studies; 29)
Includes bibliographical references.
ISBN 0-88402-183-1
1. Bible. N.T. Gospels. Armenian. Gladzori Avetaran.
2. University of California, Los Angeles. Library. Manuscript.
Arm. ms. 1. 3. Illumination of books and manuscripts, Armenian. 4. Illumination of books and manuscripts, Medieval—Armenia.
I. Sanjian, Avedis Krikor, 1921– . II. Title. III. Series.
ND3359.G46M36 1990
745.6′7′095662—dc20
90-2723

Contents

List of Illustrations

The illustrations in this volume are organized in three groups: black and white plates illustrating all the miniatures of the Glajor Gospel; color plates of select pages from the Glajor Gospel; and comparative illustrations in black and white. The illustrations of the Glajor Gospel are numbered according to their pages in the codex and are referred to in the body of the text in italics (e.g., "*page 227 and color detail*" refers to a black and white plate and the color plate designated by the same number). The comparative illustrations are designated as figures, and they have been numbered to facilitate their reference to the page of the Glajor Gospel to which they are being compared (e.g., "fig. 169c" is one of several illustrations that are compared to *page 169*). Comparative illustrations that do not refer to any particular page of the Glajor Gospel are referred to with a prefix letter "R" (e.g., "fig. R12").

The Glajor Gospel: Color Plates

The Glajor Gospel: Black and White Plates

Comparative Illustrations

Credits

The photographs of the Glajor Gospel, U.C.L.A. arm. ms. 1, are reproduced with permission of the Special Collections, the University Research Library, the University of California, Los Angeles.

The following illustrations of manuscripts in Erevan: figs. 21b, 35b, 35d, 92a, 92c, 99a, 99b, 99c, 103a, 106b, 106c, 106d, 108a, 108b, 117a, 117c, 122a, 122c, 122d, 124a, 126b, 126c, 126d, 126e, 126f, 126g, 156b, 160a, 160c, 162a, 166a, 169a, 169c, 171a, 171b, 171e, 172a, 172c, 172e, 173a, 173b, 179b, 179d, 179e, 194a, 197a, 197c, 211a, 211c, 216a, 218a, 218b, 227a, 227b, 227c, 235a, 250a, 250b, 255a, 255b, 255c, 259a, 259b, 259c, 263a, 269a, 269c, 271a, 271b, 271d, 283a, 283b, 286d, 286e, 286f, 298a, 305c, 305e, 312b, 327a, 327c, 327d, 336a, 336c, 351a, 351d, 403a, 403b, 403c, 438a, 441a, 441c, 448a, 453b, 453d, 460b, 460c, 460f, 460h, 469a, 469c, 480a, 480c, 484a, 484b, 509a, 522b, 522d, 532a, 532d, 561a, 561d, 561e, 570a, R5, R6, R7, R13, R14, are reproduced by permission of the Matenadaran, Erevan, Socialist Republic of Soviet Armenia.

Figs. 106a, 156c, 160b, 179c, 286a, 305a, 305d, 312a, 448b, 453e, 460e, 522c, 532c, R1, R11, R12, of manuscripts in the

Jerusalem collection, are by courtesy of the Armenian Patriarchate of St. James, Jerusalem.

Figs. 197b, 305b, 351b, 453c, 460a, 509b, 522a, 538b, 561c, R2, R3, R4, R15, R16 are used by courtesy of the Mekhitarist Monastery of San Lazzaro, Venice.

Figs. 35c, 122b, 124b, 169b, 211b, 235b, 250c, 263b, 269b, 271c, 286b, 441b, 469b are reproduced by courtesy of the Freer Gallery of Art, Smithsonian Institution, Washington, D.C.

Figs. 35a, 92b, 117b, 162b, 172b, 216b, 218c, 286c, 351c, 438b, 453a, 480b, 538a are reproduced by courtesy of the Walters Art Gallery, Baltimore, Maryland.

Figs. 171c, 171d, 172d, 194b, 227d, 269d, 336d, 438c, 448c, 460d, R10 are reproduced by permission of the British Library, London.

Figs. 21a, 21c, 27a, 106e, 305f, 532b, 561b, 561f, of New Julfa manuscripts, were kindly provided by Arpag Mekhitarian of the Queen Elizabeth Egyptological Foundation, Brussels.

Figs. 255d, 460g, 469d, R8, R9 are used by permission of the Case Memorial Library, Hartford Theological Seminary, from photographs of Thomas F. Mathews.

Figs. 156a, 179a, 336b, of Jerusalem, St. James 2556, are from photographs of the Library of Congress, Washington, D.C.

Figs. 103b, 327b, of the Zeytun Gospel, Istanbul, are reproduced by courtesy of the Byzantine Collection, Dumbarton Oaks, Trustees for Harvard University, Washington, D.C.

Fig. 460i was provided by the late Harutiun Hazarian.

Fig. 188a is used by courtesy of the Mekhitarist Congregation, Vienna.

Fig. 461a is reproduced by courtesy of the Metropolitan Museum of Art, New York.

Fig. 461b is reproduced by courtesy of the Pierpont Morgan Library, New York.

Fig. 126a is from a photograph by Thomas F. Mathews.

List of Maps, Diagrams, and Tables

List of Abbreviations

AJA	*American Journal of Archaeology*
ANF	*Ante-Nicene Fathers*, edited by Alexander Roberts and James Donaldson, revised edition by A. Cleveland Coxe (Buffalo, 1895–96; repr. New York, 1926)
CMH	*Cambridge Medieval History*
CSCO	Corpus Scriptorum Christianorum Orientalium
DACL	F. Cabrol and H. Leclerq, *Dictionnaire d'archéologie chrétienne et de liturgie*
DOP	*Dumbarton Oaks Papers*
EI	*Encyclopedia of Islam*
JSAS	*Journal of the Society for Armenian Studies*
Lexikon der christlichen Ikonographie	*Lexikon der christlichen Ikonographie*, edited by Engelbert Kirschbaum and Wolfgang Braunfels, 8 vols. (Freiburg, 1968–76)
NPNF	*A Select Library of the Nicene and Post-Nicene Fathers of the Christian Church*, edited by Philip Schaff and Henry Wace (New York, 1890–1900; repr. Grand Rapids, Mich., 1978)
OC	*Orientalia Christiana*
OCA	Orientalia Christiana Analecta
Ōrbēlian, *Histoire*	Stepʻanos Ōrbēlian. *Histoire de la Siounie par Stéphanos Orbélian*, trans. M. Brosset (St. Petersburg, 1864–66)
Patmutʻyun (Academy)	*Hay Žołovrdi Patmutʻyun*. Publication of the Armenian S.S.R. Academy of Sciences
PG	Patrologiae cursus completus, Series Graeca, ed. J. P. Migne
PL	Patrologiae cursus completus, Series Latina, ed. J. P. Migne
PO	Patrologia Orientalis (Paris, 1903–)
RBK	*Reallexikon der byzantinischen Kunst*
REArm	*Revue des études arméniennes*
SC	Sources Chrétiennes. Collection dirigée par H. de Lubac et J. Daniélou

Transliteration System

Ա	Բ	Գ	Դ	Ե	Զ	Է	Ը	Թ	Ժ	Ի	Լ	Խ	Ծ	Կ	Հ	Ձ	Ղ	Ճ	Մ
ա	բ	գ	դ	ե	զ	է	ը	թ	ժ	ի	լ	խ	ծ	կ	հ	ձ	ղ	ճ	մ
a	b	g	d	e	z	ē	ə	tʻ	ž	i	l	x	c	k	h	j	ł	č	m

Յ	Ն	Շ	Ո	Չ	Պ	Ջ	Ռ	Ս	Վ	Տ	Ր	Ց	Ւ	Փ	Ք	Օ	Ֆ	ՈՒ
յ	ն	շ	ո	չ	պ	ջ	ռ	ս	վ	տ	ր	ց	ւ	փ	ք	օ	ֆ	ու
y	n	š	o	čʻ	p	ǰ	ṙ	s	v	t	r	cʻ	w	pʻ	kʻ	ō	f	u

Foreword and Acknowledgments

This project had its inception in 1975 when both of us were teaching at the University of California, Los Angeles, and we had the opportunity to sit and turn the pages of the Glajor Gospel together. The splendid illuminations of the book cast a spell on us, and we felt drawn to investigating its mysteries together. The task seemed particularly suited to a collaborative venture, given the historical and art-historical implications of the subject. Indeed, as it developed, the complexity of the subject suggested further areas of collaboration, and we invited Mary Virginia Orna, professor of chemistry at the College of New Rochelle, to undertake an analysis of the pigments of the manuscript (Chapter 3, part 4), and James R. Russell, professor of Iranian studies at Columbia University, to provide a translation of the Commentaries on the Canon Tables (Appendix D). In the division of labor for the rest of the book, the responsibility for Chapter 2 on the historical setting, the translation of colophons, inscriptions, and prefaces in Appendices A and B, and the list of manuscripts executed in Glajor in Appendix C lay with Avedis K. Sanjian; the responsibility for the rest lay with Thomas F. Mathews.

During a dozen years' labor on this book we have had the good fortune of encountering exceptional generosity from a great many scholars in the field who made our work not only easier but even pleasurable. In the first place we would like to thank the librarians and keepers of manuscripts who put their precious treasures at our disposal. At Special Collections in the University Research Library, the University of California, Los Angeles, Brooke Whiting and his successor, David S. Zeidberg, were always enthusiastic in supporting our research on the Glajor Gospel. In Erevan in Soviet Armenia, Babken Choukaszian, deputy director of the Matenadaran, most kindly let us study manuscripts in his collection and supplied us with photographs and microfilms when needed. The late Onnik Eganian, curator of manuscripts at the Matenadaran, provided detailed descriptions of manuscripts of the letters of Esayi Nč'ec'i and other codices executed in Glajor. In Jerusalem, at the Armenian Patriarchate of St. James, the curator of manuscripts, the ever gracious Archbishop Norair Bogharian, gave us free access to the Surb T'oros Library, and the Archbishops Guregh Kapikian and Karekin Kazanjian facilitated our work with manuscripts in the cathedral Treasury. In Venice we are grateful to Father Nerses Nersessian for help in using the library of the Mekhitarist Fathers at San Lazzaro, and in Vienna we would like to thank the Abbot of the Mekhitarist Congregation, Grigoris Josef Manian. We were not personally able to inspect manuscripts in New Julfa in Iran, but Arpag Mekhitarian of the Queen Elizabeth Egyptological Foundation in Brussels provided us with excellent photographs. In London Vrej Nersessian helped us with the Armenian manuscripts of the British Library. At the Walters Art Gallery in Baltimore Lilian Randall gave us ample opportunity to study and analyze the Armenian manuscripts, and Esin Atil, then curator of manuscripts at the Freer Gallery of Art in Washington, was similarly generous to us with her collection. We thank also Mr. Nafih Donat, former librarian at Case Memorial Library, for letting us study manuscripts at the Hartford Seminary Foundation.

The Armenian Studies Program at Columbia University in New York provided a rich mine of background expertise in all things Armenian, to which we returned again and again for new nuggets. We are deeply grateful to its director, Nina Garsoïan, to Father Krikor Maksoudian, an endless store of ecclesiastical learning, and to James R. Russell, who was helpful with a great many Armenian texts.

We are grateful, too, for the collaboration of Robert H. Hewsen of Glassboro State College in New Jersey, who prepared the maps.

Very early in our research we consulted the late Professor Sirarpie Der Nersessian, who saved us from many false starts by her wise advice. Other art historians occupied with Armenian material also were generous with their assistance. Tatiana Izmailova of Moscow gave us leave to publish material from Erevan ms. 10780 in advance of her own publication, and Heide and Helmut Buschhausen of Vienna kindly shared their photographs with us. For taking time to discuss our problems with us, for inspiration, encouragement and occasional favors, we are indebted to many other colleagues, among whom we would like to mention Hugo Buchthal, Annemarie Weyl Carr, Levon Choukaszian, Lucy Der Manuelian, Helen C. Evans, Vigen Ghazarian, Sidney H. Griffith, Ioli Kalavrezou, Emma Korkhmazian, Dickran Kouymjian, William Macomber, Robert S. Nelson, Lucy Freeman Sandler, Alice Taylor, Gabrielle Winkler, Lilit Zakarian, Ruben Zarian. We are especially grateful to James R. McCredie, who in addition to the loyal support he gave as Director of the Institute of Fine Arts, New York University, also programmed the word processing for us. We thank Elena Quevedo Espinosa for doing much of the typing. The index was prepared by Susan Coerr.

Financial aid for the research came from several directions. Support for Thomas F. Mathews came from the John Simon Guggenheim Foundation, which named him Fellow in 1977–78, and from Dumbarton Oaks, which named him Fellow in spring 1983. The N.Y.U. Research Challenge Fund provided for the pigment analyses in 1980–81. The Hagop Kevorkian Foundation provided Mathews with funds for general research on the project in 1984, and he received travel grants from the American Council of Learned Societies in 1978 and 1986, and from the Armenian General Benevolent Union in 1986. Support for Avedis K. Sanjian came from the endowment funds of the Narekatsi Chair for Armenian Studies at U.C.L.A., which he has held since 1969, and from the U.C.L.A. Academic Senate Research Committee. For their confidence in our enterprise we offer these grantors our deep appreciation.

Thomas F. Mathews
Institute of Fine Arts
New York University

Avedis K. Sanjian
University of California
Los Angeles

Armenian Gospel Iconography

The Tradition of the Glajor Gospel

CHAPTER ONE

Introduction

Armenia, located in the high mountainous plateau where the Tigris, the Euphrates, and the Araxes originate, is of peculiar interest to the medieval historian, for while it clearly belonged to the larger world of medieval Christendom, its culture was Iranian based.[1] Ruled in the first three centuries by an Iranian Arsacid as vassal of the Roman Empire, Armenia was converted early to Christianity; the conversion of King Trdat at the turn of the fourth century must be seen as just one step—however momentous—in a process that had been long under way. In the subsequent tug-of-war then, between the Sasanian and Byzantine Empires, Armenian religious sympathies lay with Christian Byzantium while its social structures remained patterned after aristocratic Iranian feudalism, under the administration of hereditary magnates, or *naxarar*s. Accordingly, in this situation Christianity had a somewhat autonomous evolution. Eventually alienated from Byzantium by the Council of Chalcedon, the Armenian church held tenaciously to some of the earliest traditions of the new religion and developed them along its own lines. Whether one considers the Armenian creed with its expansion on the role of the Holy Spirit, or the Armenians' Epiphany calendar of the liturgy, or their hereditary clergy, or their undiluted eucharistic wine, or their practice of animal sacrifice, one is dealing with Christianity in an unfamiliar and very distinctive form. The linguistic separateness of Armenians from their neighbors and their national sense of self-identity provided an incubation for very independent patterns of thought.

The artistic evidence of Armenia is surprisingly plentiful.[2] While other artistic traditions of the Christian East, such as the Coptic or the Syrian, falter with the rise of Islam, Armenia produced abundant works throughout the Middle Ages. Only neighboring Georgia can be compared in quantity of artistic output. Illustrated manuscripts comprise the largest and most impressive body of Armenian art, occupying a place of honor not unlike that of icons in the Byzantine world. Commissioned at great expense and frequently redeemed from infidel "captivity," manuscripts were preserved as precious church treasures and family heirlooms. The exceptional wealth of Armenian manuscripts has only recently been brought to the attention of art historians with the publication of catalogues surveying the great collections of Erevan, Jerusalem, Isfahan, Venice, Vienna, Dublin, Washington, and Baltimore.[3] Only within the present generation have the overall dimensions of the subject begun to become clear, and only now do its critical problems begin to emerge.

The study of Armenian art presents an unusual challenge principally because it tests some of the fundamental concepts of how to deal with medieval art. On the surface, the image-language of Armenian art, in spite of an "eastern" cast, seems to belong to the koine of the medieval world. However exotic the style might have seemed, the images probably would have

[1] For introductions to Armenian history and its bibliography see Cyril Toumanoff, "Armenia and Georgia," *Cambridge Medieval History,* ed. J. Hussey, IV, pt. 1 (1966), 593–638; Gérard Dédéyan, ed., *Histoire des Arméniens* (Toulouse, 1982). On the Iranian substratum in Armenian culture see Nina G. Garsoïan, *Armenia between Byzantium and the Sasanians* (London, 1985).

[2] The best introduction to the subject, with current bibliography, is Sirarpie Der Nersessian, *Armenian Art* (London, 1978); also very useful is Jean-Michel Thierry, *Les arts arméniens* (Paris, 1987).

[3] L. A. Dournovo, *Haykakan Manrankarč'ut'yun,* ed. R. G. Drampyan (Erevan, 1967); Emma Korkhmazyan, Irina Drampyan, and Hravard Hakopyan, *Armenian Miniatures of the 13th and 14th Centuries from the Matenadaran Collection, Yerevan* (Leningrad, 1984); Bezalel Narkiss and Michael E. Stone, *Armenian Art Treasures of Jerusalem* (Jerusalem, 1979); Sirarpie Der Nersessian and Arpag Mekhitarian, *Armenian Miniatures from Isfahan* (Brussels, 1986); Sirarpie Der Nersessian, *Manuscrits arméniens illustrés des XIIe, XIIIe, et XIVe siècles de la Bibliothèque des pères Mekhitaristes de Venise,* 2 vols. (Paris, 1937); Mesrop Janashian, *Armenian Miniature Paintings of the Monastery Library at San Lazzaro,* trans. Bernard Grebanier (Venice, 1966); Heide and Helmut Buschhausen, *Die illuminierten armenischen Handschriften der Mechitaristen-Congregation in Wien* (Vienna, 1976); Sirarpie Der Nersessian, *Armenian Manuscripts in the Freer Gallery of Art,* Freer Gallery of Art Oriental Studies 6 (Washington, 1963); eadem, *Armenian Manuscripts in the Walters Art Gallery* (Baltimore, 1973).

been legible in Paris or Constantinople as far as general content is concerned: the chief actors in the stories would have been recognized and the narratives themselves, drawn from Sacred Scripture, would have been familiar. The reading of an image-language, or an iconography, however, is much more than the identification of figures and stories. Nuances of intention are decisive. One must understand not only what is the plot that is unfolding but how the plot is being turned or used to develop a point of view. For the same biblical subject is capable of carrying a variety of messages, whether Orthodox or Monophysite in persuasion, popular or aristocratic in outlook, secular or clerical in mentality; such differences, however, are often no more than matters of accent or emphasis in how the story is represented. Armenian art, therefore, precisely because its message does not conform to the norm, poses in a critical form the problem of how to analyze content in medieval art.

This work is the first monographic study of a single Armenian manuscript. Arm. ms. 1 in the Special Collections of the University Research Library, U.C.L.A., was produced, as will be explained, in the province of Siwnikʿ in the years 1300–1307. At this point in history it represents what might be described as the last flowering of Armenian art in its native Armenian cultural environment; the subsequent development in the Lake Van region lies within a dominantly Islamic setting, and later painting in Isfahan, Istanbul, or the Crimea belongs to a diaspora culture. The variety of styles, the quality of the workmanship, and the wealth of the iconography make the U.C.L.A. manuscript unusual and well worth publishing as completely as possible. It was the intrinsic value of the work of art and its potential interest to art historians in other areas that initially motivated the present undertaking. The further the manuscript was examined, however, the more evident it became that the manuscript is also an especially eloquent expression of a particularly Armenian way of thinking. Studied in depth it offers a unique access to the traditional religious mentality of Armenia.

Inscribed to Esayi Nčʿecʿi, abbot of Glajor in Greater Armenia and a staunch defender of Armenian orthodoxy against the pressures of Roman Catholicism, the U.C.L.A. Gospel was finished by an artist who is known by name, one Tʿoros Taronecʿi. These two historical figures, to be discussed in particulars below, provide keys to an extensive network of associations. The artist is known from a whole series of manuscripts and the U.C.L.A. Gospel turns out to be the earliest of the series. Alongside Tʿoros Taronecʿi, however, one finds the work of four other artists in the manuscript, separable into two very distinct workshops, providing a precious sampling of the artistic life of Greater Armenia at the beginning of the fourteenth century. The abbot Esayi Nčʿecʿi, on the other hand, establishes important links to the intellectual life of the monastery of Glajor, though scholarship in this area is still poorly developed. The letters of the abbot tell of his controversies with the Latinizing movement and his vigorous defense of ancient Armenian traditions. The abbot's principal work, however, was exegesis or commentary on Sacred Scripture, and this pursuit was also the most important occupation of the monastery itself; a survey of sixty-nine manuscripts traceable to Glajor in the late thirteenth and early fourteenth centuries provides a reliable picture of the scriptural studies of the monastery. Most significantly, both the abbot and the artist can be connected with a third figure at Glajor, Yovhannēs Erznkacʿi Corcorecʿi, who was a scribe and an exegete; his *Commentary on the Gospel according to St. Matthew* has fortunately survived and is one of the few Armenian works of exegesis to be published.[4] We have, then, an authoritative, contemporary commentary on the sacred text that is illustrated in the manuscript. Again and again unusual details in the iconography of the U.C.L.A. Gospel will find their rationale in the line of argument taken in the exegesis.

This study of the iconography, therefore, has involved a study of Armenian exegesis of the many subjects illustrated in the book. The importance of scriptural commentary to the monastery of Glajor and the numerous parallels of the imagery to such commentary lead one to view the work of the illuminators as a kind of continuance of the work of the exegetes. What the commentator did in parsing and embroidering a passage the painter did in illustrating it, not resting content with simply retelling the story in pictures but forging images that would direct the viewer in how to interpret the story. In taking this point of view the present study would assign manuscript illustration a somewhat different and indeed more exalted role than the literal and decorative functions often attributed to it. Manuscript illustration is not an entertainment art but a thoughtful and learned work which must be understood as part of the intellectual history of a people.

In view of the strong contacts of Armenia with Byzantium and the West it is surprising to discover in the U.C.L.A. Gospel how strong a sense the artists had of their separate cultural identity. This is most strongly documented in their reliance on a model of

[4] Yovhannēs Erznkacʿi and Nersēs Šnorhali, *Meknutʿiwn Surb Awetaranin or əst Mattʿēosi* (Constantinople, 1825).

the eleventh century—a strange Armenian manuscript of very primitive style that only recently came to the collection of the Matenadaran in Erevan. This manuscript, the so-called Vehapʻaṙ Gospel, was the immediate prototype both for the overall program and for the imagery of many individual scenes in the Glajor manuscript. The survival of both prototype and copy has offered a unique opportunity for studying the development of an important tradition of Armenian iconography. The tradition represented by these two manuscripts is by no means the only iconographic tradition in Armenia, nor did it have a very wide circulation. Yet the tradition has a certain coherence and logic, and its motifs are found to appear and reappear intermittently through the history of Armenian art. Tracing the tradition, this study tries to establish what is peculiar to it by comparison with material from Byzantium or the West; in the illustrations, however, preference has been given to the Armenian material, which is generally much less available, rather than the Byzantine and Western material.

The chapters that follow, then, have two principal goals: to give as complete an account as possible of the manuscript itself and to investigate as thoroughly as possible the implications of its image-language. The historical setting in which the manuscript was produced is the first step in this investigation. Though the picture of the intellectual life of the monastery of Glajor is far from complete, the most important intellectual accomplishment of the school of Glajor, namely, biblical commentary, is here clarified for the first time. The next step is the presentation of the manuscript and its manner of production. The sequence of work on the manuscript has been carefully followed, the contributions of separate artists distinguished, the codicology examined, and the pigments analyzed.

The central concern of this book, namely, the study of the image-language of the U.C.L.A. Gospel, opens with a methodological argument to justify the course to be followed. In the history of art the study of gospel iconography has hardly begun; the richness of allusions, the subtleties of tone, the varieties of implications are easily missed in a scholarship that mistakes the illustrations for simpleminded picture making. A method must be devised that will do justice to the complexity of the material. This method is then applied to the individual images, which have been analyzed in three sets, starting with the most complex set, that is, the narrative scenes of the life of Christ, and proceeding to the simpler iconographic sets of canon tables and evangelist portraits. In the final analysis, this study is a test of the efficacy or validity of an image-language. It comes down to a question of how far the imagery can be pressed to yield the pure wine of its content; or, from the other side, at what point does one reach a level of the simply accidental, the mechanical, or the merely conventional—the dregs, so to speak, of the imagery? What is most surprising is the depth of meaning that can be sustained in these images. Armenian art has never been approached in this fashion before, but it is only at this intensity of scrutiny that one can finally appreciate what is peculiar to Armenian art, and what makes it different from the art of Byzantium and the West. The distinctive character of Armenian art lies not in subtleties of style but in subtleties of thought. Looked at from this point of view, there is a surprising consistency and coherence to the art.

CHAPTER TWO

The Historical Setting

Avedis K. Sanjian

1. The History of the U.C.L.A. Gospel

In 1968, the University Research Library at the Los Angeles campus of the University of California acquired a major collection of mostly Persian and Armenian manuscripts, printed books, archives, and artifacts belonging to the late Dr. Caro Owen Minasian of Isfahan, Iran. This acquisition was a significant addition to the growing Near Eastern materials at U.C.L.A., now in excess of 200,000 volumes, of both source materials and secondary literature dealing with the area. The Research Library's collection of approximately 8,500 manuscripts (including some 2,000 codices in the Minasian collection) in Arabic, Persian, Turkish, and Armenian ranks second only to Princeton University among American collections of this kind.[1] The eighty-eight Armenian manuscripts of the Minasian library now make U.C.L.A. the first in the nation in the size of its Armenian holdings.[2]

When the late Professor Gustave von Grunebaum, then director of the Near Eastern Center, first heard rumors of the availability of the Minasian collection in 1966, he urged this writer to contact Dr. Minasian directly and investigate the possibility of securing the collection. At a private meeting in London in January 1967, Dr. Minasian disclosed his interest in finding a permanent home for his library and was persuaded by this writer that the U.C.L.A. Research Library would be an ideal repository. Professor von Grunebaum and Mr. Robert Vosper, then University Librarian, took part in the subsequent negotiations, and Professor Amin Banani traveled to Isfahan to inspect the collection at first hand. Chancellor Franklin Murphy, convinced of the importance of building the research resources of the University, allocated the necessary funds to purchase the collection, aided by a contribution of $25,000 from Mr. Alex Manoogian of Detroit.

Descendant of a family that had lived in the province of Isfahan for more than three hundred years, Dr. Minasian was well known in Iran both as physician and collector. Born in 1897, he attended the English College in Isfahan and studied medicine at the Universities of London, Edinburgh, and Lausanne. He began his practice of medicine in Ahwaz (1923–25) and Teheran (1925–35), but later moved to Isfahan, where he was instrumental in the establishment of a number of infirmaries and hospitals prior to his retirement in 1967. In addition to two books on medical subjects, he translated from Armenian into English *The Chronicle of Petros di Sarkis Gilanentz* (Lisbon, 1959) and wrote the archaeological study, *Shah Diz of Isma'ili Fame: Its Siege and Destruction* (London, 1971). At the time of his death in 1973 he was working on a study of "Hilltop Ruins and Stone Graves roundabout Isfahan."

The range of material in Minasian's Armenian collection is rather diverse, including manuscripts of ecclesiastical character such as gospels, psalters, menologia, and ritual books, as well as theological and philosophical works, medical treatises, and anthologies of poetry.[3] Armenian printed books in the library include hundreds of early and rare books of history and literature, and perhaps the largest collection in

[1] The Persian codices have been catalogued by Lutz Richter-Bernburg, *Persian Medical Manuscripts at the University of California, Los Angeles: A Descriptive Catalogue* (Malibu, Calif., 1978). The catalogue of U.C.L.A.'s Arabic medical and scientific manuscripts, prepared by Albert Z. Iskandar, will be published by E. J. Brill in Leiden.

[2] The next largest collection is that of the Case Memorial Library at the Hartford Seminary Foundation, Hartford, Connecticut, which counts twenty-one manuscripts. Cf. Avedis K. Sanjian, *A Catalogue of Medieval Armenian Manuscripts in the United States* (Berkeley, Calif., 1976), 73–133.

[3] This author is preparing the catalogue of the Armenian manuscripts.

the world of Indian-Armenian material.[4] The jewel of the collection, however, is undoubtedly the Glajor Gospel, which Dr. Minasian carefully excluded from the purchase price so that he might offer it as a gift to the University. When questioned by this writer why he was making so special a gift of this Gospel, Dr. Minasian explained with a solemn grin that he was motivated by the threat of the colophon on pages 579–80: "No one from among our own princes or foreign princes, be they laity or clergy, has the authority or permission to remove this gospel from Ayrivankʿ by *selling* or dividing or stealing or confiscating it. And whoever dares and endeavors to remove it, shall be judged by God and all the saints."[5]

Catalogued as Armenian manuscript no. 1, the Glajor Gospel, by reason of its extraordinary wealth of iconography and its excellent state of preservation, must be ranked as the most important manuscript from Greater Armenia to have reached the New World. Fortunately for us, the Armenian custom of entering new inscriptions or colophons in a manuscript when it changes hands permits one to trace back the history of the manuscript, step by step, from its bestowal on U.C.L.A. to its origins in the fourteenth century.

Dr. Minasian's own seal appears with the date of 1935 on pages 24b, 337, and 582; this, however, indicates the date the stamp was made rather than the year Dr. Minasian acquired the manuscript. At the beginning of this century, one learns from the inscription on page 25, the codex belonged to a certain archpriest named Xačʿ(atur) Tēr Martiros Tēr Yovakimian, who on May 1, 1901 offered it to his "beloved Mayiš Ostan," presumably a relative of his. Mayiš Ostan's name is mentioned also in two crudely written inscriptions, one of which (page 24b) informs us that he was a "servant of the holy Mother of God at (the church of) St. Karapet," which in the context of the earlier history of the manuscript must have been the church of St. Karapet, or St. John the Baptist, in New Julfa.[6] Another inscription dated 1901 (page 580) mentions a *žamarar* (officiating priest) named Tēr Yōvakim, perhaps a colleague of Mayiš Ostan.

Two inscriptions on page 25 attest that in the nineteenth century the Glajor Gospel belonged to a priest named Yōvakim Abraham. The first of these inscriptions indicates that the book was given to him by the congregation of the church of Mec Xōǰencʿ. This transfer of ownership was dated according to a local calendar in use among Armenians of Iran to the 23rd of Shamsi in the year 209, that is, March 23, 1824,[7] and it was witnessed by the priest Yarutʿiwn Yakobian, who wrote the inscription and sealed it with a stamp bearing his name. The priest Yōvakim Abraham wrote the second inscription, carrying the date of the 20th of Hameray, 209, that is, December 6, 1824. Here he refers to himself as a *žamarar* and mentions the names and ages of his five children: Barełēn, Mērxatʿun, Sarkʿis, Martiros, and Galēstan. Elsewhere the priest Yōvakim Abraham scribbled his name twice more on page 24b. Prior to 1824, then, the manuscript belonged to the church of Mec Xōǰencʿ, and this is an important piece of the history of the book.

Mec Xōǰencʿ (meaning "of the great Khoja") was the popular name for the church of St. George, built by Xōǰay Nazar in New Julfa in 1610–11.[8] New Julfa was established in the first years of the seventeenth century when Shah Abbas I forcibly relocated the Armenians of old Julfa in Greater Armenia to a tract of land situated across the Zayandehrud River south of his capital of Isfahan. Anxious to dispel Armenian hopes of returning to their homeland, the Shah had the relics, the stone altar, and other architectural fragments transferred from the cathedral at Ēǰmia-

[4] The cataloguing of the printed books is being done by Gia Aivazian, Armenian and Greek bibliographer and cataloguer in the University Research Library at U.C.L.A.

[5] Emphasis added. See Appendix A.

[6] The church of St. Karapet was built in 1620–21. John Carswell, *New Julfa: The Armenian Churches and Other Buildings* (Oxford, 1968), 40–41, 46.

[7] The calendar was devised by Azaria J̌ułayecʿi, a scholar from old Julfa in Greater Armenia. In his calendar Azaria maintained a basic computation of the "Great Armenian Era," according to which the immovable year was divided into twelve months of thirty days each, with five additional days (*Aweleacʿ*) intercalated after the twelfth month; in leap years the twelfth month had thirty-one days. Azaria moved the first day of the year from August 11 (= Nawasard 1) in the "Great Armenian Era" to March 21; he also changed the traditional Armenian names of the months into Islamic names. Azaria's calendar did not gain wide acceptance; rather, it was used mainly by the Armenian communities in Iran, especially in New Julfa, and in India. For the conversion from Azaria's calendar to the modern era, the figure 1615 or 1616 should be added to the former—1615 if the event occurred between March 21 and January 1, and 1616 if it occurred between January 1 and March 21. Accordingly, the date 23rd of Shamsi in the year 209 given in the first inscription corresponds to March 23, 1824, and the date 20th of Hameray in the year 209 indicated in the second inscription corresponds to December 6, 1824.

Regarding Azaria J̌ułayecʿi's calendar, see *Haykakan Sovetakan Hanragitaran,* I (Erevan, 1974), 100; H. S. Anasyan, *Haykakan Matenagitutʿyun,* I (Erevan, 1959), 272–76, 1177–86; B. E. Tʿumanyan, *Hay Astłagitutʿyan Patmutʿyun,* I (Erevan, 1964), 103–5. See also Édouard Dulaurier, *Recherches sur la chronologie arménienne technique et historique,* I (Paris, 1859), 81, 115–17; L. Ideler, *Lehrbuch der Chronologie* (Berlin, 1831), 441–43.

[8] Carswell, *New Julfa,* 37–40.

cin. These precious remains were placed in the care of the leader of the Armenian community, Xōǰay Nazar, who incorporated the stones into the new building of the church of St. George.[9]

If prior to 1824 the manuscript belonged to the venerable church of Mec Zōǰencʿ, the question naturally arises how long it was there. In his personal catalogue of his library Dr. Minasian states that the Glajor Gospel "once had been the property of our famous Khoǰa Nazar, known as the great Khoja,"[10] but he cites no source for this information and the internal evidence of the manuscript is silent concerning its whereabouts in the interval between the founding of the church of Mec Xōǰencʿ and 1824. The manuscript contains two inscriptions of this period but neither is very informative. On *page 156*, below the miniature of the Last Supper, there is a simple memorial inscription commemorating "*Žamarar* Ohanēs, son of the priest Yakob, in the year 104," that is, in 1719–20. Even less information can be gleaned from an inscription on page 580 stating, "This holy Gospel is 307 years old." Assuming the writer was calculating from the earliest date in the manuscript, 1377 in the colophon on page 577, the inscription must have been entered in 1684.

There is external evidence, however, that the U.C.L.A. Gospel was in New Julfa early in the seventeenth century, for a manuscript produced in that city in 1628 contains a portrait of the evangelist John (fig. 460f) that is an exact copy of the John in the U.C.L.A. manuscript, *page 460*. This manuscript in the collection of the late Harutiun Hazarian of New York City remains unpublished.[11] The portrait of John on fol. 170v copies not only the overall composition of the U.C.L.A. page, but even reproduces exactly the most trivial details, such as the roof tiles, the cloth hanging from the hand of God, and the illogical way the evangelist loses his feet in the border of the kilim. Further, the artist used the heading for the Gospel of Luke, *page 299*, as the model for his incipit page in John's Gospel, fol. 171. The other evangelists are done by a less competent artist from other models, but the dependence of these two pages on the U.C.L.A. manuscript makes it appear that the U.C.L.A. manuscript was in New Julfa at this time. It should be pointed out that the Great Xōǰay Nazar, besides erecting the church of Mec Xōǰencʿ, or St. George, also showed a lively interest in manuscripts. In 1618 he acquired a manuscript of the Gospels and Acts written at Sis in Cilicia in 1280 (now London, British Library Add. 18,549);[12] and in 1629 he acquired another thirteenth-century manuscript, a Gospel (Erevan, Matenadaran 222).[13] In addition, he commissioned a lectionary-menologium, which was recently in the collection of the late H. Kʿiwrtian of Wichita, Kansas, and is now in the Mekhitarist Library in Venice.[14] Xōǰay Nazar's family was also active in commissioning and acquiring manuscripts.[15] In other words, given the evidence indicating the presence of the U.C.L.A. manuscript in New Julfa in the early seventeenth century, and given the interest of the founder of Mec Xōǰencʿ in manuscripts, it is very likely that the manuscript was in that church's possession from the time of the resettlement of the Armenian community there.

[9] Under Shah Abbas I and his successors, the leader of the Armenians in Julfa-Isfahan was the *kalāntar*, or elder, appointed by the Shah and authorized to collect taxes; he was also responsible for the good conduct of the community as a whole. Xōǰay Nazar was the most prominent among the many Armenians who served in the capacity of Kalāntar, a position which he held until his death in 1636; hence his distinction as the "Great Xōǰay." Nazar had belonged to a well-known mercantile family in old Julfa in Greater Armenia. After settling in New Julfa, Xōǰay Nazar, a confidant of Shah Abbas I, and his brothers operated a vast network of commercial enterprises linking Iran with Europe, thereby not only amassing large wealth for themselves but also contributing significantly to the royal treasury. Indeed, so prominent was Xōǰay Nazar that he gave his name to the street in which his house stood, *Nazari Khiyaban* (Nazar Avenue). See Yarutʿiwn Tēr Yovhaneancʿ, *Patmutʿiwn Nor J̌ułayu or Yaspahan*, 2 vols. (New Julfa, 1880). Concerning Xōǰay Nazar and his family, consult H. Kʿiwrtian, "J̌ułayecʿi Xōǰay Nazar and His Family," *Hayrenikʿ Amsagīr* 4 (1943), 72–82; 5 (1943), 63–73; 6 (1943), 69–87. See also Tēr Yovhaneancʿ, *Patmutʿiwn*.

For the historical background of the Armenians in New Julfa, see John Carswell, *New Julfa*, 3–15. For details of the tribulations of the Julfa Armenians in the early eighteenth century, consult *The Chronicles of Petros di Sarkis Gilanents*, trans. C. O. Minasian (Lisbon, 1959); Laurence Lockhart, *The Fall of the Safavī Dynasty and the Afghan Occupation of Persia* (Cambridge, 1958), 150–53, 192, 485.

[10] Unpublished notes in the U.C.L.A. Research Library.

[11] The Hazarian collection now belongs to the late H. Hazarian's daughter, New York City.

[12] F. C. Conybeare, *A Catalogue of the Armenian Manuscripts in the British Museum* (London, 1913), 11–14.

[13] Vazgen Hakobyan and Ašot Hovhannisyan, *XVII Dari Hayeren J̌eragreri Hišatakaranner, 1621–1640*, vol. II (Erevan, 1978), 334–35; also Ō. Eganyan, et al., *Cʿucʿak J̌eragracʿ Maštocʿi Anvan Matenadarani*, vol. I (Erevan, 1965), col. 276.

[14] Kʿiwrtian, "J̌ułayecʿi Xōǰay Nazar," *Hayrenikʿ Amsagīr* 6 (1943), 71.

[15] Nazar's son Bałdasar sponsored a manuscript of selections of scriptural passages in 1627 (Hakobyan and Hovhannisyan, *XVII Dari*, 345); another son, Safar, commissioned a Gospel in 1658–59, New York, Pierpont Morgan 623 (Sanjian, *Catalogue*, 562–70); Nazar's sister Azat sponsored a Gospel in 1627 in Norašēn, near Isfahan (Hakobyan and Hovhannisyan, *XVII Dari*, 265–66); his grandson Xōǰay Vatʿan commissioned a menologium in Isfahan in 1659, Hartford, Case Memorial 5 (Sanjian, *Catalogue*, 94–98); and his nephew J̌alalbēk in 1629 acquired a Gospel dating to 1300 (Hakobyan and Hovhannisyan, *XVII Dari*, 346–47).

The next earlier stage in the history of the manuscript takes one to Greater Armenia, to the famous monastery of Gełard in the province of Kotaykʿ. According to the colophon on pages 578–80, "During the reign of King Gēorgi, at the time when the filthy and accursed Tʿimur plundered our lands, I, baron Martiros, son of Šahanša, and my wife, baroness Ładam, daughter of baron Arłutʿay, son of J̌um, grandson of the prince of princes Pṙoš, after much effort and expense rescued, through our honest means, this holy ancestral gospel, which had fallen captive into the hands of foreigners."[16] While the exact date was omitted from this colophon, it is clear that it refers to King Gēorgi of Georgia (1393–1407) and to Tīmūr Lang (Tamerlane), who arrived in Armenia in 1387 and died in 1405. Having rescued the Gospel from its Mongol captors, the colophon continues, Martiros and his wife deposited it in the monastery of Gełard or the Holy Lance (also known as Ayrivankʿ, the Monastery of the Caves), through the mediation of Simēon Vardapet. Simēon Vardapet is known from other sources to have been educated at Tatʿew in Siwnikʿ under Grigor Tatʿewacʿi and to have served as abbot of Gełard until 1404.[17] The rescue of the manuscript, therefore, and its donation to Gełard must date between 1393 and 1404. The absence of inscriptions mentioning other changes of place during the fifteenth and sixteenth centuries is negative evidence that may imply that the Gospel remained at Gełard through this period until it was brought with the uprooted Armenians to New Julfa.

The colophon of 1393–1404 twice refers to the manuscript as the "ancestral Gospel." The meaning of this term becomes obvious in an earlier colophon, dated 1377, in which the baroness Ładam's mother Vaxax is identified as the previous owner of the manuscript. This colophon, on pages 575–77, is the earliest in the manuscript and it provides considerable genealogical information about the proud possessors of the book.[18] Baroness Vaxax is identified as the "daughter of the majestic and royal prince baron Inanik, son of the honorable baron Biwrtʿēl, son of Ēlēkum, son of Tarsayič," the last of whom is known as a prominent member of the Ōrbēlian family.[19] Baroness Vaxax's husband, however, belonged to the Xałbakian or Pṙošian family. He is identified as the baron Arłutʿay, son of J̌um, son of Ēačʿi, son of Amir Hasan, son of Pṙoš. Their daughter Ładam, in turn, married back into the Ōrbēlian family, her husband Martiros being a distant cousin on her mother's side.[20] Both families, it will be shown, played important roles in the history of Siwnikʿ and its ecclesiastical institutions.[21]

Baroness Vaxax's colophon also contains crucial information about the place of origin of the manuscript: "This (gospel) was written in Vayocʿ Jor, at the monastery which is called Glajor. Later, however, it was acquired by the Baroness Vaxax, through her honestly earned means, in the year 826 of the Armenians (=A.D. 1377)." When Baroness Vaxax acquired the book, then, it was known to have been produced in Glajor, and indeed she may well have acquired it directly from the monastery which, as we shall see, was at this time in a state of decline.[22] Since both the Ōrbēlian and the Pṙošian families had holdings in Vayocʿ Jor, the manuscript may not have traveled very far when it was acquired by Baroness Vaxax. The baroness evidently took special pleasure in owning the Gospel, for in five other places besides the colophon she notes her ownership and asks the reader's prayers.[23] A few years later, in 1381, she records the death of a grandson Iwanē, son of her son Biwrtʿēl.[24]

The U.C.L.A. Gospel has no colophon earlier than Baroness Vaxax's colophon of 1377. The colophon of

[16] See Appendix A.

[17] From Gełard, Simēon Vardapet went to Ełoward, where he taught for ten years, and then to Jagavankʿ, where he died in 1428. See Garegin Yovsēpʿian, *Xałbakeankʿ kam Pṙošeankʿ Hayocʿ Patmutʿean Mēǰ* (2nd printing, Antilias, 1969), 215–16. See also Łewond Ališan, *Ayrarat* (Venice, 1890), 197, 291, 346, 350; idem, *Sisakan* (Venice, 1893), 241; idem, *Hayapatum* (Venice, 1901–2), 569.

[18] See Appendix A.

[19] The most important source for the history of the Ōrbēlian family is found in Stepʿanos Ōrbēlian, *Patmutʿiwn Nahangin Sisakan,* which has had several editions. In our study, reference is made to the Tiflis edition of 1910. There is a partial translation of this work in M. J. Saint-Martin, *Mémoires historiques et géographiques sur l'Arménie, suivis du texte arménien de l'Histoire des Princes Orpélians par Étienne Orpélian, archevêque de Siounie, et de celui des Géographies attribuées à Moyse de Khoren et au docteur Vartan, avec plusieurs autres pièces relatives à l'histoire d'Arménie, le tout accompagné d'une traduction française et de notes explicatives,* 2 vols. (Paris, 1818–19). For a complete translation of the text, with extensive annotations, see *Histoire de la Siounie par Stéphannos Orbélian,* traduite de l'arménien par M. Brosset, 2 vols. (St. Petersburg, 1864–66), [herafter, Ōrbēlian, *Histoire*].

[20] Martiros is identified in the colophon of 1393–1404 simply as the son of prince Šahanša; however the latter, according to several colophons written between 1314 and 1331, can be identified as son of the Ōrbēlian prince J̌alal, who in turn was grandson of the Ōrbēlian prince Tarsayič. For the genealogy of the Ōrbēlian princes, see Cyrille Toumanoff, *Manuel de généalogie et de chronologie pour l'histoire de la Caucasie chrétienne (Arménie-Géorgie-Albanie)* (Rome, 1976), 538–39.

[21] See below, pp. 12–17.

[22] See below, p. 14.

[23] These inscriptions appear on pages 1, 24a, 182, 297, and 459.

[24] This inscription appears on page 578.

the first owner may have been entered on a now missing folio before the Gospel of St. Mark and may have been removed when the monastery of Glajor disposed of the book.[25] Fortunately, inscriptions on two of the miniatures help to make good this lack. On *page 453*, under the Ascension, the painter addresses a note to the reader saying, "I beseech you to remember in the Lord Jesus the unworthy painter T'oros, who labored later"; and on *page 227* within the miniature of the Second Storm at Sea the painter addresses the original owner of the manuscript, "O great master of mine, Esayi, remember this unworthy disciple of yours T'oros." At the monastery of Glajor the "great master Esayi" can only be the famous Vardapet Esayi Nč'ec'i († 1338); the painter T'oros, it can be shown from an analysis of his style, is T'oros Taronec'i.[26] It is to the analysis of the paintings that one must turn for the various stages in the manufacture of the manuscript, as well as for a more precise date for the contribution of T'oros Taronec'i who "labored later," that is, was the last of several painters to work on the manuscript.

In summary, then, the U.C.L.A. Gospel has a most distinguished history. Executed for an important ecclesiastical figure in the early fourteenth century, it passed in 1377 into the private possession of the Ōrbēlian family who, after its capture and redemption from the Mongols, deposited it in the monastery of Gełard in 1393–1404. Here it seems to have remained until the beginning of the seventeenth century, when it accompanied the exodus of Armenians to New Julfa. At this time it was probably placed in the church of Mec Xōǰenc', or St. George, where it remained until that church gave it to a priest named Yōvakim Abraham in 1824. Thereafter it seems to have remained in the private possession of individual priests, changing hands once again in 1901, before finally being acquired by Dr. Caro O. Minasian.

2. The Political Setting

Following the ignominious defeat of the Byzantine forces at Manazkert (Manzikert) in 1071, central Asia Minor and all of Transcaucasia, including Georgia and Armenia, fell into the hands of the Seljuk Turks. Within a century, however, an independent Georgia reemerged, and between 1190 and 1209 an army of Georgian and Armenian troops under the brothers Zak'arē and Iwanē of the Zak'arian family had recovered the northern and eastern provinces of Armenia—Tayk', Gugark', Utik', Ayrarat, and Siwnik' (see Map 1).[27] Under Georgian sovereignty the two brothers divided the administration of the Armenian territories between them, with Zak'arē and his son Šahanšah controlling the northern and western portions, and Iwanē and his son Awag the southern and eastern portions. The Zak'arians, however, did not exercise direct control over their respective territories, but had recourse to the ancient *naxarar* system of hereditary principalities to reward the lords who had taken part in the military campaigns. Thus Zak'arē's domain was subdivided among the Vač'utian, the Pahlawuni, the Honenc', and other families, and Iwanē's among the Ōrbēlian, the Xałbakian or Přošian, the Dop'ian, and other families. The local princes had the responsibilities of raising troops in the event of war and paying tribute to the Zak'arians.[28]

In the region south of Lake Sevan, which especially concerns this study, the principalities of the Ōrbēlian and Xałbakian families interlocked in curious and often discontinuous geographical holdings. Step'anos Ōrbēlian, historian of the Ōrbēlian family, attests that, with the approval of King Georgi-Lasha of Georgia (1213–22), Iwanē had granted to the Ōrbēlian prince Liparit I, as domains in perpetuity, the town of "Hraškaberd and its district and a number of villages in Vayoc' Jor, [the town of] Ēlař and many villages in [the district of] Kotayk', Hamasri and many villages in Gełark'unik', and [the town of] Ałstew. . . . And because he [Liparit] had played a leading role in the capture of Siwnik' and other fortresses, he also granted him Siwnik', Orotn, Barkušat, and other fortresses."[29] At the same time, Prince Vasak I of the Xałbakian family, who had played an important role in the reconquest of Siwnik', was rewarded with the district of Vayoc' Jor and a series of fortresses and monasteries in Kotayk', Ayrarat, Šahapunik', and Varažnunik'. Among the

[25] See codicological discussion, Chapter 3.
[26] See below, Chapter 3.

[27] For the history of the liberation of Georgia and Armenia from Seljuk rule, see *Hay Žołovrdi Patmut'yun* (Armenian S.S.R. Academy of Sciences, Erevan, 1976), III, 523–40 [hereafter *Patmut'yun* (Academy)]. On Georgian history after liberation from Seljuk rule, see Dédéyan, ed., *Histoire des Arméniens*, 297–302; W. E. D. Allen, *A History of the Georgian People* (London, 1932), 95–120; Charles Burney and D. M. Lang, *The Peoples of the Hills* (London, 1971), 211–13.
[28] Concerning the reapportionment of territories among the Armenian princely families, see *Patmut'yun* (Academy), III, 541–57; G. M. Grigoryan, *Syunik'ə Ōrbelyanneri Ōrok', XIII–XV Darer* (Erevan, 1981), 43–50; Garegin Yovsēpian, *Xałbakeank' kam Přošeank' Hayoc' Patmut'ean Mēǰ*, 9–10.
[29] Step'anos Ōrbēlian, *Patmut'iwn*, 397; Ōrbēlian, *Histoire*, I, 224–25.

monasteries in their care were Gełard, Kečʿaṙis, Tʿanahat, and Glajor.

The liberation of northern and eastern Armenia from Seljuk hegemony and the reinstatement of the Armenian *naxarar* system ushered in a twenty-five year period of peace. The general revitalization of the economy was evident in the rebuilding of ruined cities and villages, bridges, fortresses, and monasteries. The province of Siwnikʿ benefited most in this revival, the Ōrbēlians and Xałbakians vying with one another in the construction and endowment of churches and monasteries.[30]

The occupation of Transcaucasia by the Mongols in the 1230s reversed much of this progress. The contemporary historian Kirakos Ganjakecʿi reflects the horrified Armenian reaction to their new conquerors, who spread over the plains and mountains "like a multitude of locusts or like a torrent of rain pouring upon the earth. . . . There was nothing that they did not plunder; they marched forth swiftly hither and thither like deer, and they themselves never grew tired of gathering booty."[31] Unable to prevent the occupation of their territories, the Georgian and Armenian princes arrived at an accommodation with the Mongols, by which they would recognize the sovereignty of the Mongol khan, pay the prescribed tribute, and provide troops for Mongol military operations. This gave the Mongol overlords effective political and economic control while preserving some autonomy for the princes in their own domains. At the same time King Hetʿum (1226–70) of the Cilician kingdom of Armenia entered into an alliance with the Mongols against the Seljuk Turks.

In the long run Mongol policies toward land ownership, taxation, and the population had disastrous effects on the Armenian principalities.[32] Large tracts of farm land were confiscated from the local lords and distributed among nomadic Mongol nobility for conversion to pastureland, destroying the agricultural base of the economy. The Ilkhanid state distinguished two kinds of ownership: *khass* lands, which were owned and controlled by the *ilkhan*; and *indjū* lands, which were technically royal property and therefore privileged. If a local lord could secure a designation of *indjū* status for his domain he might thereby secure it from census-takers and tax-collectors while paying his tribute directly to the *ilkhan*.[33]

Mongol taxation proved to be extremely onerous. Taxes were imposed on orchards, watermills, lakes, mineral mines, craft products, and animals, but the most burdensome levy was the capitation tax called *jizyah* or *ghapchur*, which was imposed on all males between the ages of ten and sixty.[34] Kirakos Ganjakecʿi describes vividly the arrival of census-takers in Armenia, Georgia, and Caucasian Albania in 1254.

> They recorded [the names of] everyone, beginning with those ten years of age and older, excepting the women. They demanded from everyone the most exorbitant taxes, more than any individual could afford . . . they subjected them to terrible torture, torment, and fetters. Those who went into hiding were seized and slain; those who could not pay the [prescribed] amount had their children taken away in lieu of their obligations . . . The princes, moreover, [that is] the lords of the districts, collaborated with them in these harassments and exactions for their own profit.[35]

It should be noted, however, that in principle women and clergy enjoyed a tax-exempt status. Kirakos Ganjakecʿi makes the observation that the census-takers "collected no taxes from the clergy, because they had received no such orders from the khan."[36]

[30] Yovsēpʿian, *Xałbakeankʿ*, 1–44; cf. also B. A. Ulubabyan, *Xačʿeni Išxanutʿyunə X–XVI Darerum* (Erevan, 1975), 176–80, 244–64; A. K. Sanjian, "The Orbelians and Proshians of Siwnikʿ: Patrons of Religious Institutions," *Handes Amsorya* 101, nos. 1–12 (1987), 911–24.

[31] Kirakos Ganjakecʿi, *Patmutʿyun Hayocʿ*, ed. by K. A. Melikʿ-Ōhanǰanyan (Erevan, 1961), 237–41; *Kirakos Gandzaketsi. Istoriia Armenii*, trans. from the Classical Armenian with notes and commentary by L. A. Khanlarian, Pamiatniki pis'mennósti Vostoka 53 (Moscow, 1976), 155–57.

[32] For a detailed discussion of the impact of these policies on Armenia, consult *Patmutʿyun* (Academy), III, 656–68. For Armenia under Mongol rule, see Dédéyan, *Histoire des Arméniens*, 302–7.

[33] For the term *khass* see Jules Theodore Zenker, *Dictionnaire Turc-Arabe-Persan* (Leipzig, 1866–76), 400a; and for the term *indjū* consult A. Boyle, article "Indjū," in *EI*, III, fasc. 59–60 (Leiden, 1971), 1208. For a detailed discussion of the system of land ownership under the Mongols, consult *Patmutʿyun* (Academy), III, 645–51; see also L. H. Babayan, *Hayastani Socʿeal-Tntesakan Kʿałakʿakanutʿyunə XIII–XIV Darerum* (Erevan, 1964), 406–17.

[34] On Mongol taxes see *Patmutʿyun* (Academy), III, 651–55.

[35] Kirakos Ganjakecʿi, *Patmutʿyun Hayocʿ*, 361–63; *Kirakos Gandzaketsi. Istoriia Armenii*, 221.

[36] Kirakos Ganjakecʿi, *Patmutʿyun Hayocʿ*, 374–75; *Kirakos Gandzaketsi. Istoriia Armenii*, 222–25. These Mongol economic policies and the system of taxation underwent no change until the reign of Ghazan Khan (1295–1304), who, after consolidating his rule, introduced a series of political and economic "reforms" that were designed to guarantee the fiscal solvency of the Mongol court's treasury and the economic welfare of the Ilkhanid dominions. These measures included the abolishment of all illegally exacted levies that had resulted from the institution of tax-farming; the establishment of a uniform system of taxation with prescribed amounts of levies; the introduction of a uniform monetary system throughout the Mongol dominions; land reforms, including the parceling out of domains to Mongol officials and military commanders; the cancellation of the

1. Map of Medieval Armenia ca. 1300

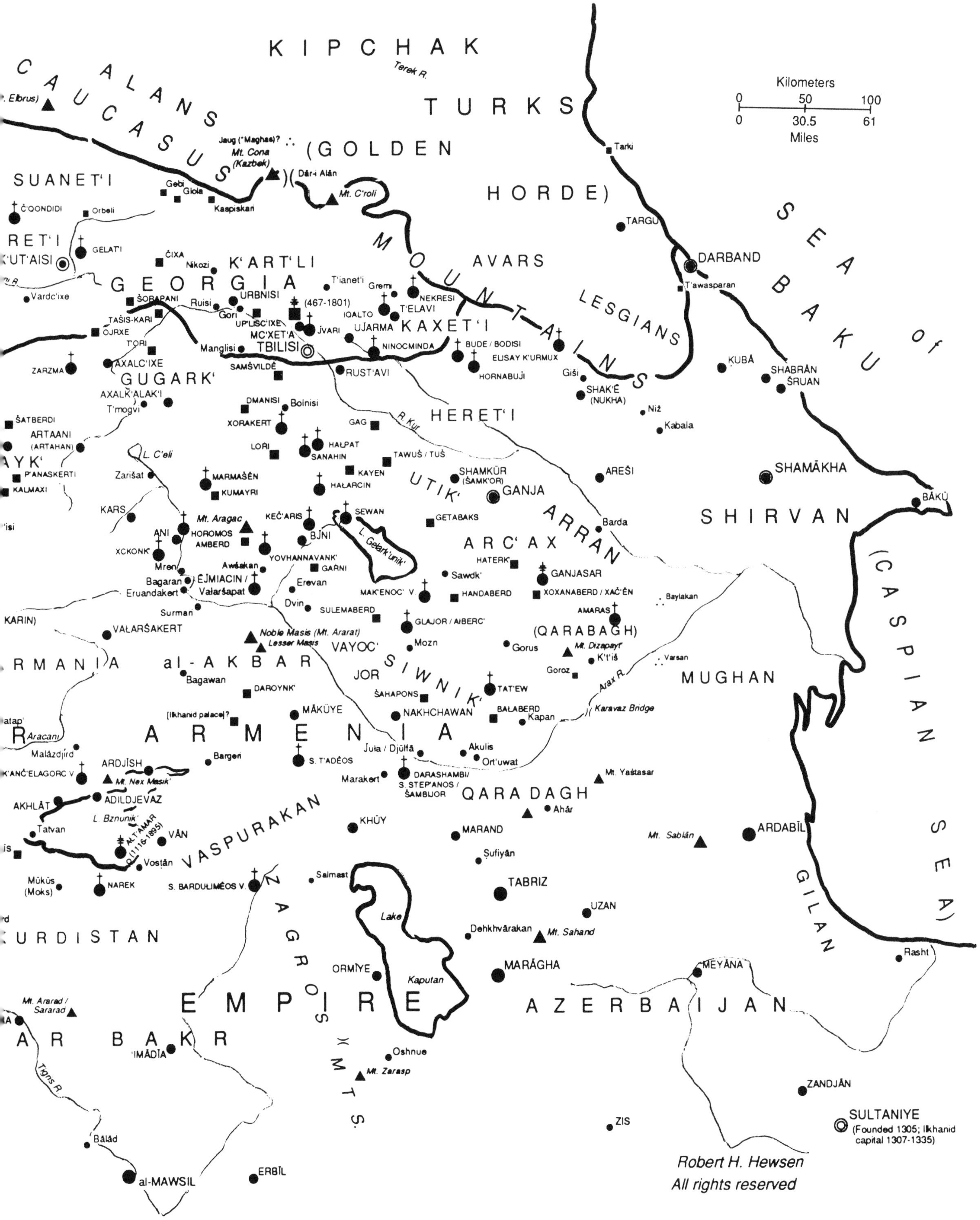
KIPCHAK
TURKS
(GOLDEN
HORDE)
Terek R.
Kilometers
0 50 100
0 30.5 61
Miles
ALANS
CAUCASUS
MOUNTAINS
Elbrus)
Jaug ("Maghas)?
Mt. Cona (Kazbek)
Dār-i Alān
Mt. C'roli
SUANET'I
Gebi
Gloła
Kaspiskari
Č'QONDIDI
Orbeli
RET'I
K'UT'AISI
GELAT'I
ČIXA
Nikozi
K'ART'LI
GEORGIA
Vardc'ixe
ŠORAPANI
Ruisi
URBNISI
(467-1801)
T'ianet'i
Gremi
NEKRESI
T'ELAVI
IOALTO
UJARMA
KAXET'I
TAŠIS-KARI
Gori
UP'LISC'IXE
MC'XET'A
JVARI
OJRXE
T'ORI
Manglisi
TBILISI
NINOCMINDA
BUDE / BODISI
ELISAY K'URMUX
ZARZMA
AXALC'IXE
SAMŠVILDĒ
RUST'AVI
HORNABUJI
GUGARK'
AXALK'ALAK'I
T'mogvi
DMANISI
Bolnisi
ŠATBERDI
ARTAANI (ARTAHAN)
XORAKERT
GAG
R. Kur
HERET'I
LORI
HAŁPAT
SANAHIN
TAWUŠ / TUŠ
P'ANASKERTI
KALMAXI
L. C'eli
Zarišat
MARMAŠĒN
KUMAYRI
KAYEN
HAŁARCIN
UTIK'
SHAMKŪR (ŠAMK'OR)
GANJA
ARRAN
KARS
ANI
XCKONK'
Mt. Aragac
HOROMOS
AMBERD
KEČ'ARIS
BJNI
SEWAN
L. Gełark'unik'
GETABAKS
ARC'AX
HATERK'
GANJASAR
Mren
Awšakan
YOVHANNAVANK'
GARNI
Bagaran
Eruandakert
ĒJMIACIN / Vałaršapat
Erevan
Sawdk'
MAK'ENOC' V
HANDABERD
XOXANABERD / XAČ'ĒN
Surman
Dvin
SULEMABERD
AMARAS
KARIN)
VAŁARŠAKERT
Noble Masis (Mt. Ararat)
Lesser Masis
GLAJOR / AIBERC'
Mozn
VAYOC'
(QARABAGH)
Gorus
Mt. Dizapayt
K't'iš
Goroz
RMANIA
al-AKBAR
Bagawan
JOR
SIWNIK'
ŠAHAPONS
TAT'EW
DAROYNK'
[Ilkhanid palace]?
MĀKŪYE
NAKHCHAWAN
BAŁABERD
Kapan
Arax R.
Karavaz Bridge
ARMENIA
Aracani
Malāzdjird
Bargeri
Jula / Djūlfā
Akulis
Ort'uwat
ARDJĪSH
K'ANČ'ELAGORC V
Mt. Nex Masik'
S. T'ADĒOS
Marakert
DARASHAMBI / S. STEP'ANOS / ŠAMBIJOR
QARA DAGH
Mt. Yaštasar
AKHLĀT
ADILDJEVAZ
Ahār
L. Bznunik'
Tatvan
AŁT'AMAR (1116-1895)
VĀN
VASPURAKAN
KHŪY
MARAND
Mt. Sablān
ARDABĪL
Vostān
Sufiyān
Mūkūs (Moks)
NAREK
S. BARDUŁIMĒOS V.
Salmast
TABRIZ
UZAN
Lake
Dehkhvārakan
Mt. Sahand
URDISTAN
ZAGROS MTS.
ORMIYE
Kaputan
MARĀGHA
MEYĀNA
Rasht
Mt. Ararad / Sararad
EMPIRE
AZERBAIJAN
AR BAKR
'IMĀDĪA
Tigris R.
Oshnue
Mt. Zarasp
ZANDJĀN
SULTANIYE (Founded 1305; Ilkhanid capital 1307-1335)
ZIS
Bālād
al-MAWSIL
ERBĪL
AVARS
LESGIANS
Tarki
TARGU
DARBAND
T'awasparan
SEA of BAKU
(CASPIAN SEA)
KUBĀ
SHABRĀN
ŠRUAN
Giši
SHAK'Ē (NUKHA)
Niž
Kabala
AREŠI
SHAMĀKHA
BĀKŪ
Barda
SHIRVAN
Baylakan
Varsan
MUGHAN
GILAN
Robert H. Hewsen
All rights reserved

While such economic policies drove many, especially of the merchant class, to emigrate, other policies took a direct and heavy toll on the population at large. The conscription of soldiers for the frequent wars waged by the Mongols, the carrying off of large numbers into slavery, and the intermittent pillaging by unruly chieftains decimated many sections of the country. Many Armenians fled into neighboring or more distant lands, especially in the Crimea. Step'anos Ōrbēlian attests that prior to the Mongol conquest the province of Siwnik' had 1,008 villages, but that by the end of the thirteenth century the number had been reduced to 677.[37]

Under Mongol rule, the history of the province of Siwnik' and the district of Vayoc' Jor in particular continued to be linked with the fortunes of the three leading princely families, the Zak'arian, the Xałbakian or Přošian, and the Ōrbēlian. Initially the Mongols divided all of Transcaucasia into five *vilayets*, one of which consisted of eastern Georgia and the Armenian provinces of Gugark', Ayrarat, Arc'ax, and Siwnik'. This *vilayet* was in turn divided into eight *tumans*, three of which, including the Awagian and Vahramian principalities, were placed under the jurisdiction of the Zak'arians.[38] Thus the Zak'arians were favored by Hulagu Khan (1255–65) over the other Armenian princes; only after their attempted rebellion in 1259–61 did the Ōrbēlian family supplant them as the leading Armenian family.

Siwnik', however, enjoyed a special status. Step'anos Ōrbēlian relates that upon the death of the prince Ēlikum II Ōrbēlian (1249/50) the Awagian branch of the Zak'arians sought to appropriate the Ōrbēlian territory. Thereupon Ēlikum's brother Smbat journeyed to the Mongol capital Karakorum, where he obtained from Mangu Khan a *yarligh* (official decree) reaffirming his family's hereditary rights, and military help to vindicate his claims. Returning to Siwnik' he "recovered the entire region of Orotn up to the boundaries of Borotn and Błen. . . . He also recovered Ełegis and the entire canton of Vayoc' Jor, as well as P'ołahans, Urc, and Vēdi with its valley up toErerawn, and many settlements and villages in [the cantons of] Kotayk' and Gełark'unik'."[39] Prince Smbat's success had far-reaching consequences. The entire province of Siwnik' was now constituted into a separate *tuman* as the Ōrbēlian hereditary domain and was granted *indjū* status. This meant that the tribute from Siwnik' was no longer collected by tax-farmers but by the Ōrbēlian prince, who was responsible directly to the Mongol court. Clergy and religious institutions were tax-exempt and properties that had been confiscated from them were restored. The Ōrbēlian control of Siwnik' inaugurated a period of new construction throughout the province,[40] and it is in precisely this period, that is, in 1271, that we first have mention of the monastery of Glajor, to be discussed below.

Smbat's successor, Tarsayič (1273–90), proved himself equally skillful in his relations with the khan and distinguished himself in several Mongol military campaigns. Arghun Khan (1284–91) made him commander of Mongol forces, and King Demetri of Georgia (1272–89) appointed him *atabek* (viceroy) and *amirspasalar* (commander-in-chief) of Georgian forces, posts which had previously belonged to Zak'arian princes.[41] During his eighteen-year rule Tarsayič's principality encompassed all of Siwnik' including the cantons of Vayoc' Jor and Gełark'unik, in which Zak'arian and Xałbakian princes were allowed to hold scattered monasteries and fortresses under Ōrbēlian sovereignty. Like his brother Smbat, Tarsayič

---

excise tax (*tamgha*) imposed upon artisans, and the installation of workshops for them with prescribed wages. These well-intentioned measures, however, failed to bring about any meaningful improvement of the economic, administrative, and fiscal practices in the occupied territories, including the Trans-Caucasus and eastern Armenia. Under Ghazan Khan's immediate successor, these "reforms" were totally ignored, due to the ingrained corruption and unruliness of the Mongol officialdom, as well as the growing weakness of the Ilkhanid central government and the ensuing civil wars (1335–54) that led to the disintegration of the Mongol-Iranian Ilkhanate. *Patmut'yun* (Academy), III, 638–39.

[37] Ōrbēlian, *Patmut'iwn*, 334, 509–23; Ōrbēlian, *Histoire*, I,190, 281–89.

[38] *Tuman*, literally "ten thousand," represented the largest administrative unit within the Mongol army. See W. Barthold, "Tuman," *EI* (Leiden, 1934), s.v. On the Mongol administration of Armenia see *Patmut'yun* (Academy), III, 614–68.

[39] Ōrbēlian, *Patmut'iwn*, 411–12; Ōrbēlian, *Histoire*, I, 231. Awagian and Georgian nobility resisted Smbat's claims by appealing to Arghun, vizir of Transcaucasia, and by resorting to arms. Smbat was compelled to make a second journey to Karakorum in 1256, and on his return it is said that he "ruled over all of his cantons and villages; but later he willingly . . . gave back to others some villages and lands here and there while he established the rest as the ancestral domains of his family and children." Ōrbēlian, *Patmut'iwn*, 405–14; Ōrbēlian, *Histoire*, I, 228–33.

[40] Smbat is said to have aspired to a general restoration of the Armenian kingdom under Ōrbēlian rule, but his death in 1273 prevented the realization of this dream. Grigoryan, *Syunik'ə*, 79.

[41] Step'anos Ōrbēlian, *Žamanakagrut'iwn*, ed. by A. Abrahamyan (Erevan, 1942), 28; Ōrbēlian, *Patmut'iwn*, 426; idem, *Histoire*, I, 238; Grigoryan, *Syunik'ə*, 83–84; *Patmut'yun* (Academy), III, 635.

sponsored the restoration or construction of many ecclesiastical and public buildings.[42]

The ascendancy of Smbat and Tarsayič coincided with the career of Prince P̣roš, the most prominent figure in the history of the Xałbakian family, which after him came to be known as P̣rošian.[43] Youngest son of Vasak I, P̣roš ruled his family domains for sixty years (1224/5–1284), distinguishing himself both in the military and diplomatic service of the Ilkhanid court.[44] Seeking to enhance Xałbakian authority in Vayocʿ Jor and Gełarkʿunikʿ, he attempted to establish an episcopal see independent of the existing bishoprics of Tatʿew and Noravankʿ in the Ōrbēlian principality of Siwnikʿ. This was blocked, however, by Tarsayič and the Catholicos Yakob I Klayecʿi. Tarsayič, moreover, arranged to unify the two existing sees by having his son, the historian Stepʿanos Ōrbēlian, appointed metropolitan bishop of the whole province, consolidating secular and ecclesiastical authority in the Ōrbēlian family.[45] Though he failed in his separatist endeavor, P̣roš nevertheless contributed significantly to monastic centers in his domains, including the monastery of Glajor, which benefited from the patronage of both of the leading families of Siwnikʿ.

Tarsayič's death in 1290 was followed by a three-way struggle among his sons Ēlikum and J̌alal and his nephew Liparit for control of the Ōrbēlian principality. The issue was submitted to the arbitration of Arghun Khan, who ruled in favor of the eldest son, Ēlikum. Nevertheless, Stepʿanos Ōrbēlian tells us that though Ēlikum "gained control of his father's domains and principality, he did not wish to deprive his brother [J̌alal]; rather, in the presence of bishops and vardapets and noblemen, he divided up all his inheritance; he offered an appropriate share to his brother J̌alal, as well as an appropriate share to his cousin [Liparit]."[46] Under Ēlikum III (1290–1300) Siwnikʿ enjoyed relative peace. While other parts of Armenia suffered from the civil strife that followed the murder of Arghun Khan in 1291, Siwnikʿ became a "Noah's ark among earth-shattering waves,"[47] receiving refugees from all sides. Among their number were Stepʿanos, the catholicos of the Albanians, many bishops and vardapets, and members of the nobility.

Ēlikum's son and successor, Prince Burtʿēl, maintained the Ōrbēlian control of Siwnikʿ through a long rule of over four decades (1300–44?). Contemporary sources refer to him as the "great prince of princes of the house of Siwnikʿ"[48] and the "great commander-in-chief of the Armenians and the Georgians,"[49] and it was under his rule that the monastery of Glajor enjoyed its most conspicuous flowering. The U.C.L.A. Gospel, as we shall see below, dates to the first years of the century, some time before 1307 (see Chapter 4). At the same time, it should be pointed out that Ōrbēlian overlordship did not preclude the local rule of other princely families. Thus, in a colophon in Erevan Mat. 9222, written at Glajor in 1334, one reads that the codex was executed "during the principality and lordship throughout the region [of Siwnikʿ] of the great prince Burtʿēl and of his sons Bēškʿēn and Iwanē, and during the lordship in our locality [that is Vayocʿ Jor] of Amir Hasan and J̌umay, grandsons of the great P̣roš."[50]

Nevertheless, while this was a period of prosperity in Siwnikʿ, ominous signs of the fragility of this prosperity were already appearing. The conversion of Ghazan Khan to Islam in 1295 gave the signal for mass conversions of his countrymen and ushered in a period of new troubles for the Christian populations. Particularly under his successors Oldjaitu (1304–16) and Abu Saʿid (1316–35), colophon evidence points to specifically anti-Christian measures and destruction of church property. A scribe in Ałtʿamar in 1307 notes the mass conversion of Mongols to Islam and adds: "They harass all the Christians to convert to their false hope; some they molest, some they torture, some they kill, and they confiscate the possessions of others. Not contented with all this, they also levied taxes upon all the Christians and made them wear symbols of opprobrium, a black linen over the shoulders, so that whoever saw them would recognize that they are Christians and would curse them."[51]

The practice of compelling Christians to wear distinctive symbols is frequently attested in the colo-

[42] Ōrbēlian, *Patmutʿiwn,* 416–18, 420, 424–25; idem, *Histoire,* I,233–34.

[43] For the most authoritative study of this family, consult Yovsēpʿian, *Xałbakeankʿ* (2nd printing, Antilias, 1969). The career of Prince P̣roš I is discussed, ibid., 45–71. See also Dédéyan, *Histoire des Arméniens,* 300, 381.

[44] *Patmutʿyun* (Academy), III, 619.

[45] Ōrbēlian, *Patmutʿiwn,* 364–66, 477–80; idem, *Histoire,* I, 206–7, 264–65; Yovsēpʿian, *Xałbakeankʿ*, 50, 254; Dédéyan, *Histoire des Arméniens,* 381–82.

[46] Ōrbēlian, *Patmutʿiwn,* 430–31; idem, *Histoire,* I, 240. On the dispute for the succession, see G. Yovsēpʿian, "Tarsayič Ōrbēliani ew Mina Xatʿuni Serundə," in *Hask Hayagitakan Taregirkʿ* I (1948), 9.

[47] Ōrbēlian, *Patmutʿiwn,* 431–32; idem, *Histoire,* I, 240.

[48] Erevan, Mat. 9222; Xačʿikyan, *XIV Dari,* 182.

[49] Xačʿikyan, *XIV Dari,* 297.

[50] Xačʿikyan, *XIV Dari,* 261.

[51] Erevan, Mat. 4881; Xačʿikyan, *XIV Dari,* 47; A. Sanjian, *Colophons of Armenian Manuscripts, 1301–1480* (Cambridge, Mass., 1969), 52–53.

phons.[52] A scribe in Glajor in 1313 remarks that Oldjaitu had extended his taxes to include nobility,[53] and in the following year another scribe in Glajor observes that taxes even extended to children a month old.[54] Scattered notices occur of the destruction of churches, as in Erzurum in 1314,[55] or the looting of monasteries, as in Varag near Van in 1318.[56] Yet the exempt status of the clergy was still generally observed; the same scribe who tells of the looting of the churches in Varag relates that taxes had been collected from the clergy "without the specific instructions of the khan. Hence the thrice-blessed pontiff Zakʿaria [I of Ałtʿamar] went to see the khan in Babelon [i.e., Baghdad] and spent a whole year there, and, obtaining an *ar̄lex* [official decree] from him, secured for the monks and priests exemption from taxation."[57]

But worse was yet to come, for after the death of Abu Saʿid Khan (1335) there followed a twenty-year period of civil wars among the Mongol princes, who vied with one another for the Ilkhanid throne. "There is anarchy, because the princes are mutineers and agitators, and they have risen against one another," relates a scribe at Aławnicʿ (exact location unknown) in 1340.[58] The monastery of Glajor falls into abrupt decline in the 1340s (see Chapter 4), and colophons record more frequently the sacking of churches and monasteries. A scribe in Siwnikʿ mentions the closing of unspecified churches in 1336,[59] and another in Mənžənkert near Erzurum the destruction of numerous churches and monasteries in the same year.[60] A decade later a scribe in Baberd, near Erzurum, saw priests so destitute that they were reduced to begging.[61] To this picture of general disorder must be added the devastation of natural disasters. A scribe records that following the death of Prince Burtʿēl of Siwnikʿ "there occurred a severe famine and one third of the inhabitants of Armenia fell victim to it; and after the famine lifted, God's wrath fell upon us, and there occurred a plague in all the land which took away half of the people."[62]

Ilkhanid rule collapsed in civil strife with the death of the last Ilkhan, Nūshirvān, in 1353. Transcaucasia in the second half of the fourteenth century became an arena of conflict between the Čobanid and Jalaʿrid tribes, and the dynastic families of Armenia saw a continued erosion of their power. In the 1350s the Zakʿarian family, which still controlled the regions of Ani and Bǰni, lost its last territories.[63] After the death of Prince Burtʿēl Ōrbēlian his family continued to control a number of districts in Siwnikʿ, but their authority was gradually restricted to limited family estates, and the same could be said of the Pṙošian holdings in Vayocʿ Jor and Gełarkʿunikʿ. In 1385 the forces of Tokhtamish Khan of the White Horde entered Siwnikʿ and, according to the contemporary historian Tʿovma Mecopʿecʿi, they "pillaged its twelve cantons and slaughtered many and carried off others into captivity;"[64] they took the Ōrbēlian fortress of Orotan and the traditional Ōrbēlian Ełegis and Vayocʿ Jor. Tamerlane's invasion the following year destroyed the Pṙošian hold on Šahaponkʿ and the Dopʿian control in southern Siwnikʿ.[65] Their authority destroyed, many of the nobility emigrated, especially to Georgia and the Crimea.

3. Ecclesiastical Patronage in Siwnikʿ

The relative political tranquility that prevailed in Siwnikʿ in the late thirteenth and early fourteenth centuries attracted to that province a migration of monks and scholars from other parts of Armenia, and the canton of Vayocʿ Jor emerged as the principal Armenian center of intellectual, literary, and artistic activity in this period.[66] Under the patronage of the Ōrbēlian and Pṙošian families the growth of monastic institutions assumed large-scale proportions. The princes and members of their families not only constructed religious edifices and educational centers; they also endowed them with lands, properties, and financial resources, as well as all kinds of precious gifts. As noted earlier, the Ōrbēlian prince Smbat (1249/50–73) secured from Mangu Khan edicts whereby properties previously confiscated from the religious institutions were restored to them and the

52 Xačʿikyan, *XIV Dari,* 46, 47, 48, 138–39, 268; Sanjian, *Colophons,* 52, 52–53, 53, 72–73.
53 Erevan, Mat. 7842, fols. 335v–336; Xačʿikyan, *XIV Dari,* 92; Sanjian, *Colophons,* 57.
54 Xačʿikyan, *XIV Dari,* 104; Sanjian, *Colophons,* 58.
55 Xačʿikyan, *XIV Dari,* 101–2; Sanjian, *Colophons,* 58.
56 Xačʿikyan, *XIV Dari,* 138–39; Sanjian, *Colophons,* 60.
57 Xačʿikyan, *XIV Dari,* 138–39; Sanjian, *Colophons,* 60.
58 Xačʿikyan, *XIV Dari,* 324; Sanjian, *Colophons,* 82.
59 Erevan, Mat. 6257, fol. 268; Xačʿikyan, *XIV Dari,* 281; Sanjian, *Colophons,* 76.
60 Erevan, Mat. 5734, fol. 335; Xačʿikyan, *XIV Dari,* 285; Sanjian, *Colophons,* 77.
61 Xačʿikyan, *XIV Dari,* 346; Sanjian, *Colophons,* 85.
62 Xačʿikyan, *XIV Dari,* 375; Sanjian, *Colophons,* 87.

63 Ališan, *Ayrarat,* 112.
64 Tʿovma Mecopʿecʿi, *Patmutʿiwn Lank-Tʿamuray ew Yaǰordacʿ Iwrocʿ* (Paris, 1860), 12, 98.
65 *Patmutʿyun* (Academy), IV, 23–25.
66 For the cultural history of Armenia in the twelfth to the fourteenth centuries see *Patmutʿyun* (Academy), III, 789–971.

clergy and their holdings were exempted from taxation.[67] His brother, Prince Tarsayič I (1273–90), likewise secured tax-exempt status for more than 150 monasteries in Siwnikʿ.[68] In view of the fact that private properties were much more vulnerable to taxation and arbitrary confiscation under the Mongols, it became customary for the nobility to safeguard their holdings by offering them, either temporarily or in perpetuity, to the monastic institutions, whose tax-exempt status was, in the main, honored by the conquerors. These property grants included villages, farms, orchards, windmills, and so forth, as attested by numerous inscriptions, and the transactions entailed securing of official edicts from the Mongol khans. The transfer of property ownership was frequently inscribed upon the walls of the churches in the presence of witnesses, the text of the inscription emphasizing that the grant had been made "free from all tax obligations."[69] Legally all such transactions were made to the monastic institutions as gifts in perpetuity, and no one except the abbot had the right to alienate such property.[70] Yet there are not a few instances in which members of the feudal families became clerics and assumed the abbacy of the monasteries to which they had transferred their estates. Such abbots became known as *paron-tēr* (literally "baron-lord"), for they were simultaneously secular princes and spiritual leaders. The metropolitan bishops of Siwnikʿ and many of the abbots of Vayocʿ Jor held the title of *paron-tēr*.[71]

The Prošian family domains were located principally in the cantons of Gełarkʿunikʿ and Vayocʿ Jor, and it is here that the benefits of their patronage were most apparent. The Prošians had their seat in the town of Srkłunkʿ (also known as Baškʿend and now called Vernašen) and in the nearby fortress of Boloraberd (also known as Prošaberd) in Vajocʿ Jor. The ruins of their palace and of two churches in Srkłunkʿ are mentioned in literary sources, but today there are no traces of these structures.[72]

Prošian patronage of monastic institutions has been reviewed by G. Yovsēpʿian in his history of the family. Their oldest religious center was the monastery of Kečʿaṙuykʿ in Gełarkʿunikʿ, which had previously belonged to the Pahlawuni princely family and which had been the second seat of the bishopric of Bǰni.[73] The Prošians' second major religious center was Ayrivankʿ, also known as Gełard. This ancient monastery had previously belonged to Prince Awag of the Zakʿarian family; it was purchased from him in the 1240s by Prince Proš I as a burial site for the members of his family. The monastery enjoyed its most prosperous period under the Prošians. Its major church had been built in 1215 during the rule of the *atabek* Iwanē and the *amirspasalar* Zakʿarē, the founders of the Zakʿarian principality, but the two rock-hewn churches were commissioned by Prince Proš I in the 1260s and 1270s and the large rock-hewn *žamatun* was completed by Prince Papakʿ I in 1288.[74] Not far from Ayrivankʿ/Gełard is the monastery of Ałǰocʿ Surb Stepʿanos, built in 1217 by the Prōšian Prince Grigor and his wife Zaz; its church of Saints Peter and Paul was constructed under their son Prince Vasak.[75]

Also closely associated with the Prošians is the monastery of Tʿanahat, just southeast of the family seat in Srkłunkʿ. According to Stepʿanos Ōrbēlian, this monastery existed as early as 735, when Stepʿanos Siwnecʿi was buried there,[76] but the fragmentary inscription in the present church of Surb Stepʿanos attests that it was constructed "during the rule of the valiant and illustrious prince Proš and his sons Papakʿ, Hasan, and the child Ēačʿi."[77] According to the inscription, the clergy were to celebrate the divine liturgy three times a year for Prince Proš. Although the date is missing in the inscription, literary sources put the construction in 1273–79.[78] Other inscriptions dated between 1284 and 1292, moreover, show that extensive lands, farms, and orchards were offered to the monastery of Tʿanahat by individuals named Xutʿlubēk, Sančar and his wife Tačmlekʿ, Utar and his wife Gurčik, and Prince Proš's daughter-in-law Tʿačer. It should be noted that members of the Ōrbēlian family as well, such as Prince Smbat, his brother Pʿaxradawla, and Smbat's son and daughter-in-law Pena and Susa, had also offered a number of properties to Tʿanahat.[79] The Prošians were also patrons of the monasteries of Kukʿi and Ocop (or Acop)

[67] See above, p. 12.

[68] See above, pp. 12–13.

[69] See, for instance, S. G. Barxudaryan, *Divan Hay Vimagrutʿyan* (Erevan, 1967), III, 55, and IV, 33.

[70] The detailed study of this system will be found in G. M. Grigoryan, *Syunikʿi Vanakan Kalvacatirutʿyunə IX–XIII Darerum* (Erevan, 1973); see also a summary discussion in Grigoryan, *Syunikʿə*, 139–40.

[71] See *Patmutʿyun* (Academy), IV, 66.

[72] See Barxudaryan, *Divan*, III, 93.

[73] The architectural monuments at Kečʿaṙoykʿ are described in detail in Yovsēpʿian, *Xałbakeankʿ*, 157–80.

[74] For detailed descriptions of these monuments, see Yovsēpʿian, *Xałbakeankʿ*, 181–223.

[75] Yovsēpʿian, *Xałbakeankʿ*, 224–34.

[76] Ōrbēlian, *Patmutʿiwn*, 139–43; idem, *Histoire*, I, 85–87.

[77] See Barxudaryan, *Divan*, III, 74.

[78] For details concerning this monastery's monuments, consult Yovsēpʿian, *Xałbakeankʿ*, 60–62, 235–43.

[79] For the descriptions attesting to these and other property grants, consult Barxudaryan, *Divan*, III, 71–92.

in the valley of Šahaponkʿ; the first of these was built by the Přošian Prince Papakʿ.[80]

Přošian patronage of Glajor and its famous school will be discussed separately,[81] but the family also sponsored another monastery in the region, with a school that rose to prominence after the decline of Glajor, namely Spitakawor Astuacacin. The church was built in 1321 by Prince Amir Hasan II, and is notable for its reliefs of the donor and of his father, now in the Historical Museum of Erevan.[82]

In the southern region of Vayocʿ Jor the Přošians were responsible for several other ecclesiastical institutions. It was at their urging that a certain individual named Martiros, son of Dełka, founded the village of Martiros in 1283. Three years later, the vardapet Mattʿēos built the rock-hewn church of Surb Astuacacin, whose inscription attests that it was constructed "during the rule of the prince of princes Přoš, of his sons Papakʿ and Hasan, of the [latter's] son Ēačʿi and his mother Tʿačer.[83] Similarly, the churches and chapels in the village of Gomkʿ were constructed in 1263 under the aegis of the Přošian princes. Two of the inscriptions mention the name of Přoš I as ruler of the region,[84] and a third inscription indicates that certain properties were offered to the monastery by Prince Hasan, son of Papakʿ.[85]

In general it might be said that Přošian patronage was stronger to the north, while the patronage of the Ōrbēlian family was stronger to the south, but their spheres of influence interlocked and overlapped. The family seat of the Ōrbēlians was situated in the ancient village of Arpʿa from the time of the founder of the Ōrbēlian principality, Liparit I (ca. 1187–1225), and in the center of Vayocʿ Jor their interests concentrated in the Arpʿa, the Ełegis, and the Herher river valleys. At the urging of Prince Tarsayič (1273–90), Bishop Sargis of Noravankʿ built a bridge over the Arpʿa River, remnants of which have survived to this day.[86] The church of Surb Astuacacin in Noravankʿ was sponsored by the metropolitan archbishop of Siwnikʿ, Yovhannēs-Awrpel of the Ōrbēlian family, in 1321; its architect was Momik, who is known as a painter and sculptor as well.[87] After the Ōrbēlians acquired the town of Ełegis they transferred their family seat there, and the princes Smbat (1249/50–73) and Tarsayič I (1273–90) built a magnificent palace there.[88] The grandson of the latter, metropolitan bishop of Siwnikʿ Stepʿanos Tarsayič I, erected the church of Surb Zoracʿ in Ełegis,[89] and the family's burial site was located on the western outskirts of the town.[90]

The records indicate that the monastery of Cʿałacʿkʿar, in the valley of Ełegis, received extensive properties from members of the Ōrbēlian family,[91] particularly during the incumbency of Yovhannēs-Awrpel as metropolitan bishop of Siwnikʿ.[92] The ancient monastery of Aratēs in the same valley was also the beneficiary of the Ōrbēlians' munificence. Its three churches were restored in 1270, and a *gawitʿ* (narthex) was added under Smbat and Tarsayičʿ I.[93] Toward the end of the century Stepʿanos Ōrbēlian restored the buildings again and offered the monastery eight villages in Gełarkʿunikʿ that were his personal domain.[94] In the valley of the Herher river the monastery of Hermon enjoyed a special flourishing under Prince Burtʿēl I (1300–ca. 1344), during which period it was sponsored by the Šahřuni princes, who were the *asparapet*s (cavalry commanders) of the Ōrbēlians.[95] Smbat, son of Liparit Ōrbēlian, made extensive gifts to the monastery in 1317.[96]

The most important religious center of the Ōrbēlians, however, was located in the southern part of Vayocʿ Jor, at the monastery of Noravankʿ. All of the monastery's four churches, its two-storied mausoleum, and its *žamatun* were constructed by the Ōrbēlians.[97] The church of Surb Karapet, completed in 1221, was built by Prince Liparit I.[98] The consecration of the church, which was held two years later, was attended by "bishops, vardapets, prominent princes, noblemen, and householders, among them the great Bupak," who offered it several villages and farms that

[80] For additional data on these two monasteries, see Yovsēpʿian, *Xałbakeankʿ*, 75, 244–50.

[81] See below, pp. 22 and 62.

[82] Barxudaryan, *Divan*, III, 94–95; Yovsēpʿian, *Xałbakeankʿ*, 106–20; for the reliefs see N. Stepʿanyan, *Dekorativnoe Iskusstvo Srednevekovoi Armenii* (Erevan, 1971), 45–46 and pl. 140; and Der Nersessian, *Armenian Art*, 190 and pl. 147.

[83] Barxudaryan, *Divan*, III, 180.

[84] Barxudaryan, *Divan*, III, 192–93.

[85] Barxudaryan, *Divan*, III, 193.

[86] Barxudaryan, *Divan*, III, 28.

[87] Barxudaryan, *Divan*, III, 29. On Momik, see Der Nersessian, *Armenian Art*, 181–82, 187, 195–96.

[88] For the inscriptions see Barxudaryan, *Divan*, III, 115.

[89] Barxudaryan, *Divan*, III, 108.

[90] Barxudaryan, *Divan*, III, 105.

[91] Barxudaryan, *Divan*, III, 148–50.

[92] Barxudaryan, *Divan*, III, 144, 150, 152–53.

[93] Barxudaryan, *Divan*, III, 124.

[94] Ōrbēlian, *Patmutʿiwn*, 493–4; idem, *Histoire*, I, 271; Barxudaryan, *Divan*, III, 125.

[95] Barxudaryan, *Divan*, III, 58.

[96] Barxudaryan, *Divan*, III, 55.

[97] Ōrbēlian, *Patmutʿiwn*, 354–68; idem, *Histoire*, I, 207–8.

[98] See the text of the inscription in Barxudaryan, *Divan*, III, 211.

had been part of his domains.[99] The church's *žamatun* was constructed in 1261 by Prince Smbat Ōrbēlian; on the same occasion he offered to Noravankʿ the villages of Awēš, Anapat, and Azat, as well as the orchards of Akoṙi, Hołocʿmacʿ, Čʿowoy, Arpʿa, and Amałvajor.[100] The monastery also received extensive properties from the domains of the Mahewanian princely family.[101] In 1275 Prince Tarsayič I built the chapel of Surb Grigor, which henceforth became the mausoleum of many of the Ōrbēlian princes, at the site where his brother, Prince Smbat, had been buried.[102] During Tarsayič I's rule, Bishop Sargis constructed the monastery's hostel.[103] The institution enjoyed its most prosperous period during the tenure of Stepʿanos Ōrbēlian as metropolitan bishop of Siwnikʿ, with his seat at Noravankʿ. Under the stewardship of this *paron-tēr,* the institution acquired extensive properties through donations and purchases.[104] Moreover, Stepʿanos himself bought the village Čʿoway and its environs from his brother, Prince Jalal, and, together with the villages of Abasašēn and Surb Sahak that were part of his own feudal domains, donated them to Noravankʿ.[105] Finally, the monastery's architectural masterpiece, the double-tiered church of Surb Astuacacin designed by Momik, was built in 1339 by Prince Burtʿēl I, the last prominent member of the Ōrbēlian family.[106]

The southern regions of the province of Siwnikʿ, comprising the cantons of Haband, Cłuk, Jorkʿ, and parts of Kʿašunikʿ and Kovsakan (now called the regions of Goris, Sisian, and Łapʿan, respectively), were also an integral part of the Ōrbēlian domains. The principal institutions that enjoyed this family's patronage were the monasteries of Tatʿew, Darabas, and Vaładn (also called Orotnavankʿ). One of the two episcopal seats in Siwnikʿ under Stepʿanos Oṙbēlian, the monastery of Tatʿew benefited the most from the Ōrbēlian family's benefactions. In 1274, for instance, Prince Tarsayič I not only furnished the large church of Tatʿew "with beautiful vessels and vestments"; he also awarded to the institution six villages that had previously belonged to it.[107] Moreover, in 1297 Stepʿanos Ōrbēlian himself rebuilt, at his own expense, the monastery's church of Surb Grigor Lusaworičʿ; in addition, he offered to the institution the village of Arit, which his brother Prince Ēlikum III had granted to him after Arghun Khan recognized the former as chief prince of the Ōrbēlian domains.[108] That the monastery of Tatʿew was one of the largest feudal institutions at this time is attested by the fact that 678 villages throughout Siwnikʿ either belonged to or paid tribute to it.[109] After the demise of Glajor, the school of Tatʿew, particularly under the leadership of Yovhan Orotnecʿi and Grigor Tatʿewacʿi, became the most prominent intellectual center in medieval Armenia.

Finally, inscriptions indicate that in 1272 Prince Tarsayič I and his wife Mamaxatʿun built the church of Surb Astuacacin in the village of Darabas; he also offered several parcels of land to it.[110] The same prince also restored the church of Surb Stepʿanos at the monastery of Vaładn.[111]

In their patronage of monastic institutions in the thirteenth and fourteenth centuries the Ōrbēlian and Pṙošian families continued a millennial tradition of church support by the Armenian nobility. The art-historical implications of this two-family patronage have been sketched by Der Nersessian,[112] and more will be said on the subject in connection with the two ateliers responsible for the U.C.L.A. Gospel. How that patronage affected the founding and growth of the monastery of Glajor is the next problem.

4. The Monastery and School of Glajor

Much of the history of the monastery and school of Glajor is still shrouded in mystery. Considerable scholarly controversy surrounds the very fundamental issues of the location of Glajor, the date and circumstances of its founding, and the nature of the studies pursued at its school. The question of the cur-

[99] See Ōrbēlian, *Patmutʿiwn,* 356–58; idem, *Histoire,* I, 203–4.

[100] Ōrbēlian, *Patmutʿiwn,* 363–64; idem, *Histoire,* I, 205–6.

[101] Ōrbēlian, *Patmutʿiwn,* 366–67; idem, *Histoire,* I, 207.

[102] See the text of the inscription in Barxudaryan, *Divan,* III, 234.

[103] Barxudaryan, *Divan,* III, 246.

[104] For details see Ōrbēlian, *Patmutʿiwn,* 490–92; idem, *Histoire,* I, 270–71.

[105] Ōrbēlian, *Patmutʿiwn,* 492–96; idem, *Histoire,* I, 271–72.

[106] See the text of the inscription in Barxudaryan, *Divan,* III, 240.

[107] See Ōrbēlian, *Patmutʿiwn,* 416–18; idem, *Histoire,* I, 233–34.

[108] Ōrbēlian, *Patmutʿiwn,* 483–85; idem, *Histoire,* I, 267. See also Barxudaryan, *Divan,* II, 25.

[109] The list of these villages will be found in Ōrbēlian, *Patmutʿiwn,* 509–23; idem, *Histoire,* I, 281–89.

[110] See Barxudaryan, *Divan,* II, 114.

[111] Barxudaryan, *Divan,* II, 102.

[112] Der Nersessian, "L'Évangile du Matenadaran no. 10.525 de l'an 1306: Contribution à l'étude de la miniature en Siwnikʿ au XIVe siècle," *REArm,* n.s. 16 (1982), 337–39; Der Nersessian, *Armenian Art,* 163–225.

riculum of studies at Glajor has been discussed with special passion by those who would like to find in the school close parallels to the medieval university system in Western Europe. Each of these issues must be taken up in turn, while at the same time some sketch of the history of Glajor must be attempted. The picture that emerges of the monastery and its intellectual pursuits is essential background to the understanding of the iconography of the U.C.L.A. Gospel and other manuscripts belonging to that tradition.

The canton of Vayocʿ Jor (previously known as Daralageaz, and now comprising the regions of Ełegnajor and Azizbekov in Soviet Armenia) is a veritable museum of medieval architectural monuments which, relatively speaking, have been spared the ravages of conquerors and marauders. Indeed, many of the canton's monasteries, churches, schools, and secular structures belong to the thirteenth and fourteenth centuries, that is, the heyday of the Ōrbēlian and Xałbakian princely families. The region's relative safety is attributable to several factors. Its valleys were protected by a chain of lofty mountains, and its link to the outside world was by means of deep gorges and passes that were difficult to traverse. Vayocʿ Jor never developed large cities that would have attracted the rapacity of conquerors. Nevertheless, the exact site of Glajor remains uncertain (see Map 2). The name of Glajor (which is variously spelled Gaylajor, Gaylejor, Gaylijor, Gaylujor, Galijor, Galoy Jor, and Galu Jor) probably means etymologically "the valley of the wolf." Part of the problem in locating the site is that occasionally it is referred to by another name, Ałbercʿ, which means "of the springs." This designation for Glajor is used in the colophons of six manuscripts written between 1284 and 1328;[113] moreover, in two of the manuscripts the scribes leave no doubt about the identity of the two toponyms, remarking that the work was done at "Glajor, which is called the monastery of Ałbercʿ."[114] Ałbercʿ is evidently a nickname or a popular designation for Glajor.

The commonest theory on the localization of Glajor is that proposed at the beginning of the century by Eruand Lalayan, who identified Glajor with a medieval site called Tʿanahat, which is found a few miles northeast of the village of Ōrtʿakʿend.[115] In 1970 a team of archaeologists from the University of Erevan, under the direction of I. Łaribyan, conducted excavations at Tʿanahat and claimed to have found evidence for its identification with Glajor.[116] Within the monastic compound the team uncovered the ruins of many structures which, they maintained, must have supported the needs of a large academic institution. Łaribyan proposed that the main church, which was erected in 1215, was turned into a school hall in 1273–79, when the new church of Surb Stepʿanos was built.[117] The archaeologists also claimed to have found the tombs of three of the principal figures of Glajor, Nersēs Mšecʿi, Esayi Nčʿecʿi, and Dawitʿ Sasnecʿi.[118] Łaribyan also cites in support of his position a colophon of 1284 in which the scribe Mattʿēos Kilikecʿi relates that he came to Vayocʿ Jor, "near the tomb of Siwnecʿi, in the monastery of Ałbercʿ Vank, the glorious second Athens," to study with Nersēs Mšecʿi, who was a vardapet at Glajor.[119] The names Glajor and Ałbercʿ, according to Łaribyan, were secondary or nicknames for the monastery; its formal name was Tʿanahat. Hence, he continues, Stepʿanos Ōrbēlian, who studied with Nersēs Mšecʿi, does not mention either Glajor or Ałbercʿ in his list of monasteries, but he does mention Tʿanahat.[120]

Other scholars have endorsed the identification of Glajor with Tʿanahat for the same or similar reasons. A. N. Avetisyan has suggested that the monastery, which was earlier known as Tʿanahat, acquired the name of Glajor during the rectorship of Nersēs Mšecʿi who named the monastery Glajor after a monastery in his home town called Glajor.[121] A. G. Abra-

[113] See New Julfa ms. 373 in Smbat Tēr-Awetisian, *Cʿucʿak Hayerēn Jeṙagracʿ Nor Jułayi Amenapʿrkičʿ Vankʿi,* I (Vienna, 1970), 567–69; Vienna Mekhitarist 382 in Y. Tašian, *Cʿucʿak Hayerēn Jeṙagracʿ Matenadaranin Mxitʿareancʿ i Vienna* (Vienna, 1895), I, 833–35; Erevan, Matenadaran 1409 in Eganyan, *Cʿucʿak Jeṙagracʿ Maštocʿi Anvan Matenadarani,* vol. I, col. 545. There are also three mss. whose locations are unknown: Ališan, *Sisakan,* 131; Yovsēpʿian, *Xałbakeankʿ,* 274–75, 350–51.

[114] See Ališan, *Hayapatum,* 525; Yovsēpʿian, *Xałbakeankʿ,* 274–75, 350–51.

[115] Eruand Lalayan, "Šarur-Daralageazi Gawaṙ. I Masn, Vayocʿ-Jor kam Daralageaz," in *Azgagrakan Handēs,* vol. 12 (Tiflis, 1904–5), 267, 271.

[116] I. Łaribyan, "Glajori Hamalsarani Pełumnerə," in *Banber Erevani Hamalsarani* 2 (1971), 251–60. The complete report was published in I. Łaribyan, *Glajor* (Erevan, 1983).

[117] Łaribyan, "Glajori Hamalsarani Pełumnerə," 257.

[118] Łaribyan, "Glajori Hamalsarani Pełumnerə," 257–60.

[119] The text of this colophon will be found in Yovsēpʿian, *Xałbakeankʿ,* 259; Tašian, *Cʿucʿak Hayerēn Jeṙagracʿ,* 1039; Ališan, *Sisakan,* 130.

[120] Łaribyan, "Glajori Hamalsarani Pełumnerə," 260.

[121] See A. N. Avetisyan, *Haykakan Manrankarčʿutʿyan Glajori Dprocʿə* (Erevan, 1971), 11–17. Avetisyan has provided no documentation for his conjecture. The same is true of Xačeryan, whose assertion of this is even more emphatic; see *Glajori Hamalsaranə Hay Mankavaržakan Mktʿi Zargacʿman Mēǰ, XIII–XIV Darerum* (Erevan, 1973), 45–49. A. Matʿevosyan remarks that there is a colophon indicating that a ms. had indeed been written in 1521 "in the canton of Taron, in the monastery of Glajor, at the church of Surb Aṙakʿelocʿ," but he too fails to cite his source. In any event, Matʿevosyan argues that this is the only source attesting that the monastery at Muš was also called Glajor. He not only rejects Xačʿeryan's assertion that Nersēs Mšecʿi and his pupils, who came from the monastery of Surb Aṙakʿelocʿ to

2. Map of the Province of Siwnikʿ ca. 1300

hamyan expresses himself in full agreement with Łaribyan's view and reiterates many of his archaeological arguments.[122] At the same time, he adds a misrepresentation of his own, contending that "most of the extant manuscripts of Glajor clearly indicate that the university of Glajor operated under the aegis of the monastery of Surb Step'anos at T'anahat."[123] But in point of fact, none of the manuscripts of Glajor ever mention T'anahat. Another scholar, P'aylak Ant'abyan, is also in general agreement with the conclusions of the archaeologists.[124]

Nevertheless, the archaeological evidence is far from compelling. Levon Xač'eryan has accused Łaribyan of excessive haste in his excavation; none of the tombstones found at T'anahat, he points out, actually belonged to figures associated with the school of Glajor. While he proposes no exact location for Glajor, Xač'eryan makes the important observation that subsequent to the death of Esayi Nč'ec'i in 1338 sources referring to Glajor virtually cease, whereas references to T'anahat continue for another century and a half.[125] The epigrapher S. G. Barxudaryan, editor of several volumes in the series *Corpus Inscriptionum Armeniacarum,* has also declared the identification of Glajor as T'anahat unsubstantiated.[126] Neither inscriptions nor colophons, he observes, ever refer to T'anahat by any other name; only in modern times did the local Turkish villagers start referring to it as Karavank'. Further, none of the inscriptions from T'anahat refer to Glajor and none of the tombstones name any figures connected with Glajor. On the other hand, manuscripts from Glajor name their place of origin as Glajor and/or Ałberc', but never T'anahat. To these arguments G. Grigoryan adds another, based on the self-evident meaning of the toponym Ałberc'.[127] Genitive plural of *ałbiwr,* "spring" or "brook," the name implies that the monastery was built in a location abundant with springs; but there are no springs on the slopes of T'anahat.

If one turns to the historical sources, the identification of Glajor with T'anahat misrepresents the meaning of a number of texts. Part of the confusion arises over the existence of a church of Surb Step'anos in both monasteries. However, A. Mat'evosyan has shown that they were dedicated to two different saints.[128] Step'anos Ōrbēlian testifies that the church of T'anahat was dedicated to the eighth-century bishop Step'anos Siwnec'i and that it was rebuilt on a larger scale in 1279.[129] The church of Glajor, however, was dedicated to Surb Step'anos Naxavkay, that is, St. Stephen the Protomartyr, as witnessed by three colophons.[130]

The oldest historical reference to Glajor appears in the *Ašxarhac'oyc'* by Vardan Arewelc'i, and the full significance of the text has not been appreciated. The text survives in two versions as follows:

> Vayoc' Jor is the valley of Ełegec', where is found the life-giving Holy Cross; and Galoy Jor, where is found the seat and the school [*varžaran*] of our holy vardapets; and the mountain in the region called Holy Sion, and at the summit of the mountain the monastery of the hermit Noy. There also are the most sacred relics of the lord Step'anos of Siwnik' interred in the monastery of T'anahat.[131]
>
> Vayoc' Jor is the valley of Ełegec', where is found the life-giving Holy Cross and the monastery of Hermon; and there also are the relics of the lord Step'anos of Siwnik' in the monastery of T'anahat. And Galu Jor, where is found the seat and the school of our holy vardapets.[132]

It is evident that the author, in both versions, meant to offer an enumeration of the various sites along the valley of Ełegec' in Vayoc' Jor; both Glajor and T'anahat were found in the same valley but they are by no means identified. It is in this way that the colophon of Matt'ēos Kilikec'i should also be interpreted.[133] Equally important is the early date of the document, for the *Ašxarhac'oyc'* of Vardan must date before his

Vayoc' Jor, named their school Glajor after their former institution; rather he conjectures that in the early sixteenth century the monks of Surb Aṙak'eloc' may have nicknamed it Glajor in memory of their predecessors who founded an eminent school in Vayoc' Jor, or they may have founded a separate school by that name which had a brief lifespan. (Artašes Mat'evosyan, "Hiravi, Erb ev Orteł ē Himnadrvel Glajori Hamalsaranə," *Garun* 7 [1980], 58–59.)

[122] A. G. Abrahamyan, "Glajori Hamalsarani Telə ev Himnadrut'yan Taret'ivə," *Patma-Banasirakan Handes* 1 (1982), 159–76. The same article also appeared in *Garun* (September 1978), 76–84.

[123] Abrahamyan, 163–65. The colophons he has cited are from Xač'ikyan, *XIV Dari,* 96, 261. See also L. G. Minasian, *C'uc'ak Jeṙagrac' Nor-Jułayi S. Amenap'rkč'ean Vanac' T'angarani,* II (Vienna, 1972), 177; Norayr Połarian, *Mayr C'uc'ak Jeṙagrac' Srboc' Yakobeanc',* V (Jerusalem, 1971), 71–73.

[124] P'aylak Ant'abyan, "Ardyok' Hay Aṙajin Hamalsaranə Glajorn ē," *Banber Erevani Matenadarani* 2 (1974), 200–203.

[125] Xač'eryan, *Glajori Hamalsaranə,* 15–18. The single exception is a manuscript executed in Glajor in 1346, Erevan, Mat. 2187. See Appendix C, no. 23.

[126] Barxudaryan, *Divan,* III, 71–73.

[127] Grigoryan, *Syunik'ə,* 158–59.

[128] Mat'evosyan, "Hiravi, Erb ev Orteł ē Himnadrvel Glajori Hamalsaranə," 55–59.

[129] Ōrbēlian, *Patmut'iwn,* 131–44; idem, *Histoire,* I, 81–88.

[130] Xač'ikyan, *XIV Dari,* 92, 261, 351.

[131] Vardan Arewelc'i, *Ašxarhac'oyc' Vardanay Vardapeti,* critical edition by Hayk Pērpērian (Paris, 1960), 15.

[132] Ibid., 31–32.

[133] See above, p. 18.

death in 1269 or 1271.[134] Since the document refers explicitly to the "school (*varžaran*) of our holy vardapets," the school must have existed some time before the arrival of Nersēs Mšecʻi, who is usually credited with founding the school in 1280 or 1282.[135]

Finally, the fact that the historian Stepʻanos Ōrbēlian who studied at Glajor failed to mention either Glajor or Ałbercʻ in his list of the monasteries of the area is by no means an argument for identifying Glajor with Tʻanahat. G. Grigoryan has offered a much more plausible explanation.[136] He argues that in the 1270s and 1280s the Ōrbēlians and Pṙošians were engaged in a struggle for political supremacy in the province of Siwnikʻ, culminating in Prince Pṙoš I's abortive attempt to establish within his domains in Vayocʻ Jor an episcopal seat independent of those at Tatʻew and Noravankʻ, which were located in the Ōrbēlian family's domains. Not only did the Ōrbēlian Prince Tarsayič I prevent this apparent encroachment upon his family's authority; he also managed to have his own son, Stepʻanos Ōrbēlian, proclaimed as the sole metropolitan bishop of Siwnikʻ after the unification of the episcopal sees of Tatʻew and Noravankʻ into a single hierarchy. Under these circumstances, therefore, Grigoryan argues, Stepʻanos Ōrbēlian's failure to mention Ałbercʻ/Glajor must have been a deliberate omission, because he did not wish to give credit to the Pṙošians for their role in the establishment of the school of Glajor. In support of this view, one must also point out that, in connection with the construction of the church of Surb Stepʻanos at Tʻanahat in the years 1273–79, Stepʻanos Ōrbēlian again failed to record the fact that the edifice had been built by Prince Pṙoš I and his sons, even though this event had occurred during his lifetime.

Concerning the location of Glajor, then, neither historical nor archaeological sources provide exact information. It is clear that it was located in the Ełegecʻ valley. The most likely site suggested so far is a ruined monastery some four kilometers southeast of the ancient village of Ełegis, which on account of the presence of springs in the area would well deserve the appellation Ałbercʻ, as suggested by Grigoryan.[137]

Much of the history of Glajor revolves around the careers of two vardapets, and it was their instruction that determined the intellectual character of the school of Glajor. The first was Nersēs Mšecʻi, whose biography has survived in two versions. One version, found in the Armenian Menologium for the 6th of February, provides the following data:

> On this day, in the year 1284 of our era, the great and renowned Nersēs vardapet passed away in Christ at the monastery of Glajor. He was from the canton of Tarōn, from the city of Muš. He had been nurtured and trained at the famous monastery of Łazar, which is also [known as the monastery of] Surb Aṙakʻelocʻ [Holy Apostles]. He was deeply versed in the literature and learning of the Greeks, and he had an intimate knowledge of the language of the Romans and of their priesthood [that is, doctrinal writings]. He then met the great and divinely inspired Vardan vardapet and became his pupil. And after his [that is, Vardan's] departure from this earth, he occupied his seat, and he enlightened our Armenian nation with the knowledge of the books. And, reaching a ripe old age, he passed away in Christ in the same monastery of Glajor.[138]

Another version of the life of Nersēs Mšecʻi relates that after leaving the monastery of Surb Aṙakʻelocʻ in Muš he established a school in the canton of Kʻaǰberunikʻ; fifteen years later he moved to the plain of Ararat, where he became a disciple of the scholar Vardan. He later returned to Surb Aṙakʻelocʻ, and finally, in 1280, established himself in Glajor.[139] The Vardan referred to is Vardan Arewelcʻi who had a school with some forty students at the monastery of Xor Virap.[140] It is assumed that it was here that Nersēs received the title of vardapet, and on Vardan's death in 1269 or 1271 he succeeded him as head of the school. He must have had a similar position when

[134] Hayk Pērpērian, the editor and publisher of the critical text of the *Ašxarhacʻoycʻ*, claims that Vardan Arewelcʻi died in 1269 (see ibid., xxiii, xxix).

[135] There is no consensus among scholars about the year in which the school of Glajor was founded. Most scholars are of the opinion that it occurred in 1280 (e.g., A. G. Abrahamyan, *Glajori Hamalsaranə* (Erevan, 1983), 31–43; idem, "Glajori Hamalsarani Tełə ev Himnadrutʻyan Taretʻivə," *Patma-Banasirakan Handes* 1 (1982), 159–76; Ališan, *Sisakan,* 131; Yovsēpʻian, *Xałbakeankʻ*, 252; Xačʻeryan, *Glajori Hamalsaranə,* 34. Other scholars contend that the school was founded in 1282 (e.g., A. S. Arevšatyan and A. S. Matʻevosyan, *Glajori Hamalsaranə Miǰnadaryan Hayastani Lusavorutʻyan Kentron* (Erevan, 1984), 11–13; Matʻevosyan, "Hiravi, Erb ev Orteł ē Himnadrvel Glajori Hamalsaranə," 55–59.

[136] See Grigoryan, *Syunikʻə*, 160.

[137] Ibid., 158–59.

[138] *Girkʻ or Kočʻi Yaysmawurkʻ* (Constantinople, 1730), 358; also Yovsēpʻian, *Xałbakeankʻ*, appendix II, 59.

[139] See Łewond Ališan, *Sisakan,* 131; also Yovsēpʻian, *Xałbakeankʻ*, 252.

[140] Vardan Arewelcʻi's prolific works include commentaries on several books of the Old Testament, a history of the Armenian people, a commentary on grammar, theological and philosophical treatises, encomiums, epistles, hymns, and other miscellaneous works. For details see G. Zarbhanalian, *Patmutʻiwn Hay Hin Dprutʻean, IV–XIII Dar* (Venice, 1932), 735–45; Norayr Połarian, *Hay Grołner* (Jerusalem, 1971), 294–300; Yovsēpʻian, *Xałbakeankʻ*, 252–53; Pʻ. Antʻabyan, "Vardan Arewelcʻi," *Hay Mšakuytʻi Nšanavor Gorcičʻnerə, V–XVIII Darer* (Erevan, 1976), 317–25.

he returned to Surb Aṙakʿelocʿ.[141] When he left this monastery he took with him Esayi Nčʿecʿi and several other young scholars, arriving at Glajor in 1280.

Although Nersēs Mšecʿi cannot be credited with founding the school of Glajor, his career reaches its climax at Glajor. Exactly what brought him to Glajor is uncertain. Yovsēpʿian suggests that Prince Pṙoš I, after failing in his attempt to establish in Vayocʿ Jor an episcopal see independent of the Ōrbēlian bishop of Siwnikʿ, decided instead to install an important vardapet in his own domain of Vayocʿ Jor.[142] Whatever the immediate motive for his move to Glajor, Nersēs very soon started attracting students from near and far. In addition to disciples from eastern Armenia, one hears of students from Tarōn, Sasun, and even Cilicia. Upon his death in 1284 Nersēs was succeeded by his pupil, Esayi Nčʿecʿi, who remained the leading vardapet of Glajor down to his death in 1338. The date of his birth is unknown, but it is supposed that he was born in the middle of the thirteenth century.[143] His place of origin was Ničʿ, or Nič, in the region of Sasun. Educated under Nersēs Mšecʿi at Muš and then at Kʿaǰberunikʿ, his fifty-four-year career as principal vardapet coincided with the period of greatest prominence of Glajor as a center of learning. Indeed, in this period Glajor must be counted the most important intellectual center in Armenia.

In spite of the rivalry between the Pṙošians and Ōrbēlians, support for Glajor in this period came from both families. In a colophon of 1323 Esayi Nčʿecʿi acknowledges the patronage of Prince Burtʿēl Ōrbēlian (1300–ca. 1344). Esayi extols the Ōrbēlian family for their faith and virtuous deeds, including the construction of unspecified buildings at Glajor, and remarks that the Ōrbēlians had "gathered those of us who are from strange places, and received us not as strangers but as their own genuine children, and accepted us . . . with compassion and love."[144] Two manuscripts contain dedications to Ōrbēlian ecclesiastics, one executed in 1314 for Bishop Stepʿanos-Tarsayič (Erevan, Mat. 9150; below, Appendix C, no. 36) and the other begun for Iwanē Ōrbēlian in 1307 and completed with illuminations in 1331 for Bishop Stepʿanos (Hartford, Case 3; Appendix C, no. 38). That the Pṙošians never ceased to support Glajor is affirmed by a number of colophons that mention both families as benefactors. One of these, written by Aṙakʿel Hałbatecʿi in 1327–28, while mentioning the Ōrbēlian Prince Burtʿēl I and other members of his family as masters of Siwnikʿ, also refers to the progeny of Prince Pṙoš I, "who are the lords and rulers of their ancestral domains, [namely], the affable and judicious Amir Hasan, the brave and valiant Vasak, and the sagacious Amir Asatʿ . . . who are the lords and rulers of our holy monastery [of Glajor] and the pupils assembled therein."[145] None of these sources, however, gives specific information about the kind of income-producing grants that must have been made in support of the monastery.

The character of the school of Glajor, its internal organization, and its curriculum of instruction have been the subject of considerable debate. The controversy was precipitated by the publication in 1973 of L. G. Xačʿeryan's monographic study, in which the author contended that, as an academic institution, Glajor had been a university comparable to those in medieval Europe, having similar faculties, curricula of instruction, and utilizing similar instructional materials. He not only claimed that the graduates of Glajor, as those of the European universities, acquired training in the theoretical and practical sciences; he even asserted that the seven liberal arts (*septem artes liberales*) offered at Glajor had been a tradition in Armenian schools of higher learning as far back as the fifth century A.D.[146] He imagined instruction divided in traditional Western fashion into the *trivium*, consisting of grammar, rhetoric, and logic, and the *quadrivium*, comprising arithmetic, geometry, astronomy, and music. In addition, according to Xačʿeryan, Glajor offered training in theology, philosophy, exegetical literature, and Latin and Greek. While many of these subjects were known at Glajor, the attempt to find a Western university structure in Glajor has no basis in fact, as Pʿ. Antʿabyan and Ē. Pivazyan have demonstrated.[147]

141 See Xačʿeryan, *Glajori Hamalsaranə*, 19–28; Yovsēpʿian, *Xałbakeankʿ*, 252–53.

142 Yovsēpʿian, *Xałbakeankʿ*, 254.

143 Xačʿikyan (see "Glajori Hamalsaranə ev Nra Saneri Avartakan Atenaxosutʿyunnerə," *Erevani Petakan Hamalsarani Gitakan Ašxatutʿyunner*, vol. III [1946], 426–27) has surmised that Esayi was born between the years 1248 and 1253, while Xačʿeryan (*Glajori Hamalsaranə*, 50–51) has proposed a date between the years 1254 and 1259.

144 The text of this colophon will be found in Xačʿikyan, *XIV Dari*, 182–83; see also Yovsēpʿian, *Xałbakeankʿ*, 384–85.

145 See the text of this colophon in Yovsēpʿian, *Xałbakeankʿ*, 350–51. Cf. also Xačʿikyan, *XIV Dari*, 261–62.

146 See Xačʿeryan, *Glajori Hamalsaranə*, 8–10. The same assertions are reiterated in other sections of the monograph. It should be noted that Xačʿikyan (see "Glajori Hamalsaranə ev Nra Saneri," 449–50) had, a quarter of a century earlier, arrived at conclusions similar to those advanced by Xačʿeryan.

147 Antʿabyan, "Ardyokʿ Hay Aṙaǰin Hamalsaranə Glajorn ē," 192–205; Ē. Pivazyan, "Darjyal Glajori Dprocʿi Hamalsaranakan Bnuytʿi Masin," *Banber Erevani Hamalsarani* 3 (1975), 154–69. For monographic studies dealing with the history of Armenian educational institutions, consult Kevork A. Sarafian, *History of Education in Armenia* (Los

Something of the structure of the school of Glajor can be inferred from the hierarchy of terms used for teachers, though one must be careful not to try to translate these into ranks of modern university professors, as Xačʿeryan has done.[148] Lowest in the hierarchy was the *rabuni* or "master," a term borrowed from the Hebrew; somehow more accomplished was the *rabunapet* or "headmaster"; and still more distinguished was the *vardapet*, literally "head teacher." There is considerable overlapping in the use of these terms, and in many instances *rabunapet* and *vardapet* seem interchangeable.[149] It is clear that there was a certain formality involved in the training and promotion of a person to the rank of vardapet. Mxitʿar Goš lays down in his *Law Book* that a cleric could be admitted to the rank of vardapet only after he had satisfied a panel of two or three vardapets about the level of his learning, though his training might have been under just a single vardapet.[150] The vardapet was regarded as having a special authority to teach. Grigor Tatʿewacʿi, in his treatise on priestly ordination, remarks that only clerics who had attained the rank of vardapet "could sing the psalms (perhaps this means "intone or lead the psalms") and reveal the divine words and speak with tongues and interpret them for the profit of the brethren and for the perfection of the church."[151]

In the course of examining the manuscript of a miscellany (Erevan, Mat. 631) L. S. Xačʿikyan ascertained that what at first sight appeared to be a collection of homilies was actually a compilation of orations by students upon completing their course for the rank of vardapet at Glajor.[152] A quarter of a century later, L. G. Xačʿeryan, too, found similar texts in a collection of homilies (Erevan, Mat. 734).[153] The study of these texts reveals that the school of Glajor, unlike other medieval Armenian institutions, had developed an elaborate system, whereby the candidate, having already fulfilled the academic requirements, would deliver his "maiden oration" before an assembly presided over by the rector Esayi Nčʿecʿi, and attended by the members of the faculty, the student body, and other clerical and lay dignitaries, following which Esayi would formally and ceremonially confer upon the candidate the title of vardapet. The texts also show that these orations dealt with specific theological and philosophical themes.[154]

The actual course of studies pursued at Glajor is difficult to reconstruct. Perhaps the kind of studies described a generation later at the school of Tatʿew in Siwnikʿ can be taken as a reflection of the curriculum at Glajor insofar as its eminent vardapet, Yovhan Orotnecʿi, received his training at Glajor. One suggestive text says of Yovhan Orotnecʿi that, having assembled students from near and far, "he labored over them and taught them and placed them on seats by rank of honor, some as *rabunis* and priests, some as musicians and philosophers, and others as painters and scribes."[155] Somewhat more specific is the information in a second source, which states that there were three "areas of instruction" (*usumnaran*) at Tatʿew: "In one of these, he [Grigor Tatʿewacʿi] taught the sweet-sounding melodies of the music composed by former musician vardapets . . . and in the other, the painting of pictures and other forms of painting. In yet another [he taught] the internal and external

Angeles, 1930); A. X. Movsisyan, *Urvagcer Hay Dprocʿi ev Mankavaržutʿyan Patmutʿyan, X–XV Darer* (Erevan, 1958); and Aršak Alpōyačian, *Patmutʿiwn Hay Dprocʿi* (Cairo, 1946).

148 Xačʿeryan, *Glajori Hamalsaranə*, 131–71.

149 At Glajor the vardapets Dawitʿ Sasnecʿi, Grigor, Martiros, Yovhannēs, Kirakos, Kiwrion, Nersēs, and Tiratur are also referred to as *rabunapet*, and the inscription on page 227 of the U.C.L.A. Gospel addresses the vardapet Esayi Nčʿecʿi as "great rabunapet." Dawitʿ Sasnecʿi is known to have been versed in theology, philosophy, and exegesis (Ališan, *Sisakan*, 135); Tiratur is known for his collection of homilies (Artawazd Siwrmēian, *Cʿucʿak Hayerēn Jeṙagracʿ S. Kʿaṙasun Mankunkʿ Ekełecʿwoy ew Masnaworacʿ* [Jerusalem, 1935], 370–73). Only a single *rabuni* is known by name at Glajor, and that is Yovhannēs Erznkacʿi Corcorecʿi, who distinguished himself as the author of a commentary on the Gospel of Matthew and a grammar.

150 Mxitʿar Goš, *Girkʿ Datastani*, ed. Xosrov Tʿorosyan (Erevan, 1975), 34.

151 *Maštocʿ Jeṙnadrutʿean* (Vałaršapat, 1876), 111.

152 Levon Xačʿikyan, "Glajori Hamalsarani ev Nra Saneri Avardakan Atenaxosutʿyunnerə," 423–50.

153 Xačʿeryan, *Glajori Hamalsaranə*, 180–202.

154 Contemporary data seem to be lacking on the number of students who were promoted to vardapet under Esayi Nčʿecʿi. The seventeenth-century Catholic missionary Clement Galanos appears to have been the first author to assign a figure to the number of graduates, placing it between 360 and 365. See Klemēs Galanos, *Miabanutʿiwn Hayocʿ Surb Ekełecʿwoyn ənd Meci Ekełecʿwoyn Hṙovmay*, vol. I (Rome, 1648), 347–48. Several other sources have claimed that 360 students received their training as vardapets with Esayi. Yovsēpʿian has cited a certain Gēorg vardapet, who claimed that Esayi had "trained 360 pupils" (see *Xałbakeankʿ*, 256, note 3, citing Ējmiacin ms. 4226, fol. 300a). M. Čʿamčʿian has suggested that Esayi alone had 363 pupils, but does not indicate whether this number represented those who had studied under him or had earned their doctorate under his supervision (see Čʿamčʿian, *Patmutʿiwn Hayocʿ*, III [Venice, 1786], 326). Ł. Ališan, on the other hand, claims that the number of recipients of the doctorate totaled 360 (*Sisakan*, 23). Finally, A. X. Movsisyan asserts, without any substantiation, that Glajor had graduated an aggregate of 723 pupils, of whom 360 had earned their doctorate (*Urvagcer*, 176); this view is shared by two other scholars (see Tʿ. X. Hakobyan and S. T. Melikʿ-Baxšyan, *Stepʿanos Ōrbelyan* [Erevan, 1960], 31).

155 Xačʿikyan, *XIV Dari*, 560.

commentaries and translations."[156] It must be pointed out, however, that these three "areas of instruction" seem to be alternatives rather than sequential courses of study, for the students were assigned to one or the other area; they are, moreover, areas of widely different intellectual requirements. Singing is a practical skill useful in the divine services, and painting and writing are crafts depending more on manual dexterity than on a theoretical grasp of the subject. The areas of book-learning, insofar as they are described at Tat'ew, comprise the study of Sacred Scripture and the tradition of commentaries on Sacred Scripture. The evidence would seem to indicate that the chief subject of study at the school of Tat'ew was exegesis.

The same seems to have been true of Glajor. The principal contribution to learning made by Nersēs Mšec'i and Esayi Nč'ec'i was their work on the interpretation of Sacred Scripture. Nersēs' writings have not survived, but he collaborated with his mentor Vardan Arewelc'i in the composition of a commentary on Daniel,[157] and he was responsible by himself for a commentary on Proverbs and another on the Song of Solomon.[158] The literary output of Esayi was somewhat broader, including a grammar, a commentary on the works of Pseudo-Denis, and a number of letters,[159] but his major works were his verse-by-verse exegetical studies of Ezekiel and Isaiah.[160] These commentaries, composed in 1302–3 and dedicated to bishop Step'anos Ōrbēlian of Siwnik', have unfortunately never been edited and remain virtually unknown, but to his contemporaries the fame of Esayi rested chiefly on his skill as a commentator. Step'anos Ōrbēlian, for example, praises the breadth of Esayi's learning, embracing both sacred and secular literature, but his highest tribute is his assertion that Esayi had outdone his namesake the prophet Isaiah, for while Isaiah's fame rested with a single book, Esayi's fame rested on his profound knowledge of all the books of the Bible.[161] Esayi's abilities as an exegete are likewise extolled by his disciple Mkrtič', who calls him the "most learned philosopher and eloquent orator, deeply versed in theological works . . . who in these oppressive times shines on earth like a sun through the brilliance of his pious life and the abundance of his knowledge of Sacred Scripture."[162] In a colophon of 1318 a scribe named Yakob T'agorc'i informs us that he labored "in the angel-inhabited monastery of Glajor, which I dare call the second Athens and the capital of all wisdom," under the direction of Esayi, "the receptacle of the Spirit, a prudent, affable, magnanimous soul, at whose door we his pupils toil in search of knowledge and the truth of scripture." Esayi, he goes on to say, is able to elucidate "the intricate, incomprehensible, and obscure meanings found in books of the Old and New Testaments" as well as in the writings of the Fathers.[163] Another scribe, Aṙak'el Hałbatec'i, writing in 1327–28, describes how Esayi, although burdened with old age, spent all his time in strenuous labors and nocturnal vigils, studying and explaining Sacred Scripture.[164] The portrait of Esayi and his monastic community in Jerusalem, St. James 365 (fig. R1), shows the master engaged in this labor; heavenly inspiration flows into his ear and out of his mouth to the encircling brethren, many of whom hold their own copies of Sacred Scripture cradled in a cloth of honor. The interpretation of Scripture, then, seems to have been the principal focus of scholarship for the two vardapets who directed the school of Glajor.

But there is better and far more concrete evidence of the nature and scope of studies pursued at Glajor in the manuscripts that were produced at Glajor. A total of sixty-nine manuscripts can be reliably attributed to Glajor, and an account of the contents of these manuscripts is presented below in Appendix C. Since this list depends on catalogues, the entries are sometimes more general than one might like, mentioning simply a "work" of Gregory Nazianzenus, for

[156] See the text of this colophon in Xač'ikyan, "Glajori Hamalsaranə ev Nra Saneri," 428; and Xač'eryan, *Glajori Hamalsaranə*, 96–97.

[157] Yovsēp'ian, *Xałbakeank'*, 253.

[158] Hamazasp Oskian, *Mayr C'uc'ak Hayerēn Jeṙagrac' Mxit'arean Matenadaranin i Vienna* (Vienna, 1963), II, 478.

[159] See discussion of Esayi's literary output below, p. 29.

[160] The *Commentary on Ezekiel* is found in the following mss. at the Matenadaran in Erevan: nos. 1240–1243, 1273–1277, 1311, 2511, 2885, 2972–2973, 3120, 3915, 4349 (Ō. Eganyan et al., *C'uc'ak Jeṙagrac' Maštoc'i Anvan Matenadarani*, 2 vols. [Erevan, 1965–70] hereafter *Matenadaran Catalogue*), I, cols. 507, 508, 515, 516, 523, 815, 895, 913, 945, 1109, 1196), and nos. 5566, 5717, 5906, 6573, 6730, 10083 (*Matenadaran Catalogue*, II, cols. 135, 170, 208, 347–48, 382, 1044). There are also two copies of the same text in Jerusalem: no. 152 (Norayr Połarian, *Mayr C'uc'ak Jeṙagrac' Srboc' Yakobeanc'*, I [Jerusalem, 1966], 426–27), and no. 1159 (ibid., IV, 252–53). Yovsēp'ian has studied the sources used by Esayi in this commentary; see *Xałbakeank'*, 289–92; idem, "Esayi Nč'ec'i's Commentary on Ezekiel," in *Ararat* (Vałaršapat, 1917), 193 ff. Esayi's *Commentary on Isaiah* is found in Matenadaran 167 (see *Matenadaran Catalogue*, I, col. 263) and Mat. 7581 (ibid., II, cols. 563–64). Garegin Zarbhanalian states that the original ms. of this work, written by Esayi himself, was found at the monastery of Ktuc' on the homonymous island in Lake Van (*Patmut'iwn Hayerēn Dprut'ean, Nor Matenagrut'iwn* [Venice, 1905], 149).

[161] The text of this document is found in Matenadaran 848, fols. 78–82; see its summary in Xač'eryan, *Glajori Hamalsaranə*, 66–67, 141–47.

[162] Xač'ikyan, *XIV Dari*, 5.

[163] See the text of this colophon in Minasian, *C'uc'ak Nor Jułayi*, II, 177.

[164] The text of this colophon is found in Yovsēp'ian, *Xałbakeank'*, 350–51.

example, or naming a work without an author; but in large measure this reflects the state of Armenian studies, in which much more basic research remains to be done with primary sources.

Within these limits, and with the reservation that other Glajor manuscripts probably remain to be discovered, the list provides a fairly realistic profile of the interests of the school of Glajor. Statistically there are two areas where the sixty-nine manuscripts may somewhat misrepresent the original total output of Glajor. Sacred Scripture, which accounts for thirty-two percent of the list, with sixteen Gospels and six Bibles, may be over-represented due to a better survival rate. A greater value was always assigned to the Word of God than to works of mere human authorship, and Sacred Scripture had a much wider usefulness to the general public. Furthermore, manuscripts of Scripture were much more likely to be illuminated than others, and this would further increase their worth and consequently their survival rate. On the other hand, liturgical manuscripts seem to be under-represented. Only a single manuscript on the list, a book of hymns, can be classed as a liturgical book; lectionaries, rituals, breviaries, and other books of daily liturgical use are all missing from the surviving manuscripts made at Glajor. It is conceivable that the production of manuscripts was marked by a certain degree of specialization and liturgical manuscripts were generally produced in another center; but it is more likely that the lack should be ascribed to the strictly utilitarian function of the books.

Outside of Sacred Scripture and the single liturgical manuscript, the manuscripts of Glajor can be divided into two large categories, philosophical and theological. In the former category, works of speculative philosophy are remarkably few. Plato is represented by a single dialogue, the *Timaeus* (no. 6), and Aristotle's vast output is represented by two brief handbooks commonly ascribed to him in the Middle Ages, *On the Cosmos* (no. 22) and *Virtues and Vices* (nos. 22, 32), and his logical works. The philosophical works that most interested the scholars of Glajor were the very practical works on grammar, logic, and rhetoric, which must have been viewed as propaedeutic to the study of theology. Aristotle's *Categories* and *On Interpretation* were regarded in Armenia as the foundation of all logical thinking, and they exist in several Glajor manuscripts (nos. 22, 32, 40, 53); in addition, several commentaries on Aristotelian logic were in circulation, including Porphyry's *Introduction to Aristotle's "Categories"* (nos. 22, 32, 40, 53), and four works of the Armenian philosopher David the Invincible: *Interpretation of Aristotle's "Categories"* (nos. 32, 40, 53), *Interpretation of Aristotle's "Analytics"* (no. 40), *Commentary on Porphyry's "Introduction"* (nos. 22, 32, 40, 53), and *Definitions of Philosophy* (nos. 6, 21, 22, 32, 42, 53, 60, 65).[165] This last, beyond treating questions of logic, attempts a classification of the theoretical and practical, that is, ethical, branches of philosophy, was the most frequently copied philosophical work at Glajor, and was the subject of a commentary by Nersēs Šnorhali which survives in two copies (6, 22).[166] The basis for the study of grammar in Armenia was always Dionysius Thrax, whose *Art of Grammar* occurs in one manuscript (no. 32);[167] two Armenian commentaries on the same also survive in Glajor copies, one by David the Philosopher (no. 6)[168] and another by Esayi Nčʻecʻi (no. 32).[169] The standard work on rhetoric was the *Girkʻ Pitoyicʻ*, an Armenian version of the *Elements of Rhetoric* of Aphthonius, an author of fourth-century Antioch, which appears in three copies (nos. 21, 32, 57).[170] On the basis of this kind of a library, the scholar of Glajor could not have gotten very far in the study of philosophy as such, but he could have learned a great deal about the art of reasoning and the logical presentation of an argument. It should be noted in this connection that one of the commonest honorary titles accorded scholars in Armenia was the Greek term *rhetor*, by which they meant someone who was eloquent in his exposition of orthodox doctrine.

Works of a theological nature outnumber philosophical works by a proportion of better than three to one. Exact and comprehensive statistics are diffi-

[165] The Greek versions of two of David the Invincible's works will be found in Adolfus Busse, *Davidis Prolegomena et in Porphyrii Isagogen Commentarium* (Berlin, 1904). The critical editions of the Armenian versions of the four works attributed to David are published by S. S. Arevšatyan in *Dawitʻ Anyałtʻ, Erkasirutʻiwnkʻ Pʻilisopʻayakankʻ* (Erevan, 1980), and the modern Armenian versions in S. S. Arevšatyan, *Davitʻ Anhałtʻ, Erker* (Erevan, 1980).

[166] See *Definitions and Divisions of Philosophy by David the Invincible Philosopher*, trans. Bridget Kendall and Robert W. Thomson, University of Pennsylvania, Armenian Texts and Studies 5 (Chico, California, 1983). For a study of Nersēs Šnorhali's commentary, consult A. Madoyan, "Davitʻ Anhałtʻ ev Nersēs Šnorhali," in *Davitʻ Anhałtʻ, Hodvacneri Žołovacu* (Erevan, 1980), 123–42.

[167] The text will be found in Nicolas Adontz, *Denys de Thrace et les commentateurs arméniens* (Louvain, 1970).

[168] For David's commentary on Thrax's Grammar, see G. J̌ahukyan, "Davtʻ i kʻerakanakan ašxatutʻyan norahayt ambołǰakan jeṙagir tekʻ stə," *Banber Matenadarani* 3 (1956), 242–64. This text has been reproduced in N. Adontz, *Denys de Thrace*, 312–32, as an appendix. Adontz had previously published a reconstruction of David's text based on later quotations of it scattered through other Armenian grammatical treatises (see *Denys de Thrace*, 77–124).

[169] The text was published by L. G. Xačʻeryan in *Esayi Nčʻecʻi, Verlucutʻiwn Kʻerakanutʻean* (Erevan, 1966).

[170] See text in *Girkʻ Pitoyicʻ Movsisi Xorenacʻwoy*, published by Y. Zōhrapian (Venice, 1796; repr. 1843).

cult to derive from the list of manuscripts, since many of the manuscripts are composed of heterogeneous material. Nevertheless, it can be observed that there are nine manuscripts of exclusively philosophical content while there are thirty-two exclusively theological; and this proportion generally holds in the manuscripts of a composite character. While the philosophical manuscripts were dominated by treatises on logic, the theological manuscripts are overwhelmingly exegetical.

In the realm of analytic or speculative theology Pseudo-Denis the Areopagite appears to have been the favorite Greek author in Glajor. His works had been translated into Armenian by the eighth-century Step'anos Siwnec'i, and all of them were available in Glajor in several copies (nos. 2, 3, 6, 42, 53). Esayi Nč'ec'i wrote a commentary of his own on the works of Pseudo-Denis. Next frequent is Gregory of Nyssa's treatise *On the Creation of Man,* which is found in four manuscripts (nos. 9, 26, 47, 63). On the same subject there are two copies of Nemesius of Emesa's neo-Platonic work *On the Nature of Man* (nos. 9, 26). Gregory of Nyssa's *Against Eunomius* and his treatise *On Virginity* were also known in Glajor (nos. 20, 26), and the *Orations* of Gregory Nazianzenus (no. 41).

While works of a more strictly theological nature such as these are by no means unimportant in the list of Glajor manuscripts, they do not seem to have been collected and studied with the same passion as works of an exegetical nature. Works of exegesis outnumber other theological works by a proportion of two to one. What is more remarkable, among the surviving manuscripts of Glajor, commentaries can be found on virtually every book of the Old and New Testaments, and many of them are the works of Armenian commentators. As far as one can judge from the manuscripts that were produced in Glajor, the interpretation of Sacred Scripture was pursued with system and thoroughness and constituted the main curriculum of the school. From the colophons, moreover, it is clear that the bulk of this manuscript production was intended for the internal use of the monastic school of Glajor. Only five of the sixty-nine manuscripts can be identified as made for outsiders: four for distinguished members of the clergy (no. 18, an exegetical collection for Archbishop Grigor of Sararad; nos. 36, 38, Gospels for Bishop Step'anos-Tarsayič Ōrbēlian; no. 51, a collection of spiritual treatises for the vardapet Nersēs, son of Vahra, of Taron), and one for a lay member of the nobility (no. 44, a Gospel for the princess Vaxax Ōrbēlian). Names of the original owners are supplied in thirty-six other manuscripts, and in twenty-six of these cases the owners can be identified as certainly living and working at Glajor, for they are named as scribes in the same or other manuscripts. These twenty-six manuscripts belonged to fifteen owners. The ten remaining manuscripts belonged to a total of six or eight owners, who may or may not have belonged to the monastery. In other words, manuscript production at Glajor was largely for internal consumption, monks writing works for their own use or that of their brethren. Even the eminent teachers of Glajor were occupied with the labor of the scriptorium; Esayi Nč'ec'i and the exegete Yovhannēs Erznkac'i Corcorec'i are both responsible for writing manuscripts. There is no sense in which the school of Glajor can be interpreted as a kind of lay university; it was a monastic school, the main business of which was the study and interpretation of Sacred Scripture. The nature and content of these exegetical studies will be considered below.

5. Glajor and the Defense of the Faith

Historically, perhaps the most important contribution of the monastery of Glajor was the part it played in resisting the Latinizing of the Armenian church. Esayi Nč'ec'i, principal vardapet of Glajor and first owner of the U.C.L.A. Gospel, assumed a leading role in this cause alongside the metropolitan bishops of Siwnik', who had been trained at Glajor. Since this struggle to maintain Armenian traditions, both in doctrine and in ritual, forms essential background to the iconography of the U.C.L.A. Gospel, some discussion of the issues involved is necessary.

The contacts of the Armenians in Cilicia with the Roman Catholic church began with their involvement in the Crusades. The Crusaders found the Armenians their natural allies in the Near East, and the Armenian court in Cilicia took as its model the conduct of the Latins in their kingdoms of Jerusalem, Antioch, and Edessa. Diplomatic relations were close and intermarriage among the princely houses was frequent. When Leo I was crowned first king of Cilician Armenia in 1198, he received royal insignia from Emperor Henry VI at the hands of the papal legate, the Archbishop Conrad of Mainz. The fall of each of the Latin kingdoms in the course of the twelfth century, however, left the fledgling Armenian kingdom isolated between the Seljuks of Anatolia and the Mamluks of Egypt and desperate for assistance from the West. What had originally been fashionable eventually became a matter of survival, for aid promised by the papacy was always made contingent on unity with Rome in religion. A Council of Union in Sis in

1252 may have spelled out the terms under which the Armenian church was to be united with Rome, but the acts of the council have not survived and its content is disputed. Whatever its terms, Catholicos Yakob I (1268–86) and his successor Kostandin II (1286–89) resisted strongly its implementation, at least in strictly ecclesiastical matters; in manners, dress, and art Western fashions set the pace.[171]

Under King Het῾um II (1289–97) Cilician policy toward the papacy underwent a significant change. Assuring Pope Nicholas IV of his loyalty, Het῾um II took the Franciscan habit himself and replaced Catholicos Step῾anos IV with Grigor VII Anawarzec῾i, who proposed a synod to bring the Armenian church into conformity with that of Rome.[172] The changes proposed included the acceptance of the seven ecumenical councils (the Armenian Church had accepted only the first three), including the creed as formulated at Chalcedon; the adoption of the Latin calendar of feasts with Christmas on the 25th of December instead of on the 6th of January; the addition of water to the eucharistic wine; and the deletion from the Trisagion hymn of the words "who was crucified for us."[173]

The situation in Greater Armenia, more relevant to this study, was always quite different from that in Cilicia. Contacts with the Crusades were few and the occasional missionaries and ambassadors who reached the landlocked mountainous country were generally in transit to the Ilkhanid court in Tabriz or Maragha. Der Nersessian has surveyed these sporadic encounters in the course of the thirteenth century.[174] The initiative of Het῾um II and Grigor VII, however, was felt in Greater Armenia, and before the proposed synod was convoked the lines of resistance were being drawn up. Having learned of Grigor's intentions through his legate, Bishop Kostandin Kesarac῾i, the bishops and vardapets of Siwnik῾ met to formulate a response. Drafted by Step῾anos Ōrbēlian, the metropolitan of Siwnik῾, the document deplored the rumor that the "catholicos is a Latin and has become their ally."[175] The clergy of Siwnik῾ rejected all innovations, and condemned the Chalcedonian creed, reiterating what Armenian synods had said on this subject. Appended to the document were excerpts from Gregory Thaumaturgus and Athanasius of Alexandria supporting the "one nature united" formula that the Armenian church had adopted as its christological position.[176] On this subject Step῾anos Ōrbēlian subsequently wrote a staunch defense of Armenian Monophysitism in his treatise *Hakačaṙut῾iwn ənddēm Erkabnakac῾*, or a "Refutation against those who believe in two natures."[177] The church of Siwnik῾ also rejected all proposed modifications of Armenian liturgical practice. So as to leave no question about where they stood they concluded by affirming, "We are willing to go to hell with our forefathers rather than ascend to heaven with the Romans"; and, "if you punish us with a royal rebuke, we are prepared to suffer torment and exile and imprisonment and death for the traditions bequeathed by the holy and apostolic fathers."

This ringing rebuke of the catholicos was signed by nine bishops: Step῾anos Ōrbēlian, Sargis and Grigor of Siwnik῾, Yovhannēs and Grigor of Bǰni, Yovhannēs of Hałbat, Mxit῾ar of Hawuc῾ T῾aṙ, Margarē the nephew of Vanakan Vardapet, and Sarkawag of Gołt῾n; by two vardapets: Esayi Nč῾ec῾i and Dawit῾ Sasnec῾i of Glajor; and by four princes of Siwnik῾: Ēlikum and Liparit Ōrbēlian, and Papak῾ and Ēač῾i Pṙošian. In signing, the princes expressed the concurrence of their families and nobility, and Esayi Nč῾ec῾i that of his monastery: "I, Esayi, the least among scholars and a lowly teacher, together with my pupils, am in agreement and in accord with this letter

[171] Der Nersessian, *Arm. Mss. Freer*, 49–50. Helen C. Evans has traced an extensive pattern of Franciscan borrowings in Cilician art, *Armenian Manuscript Illumination at the Patriarchate in Hṙomkla and the West*, diss., Institute of Fine Arts, New York University, 1990.

[172] Galanos, *Miabanut῾iwn*, I, 403–10; Ōrbēlian, *Patmut῾iwn*, 437–39; idem, *Histoire*, I, 243–44.

[173] Galanos, *Miabanut῾iwn*, I, 439; Małak῾ia Ōrmanian, *Azgapatum*, II (Beirut, 1960), para. 1205. For a summary of Armenian church doctrines, discipline, and liturgy, consult Malachia Ormanian, *The Church of Armenia*, trans. G. Marcar Gregory and ed. Terenig Poladian (London, 1955). For an extensive bibliography on the early period of the Armenian church, consult Gabriele Winkler, *Das armenische Initiationsrituale*, OCA 217 (Rome, 1982), 15–44. For a comprehensive listing of works dealing with various aspects of the Armenian church, see also A. Salmaslian, *Bibliographie de l'Arménie* (Erevan, 1969), 136–75. Among the more important works in western languages, consult: Leon Arpee, *A History of Armenian Christianity* (New York, 1946); J. Issaverdenz, *Rites et cérémonies de l'église arménienne* (Venice, 1876); K. Kassardjian, *L'Église apostolique arménienne et sa doctrine* (Paris, 1943); J. Mécérian, *Histoire et institutions de l'Église arménienne* (Beirut, 1965); A. Ter-Mikelian, *Die armenische Kirche in ihren Beziehungen zur byzantinischen, vom IV. bis XIII. Jahrhundert* (Leipzig, 1892); F. Tournebize, *Histoire politique et religieuse de l'Arménie depuis les origines des Arméniens jusqu'à la mort du leur dernier roi l'an 1393* (Paris, 1910); S. Weber, *Die Katholische Kirche in Armenien* (Freiburg, 1903).

[174] Sirarpie Der Nersessian, "Western Iconographic Themes in Armenian Manuscripts," *Études*, I, 617–25.

[175] The text of this letter will be found in Ōrbēlian, *Patmut῾iwn*, 449–60; idem, *Histoire*, I, 250–55.

[176] Ōrbēlian, *Patmut῾iwn*, 463–67; idem, *Histoire*, I, 256–58. On the christological question in this period, see Pascal Tékéyan, *Controverses christologiques en Arméno-Cilicie dans la seconde moitié du XIIe siècle (1165–98)*, OCA 126 (Rome, 1939).

[177] Published in Constantinople, 1756.

and with the above persons, and we excommunicate with anathemas those who dissent."[178]

This uncompromising stand by the church of Siwnikʿ seems to have given pause to the Latinizing efforts of Grigor VII. Though he insisted that his reform of the Armenian church should be accomplished through a synod of the whole church, he delayed in convening it.[179] The Synod of Sis was finally called under his successor, Kostandin III Kesaracʿi, in 1307. The Latin reforms proposed by Grigor VII were dutifully signed by the bishops present.[180] Ōrmanian has questioned the canonical validity of the synod, pointing out that it was convened by the eighteen-year-old King Leon III, not by the catholicos, for Kostandin Kesaracʿi was elected to that office only after the synod. Moreover, the twenty-six bishops who signed were principally from Cilicia; no representatives from Greater Armenia were present. Finally the procedures were irregular in that, under duress from the royal court, the resolutions were adopted without debate.[181]

The resolutions of the synod proved difficult to implement for it provoked popular uprisings in Adana and Sis in 1308 and 1309. A conclave in Adana rejected the synod and a massive popular protest at Sis was followed by a meeting of traditionalist clergy, who categorically rejected the synod.[182] The authorities resorted to force; some resisters were actually executed and others were imprisoned or banished to Cyprus.[183] Nevertheless, as far as changing Armenian church practice is concerned, the synod had little effect. Even the Catholic historian Čʿamčʿian admits that the synod's resolutions were implemented nowhere in Cilicia outside the royal court and the palace of the catholicos.[184] These developments gave to the Armenian church of Cilicia a peculiar split personality, professing one set of principles as official policy and winking at popular practice at variance with the policy.

Ten years later the same scenario was repeated; a synod was convened at Adana at the insistence of Pope John XXII. The resolutions of the Synod of Sis concerning the Chalcedonian creed, the dilution of the eucharistic wine and the celebration of Christmas on the 25th of December were reaffirmed by a gathering of Latinizing bishops.[185] The Synod of Adana, however, was no more effective than its predecessor; the resolutions were widely ignored and King Ōšin and Catholicos Kostandin III did not insist on putting them into effect.[186] But new pressures were brought to bear on the church in Siwnikʿ. In 1317–18 Kostandin III threatened to deny them the holy chrism if they did not conform to the official policy of the Cilician church. This threat evoked a new response signed by the bishops Yovhan Awrpēl and Stepʿanos-Tarsayič, along with the vardapets Esayi Nčʿecʿi and Dawitʿ Sasnecʿi of Glajor.[187] In defense of the practice of celebrating the Eucharist with undiluted wine they contended that this was in fact the original practice of both the Greek and Roman churches to the time of Honorius and Arcadius. As proof they cited passages from Pseudo-Denis the Areopagite, Pope Celestine, and Chrysostom's *Commentary on the Gospel.*

In 1318 a new initiative was taken toward Greater Armenia by Pope John XXII, who divided up all of Asia as potential mission territory between the Franciscans and the Dominicans, and assigned the latter a metropolitan see in Sultaniya. The new see in turn established six suffragan bishoprics; that of Maragha, occupied by Bartolomeo degli Abbagliati, became the beachhead for the Latinizing of Greater Armenia. The history of this development and the founding of the Armenian Catholic order of the Fratres Unitores has been traced in detail by van den Oudenrijn.[188] It was a monk of Glajor and pupil of Esayi Nčʿecʿi, Yohan Kʿṙnecʿi, who founded the order. Upon completion of his studies in Glajor, Yohan was appointed abbot of the monastery of the Mother of God in Kʿṙna, in the region of Ernǰak. In 1328 Yohan traveled to Maragha along with several of his monks, where he entered into dialogue with bishop Bartolomeo, translated a number of Latin works into Armenian, and converted to Roman Catholicism. In 1330 Yohan and his companions returned to Kʿṙna, where they established the order of the Fratres Unitores. The order

178 Ōrbēlian, *Patmutʿiwn,* 462; idem, *Histoire,* I, 255–56.

179 Galanos, *Miabanutʿiwn,* I, 438.

180 Ibid., I, 456–57; Ōrmanian, *Azgapatum,* II, paras. 1230–35.

181 Ōrmanian, *Azgapatum,* II, paras. 1233, 1235.

182 Galanos, *Miabanutʿiwn,* I, 472–76; Čʿamčʿian, *Patmutʿiwn Hayocʿ,* III, 311.

183 *Samuēli Kʿahanayi Anecʿwoy Hawakʿmunkʿ i Grocʿ Patmagracʿ,* published by Aršak Tēr-Mikʿēlian (Vałaršapat, 1893), 156; see also Čʿamčʿian, *Patmutʿiwn Hayocʿ,* III, 312–13.

184 Čʿamčʿian, *Patmutʿiwn Hayocʿ,* III, 313; see Galanos, *Miabanutʿiwn,* I, 472.

185 Galanos, *Miabanutʿiwn,* I, 472–518; Ōrmanian, *Azgapatum,* II, paras. 1253–57.

186 Čʿamčʿian, *Patmutʿiwn Hayocʿ,* III, 314.

187 The text of the letter will be found in Yovsēpʿian, *Xałbakeankʿ,* appendix III.9, 397–99.

188 M. A. van den Oudenrijn, "Uniteurs et Dominicains d'Arménie," *OC,* ser. 4, 40 (1956), 94–112; 42 (1958), 110–33; 43 (1959), 110–19; 45 (1961), 95–108; 46 (1962), 99–116.

was recognized by the papacy in 1334 and Yohan served as its superior until his death in 1348. In K'ṙna the Fratres Unitores devoted themselves to translating into Armenian the works of the Dominican theologians and exegetes of the thirteenth century and some liturgical books.[189] Their proselytizing had considerable success; by 1356 the Order had established some fifty monasteries in Armenia, with a total of seven hundred monks and thousands of lay converts.

Although earlier Dominican scholars claimed that Esayi himself had taken part in the founding of the Fratres Unitores, van den Oudenrijn has demonstrated that this tradition had its origins only in the fifteenth century and has no foundation in contemporary sources or in the extant writings of Esayi.[190] Quite the contrary, Esayi must be counted the mainstay of the opposition to Latinizing in Siwnik' during his lifetime. It is unfortunate that of Esayi's considerable literary oeuvre nothing has been edited and published save his work on grammar.[191] For present purposes this is the least interesting of his works. Esayi authored five theological works: (1) "A Commentary on the Book of Ezekiel," composed in 1302/3 for bishop Step'anos Ōrbēlian;[192] (2) "A Commentary on the Book of Isaiah," written in 1303, probably also for Step'anos Ōrbēlian;[193] (3) "A Brief Commentary on the Works of Dionysius the Areopagite";[194] (4) "A Commentary on Gregory of Nyssa's Treatise on the Nine Beatitudes"; and (5) "A Commentary on Gregory of Nyssa's Treatise on the Pater Noster."[195] Seven homilies by Esayi also survive.[196]

All of these works await the attention of text editors and theologians.[197] It makes more sense, however, to look at the letters of Esayi for some idea of the day-to-day concerns that preoccupied him. In addition to the role he may have played in drafting the two letters referred to above, Esayi Nč'ec'i is the author of at least nine other letters dealing with church doctrine and discipline. Four of these are immediately pertinent to this discussion.

The earliest of Esayi's letters seems to be his "Response to the letter from the Catholicos and the King," which was written in reaction to the Synod of Sis in 1307.[198] While admitting the theoretical desirability of the union of all Christian churches, Esayi contends that its realization has been "obstructed by the machinations of Satan," and as long as the preconditions for such union are missing each church must retain its only historical traditions while respecting those of other churches. The Synod of Sis, he objects, had been attended by very few, with no representatives from Greater Armenia. Church canons cannot be changed by kings and princes, he remarks. Two issues are treated at some length in the letter, the dilution of the eucharistic wine and the elimination of the clause "who was crucified for us" from the Trisagion.

Concerning the eucharistic wine Esayi points out that neither the Old Testament allusions to the sacrament nor the New Testament accounts of its institution, whether in the synoptics or in Paul, ever mention a diluting of the wine with water. The early fathers of the church also knew of no such custom, he claims, citing Athanasius, Basil, and John Chrysos-

[189] For a comprehensive study of the Latin works translated into Armenian, consult M. A. van den Oudenrijn, *Lingua Haicane Scriptores, Ordinis Praedicatorum Congregationis Fratres Unitorum* (Bern, 1960); idem, *Uniteurs, OC*, ser. 4, 40 (1956), 111–15, 118–24. See also Yovhannēs K'ṙnac'i, *Yałags K'erakanin*, ed. L. S. Avagyan (Erevan, 1977), 19–20, 30–39.

[190] M. A. van den Oudenrijn, "Uniteurs," *OC*, ser. 4, 40 (1956), 104; idem, "La lettre encyclique de Jean de Qrhnay dans la 'Conciliatio' de Galanus," *Neue Zeitschrift für Missionwissenschaft* (Beckenried, Switzerland), 1 (1947), 25–39.

[191] For a partial list of Esayi's works, see H. Ačaṙyan, *Hayoc' Anjnanunneri Baṙaran* (Erevan, 1944), II, 128. Esayi's grammatical work was published with analytical introduction by L. G. Xač'eryan, *Esayi Nč'ec'i, Verlucut'iwn K'erakanut'ean* (Erevan, 1966), with summaries in Russian and English.

[192] There are numerous copies of this in Erevan, Matenadaran; see Eganyan, *C'uc'ak Jeṙagrac'*, I, 507, 508, 515, 516, 523, 815, 895, 913, 945, 1109, 1196, and II, 135, 170, 208, 347–48, 382, 1044. Two more copies exist in Jerusalem, St. James; see Połarian, *Mayr C'uc'ak*, I, 426–27 and IV, 252–53.

[193] This survives in two manuscripts, Erevan, Mat. 167 and 7581. Eganyan, *C'uc'ak Jeṙagrac'*, I, 263 and II, 563–64.

[194] Manuscripts of this survive in Erevan, Matenadaran (Eganyan, *C'uc'ak Jeṙagrac'*, I, 239, 263, 675); Jerusalem, St. James (Połarian, *Mayr C'uc'ak*, III, 162–63); and Vienna, Mekhitarist Congregation (Tašian, *C'uc'ak Hayerēn Jeṙagrac'*, I, 454–55).

[195] These last two works survive in a single manuscript in Venice (Barseł Sargisian, *Mayr C'uc'ak Hayerēn Jeṙagrac' Matenadaranin Mxit'areanc' i Venetik* [Venice, 1914–24], II, 848–50).

[196] Eganyan, *C'uc'ak Jeṙagrac'*, I, 396, 474, 540, 678, 739, 741, 758, 762, 774, and 988.

[197] A single modern study has appeared, devoted to Esayi's "Commentary on Ezekiel," but this fails to discuss any of the theological issues and concentrates instead on counting the source references. Esayi is shown to have relied most heavily on the commentaries of Chrysostom, Ephraem Syrus, Cyril of Alexandria, and Origen. Yovsēp'ian, "Esayi Nč'ec'i's Commentary on Ezekiel," *Ararat* (Vałaršapat, 1917), 193 ff; idem, *Xałbakeank'*, 289–92.

[198] We have used two manuscripts for the study of this letter: (a) Jerusalem, St. James 773, a Miscellany written in 1359 (?) by the scribe-priest Anton (the letter is found on fols. 115–121v); (b) Erevan, Mat. 9622, a Miscellany copied in 1858 in Jerusalem by the scribe Yakobos Č'ilinkirian (the letter is found on pp. 734–54).

tom. Concerning the passage cited by the Latins as adumbrating the mixed cup, "One of the soldiers pierced his side with a spear, and at once there came out blood and water" (John 19:34), Esayi remarks that it was not on the cross but in the upper room that Jesus instituted the sacrament.[199]

On the addition to the Trisagion, introduced by the Monophysite bishop Peter the Fuller of Antioch in the fifth century, Greek and Latin theologians had always objected that the clause implied that the Trinity was crucified. Esayi takes the traditional Armenian defense that the hymn is not addressed to the Trinity but to Christ alone, and therefore the addition is perfectly appropriate. The hymn, he maintains, was authored by Joseph of Arimathea, who took the body of Christ from the cross, and the clause "who was crucified for us" was added to it by one of the first followers of the apostles, Ignatius of Antioch.

Perhaps Esayi's most important doctrinal statement is found in a letter called "The doctrine and confession of faith in the Holy Trinity." Without date, the letter was addressed to some "illustrious person honored by God," very likely a bishop of the Armenian church, who had requested his views on the subject.[200] Professing faith in the "Divine nature, the holy Trinity, blessed, infinite, in three equal hypostases, the Father and the Son and the Holy Spirit," Esayi defines the properties of each person. The Father is omnipotent, all-powerful, creator, incomprehensible, unbounded, without accident, without measure, eternal, without beginning and without end; the Son is the begotten Word; the Holy Spirit proceeds from the Father and from the Son. In confirmation of this last, anti-Greek position he cites Paul's reference to the Holy Spirit as "the Spirit of Christ" (Rom. 8:9). The Incarnation is discussed at some length. Esayi asserts that the Armenian church professes the only-begotten Son was sent by the Father and born of the Virgin Mary as a true man. Jesus became a perfect man without confusion, and he remained a man without confusion; yet his divine nature did not dissolve into the flesh. The Mother of God remained ever a virgin, according to Ezekiel's verse on the gate by which only the Lord should enter (Ezek. 44:2). Born of the Virgin, Christ was perfect in his humanity and perfect in his divinity. Yet Esayi insists on the traditional Monophysite expression of this unity: one must not speak of the division of his nature into two; rather he is the one incarnate Word of God, one in nature, hypostasis, and singularity. In him "the divine are human and the human are divine," the immortal is mortal and the mortal is immortal; hence Paul could write that God "did not spare his own Son but gave him up for us all" (Rom. 8:32).

In the early 1320s one finds Esayi Nčʿecʿi addressing an "Epistle to Bishop Mattʿēos of Tabriz" concerning a wide range of matters of church discipline in direct response to the proselytizing of the Dominican missionaries. Mattʿēos had been Esayi's pupil at Glajor. Frankish, Greek, or Syrian clergy who urge them to renounce their traditions should not be welcomed by Armenians but be treated as "sowers of discord within the Church of Christ, as enemies of the truth, and as wolves hiding in sheep's clothing." Armenians who defect to them should not be received into one's home. The tone is firm yet not intolerant. On the subject of the eucharistic wine, he believes that the Armenians are following the apostolic tradition, but he allows that if mass is celebrated "with perfect faith and piety, both (diluted and undiluted wine) would be acceptable and pleasing to God." Esayi also shows considerable toleration on the subject of christological formulae. He advises the bishop not to be irrational in this respect because "the holy vardapets also spoke of two natures," that is, of Christ "as perfect God and perfect man, without confusion and without alteration." The issue should not be used to anathematize others. "If, following the holy fathers, one speaks with integrity about the one or the two natures in Christ, one cannot speak of heresy but rather of following the truth." This may sound like a softening of his position, but Esayi goes on to say that the Latin missionaries, like Nestorius, have divided the one Christ into two natures. The letter discusses other matters of church discipline, such as fasting, marriage, confession, and communion. All should confess every week, he says, and receive communion every forty days.

The fourth letter, "On the consecration of priests, at the request of Bishop Sargis," metropolitan of Siwnikʿ, was written sometime after 1337, toward the end of Esayi's life.[201] The style is uncharacteristic of

[199] Esayi defends the Armenian use of undiluted wine in another letter, "Against those who err in the matter of the Eucharist." We have used the text in Jerusalem, St. James, 773, a Miscellany written by the scribe-priest Anton in 1359 (?) (see Połarian, *Mayr Cʿucʿak*, III, 218–22). The letter was published in *Sion*, old series (Jerusalem, 1866), no. 1, 6–9.

[200] We have used the text in Erevan, Matenadaran, 614, fols. 29–33. The manuscript is a Miscellany dated 1625, written by the scribe Simēon for one Pałum Julecʿi. Other copies can be found in Erevan, Mat. 571, 614, 1043, 1337, 1476, 2283, 4063, 7255, and 8389 (cf. Eganyan, *Cʿucʿak Jeṙagracʿ*, I, cols. 351, 364, 464, 529, 560, 766, 1140; II, cols. 492–93, 734).

[201] We have used the text in Erevan, Mat. 3937 (fols. 133–39), a Miscellany written in 1370 by the scribe Stepʿanos. See Eganyan, *Cʿucʿak Jeṙagracʿ*, I, 1114. Other copies can be found in Erevan, Mat. 3276 (ibid., I, 978) and Jerusalem, St. James, 69 and 1279 (see Połarian, *Mayr Cʿucʿak*, I, 224–39 and IV, 465–68).

Esayi's other works; besides a number of passages that are quite obscure, the text contains many grammatical infelicities. Either the original has been tampered with or Esayi must have dictated the letter to a pupil of limited skills. But the theme is entirely in keeping with Esayi's known interest in Pseudo-Denis the Areopagite, for it takes its ecclesiology from him by way of frequent direct quotations. As in Pseudo-Denis the hierarchy on earth is said to reproduce the order of the three-times-three ranks of angels. The earthly orders are: archbishop, bishop, and priest; deacon, psalm-singer, and reader; and monk, congregant, and catechumen. According to Pseudo-Denis, the purpose of hierarchy is "assimilation and union, as far as attainable, with God, having him leader of all religious knowledge and operation, by looking unflinchingly to his most divine beauty and copying it."[202] Not found in Pseudo-Denis, however, is Esayi's belief that the church was created in the Garden of Paradise. The Word, he says, created the church on earth by endowing Adam with priestly graces. He placed him upon the illumined altar that stands on high on the eastern side of paradise as the symbol of his spiritual and incorruptible wisdom. God instilled in Adam the breath of wisdom, by which he could serve forever as priest to the immortal God. Priesthood, therefore, is eternal, one of the fundamental works of creation.

Esayi seems to have been occupied with three principal themes: the defense of Armenian Christology, the preservation of Armenian traditions in liturgy, and the definition of the nature of the church. As discussed subsequently, these are also the principal themes enunciated by the iconography of the U.C.L.A. Gospel and the exegetical literature associated with it.

[202] Pseudo-Denis, *Celestial Hierarchy*, chap. 3. Cf. John Parker, *The Works of Dionysius the Areopagite* (Merrick, N.Y., 1897–99; repr. 1976), pt. II, 13–14.

CHAPTER THREE

The Archaeology of the U.C.L.A. Codex

1. Introduction

The production of an illuminated codex was a process of considerable complexity, involving the successive employment of several artists or artisans of diverse skills. First the parchment had to be prepared by the parchment maker, who cured, stretched, blanched, and trimmed the animal skin in specified standard sizes. The scribe or scribes then ruled the pages and assembled them into quires or gatherings. Working from a chosen exemplar, they copied the text, planning the layout of the book as they proceeded, deciding where decorations or illustrations were to fall. The painting of the manuscript usually went forward in stages, decorative work preceding the painting of figures, and these stages were frequently the work of separate artists. After the painting was completed a scribe was again called upon to fill in the Eusebian preface and the columns of numbers in the canon tables. Finally the manuscript went to a binder who stitched the book into a cover of leather stretched over wood, and who might employ still another artist to decorate it with silver and gems.

The critical study of the making of such a work is called the archaeology of the codex, insofar as it involves the separate study, as if layer by layer, of the stages by which the product acquired its final form, as well as of the subsequent changes that may have modified the manuscript. The archaeology of the U.C.L.A. manuscript has involved the dismantling of the binding, a complete codicological analysis, the separation of the contributions of the various painters, and a chemical analysis of the pigments employed. A detailed understanding of how the different components of the manuscript came together is especially critical in the study of the U.C.L.A. Gospel because it can be shown that the manuscript is the product of two distinct workshops, involving five different artists. Ultimately, however, despite its complicated history the Glajor Gospel has a programmatic or conceptual unity that reconciles the diversity of artistic material it contains.

2. The Binding, the Codicology, and the Work of the Scribes

When the Glajor Gospel came to U.C.L.A. it was bound in Persian lacquered covers of the Qajar period. These are decorated inside and out with floral bouquets and birds in designs that repeat in precise mirror images on the front and back (figs. 1–2, 87–88). On the outside a black central field is strewn with a profusion of flowers that spread out from the center in all directions. Iris, tulips, carnations and a variety of roses can be recognized along with some blossoms that are purely fanciful. The lack of orientation in the floral composition is reflected in the placement of four yellow birds that perch, somewhat insecurely, in various directions; two of the birds are grouped so closely that they appear as a single bird with two heads. The framing of this bouquet consists of a broad border of repeating yellow and green blossoms between bands of smaller geometric motifs in black and gold. Inside the cover, the decoration of the doublures is somewhat more restrained. Against a gold background a single spray of roses and rosebuds is painted in a graceful S-curve, growing up from the lower border, with two yellow birds on it. The border is a simplified variant of that on the outside of the covers.

The lacquerware technique involved in the covers consists of layering and pressing cardboard and decorating it with successive coats of paint and varnish until a high glossy finish is obtained. This technique was introduced in Persia in the sixteenth century, and although Persian lacquerware has not been systematically collected and studied, the U.C.L.A. covers can be dated to the first half of the nineteenth century.[1] The decoration of the exterior of the covers should be compared to the covers published by Gratzl, on which one finds the same repertoire of flowers,

[1] On Persian lacquerware see Emil Gratzl, *Islamische Bucheinbände des 14. bis 19. Jahrhunderts* (Leipzig, 1924); idem, "Lacquer Bindings of the 16th to the 19th Centuries," *Survey of Persian Art* (London, 1938), 1984–86.

within borders that are virtually identical in design to those of the U.C.L.A. Gospel; Gratzl dates his example to the second quarter of the nineteenth century.[2] Another example, dated precisely to 1819, displays similar flowers on a gold field, again with the same borders.[3] The yellow birds can be found on the bouquets that decorate a rectangular mirror case, which is dated to the beginning of the nineteenth century.[4] If on this basis the U.C.L.A. book covers can be assigned to the first half of the nineteenth century, they should in all probability be assigned precisely to the year 1824–25 on the basis of the inscription on page 25. In that year, as noted above, the priest Yōvakim Abraham of Isfahan received the book from the congregation of the church of Mec Xōǰencʿ and proudly inscribed his name and the names of his children; very likely this change of ownership was the occasion for the pious work of restoring the book by having it newly bound.

When the University of California, Los Angeles, acquired the manuscript it was found that the first few gatherings were breaking loose from the stitching while the rest of the book was stitched so tightly that it would not lie open. Accordingly Brooke Whiting, then curator of manuscripts, decided that the proper conservation of the manuscript required that it be bound anew. The dismantling of the codex afforded a unique opportunity to study the binding and codicology, and a chance to correct four mistakes or revisions in pagination that were made in the nineteenth century and one that had been made by the original fourteenth-century binder (pages 1–2, 24a-b; 29–30 and 39–40; 295–96; and *403–4*, as discussed below).

When the lacquered covers were removed it was found that they were not stitched to the book in medieval fashion but had been attached to a pair of black leather hinges, which were glued flat on the spine of the book, overlapping in the middle (figs. 1–2, 87–88).[5] Beneath these black hinges two little wedges of cardboard created artificial horizontal ridges, or hubs, across the spine in imitation of the ridges that would be created by the stitching in a medieval binding. On the inside, hinges of printed cotton cloth connected the covers to the first and last folios of the book. Beneath this artificially constructed spine the individual gatherings of the book were stitched together with red and green silk thread through four needle holes in the fold of each gathering; all the stitching was then covered with a generous coat of glue to receive the leather flaps of the spine. No evidence remained of earlier bindings of the manuscript except for the stitching holes cut in V-shaped notches in the fold of each gathering (*page 529*). These notches offered a valuable additional control in checking the original order of the folios within each gathering, for since they were chopped through the fold of the entire gathering together they diminish in size from the outer bifolium of a gathering to the innermost bifolium.

The pages of the U.C.L.A. Gospel now measure an average of 235 x 176 mm, but this is the result of trimming during the nineteenth-century rebinding, when the fore-edges were painted in a flower pattern. The original measurements must have been close to 270 x 180 mm, a standard measurement in Byzantine manuscripts.[6] The writing surface is justified to 165 x 119 mm (see diagram). Unfortunately Armenian palaeographic studies have not yet developed the kinds of paradigms for ruling and pricking that have been worked out for Byzantine manuscripts;[7] nevertheless one can observe that the manuscript is ruled with a stylus for 21 lines of text in two columns and the first line of text sits on the first ruled line, rather than under it as in Greek manuscripts. Prickings appear near the outer edges of many folia (for example, see *pages 28, 92, 103, 106*), but in other places they have been trimmed off.

The U.C.L.A. Gospel is composed of twenty-four gatherings, which as a rule are gatherings of six bifolia (see diagrams). It should be noted that in Byzantine manuscripts the normal gathering is four bifolia, and larger gatherings are rare;[8] but in Armenia, while gatherings of four sheets is the more common practice, some important scriptoria of Cilicia used six sheets.[9] Ten of the gatherings in the U.C.L.A. manuscript are perfectly regular; the irregularities in the remaining fourteen are due in three

[2] Gratzl, *Islamische Bucheinbände*, pl. 22.

[3] Sotheby Parke Bernet, Inc., *Catalogue of Fine Oriental Miniatures Manuscripts and Printed Books* (London, 28 April 1981), lot 352, p. 133.

[4] Hôtel Drouot, *Art d'Iran, Art d'Orient* (Paris, 20 November 1974), lot 117, pp. 68–69.

[5] Very little has been done on the history of Armenian book binding; it is hoped that a dissertation now in preparation at Columbia University by Sylvie Merian will remedy this situation. Meanwhile see Berthe van Regemorter, "La reliure arménienne," *Bazmavep* 8–10 (1953), 200–204; B. Aṙakʿelyan, "Kazmeri zardarman arvestə miǰnadaryan Hayastanum," *Banber Matenadarani* 4 (1958), 183–203.

[6] Jean Irigoin, "Pour une étude des centres de copie byzantins," *Scriptorium* 12 (1958), 212.

[7] Ibid., 208–27; 13 (1959), 177–209; Julien Leroy, *Les types de reglure des manuscrits grecs* (Paris, n.d.).

[8] Irigoin, "Centres de copie byzantins," 220–21.

[9] For example, Washington, Freer 32.18, of Tʿoros Ṙoslin, the Gospel of Baron Vasak, and Freer 56.11, dated 1263, are composed of gatherings of six bifolia. Der Nersessian, *Arm. Mss. Freer*, 26 and 55.

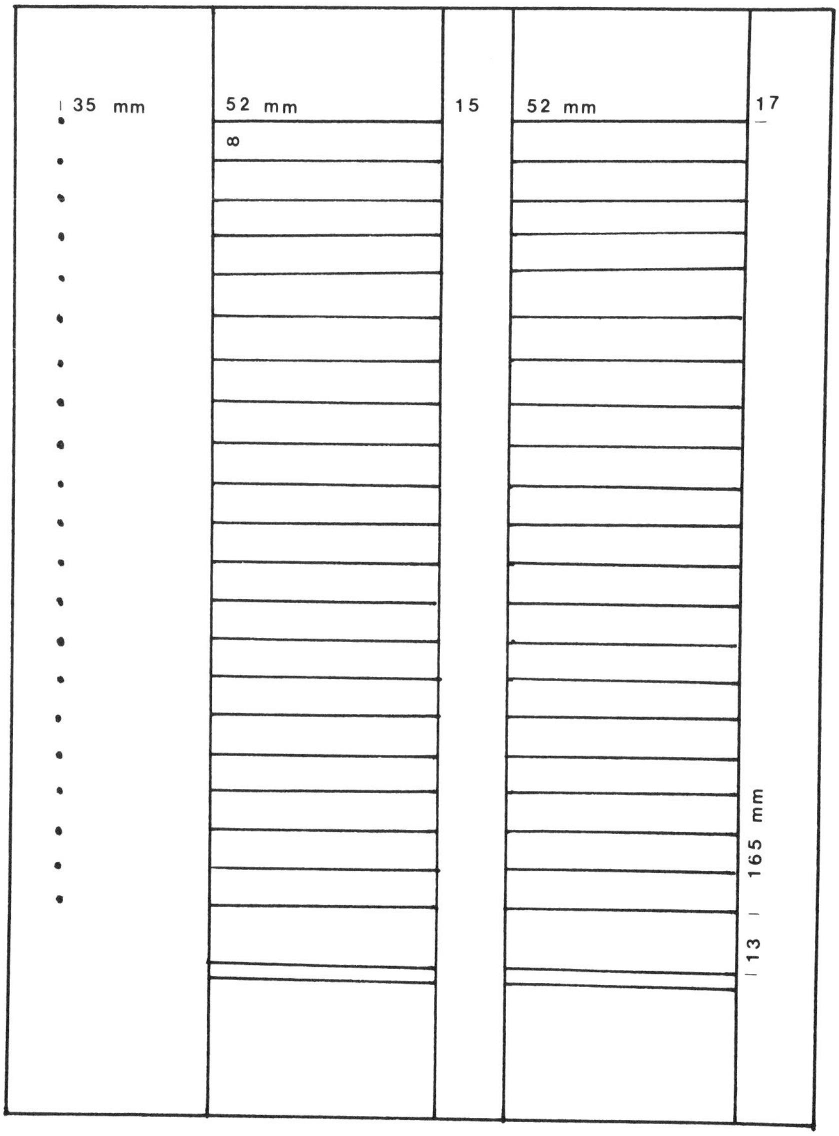

Diagram of Rulings and Prickings

instances to missing leaves, but otherwise they are due to the use of single leaves that were employed from the outset exactly as they now appear, sometimes carrying text and sometimes miniatures. Parchment was a precious commodity, and when the parchment maker had pieces smaller than the bifolium format he made single leaves, which were slightly wider than half a bifolium to allow for a folded stub by which they could be stitched into the gathering. In the nineteenth-century rebinding many of the stubs of these leaves were cut off and the leaves were glued in. The use of these single leaves sometimes results in a gathering being smaller than standard (gathering 6), sometimes larger (gathering 13). In one instance two single leaves were paired to make a bifolium (pages 461–64 in gathering 20).

As a rule the first and last page of each gathering carry the quire signature in the middle of the lower margin. However, the initial gathering, which contains the canon tables and is made of a finer and more supple parchment, is unnumbered, as usual in both Greek and Armenian manuscripts.[10] But signatures are also missing from the beginning of the second and ninth gatherings, due to the loss of pages, and from the end of the eighth and twenty-fourth gatherings for no clear reason. In assembling each gathering the scribe alternated the hair and smooth sides of the parchment, starting with hair sides facing one another in the center fold. The traditional end leaves, which in Armenia were reused from older manu-

[10] Der Nersessian, *Manuscrits*, 15.

scripts as a way of sanctifying the new one, are missing from the U.C.L.A. Gospel, possibly a casualty of the nineteenth-century rebinding.

An inspection of the gatherings in order reveals that the first gathering was evidently originally composed of seven bifolia. Two changes were made in 1982 to restore the primitive pagination of this gathering. When the Gospel book came to U.C.L.A. the solitary first leaf (pages 1–2), which is blank except for the inscription of the baroness Vaxax, was bound in upside-down at the very back of the book. But this leaf is of the same fine white parchment as the first gathering (the rest of the book is heavier and brownish parchment) and the burn stains along its outer edge exactly match those on page 3 (these stains continue, gradually diminishing, through the first two gatherings). This leaf has therefore been restored to its proper position. Its conjugate leaf, which is now missing, must have carried the prefatory material for Matthew's Gospel, which continued onto the missing first leaf of the next gathering. In the seventeenth century someone started to make good this loss by entering the Preface and Contents of Matthew (the usual order is Contents and then Preface) onto pages 22–23, but he left the task unfinished. The other change in pagination concerns the leaf pages 24a-b. Having moved the initial blank leaf to the back of the book, the nineteenth-century binder needed another blank for the front flyleaf; this he found in pages 24a-b, which he folded forward to take the place of the first page. It was in this position when Dr. Minasian acquired the book and put his library stamp on it, but it has now been restored to its original position.

The second gathering carries the signature *ayb* at the end on page 46; it evidently lacks its initial leaf, which would have carried another *ayb* along with the continuation of the prefatory material of Matthew. Here again a correction in pagination was made in 1982. In the nineteenth century the bifolium of *pages 29–30* and 39–40 was exchanged with that of *pages 31–32* and 37–38. The text leaves no question about the correct order, and this has been restored and the page numbering revised. More significant is the loss of a miniature which is attested by offset smudges of pigment on page 41—red, blue, green, yellow, and magenta. The subject must have been the Baptism, since page 41 begins with the text of Matt.3:4. Nothing is missing in the text at this point, hence the miniature must have been assigned a full page, the other side being left blank.

The third, fourth, and fifth gatherings are regular, with the signatures *ben, gim,* and *da* on their first and last pages. The sixth gathering is one leaf short of regular, but nothing is missing. The signature *yečʿ* appears on pages 119 and 140. The seventh gathering is regular with the signature *za* on pages 141 and 164. In the eighth gathering, which is regular, the signature *ē* appears on page 165, but it is missing on the conjugate concluding page 186.

The ninth gathering, embracing the portrait of Mark and the beginning of his Gospel, is very peculiar, for it consisted of only two bifolia. The signature *ətʿ* is found on page 192 at the end of the gathering, but the conjugate leaf at the start of the gathering is missing. Since the prefatory material to Mark is complete on pages 183–86 this missing leaf must have contained something else, and the most likely supposition is that this was the original dedicatory colophon of the manuscript. A colophon is to be expected in the manuscript, and there is no other missing leaf where it is likely to have occurred.

The tenth gathering is regular with the *tʿo* on pages 193 and *216*. The eleventh gathering, with *žē* on pages 219 and 242, would be perfectly regular were it not for the addition of the single leaf, pages 217-*18*. This insertion, which is blank on one side and carries the Raising of Jairus' Daughter on the other, calls one's attention to the beginning of Tʿoros Taronecʿi's work on the manuscript, as will be explained below. By mistake, Tʿoros painted his first miniature, the Woman with Hemorrhage and Jairus' petition, on *page 216* instead of where it belonged—in page 214 where the scribe had left a full page blank for it. Realizing the mistake and unwilling to omit the next scene from the program, Tʿoros inserted the extra single leaf, pages 217-*18*.

The twelfth gathering is again regular, with the signature *žē ayb* on pages 243 and 266. The thirteenth gathering has the signature *žē ben* on pages 267 and 292. The last folio is a single leaf, but since it carries the signature it is clear that this is how the scribe assembled the gathering.

The fourteenth gathering is oversize—seven bifolia plus the single sheet pages 295–96. This sheet, carrying part of the Contents of the Introduction to Luke, had been misbound in the preceding gathering in the nineteenth century (between the present pages 290 and 291). The error was corrected in 1982. The signature *žē gim* appears on pages 293 and 322.

The fifteenth gathering has fourteen leaves, two of which are single leaves with full-page miniatures of the Annunciation and the Visitation, the reverse of the miniatures being blank (*pages 327–28* and *335–36*). The signature *žē da* appears on page 323 and page 350. The sixteenth gathering is regular except for the insertion of *pages 351–52,* with a full-page miniature, the Anointing at Simon's, on one side. The signature *žē yečʿ* appears on pages 350a and 374. The seventeenth gathering is regular and without miniatures. It has the signature *žē za* on *page 375* and page 398.

The eighteenth gathering is regular except for the insertion of the leaf pages 403–4. This folio has the Parable of the Cunning Steward on one side, and it was previously found at the start of the next gathering, between pages 424 and 425, where it was evidently misbound from the very start. As will be explained below, the iconography associates the miniatures with the text of Luke 16:1–9 which is found on pages 402–5, rather than with the questions of tribute and of the resurrection, which are found on page 424 (Luke 20:21–38). The fact that the miniature was out of place was recognized from the outset and an inscription was entered in the upper margin saying: "This is the rich man and his steward and it is not in its proper place." This mistake was rectified in 1982 and the page numbering adjusted accordingly. The signature *žē ē* appears on pages 399 and 424.

The nineteenth gathering is regular, with *žē ətʿ* on pages 425 and 448. The twentieth gathering is irregular only insofar as the innermost pair of leaves are two single leaves rather than conjugate leaves. The signature *žē tʿo* appears on pages 449 and 476. The twenty-first gathering consists of seven regular bifolia; it has the signature *ini* on pages 477 and 504. The twenty-second and twenty-third gatherings are regular, with signatures *ini ayb* and *ini ben* at the beginning and end.

The twenty-fourth gathering has the signature *ini gim* on page 553 but lacks a concluding signature, perhaps because it would have no use in the process of assembling the gatherings for binding. This is a regular six-sheet gathering, with two extra single leaves. One leaf carries the full-page miniature of the Crucifixion, pages *561*-62, and is blank on the other side; the other leaf, pages 579–80, was added at the end of the gathering to accommodate the colophon of Baron Martiros of 1393–1404.

In addition to guaranteeing that very little has been lost from or added to the original manuscript, the detailed examination of the codicology of the U.C.L.A. Gospel puts one in a position to appreciate exactly what shape the manuscript had when the scribe turned it over to the painters. Since the layout of the book was basically determined in the scribal phase, it is important to understand the work of the scribe. As remarked above, the principal work of the scribe was done before any of the decoration; this sequence is required by the logic of interrupting text to leave room for inserting miniatures, but it can also be demonstrated by the manner in which painters of the U.C.L.A. Gospel conscientiously tried to fill up the uneven spaces left by the scribe for the miniatures (for example, see *pages 124, 169, and 193*). On the other hand, the completion of the "text" material of the canon tables logically had to follow the painting of the enframing architecture, and the way the columns of numbers bend to fit around capitals and bases demonstrates this work sequence in the U.C.L.A. Gospel (for example, see *pages 8, 9, 13, and 21*). The manuscript was begun by a scribe, it was passed to painters for decoration, and it was returned to a scribe for completion of canon tables.

Examination of the script reveals that, apart from colophons and inscriptions and the rewriting of the prefatory material before Matthew remarked above, all of which material is clearly later than the original production, the manuscript is the work of two scribes. The scribe of the canon tables is not the same as the scribe of the body of the text; his hand slants at a sharper angle and his letter forms are not as full and well rounded as those of the principal scribe. This is especially evident in the larger letters, such as the *tʿo*, *ǰē* and *ša*. No such changes, however, can be detected in the body of the manuscript. The principal scribe wrote the entire text of the four Gospels, as well as the prefatory material that stands before each Gospel. He also entered the quire numbers into the bottom margins and the Easter lection numbers in the side margins (*page 375*). The scribe of the canon tables, however, was responsible not only for the text of the Eusebian Introduction and the numbers within the tables themselves but for corresponding Eusebian numbers throughout the manuscript.

It is characteristic of Armenian Gospel manuscripts that in addition to numbering Eusebius' divisions of

CODICOLOGICAL DIAGRAMS

Key to Codicological Diagrams

c	canon table pages
col.	colophons and inscriptions
(col.)	missing original colophons
e	evangelist portrait
i	incipit page
m	page carrying a miniature
(m)	miniature missing or unexecuted
o	page originally left blank
p	prefatory material (i.e., chapter lists and Gospel prefaces)
(p)	missing prefatory material
#	quire signature number
-------	conjectural leaf

QUIRE 1

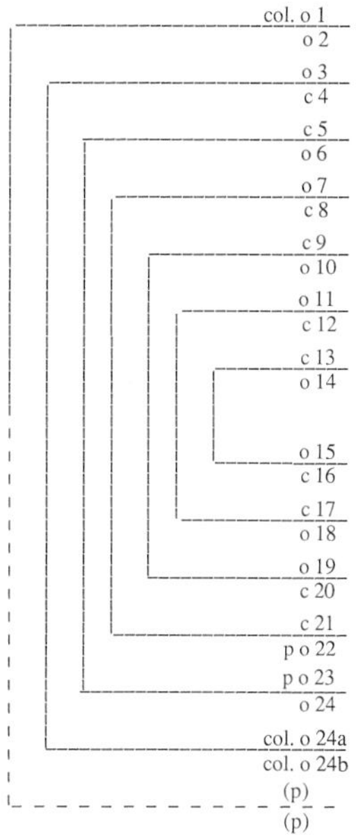

QUIRE 2

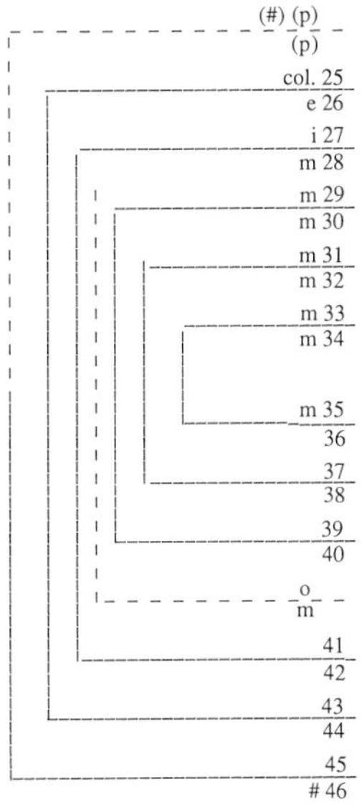

QUIRE 3

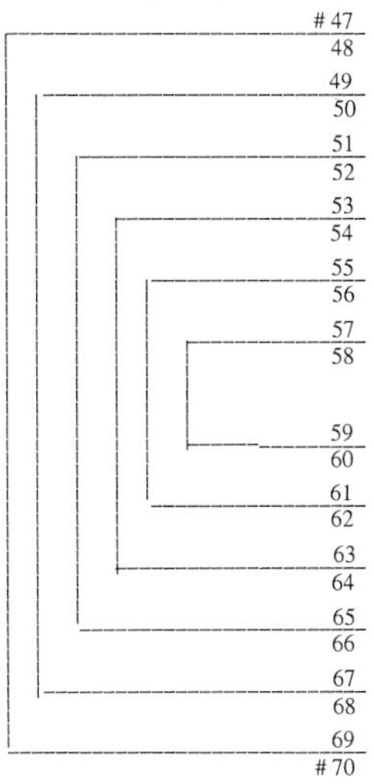

QUIRE 4

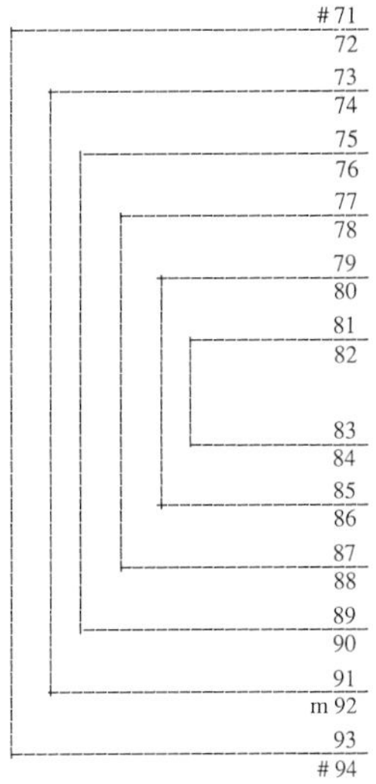

QUIRE 5

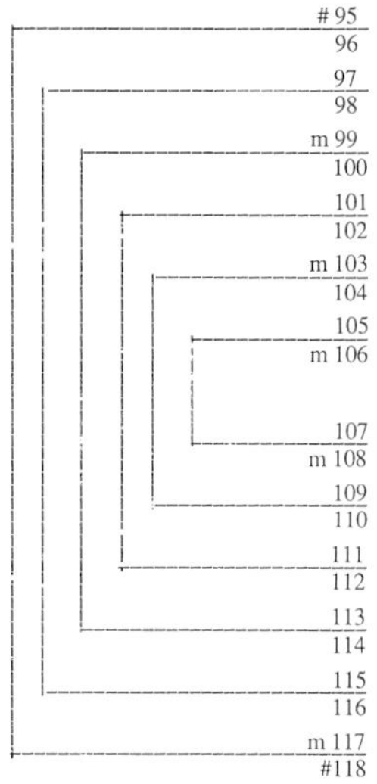

QUIRE 6

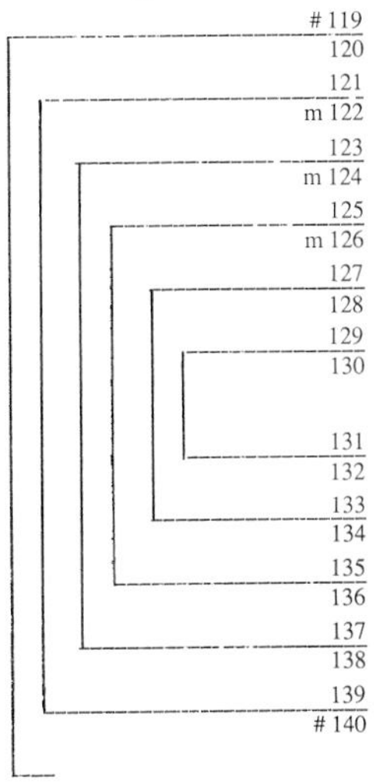

QUIRE 7

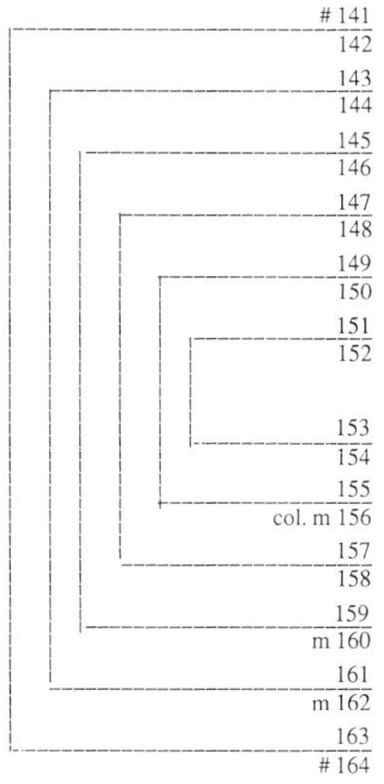
141
142
143
144
145
146
147
148
149
150
151
152
153
154
155
col. m 156
157
158
159
m 160
161
m 162
163
164

QUIRE 10

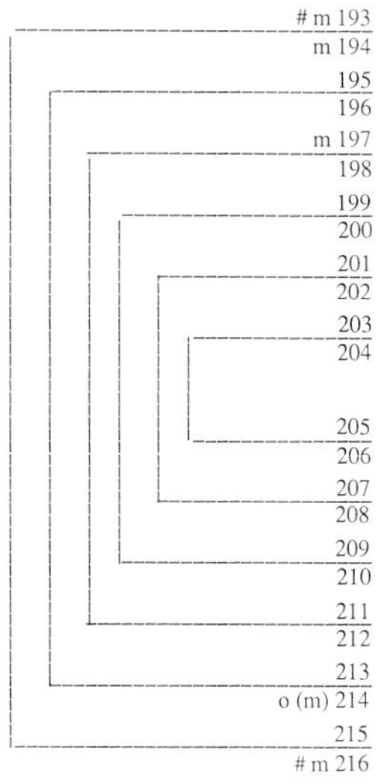
m 193
m 194
195
196
m 197
198
199
200
201
202
203
204
205
206
207
208
209
210
211
212
213
o (m) 214
215
m 216

QUIRE 8

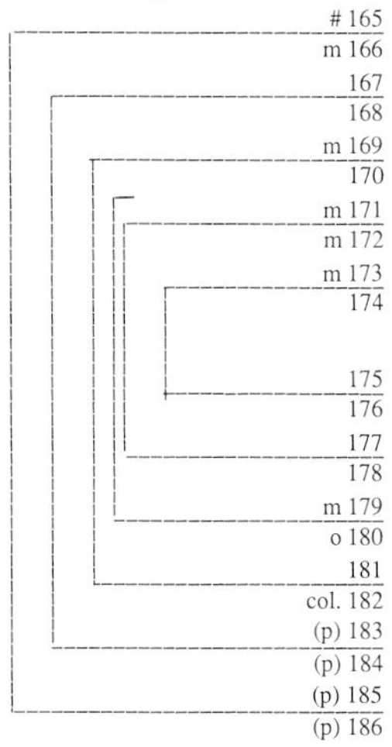
165
m 166
167
168
m 169
170
m 171
m 172
m 173
174
175
176
177
178
m 179
o 180
181
col. 182
(p) 183
(p) 184
(p) 185
(p) 186

QUIRE 11

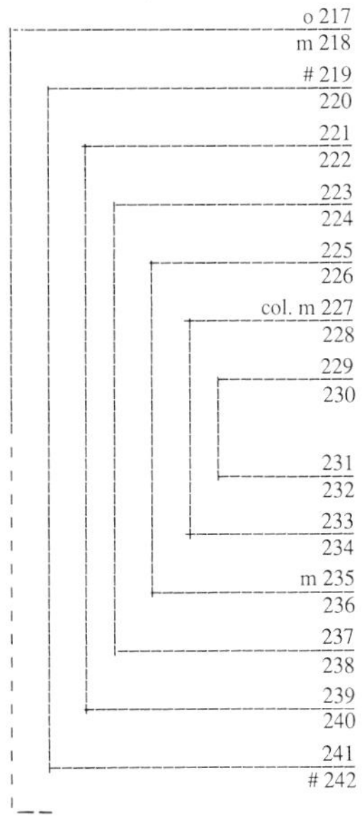
o 217
m 218
219
220
221
222
223
224
225
226
col. m 227
228
229
230
231
232
233
234
m 235
236
237
238
239
240
241
242

QUIRE 9

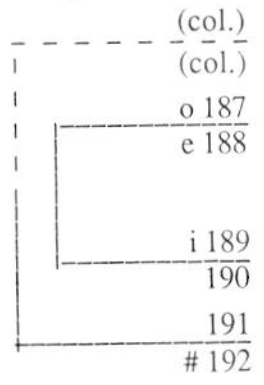
(col.)
(col.)
o 187
e 188
i 189
190
191
192

QUIRE 12

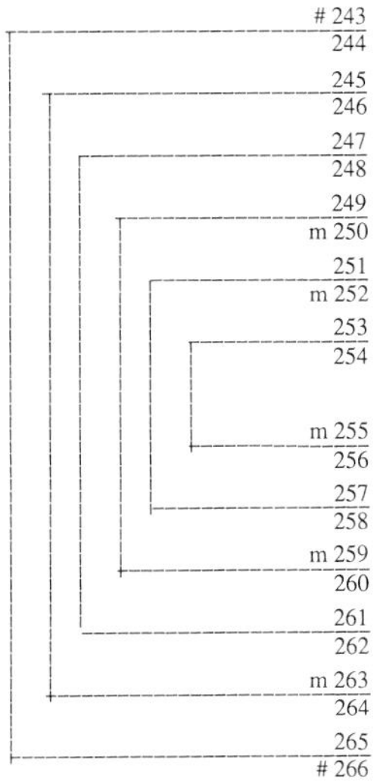
243
244
245
246
247
248
249
m 250
251
m 252
253
254
m 255
256
257
258
m 259
260
261
262
m 263
264
265
266

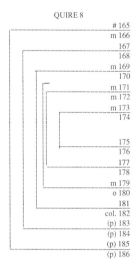

QUIRE 13

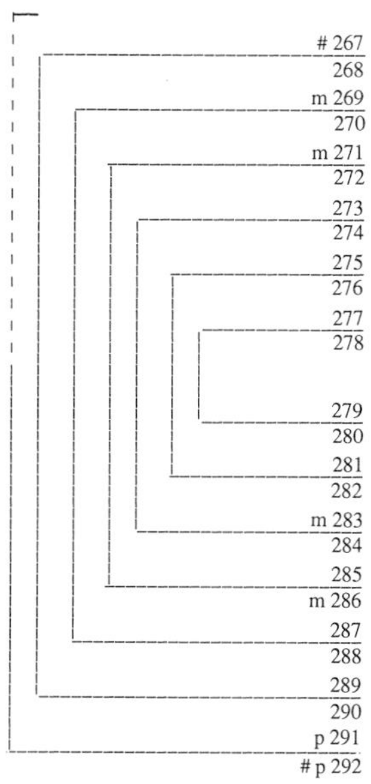

267
268
m 269
270
m 271
272
273
274
275
276
277
278
279
280
281
282
m 283
284
285
m 286
287
288
289
290
p 291
p 292

QUIRE 14

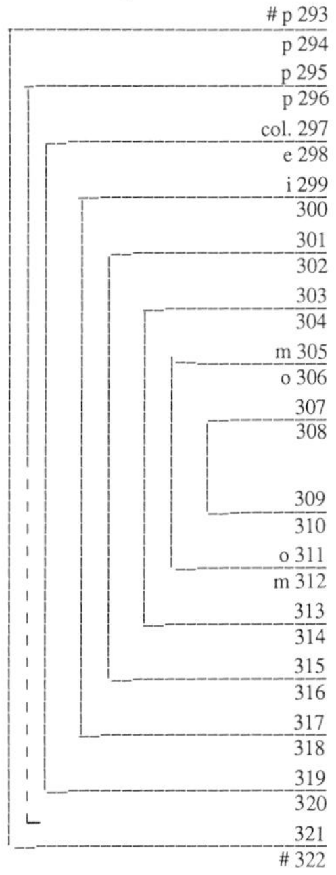

p 293
p 294
p 295
p 296
col. 297
e 298
i 299
300
301
302
303
304
m 305
o 306
307
308
309
310
o 311
m 312
313
314
315
316
317
318
319
320
321
322

QUIRE 15

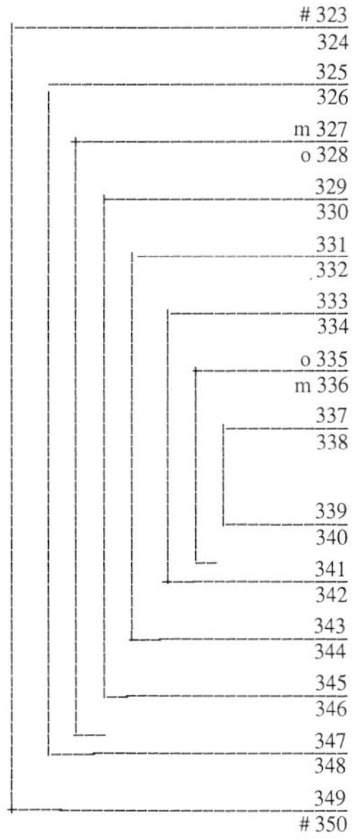

323
324
325
326
m 327
o 328
329
330
331
332
333
334
o 335
m 336
337
338
339
340
341
342
343
344
345
346
347
348
349
350

QUIRE 16

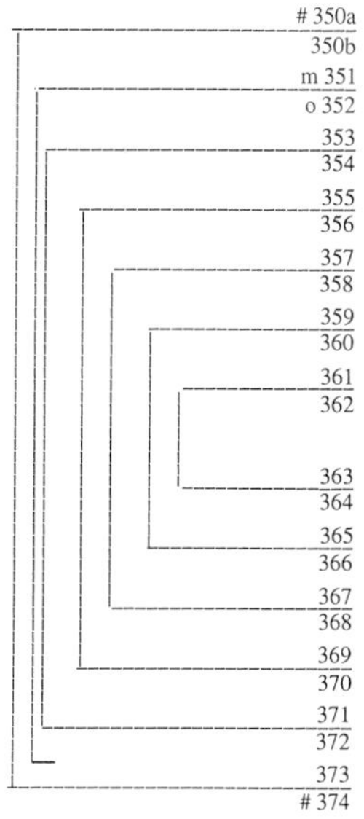

350a
350b
m 351
o 352
353
354
355
356
357
358
359
360
361
362
363
364
365
366
367
368
369
370
371
372
373
374

QUIRE 17

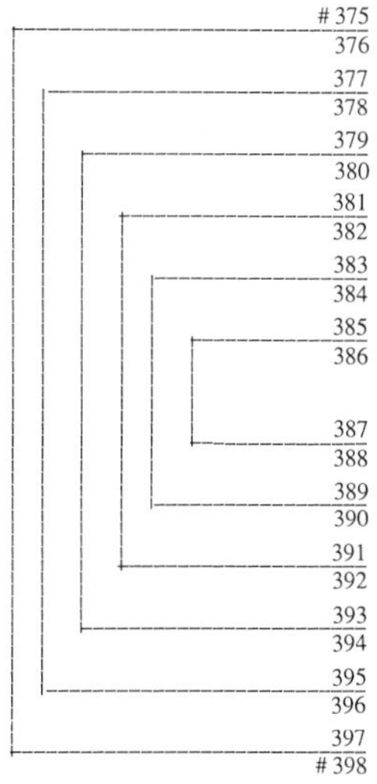

375
376
377
378
379
380
381
382
383
384
385
386
387
388
389
390
391
392
393
394
395
396
397
398

QUIRE 18

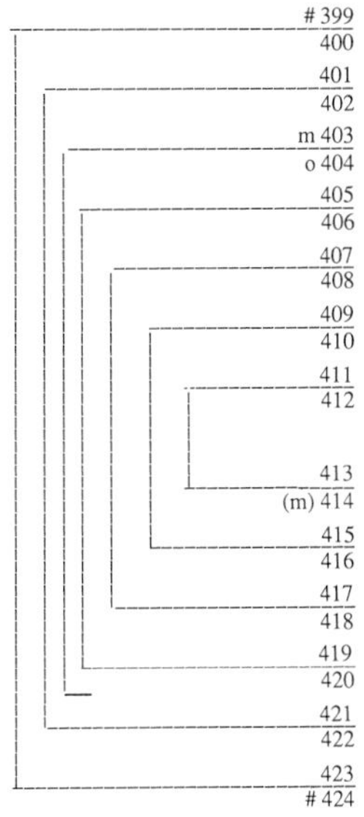

399
400
401
402
m 403
o 404
405
406
407
408
409
410
411
412
413
(m) 414
415
416
417
418
419
420
421
422
423
424

QUIRE 19

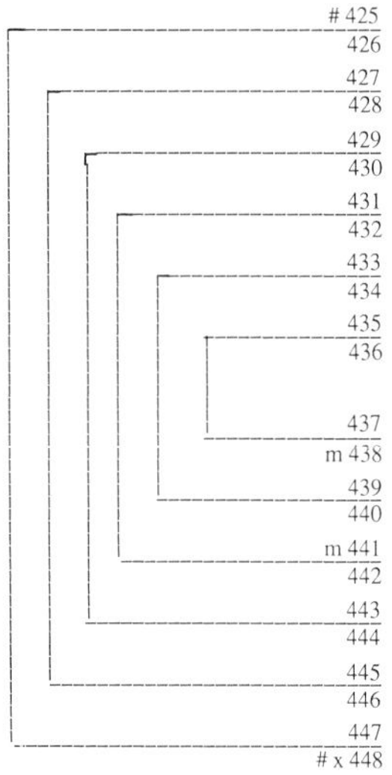

425
426
427
428
429
430
431
432
433
434
435
436
437
m 438
439
440
m 441
442
443
444
445
446
447
x 448

QUIRE 22

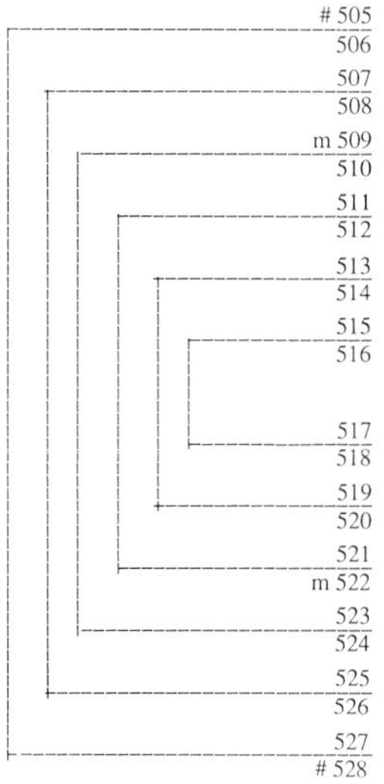

505
506
507
508
m 509
510
511
512
513
514
515
516
517
518
519
520
521
m 522
523
524
525
526
527
528

QUIRE 20

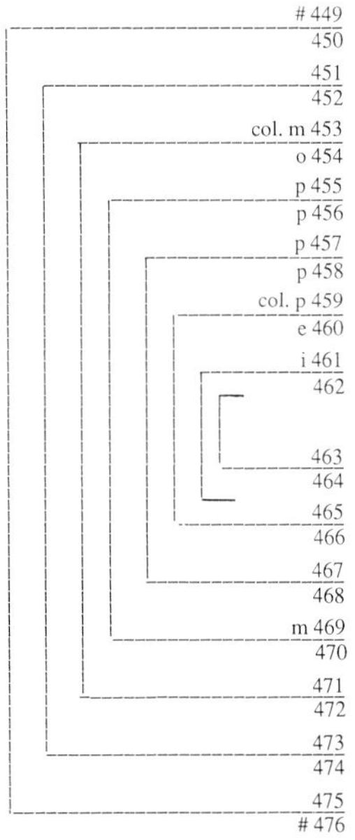

449
450
451
452
col. m 453
o 454
p 455
p 456
p 457
p 458
col. p 459
e 460
i 461
462
463
464
465
466
467
468
m 469
470
471
472
473
474
475
476

QUIRE 23

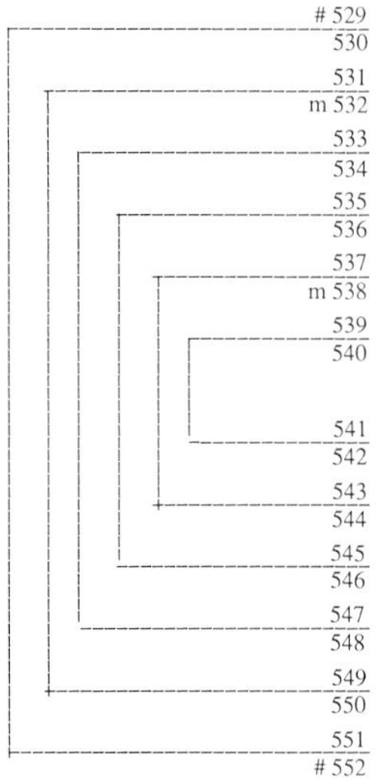

529
530
531
m 532
533
534
535
536
537
m 538
539
540
541
542
543
544
545
546
547
548
549
550
551
552

QUIRE 21

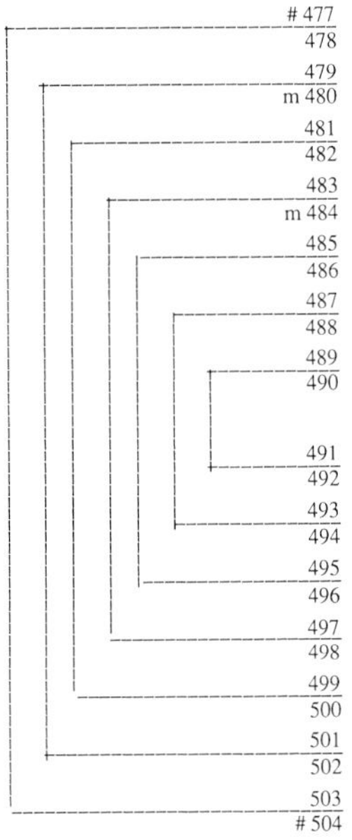

477
478
479
m 480
481
482
483
m 484
485
486
487
488
489
490
491
492
493
494
495
496
497
498
499
500
501
502
503
504

QUIRE 24

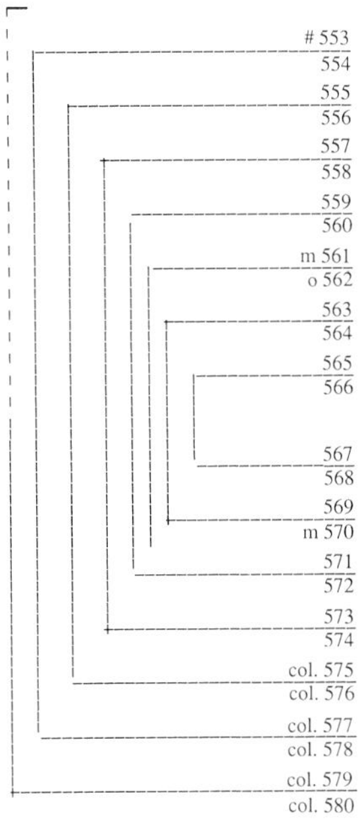

553
554
555
556
557
558
559
560
m 561
o 562
563
564
565
566
567
568
569
m 570
571
572
573
574
col. 575
col. 576
col. 577
col. 578
col. 579
col. 580

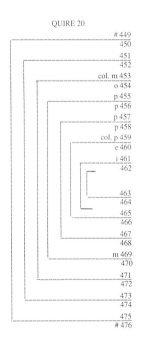

the text—without which the canon tables would be useless—the scribe provided two other aids to the use of the Eusebian system: beneath the number of the Eusebian section in black he supplied in red the number of the canon table one ought to consult to locate the passage in question, and at the foot of the page he supplied an excerpt of the data one would obtain by consulting that particular canon table (*page 375*). It is only logical that all of these Eusebian numbers should be entered into a manuscript by the same scribe, and in the U.C.L.A. Gospel they are all done in the angular script and finer pen of the second scribe. One other set of numbers also runs continually through the manuscript and they are the chapter numbers, written in blue within a blue circle; these correspond to the lists of chapters that are given at the beginning of each Gospel. These also seem to be the work of the principal scribe, for it is clear that they are done before the painted decoration, which often overlaps them. The second scribe probably never knew the first, for as we shall see the painting of the manuscript that intervened involved a number of discontinuities.

When the principal scribe had finished the body of the text (with the prefatory material before each Gospel and the numbering of quires, chapters, and lections) it is clear that much of the program of illumination had already been determined. Obviously the placement of textual ornament was rigidly tied to the text; the scribe's placement of the lection number in the margin determined the placement of the ornament with which the illuminator would enframe it, and the scribe must have sketched in the capital letter at the start of each lection for the illuminator to decorate. At the beginning of each Gospel the scribe had to leave space for the headpieces and the ornamented letters with which the first few words of the Gospel would be presented, and the verso facing this page was left blank for the portrait of the evangelist. The scribe's plan for the narrative illuminations, however, raises some problems, for it exhibits some curious inconsistencies.

It is perfectly understandable that the scribe should have assigned some miniatures less than full-page format, so that they share the page with the text which they interrupt (for example, *pages 103, 108*) while he gave other miniatures full-page format, using the other side of the folio for text (for example, *pages 99, 106*). However, examining the codicology one cannot but be struck by the fact that in Luke six miniatures in succession are painted on single leaves that have no text on the other side—from the Annunciation (*page 305*) through the Clever Steward (*page 403*). One might logically ask whether the scribe had in fact intended these miniatures, or whether they represent an effort on the artists' part to fill out an earlier program that they found inadequate. There are four other miniatures that were treated in the same fashion, that is, single leaves blank on one side, namely, the missing miniature of the Baptism (between pages 40–41), the Women at the Tomb (*page 179*), the Raising of Jairus' Daughter (*page 218*), and the Crucifixion (*page 561*).

We have seen that one of these miniatures, the Raising of Jairus' Daughter, does represent an addition by the artist to the scribe's layout, but this was done to make good his mistake four pages earlier, and the subject was part of the scribe's original plan. The other miniatures seem to have been planned by the scribe the way they now occur. It is a priori unlikely that he would have designed a program of illumination that would have omitted such momentous subjects as the Annunciation and the Crucifixion. It will be argued below, in fact, that the program of the U.C.L.A. Gospel belongs to a venerable tradition in Armenia going back to the eleventh century and this tradition determined the selection, even if not the size, of most of the miniatures. One decisive piece of evidence is offered by the codicology in the scribe's handling of the miniature for the Ascension (*page 453*), for here he located the miniature on a folio that was conjugate with a folio of text but still he left the reverse of the miniature blank. One can only conclude that the scribe had no fixed rule of procedure for full-page miniatures; sometimes he planned them on leaves that were an integral part of the gathering and sometimes he assigned them single leaves. Sometimes he left the other side of the page blank and sometimes he used it for text. Some single leaves, it should be noted, carry only text (pages 119–20, 291–92, 295–96, 463–64), and the full-page illumination of the beginning of John is on a single leaf with text on the reverse (pages 461–62).

The relationship of the principal scribe to the artists of the U.C.L.A. manuscript cannot be fixed with precision. It is not impossible that once he finished copying the text, the scribe himself began working on the illumination of the manuscript, a situation often encountered in Armenia. Or, having finished the text, the scribe may have delivered it and the model manuscript from which he was copying to the artist's workshop. But by the time the artist of *pages 216 and 218* received the manuscript, contact between scribe and artists seems to have been broken. Another sign of this break can be found on page 414, where the scribe had allotted a small space for a miniature of Zacchaeus, but the artist neglected to paint a miniature in the space. The painting of the manuscript, the evidence seems to show, was done in two very separate workshops.

3. The Distinction of Artists' Hands

While the text and layout of the U.C.L.A. Gospel is the work of a single scribe, the painting of the manuscript was a more complex affair. In general it might be expected that the purely decorative painting of initials and lection markers would be completed before the painting of the figurative miniatures, and this is confirmed on *page 259,* where the miniaturist painted around the decorated initial *gim,* even though he sacrificed the right foot of one of the figures. But there are more than two stages involved in the painting. Even a cursory examination of the figurative miniatures discloses that they are the work of several hands. The artist responsible for the refined portrait of the evangelist St. Matthew on *page 26* (see also color) could never have painted the rough-and-tumble Beheading of John the Baptist on *page 92;* differences abound not only in the manner but in concept, whether one looks at the way the figures are conceived, the setting of the figures in their space, or the handling of decorative details of architectural ornament. Two subjects are presented twice, the Entry into Jerusalem on *page 126* (see also color and color detail) and *page 252,* and Peter's Denial on *pages 166 and 438,* and in both cases it is clear that different artists are involved in the two versions. Often the differences are most remarkable in secondary details, such as the way lions are represented on *pages 4* (see color), *12, 27* (see color), *189,* and *469,* or the way fishing vessels are represented on *pages 193, 194, 211, 227* (see color), and *570.* Often, too, within a single painting discontinuities of style reveal the work of more than one artist, as in the Annunciation, *page 305* (see color), in which the face and much of the figure on the Virgin was painted over by an artist who was intent on revising the work of his predecessor.

The task, then, is to sort out the contributions of the separate artists in order to understand how the finished work came into being. Once the individuality of the separate artists is clear it is possible to press the analysis further in the following chapter and inquire how these artists were connected to the larger art world around them at the beginning of the fourteenth century. Fortunately, each artist's manner is sufficiently distinct that his contribution can usually be readily recognized. The artists can best be described in the order in which they are encountered in the manuscript, and this will prove to be in general the order in which the miniatures were painted.

The painter of the canon tables is the First Painter. By its very nature the largely abstract character of canon table decoration offers limited points of stylistic comparison with the narrative program of the Gospel. However, the inclusion of a pair of portraits on the first two canon pages, *4 and 5* (see color and color detail of *page 4*), namely, Eusebius of Caesarea, author of the tables, and Carpianos, his correspondent, provides a starting point for distinguishing the First Painter from the artist who did the four evangelists, the Second Painter. Although the scale is quite different, one is still dealing with the same genre of figure painting, that of author portraits. The aged Eusebius can be compared with the two senior evangelists, Matthew and John (*pages 26, 460,* and color *page 26*), and the younger, brown-haired Carpianos can be compared with Mark and Luke (*pages 188, 298,* and color detail *page 188*). Both artists are highly accomplished and both work within a tradition that requires a tightly controlled manner, but the First Painter allows himself to be slightly looser and more painterly in his handling of surfaces. The Second Painter is immaculate in his handling of surfaces; he modulates each color area smoothly from its most saturated intensity to a bright white as if he were intent on eliminating every trace of the brush. The First Painter is content with a sketchier handling of the gradations of color, finishing with streaky white highlights as in Eusebius' garments or in his exposed forearm. While the First Painter can generalize in his handling of drapery, the Second Painter can leave nothing to the imagination: he must give every fold a firm, hard edge and a well-defined shape.

Features too are remarkably different in the work of the two artists. The First Painter gives his figures delicate features—thin noses, beady eyes, fragile fingers; the Second Painter gives the evangelists wide almond eyes and strong, prominent noses; their hands are long and well structured and the two bones of the forearm are separated by a distinct shadow. The fact that the portraits by the First Painter are only half-length may make the comparison a little unfair, but in total effect the Second Painter's style seems much stronger. His strong graphic sense of design and his interest in the firm curvilinear contours of his figures lend them a kind of sculptural presence that is missing in the more restrained figures of the First Painter. As will appear in following his work through the manuscript, the contribution of the Second Painter is probably the most significant artistic accomplishment of the U.C.L.A. Gospel.

The contrasts between the first two painters must also be observed in their handling of decoration, for the chief contribution of the First Painter is in decoration. The uniform quality of execution throughout the ten canon tables warrants our conclusion that they are all the work of the same First Painter, without the intrusion of any collaborator. It is painting of the utmost crispness. The sureness of hand is especially impressive under magnification in the fine lines and dots of the highlights, which stand up like threads and beads on the painted surface. The hand never wavers. Every leaf and blossom comprises three or four values of the same hue, and these are laid on separately so that each value maintains its identity without blending or muddying. Further indications of the uniformity of hand throughout the canon tables could be found in the study of fauna. For example, the peacocks on *pages 8, 9, 12, and 13* are virtually identical, and the lions on *pages 4, 5, 12, 13, 20, and 21* are all of the same litter, even though they are put to widely different uses in bases, capitals, spandrels, and margins and are rendered at different scales.

These same features of fauna and flora can be used to distinguish the decoration of the Second Painter from that of the First. The sharp-clawed lions that compose the first initial of Mark's Gospel on *page 189*, with their enormous almond eyes, broad forehead, and tufted ears, are quite a different strain of beast from the lions of the First Painter; they are entirely consistent, however, with the lion heads that support the arch over the portrait of Mark on the facing page. In all four Gospels the identity of the evangelist symbols on the incipit pages with those in the portraits of the evangelists indicates that the Second Painter was responsible for both.

The Second Painter's preference for smoothly modulated color is also evident in his handling of leaf and blossom forms. Where the First Painter kept each value distinct, the Second Painter handled the forms more broadly—the way he did his draperies—and the same manner characterizes his treatment of the marginal decoration around the headpiece of each Gospel. The ornament of the Second Painter is marked by a kind of freedom and exuberance that is missing in that of the First Painter. Nowhere is this freedom more evident than in his highly imaginative trompe l'oeil transformation of flora into fauna in the incipit page of Luke (*page 299* and color detail). In the pi-shaped headpiece a traditional pattern of interlaced vines turns into a wild profusion of creatures: the leaves become birds' wings and the stems their beaks, while the blossoms are human faces—all within a border of svelte little hares in wild flight with lion heads at the corners. In the margin at the right, fish and birds constitute the leaves of the foliate support of the cross, and the affronted birds at the top of the page are themselves made up of smaller birds. Nothing this wild and bold happens in the decorative work of the First Painter.

Given the fact that the canon tables occupy a separate gathering on a parchment of higher quality than the rest of the manuscript, one might well ask whether they did not constitute a completely separate work assignment, the First Painter having nothing whatever to do with the Second. The initials and marginal ornaments of the manuscript, however, give proof that the two worked side by side. Most of the decorated initials and marginal ornaments in the manuscript exhibit the crisp manner of the First Painter, the master of the canon tables. His way of treating leaves and blossoms is unmistakable, and when trees and birds are called for in the margins they are of the same garden varieties that occur in the margins of the canon tables (*page 346, 375*, color details *pages 111, 319*).[11] The uniformity of this decorative work, however, is interrupted at the beginning of the twenty-second gathering, where the hidden creatures observed on the opening page of Luke suddenly reappear. The lection markers in the margins now sprout leaves that are in fact little birds and fish, and the shapes of letters and other ornaments are executed in the smoothly modulated style that is the hallmark of the Second Painter (see color detail *page 514*). Just as abruptly, at the end of the twenty-third gathering the Second Painter leaves off his work on the ornaments and turns the job back over to the First Painter.

It is clear, therefore, that the two artists are collaborators in a very real sense of the term, despite the differences in style between them. Whether these differences stem from training in different locales or with different masters, the notion of a "workshop" in Armenian manuscript production has to be loose enough to contain this kind of diversity. The First Painter seems to have been a specialist in ornamentation. Although he worked closely alongside the Second Painter he was not asked to share in the work of the narrative paintings of the book; the style of the portraits of Eusebius and Carpianus does not reappear.

[11] For example, the marginal tree of *page 124* compares closely with trees on pages *13–14* of the canon tables, and the golden palm trees of *page 252* compare well with those on *pages 8–9* of the canon tables.

The Second Painter was not only an innovative ornamentor but also a figural painter of great distinction, and at the start of the project he seems to have undertaken the assignment of supplying all the narrative miniatures of the Gospel, although he was soon interrupted in his work. The characteristics that distinguish the Second Painter's style in the portraits of the four evangelists—the strong sculptural heads with large almond eyes, the immaculate handling of surfaces, the love of graphic detail—constitute a ready key for tracing his hand throughout the manuscript. Following these key characteristics one can identify the work of the Second Painter in nine narrative subjects, counting the eight pages of the Genealogy of Christ in Matthew as a single subject (see Table 1). These nine subjects comprise a wide range of iconographical and compositional types, and the stark contrast of their painting with that of the remaining miniatures helps to further define the style of the Second Painter.

The Second Painter is a draughtsman of extraordinary precision, modeling his figures with long flowing drapery, every fold of which is as carefully placed as if it had been cast in bronze. While the other narrative painters work with a limited repertoire of short, stocky figures drawn with jerky, often uncertain, strokes, the figures of the Second Painter are carefully composed and have an air of great dignity. One might contrast the commanding figure of Christ in the Raising of Lazarus (*pages 522*) with any number of attempts at a similar pose in the work of the later painters, as in the Second Storm at Sea (*page 227*, see color); or one might compare the handling of the citizens of Jerusalem in the two versions of the Entry into Jerusalem (*pages 126, 252*, color and color detail *page 126*). The Second Painter even manages to catch figures in action in a convincing fashion, such as the children clambering in trees or falling on their knees in the Entry (*page 252*) or the angels flying in the Crucifixion (*page 561*, see color), while the later artists have a great deal of trouble finding hip or knee joints that would allow their figures to move (see the kneeling figures on *pages 197* or *351*, or the flying angels in the Ascension, *page 453*, see color). In the modeling of heads, moreover, the Second Painter achieves effects that are truly remarkable. While the other painters are satisfied with stereotypical faces, the Second Painter creates individuals of convincing character. St. John the Evangelist is not just an aged saint, he is a bone-headed ascetic deep in concentration (*page 460*), and St. Luke is rendered as a sharp-featured intellectual of sensitive temperament (*page 298*). The youthful John is a round-faced innocent of child-like simplicity (*pages 522, 561*, and color *561*), and something of the complexity of Peter's ardent yet insecure personality can be seen in his face (*pages 522 and 156*). Even figures in a crowd appear not just collections of heads but persons reacting in highly individual ways, whether one considers the witnesses of Lazarus' resurrection (*page 522*) or the three reserved, somewhat suspicious elders who welcome Christ into Jerusalem (*page 252*). Christ himself is given a special dignity, emphasized by making his head slightly larger than those of the figures around him. The blocky cast of his head, with broad brow and thick neck, conveys a sense of power, while his luxurious hair, falling in free and copious curls on his shoulders, adds an aspect of alarming tenderness (*pages 28, 35, 156, 252, 522, 561*, and color *561*).

In composition, too, the Second Painter differs markedly from the other narrative painters. In contrast to the busy, many-windowed cityscapes used as stock settings by the other painters (for example, see *pages 99, 271, 312*), the Second Painter employs broad, windowless masses of architecture, immaculately rendered in gradually modulated values of a given hue (for example, see the Last Supper, *page 156* and color detail, and the Annunciation, *page 305* and color). On the other hand the Second Painter frequently introduces rich decorative patterns into his settings, such as the tile background of Matthew (*page 26* and color) or the brick backgrounds of Mark (*page 188* and color detail) and the Washing of the Feet (*page 532*). These patterns are painted with meticulous precision, and however brilliant the color of the individual unit of pattern may be, its repetition creates a unified field. No such effects are attempted by the later painters. In the miniatures of the Second Painter landscapes are reduced to a bare minimum, as in the Entry into Jerusalem (*page 252*), or are treated in a perfectly abstract mode, as in the Cure of the Man Born Blind (*page 509*), where broad horizontal bands of gold, pink, and green constitute the entire setting. The other artists sometimes attempt this abstract mode, as in the Cure of Blind Bartimaeus (*page 250*) or the Apparition in Galilee (*page 570*), but the uneven rendering of the bands of color makes them appear more solid than abstract; more frequently outdoor landscape is shown as rough mountainous terrain with streaky white highlights, as in the Agony in the Garden (*page 160*) and the Curse of the Fig Tree (*page 255*).

The handling of color also distinguishes the Second Painter from the other narrative artists. The latter are fond of a somber purple and use black generously for shading, neither of which characterize the Second Painter. His continuous modulation of hues with white gives his painting a much brighter tonality in general. He also shows a considerable subtlety in playing one color against another. The ancestors of Christ (*pages 28–35* and color *30*) and the apostles in Pentecost (*page 538*) alternate red and blue, then blue and red in their mantles and tunics; the first and third apostles in the Cure of the Man Born Blind (*page 509*) have blue tunics and yellow cloaks, while the one in the middle has a pink tunic and a blue cloak. In a similar way the color of the brick background behind Mark (*page 188* and color detail) is made to change on either side from blue to red in order to contrast with the change from the red tunic on his right shoulder to the blue cloak over his left. The Second Painter achieves his richest color effects in the settings he provides for the four evangelists, in which vibrant patterns of bricks, tiles, and kilims are juxtaposed with the shimmering gold of the background; the total effect is one of sumptuous elegance (*pages 26, 188, 298, 460* and color *page 26*).

For some unknown reason the work of the Second Painter was abruptly broken off, as can be seen in two miniatures that he left incomplete. In the Cure of the Man Born Blind (*page 509*) and the Washing of the Feet (*page 532*) all of the faces and hands have been executed by a later painter. While it is possible to imagine that this later painter (to be identified as T'oros Taronec'i) was painting over faces already finished by the Second Painter, this is a less likely explanation. When this later painter repaints a face, as he does in the Annunciation (*page 305* and color), it is with a specific purpose in mind, namely, to make the Virgin match his painting of the Virgin in the nearby miniature of the Visitation (*page 312*); to repaint all the faces in these two miniatures would seem gratuitous. Moreover the Washing of the Feet gives other proof of having been left incomplete by the Second Painter, for the chair of Peter and the area beneath the arch have been left the white of the naked parchment, an effect quite inconsistent with the finished work of the Second Painter, though perfectly allowable in the aesthetic of the later artist (for example, Christ Teaching in the Synagogue, *page 327*, and the Wedding at Cana, *page 469*). The Second Painter had finished most of the architectural setting in his miniature—including the visual double take of an exterior cityscape in the spandrels of the arch overhead—and had painted the garments of the apostles, but the rest was left unfinished, including the entire figure of Christ. This is perfectly in keeping with the normal procedure in Byzantine and Armenian miniature painting, in which the most important figures and the faces of all figures are generally executed last.[12]

Evidently, then, the Second Painter was interrupted midcourse in his labor on the manuscript. His completed work offers something of a shock to modern preconceptions about the working methods of the medieval artists, for it is impossible to explain what method he was pursuing in doing these miniatures first. The four evangelists and the decorated incipit pages formed an obvious set, and these may have been done first as more important than the narrative miniatures. Among the narrative subjects, after the Genealogy of Christ, which was the first subject in Matthew, the Second Painter skipped in eclectic fashion, doing one full-page miniature in each of the synoptic Gospels before he finally settled down to paint a consecutive series of miniatures in the Gospel of John (see Table 1). But not even these five miniatures were executed in order, for the first and the third of them are the unfinished miniatures (*pages 509 and 532*). Perhaps one should imagine that the artist, having a fairly long work assignment before him, simply started with subjects that appealed to him. Only one of the Second Painter's miniatures is less than full-page, namely, the Cure of the Man Born Blind.

How long the manuscript lay idle and incomplete before work was resumed on the narrative miniatures it is impossible to say. The artists who brought the work to completion, however, represent so different a manner of painting that they must be considered a separate workshop, and chemical analysis of their pigments seems to confirm this stylistic analysis. Although three artists can be distinguished in this second workshop, they share a number of characteristics in common. Backgrounds are far more active than in the work of the Second Painter; space is often broken up into arcades or zones enframing separate figures or separate moments in the story; and figures and objects often break through the rectilinear borders of the miniatures. The drawing is shaky and full of revisions, the painting rough and uneven. Figures move with considerable awkwardness, their arms often growing from their bellies with little sense of where shoulder and elbow should be. Solids of color are streaky, and shadows are laid on in heavy black lines. The gold is applied in a rougher, powdery form, and blank parchment is used to set off certain figures. The coloration, on the whole, is much more

[12] A good example of this procedure can be seen in the unfinished miniatures of the Istanbul Octateuch, Jeffrey C. Anderson, "The Seraglio Octateuch and the Kokkinobaphos Master," *DOP* 36 (1982), fig. 7.

somber than in the first workshop, modeling forms with black rather than with white. All of these contrasts seem to confirm the impression that the artists who resumed work on the manuscript had no direct contact with the artists who started it and very likely worked in another location.

When the second workshop received the manuscript only nine narrative subjects, or about one-sixth of the eventual program, had been painted and two of these subjects were still unfinished. Three artists can be distinguished in the second workshop, each in turn working on a consecutive run of miniatures (Table 1). Since the divisions in their work do not correspond to breaks between gatherings, they do not seem to have been working on the manuscript at the same time; rather the manuscript passed from artist to artist. There are indications, moreover, that another interruption in the production of the manuscript took place between the fourth and fifth artists, as we shall see.

The three artists are most readily distinguished by their handling of faces. Although all three are working with faces of the same very round cast and with the same range of types, each has a very different manner of constructing the face. The artist who illuminates seven subjects between *pages 92 and 122*, who is the Third Painter, begins his faces by painting the shadow layer first in a dark yellow-green, or olive (see color and color detail *page 106*). On this ground he builds with lighter colors, first by sketching in the features in grey, then by adding in order: the brown beard and hair, the white of cheeks, chin and forehead, and the red of lips. Finally, the whole face is sharpened with an over-drawing in black, producing a face of stark, rugged contrasts. The Fourth and Fifth Painters start with lighter grounds and produce effects that are much less harsh. The Fourth Painter executes fourteen subjects between *pages 124 and 211*. The ground with which he starts is an olive color that is so drab it is almost grey beside the warmer facial tones (see color and color detail *page 126*). On this he builds by adding alternately layers of creamy pink, shadows of a slightly darker value of the ground color, and highlights of white. This is enlivened with touches of red on nose, lips, and cheeks—the red on cheeks is always applied in a speckled fashion. Finally, the features are over-drawn in a sepia color, to which the black lines of eyes, nose and mouth are added. The faces have an overall swarthy complexion. The Fifth Painter begins with a creamy yellow ground, on which he makes a rough brown sketch of the features. Next he adds green shadows beneath the hair line, under the eyes and along the nose, and a ruddy tone to the cheeks (see color *pages 227, 250, 327, and 453*, and color details *227, 453*). Over this he adds white highlights in a fairly linear fashion along brow, nose, and chin, and finally the over-drawing in black that completes the definition of features. Compared to the other artists his faces are youthful and rather bland. It is this bland master who identifies himself on *pages 227 and 453* as "T'oros," to be identified as T'oros Taronec'i (see below). He is responsible for the largest number of narrative scenes in the Gospel, some twenty-three in total.

Having distinguished the three artists of the second workshop on the basis of their painting of faces, one cannot help but notice that there is a certain amount of overlapping in their work. For example, on *page 92*, in the Beheading of John the Baptist, some faces are attributable to the third artist while others are attributable to T'oros. Furthermore, there occasionally appear faces done in still another manner, such as the soldiers in the Betrayal, *page 162* (see color). Sorting out these problems involves pursuing the differences among the three artists a bit further.

While his painting of faces tends toward the bland, T'oros' drawing in general is more supple and flexible than that of the other two artists. If one compares his rendering of figures in Christ's Apparition at the Sea of Galilee (*page 570*) to a lakeside scene of the Fourth Painter, the Call of James and John (*page 194*), the differences are easily detected. The figure of Christ is more slender and fluid; with one foot pointed toward the viewer, he actually makes a cautious step; his neck is longer and his gesturing arm freer, and on the whole the artist seems a good deal more secure in his construction of the human body. The same contrast emerges to some extent in the other figures; the Fourth Painter made John and James seem in danger of being pulled overboard by their fish—if indeed the artist had not forgotten to paint in their fishing net. In painting the boats, the Fourth Painter has not understood the structure of the vessel; and in painting the background, his handling of solid areas of color tends to be more blotchy and streaky. Similar figure contrasts should be made in the two scenes of Peter's Denial (*pages 166 and 438*). T'oros' standing figure of Christ actually turns and looks over his shoulder; in the miniature of the Fourth Painter, Peter walks very awkwardly, with one foot crossed in front of the other and the right shoulder hunched up in back. One should contrast, too, the expression of Peter's grief in the two miniatures: T'oros' Peter shows grief in a furrowed brow; the Fourth Painter has simply inverted the natural curve of the brow. Both painters use arcades to define the space, but the foliate moulding in T'oros' arches has a crispness and definition that is wanting in the

Fourth Painter's, and his marble columns are stippled in three colors while the Fourth Painter's are done in a coarser two-color texture. If one looks at the cityscape backgrounds of the two artists (one might compare the curing scenes on *pages 124 and 235*), T'oros is freer and more imaginative, breaking his towers into successive stories and contrasting the roof lines of different structures.

While the contrasts between the Fourth and Fifth Painters can be followed with some consistency from miniature to miniature, the contrasts between the Third and Fourth Painters are less marked, especially in background details, which are not consistently distinguishable. The two may have shared their work, the Third Painter doing most of blocking out of the miniatures with rough sketches and backgrounds, leaving the work after *page 122* to be finished by the Fourth Painter. But in their figure painting certain differences do emerge. If one compares, for example, the similarly placed apostles on *pages 99 and 197* or the separate figures of Peter on *pages 103 and 166*, the work of the Third Painter is more solid and better finished, even if his drawing has similar uncertainties and infelicities. The lines of his figures have been better thought out and the modeling has been brought to a smoother finish. Highlights and shadows of figures tend to be much harsher in the work of the Fourth Painter, conveying a somewhat jagged tactile quality. The Third Painter seems to have labored longer on his figures, until he gradually softened their rough edges.

These distinctions permit one to draw a few conclusions. In the first place three artists working this closely must in fact have belonged to the same "workshop." All share the same principles of design—a clarity and simplicity of composition animated by brilliant patches of background color—and all share the very same palette (see pigment analysis below). They share the same basic figure types and use the same kinds of poses and gestures, although T'oros' repertoire is somewhat larger than that of the other two. Indeed, in their figure painting they even share the same weaknesses: all three artists are uncertain where the limbs should bend when the figure sits or kneels; when the figure faces to the left the arm tends to emerge from the belly in a most uncomfortable fashion; and hands are revised over and over, the earlier attempts being left as shadows to the later versions. This workshop situation is important because, as will appear, it defines the situation in which T'oros' style was formed.

On the other hand there is evidence that T'oros' work on the manuscript is somewhat independent of the work of the other two artists, and was begun after a second interruption in the manufacture of the book. In the first place, the distinction of hands observed above indicates that T'oros finished or repainted faces in many of the miniatures of the Third and Fourth Painters. In the Third Painter's Beheading of John the Baptist (*page 92*) it is clear that the faces of the banqueters, the servant, and the second Salome belong to T'oros' bland manner rather than to the green-shadow manner of the Third artist. A similar intrusion of T'oros' style can be traced in nine of the fourteen miniatures of the Fourth Painter (*pages 124, 126, 160, 162, 166, 169, 171, 173, 179* and color *162*). Some of these faces may have been left unfinished, but it seems unlikely that the Third and Fourth Painters would have left so many scattered gaps in their work; rather the freedom T'oros took in redoing these faces seems to indicate that by the time he received the manuscript he was solely responsible for its finished state and wanted to bring certain parts up to his personal standards. A second sign of an interruption between T'oros and his predecessors is to be found in his first complete miniatures in the manuscript, the Woman with Hemorrhage and Jairus' Petition (*page 216*) and the Raising of Jairus' Daughter (*page 218*). As the codicology reveals (see above), T'oros began with a mistake, for the scribe had left a full blank of page 214 for the first of these scenes, but T'oros instead placed it where the second scene belonged; then, realizing his error, he was obliged to add another leaf of parchment to make room for the Raising of Jairus' Daughter. A mistake such as this, of course, is possible at any point in the work; but an interruption in production would make it all the more understandable, especially if his predecessors were not immediately at hand. Finally, T'oros seems to imply an interruption in the work in his own inscription on the miniatures of the Ascension (*page 453*, also color and color detail), where he asks: "I beg you to remember in the Lord Jesus the unworthy painter T'oros who labored later." The "later" implies a comparison with artists who are not strictly contemporary with T'oros, but who labored earlier and left the work for T'oros to bring to completion.

Since the distinction of the three hands in this second workshop was based first of all on three distinct manners of painting faces, the occurrence of still one other manner of painting faces must be noted in a scattering of figures. The question is whether this other manner of painting faces is evidence of the involvement of still another artist, a sixth painter. These faces first appear in the scene of the Betrayal, a painting of the Fourth Painter in which T'oros Taronec'i added the faces of the two soldiers on the right in the second row. T'oros' manner may also be detected in the first three soldiers in the front row, insofar as they have his usual bland, creamy undercoat and the same light green shadows, even though they are turned in profile and handled much more summarily than is customary in his painting, with rather crude black outlines. Other faces painted in this ugly manner, almost always in profile, appear on the following pages: *169, 172, 179, 197, 283, 286, 336, 351, 438, and 441*. It is significant that all of these are either miniatures painted entirely by T'oros or ones in which he finished some faces. The situations in which this manner of painting is used are also significant, for this treatment is reserved for Christ's adversaries, whether the soldiers who accompany him through his Passion or the Jews who oppose him. The only exception to this rule is the Anointing at Simon's, *page 351*, where, perhaps through some confusion, the artist painted two disciples in a modified version of the ugly, livid manner, their faces turned in three quarters. The ugly faces, therefore, do not seem to be evidence of another painter but of a special manner of painting that T'oros adopted to express the ugliness of character appropriate to the enemies of Christ.

The discussion of the styles of painting of the U.C.L.A. Gospel will be resumed in the following chapter in order to situate the manuscript in the larger context of Armenian painting of the period. The place of the manuscript within the evolution of the painting style of T'oros Taronec'i provides the most accurate means of dating the manuscript.

4. Pigment Analysis, by Mary Virginia Orna, O.S.U.

While the above "Morellian" stylistic analysis leads to a fairly secure explanation of the stages of work involved in the U.C.L.A. Gospel and the manner in which the five painters collaborated in its production, methods of scientific analysis can add further evidence.[13] An analysis of the pigments was undertaken in the first place to provide as complete a description as possible of the materials used in the painting of the manuscript. However, the separation of the work of the five painters provided a specific agenda for the analysis. One must ask whether the two workshops that produce such different effects might in fact be using different pigments or whether individual painters, whose manners are so markedly distinguished, might also be distinguished by their pigments. Further, one might look to the larger situation and ask how the palette being employed in this manuscript relates to painting practices elsewhere in Armenia or elsewhere in the medieval world.

The analysis of the pigments contained in illuminated manuscripts can be approached in various ways. The final decision regarding approach must be made on the basis of availability of samples, the equipment at the disposal of the analyst, and the amount of information that can be gained.

One creative approach to pigment analysis based upon methods of physical examination is that described by Roosen-Runge and Werner in their examination of the Lindisfarne Gospels.[14] The heart of this method is a visual comparison of the various pigment surfaces contained in a manuscript with pigments manufactured according to the recipes of the major medieval painters' manuals. The sources of recipes that Roosen-Runge and Werner consulted included the "Lucca Manuscript,"[15] the "Mappae Clavicula,"[16] the "De Diversis Artibus" of Theophilus,[17] and the manuscript of Heraclius.[18] The prepared

[13] This study of the pigments of the U.C.L.A. Gospel was first published as an article, Mary Virginia Orna and Thomas F. Mathews, "Pigment Analysis of the Glajor Gospel Book of U.C.L.A.," *Studies in Conservation* 26 (1981), 57–72. For further studies of pigments, see Thomas F. Mathews, "A Pigment Analysis of Medieval Armenian Manuscripts," *XVI Internationaler Byzantinistenkongress = Jahrbuch der Österreichischen Byzantinistik* 31 (1981) section 3.2, pp. 1–4; Diane E. Cabelli and Thomas F. Mathews, "The Palette of Khatchatur of Khizan," *Journal of the Walters Art Gallery* 40 (1982), 37–40; Diane E. Cabelli, M. Virginia Orna, Thomas F. Mathews, "Analysis of Medieval Pigments from Cilician Armenia," *Archaeological Chemistry* 3, Advances in Chemistry Series 205 (Washington, D.C., 1984), 243–54; Diane E. Cabelli and Thomas F. Mathews, "Pigments in Armenian Manuscripts of the Tenth and Eleventh Centuries," *REArm* 18 (1984), 33–47; M. Virginia Orna and Thomas F. Mathews, "Uncovering the Secrets of Medieval Artists," *Analytical Chemistry* 60 (1 Jan., 1988), 47A-56A; M. Virginia Orna, Patricia L. Lang, J. E. Katon, Robert S. Nelson, and Thomas F. Mathews, "Applications of Infrared Microspectroscopy to Art Historical Questions about Medieval Manuscripts," *Archaeological Chemistry* 4 (Washington, D.C., 1989), 265–88.

[14] H. Roosen-Runge and A. E. A. Werner, "The Pigments and Medium of the Lindisfarne Gospels," *Codex Lindisfarnensis*, vol. 2 (Basel, 1960), 263–72; H. Roosen-Runge, *Farbgebung und Technik frühmittelalterlicher Buchmalerei*, I (Munich, 1967), 11–17.

[15] H. Hedfords, ed., *Compositiones ad Tingenda Musiva* (Uppsala, 1932).

[16] Cyril Stanley Smith and J. G. Hawthorne, *Mappae Clavicula: A Little Key to the World of Medieval Techniques* (Philadelphia, 1974).

[17] Albert Ilg, *Theophilus Presbyter Schedula Diversarum Artium* (Vienna, 1874).

[18] Albert Ilg, *De Coloribus et Artibus Romanorum* (Vienna, 1873); this manuscript is now available in M. P. Merrifield, *Original Treatises on the Arts of Painting*, I (New York, 1967), 166–257.

pigments were painted out on small pieces of parchment according to the instructions given in the above-mentioned references using three different binding media—white of egg, fish glue, and gum. The microscopical structures of the pigments in the manuscript were then compared with these known samples using polarized light, supplemented by visual observation in ultraviolet light. Furthermore, the authors were able to take color photomicrographs of the pigments in both reflected and transmitted light.

Another approach is that described by Muether, Balazs, and Cotter, utilizing neutron irradiation of the whole manuscript in a nuclear reactor, followed by gamma-ray analysis and autoradiography.[19] The gamma-ray spectrum permits the researcher to identify the elements contained in the manuscript, and the autoradiographical analysis provides the specific locations of these elements in the manuscript.

While both these methods are non-destructive in the sense that the manuscript remains intact after analysis, some serious shortcomings accompany both. With respect to the method of Roosen-Runge and Werner, the sheer number of pigments that need to be manufactured before examination of the manuscript confronts the investigator with a staggering task. Secondly, one must assume that no pigments were used in the manuscript that were not described in one of the painters' manuals consulted. Since all of the painters' manuals originated in the Latin West, their applicability to Byzantine and Armenian painting cannot be taken for granted. Thirdly, the assumption would have to be made that the pigments reproduced from modern starting materials exactly resemble their medieval counterparts and that the medieval pigments have undergone little or no change through the centuries. On the other hand, analysis by neutron activation entails problems of the limited availability of reactor facilities, the necessity of bringing the manuscript to the facility, the multiple handlings of the manuscript in order to take autoradiographs after longer and longer time intervals, the continuing radioactivity of gilded areas, as well as the security problem due to transporting the manuscript to the reactor site and its subsequent "long sojourn" in the analytical laboratory. But the most serious drawback of all is the fact that neutron activation analysis only provides information regarding the elements contained in the pigments, but no information regarding their chemical formulas.

[19] H. R. Muether, N. L. Balazs, and M. J. Cotter, "Neutron Activation Analysis of Manuscripts," *College Art Association Abstracts* (New Orleans, 1980), 133; eidem with W. Voelkle, "Neutron Autoradiography and the Spanish Forger," *MASCA Journal*, I, 4 (June 1980), 112–13.

For these reasons, in the study of the U.C.L.A. Gospel it was decided to employ "good old-fashioned" methods of analysis of microscopic particles. With proper safeguards the taking of pigment samples from a manuscript can be as non-destructive as the methods described above. First, sample taking does not require removal of the manuscript from its permanent location. Secondly, the sampling, if well planned, is a one-time operation, which need never be repeated. Thirdly, sample taking involves much less handling of the manuscript than the other methods. Fourthly, only the samples, and not the entire manuscript, are subjected to high-energy irradiation, whether it take the form of ultraviolet light or neutron flux. Fifthly, the samples can be taken in such a way that the lacunae left by the incision of the pigment particles are not discernible by the naked eye. However, the most compelling reason for taking samples is the wealth of information that can be obtained by this method, including particle size and refractive index measurements, microscopical chemical test results, and unambiguous chemical identification.

In July 1979, through the courtesy of Mr. Brooke Whiting, Curator of Special Collections at U.C.L.A., seventy-six samples, selected to yield the spectrum of hues from each artist, were taken from the Glajor Gospel Book. The hues were differentiated by both visual assessment and by comparison with color chips from the Munsell Book of Colors.[20] The samples were abstracted with a fine surgical scalpel (Steri-sharps No. 11 blade) under a forty-power binocular microscope, stored for transport between two pre-cleaned 75 x 25 mm microscope slides (Fisher), and sealed with transparent tape. In many instances, samples were taken from smudges of pigments which had transferred onto the opposite page, thus allowing for procurement of the relatively large amount of sample without disturbing the corresponding miniature. In those instances where samples were excised directly from the paintings, the lacunae were hardly discernible under the microscope, much less by the naked eye. Each sample was coded according to painter, hue, page number, and x-y coordinates in millimeters as measured from the bottom-left corner of each page with a transparent grid. For example, a code of 2.M.305(35,65) identifies a magenta sample taken from page 305, 35 mm from the left edge and 65 mm from the bottom of the page, and attributed to the Second Painter, the Evangelist Painter. The location of each sample was also marked on photo-

[20] *The Munsell Book of Color, Neighboring Hues Edition, Matte Finish Collection* (Baltimore, 1976).

graphs made of each page in the manuscript. The average size of the "smudge" samples was 50–100 micrometers; the others ranged in size from 4 to 30 micrometers.

These samples were subsequently analyzed by polarized light microscopy and X-ray diffraction according to the methods outlined by McCrone and Delly.[21] The microscope was an Olympus Model POS-1 equipped for photomicrography in transmitted light. The opaque samples were photographed at 180X magnification in reflected light on a Reichert Me F 2 metallograph. The X-ray diffraction patterns were obtained by mounting the sample particles on a glass filament in a 114.59 mm diameter Debye-Scherrer powder camera and irradiating with Cu-K_α (= 1.54050 Å) X-rays for twenty-four hours at 30 kV and 15 ma. Only the gold samples were analyzed by X-ray fluorescence (Kevex Non-dispersive XRF Unit at 2 ma and 40 kV), since they were the only ones large enough to yield usable results by this method. The magenta samples suspected of being lake pigments were also subjected to the microchemical tests described by Hofenk-de Graaff.[22]

The data taken for each sample included refractive index (η) relative to the mounting medium, "Arocolor," (η = 1.66), average particle size, behavior in polarized light, and the X-ray diffraction pattern. The data for some representative samples is listed in Table 2. A photomicrograph of each sample was also taken on Ektachrome ASA 160 tungsten film with an Olympus Om-1 SLR 35 mm camera equipped with an FK3.3X eyepiece adapter through a 40X objective (55X for the samples photographed in reflected light). These photographs were particularly helpful in examining the purple, brown, flesh color, and green pigments, which were mixtures. Tables 3, 4, and 5 illustrate the excellent correlation in X-ray diffraction patterns that could be achieved between the sample and the ASTM powder diffraction file.[23]

The general results of the analysis, broken down according to hue and painter, are represented in Table 6, and the overall palette of the U.C.L.A. Gospel is presented in Table 7. The most striking result that emerges from the analysis is the discovery that the stylistic distinction drawn between the painting of the two workshops coincides with differences in the chemistry of the palette. While the two workshops have a great many pigments in common, in some pigments they are consistently different. The strong purple (Munsell 5P 4/4) that is used in virtually every miniature of the second workshop consists of a mixture of red lake and ultramarine that occurs nowhere in the pigments of the first workshop. The second workshop was also found to use gamboge rather liberally, by itself and as an ingredient in mixtures where yellow was needed, but again this was found nowhere in the pigments of the first workshop. Gamboge is a yellow gum resin produced in parts of India and Southeast Asia. White also seems to be different in the two workshops. The artists of the second workshop used white lead for a pure white and used gypsum and anhydrite for white in mixtures. It was not possible to get a complete sampling of the whites of the first workshop, since samples were not taken except from already damaged areas of the miniatures. However, in the samples obtained the First Painter was found to use calcined bone for his pure white and the Second Painter used gypsum in mixtures.

Most interesting of all were the differences found in the blue pigments, for these show distinctions between the two workshops and between the two painters of the first workshop. The blue used by the painters of the second workshop is a very poor quality ultramarine containing up to 80% colorless silicate-aluminate substrate. The extraction of ultramarine pigment from lapis lazuli involves repetition of a settling process, in which the first wash produces pigment of the highest purity while the second and third washes include increasingly high admixtures of ash.[24] The pigment of the second workshop is clearly of a second or third wash. In the first workshop, on the other hand, there are two blue pigments in use, and the blue of the First Painter is an ultramarine of the highest purity. The refinement observable in his style is matched by the refinement in his pigments. At the same time, the Second Painter, working at his side, chose azurite for his blue. In their use in the U.C.L.A. Gospel the two colors are virtually indistinguishable to the naked eye, yielding a Munsell reading of 5PB 3/6. The choice, then, must have been a matter of diversity of training of the First and Second Painters. While azurite was a far more common blue in the medieval West, in Armenia the situation was reversed, doubtless because of the relative proximity of the source of the pigment in the mines of Badakshan in Afghanistan. The Second Painter's preference for azurite can be followed consistently through the man-

[21] W. C. McCrone and J. G. Delly, *The Particle Atlas*, 2nd ed., 6 vols. (Ann Arbor, 1974–78); W. C. McCrone, L. B. McCrone, and J. G. Delly, *Polarized Light Microscopy* (Ann Arbor, 1978).

[22] J. H. Hofenk-de Graaff, *Natural Dyestuffs for Textile Materials: Origin, Chemical Constitution, Identification* (Brussels, 1967), 13.

[23] American Society for Testing and Materials, *X-ray Powder File*, revised (Philadelphia, 1960).

[24] Joyce Plesters, "Ultramarine Blue: Natural and Artificial," *Studies in Conservation* 11 (1966), 62–91.

uscript, and when in the two penultimate gatherings he takes over the work of painting the marginal ornaments—a change signaled by the presence of his hidden birds and fish—the blue is again azurite, in contrast to the ultramarine in the ornaments elsewhere. This distinction can also be found in the greens; the Second Painter obtains green by mixing orpiment with azurite, while the First Painter (and those of the second workshop as well) mixes orpiment with ultramarine.

Other results of the pigment analysis are worth noting in passing. There are two reds throughout the manuscript, a vibrant intense red (Munsell 7.5R) and a magenta or slightly purple red (Munsell 7.5RP); the former is always vermilion of mercuric sulfide, and the latter is an organic pigment, a red lake. The brown, yellow-brown, flesh tone pigments, and one of the orange pigments, have been found to be mixtures. One sample taken from the Fourth Painter indicates the use of iron oxide hydrate as a pigment, the only instance of an earth pigment in use in the manuscript. It is also interesting to note that the Fifth Painter, T'oros Taronec'i, used a mixture avoided by experienced artists because of the incompatibility of arsenic sulfide with lead oxide. A trace of massicot was also found in the yellow of the Third Painter.

CHAPTER FOUR

The Development of Armenian Painting

1. The Tenth and Eleventh Centuries

The chief problem in writing the history of painting in medieval Armenia is its radical discontinuity. The art historian is confronted with a multitude of styles that cannot reasonably be construed as a linear developmental sequence. While certain works exhibit close stylistic interrelationships that allow one to group them together, it is impossible to connect such groups of works into a larger, coherent whole. In part this disjointed appearance may be attributed to the loss of a large percentage of the original artistic output of medieval Armenia. For example, from the independent Bagratid and Arcruni kingdoms of the tenth and eleventh centuries only a single manuscript can be documented as a royal commission, namely, the Gospel of King Gagik of Kars, dated 1045–54 (Jerusalem, St. James 2556), and barely five percent of its splendid narrative program survives.[1] The survival rate of fresco decoration is equally poor; although churches are often said to have been decorated, very little remains beyond the frescoes of Ałtʿamar in Vaspurakan (915–920) and some fragments at Tatʿew in Siwnikʿ.[2]

But gaps in the surviving corpus can only partly explain the fitful course of Armenian art. Much of the blame must be laid to the geographical and political fragmentation of the Armenian people, a condition that was scarcely conducive to the uniform and tranquil development of the arts. In the post-Arab period, the Bagratids regained sovereignty in 884 with the compliance of the Moslem and Byzantine superpowers that hedged them in on either side; but this sovereignty was shared among more or less independent princes in the clan. In Vaspurakan to the south, moreover, the Arcrunis broke with the Bagratids and established a rival principality in 908.[3] At the same time, in the midst of these Armenian principalities there continued to exist a constellation of minor Arab emirates.[4] Medieval Armenia did not constitute a single state but a set of small kingdoms, which were often in conflict among themselves and had different ways of dealing with international politics.

From such a situation a single style of painting should hardly be expected to emerge. In fact, a series of distinct styles appeared, side by side or in sequence, without causal connections among them. Thus the Gospel of Queen Mlkʿē (Venice, S. Lazzaro 1144/86), which was donated to the Church of the Mother of God in Varag in the early tenth century (and was probably executed a little earlier in Varag), exhibits a style with strong echoes of Early Christian art in the poses and settings of the evangelists and in the Nilotic motifs of the canon tables.[5] Graceful figures, bright strong colors, and modeling in layers of pigment characterize the work. Such a style may have reached Armenia by way of the contemporary Macedonian revival in Constantinople, but however it reached Armenia it bears no relationship to the style of the frescoes of Ałtʿamar, which were executed 915–920, barely forty kilometers away. According to the historian Tʿovma Arcruni, when Gagik of Vaspurakan erected his palace and church on this little island in Lake Van, "there were many artisans assembled at the royal court, honourable men gathered from all nations of the earth who could unerringly carry out the king's plan."[6] If the fresco painters were

[1] This manuscript is described briefly in Połarian, *Mayr Cʿucʿak,* VIII, 245 ff. See also Narkiss and Stone, *Jerusalem,* 32–33, 147; S. Der Nersessian, *Armenian Art,* 108–14. On the extent of the program see Mathews, "Gospel Iconography in Greater Armenia," *Fourth International Symposium of Armenian Art* (Erevan, in press).

[2] Sirarpie Der Nersessian, *Aghtʿamar, Church of the Holy Cross,* Harvard Armenian Texts and Studies 1 (Cambridge, Mass., 1965); N. and M. Thierry, "Peintures murales de caractère occidental en Arménie: Église Saint-Pierre et Saint-Paul de Tatev (début du Xme siècle)," *Byzantion,* n.s. 38 (1968), 180–242.

[3] Cf. Nina G. Garsoïan, "L'indépendance retrouvée: Royaume du Nord et royaume du Sud (IXe–XIe siècles)," in *Histoire des Arméniens,* ed. Gérard Dédéyan , 215–68.

[4] Aram Ter-Ghewondyan, *The Arab Emirates in Bagratid Armenia,* trans. N. G. Garsoïan (Lisbon, 1976).

[5] Janashian, *Armenian Miniature Paintings,* 16–23, pls. 1–11.

[6] Tʿovma Arcruni, *History of the House of the Artsrunikʿ,* trans. Robert W. Thomson (Detroit, 1985), IV, chap. 7, 356–57.

non-Armenian, this does not seem to have prevented their developing a program of particularly Armenian resonance;[7] but whatever their country of origin, the painters worked in a severe style, modeling heavy-set figures in a technique that relies on linear rather than painterly effects (fig. 126a).

A similar disparity might be observed between the frescoes of Sts. Peter and Paul in Tatʿew in Siwnikʿ, for which the bishop Yakob invited "Frankish" artists in 930, and the miniatures of the Ēǰmiacin Gospel, executed in Siwnikʿ in 989 (Erevan, Matenadaran 2374).[8] The closest parallels for the Tatʿew frescoes are found in Reichenau, while the Ēǰmiacin Gospel must be seen as a very faithful copy of an Early Christian manuscript.[9] Yet it would be difficult to argue a direct link between the Gospel of Queen Mlkʿē and the Ēǰmiacin Gospel. The painting of the latter is in much thinner washes and its figure drawing is delicate and sketchy, entirely lacking in the solidarity and weight of the figures of the Queen Mlkʿē Gospel. While it is theoretically possible that they represent two stages in the development of a single painting tradition, the intermediate steps in the development are lacking.

This fragmentation continues into the eleventh century, although many more manuscripts survive from this period and some of them fall into fairly coherent groups. The largest single group—and the most interesting iconographically—is the so-called Melitene group of manuscripts, many of which can be located by colophons quite outside the Armenian principalities, in Lesser Armenia, that is in Armenian communities found west of the Euphrates around Melitene and Sebasteia.[10] There had always been a substantial Armenian population in these provinces of the Byzantine Empire, known as the Armeniakon theme, but in the course of the eleventh century it was much augmented by the influx of Armenians resettled from Greater Armenia. In 1022, already sensing the pressure of Turkish incursions from the east, King Senecherim of Vaspurakan accepted the offer of Basil II of territory around Sebasteia in return for his kingdom, and the royal family with 14,000 subjects set out for their new homeland.[11] The same year the Bagratid king of Ani, Yovannēs Smbat, finding himself now encircled by Basil II (who had claimed Georgia in 1001), deeded his kingdom to the Byzantine emperor. The Byzantine claim to Ani was enforced in 1045, when King Gagik II resigned and emigrated to Caesarea in Cappadocia. A third Armenian king, Gagik Abas of Kars, owner of the famed Gospel referred to above, joined the Armenian migration in 1065, when he too abdicated in favor of the Byzantine emperor. Finally, when the Turks overran the Byzantine defense system at the Battle of Manazkert in 1071, a large Armenian population migrated west.

Curiously enough, the manuscripts of the Melitene group, executed on Byzantine territory, are the least byzantinizing of Armenian manuscripts. Erevan, Matenadaran 6201 may be taken as typical of the group.[12] Executed in 1038, its colophon mentions the Byzantine emperor Michael IV rather than any Armenian prince. But rejecting Byzantine subtleties of shading, modeling, or displaying figures against an architectural background, the artist presents flat figures painted in light washes within dark outlines, which are set boldly against the unpainted ground of the parchment. A number of evident connections to Syrian manuscript illumination appear: the miniatures are turned sideways, that is, they run the height of the page, with the feet of the figures toward the gutter of the book; the action of the composition often moves from right to left; and the four evangelists are presented together on a single page, standing.[13] The Syrians, it should be observed, were natural allies of the Armenians in this situation: as Christians they resisted the Turks and as Monophysites they resisted the Byzantines. The two nationalities were often neighbors in the same cities, and Armenian interest in Syrian exegesis will be commented on below.[14]

One manuscript of the Melitene group is of crucial importance to this study, since it is the immediate model of the U.C.L.A. Gospel. Erevan, Mat. 10780 is

[7] For the current debate concerning the meaning of the iconography, see Mathews, "The Genesis Frescoes of Ałtʿamar," *REArm*, n.s. 16 (1982), 245–57; Nicole Thierry, "Le cycle de la création et la faute d'Adam à Ałtʿamar," *REArm*, n.s. 17 (1983), 289–329; Bernard Outtier, "Le cycle d'Adam à Ałtʿamar et la version arménienne du commentaire du S. Ephrem sur la Genèse," *REArm*, n.s. 18 (1984), 589–92; Nicole Thierry, "Les peintres d'Ałtʿamar (915–21), le cycle de la passion et de la résurrection," in press.

[8] N. and M. Thierry, "Peintures murales," 180–242; Frédéric Macler, *L'évangile arménien. Édition phototypique du ms. 229 de la Bibliothèque d'Etchmiadzin* (Paris, 1920); Lydia A. Dournovo, *Miniatures arméniens* (Paris, 1960), 26–33.

[9] See especially the discussion of the canon tables in Carl Nordenfalk, *Die spätantiken Kanontafeln: Kunstgeschichtliche Studien über die eusebianische Evangelien-Konkordanz in den vier ersten Jahrhunderten ihrer Geschichte*, 2 vols. (Göteborg, 1938).

[10] For discussions of the Melitene group of manuscripts see: Der Nersessian, *Arm. Mss. Freer*, 1–6; Narkiss and Stone, *Jerusalem*, 36–40; Tatiana Izmailova, *Armianskaya miniatjura XI veka* (Moscow, 1979), 21–102.

[11] N. G. Garsoïan, "Indépendance retrouvée," 237–42, 250–52.

[12] Izmailova, *Arm. miniatjura XI veka*, 45–64, pls. 20–29.

[13] For Syrian examples of these features, see J. Leroy, *Les manuscrits syriaques à peintures conservés dans les bibliothèques d'Europe et d'Orient* (Paris, 1964), passim.

[14] N. G. Garsoïan, "Indépendance retrouvée," 254.

a recent acquisition of the library, which was donated in 1978 by the Catholicos of Armenia Vazgen I, whence its name the "Vehapʿaṙ Gospel," meaning the Gospel of his Holiness. The Vehapʿaṙ Gospel is the earliest Armenian example of a Gospel with a running narrative set of illuminations. After canon tables and two prefatory miniatures (the Hospitality of Abraham and a donor portrait) the book contains a relatively dense set of sixty-four illustrations within the text itself, breaking the columns of text exactly where the illustrations belong in the narrative (figs. 92a, 99a, 103a, 108a, 117a, 122a, 124a, 126b, 160a, 162a, 166a, 169a, 171a, 172a, 173a, 194a, 197a, 211a, 216a, 218a, 227a, 250a, 255a, 259a, 269a, 271a, 283a, 327a, 336a, 351a, 403a, 403b, 438a, 441a, 448a, 469a, 480a, 484a, 509a, 532a). The term "running narrative" will be used for this kind of set to distinguish it from other kinds of narrative sets: the preface-page set, which groups the narrative subjects together at the beginning of the Gospel, as frequently in Melitene manuscripts; the frieze-format set, which groups successive moments of the story in horizontal strips across the page, as in the famous eleventh-century Byzantine manuscripts;[15] and the "festival" set, which selects only a dozen or so of the chief subjects and illustrates them on full pages scattered through the book. The typical proximity of the illustrations to their related texts is especially characteristic of running narrative Gospels, and, as will be seen, the U.C.L.A. Gospel follows the Vehapʿaṙ Gospel closely in this respect.

An article by A. S. Matʿevosyan sets out the principal facts of the Vehapʿaṙ Gospel, while a more complete publication of the manuscript by Matʿevosyan and Izmailova is anticipated.[16] The earliest colophon of the manuscript, on fol. 79, documents its restoration by a secondary owner: "In the year 1088 I, Sargis the priest, with much labor repaired this holy gospel as intercession on behalf of myself, my son Vard, and his mother. Those of you who are enlightened by it consider us worthy of commemoration."[17] The manuscript therefore antedates 1088, but the precise date and the location are unknown. It is theoretically possible that the miniatures postdate the text of the manuscript; but paleographic and stylistic considerations make it impossible to date the miniatures much later than the rest of the manuscript. The Armenian inscriptions that are entered into the miniatures themselves are in an eleventh-century *bolorgir* very similar to the script of the colophon of Sargis the priest later in the century.[18] Moreover, they appear to be entered in the same faded brown ink as the text itself. The Greek inscriptions on three of the miniatures also conform to an eleventh-century dating.[19]

The stylistic parallels with works of the Melitene group of manuscripts, particularly with Erevan, Mat. 6201, justify Matʿevosyan's association of the manuscript with that group and his dating in the early years of the eleventh century. The Syrian features that often characterize the Melitene group of manuscripts are strongly in evidence. All sixty-four of the narrative miniatures and the four evangelist portraits are turned at a right angle to the text. The action of the individual scenes generally reads in reverse, from right to left, and in one scene, the Petition of the Canaanite, even an inscription in Armenian has been made to read in reverse (fig. 99a). The evangelists are depicted on separate pages, but they are of the standing Syrian type.[20] In general, the figures are short and stocky, and painted against the blank parchment without even the indication of a ground line for them to stand upon (e.g., figs. 117a, 122a). They have large heads and great staring eyes, the whiteness of which is emphasized by the swarthy coloring of the faces. The painting technique is that common to the Melitene group: the figures are drawn in ink and filled in with light washes, and sometimes the lines are gone over with a darker shade of paint. The pigments too appear to be those of the Melitene group—thin washes of organic pigments of variable intensity and uneven covering power.[21]

To these general associations of the Vehapʿaṙ Gospel with the Melitene group of manuscripts one can add a number of very specific connections. In the handling of drapery the folds usually follow the plan

[15] Tania Velmans, *Le Tétraévangile de la Laurentienne, Florence, Laur. VI.23* (Paris, 1971); Henri Omont, *Évangiles avec peintures byzantines du XIe siècle* (Paris, 1908).

[16] A. S. Matʿevosyan, "Vehapʿaṙi Avetaranə," *Ējmiacin* 5 (1978), 34–51. T. Izmailova has proposed that the miniatures reproduce a model of Early Christian date; see "Quelques miniatures de l'évangile du Catholicos (Vehapar)," *Fourth International Symposium on Armenian Art: Theses of Reports* (Erevan, 1985), 171–73. We are most grateful to Tatiana Izmailova and A. S. Matʿevosyan for sharing their material with us prior to their final publication of it.

[17] Matʿevosyan, "Vehapʿaṙi Avetaranə," 35.

[18] For analysis of the palaeography, see ibid.

[19] The Greek inscriptions are found on fols. 130 ("Zacharias"), 130v ("The Annunciation"), and 210 ("John"). Prof. Ihor Ševčenko of Harvard University was consulted on the Greek palaeography.

[20] Matʿevosyan, "Vehapʿaṙi Avetaranə," 49.

[21] One can distinguish a magenta, a blue/green, and a brown/tan/yellow (probably varying intensities of the same pigment). Only a single color seems clearly inorganic and that is a red/orange, which in most of the miniatures is deteriorating into a brown black, a change that probably identifies the pigment as a sulfur compound. Cf. Diane E. Cabelli and T. F. Mathews, "Pigments in Armenian Manuscripts of the Tenth and Eleventh Centuries," *REArm.*, n.s. 18 (1984), 33–47.

of a branch with a series of twigs running off it (e.g., figs. 160a and 172a), as in Jerusalem, St. James 3624, from Melitene in 1041 (fig. 312a).[22] The high-backed chair with one or more knobs on top (figs. 117a, 169a, 171a, 336a, 403b, 469a) has a very close parallel in Erevan, Mat. 6201, and the flanged cross of Christ's halo is close to his halo in the same manuscript.[23] The decorative panels of leaf-work (figs. 92a, 166a, and 351a) repeat patterns used in the canon tables of Erevan, Mat. 4804 of 1018.[24] Moreover, the L-shaped corner decorations of the codices held by the evangelists and by St. Peter (fig. 103a) are exactly like those of the evangelists in Erevan, Mat. 6201.[25] Finally, one should note a most interesting iconographic feature of the Vehapʿaṙ Gospel, namely, the clericalization of Christ and the apostles by clothing them in stoles (e.g., figs. 99a, 108a, and 117a). This is a most unusual feature, which occurs in two other Melitene group manuscripts, Erevan, Mat. 4801 (of 1018) and Jerusalem, St. James 1924 (of 1064), in which the evangelists are clothed in stoles.[26] In the Vehapʿaṙ Gospel this iconography must be connected with the priestly status of the first owner of the book, who is illustrated in the donor portrait with his wife and children, wearing chasuble and stole and raising his hands in prayer.[27] It is worth noting, too, that the dress of the donors must be pre-Mongol, without the fur caps, fur-lined coats, and loose-hanging sleeves that come into style in the thirteenth century (fig. R4).[28]

Matʿevosyan's date in the early eleventh century and his location of the manuscript in Lesser Armenia can therefore be accepted with confidence. This is a conclusion of considerable importance to the history of iconography, for the Vehapʿaṙ Gospel thus becomes one of the earliest surviving Gospels with a running narrative set of illustrations interrupting the text. No earlier Armenian manuscript of this kind exists; the Gospel of Gagik of Kars (to be discussed momentarily) belongs to the middle of the century. Among Greek manuscripts the only earlier instance of a Gospel book with text interrupted by narrative illustrations is the very fragmentary Sinopensis Gospel of the sixth century, Paris, B.N. Suppl. gr. 1286, and all its illustrations are two-column miniatures placed at the bottom of the page.[29] The eleventh century witnessed an explosion of Gospel iconography in Byzantium, and the Vehapʿaṙ Gospel stands chronologically at the beginning of this development. It also stands quite independent of the Byzantine development, as will be seen in the analysis of its program and its iconography.

Alongside the homely style of the Melitene group of manuscripts, the eleventh century also produced a brilliant series of manuscripts of Byzantinizing tendencies, but as in the tenth century it remains difficult to establish links among them.[30] One of the most accomplished of these manuscripts is the now mutilated Gospel of King Gagik of Kars (Jerusalem, St. James 2556). In her recent study, Der Nersessian argues for a date early in the reign of the humanist king, in the years 1045–54.[31] A manuscript of grand dimensions, 46 × 35cm, this Gospel was planned with a set of over 227 running narrative illustrations, in addition to the usual canon tables and evangelist portraits. Unhappily, the manuscript was hideously mutilated by a collector who excised almost all the miniatures. Examining the fifteen surviving narrative miniatures, or fragments thereof, Der Nersessian identifies a master of great ability whose style closely resembles that of the Byzantine lectionary of Mount Athos, Dionysiou 587, of around 1059, a connection that should not surprise one in view of Gagik's contacts with Constantinople.[32] This master is capable of very delicate, small-featured faces and figures that move with considerable grace (fig. 156a). Other miniatures, however, are far less sensitive, with rigid figures poorly drawn or in a style far more linear, and these Der Nersessian attributes to less competent collaborators (figs. 160b, 179a, and 336b). The most famous miniature, however, that showing the king with wife and daughter, Goranduxt and Marem, seated in cross-legged oriental style on rich carpets, is not part of this manuscript at all, as an inspection of the colophon on its reverse demonstrates.[33]

22 Narkiss and Stone, *Jerusalem*, figs. 49–53.

23 Izmailova, *Arm. miniatjura XI veka*, pl. 27 for the chair; pls. 24–28 for the halo.

24 Izmailova, *Arm. miniatjura XI veka*, pls. 1 and 2.

25 Izmailova, *Arm. miniatjura XI veka*, pl. 29.

26 Izmailova, *Arm. miniatjura XI veka*, pl. 4; Narkiss and Stone, *Jerusalem*, fig. 56

27 Matʿevosyan, "Vehapʿaṙi Avetaranə," 46.

28 See the donor portraits of New Julfa, All-Savior 36 (1236) and 481 (1330), Der Nersessian and Mekhitarian, *Isfahan*, figs. 45 and 66.

29 Antonio Muñoz, *Il codice purpureo di Rossano e il frammento Sinopense* (Rome, 1907).

30 Izmailova, *Arm. miniatjura XI veka*, 103–214.

31 Sirarpie Der Nersessian, "Évangile du roi Gagik de Kars: Jérusalem, no. 2556," *REArm.*, n.s. 18 (1984), 85–107.

32 S. M. Pelikanidis et al., *The Treasures of Mount Athos, Illuminated Manuscripts* (Athens, 1974), vol. I, 162–219. Der Nersessian cites Matthew of Edessa's remark about Gagik's visit to Constantinople (*Armenian Art*, 109).

33 For a good color plate see Der Nersessian, *Armenian Art*, pl. 75. This miniature was found separately from the Gospel in 1911 by Mesrop Nšanian, who argued that it must have belonged to the manuscript because it represents the royal owner of the manuscript. ("The Portrait of King Gagik of Kars," *Ararat* [August 1911], 683–87.) But the rul-

With the Gospel of King Gagik, Der Nersessian associates another splendid manuscript, the Trebizond Gospel (Venice, San Lazzaro 1400/108) on the basis of its style.[34] The Venice manuscript shares much of the decorative vocabulary of the Jerusalem manuscript, and a figure style with delicate, small-featured faces similar to those of the master painter of the Gospel of King Gagik. The relationship between the two manuscripts, however, is more complicated than this. The painting technique of the Trebizond Gospel is smoother, so that brush strokes cannot be distinguished, and the palette is less brilliant and closer to the Byzantine.[35] The presence of Greek inscriptions on all but one of the miniatures also speaks for closer ties to Byzantium.

At the same time, other eleventh-century manuscripts transform Byzantine painting into quite a different aesthetic. The Mułni Gospel, for example, derives its figures and compositions out of Byzantine models but eliminates all atmospheric and space-creating effects, so that the paintings take on a flat, decorative quality (fig. 156b and 561a).[36] Figures have bright patches of rouge on their cheeks, landscapes are enlivened with leaf-dotted trees, and architecture becomes surface decoration. Izmailova places this manuscript at Ani in the second half of the eleventh century, along with Erevan, Mat. 3793 and 10099, but none of these manuscripts has its original colophon, and if this style was characteristic of Ani it is impossible to relate it to the style of the Gospel of Gagik only a few years earlier and a few kilometers to the west.[37]

Looked at from the point of view of stylistic development, then, the painting of the Armenian kingdoms of the tenth and eleventh centuries is marked by discontinuities, and the Seljuk invasion that concludes the period is a still greater discontinuity that cuts across all cultural activities. Nevertheless, there are specifically Armenian developments in this painting that are worth noting, and they lie in the realm of program and iconography rather than in style. In canon tables the manuscripts exhibit the consistent Armenian ten-table set embellished with a richer and more varied range of motifs than appears in Byzantine manuscripts. In narrative program some manuscripts (such as the Mułni Gospel) explore a special Armenian system, namely a set of preface miniatures that stand between the canon tables and the Gospels, and others (the Vehap'aṙ and Gagik Gospels) develop very extensive sets of running narrative illustrations within the text of the Gospel. Finally, in the iconography of individual subjects they continue to tamper with standard formulae and invent new formulae of their own. As Der Nersessian has noted, of the surviving miniatures in the Gospel of King Gagik, hardly one is a straightforward copy of its Byzantine counterpart.[38] Some of these idiosyncrasies will be explored below.

2. Painting in Cilicia, the Late Twelfth to the Mid-Fourteenth Century

Sweeping into Asia Minor after the battle of Manazkert, the Seljuk Turks bypassed Cilicia to establish their sultanate at Konya, ancient Iconium. The former Byzantine province of Cilicia, on the Mediterranean Sea south of the Taurus Mountains, was seized as a place of refuge by Armenians, who established themselves in the mountain passes that protected the area.[39] Under the princely Rubenid family, who came from Ani by way of Cappadocia, the Armenian presence was increased and secured in the course of the twelfth century until, in 1198, the baron Leon II was crowned king, by grace of the Holy Roman Emperor Henry VI and Pope Celestine III.

Politically and geographically, Cilician Armenia moved in quite a different orbit from that of the landlocked kingdoms of Greater Armenia. Its Mediterranean ports became the chief European access to the overland route to China, putting Armenia in imme-

ing of the colophon on the reverse is irreconcilable with the ruling of the Gospel of Gagik and the colophon is written in a slanted hand that shows up nowhere else in the manuscript. Further, the reconstruction proposed by Nšanian, placing four such donor portraits at the *end* of each of the four Gospels, is an arrangement for which absolutely no precedent exists (see Der Nersessian's discussion of this point, "Évangile du roi Gagik," 89–90).

[34] Janashian, *Armenian Miniature Painting*, 23–27, pls. 12–33. Der Nersessian, *Armenian Art*, 114; eadem, "Évangile du roi Gagik," 98.

[35] The pigments of this manuscript are under study by M. Virginia Orna and will be reported on along with other manuscripts of San Lazzaro.

[36] Tatiana A. Izmailova, "Le cycle des fêtes du tétraévangile de Mougna: Maténadaran, no. 7736," *REArm*, n.s. 6 (1969), 105–39; eadem, "Les racines prébyzantines dans les miniatures arméniennes: Les canons du tétraévangile de Mougna," *Armeniaca: Mélanges d'études arméniennes* (Venice, 1969), 28–41; eadem, *Arm. miniatjura XI veka*, 124–70, pls. 81–106.

[37] Izmailova, *Arm. miniatjura XI veka*, 103–24.

[38] Der Nersessian, *Armenian Art*, 109.

[39] Jacques de Morgan, *Histoire du peuple Arménien* (Paris, 1919), 161–239; Sirarpie Der Nersessian, "The Kingdom of Cilician Armenia," *A History of the Crusades*, ed. Kenneth M. Setton (Madison, Wis., 1969), II, 630–59, repr. in Der Nersessian, *Études*, 329–52; Gérard Dédéyan, "Le temps de la croisade," *Histoire des Arméniens*, 297–339.

diate touch with merchants from Venice, Genoa, and France. The royal Rubenid, and then Het'umid, line made marriage alliances with all the Crusader states, and the court and ecclesiastical hierarchy tried to work out a series of compromises with Rome to bring Armenian religious practice into conformity with that of the Latins. Although the effects of such changes on the populace at large are open to question, at least among the nobility Western customs and ways of dress came to predominate, and this was the class that commissioned the illuminated manuscripts.[40]

The artistic world of the Mediterranean in this period was characterized by the most extensive circulation and interchange of ideas stimulated by the Crusades. In Jerusalem and Acre manuscripts were being illuminated by French artists brought to the Holy Land, working almost as if they had never left their studios in the Ile de France.[41] In Constantinople the Latin occupation (1204–61) produced related work in the apse decoration of the Kalenderhane Camii, in which a Life of Francis of Assisi was flanked by Byzantine church fathers.[42] At the same time, icons were being produced in the Holy Land in very curious mixtures of French, Italian, and Byzantine styles, which Weitzmann has been studying and publishing in recent years.[43] While contact with Islamic painting was generally resisted in Crusader circles, among native East Christian communities both in Egypt and Syria another kind of amalgam was emerging, in which both figurative styles and the wide repertory of abstract decoration were being assimilated from Islamic art.[44] Similar cross-fertilization of styles could be found along the western shores of the Mediterranean, as has been documented in recent studies of Italian art of this period.[45] Almost anything seems possible in this vast circulation of books and artists and their patrons. In one famous example, the Conradin Bible produced in Sicily in the mid-thirteenth century, English traditions of manuscript illumination encounter the modern Paleologan fashions from Constantinople.[46]

This is the cosmopolitan setting in which Cilician painting must be situated.[47] Stylistically this development is the most cohesive in the history of Armenian art. The comparative stability of the ruling families, the extremely high percentage of princely commissions, and the workshop continuity of manuscript production from one generation to the next combined to produce much greater uniformity and a smoother growth of stylistic change.[48] The large number of surviving manuscripts of the highest quality, especially in the second half of the thirteenth century, make this the most exciting period of Armenian art to study. Since more comprehensive studies of Cilician painting are presently under way, for the present purposes one need only sketch the evolution in order to observe the principal developments in Gospel illustration.[49]

Cilician painting is in origin continuous with painting in the Armenian kingdoms of the tenth and eleventh centuries, and nowhere is this more striking than in matters of technique. The palette retains all of the brilliance and strength of earlier works in Greater Armenia, using rich, saturated colors that immediately distinguish Armenian painting from the pastel tints favored in Byzantine painting. The basis of this difference, it has been demonstrated, lies in continued use of exactly the same mineral pigments as were employed earlier, in contrast to Byzantine re-

[40] Drampyan notes the predominantly aristocratic nature of Cilician patronage, but she makes the unlikely supposition that "by a peculiar whim of fate" non-aristocratic commissions simply have not survived. Korkhmazyan, *Armenian Miniatures of the 13th and 14th Centuries,* 21.

[41] Hugo Buchthal, *Miniature Painting in the Latin Kingdom of Jerusalem* (Oxford, 1957); Jaroslav Folda, *Crusader Manuscript Illumination at Saint-Jean d'Acre, 1275–1291* (Princeton, 1976).

[42] C. L. Striker, "Work at the Kalenderhane Camii in Istanbul: Preliminary Reports," *DOP* 22 (1968), 191, figs. 19–29; 25 (1971), 257–58.

[43] Kurt Weitzmann's articles on Crusader icons have been gathered in his *Studies in the Arts at Sinai* (Princeton, 1982), 291–422; more recently see idem, "Crusader Icons and Maniera Greca," *Byzanz und der Westen: Studien zur Kunst des europäischen Mittelalters,* Österreichischen Akademie der Wissenschaften, phil.-hist. Klasse 432, ed. Irmgard Hutter (Vienna, 1984), 143–70.

[44] Leroy, *Mss. syriaques,* passim; Robert S. Nelson, "An Icon at Mt. Sinai and Christian Painting in Muslim Egypt during the Thirteenth and Fourteenth Centuries," *Art Bulletin* 65 (1983), 201–18.

[45] Wolfgang Grape, *Grenzprobleme der byzantinischen Malerei,* diss., University of Vienna, 1973; Ann Derbes, *Byzantine Art and the Dugento: Iconographic Sources of the Passion Scenes in Italian Painted Crosses,* diss., University of Virginia, 1980.

[46] Rebecca Corrie, "The Conradin Bible: Since 'Since deRicci,'" *Journal of the Walters Art Gallery* 40 (1982), 13–24.

[47] On Armenian painting in Cilicia in general, see Der Nersessian, *Armenian Art,* 123–62; L. Ṙ. Azaryan, *Kilikyan Manrankarč'ut'yunə XII–XIII dd.* (Erevan, 1964); Narkiss and Stone, *Jerusalem,* 41–73; Korkhmazyan, *Armenian Miniatures of the 13th and 14th Centuries,* 19–29 and notes on pls. 79–152.

[48] On workshop continuity see Helen C. Evans, "Canon Tables as an Indication of Teacher-Pupil Relationships in the Career of T'oros Ṙoslin," in T. Samuelian and M. Stone, eds., *Medieval Armenian Culture,* University of Pennsylvania Armenian Texts and Studies 6 (Chico, Calif., 1983), 272–90.

[49] Sirarpie Der Nersessian, *Miniature Painting in the Armenian Kingdom of Cilicia from the Twelfth to the Fourteenth Century* (Washington, D.C., forthcoming); and Helen C. Evans, *Armenian Manuscript Illumination.*

liance on organic substances.[50] Evidently the workshop traditions remained intact despite the uprooting and emigration from Greater Armenia to Cilicia.

This continuity may also be observable in style in the relationship of the Theodore Gospel (Jerusalem, St. James 1796) of the late twelfth century to the Gospel of King Gagik of Kars of the eleventh. Named for the artist who signed himself under the portrait of Matthew, the Theodore Gospel has only two narrative miniatures—scenes of the Resurrection—along with canon tables, evangelists, and a donor portrait.[51] Still, there are evident links with the Gagik Gospel in the solemnity and monumentality of the figures, the uncluttered compositions, and the deep blue backgrounds, and one is tempted to imagine a painting tradition bridging the century between them.[52] A similar monumental style has been traced in a handful of manuscripts that Der Nersessian associates with Washington, Freer 50.3.[53]

In the first half of the thirteenth century this grand style disappears. A pair of manuscripts of 1237 and 1251 show a distinct softening of style toward a smooth and elegant manner in much lighter colors.[54] The first, Erevan, Mat. 7700, introduces a smooth, almost unwrinkled handling of the evangelists' garments, modulating large areas from highlight to shadow in continuous gradations. The second, Erevan, Mat. 3033, enlarges the evangelists relative to the frame and renders the figures in the lean proportions and harder graphic manner characteristic of Byzantine painting of the Comnenian period. In both, the architecture of the background is simplified to unadorned geometric shapes. The negotiations of Levon II with Constantinople and the intermarriages with the ruling house of Nicaea must have brought with them an exchange of gifts, among which manuscripts would have been very appropriate.

None of the early thirteenth-century manuscripts contain narrative subjects. The appearance of T'oros Ṙoslin in the third quarter of the century, with his great store of lively and new narrative imagery, then, comes somewhat as a surprise. Stunning, too, is the enormous variety of figure types and poses, the delicate sense of movement, and the strong, dramatic effects he manages to achieve (figs. 92b, 103b, 117b, 124b, 162b, 169b, 172b, 211b, 216b, 218c, 235b, 250c, 263b, 269b, 271c, 286b, 286c, 327b, 351c, 438b, 453a, 469b, 480b, 522c, 532c). Though the work of separating the master's painting from that of his collaborators has not yet been completed, it is clear that Ṙoslin was one of the most accomplished painters of the entire Middle Ages.[55] Ṙoslin was also extremely receptive to imagery he found in manuscripts arriving from the West. Der Nersessian noticed Western sources for a number of motifs, such as Ecclesia and Synagoga at the Crucifixion, and Western women's headdresses in Washington, Freer 32.18, and the Mocking of Christ in Baltimore, Walters 539, but she viewed this as a rather limited phenomenon.[56] A closer study, however, of both Ṙoslin and his contemporaries, begins to reveal a fairly extensive pattern of imported Western motifs, which made their way to Cilicia with Franciscan missionaries.[57] The missionaries were well received and contemporary sources mention the books they carried.

As in Greater Armenia, the bulk of the Cilician manuscripts that were illustrated were Gospel books. Some features of Gospel production remained constant with only accidental changes, while others were reshaped extensively or simply dropped. The ten-page set of canon tables is one of the most stable features—this remained standard, with two pages for the Eusebian prologue and eight for the tables themselves—though many innovations were made in its page format and decoration. The page format had evolved in the eleventh century from being an arched structure with a decorated tympanum to a column-supported rectangular headpiece, which might contain arches or other subdivisions of the field within it. A great many solutions were found to the problem of decorating the field, some stressing the architectural membering of the field, others the overall patterns within the field, whether of flowers or palmettes or Islamic interlace. Half-length portraits of Eusebius and Carpianos were standard on the first two pages; T'oros Ṙoslin boldly extended the portraits by adding prophets throughout the canon tables in some of his manuscripts.[58] In Cilician painting all parts of the

[50] Cabelli and Mathews, "Pigments in Armenian Manuscripts of the Tenth and Eleventh Centuries," 33–47; D. E. Cabelli, M. V. Orna, and T. F. Mathews, "Analysis of Medieval Pigments from Cilician Armenia," *Archeological Chemistry* 3, ed. Joseph B. Lambert, Advances in Chemistry Series 205 (Washington, D.C., 1984), 243–54.

[51] Narkiss and Stone, *Jerusalem*, 41–42, 148, figs. 57–60.

[52] Compare Der Nersessian, *Armenian Art*, pls. 76–77.

[53] Der Nersessian, *Arm. Mss. Freer*, 7–17.

[54] Korkhmazyan, *Armenian Miniatures of the 13th and 14th Centuries*, 21–22 and pls. 79–83.

[55] On the distinction of Ṙoslin's style from his collaborators', see Der Nersessian, *Arm. Mss. Freer*, 33–35; eadem, *Arm. Mss. Walters*, 15–18.

[56] Der Nersessian, *Arm. Mss. Freer*, 49–50; eadem, *Arm. Mss. Walters*, 18.

[57] Helen C. Evans, *Armenian Manuscript Illumination*.

[58] Baltimore, Walters 539 (Der Nersessian, *Arm. Mss. Walters*, pls. 30–39); Erevan, Mat. 10675 (Korkhmazyan, *Armenian Manuscripts of the 13th and 14th Centuries*, pls. 90–92); Jerusalem, St. James 2660 (Narkiss and Stone, *Jerusalem*, fig. 65).

canon page admitted of embellishment: columns could be treated as panels or plaited like ribbons; capitals and bases could assume animal forms; and the margins could be filled with trees and birds and beasts of the hunt. Hence, while the ten-page set remained unchanged, it provided a vehicle for the artist to integrate decorative elements that can often be shown to derive from Cilicia's contacts with Islam and Europe.

The evangelists' portraits, placed before each Gospel, are another stable feature. These were updated in the painting of Cilicia by the substitution of more current Byzantine models in the Comnenian style.

In the program of Gospel illustration, however, a number of substantial changes were introduced. The old preface-page system, which placed a set of subjects from the Life of Christ between the canon tables and the beginning of Matthew, was much less commonly used; perhaps it was seen as archaic. Instead, several ways of integrating the narrative miniatures with the text were developed. One way was to scatter a select set of subjects, more or less equivalent to the Byzantine festival set, through the four Gospels, as Ṙoslin did in Erevan, Mat. 10675. These illuminations would be placed on full pages and would be located as near as possible to the appropriate texts. Another way was to develop the running narrative system introduced in Greater Armenia with the Vehapʿaṙ Gospel and the Gospel of King Gagik. Tʿoros Ṙoslin explored the possibilities of this system in three very important manuscripts, occasionally interrupting the sequence of smaller miniatures by full-page illuminations, as in the festival set.[59] A third system relegated the narrative illustrations to the rather abbreviated representations confined to the margins of the page. While Ṙoslin occasionally takes advantage of this way of illustrating (fig. 103b), he never follows it with the thoroughness seen in the splendid Cilician manuscript of 1263, Washington, Freer 56.11, which has fifty-six little marginal vignettes.[60]

Still another system of Gospel illustration appears in the very important frieze Gospel, Erevan, Mat. 7651, sometimes called the Gospel of the Eight Painters. The page layout of this manuscript called for text arranged in a single wide column, interrupted by miniatures of multiple scenes that stretch across the page (figs. 35b, 92c, 99b, 108b, 117c, 122c, 126d, 160c, 171b, 172c, 179d, 197c, 211c, 218b, 227b, 227c, 235a, 250b, 255c, 259b, 263a, 269c, 271b, 327c, 336c, 351d, 403c, 453b, 469c, 480c, 484b, 561e). Begun in Sis in the 1270's, this manuscript still languished incomplete in the palace treasury of King Ōšin in 1320, when Bishop Stepʿanos of Sebasteia picked it out as a present. According to the bishop's colophon, the book "was written in a beautiful cursive hand and adorned with many-colored pictures, but was not complete in its illustration, with some pictures merely outlined and still more entirely blank."[61] Accordingly the bishop commissioned the painter Sargis Picak to finish the manuscript, for the sum of 1,300 dram.[62] Another manuscript of this format is found in Isfahan, All-Savior 546, completed only through the Gospel of Matthew in the late thirteenth century.[63] However, what makes Erevan 7651 most valuable for the study of Armenian Gospel iconography is the possibility of comparing it to its Greek model, the frieze Gospel in Florence, Laurentiana VI,23. Many of the Armenian miniatures are literal, figure-for-figure copies of the Greek model. But the fact that the Armenian manuscript derives from the Greek one without any intermediary can be demonstrated from the existence of Armenian signature numbers that were added to the Greek manuscript when it was taken apart for copying, and from the Armenian inscription on fol. 27 telling the copyist, "This is the image that should be omitted"; in fact, the corresponding section of the Armenian manuscript, fols. 40–41, omits the image.[64] Comparison of the two manuscripts, then, gives one a most interesting barometer of Armenian preferences in Gospel imagery, for beyond the copied miniatures are countless miniatures where the painters transformed the original iconography, sometimes in subtle ways, sometimes in drastic revisions and additions. We will appeal to the manuscript frequently in examining the peculiarities of Armenian Gospel iconography.

The Armenian frieze Gospel could also be used as a measure of the last two stylistic phases of Cilician painting. Sargis Picak was responsible for approximately two-fifths of the miniatures.[65] The first artist, responsible for the Infancy and Passion miniatures in

[59] Baltimore, Walters 539; Erevan, Mat. 5458; Washington, Freer 32.18.

[60] Der Nersessian, *Arm. Mss. Freer,* figs. 204–56.

[61] Korkhmazyan, *Armenian Painting of the 13th and 14th Centuries,* 28.

[62] Compare this sum to 1,800 dram spent by the vardapet Nersēs of Taron for the scribes' work on a Bible executed in Glajor in 1332, in addition to another 400 dram for the binding. For this and some later figures on costs of manuscripts, see Sanjian, *Colophons,* 10–12. For the dram see Paul Z. Bedoukian, "Armenian Mints and Money," *Dictionary of the Middle Ages* 8, 417–18.

[63] Der Nersessian and Mekhitarian, *Isfahan,* 39–57.

[64] Velmans, *Le Tétraévangile,* 12; Der Nersessian, *Armenian Art,* 156.

[65] Picak did 99 out of 245 miniatures. His work is found in all four Gospels, usually in continuous runs; a codicological analysis of the manuscript might reveal much about artists' working methods.

Matthew, exemplifies the exuberant style of the post-Ṙoslin decades, working in a mannerist style of turbulent, crowded composition; figures twist and turn and break through the borders of the images, and some assume the inflated proportions of contemporary Palaeologan painting, as in Erevan, Mat. 197 and 9422.[66] Other painters are somewhat more restrained, but still lively, with an interesting range of figure types (fig. 480c, 484b). The style of the last painter, Sargis Picak, is by contrast tame, staid, and formulaic. From his painting at Drazark and Sis, his work can be followed in over thirty manuscripts from 1301 to 1353.[67] While the overall compositions have a brilliant decorative quality, individual figures are short and doll-like, proportions are squat, with large heads, and everyone has identical facial features; by contrast, the patterns of materials and fanciful architecture play a large role in the pictorial effect (figs. 227c, 250b, 263a, 269c, 271b, 403c, 561e). This somewhat bankrupt ending of the Cilician school is contemporary with the development of painting in Glajor.

3. The Thirteenth Century in Greater Armenia

After more than a century under the Saltukids and the Shaddadids, with nominal allegiance to the Seljukid dynasty of Iran, the Armenians achieved a brief new period of independence in their native homeland. As outlined above (see Chapter 2), liberation came from the north, from Georgia, where the royal Bagratid family, joined by the Zakʿarians, led the struggle for independence from the Seljuks. In 1199 Dwin, Kars, and Ani were liberated and thereafter the northern and eastern provinces of ancient Armenia were gradually recovered. However, all of this fell to the Mongols in the 1230's, and although the Mongols left in place the local structures of government through princely families, the disruption was enormous. Very few illuminated manuscripts survive from the second half of the thirteenth century. Hence the manuscripts of early in the century seem somewhat isolated both from what preceded and from what followed.

The new resumption of artistic activity in Greater Armenia followed a great hiatus of over a century. In spite of the continuity of artistic traditions maintained in Cilicia to the south, in Greater Armenia traditions remained quite fragmented. Perhaps it was their ingrained suspicion of Cilician compromises with the West that made the Armenians in their homeland less ready to accept the cosmopolitan painting styles of Cilicia as normative. At any rate, the new painting seems to lack a center stylistically. Instead one finds a series of fitful attempts at synthesis of very disparate material. In the uncertain political situation it must have been rather unpredictable what a given artist would have at hand as models or what he would regard as his native tradition. Alongside the older manuscripts of Greater Armenia, an artist might come across Islamic manuscripts, for elements of Moslem decoration are common; but he might equally be influenced by Syrian manuscripts belonging to his Monophysite neighbors. At the same time, contemporary manuscripts from Cilicia were always arriving, complete with their baggage of Western additions. No single style can be said to dominate the period, but each manuscript has to be approached on its own terms.[68]

At the start of the period one finds the largest surviving Armenian manuscript, the Homilary of Muš, Erevan, Mat. 7729, with folios measuring 70.5 × 55 cm. Produced in 1201–2 under the Mangujakid dynasty in Awagvankʿ, near Erznka on the Euphrates, the manuscript echoes its Islamic surroundings. The incipit title page at the beginning of the manuscript is composed of intricate interlace designs, affronted animals, and plants that derive from an Arabic Dioscorides.[69] The style of the narrative scenes, however, comes from other sources. Mountainous landscapes are rendered in oriental conventions, figures tend to be squat in proportions and faces have the oriental cast found in contemporary Syrian manuscripts.[70] Christ has a small mouth and delicate moustache and rich flowing curls of hair.

A few years later, in the liberated zone north of Lake Sevan, the artist of the Hałbat Gospel (Erevan, Mat. 6288) was even more obviously dependent on Syrian models. Painted in 1211, the manuscript con-

[66] See fol. 12a, the Magi before Herod, in Dournovo, *Haykakan Manrankarčʿutʿyun,* fig. 52; and fols. 79v–80, the Crucifixion, in Der Nersessian, *Armenian Art,* fig. 113; cf. Korkhmazyan, *Armenian Miniatures of the 13th and 14th Centuries,* pls. 126–39.

[67] Der Nersessian, *Manuscrits,* 137–66; Narkiss and Stone, *Jerusalem,* 80–87.

[68] The best introduction to the art of this period is Der Nersessian's chapter on "The Great Feudal Families" in *Armenian Art,* 163–225; on manuscript illumination in particular, see 209–25.

[69] Der Nersessian, *Armenian Art,* 209–14, pl. 163; Korkhmazyan, *Armenian Miniatures of the 13th and 14th Centuries,* pls. 1–2.

[70] Compare the nearly contemporary illustrated Syrian lectionaries, Vatican City, Bibl. Apost. Syr. 559 and London, B.L. add. 7170, in Leroy, *Mss. syriaques,* pls. 83–99.

tains an Entry into Jerusalem in which the direction of the action is reversed, Syrian fashion; the rendering of the battlements of Jerusalem, the figures who appear in the merlons extending their hands to the men in the trees, the boy and the man in the gate, the blessing gesture of Christ, all these motifs are paralleled in the Entry in the Syrian lectionaries.[71] Discs of Islamic interlace decorate the headings and canon tables.[72]

Some notion of the kind of painting that was taking place in Ani at this time may be gained from New Julfa, All-Savior 36, which was executed in 1236, probably in Hoṙomos (figs. 532b, 561b).[73] Though he has taken Byzantine compositions for his point of departure, the artist, Ignatios of Ani, shows a special interest in strong, sculptural heads, with deep shadows below the brows and below the eyes and marked contours in the cheeks; the eyes are frequently extended to a line on the outside, in Mongol fashion. Christ is often shown enlarged out of scale with the rest of the figures. Modeling is achieved with harsh bright whites laid on in sharp angular lines or comb patterns. Another manuscript associated with Ani, the Tʿargmančʿacʿ Gospel of 1232, seems to be a less competent realization of the same style.[74] The painter has a similar interest in strong sculptural faces, but he achieves this with simpler means, giving them all dark, sunken eye sockets, and his figures are awkward, if not actually uncomfortable in design.

Yet none of these manuscripts can be connected with the splendid Erznka Bible produced in that city in 1269 (Jerusalem, St. James, 1925).[75] Though illustrated Bibles from Cilicia with which to compare it are lacking, the style is very purely Cilician, very likely done by a traveling artist. Windblown draperies, lively figures, and a solid painterly manner of modeling link this work to counterparts in the circle of Tʿoros Ṙoslin. Perhaps the revival of trade under Mongol rule made such contacts more natural. Yet this manuscript stands very much alone; when painting activity resumes in Siwnikʿ at the end of the century it starts with a different mix of traditions.

[71] Compare Der Nersessian, *Armenian Art,* pl. 165 to Leroy, *Mss. syriaques,* pl. 86.

[72] Korkhmazyan, *Armenian Miniatures of the 13th and 14th Centuries,* pls. 11–12.

[73] On Ignatios of Ani see Der Nersessian and Mekhitarian, *Isfahan,* 60–64; Der Nersessian, "L'Évangile Matenadaran no. 10.525," 333; Janashian, *Armenian Miniature Paintings,* 45–46.

[74] Der Nersessian, *Armenian Art,* 218, pl. 167; Dournovo, *Haykakan Manrankarčʿutʿyun,* pls. 24–28; Korkhmazyan, *Armenian Miniatures of the 13th and 14th Centuries,* pl. 7–10.

[75] Narkiss and Stone, *Jerusalem,* 66–68, 150, figs. 84–86; Der Nersessian, *Armenian Art,* 218–19, pl. 166.

4. Siwnikʿ in the Fourteenth Century: Ełegis and Noravankʿ

The diversity of artists at work in the U.C.L.A. Gospel presents a confusing impression: the two workshops paint in conflicting styles, and within each workshop there is considerable stylistic disagreement among artists. When placed in the larger situation of painting activity in the province of Siwnikʿ in the early fourteenth century, however, the inconsistencies become more understandable; in fact, the manuscript is symptomatic of the stylistic conflicts of this province of Armenian painting and offers a kind of compendium of its two most significant developments.

The art-historical situation in Siwnikʿ around the beginning of the fourteenth century is obscure and has only begun to be clarified very recently. Two conflicting interpretations of the material have been proposed. In a pioneering effort to describe the painting of Glajor, in Siwnikʿ, Avetisyan grouped the painters in two generations.[76] According to Avetisyan, the first generation was dominated by Momik, whom he described as the founder of the Glajor school of painting, and the second generation was dominated by Tʿoros Taronecʿi, whom Avetisyan saw as a pupil of Momik. Der Nersessian has demonstrated, however, that there is no evidence that Momik was ever employed as a painter in Glajor.[77] Although Momik is signed in one Glajor manuscript of 1283–84, the manuscript has no painted decoration beyond a single monochrome chapter heading. Momik has left two signed illuminated manuscripts: one, Matenadaran 2848, painted in 1292 in Noravankʿ, and the other, Matenadaran 6792, painted in 1302, very likely in the same place, for Ivanē, the bishop of Noravankʿ (fig. 106c). His other attested works show him employed as a sculptor in 1304 and 1308 in Noravankʿ, as a scribe in 1307 and 1331 in Noravankʿ and Ełegis, and as an architect at Arpʿa Areni, near Noravankʿ, in 1321. He died and was buried in Noravankʿ in 1333.[78] It is not possible, then, to make Momik into a Glajor painter, much less the founder and initiator of an artistic school there. Moreover, visual connections between the work of Momik and Tʿoros would be extremely difficult to establish; in contrast to the rough and somewhat spontaneous style of Tʿoros, Momik's work has a frozen formality about it. Rather, his smooth surfaces, hard edges, and patterned back-

[76] A. N. Avetisyan, *Haykakan Manrankarčʿutʿyan.*

[77] Der Nersessian, "L'Évangile du Matenadaran no. 10.525," 337–39.

[78] Ibid., 338–39.

ground place him much closer to the Second Painter of the U.C.L.A. Gospel than to Tʿoros.

Momik does not represent an early phase of the Glajor style but rather a different style, and this manner of painting he practiced at Noravankʿ. Momik's style, moreover, is not an isolated, personal phenomenon, but part of a somewhat larger development described by Der Nersessian in her analysis of Matenadaran 10525 (figs. 21b, 179e, 286e, 522d). This tattered but very fine manuscript was executed by the scribe and painter Sargis, a painter of far greater ability than Momik, at Ełegis in 1306. The two localities are only a few kilometers apart, situated on either side of Glajor. According to Der Nersessian, the stylistic dichotomy between Glajor and its two neighbors is less one of regional differences than it is one of family patronage; the style of Noravankʿ and Ełegis is associated with the Ōrbēlians while that of Glajor is linked with the Pṙošians. In fact, both families were interested in Glajor, as mentioned above; it is nevertheless true that the Pṙošians were the founders of Glajor while the other two centers belonged to the Ōrbēlians, and this may well explain the different artistic directions they took. The colophon of Matenadaran 10525 informs us that it was executed for one Daniel, for the salvation of his family, under the archbishop Yovhannēs Ōrbēlian of Noravankʿ.

The style of Sargis and Momik gains much of its strength from a process of simplification. Secondary figures are sometimes omitted to focus attention more sharply on the principal actors in a scene. Thus Sargis omits servants and bystanders in his Raising of Lazarus (fig. 522d), and Momik includes only John and the Virgin in his Crucifixion.[79] The figure of Christ is often enlarged out of scale with the rest of the figures, further strengthening the dramatic focus; at the same time backgrounds are simplified, landscapes sometimes being reduced to abstract bands of solid color.[80] This abstraction of backgrounds extends to the introduction of arbitrary fields of patterned decoration of brick, tile, or textile motifs. Momik reduces the mountains of his Ascension (fig. 106c) and his Descent of the Holy Spirit to a pattern of repeated arcs, and he fills the arched background of his author portrait of St. James with hexagonal tiles; in Sargis' Women at the Tomb, Christ stands on a panel of octagonal tiles.[81]

In their treatment of figures Sargis and Momik show a preference for clean, smooth surfaces shaded very gradually from light to dark. Draperies are artificially arranged in carefully contrived parallel folds that often break in a kind of hook fold around the shoulders and T-form folds at the hems (fig. 522d).[82] Faces have an expression of wide-eyed astonishment. They are given large, almond eyes, extended to a line at the outer corner, small delicate mouths, and prominent noses. Hands are often too large, with long, tapering fingers; and the articulation of forearms is shown in an unusual fashion, with a shadow line down the middle defining the two bones, and another line defining the wrist. Christ is generally given a youthful appearance, with piles of rich dark hair falling on his shoulders.

A further feature of the style is analyzed by Der Nersessian in the decorative vocabulary of Sargis (comparable pages in Momik's work have not been published). In his canon tables Sargis introduces sinuous, long-necked winged bulls and lions into the lunettes (fig. 21b). Furthermore, while Cilician manuscripts had occasionally used lion and bull heads as column capitals in the canon tables,[83] Sargis uses them systematically both as capitals and bases, giving them always large human eyes. One further animal innovation appears in the unique decorated initials, which carry the symbolism of the beasts of the evangelists throughout the Gospel text. The customary bird letters that mark the beginning of each reading are given human heads in Matthew's Gospel, lion heads in Mark, bull heads in Luke, and eagle heads in John.[84]

Taken together these features comprise a style of considerable distinction. The style has great force and clarity and the artists who practiced it seemed capable of interesting innovations. A few other manuscripts can be associated with this style, the most important of which is New Julfa, All-Savior 477, executed for Bishop Ivanē Ōrbēlian in Noravankʿ in 1300.[85] Since this manuscript lacks evangelist portraits and narrative scenes, its figure style must be judged from the diminutive figures on the incipit pages. Above the headpiece of Matthew's incipit (fig. 27a) appears the bust of Christ set in a little reservoir of water; his garments are executed in the soft, immaculate style of Sargis and Momik, his hair bunches

[79] Avetisyan, *Haykakan Manrankarčʿutʿyan*, fig. 13.

[80] See also Momik's Burial of Christ and Women at the Tomb, Avetisyan, *Haykakan Manrankarčʿutʿyan*, pl. 1.

[81] Ibid., figs. 10, 15, 17; Der Nersessian, "L'Évangile du Matenadaran no. 10.525," pl. LXVI, fig. 8 and pl. LXX, fig. 12.

[82] See comparable features in Momik's Women at the Tomb, Der Nersessian, "L'Évangile du Matenadaran no. 10.525," LXXI, fig. 13.

[83] For example see Erevan 8321 and 7644, Korkhmazyan, *Armenian Miniature Painting of the Thirteenth and Fourteenth Centuries*, figs. 87, 108, 109.

[84] Der Nersessian, L'Évangile du Matenadaran no. 10.525," 331 and pls. LXIV and LXV, figs. 4–7.

[85] Der Nersessian and Mekhitarian, *Isfahan*, 64–73.

in three great ringlets on either side, and he makes a blessing gesture with two long fingers. To the right and left, figures of the Blessed Virgin and John the Evangelist stretch out their hands in prayer toward Christ. A very similar Christ is found on the incipit of John, seated in a chalice atop the four living creatures in the letter *ini.*

A hitherto unpublished leaf in the collection of the Metropolitan Museum of Art in New York, no. 388.171.2, belongs to this same style.[86] The headpiece of John's incipit contains five pairs of paired beasts—eagles, bulls, and lions, the latter performing a kind of dance on one foot (fig. 461a). Above, a pair of human faces complete the sacred four symbols, nestled close on either side of a bird-throne that contains Christ in the center while it spouts water to either side. The faces show the same surprised eyes, tiny mouths, and prominent noses observed in the work of Sargis and Momik; Christ's hair falls in copious locks on his shoulders, and his draperies are arranged in soft rounded folds. He blesses with two very long fingers. A very similar Joannine incipit page, with paired dancing beasts, occurs in another New York manuscript, Morgan 620. G. Hovsepian, whose opinion is cited by Sanjian, thought that a "baron Dawitʿ" mentioned in six inscriptions should be identified with a prince of that name active in Gugarkʿ in northern Armenia in the early thirteenth century.[87] But Dawitʿ is a common name and the style does not fit a thirteenth-century date. Paleographically the manuscript must be dated in the seventeenth century.[88] Nevertheless, it copies the Ełegis-Noravankʿ style so successfully that it might be taken as an accurate witness to a model manuscript of around 1300 (fig. 461b). Finally, one other manuscript has been very plausibly ascribed to the group by the Buschhausens on the basis of its similarities to Erevan, Mat. 10525. Only a single evangelist survives in this manuscript, Vienna, Mekhitarist 460, and it is the work of a somewhat less talented artist (fig. 188a).[89] Unfortunately these manuscripts lack colophons.

In an effort to describe this style more fully Der Nersessian has proposed to trace its origins to the painting of Ignatios of Ani early in the thirteenth century, and in the other direction she has followed its sequel in the work of Kirakos of Tabriz a generation later.[90] The precedent is less convincing than the sequel. Though the proportions of the figures have something in common, the soft modeling that is the hallmark of the painting of Sargis and Momik does not appear in the work of Ignatios. In his manuscript of 1236 (New Julfa, All-Savior 36), Ignatios models the evangelist's garments in graphic comb patterns and sculpts his face in harsh shadows (figs. 532b, 561b). In general his effects are stark and severe while the style of Sargis and Momik is gentle and reserved. The origins of the soft modeling style must lie rather in Cilicia, in manuscripts such as Erevan, Mat. 7700 and 3033, discussed above.

The sequel presents a far more decorative development of the style. In a manuscript of 1330 (New Julfa, All-Savior 47), the painter Kirakos of Tabriz repeats many of the iconographic types used by Momik; but the compositions lose their simplicity in a proliferation of decorative patterns; brick and tile patterns cover every available surface including the sky (figs. 106e, 305f, 561f).[91] Faces have become distinctly oriental in a Far Eastern fashion, evangelists and apostles taking on the looks of Chinese sages.

Even if other manuscripts should eventually be added to those already discovered, one may reasonably conclude that the painting of Sargis and Momik at Ełegis and Noravankʿ was part of a fairly limited development. The style was well established in Siwnikʿ around the turn of the century and had a few highly skilled and imaginative practitioners. It is to this group that the painting of the Second Painter of the U.C.L.A. Gospel clearly belongs. One can make a stronger claim: the Second Painter is, as far as surviving evidence permits one to judge, the most accomplished master of the Ełegis-Noravankʿ style.

A general picture of the Second Painter's style has been drawn in order to distinguish him from the other artists of the U.C.L.A. Gospel. His personal style can be defined more fully, however, in relationship to the artists who stand closer to him. His figure of Christ is perhaps the best index of his place in the Ełegis-Noravankʿ style. The Genealogy contains representations of the seated Christ blessing at the beginning and at the end of the series (*pages 28 and 35*), both of which use the beardless or Emmanuel-type image. The expression is slightly different in the two figures; but both faces have large eyes, prominent noses, and tiny, delicate mouths; the hair falls copi-

[86] Sanjian, *Catalogue,* 474.

[87] Ibid., 510.

[88] Der Nersessian, in private correspondence, remarks that the extended ligatures in the *erkatʿagir* letters belong to the 17th century.

[89] Heide and Helmut Buschhausen, *Armenische Handschriften der Mechitaristen-Congregation in Wien: Katalog zur Sonderausstellung in der Österreichischen Nationalbibliothek* (Vienna, 1981), 120–21.

[90] Der Nersessian, "L'Évangile du Matenadaran no. 10.525," 340–42.

[91] Der Nersessian and Mekhitarian, *Isfahan,* 88–93, figs. 51–63; Der Nersessian, "L'Évangile du Matenadaran no. 10.525," 340–42, pl. LXXII, fig. 16.

ously on the shoulders, and the bone structure of the forearm and wrist is outlined. Furthermore, a very strict parallel can be drawn with the frontal half-length figure of Christ that appears at the top of the incipit page of New Julfa 477 (fig. 27a). The structure of the figures is virtually identical, the faces are extremely close, and on *page 28* Christ has exactly the same blessing gesture with two long bent fingers. It should be noticed, however, that the Second Painter is using the figures in a different context and on a larger scale, and he has dressed them more richly, outlining their garments in gold and giving the Christ on *page 35* a brocaded tunic. He uses such Islamic-derived brocades again in the Annunciation and the Cure of the Man Born Blind, *pages 305 and 509*.

The genealogical context of these figures restricts them to frontal, emblematic poses; the true power of the Second Painter's Christ is better seen in the narrative subjects. It is readily apparent in examining the subjects of the Life of Christ that the Second Painter is following a different iconographic tradition from that familiar to Sargis or Momik. The iconography of each subject will be studied below in some detail, but it can be noted here that the Entry into Jerusalem on *page 252* has little to do with Momik's composition of this subject, and the Raising of Lazarus (*page 522* and fig. 522d) is radically different from Sargis' painting of the subject.[92] Yet the painting of the narrative subjects stands very strictly within the Ełegis-Noravankʿ style. Backgrounds are simplified by the reduction of landscape, as in the Entry, or by abstraction into horizontal panels of solid color as in the Cure of the Man Born Blind (*page 509*), and architectural backdrops tend to be simple and massive (*pages 305 and 156*, and fig. 532d).[93] Garments are smoothly modeled in rounded folds with occasional hook folds and T-form folds (*pages 509 and 522*). Finally, the Second Painter's faces and hands, his postures of figures, and his group of figures, all have close parallels in the Ełegis-Noravankʿ tradition.

But while the Second Painter of the U.C.L.A. Gospel is firmly rooted in the Ełegis-Noravankʿ tradition he also stands out within the tradition. Momik's Christ in the miniature of the Entry into Jerusalem is so similar to the apostles around him in cast of head and expression that he is hardly distinguishable from the crowd, and while Sargis has distinguished Christ from the other figures by his scale, his head has the same sharp chin and delicate features as the women or angels (fig. 179e). By contrast, the Second Painter gives us a figure of Christ of unmistakable power and dignity. While continuing the tradition of luxurious hair, he paints Christ's head in strong blocky lines with broad brow and a full, rounded beard, set upon a thick neck. Moreover, Christ's face has an impressive range of expression, from his severe, firm gaze in the Raising of Lazarus (*page 522*), to his tender and anxious regard for his apostles in the Last Supper (*page 156*), to his peaceful repose in death in the Crucifixion (*page 561*). In all images, by scale, stance, and composition the Second Painter has given the Savior a grandeur that easily sets him apart from the rest of mankind.

Beyond the figure of Christ, the U.C.L.A. Second Painter gives repeated demonstrations of the versatility of his powers as an artist. The range of expression he achieves in rendering bystanders, whether they be ardent apostles or suspicious Jews, was remarked above. This skill in characterization should be contrasted to the homogeneity of the apostles' faces in Sargis' Raising of Lazarus or in Momik's Entry into Jerusalem.[94] In addition, one could contrast the tension in the faces of the grieving women in the Crucifixion (*page 561*) with the remote and passive expression of sorrow of the Virgin in Sargis' Descent from the Cross (fig. 286e). In rendering the angel Gabriel in the Annunciation (*page 305*), the Second Painter seems to be searching for a facial type that will carry something more than the innocence implied in the childlike face employed by Momik in the same subject.[95]

To the sense of drama observed in Sargis and Momik, the U.C.L.A. Second Painter has added a sense of monumentality in composition and an understanding of the personal pathos of his subjects. He is, at the same time, a master of the decorative repertoire developing in the Ełegis-Noravankʿ style. The brick, tile, and textile motifs noticed in the work of Sargis and Momik are used with special brilliance in the U.C.L.A. evangelists. In the portraits of Matthew and John, the Second Painter has covered the floor with a kilim or carpet of bright chevron pattern—vermilion and azurite blue in one, vermilion and green in the other. This chevron carpet appears later in the work of Tʿoros Taronecʿi, under the influence of the Second Painter, and in the work of Kirakos of Tabriz, where it is used with compelling illogic

[92] Avetisyan, *Haykakan Manrankarčʿutʿyan*, fig. 11; Der Nersessian, "L'Évangile du Matenadaran no. 10.525," pl. LXVI, fig. 8.

[93] Avetisyan, *Haykakan Manrankarčʿutʿyan*, fig. 12.

[94] Der Nersessian, "L'Évangile du Matenadaran no. 10.525," pl. LXVI, fig. 8; Avetisyan, *Haykakan Manrankarčʿutʿyan*, fig. 11.

[95] Avetisyan, *Haykakan Manrankarčʿutʿyan*, fig. 6.

to cover rooftops.[96] While Sargis uses a panel of octagonal tiles for Christ to stand on in his raising of Lazarus (fig. 522d), the Second Painter applies a brilliant pattern of cruciform tiles to the architecture behind Matthew (*page 26*) which is also picked up by Kirakos a generation later, who uses it to pave the sky in his Annunciation (fig. 305f). The brick pattern that serves as background to Mark (*page 188*) and reappears in the lower story of the cenacle in the Washing of Feet (*page 532*), has its parallel in the brick manger in the Nativity by Momik (as well as in Kirakos' version of the same).[97] In general the Second Painter's employment of decorative geometric patterns is marked by its appropriateness or plausibility, as well as by a certain restraint; given free rein such brilliant patterns would quickly dominate the composition, but the U.C.L.A. artist carefully balanced them against the equally strong brilliance of gold ground.

Beyond the geometric range of decoration, the U.C.L.A. Second Painter proves himself equally adept in the animal decoration of the Ełegis-Noravankʿ style. While Sargis incorporated the four living creatures of the evangelists in capital and bases in his canon tables, the Second Painter introduced them into the capitals of the frame around his evangelists, where they had not appeared earlier. Since each of these four creatures is repeated again in the zoomorphic letter with which the text of the Gospel begins, the innovation has the effect of integrating the design of the evangelist page with the design of the facing incipit.[98] This motif is further developed in the St. Mark incipit page, in which the marginal cross surmounts a fantastic vine containing the four living creatures framed by birds, fish, monkeys, and men. This grouping of a variety of animals around the canonical four implies a world view in which all creatures have a spiritual meaning. It is in this vein that the Second Painter develops his triumph of animal design in the heading of Luke, in which flora and fauna interchange their forms in a marvelous composition of lions and hares, birds and men (*page 299*). In subtlety of design and ambiguity of form this composition goes a step beyond the elaborate dance of the four living creatures in the Metropolitan Museum page. The Second Painter carries this flora-fauna illusion into the marginal cross decoration on the same page and then into the pericope markers of the two penultimate gatherings in the manuscript. This experimentation should be compared to that of Sargis, who joined the heads of the four living creatures to the bodies of birds in his initials. But while Sargis' experiment seems to manifest a rather narrow pursuit of system—heads of bulls don't sit well on birds' bodies—the experiments of the Second Painter show a true artist's insight into nature, in the discovery that the shapes of leaves and blossoms can be readily exchanged for those of birds or fish.

In all aspects of his art, then, the Second Painter of the U.C.L.A. Gospel is firmly rooted in the style of Ełegis-Noravankʿ and demonstrates an exceptional mastery of manifold possibilities of that style. But the same tradition that explains the work of the Second Painter also tells a good deal about the work of his collaborator, the First Painter—the artist responsible for all the canon tables, and the decorated letters and pericope markers through most of the manuscript.

It is of the essence of the art of canon tables to present ever new variations on what is basically no more than an architectural framing device.[99] From its very inception in the sixth century the decoration of these tables afforded an opportunity for free and rich invention. All elements of the design were open to reworking by the artist; the architecture could be restructured or its ornament changed, new pattern fields could be introduced within the architecture, trees and plants might sprout from it and men and animals might climb on it. Even if he copied a design very literally the artist seems to have felt obliged to introduce at least a new color scheme. Hence no two sets of canon tables are exactly the same. Fortunately for the art historian, however, certain sets of designs enjoy considerable stability and permit one to distinguish separate traditions within the art form.

In the U.C.L.A. Gospel, the canon tables, along with Eusebius' Preface, are distributed on ten pages which are designed as five pairs according to the constant Armenian tradition. Except for the first pair, which enframe Eusebius' Preface, all the headpieces are carried on three columns. If one looks simply at the architectural design of these rectangular head-

96 See Tʿoros' manuscript of 1318, Matenadaran 206, fol. 443, ibid., fig. 31; for Kirakos, see Der Nersessian and Mekhitarian, *Isfahan*, fig. 55.

97 Matenadaran, 6297, fol. 2 and New Julfa, 47, fol. 2., Der Nersessian, "L'Évangile du Matenadaran no. 10.525," pl. LXXII, figs. 15 and 16.

98 Evangelists' symbols are commonly used to form the first letter of the text in manuscripts of the Cilician period. On their development see Der Nersessian, *Manuscrits*, 42–43, and *Arm. Mss. Freer*, 71–72, and Helen C. Evans, *Armenian Manuscript Illumination*.

99 The history of canon table decoration has not been written beyond the early centuries of its development; see Carl Nordenfalk, *Die spätantiken Kanontafeln*. On Armenian canon table decoration, see Der Nersessian, *Manuscrits*, 53–61, 113–15, 144–45.

pieces, disregarding the fields of decoration and the flora and fauna around them, one may distinguish the following sequence in the five pairs of tables: (1) lunette; (2) triangle; (3) cinquefoil arch; (4) chevron arch intersected by radiating bands; (5) two concentric rainbow arches. This sequence of designs clearly goes back to Cilician precedents, such as the famous Queen Keṙan Gospel of 1272. In the Queen Keṙan Gospel the design sequence runs as follows: (1) lunette encircled by inhabited scroll; (2) triangle with circle inside; (3) lunette containing paired animals; (4) chevron arch intersected by radiating bands; (5) two concentric rainbow arches.[100] In addition, the trees that flank the tables, always with birds in them, and the general repertoire of birds and beasts around the headpieces in the manuscript also have frequent parallels in Cilician material, to be discussed in connection with the symbolism of the tables.

There is, however, a manuscript in which the canon tables match very closely those of the U.C.L.A. Gospel, not only in general sequence but bird for bird, and that manuscript, significantly, belongs to the Ełegis-Noravankʿ group. The canon tables of New Julfa ms. 47 of 1330, by Kirakos of Tabriz, are not of the same high quality as those of the U.C.L.A. Gospel; the painting is not as delicate, the tables are asymmetrical in layout, and insufficient space was left in the inner margins to allow for the ornament on that side (fig. 21c).[101] Nevertheless, in all the other features the designs are so close that the two manuscripts must come from the same workshop tradition (*page 17*).[102] Der Nersessian has demonstrated that in its scenes from the Life of Christ Kirakos' manuscript follows very closely the iconography of Momik in his Gospel of 1302. But what Momik's canon tables were like is unknown, since they are missing from the manuscript. What is significant is that in both manuscripts—Kirakos' Gospel and the U.C.L.A. Gospel—the same set of canon tables is being used in conjunction with figure painting of the smoothly modeled Ełegis-Noravankʿ style. At the same time, it should be noticed that this is a different set of canon tables from that used in Erevan 10525, which seems to belong to a tradition that had some antiquity in Greater Armenia (fig. 21b). As Der Nersessian remarks, the painting of Siwnikʿ at the beginning of the fourteenth century drew on sources from Cilicia and Greater Armenia with equal ease.[103] Therefore, the collaboration of the First Painter, an artist personally trained in the meticulous style of Cilician ornamental painting, with the Second Painter, representing a local development in Greater Armenia with more remote contacts with Cilicia, is by no means anomalous, but is characteristic of what is happening in Siwnikʿ at this time. The relative tranquillity and prosperity of Siwnikʿ was attracting monks and scholars from all sides, and this accounts for the coexistence there of markedly different traditions.

In the tradition to which he belongs, namely the Cilician tradition transplanted to Siwnikʿ, the First Painter of the U.C.L.A. Gospel is a practitioner of the highest skill. So sure is his hand that his work can be magnified many times over without losing the least crispness or showing the least hesitancy. Kirakos' canon tables are by contrast slightly insecure. Apart from his problems in symmetry, Kirakos seems incapable of the precision of the First Painter and shies away from his miniaturization of design, as for example in the globe from which the bands radiate (fig. 21c). Similar limitations appear in the canon tables of New Julfa 477, which, as seen above, was executed in Noravankʿ in 1300 (fig. 21a). The artist of this manuscript combines figure painting of the smooth style with canon tables very close to the tradition of Kirakos and the U.C.L.A. First Painter. He seems not to have understood, however, the grace and logic that underlie the support system in the U.C.L.A. columns, bases, and capitals, and his birds lack the animation of those of the First Painter.

The First and Second Painters of the U.C.L.A. Gospel constituted an artistic team of special talent and skill. Our examination of the painting of Ełegis and Noravankʿ in the early fourteenth century provides the setting in which their work belongs and offers a basis for locating and dating the first phase of the painting of the U.C.L.A. manuscript. Concerning the place, one has a choice between Ełegis and Noravankʿ. The canon tables of the First Painter are clearly in the Noravankʿ tradition of the Gospel commissioned by bishop Ivanē Ōrbēlian in 1300 and that painted by Kirakos in 1330; they have nothing in common with the tables of Sargis of Ełegis. At the same time, the Second Painter's manner of painting has more in common with the work of Sargis in Ełegis than it does with the work of Momik in Noravankʿ.

[100] These tables remain unpublished, except for the first two. Helen C. Evans, "Canon Tables as an Indication of Teacher-Pupil Relationships," fig. 12.

[101] The problems in layout seem to be due to the writing of the columns of numbers before the painting of the tables, a reversal of the usual practice.

[102] Also compare page 8 to New Julfa 47, fol. 15v, Der Nersessian and Mekhitarian, *Isfahan*, fig. 60.

[103] Der Nersessian, "L'Évangile du Matenadaran no. 10.525," 330–32.

Since the places are within a day's travel of one another, the issue is not critically important.

Concerning the date the evidence is simple. There are three related manuscripts firmly dated in the first years of the century (New Julfa 477 in 1300; Matenadaran 6792 in 1302; and Matenadaran 10525 in 1306), and there is Kirakos' manuscript in 1330 (New Julfa 47). The U.C.L.A. Gospel must be associated with the earlier group; as remarked above, the simplicity and force of the style becomes dissipated in Kirakos' work in the proliferation of tile patterns, and the faces become markedly oriental. A date in the first years of the century would also fit well with the evidence for dating T'oros Taronec'i's role in completing the manuscript, as will be seen presently.

5. Glajor in Siwnik'

Having been begun at Ełegis or Noravank' in one of the provincial centers of Ōrbēlian influence, for some unknown reason work on the U.C.L.A. Gospel was suddenly suspended, and when it was resumed the manuscript was in the monastery of the Pŕošian family at Glajor, a short distance away but under very different artistic circumstances. The colophon of 1377 and the inscription on *page 227* leave no doubt about the place. Continuity was maintained, insofar as the later artists were perfectly familiar with the program with which the book had been begun; hence, the iconographic model must have been conveyed to the new workshop along with the unfinished manuscript. But in style the new workshop had little in common with the old.

It would be misleading to talk of the "school" of Glajor as if there was some academy or assembly of artists attached to the monastery; when Momik is removed from consideration, the development of manuscript illumination at Glajor becomes the story of a single artist, T'oros Taronec'i, and his immediate associates, the Third and Fourth Painters of the U.C.L.A. Gospel. Although others occasionally execute a few pages, they never emerge as distinct personalities. T'oros' only true successor is Awag, a painter who in fact surpasses him in flair and imagination (figs. 35d, 99c, 122d, 126g, 169c, 171c, d, and e, 172d and e, 173b, 194b, 227d, 259c, 269d, 271d, 283b, 286f, 327d, 336d, 438c, 441c, 448c, 453e, 570a). Awag's painting has a fluidity and dynamism that matches the best of Cilician painting; but though he was trained in Glajor and depends heavily on the iconography he saw there, all his surviving manuscripts were done after he left the monastery.[104] T'oros' work over a period of four decades was the chief artistic accomplishment of Glajor. As the earliest work of T'oros, the U.C.L.A. Gospel puts one in a unique position to reconstruct his beginnings and the situation of painting in Glajor.

The inscriptions of the painter T'oros on *pages 227 and 453* are not in themselves adequate grounds for attributing the U.C.L.A. manuscript to T'oros Taronec'i; the artist's toponym is omitted and T'oros, which is the Armenian for Theodore, is a common name in medieval Armenia. Logically one ought to begin by identifying the style of T'oros Taronec'i in those manuscripts that carry his full name. These are only two and their decoration is extremely sparse, but they tell something about the artist's biography and they offer a starting point for the attribution of other paintings to the same T'oros.

The first is a Treasury of patristic and homiletic material, Venice 1108/265, dated 1317–18. On fol. 261 the scribe added a personal but anonymous note to the colophon, saying, "Remember in (your) prayers the sinful and vile scribe." Later, however, he returned to this note and inserted his own name above the line and continued thus: ". . . Sargis, and my brother Davit' Hałbatec'i, and T'oros the decorator Taronec'i."[105] This inscription faces the incipit page of the Encyclical Letter of Nersēs Šnorhali, which is ornamented in magenta monochrome with a headpiece, marginal cross and initial letter. The placement of the inscription opposite the decorated page strongly suggests that the decoration belongs to T'oros Taronec'i, and inspection of the rest of the volume confirms this impression, for the only other decoration in the manuscript is a pair of monochrome decorative bands that serve as chapter headings in fols. 1 and 183, and a rather ambitious full-color donor portrait on fols. 181v–82 (figs. R3, R4). The latter, however, is in a totally different style and carries the inscription of another artist: "I beg you to remember the worthless Yohanēs."[106] Therefore, it is the monochrome decorations of the manuscript that must be ascribed to "T'oros the decorator Taronec'i."

The situation attested to by Venice 1108/265 is quite interesting. The years 1317–18 are peak years

[104] Avetisyan has included Awag in his study of the Glajor "school" of manuscript painting, *Haykakan Manrankarč'ut'yan*, 140–51. See also Der Nersessian, *Armenian Art*, 224–25.

[105] The revision in this inscription is not noted by Barseł Sargisian, *Mayr C'uc'ak Hayerēn Jeŕagrac'*, II, col. 859.

[106] Sargisian (ibid.) omits to note the inscriptions on the donor portrait.

in the career of T'oros Taronec'i, in which he was doing his most important commissions. Nevertheless, he accepted the very routine assignment of decorating a few headpieces in magenta in this very modest Treasury. This he did, moreover, when the only important painting in the volume, the portrait of the donor Grigoris and his wife Mamaxat'un kneeling before the Mother of God, was assigned to Yohanēs, whose work is certainly far less elegant than his own. Yohanēs works in bold forms and sharply contrasting colors. His painting of faces starts with a light pink wash on which he shadows the main features in strong green lines (nose, brows, lower lids, chin). Thin black lines are then applied to sharpen these features and unmodulated patches of red are applied to the cheeks. The figure drawing is strangely discontinuous; though the Virgin sits frontally on her bench her knees are in profile, and the piles of folds that encompass her and her Child are more like the random crags of a mountain than the logical curves of the human body. Colors are applied unmixed in their full strengths in unorthodox combinations—the shadows of Mamaxat'un's green veil are painted red.

T'oros Taronec'i's drawing, on the other hand, shows a curious mixture of competence and carelessness (fig. R2). He shows a good draughtsman's sense of how to articulate the limbs of the sinuous addorsed lions, glowering fiercely at one another, but the shading of these beasts he does in a very uneven hatching stroke. The medallion contains a fairly complicated vine interlace, but it is placed off-center in the headpiece so that the lion on the left has less room than his mate. The shape of the shoulder arch beneath the headpiece is a contemporary Islamic-derived design, but the scroll that decorates the headpiece is ill-suited to its shape. The drawing is fairly free, with firm, confident lines, but the painting that fills in the background is often blotchy and uneven. This kind of roughness in execution seems not to spring from incompetence but carelessness, as if the artist knew his manner well enough to allow himself to be sloppy in its execution.

The second manuscript that carries the full name of T'oros Taronec'i tells less about the style of the artist, for its only decoration is a single, very perfunctory chapter heading (fig. R5). It is the last dated manuscript of Glajor, a collection of sermons, Erevan, Mat. 2187.[107] On fol. 245, at the conclusion of a chapter the scribe found room to add: "I beg you to remember us in your pure prayers, the owner of this book of holy sayings, Martiros the priest Sanahnec'i, and the painter T'oros Taronec'i. In the Armenian year 795 [i.e., 1346]." A similar note on fol. 162v asks the reader to "remember the painter T'oros, and say continually, 'Lord, have mercy.' In the year of the Armenians 795." The fact that there is practically no decoration in the manuscript, and the fact that these memorials are written in the same hand as the rest of the manuscript leads to the conclusion that in this manuscript T'oros Taronec'i was the scribe. While it adds little to the picture of his style, this manuscript is important in that it documents the continued activity of T'oros Taronec'i in Glajor three decades after Venice 1108/265.

On the basis of these two manuscripts signed with the full name of T'oros Taronec'i it would be extremely difficult to form any adequate definition of his artistic personality. Not only is their decoration extremely limited and without a human figure, but it is also executed in monochrome and therefore gives no idea of the artist's manner of working with a full palette. Fortunately another manuscript, also in monochrome, can be added to these, which by its wider range of decoration offers a bridge to his painted oeuvre.

Erevan, Mat. 6897 is a Philosophical Collection dated 1317, contemporary with Venice 1108/265.[108] The two manuscripts are both on paper and are virtually identical in size and format. The scribe Karapet Vardapet fails to mention the place, but the fact that the manuscript contains a commentary on Denis the Grammarian by the Abbot of Glajor, Esayi Nč'ec'i, and the fact that Karapet is the scribe of another Glajor manuscript in 1317, Erevan, Mat. 353, justify our attributing Mat. 6897 to Glajor. On fol. 85v, opposite the headpiece of the work of David the Invincible, is found the inscription: "Remember in the Lord Jesus the painter T'oros," and at the start of Esayi Nč'ec'i's commentary on fol. 13 is found an ornamental band of foliate letters reading "Remember T'oros." It is not impossible that there were two artists named T'oros in Glajor in the year 1317; but the style of this manuscript is so close to that of Venice 1108/265 that one must attribute them to the same artist. The headpieces of fols. 2 and 86 contain the same kind of irregularities in planning as noticed in Venice 1108/265. On fol. 86 (fig. R7) the quatrefoil frame is drawn of unequal arcs and the Eleousa-type Madonna is placed to one side in the frame; the steps on either side of it provide unequal spaces for the attendant angels. The vinescroll in this headpiece is virtually identical in drawing and shading to that of

[107] A brief description without the text of the colophons can be found in Eganyan, *C'uc'ak Jeṙagrac'*, I, col. 741.

[108] Described briefly in Eganyan, *C'uc'ak Jeṙagrac'*, II, cols. 416–17.

Venice 1108/265, and it fits the shape of the arch just as poorly. The arches of fol. 2 and fol. 86 (fig. R6) are of the same general character, variants on a shouldered arch, supported by consoles on either side. The marginal vine-and-cross decoration on fol. 86 is more complex than those in Venice 1108/265, full of birds and lions; but if one compares the range of marginal ornaments in the two manuscripts it is clear that the same hand is at work. The Tʿoros of Erevan 6897 is clearly Tʿoros Taronecʿi.

Erevan 6897, therefore, adds a sampling of human figure drawing to the definition of the style of Tʿoros Taronecʿi—the author portrait of Denis of Thrace on fol. 2 and the Virgin and Child with angels on fol. 86. Black hair and beard were added at a later date to the portrait of Denis of Thrace; originally his face was very close to the faces on fol. 86. All were drawn in three-quarters pose with a single sweeping line describing the curve of full chin and cheek. Nose, eyes, and mouth are practically identical from figure to figure; the male portrait is drawn with slightly more severe lines, while the Virgin was given wider and more thoughtful eyes. In drawing the eyes, Tʿoros has left a corner open and indicated pupils by a dot against the upper lid. Hands have long slender fingers, which convey no sense of strength when they grasp a pen or a chalice. What can be seen of the drapery of the figures is clear and simple.

None of the full-color painted works attributed to Tʿoros Taronecʿi bears his full name, but the firm attribution of this small nucleus of monochrome works offers a norm for identifying his hand in the painted manuscripts, including the U.C.L.A. Gospel. Obviously the identification of Tʿoros' hand in a manuscript does not necessarily imply that all the paintings in the manuscript were by him; he might collaborate with other artists. A *catalogue raisonnée* of the works of Tʿoros would therefore require a page-by-page discussion of the miniatures in all the manuscripts attributed to him, an undertaking which would take one far afield. The object is rather to examine a few works that might establish the manner characteristic of the artist. This personal manner of painting is the true signature of Tʿoros Taronecʿi, more reliable than any inscriptions or colophons, and this alone justifies our attributing or denying a work to him. In Tʿoros' oeuvre this personal signature has a surprising consistency, considering the length of his career, the range of material that he assimilates, and the varying quality of his output.

Closest to these monochrome works are two manuscripts that have headpieces with enthroned Madonnas. Hartford, Case Memorial Library 3 is, like the U.C.L.A. Gospel, another instance of exchange between Glajor and the neighboring monasteries.[109] According to the colophon, Momik and the vardapet Pōłos began copying the text of the manuscript in the fall of 1307, but the troubles caused by the Mongol Khan, Olčaitu Khudābanda, and the deteriorating eyesight of Momik, forced them to leave the work unfinished. Momik says: "I was unable to bring to completion the concordance tables and the ornament and the gold painting. But later the scribe Yohanēs filled in the incomplete (parts) and Tʿoros the gold painting. The light of my eyes returned to me in 1331, after many years, through my hope which was in Jesus, and I made the colophon, writing by command of Lord Tarsayič, surnamed Lord Stepʿanos, son of J̌alal. In this year through the order of and by the provision of the great baron Biwrtʿel they ornamented this gospel with gold and silver in the chief city of Ełegis, in Noravankʿ, having founded which new church by himself, he consecrated it to the name of the holy Mother of God, St. Nicholas and St. Christopher."[110] Momik's account leaves it vague exactly when Tʿoros worked on the manuscript, but one presumes it was part of the effort that led to its completion in 1331. The colophon of Momik seems intended to commemorate the provision of a gold and silver cover for the manuscript in Ełegis and its donation to the church of the Mother of God there. Perhaps this intended donation suggested the inclusion of images of the Mother of God in the headpieces of the Gospels of Matthew and Luke (fols. 14 and 153).[111] The headpiece on fol. 153 (fig. R8) repeats the Eleousa-type Madonna of Erevan 6897 (fig. R6), with many of the same peculiarities. Starting with another variant of shouldered arch, the painter again places the central motif slightly to one side and seats the Virgin somewhat uneasily to one side within her throne. Again the diaper pattern conflicts with its frame, which sometimes bisects the lozenges and sometimes cuts off corners. The drawing of the figures in the two headpieces can be matched in many details, allowances being made for the larger scale of the Hartford manuscript. The hands, the cast of the faces, the way the Virgin's maphorion falls around her ear, or the way the Child's draperies fall across his knees all argue that the Tʿoros who painted the Hart-

[109] S. Der Nersessian, "An Illustrated Armenian Gospel of the XIV Century," *Études*, 631–35 (originally published in *Hartford Seminary Foundation Bulletin* 19 [1955], 1–7); "Western Iconographic Themes in Armenian Manuscripts," *Études*, 611–30 (originally published in *Gazette des Beaux Arts*, ser. 6, 27 (1955), 71–94.

[110] The Armenian text of the colophon is published by A. K. Sanjian (*Catalogue*, 85–87).

[111] Reproduced in Der Nersessian, *Études*, figs. 389 and 390.

ford manuscript was the T'oros Taronec'i of Erevan 6897.

Even closer to the Erevan headpiece is the headpiece to the Gospel of Mark in London, B.L. add. 15,411.[112] According to the colophon, the manuscript was executed in 1321 at St. Stephen's of Glajor under the enlightened leadership of David and Esayi, "twin guardians of our true faith," for a certain priest Martiros, who should probably be identified with the priest "Ma(r)tiros" who twenty-five years later commissioned T'oros Taronec'i to execute Erevan 2187.[113] In other inscriptions the scribe is identified as Kerion and the painter as T'oros. The format of the headpiece on fol. 92 (fig. R10) is virtually identical to that of Erevan 6897 (fig. R7) in the design of the arch and the placement and poses of the attendant angels. Now the Madonna is the crowned Virgo Lactans, a type introduced from the West as Der Nersessian has shown, but the drawing is very close to the Madonna of Erevan 6897. The loros-clad angels are shoulderless and their hair is swept back in the same fashion, their fillets fluttering in S-forms. The very generalized feathering of their wings is sketched in similar strokes, and the strokes that define facial features have the same lightness and delicacy. Here, too, the whole composition is slightly off-center, shifted now to the right.

The impression that this is the same painter is strengthened when one compares the two full-palette Madonnas to one another. The angels' feathers are now even closer; the thrones are similarly constructed; and although the Virgins are holding the Child very differently, the draperies fall over their laps in exactly the same fashion (the draperies are less fully modeled in the London example because it is much smaller in scale). The differences between the artist's monochrome style and his full-palette style must be ascribed to the difference in medium. In the monochrome style the pen predominates over the brush and gives the image crispness and vigor; color is suggested by linear effects such as hatching, veining, or serrating. In the full-palette style even the original underdrawing is done with brush, as can be seen in the variable width of the strokes, and this drawing is totally painted over. The whole image takes on the softness of brushed edges. This is especially obvious in the transformation that takes place in the marginal cross ornaments, where now every leaf and face is rimmed in gold. But whether painting or drawing, T'oros Taronec'i's competence remains the same: he has a certain self-assurance born of having learned his trade in an established tradition, but he is not at all fastidious. Irregularities and unfinished or unresolved details abound. At the same time, there is a certain experimental quality about the style of T'oros Taronec'i; within the limits of these three Madonnas it is clear that the artist is always ready to tinker with the formula he has at hand, whether in poses or in decorative details. This impression is confirmed in the wider survey of his oeuvre. What remains most constant amid these variations is his handling of faces, and it is this that provides the firmest link to the U.C.L.A. Gospel.

In distinguishing the five artists of the U.C.L.A. Gospel the manner of building up the painting of the faces from initial ground to final definition of features proved to be the most constant and reliable index for telling one artist from the other. The T'oros of the U.C.L.A. Gospel began with a rough sketch in magenta (best visible in the damaged area of *page 286*), over which he painted his basic ground in cream color (see color *pages 227, 250, 327, 453,* and color details *pages 227, 453*). On this ground he sketches the face a second time in brown. He then proceeds to build up the shadows and highlights of the face. The shadows are a series of green lines applied under the hairline and beneath the eyebrow and lower lid, along the near side of the nose, and around the curve of the cheek. The highlights consist of a ruddy pink to give life to the cheeks and forehead and a series of white lines along the brow, nose, and chin. Finally, the features are given a redefinition with black lines and a touch of red to the lips. This sequence is capable of considerable adaptation, from bland and almost expressionless faces in which it has been used more summarily, as in spectators in some scenes, to the very complex and emotion-strained faces of Christ and Joseph of Arimathea (*page 286*), in which the system of lines and shadows is stretched to approximate a contemporary Byzantine model. Yet the basic manner of proceeding in the painting remains the same throughout his work in the manuscript, and it is this manner that firmly links the T'oros of the U.C.L.A. Gospel to T'oros Taronec'i in the Hartford and London manuscripts.

Although there are a variety of modifications of this procedure of painting in the Hartford and London manuscripts, the "typical" face remains very close to the procedure described above. The Virgin in the London manuscript is a good instance (fig. R10) as well as the figures of John and Prochorus in both manuscripts (figs. R8, R9). The painting of these faces is somewhat more sure and polished than the faces in the U.C.L.A. Gospel, but basically they are

[112] Conybeare, *Catalogue,* 22–24.

[113] For transcriptions and translations of colophons and inscriptions, see Conybeare, loc. cit.

painted in the same succession of layers. It is this formula of face-painting more than any other single detail that allows one to follow a continuity through the painted oeuvre of the artist and conclude that the "T'oros" referred to repeatedly in the colophons and inscriptions is one and the same person, T'oros Taronec'i. Applying this test, then, ten full-palette manuscripts and another monochrome one can be added to the three monochrome works, giving the following list of the works of T'oros Taronec'i. As cautioned earlier, the fact that T'oros' hand is present in all these manuscripts does not guarantee that other artists are not also at work on them; a page-by-page sorting of the material is beyond the present scope of this work.

Chronological List of Manuscripts
Containing Decoration by T'oros Taronec'i

1. Los Angeles, University of California, Arm. ms. 1, Gospel (before 1307).
2. Venice, San Lazzaro, ms. 1917, Gospel (1307).[114]
3. Erevan, Matenadaran, ms. 353, Bible (1317).[115]
4. Erevan, Matenadaran, ms. 6897, Philosophical Collection (1317).[116]
5. Erevan, Matenadaran, ms. 8936, Gospel (1317).[117]
6. Venice, San Lazzaro, ms. 265, Treasury (1317–18).[118]
7. Erevan, Matenadaran, ms. 206, Bible (1318).[119]
8. Jerusalem, Patriarchate of St. James, ms. 2360, Gospel (1321).[120]
9. London, British Library, ms. add. 15,411 (1321).[121]
10. Erevan, Matenadaran, ms. 6289, Gospel (1323).[122]
11. Erevan, Matenadaran, ms. 560, On the Seven Sacraments by Thomas Aquinas (1325).[123]
12. Hartford, Case Memorial Library, arm. ms. 3, Gospel (1307–31).[124]
13. Erevan, Matenadaran, ms. 2187, Collection of Sermons (1346).[125]
14. Erevan, Matenadaran, ms. 6348, Gospel (undated).[126]

Previous lists of the works of T'oros Taronec'i have been more generous than this, including four lost works the colophons of which have survived; but since the painting style of these cannot be checked they are omitted here.[127] Three other manuscripts have been rejected on stylistic grounds. Połarian ascribes to T'oros a lectionary, Jerusalem ms. 95, dated 1331. Inscriptions of a decorator "T'oros" appear on fols. 61, 174, and 556, but according to the colophon on fol. 556 the manuscript was executed far from Glajor, in T'onrak in the canton of Apahunik, northwest of Lake Van. Narkiss has recently rejected the Taronec'i attribution on the basis of a comparison with the painting style of T'oros Taronec'i, and a comparison with his monochrome work would confirm this conclusion.[128]

Even further removed stylistically is a commentary of Chrysostom on St. Paul, Matenadaran 1379, which Avetisyan lists with the work of T'oros Taronec'i.[129] Apart from a pair of genealogical diagrams (fols. 355v–356r), the manuscript has only two full pages of decoration, an incipit page on fol. 2 (fig. R13), executed in magenta, and a donor portrait on fol. 160v (fig. R14) executed in color, showing Kirakos Vardapet and his disciples. The latter is by a naive painter named Manuel; the former, the work of T'oros the Deacon, is a complex linear design (retouched later by a less competent artist in heavier lines) much too

[114] Complete description and analysis in Der Nersessian, *Manuscrits*, 110–36.

[115] Brief description in Eganyan, *C'uc'ak Jeṙagrac'*, I, cols. 304–5.

[116] Brief description ibid., II, cols. 416–17.

[117] Brief description ibid., II, col. 840.

[118] Complete account in Sargisian, *Mayr C'uc'ak*, II, cols. 847–60.

[119] Brief description in Eganyan, *C'uc'ak Jeṙagrac'*, I, col. 272; see also Der Nersessian, "Western Iconographic Themes," *Études*, 611–12.

[120] Połarian, *Mayr C'uc'ak*, VII, 510–14; Narkiss and Stone, *Jerusalem*, 75–76, 150.

[121] See above, note 112.

[122] Brief description in Eganyan, *C'uc'ak Jeṙagrac'*, II, col. 288.

[123] Brief description ibid., I, col. 348.

[124] See above, note 109.

[125] Brief description in Eganyan, *C'uc'ak Jeṙagrac'*, II, col. 741.

[126] Brief description ibid., II, col. 300.

[127] Norayr Połarian, "T'oros Taronac'i," *Sion* (1970), 454–55.

[128] Narkiss and Stone, *Jerusalem*, 77–79. There is a fineness and delicacy of line in the lectionary (figs. R11, R12) drawings that is missing in the somewhat rough manner of T'oros Taronec'i's drawings. At the same time there is a compulsive search for complications in the decoration of the lectionary. For example, every turn in the vine scroll of fol. 4 has to make an extra circle, and every circle is punctuated with repeated little knobs. Figures consistently wear doubled tunics showing sleeve inside sleeve, hair is drawn in repeated curls and haloes are indicated by lines of incessant wobbles. This repertoire of mannerisms seems to stand outside the range of the work of T'oros Taronec'i.

[129] Brief description in Eganyan, *C'uc'ak Jeṙagrac'*, I, col. 538; A. N. Avetisyan, *Haykakan Manrankarč'ut'yan*, 88–89. According to the inscriptions and principal colophon (fols. 354v–355r) the vardapet Kirakos received this book in Erznka, where it was made by the scribes Manuēl and T'oros the Deacon in 1334.

fragile to be Taronec'i. Again the distance of the place of manufacture from Glajor makes the ascription to T'oros Taronec'i improbable.

A third monochrome manuscript that has generally been ascribed to T'oros Taronec'i is somewhat more problematical. In a very voluble colophon on fol. 188 of Venice 1007/12, the Vardapet Nersēs of the monastery of S. Lazar in Kor, Taron, tells all the troubles he had in the making of this Bible, from the raising of funds among friends and relatives, to the purchase of the paper in Tabriz, to the employment of two scribes, Ep'rem and Dawit', at the monastery of Glajor.[130] The transcribing of the text was begun in December 1331 and finished in October 1332, but to have the book bound Nersēs had to take it to Kṙnay, a center of the Unitores. Typically, though the exact cost of each part of this enterprise is accounted for, no mention is made of the artist employed. The artist tried to make good this omission with an inscription of his own on fol. 358v, at the bottom of the second page of canon tables. "Vardapet Nersēs, remember in your prayers T'oros, the decorator, and my grandfather Miar and my father Sargis the priest, and my mother Mariam from the city of Muš." Given the fact that Muš is in the province of Taron, it has always been assumed that the T'oros in question must be identified with T'oros Taronec'i, and indeed it is hard to imagine a second artist named T'oros from the province of Tarōn working at Glajor at the same time. Nevertheless, it is hard to find T'oros' hand in the painting. The principal headpieces of the manuscript were incompetently overpainted in the seventeenth century, but where the original decoration remains the drawing is tidier, fussier, and generally weaker than T'oros' usual work (fig. R16). The sinewy quality of T'oros Taronec'i's lions is transformed into something cute and sweet by the artist of 1007, and the energetic Carpianos of Hartford (also executed in 1331) becomes shaky and uncertain in his counterpart in 1007. Perhaps one should attribute this work to an understudy and imagine T'oros' work to be hidden by the overpainting.

Having established the identity of T'oros Taronec'i in the U.C.L.A. Gospel, one is now in a position to define its place relative to his dated oeuvre. T'oros is an artist in whom it is difficult to define a genuine stylistic evolution. Variations in his painting often appear to be vacillations rather than purposeful explorations of an artistic concept. In his successive portraits of John the Evangelist (figs. 460a–g), for example, once he decided on the rocky landscape setting with the evangelist on the right and Prochorus seated on the left, he remained content with this formula and played only with minor variations. John may look to the right or to the left for his inspiration; he may stand immobile or stride ahead; his drapery is at times sharp and angular, at times curvilinear; the modeling may be fussy or generalized. Similar vacillations appear in the handling of Prochoros, the landscape setting, and the segment of heaven above. These variations, however, seem to reflect not the intentional unfolding of some hidden potential in the subject but simply the relative importance or unimportance of the commission. The grand commissions of full Bibles for Esayi Nč'ec'i (Erevan 353 and 206, 26 × 18 cm) gave the artist a larger format to work in and inspired a care and attention that lesser commissions did not. In the two small-scale Gospel manuscripts of 1321 (Jerusalem 2360 and British Library add. 15,411, 11 × 8.5 cm) the treatment of figures is greatly simplified and figures occupy proportionately much more of the field. On the other hand, a book could be large in scale without being expensive in production—such as Erevan 8936, in which the headpieces were painted in monochrome magenta and the evangelists lack gold backgrounds. In this manuscript T'oros' painting is much more summary and the modeling is sketchy. T'oros might then be said to have an expensive manner and an inexpensive one, but this is not a linear development.

In T'oros' successive versions of the Ascension, however, some evidence of an evolution of his painterly skills can be traced (*page 453* and figs. 453c–d). Moreover, since this is one of the two miniatures he signed in the U.C.L.A. Gospel, it affords a firm starting point. The U.C.L.A. Ascension is the least competent of the series. The figures below are rigidly grouped in symmetrical files, and the apostles seem to be not organically constructed but almost glued together—standard torsos with heads, hands, and feet attached. In the front row the figures on the left are supposed to hold their books with one hand and salute Christ with the other, but T'oros is confused as to which hand is doing what; Paul has two left hands and his companions have lost their right arms entirely. In 1307, however, T'oros has understood the figures well enough to show them at once holding books and gesturing without inconvenience (fig. 453c). Each figure now has a modicum of independent life and movement, and instead of simply pasting toes on their tunics T'oros now shows feet and ankles involved in the action of the figures. The figures are slenderer, and liveliness is added by varying the grouping right and left. A decade later, in the splendid Bible of Esayi Nč'ec'i of 1318, the figures

[130] Sanjian, *Colophons*, 11–12.

are still better understood; the regular rhythm of poses is broken by allowing more interesting spacing of figures, and the gestures and costumes vary from figure to figure (453d). A parallel development can be followed in the circle of angels in the sky, from the conservative composition of the U.C.L.A. Gospel to the more ambitious, even if not entirely successful, composition of the Venice manuscript, in which a pair of golden angels with trumpets are introduced while another pair try to hold the mandorla with both hands while flying. When he attempts the composition again, T'oros succeeds in adding a fifth angel to the group and creating an extraordinary composition. The angels now have long, lithe bodies and delicate limbs, they are dressed in rich apparel, and they beat the air wildly with their outspread wings.

This comparison would suggest that the U.C.L.A. Gospel was the earliest of T'oros' manuscripts, antedating the Venice manuscript of 1307. While there are few subjects in the U.C.L.A. Gospel that admit of similar comparisons (T'oros never works on another Gospel with running narrative illustrations) his competence in handling figures in general could be followed with similar results. One might compare the stiff and robot-like Virgin in the U.C.L.A. Visitation (*page 312*) with her gradually more relaxed poses in the sequence of dated examples of the Annunciation (figs. 305c–e). Her draperies are crude, unmodulated striations in the U.C.L.A. example; they take on clear shape and become gradually softened and loosened in the dated sequence. This is a real progress, and it is hard to imagine reversing it chronologically; the U.C.L.A. painting seems to represent T'oros in his most formative stage.

This conclusion is confirmed in a remarkable way if one examines closely the relationship between the U.C.L.A. Gospel and T'oros' earliest dated work, Venice 1917, of 1307. This manuscript stands rather apart from the rest of T'oros' later works—to such an extent that T'oros' artistic "signature," namely, his system of painting faces, is virtually the only common denominator between the two. In the portrait of John, for example, the composition and figure treatment are radically different from later versions (figs. 460a–g). Seated before a lofty building, Prochorus turns toward the viewer and writes in a codex instead of a scroll. John is stiff and awkward, his garments heavy and confining, and his feet are cut off by a kind of platform. The whole composition is set with an arch. Finally, and most tellingly, the whole range of colors is shifted away from the simple red-and-blue or blue-and-ochre figures, set against blue mountains, to a much higher range of tones dominated by pinks and light blues. In fact, both in composition and in tonality this painting is extremely close to the portrait of John by the Second Painter of the U.C.L.A. Gospel (*page 460*).

Nine of the miniatures of Venice 1917 are very close to the corresponding subjects in the U.C.L.A. Gospel: the four evangelists, the Annunciation, the Raising of Lazarus, the Entry into Jerusalem, the Last Supper, and the Descent of the Holy Spirit. It is noteworthy that in the U.C.L.A. Gospel all of these miniatures were the work of the Second Painter. In these shared subjects it can be established that the U.C.L.A. Gospel does not depend on the Venice manuscript, but the other way around.

Misunderstandings are sometimes the most telling index of which painting depends on which. In the U.C.L.A. portrait of John, the Second Painter sacrificed the feet of the evangelist to his interest in developing the pattern of the kilim on which he stands; in the Venice manuscript this peculiarity is copied without the kilim and the evangelist is cut off at the knees, giving the impression that he stands in a box (*page 460* and fig. 460a). The copy in this case has also lost some of the iconographic richness of the original by omitting the seraphim of the capitals and the spandrels of stars. One can derive the Venice rendition of the subject from the U.C.L.A. version, but not vice versa.

The Annunciation is a decisive demonstration of the procedure of copying, since in the U.C.L.A. Gospel T'oros was responsible for retouching this miniature of the Second Painter, adding the dove and the descending rays, and redoing the Virgin's face (*page 305* and color). When he copied the iconography in Venice 1917 (fig. 305b), he repeated all the features of the U.C.L.A. version—the poses, the architecture, the tree, the well—plus his own additions to the subject, though he omitted the water flowing from the well into the amphora. Since he was able to plan this miniature from the start, he was able to shorten the tree to make room for the dove in the center of the composition, descending from a segment of heaven with the hand of God. Clearly the Second Painter was not working from Venice 1917, but the other way around. T'oros' effort to copy the formal style of the Second Painter also explains the peculiar style of his work in Venice 1917. His figures in the Venice Annunciation are extremely rigid and immobile, approximating those in the U.C.L.A. version; but the personal style of the mature T'oros is much more fluid and loose, as can be seen in later versions of the subject. In Erevan, Mat. 6289 of 1323, the angel strides with considerable self-confidence and the Virgin holds her spinning comfortably before her instead of unnaturally to one side (fig. 305e). The architecture of the separate, simple masses is abandoned for a screen of city architecture, which is T'oros' preferred backdrop. Finally, giving up on the misunderstood well, T'oros introduces a two-spigot well with a new symbolic meaning of its own.[131]

Generally speaking, those points in which the Venice manuscript departs from the standard Byzantine iconography of a subject are points of dependence on the U.C.L.A. Gospel. In the evangelists one might note the arched framing and the architectural backgrounds (fig. 460a); in the Raising of Lazarus, the curious confrontation between Christ and the Pharisee; in the Entry into Jerusalem, the peculiar domed temple containing an altar; or in the Pentecost one might note the peculiar shape of the tongues of fire and the panelled benches on which the apostles sit (fig. 538b).[132] In all of these subjects T'oros copies only the work of the Second Painter, even when in the case of the Entry into Jerusalem there was another version of the subject available in the U.C.L.A. Gospel. Clearly he saw the work of this master as the finest painting in the U.C.L.A. manuscript and an example especially worthy of imitation.

We therefore find T'oros Taronec'i at the very start of his career in the U.C.L.A. Gospel, which he must have finished before 1307. Following his development from the U.C.L.A. Gospel to the Venice manuscript, to his mature works of 1317–31, one witnesses not only a growing mastery of individual compositions but a general expansion of the painter's skills. In the U.C.L.A. Gospel, apart from the two ambitious compositions of Christ ascending and removed from the cross (*pages 283 and 286*) in which he is struggling with fairly sophisticated models, T'oros had an extremely limited stock of figures. Most of the figures stand or sit in three-quarters pose and stick out an arm in a kind of all-purpose gesture that denotes speech, blessing, surprise, etc., depending on the context. This, of course, is the repertoire in which his colleagues, the Third and Fourth Painters, also worked. When he reached Venice 1917, T'oros largely abandoned these mechanical figures; exploring a variety of other models, including the legacy of the Second Painter of the U.C.L.A. Gospel, he began forming a far more flexible figure style. His palette too underwent a gradual development. In the U.C.L.A. Gospel he preferred a limited range of colors employed in full strength, shaded with black. In the Venice manuscript he made a conscious effort to imitate the tonalities of the Second Painter, and what he learned by this became standard in his later work, in which he shows himself to be a colorist of some subtlety. Pinks and mauves and light greens expand his palette, and symptomatic of this interest in a wider color range he introduced azurite in Jerusalem 2360 of 1321.[133]

This picture of the artistic career of T'oros Taronec'i also affords a clearer notion of painting at Glajor in general. The Third and Fourth Painters of the U.C.L.A. Gospel may have come to Glajor with some professional training; at least they knew set formulae of laying on pigments and of composing figures. T'oros clearly learned a great deal from them, though it is not clear that he was their pupil; from the outset he seems to have had a lighter and more flexible style and great deal of curiosity about other ways of painting.

Someone in the immediate circle of these three was the artist responsible for the exceptional group portrait of Esayi Nč'ec'i and his monks in Jerusalem, St. James 365 of 1301 (fig. R1). This manuscript, a commentary on Isaiah by Gēorg Skewṙac'i (based on Ephraem, Chrysostom, and Cyril of Alexandria), was written in 1299 for bishop Kostandin of Drazark in Cilicia, who donated it to the revered abbot of Glajor.[134] The faces here are painted in a light grey undercoat and modeled with dashes of green and red pigment; the heads are piled one on the other the way groups sometimes appear in the U.C.L.A. Gospel. The arbitrary coloring and the craggy modeling of Esayi's draperies bears a strong resemblance to the donor portrait done by Yohanēs in Venice, San Lazzaro 1108/265, in 1317–18, and indeed Yohanēs may have painted both portraits (figs. R3–R4). Still another Glajor painter appears in Erevan, Mat. 3393, executed in 1309 by the scribe Tiratur Kilikec'i (fig. 460h).[135] Like T'oros in his Gospel of 1307, this painter is trying to work in the style of Ełegis and Noravank', though the results are less successful.

A search of T'oros' later manuscripts for other, auxiliary hands might add a little more to one's knowledge of painting in Glajor, but the situation is not liable to change substantially. T'oros' fellow painters are few, and beyond occasional pages they have left no works of importance. Glajor was simply not a

[131] Mathews, "The Annunciation at the Well: A Metaphor of Armenian Monophysitism," *Medieval Armenian Culture*, University of Pennsylvania Armenian Texts and Studies 6, ed. T. Samuelian and M. Stone (Chico, Calif., 1983), 343–56.

[132] Der Nersessian, *Manuscrits*, pls. 46–58.

[133] Analyses by Diane Cabelli, to be published, have found azurite in several Armenian manuscripts of the mid-fourteenth century.

[134] The portrait is inscribed: "Our chief master Esayi and his disciples." Cf. Połarian, *Mayr C'uc'ak*, III, 269–71; Narkiss and Stone, *Jerusalem*, 76–77, 151.

[135] This manuscript is missing its canon tables; the four evangelists are the only miniatures.

major center of manuscript painting. T'oros Taronec'i was its most skilled and most prolific painter, and his work is uneven. His most productive years were 1317–23, when he produced eight surviving manuscripts, including his masterpieces, Erevan, Mat. 353 and 206. In his best work he manages to achieve a brilliance of color and a tenderness of expression; but he rarely manages an intensity of emotion. In his lesser works he is often superficial and even careless in execution. Perhaps his greatest virtue as a painter is his curiosity about the wide variety of material that passed his way and his readiness to explore new forms. Der Nersessian noticed some of his borrowings of Western material, and Korkhmazian has recently demonstrated that his Old Testament iconography is almost entirely taken from Latin manuscripts.[136] Yet, insofar as the present evidence goes, T'oros generally shows himself to be a painter who understood what he was doing; when he borrows it is with a sense of what is appropriate, and he generally keeps in view the traditional themes of Armenian Christianity which he is trying to enunciate. He must always have been conscious of the fact that the principal work of the monastery was not painting but scriptural commentary.

About the artist personally, however, very little is known, and this is typical of the situation of Armenian artists. His inscription on *page 227* proclaims pride he took in being a disciple of Esayi Nč'ec'i, and his frequent engagement in writing and decorating manuscripts for the abbot may indicate a special relationship. In addition, in the colophon of a now lost manuscript, one contemporary of his, Mxit'ar Eznkayec'i, mentions meeting in Glajor "the innocent and sweet-mannered brother, full of all wisdom and much book learning and art, named T'oros of the province of Taron."[137] In context the term "brother" must refer to his monastic state, and perhaps the mild disposition referred to can be read in the gentle style of painting.

[136] Emma Korkhmazyan, "The Sources of the Old Testament Illustrations in the Bible Illuminated by T'oros Taronatsi (Matenadaran no. 206)," *Fourth International Symposium on Armenian Art: Theses of Reports* (Erevan, 1985), 209–10; full publication in press.

[137] Xač'ikyan, *XIV Dari,* 104.

CHAPTER FIVE

Iconographic Method

1. Exegetical Method in the Study of Gospel Iconography

The study of illuminated manuscripts differs substantially from the study of other works of art in that it involves images in large sets. Gospel illustration is comprised of three different sets—the canon tables, the portraits of the evangelists, and narrative illustrations of the Life of Christ—each of which has a separate history and poses separate problems for the art historian. It is the narrative set, however, which by virtue of its size poses special methodological problems. As the number of components in a narrative set increases, the complexity increases geometrically, for one must constantly ask not only what is the meaning of each component—how, for example, this particular representation of the Transfiguration differs from other versions of the subject and how those differences are to be interpreted—but one must also ask how each component relates to the others, that is, to what extent modifications of a single image should be taken as programmatic modifications of the entire series of images. Approached item by item the task soon becomes unmanageable. When the number of images ranges between 50 and 250 (the Gospel of King Gagik of Kars had over 227 separate illustrations), it is imperative that one begin with the basic principles that governed the choice and constitution of the iconography.

To date, the most ambitious attempt to deal with Eastern Gospel iconography is still Gabriel Millet's pioneering work *Recherches sur l'iconographie de l'évangile.* [1] Attacking the problem of Late Byzantine fresco painting, Millet found it necessary to review the entire history of Gospel iconography in the East, much of which he found in Gospel manuscripts. But while Millet's work remains valuable for the wide range of material encompassed (it contains 670 figures from all kinds of media), the categories into which he forced the material are no longer useful. Preoccupied with the question of regional sources for Early Christian art, Millet made everything fit into either of two schools: an idealistic hellenistic school, which had its roots in Alexandria and its flowering in Byzantium, and a realistic oriental school stemming from Syria and Anatolia. There is no basis, however, for such a geographical sorting of the material; the iconographic tendencies within Byzantine and East Christian art are much more diverse than his two-fold scheme would allow. Moreover, when one raises concrete questions of how to read the iconography under discussion, Millet's categories offer very little assistance. To say that a given example of iconography is colorful and picturesque and represents a long "hellenistic" tradition within Byzantine art does not explain anything specific about the content of the imagery. The task of extracting the meaning from specific iconographic variants therefore is largely avoided.

Nevertheless, the Millet approach has dominated the study of iconography. Typically the art historian regards iconography as a useful tool in tracing filiation among works of art; iconographic analysis in this understanding of the term consists in discerning a distinctive configuration of gestures and motifs in a subject and following it back to its sources. By tracing such filiation, an art historian is able to link a given mosaic in Italy, for example, to mosaics in Greece that can in turn be traced to manuscripts produced in Constantinople. This is, admittedly, of special importance in establishing the lines by which artistic ideas are transmitted and diffused. Still, issues of specific meaning are often sidestepped; one can follow lines of filiation across seas and centuries without ever confronting the problem of the meaning of the particular configuration of gestures and motifs in question. It is as if a philologist were to parse all the sentences in a given text but never bother with the meaning of the passage, being more interested in classifying grammatical structures.

Equally influential for the study of Byzantine man-

[1] *Recherches sur l'iconographie de l'évangile aux XIVe, XVe, et XVIe siècles d'après les monuments de Mistra, de la Macédoine, et du Mont Athos* (Paris, 1916).

uscript iconography has been the method developed by Kurt Weitzmann.[2] Weitzmann proposed a parallel between the work of the miniaturist and that of the scribe, insofar as each was thought to be copying a given model. This is an approach that strongly emphasizes the mechanical and fortuitous aspects of manuscript illustration; changes in iconography are frequently explained as casual rearrangements of material, in which the artist combined elements that had previously been separate ("conflation"), or split elements that were previously together ("excerpting"). The task of the art historian, then, is parallel to the task of the text critic: he must try to detect whatever "corruptions" have crept into the picture cycle so that he may rearrange the images as they appeared in the hypothetical original model, just as the text critic tries to restore the reading of the hypothetical autograph text. But like Millet's, this approach generally avoids dealing with the specific content of specific miniatures. Because the changes introduced into the iconography are accidental they can be regarded as not significant carriers of meaning. The reconstructed original cycle, moreover, is regarded as naive storytelling, inasmuch as Weitzmann regards the closeness of the iconography to the literal story of the text as the constant measure of iconographic genuineness. Since the miniatures are not expected to add anything to the text, the iconographic analysis generally does not go beyond literal text.

Lexicons of iconography, a contribution of modern German scholarship, also avoid the difficult work of squeezing meaning out of the picture-language they describe.[3] The task of the encyclopedist is conceived as one of cataloguing the infinite variety of images rather than interpreting them. The reader is told how one version of a subject differs from another and is provided with long lists of the occurrences of each version, but he is seldom told what these differences mean. While modern scholarship has accomplished a great deal in the sorting and stylistic analysis of manuscript illustration, the careful and thorough reading of the iconography of the Gospels is still in its infancy. It remains unknown how far one can press the symbolic language of these images. Maguire's very provocative study of the relationship between Byzantine painting and rhetoric has demonstrated the remarkable subtleties of meaning that Byzantine art is capable of carrying; his material, however, was chiefly monumental or public art, matching the public dimension of the rhetorical sources to which he appealed.[4] To what sources one ought to turn in interpreting Gospel miniatures is the question at hand.

Perhaps more attention should be paid to a very fundamental difference in attitude toward Gospel illustration that can be observed between Eastern and Western Christendom. It should be noted that the wide variety of ways of connecting the illustrations to the relevant Gospel text in Armenian manuscripts is virtually unknown in the West. In Armenian Gospels four distinct systems of intra-textual illustrations were noted that attempt to place the miniatures beside the text they illustrate: a running narrative system, which interrupts the columns of text to insert the illustration; a frieze system, which places dense, moment-by-moment strips of scenes across the page; a marginal system, placing vignettes beside the text; and a system of "festival" images, that is, select scenes from the Life of Christ scattered through the book. By contrast, in the West one is struck by the detachability of Gospel illustration from Gospel text. A preface-page set of the Life of Christ was sometimes introduced into Gospels, but such a set was equally appropriate to the first pages of psalters, epistularies, and lectionaries, in which situations a typological meaning was often implied. Indeed the most extensive collection of Gospel iconography in the West was the *Bible Moralisée,* which rearranged the Gospel subjects to fit a vast typological system linking Old Testament, New Testament, and ecclesiastical history.[5] In the West, the passion for order and system, for schemes that would match parallel scenes in some numerological total, usually dictated the setting in which Gospel iconography was to occur. Accordingly, the best approach to such iconography is probably one which follows the structure of a medieval text-

[2] Kurt Weitzmann, *Illustrations in Roll and Codex: A Study of the Origin and Method of Text Illustration,* 2nd printing with addenda (Princeton, 1970). For a bibliography of Weitzmann's prolific contributions to manuscript studies, see his *Studies in Classical and Byzantine Manuscript Illumination,* ed. Herbert L. Kessler (Chicago, 1971), 335–39.

[3] Engelbert Kirschbaum and Wolfgang Braunfels, eds., *Lexikon der christlichen Ikonographie,* 8 vols. (Freiburg, 1968); Gertrud Schiller, *Ikonographie der christlichen Kunst,* 4 vols., 2nd ed. (Gütersloh, 1969); Klaus Wessel and Marcell Restle, *Reallexikon zur byzantinischen Kunst* (Stuttgart, 1963 ff).

[4] Henry Maguire, *Art and Eloquence in Byzantium* (Princeton, 1981).

[5] Alexandre de Laborde, *La Bible Moralisée conservée à Oxford, Paris et Londres,* 5 vols. (Paris, 1911–27); Reiner Haussherr, *Bible Moralisée, Faksimile-Ausgabe in Originalformat des Codex Vindobonensis 2554 der Österreichischen Nationalbibliothek,* 2 vols. (Graz, 1973); Robert Branner, *Manuscript Painting in Paris during the Reign of St. Louis* (Berkeley, 1977), 32–57.

book, such as a *Speculum humanae salvationis* or a *Summa theologica*, as Émile Mâle maintained.[6]

In the East such iconographic schemata are virtually unknown. Instead, Gospel illustration tends to be situated in the text and intimately bound to it. Gospel miniatures stand, then, as a visual commentary on the text that they accompany, and for this reason it is proposed here that the best approach to such iconography is one which follows the structure of exegesis, that is, the literature of commentary on the Gospels. In dealing with the monastery of Glajor in Armenia one is in the fortunate situation of being able to document the artist's close familiarity with a circle of exegetes. T'oros Taronec'i worked as scribe and as painter side by side with the exegetes Yovhannēs Erznkac'i and Esayi Nč'ec'i, and the latter he saluted as his teacher. The surprising extent to which concrete links can be demonstrated between the iconography of the U.C.L.A. Gospel and the traditions of Armenian exegesis permits one to infer a lively interchange of ideas between artist and exegete. It is exegesis that supplied the principles by which subjects were chosen and developed. To what extent the same processes may have been operative in Byzantine art is as yet unknown; unfortunately, little has been done to explore the imagery from this point of view.

The premise of the present undertaking is that everything in the iconography, insofar as it is deliberate, is meaningful. This does not deny that the artist may be involved in a process of copying, but it assumes that the end product is the work of intelligence, whether that be the individual intelligence of the single artist or the collective intelligence of a tradition of scribes and artists who have shaped and reshaped the imagery over the course of time. Each step in the process manifests a mind at work, starting with the most basic step of the decision to illustrate the book. Gospel iconography cannot be regarded as simple decoration, corresponding to some need of display or embellishment; if one simply wanted to decorate or enrich a book, an abstract vocabulary was always available, such as that employed in canon tables and initial pages. The decision to "decorate" a Gospel by adding figures to the text constitutes a decision to say something about the text.

The decision to say something about *this* text, as opposed to the text on the next page, represents a purposeful intervention. The choice of a passage is of great significance, for it necessarily gives a special importance to the passage chosen and sets it apart from the unillustrated passages. Hence, in an iconographic program, which may be regarded as an accumulation of such choices, both omissions and inclusions are significant. The program constitutes a set of markers calling the reader's attention to those passages that are thought to be of greater importance. The program, therefore, even before its individual components have been examined, already indicates a bias, a particular way of reading or interpreting the Gospel, and no set of illustrations can be taken as neutral storytelling, or picture-making for the sake of filling up space or for entertaining the eye. Even in the case of the frieze Gospels, in which one might imagine an impartial decision had been made to illustrate "everything" indiscriminately, considerable discretion can be detected in the choice of subjects. Indeed it is hard to conceive even theoretically what an absolutely complete illustration of the Gospels would involve. One might ask, for example, how many pictures it would take to illustrate completely every phrase of the Lord's Prayer.

In confronting the illustrated Gospel, then, the first task is program analysis. By tabulating the selection of subjects one can make comparisons among the programs of different manuscripts that will reveal continuities in selection of subjects for illustration. To make such comparative tabulations, it is important to identify by chapter and verse the break in the text where the miniature was inserted. Naturally the proximity of miniature to the verse it illustrates is closer in single-column illustrations and looser in full-page illustrations; and when an illustration cuts across a half page it can be counted as following two breaks in the text. In either case, however, the data must be reported in the table without interpretation. Only then can one meaningfully compare program with program and look for the interrelationships.

To analyze the program of the U.C.L.A. Gospel, a table has been prepared comparing it to three other manuscripts: the Gospel of King Gagik of Kars (Jerusalem, St. James 2556); the Vehap'aṙ Gospel (Erevan, Mat. 10780); and the Awag Gospel (Erevan, Mat. 212). Such a presentation of the programs permits one to draw a number of conclusions. Looking first at the U.C.L.A. manuscript, it is clear that the designer of the layout (that is, the scribe and perhaps the first two artists) strove for some sort of balance among the four Gospels with 56 subjects divided as follows: Matthew 20 (including the robbed Baptism); Mark 17; Luke 11 (including the space left for the Zacchaeus miniature that was not executed); and John 9. This contrasts with the method often pursued in Byzantine Gospels of illustrating Matthew fairly densely

[6] Émile Mâle, *L'art religieux du XIIe siècle en France* (Paris, 1910); *L'art religieux du XIIIe siècle en France* (Paris, 1922).

and then adding some of the missing subjects in the other Gospels.[7]

If one then compares the program of the U.C.L.A. Gospel to the early eleventh-century Vehapʿaṙ Gospel one is immediately struck by the frequent coincidence of subjects. Seventy-five percent (forty-two of the fifty-six subjects) correspond exactly to the Vehapʿaṙ Gospel. Indeed, where the illustrations are single-column format the break in the text is frequently at exactly the same verse, sometimes at the same word. Also striking are correspondences in subjects that are out of the ordinary, such as the Petition of the Canaanite, the Cunning Steward, or the Message from Pilate's Wife; on the other hand, common subjects are sometimes given unusual treatment, so that instead of illustrating the Curse of the Fig Tree (Mark 11:12–14), both Gospels illustrate the subsequent lesson Christ draws from the miracle (Matt. 11:20–24). Of the twenty-five percent of the subjects in the U.C.L.A. Gospel that do not exactly match the Vehapʿaṙ program, three subjects have been moved to different Gospels (the Raising of Jairus' Daughter, Christ Ascending the Cross, and the Crucifixion); six other subjects can be seen as borrowings from the more usual "festival" set of images (Baptism, the Last Supper, the Deposition, the Women at the Tomb, the Descent from the Cross, the Promise of the Holy Spirit or Pentecost, and the Ascension), all of which were assigned full-page format.

In other words, the designer of the U.C.L.A. Gospel took the Vehapʿaṙ Gospel as his model and tried to enrich it with several images that were in more general circulation; but that the Vehapʿaṙ Gospel was the primary model is inescapable. This conclusion will be repeatedly reinforced by examining the borrowings in individual images, but two very striking instances can be cited here: the unparalleled image of Christ leaning on a staff in the Raising of the Daughter of Jairus (*page 218* and fig. 218a); and the iconography of Paul in the scene of Christ on the Way to Emmaus, in which scene the artist depended not on the facial type used in the Vehapʿaṙ Gospel but on an inscription identifying one of the disciples as Paul (*page 448* and fig. 448a).

The choice of the Vehapʿaṙ Gospel as program model, at a time when more sophisticated Cilician books were much appreciated, implies that a special authority was attributed to the Vehapʿaṙ Gospel. Its antiquity may have given it a certain venerability in the eyes of the monks of Siwnikʿ; but it can also be argued that the copiers in the U.C.L.A. Gospel understood the program and found it especially relevant to their contemporary needs. To what extent this program was a standard program in Greater Armenia can be judged by comparison with other manuscripts. Virtually the entire program of the U.C.L.A. Gospel, fifty-one of its fifty-six subjects, was incorporated in a handsome Gospel executed a generation later, in 1337, in Sultaniye, the Ilkhanid capital.[8] Awag, the painter of manuscript Erevan, Mat. 212, was also the scribe and hence the designer of its layout and program. Having begun his career in Glajor (he was a scribe of Erevan, Mat. 7650 in 1329), Awag was evidently familiar with the program of the U.C.L.A. Gospel and took it as the model of his manuscript. Although it was not possible to compile the data on exact breaks in text where the miniatures fall (they are listed simply by folio number) it is clear that the program of the U.C.L.A. Gospel, including the subjects that it added to the Vehapʿaṙ program, was followed closely. It is not inconceivable that he even borrowed the U.C.L.A. Gospel for this purpose, since, as will be seen, they share many peculiar features of iconography; or he may have had a third, intermediary manuscript. To the U.C.L.A. program Awag added a few more scenes, notably a series of parables in Luke. A second Awag Gospel, with both running narrative illustrations and marginal vignettes, also depends closely on the U.C.L.A. Gospel. Although less copiously illustrated, London, B.L. Or. 5304, containing the Gospels and the Apocalypse, shows many points of contact with the program (and iconography) of the U.C.L.A. Gospel.[9]

The program of the Vehapʿaṙ and U.C.L.A. Gospels therefore can be said to have enjoyed a certain amount of popularity in the fourteenth century. What its circulation was earlier, apart from the Vehapʿaṙ Gospel itself, is hard to say. Comparison with the Gospel of King Gagik of Kars yields ambiguous results.[10] The Vehapʿaṙ and the U.C.L.A. Gospels have relatively the same size program, 62 and 56 sub-

[7] Annemarie Weyl Carr, *The Rockefeller McCormick New Testament: Studies toward the Reattribution of Chicago University Library, ms. 965*, diss., University of Michigan, 1973; eadem, *Byzantine Illumination 1150–1250: The Study of a Provincial Tradition* (Chicago, 1987).

[8] A. N. Avetisyan, *Haykakan Manrankarčʿutʿyan*, 140–50; Der Nersessian, *Armenian Art*, 224–25; Korkhmazyan, *Armenian Miniatures of the 13th and 14th Centuries*, 12 and notes on pls. 18–20; Lilith Zakaryan, *Awag* (Erevan, 1984). Zakaryan is presently preparing a full-length study of Erevan, Mat. 212.

[9] F. C. Conybeare described the manuscript incompletely and misdated it to the fifteenth century (*Catalogue*, 27–28). V. Nersessian, *Armenian Illuminated Gospel-Books* (London, 1987).

[10] Mathews, "Gospel Iconography in Greater Armenia."

jects respectively, while the Gagik Gospel had 227 subjects and perhaps a few more on the final missing folios. It can be observed that eight of the subjects that the U.C.L.A. Gospel added to the program of the Vehapʻaṙ Gospel occurred also in the Gagik Gospel; but this is not surprising, since the added subjects were generally not unusual ones. Moreover, in the absence of the robbed miniatures of the Gagik Gospel few iconographic connections can be established. The most significant programmatic connections with the U.C.L.A. Gospel are those subjects that are specifically non-Byzantine, such as the Genealogy, the Mocking of Christ, the Carrying of the Cross. Even though these are sometimes in different Gospels, the fact that these themes occurred in the Gagik Gospel points to a special and persistent Armenian interest in them. While one lacks evidence, then, to prove that the Vehapʻaṙ-U.C.L.A. program was a standard one in medieval Armenia, its correspondences with the Gagik Gospel demonstrate that it was not an aberration; and in the fourteenth century, on the other hand, it enjoyed a special popularity.

Beyond program analysis, the next step must be the analysis of the individual units of the narrative iconography. Certain rules or guidelines can be drawn up for this analysis, and while in some points they may seem obvious they deserve to be made explicit for the sake of clarity. In the first place it is important to observe what moment or moments in the Gospel narrative are being illustrated. For example, if the subject is a miraculous cure one must notice whether it is the petition of the sick man that is illustrated or the cure itself or the reactions of the public to the cure; for each of these would point to a different lesson to be drawn from the narrative, depending on whether the painter sought to draw attention to the faith of the petitioner or the power of Christ or the stubbornness of the Jews. Each such conscious choice makes a comment on the text, and this is precisely the work of the exegete, telling the reader what is significant in a passage.

Secondly, one must look carefully for those features in which the iconography departs from or adds to the naked narrative of the Gospel, for these are even more striking signals of the intervention of the exegetical mind. It is of the nature of the commentator to embroider the text, to add details to the story that will make his own interpretation of the text more convincing. Had the simple text been adequate there would have been no need for commentary, and, for that matter, no need for illustration. In the third place, one must listen to the emphases and intonations the illustrator gives in his retelling of the story. These potential modulations of meaning are infinite, whether in the gestures, in the way figures are grouped, the way they are clothed, the colors, the scale, and even the style of the painting.

In the fourth place (though obviously the sequence is immaterial) the relationship of the iconography to the history of iconography must be examined. One must understand the tradition in which the artist worked in order to measure the freedom with which he reworked the tradition. The sources of motifs and the lines by which motifs were transmitted are all indications of the development of the artist's language. But in dealing with iconography of the year 1300 the question of the ultimate source of a given motif—whether it was first employed in Palestine or in Constantinople a millennium earlier—is generally academic; the question is rather the state of the tradition as received by the artist.

What departs from the norm is often more revealing than what conforms to the norm, for it shows the individual artist making his own decisions. On the other hand, the fact that a traditional version of a subject has been chosen should not be taken to mean that the subject was trite and less significant; quite the contrary, the fact that a given formula is repeated with a regularity that the modern viewer finds boring is probably due to the fact that medieval man found it so perfectly satisfying for the situation. At the same time, the exact repetition of an iconographic formula over a given interval of time does not guarantee that the meaning attached to that formula has remained static. Obviously, to define such shifts in meaning one must look beyond the iconography itself and beyond the immediate Gospel text that the iconography ostensibly illustrates to sources that discuss the import of the passage in question. Indeed, at each stage in the iconographic analysis a parallel exegetical analysis must also be taking place.

To understand the intent of Gospel iconography one must be ready to go beyond works of art into the literary sources of the period. Although the art historian may be wary of having recourse to arcane sources beyond the ken of the "simple" artist, it would be a mistake to imagine that the illustration of a Gospel book was a democratic or folk art made by simple artists for the eyes of uneducated peasants. Evidence from Armenia indicates rather that one is dealing with a monastic art made for a highly literate monastic circle; in Glajor a survey of the surviving manuscripts demonstrates that the principal intellectual activity of the monks was studying and commenting on Sacred Scripture. In this tradition Gospel iconography was the visual component of a larger process, namely exegesis, and that process must be studied in the surviving literary sources.

The place of Sacred Scripture in the intellectual life of medieval man is hard to overestimate. Beryl Smalley has described this situation in the West, where down to the twelfth century a separate term for "theology" still did not exist; it was simply called "sacra pagina" or "lectio divina", meaning the study of the text of Sacred Scripture.[11] A parallel situation maintained in the East a good deal longer, since there a scholastic systematization of doctrine was never introduced. In Constantinople in the twelfth century the patriarchal school divided all theology among three chairs of exegesis: the Gospel, St. Paul's Epistles, and the Psalter.[12] Christian doctrine was in a sense coterminous with the interpretation of the revelation of Sacred Scripture. The four Gospels, of course, were preeminent among the books of the Bible, since they gave meaning to all the rest. A great part of the medieval reasoning process took the form of rethinking the familiar passages of the Gospels. One reasoned toward new positions or developed arguments to deal with new situations by rehearsing familiar stories and finding new content in them. Gospel iconography is the extension of this process into images.

2. Gospel Exegesis in Armenia

Although much has been written on the history of exegesis, particularly in the patristic period, the history of Armenian exegesis has hardly been begun; the commentaries themselves, on which such a study must rest, remain unedited and unstudied.[13] It is possible to draw up a rough list, as Eznik Petrosyan has done, of the Armenian literature of Gospel exegesis, and this is of some use in the investigation.[14] But listing the authors still leaves one far from defining their separate contributions, and much is still obscure about the overall shape of Armenian exegetical writing. However, some of the main lines of the development are clear, and luckily for this investigation there are some sources that have a direct bearing on the iconography of the U.C.L.A. Gospel.

Like other branches of Armenian literature, Armenian exegesis took its start from a series of translations made from Greek and Syriac patristic sources in the fifth and sixth centuries, the Golden Age of Armenian literature.[15] Most important for the interpretation of the gospels were the translations made of Ephraem Syrus' *Commentary on the Diatessaron* and John Chrysostom's *Homilies on Matthew.* Ephraem, writing in Edessa in the years 363–373, and Chrysostom, writing in Antioch before his appointment to the see of Constantinople in 398, must be considered the founding fathers of Armenian Gospel exegesis, and the availability of their works in critical editions and translations provides the modern scholar with a secure starting point in defining the Armenian exegetical tradition.[16] Two distinct translations of Chrysostom's work on Matthew were in circulation in Armenia before the seventh century, and his continued popularity is attested by numerous surviving manuscripts and by frequent citations in Armenian au-

[11] Beryl Smalley, *The Study of the Bible in the Middle Ages,* 2nd edition (Oxford, 1952).

[12] Ibid., 361.

[13] On the history of exegesis in general, see P. R. Ackroy and C. F. Evans, eds., *The Cambridge History of the Bible,* I, From the Beginnings to Saint Jerome (Cambridge, 1970), II, The West from the Fathers to the Reformation (Cambridge, 1969); A. J. Maas, "Exegesis," *The Catholic Encyclopedia* (New York, 1909), V, cols. 692–706; Jean Daniélou, *From Shadow to Reality: Studies in the Biblical Typology of the Fathers* (London, 1960). On the history of exegesis in the Latin West, see P. C. Spicq, *Esquisse d'une histoire de l'exégèse latine au moyen âge,* Bibliothèque Thomiste 26 (Paris, 1944); Smalley, *Study of the Bible;* Henri de Lubac, *L'exégèse médiévale. Les quatre sens de l'écriture,* 4 vols. (Paris, 1959–64). The history of Byzantine exegesis has been less studied, but see the important work of Robert Devreesse, "Chaines exégétiques grecques," *Dictionnaire de la Bible, Supplément* (Paris, 1928), I, 1084–1233.

[14] Eznik Petrosyan, "Avetarani Miǰnadaryan Haykakan Meknut'yunner" [Medieval Armenian Interpretations of the Gospels], *Eǰmiacin* 1 (1982), 35–41. See also the article by Irénée Hausherr, "Spiritualité arménienne," *Dictionnaire de Spiritualité* (Paris, 1933), 862–76.

[15] Concerning the non-Armenian exegetical literature that was available in translation in medieval Armenia, see Robert Thomson, "The Fathers in Early Armenian Literature," *Studia Patristica* 12.1 (Berlin,1975), 457–70, as well as the fundamental but less up-to-date work of G. Zarbhanalian, *Matenadaran Haykakan T'argmanut'eanc', 4–13 dd.* [Catalogue of Early Armenian Translations, 4th–13th Centuries] (Venice, 1889).

[16] Ephraem's *Commentary on the Diatessaron* was unknown before modern times and was first discovered in its Armenian version, which was edited and translated into Latin by Louis Leloir, *Commentaire de l'évangile concordant,* CSCO 137–38, Scriptores Armeniaci 1–2 (Louvain, 1953–54). This is the version used here in order to stay closer to the wording available to the Armenian reader, in preference to Leloir's subsequent edition and translation of the original Syriac, *Commentaire de l'évangile concordant, texte syriaque,* Chester Beatty Monographs 8 (Dublin, 1963), and SC 121 (Paris, 1966). For Chrysostom the translation of George Prevost was used, *Homilies on the Gospel of St. Matthew,* Nicene and Post-Nicene Fathers, ser. 1 (New York, 1888), controlled when necessary against the Greek edition of F. Field in PG 57–58. Citations occasionally take the liberty of modernizing Prevost's English.

thors.[17] Evidence of the continued use of Ephraem in medieval Armenia will be mentioned below.

Both Chrysostom and Ephraem may be taken as representative of Syrian exegesis, but they represent two very different traditions. Chrysostom learned from Diodorus of Tarsus the Antiochene method of interpretation. In contrast to the Alexandrian approach introduced by Origen, which put great stock in number symbolism, hidden etymologies and the allegorical reading of narratives, Chrysostom insists on the literal reading of the text. His *Homilies on Matthew* are addressed to the general lay public of Antioch, where he was appointed to preach, and they reflect the pastor's practical concern for the welfare of his parishioners. Theological speculation gives place to the cultivation of the everyday virtues of the Christian way of life. The stories of the Gospel are therefore seen as the source of instruction for Christian behavior, providing countless *exempla* for imitation. The faithful are urged to observe and imitate the faith of the woman with hemorrhage, the sobriety of the apostles at Cana, the humility of Christ in his suffering. Chrysostom missed no opportunity for criticizing the luxury he saw around him and for urging his listeners to look to their final purpose rather than their immediate gratifications.

Ephraem Syrus represents still a third method of exegesis, quite distinct from the Alexandrian and the Antiochene.[18] Ephraem was a poet of great power, who was perfectly at home in the world of signs and symbols. He constantly sees in the events of the Gospel the echoes of Old Testament history and the foreshadowings of the end of time; nevertheless, it would be unfair to call his method allegorical. The correspondences he traces are not exactly types and antetypes; the realities are too close to be separable in such artificial categories. For Ephraem Christ already existed in the Old Testament, and Jahweh's revelations of himself to the patriarchs were manifestations of Christ's form. Sacred history takes on a kind of transparency, in which everything is foreseen and planned from the beginning and everything belongs to a single pattern. Perhaps the best name for Ephraem's method would be "symbolic synecdoche," or part-for-whole symbolism. Since all of Christ's life and death is a single grand act of man's salvation, each individual event in his life somehow contains and reveals the whole. Thus, as discussed below, in making mud to cure the blind man, Christ is said to be recreating Adam out of the mud of the earth, but this time it is the second and redeemed Adam; or, in appearing transfigured before his disciples Christ is manifesting his coming resurrection, which in fact involves the restoration of redeemed man to paradise. In this way Ephraem describes each part of Christ's life as if it stands for and encapsulates the entire work of salvation. No Gospel event is to be seen as an isolated incident; all is interrelated, as if all of history were simultaneous.

While both the practical literal method of Chrysostom and the symbolic synecdoche of Ephraem were enthusiastically received in Armenia, it is Ephraem's approach that seems to prove more decisive for the development of native Armenian exegesis. The oldest and most influential document of native Armenian exegesis is the extended catechism called *The Teaching of Saint Gregory*, which is contained within the late fifth-century *History of the Armenians* by Agatʿangelos.[19] While not systematically a work of exegesis, *The Teaching of Saint Gregory* is an introduction to Christian doctrine that is thoroughly biblical in method of exposition. As in Ephraem, Gospel events are interpreted in the widest possible view of their implications. For example, the transformation of water into wine at Cana looks backward to creation, when God made water out of nothing, and forward to Christ's passion, when he transformed his sufferings into man's well-being. Or, the giving of the keys to St. Peter is a link in a much larger chain, which includes Christ's inheritance of priestly, prophetic, and royal power that he had received from Abraham through John the Baptist, as well as his transfer of these powers to the apostles and their successors in the church. Each event somehow contains the entire process of salvation history, and therefore the exegete is justified in appealing to a rich pattern of Old Testament associations for every event.

The subsequent history of Armenian exegetical writing is known very imperfectly. The cultivation of exegesis as a special branch of theological learning seems to have been particularly intense in the province of Siwnikʿ in the sixth to the eighth centuries. Petrosyan singles out for mention the gospel commentaries of Petros Siwnecʿi († 557), Matʿusałay († 651), Movsēs Siwnecʿi († 725), and Stepʿanos

[17] R. Thomson, "The Fathers in Early Armenian Literature," 464–65.

[18] Ignatius Ortiz de Urbina, *Patrologia Syriaca*, 2nd ed. (Rome, 1965), 56–83; Louis Leloir, *Doctrines et méthodes de S. Ephraem d'après son commentaire de l'évangile concordant*, CSCO 220, Subsidia 18 (Louvain, 1961); Robert Murray, *Symbols of Church and Kingdom* (Cambridge, 1975), passim. The first two of these studies are concerned with proving Ephraem's orthodoxy in terms of the trinitarian debates of the Greek-speaking world, in which Ephraem took no part; Murray's treatment is much more sympathetic to Ephraem's own method of theologizing.

[19] See the recent translation and commentary by Robert W. Thomson, *The Teaching of Saint Gregory, An Early Armenian Catechism* (Cambridge, Mass., 1970).

Siwnec'i († 735), the last of whom composed a commentary on all four Gospels.[20] Unfortunately, there exist no editions or modern studies of any of this material.

The twelfth century witnessed a renewed enthusiasm for translating Greek and Syriac sources.[21] A commentary on John attributed to the seventh-century Andrew of Crete (but otherwise unknown) was translated at this time, as well as Chrysostom's commentaries on Luke and John.[22] From the Syriac a commentary on John attributed to "Nana the Syrian," very likely the Monophysite theologian Henana of Nisibis († 610), was added to the Armenian library.[23] Perhaps it was this wider contact with outside sources that stimulated the new Armenian ventures into exegesis in this period: a commentary on Luke by Ignatios Sewleṙnec'i († 1160); another commentary on Luke by Sargis Kund († ca. 1190); and, most important, the commentary on Matthew begun by the famous Nersēs Šnorhali.[24] A poet whose hymns enriched the Armenian liturgy and a zealous catholicos of Armenia who entered dialogue with the Greek church toward reconciling their differences, Nersēs († 1173) completed his commentary only as far as Matthew 5:17. The work is of special importance for two reasons: first, because he prefaced it with an extended commentary on the decoration of canon tables, and this key document is translated in Appendix D and discussed at length in Chapter Seven; in the second place, the commentary itself was brought to completion in the fourteenth century by Yovhannēs Erznkac'i, the exegete of Glajor. Fortunately, it is available in a printed edition of the last century.[25]

The fourteenth century seems to have witnessed a special flowering of gospel commentary; in addition to Erznkac'i, a commentary on Mark was composed by Barseł Maškeworc'i († ca. 1345) and Yovhan Orotnec'i († 1397) wrote commentaries on Matthew and John, as did Gregory of Tat'ew († 1409).[26] All this activity seems to have been sparked by the learned biblical studies of the monastery of Glajor, where Erznkac'i worked and where the U.C.L.A. Gospel was brought to completion. The career of Yovhannēs Erznkac'i, also known as Corcorec'i, was confused in earlier literature with the career of his namesake Yovhannēs Erznkac'i Pluz, a somewhat older contemporary of his.[27] But Levon S. Xač'ikyan, in his study of the colophons of the period, succeeded in disentangling the two men.[28] The older man was born in the 1230s and spent most of his life in the vicinity of Erznka, where he reorganized the monastery of St. Minas.[29] Yovhannēs Erznkac'i the exegete, on the other hand, spent most of his life in Siwnik'. Born perhaps in the 1260s, he appears as scribe in three manuscripts executed at Glajor. The first, dated 1306 (Erevan, Mat. 2520), is a manuscript that he copied for his own use, and significantly enough it contains three exegetical treatises: the commentaries on John by Step'anos Siwnec'i and Nana the Syrian, and a commentary on the Apocalypse attributed to one John of Cappadocia. The second, dated 1308 (Erevan, Mat. 206), provides a most significant network of connections, for it is the splendid Bible executed for the great vardapet of Glajor, Esayi Nč'ec'i, in which T'oros Taronec'i executed the miniatures.

We have, therefore, the unusual situation in which a documented artist, the painter who brought to completion the iconography of the U.C.L.A. Gospel, can be closely linked to a known theologian who left a treatise on the meaning of the Gospel. The two knew one another and worked side by side in the same scriptorium; but while T'oros would interrupt his scribal work to paint, Yovhannēs would alternate his scribal work with his activity as theologian and exegete. He completed his commentary on Matthew in 1316. The following year he was present at the local council convoked in Adana, in Cilicia, to try to achieve some measure of compliance with the agreement of 1307–8 to bring Armenian church observances into conformity with Roman Catholic usage. Modern authors interpret this as a sign of his having

20 Petrosyan, "Avetarani Miǰnadaryan Haykakan Meknut'yunner," 35–36.

21 Ibid., 38–40.

22 See the translation by Philip Schaff, *Homilies on the Gospel of John,* Nicene and Post-Nicene Fathers, ser. 1, 14 (New York, 1889), and the de Montfaucon edition in PG 59.

23 Petrosyan, "Avetarani Miǰnadaryan Haykakan Meknut'yunner," 41; on Henana see Ortiz de Urbina, *Patrologia Syriaca,* 168–69.

24 Petrosyan, "Avetarani Miǰnadaryan Haykakan Meknut'yunner," 37–39. Ignatios Sewleṙnec'i's commentary has been published: *Meknut'iwn Srboy Awetaranin or əst Łukasi* (Constantinople, 1824). Sargis Kund has never been edited. Nersēs Šnorhali was published with its completion by Yovhannēs Erznkac'i (see following note).

25 Yovhannēs Erznkac'i and Nersēs Šnorhali, *Meknut'iwn Surb Awetaranin or əst Matt'ēosi* (Constantinople, 1825).

26 Barseł Čon Maškevorc'i, *Meknut'iwn Srboy Awetaranin or əst Markosi* (Constantinople, 1826). The commentaries of Yovhan Orotnec'i and Gregory of Tat'ew remain unpublished.

27 For two recent, and sometimes conflicting, biographies of Yovhannēs Erznkac'i, see H. Ačaṙyan, *Hayoc' Anjnanunneri Baṙaran,* III, 610–13, and entry by Armenuhi Srapyan in *Haykakan Sovetakan Hanragitaran,* VI, 558–59.

28 Xač'ikyan, *XIV Dari,* 649n.

29 For Yovhannēs Erznkac'i Pluz, see entry by Armenuhi Srapyan et al. in *Haykakan Sovetakan Hanragitaran,* VI, 2559–60.

gone over to the Catholic side, but perhaps the lines of division appear clearer now than they actually were in the fourteenth century, for a few years later he was still a scribe at the firmly anti-unionist monastery of Glajor, collaborating on another manuscript for Esayi Nčʿecʿi. This manuscript (Erevan, Mat. 6558), completed in 1320, contains several theological treatises, the principal one of which is another exegetical work, Nersēs Lambronacʿi's *Commentary on the Psalms.*

In his later career Yovhannēs appears in Corcor, in the province of Artaz, a center of Catholic activity. Here, at the monastery of the Mother of God, he collaborated in 1321 with one Tēr Bartʿolimēos, in the circle of the Latin archbishop Zakʿaria of Corcor, to produce an Armenian translation of the fourth book of Thomas Aquinas' *Commentary on the Sentences of Peter the Lombard,* a work on the sacraments. Insofar as this was an enterprise commissioned by Pope John XXII, it might be assumed that Yovhannēs had by this time clearly gone over to the Catholic cause; but this is only an assumption. A translator is not responsible for the contents of what he translates, and it is interesting to notice that four years later, in 1325, Esayi Nčʿecʿi himself, who is not suspected of Catholicism, commissioned a copy of this same translation of Aquinas, to be made at Glajor by Tʿoros Taronecʿi (Erevan, Mat. 560). But regardless of Yovhannēs Erznkacʿi's later position on union with Rome—and a great many of his colleagues who studied in Glajor did end up in the Catholic center in Kʿṙnay in the 1330s[30]—the contents of his *Commentary on Matthew* are firmly in the Armenian tradition, as shall be seen below.

Because of his association with the school of Glajor and with Tʿoros Taronecʿi, Yovhannēs Erznkacʿi is the most important exegetical source for interpreting the iconography of the U.C.L.A. Gospel. The procedure of his *Commentary on Matthew* follows closely the pattern that Nersēs Šnorhali established in his work on the first five chapters—a thorough, verse-by-verse explanation of the entire Gospel—and this immediately puts the work in a different category from the popular sermons of Chrysostom and Ephraem. Erznkacʿi's *Commentary* is a scholarly work intended for the classroom or for other scholars—the same scholarly monastic circle for which the product of the Glajor scriptorium in general was intended. No verse, however plain its meaning, can be bypassed, though such an approach would be far too tedious for instruction of the laity; and when several opinions exist on a point Erznkacʿi sets them all down like an objective scholar and numbers them. On the other hand, his procedure differs sharply from that of the Byzantine catenists, whose aim was simply to collect and who were content to set mutually contradictory interpretations side by side.[31] Unlike the catenists Erznkacʿi does not name his sources—the opinion being more important than the person who formulated it—and he feels compelled to resolve the contradictions when they arise, often introducing it as an opinion of his own. So too with contradictions among the evangelists; these he usually resolves by saying both were true. Thus when Matthew says Simon of Cyrene carried Christ's cross, but John says Christ himself carried it, Erznkacʿi decides that Simon carried it first and then Christ.

How much of Erznkacʿi's Commentary is original it is difficult to say, since the other Armenian commentators of the Middle Ages remain unpublished. But his wholesale dependence upon Chrysostom and Ephraem is striking; perhaps as much as a half of his commentary can be traced to these two sources, either in paraphrase or in verbatim quotations. It is important to notice too that when he voices a line of exegesis independent of these two sources he tends to prefer Ephraem's method of symbolic synecdoche. Thus, in trying to resolve the difference of opinions on where the Transfiguration took place, he hits on the happy solution that it happened in the Garden of Eden, for by Christ's death and resurrection he restored man to paradise: the beginning and end of salvation history are encapsulated in the moment of the Transfiguration.

Needless to say, not everything in the exegetical sources is of equal relevance to the student of iconography. Yovhannēs Erznkacʿi comments on every verse but not every verse is illustrated. The inquiry must always start with the imagery itself; the peculiarities of the iconography motivate our reading of the literature. The goal, then, is twofold: to understand the importance attached to certain subjects in the Armenian program of Gospel iconography, and to interpret the nuances of specific subjects as developed in Armenian iconography.

Our contention that the iconography of the U.C.L.A. Gospel and related manuscripts served a fundamentally exegetical purpose, enlarging on the process of Gospel commentary, necessarily puts other possible purposes in second place at best. This must be noted particularly of the liturgical aspects of the manuscript; for it is clear that the text of the U.C.L.A.

[30] M. A. van den Oudenrijn, "Uniteurs et Dominicains d'Arménie," *Oriens Christianus,* ser. 4, 40 (1956), 94–112, and 42 (1958), 110–33.

[31] See Devreesse, "Chaines exégètiques grecques."

Gospel was devised for liturgical use, containing as it does the numbering for the Easter series of lections in the liturgy (*page 375*). The question naturally arises, then, whether the liturgy may have governed the development of the iconographic program. This is basically a problem of the relationship of the program to the lectionary of the Armenian church: one must ask to what extent the selection of subjects follows the selection of texts for readings in the calendar. The origins of the Armenian lectionary are well documented in the famous Jerusalem lectionary, which witnesses the calendar of readings in Jerusalem in the fifth century.[32] The Armenians adapted this nucleus to a hebdomadal calendar with a much enriched sanctoral cycle, which is the lectionary in current use.[33] The antiquity of this calendric system, in which saints' days are not fixed, but move with the date of Easter, can be demonstrated by the discussion of the issue with the Greek church in 1172.[34] The sanctoral cycle, and therefore the lectionary, underwent a considerable expansion between the eleventh and the thirteenth century, but has remained practically the same since then. It is therefore possible to analyze the liturgical uses of all the passages that are singled out for illustration in the U.C.L.A. Gospel (see Table 9).

While virtually every Gospel text has some liturgical importance, insofar as the text is read on some occasion in the church year, it soon becomes evident that the selection of readings is not the governing factor in the illustration of the text. For example, the reading for the Feast of the Transfiguration is taken from Luke 9:27–36; illustration of the Transfiguration (*page 106*), however, accompanies the reading in Matt. 17:1–8. Similarly, the size of the miniature in the U.C.L.A. Gospel has nothing to do with its role in the lectionary: the Petition of the Canaanite is accorded a full page (*page 99*), though this story never figures as a Gospel reading in the Mass, while the subject of Peter Receiving the Keys (*page 103*), which is a common reading, receives only a quarter of a page. The Petition of the Canaanite does count as one of the "Gospels of Healing," a series of readings that are used to conclude Sunday Matins; but not all those readings are illustrated. Naturally, some of the most prominent miniatures in the U.C.L.A. Gospel do coincide with some of the most important liturgical feasts, and this will be duly noted. But the feasts do not seem to control the illustrations. Rather, the most important liturgical dimension of the U.C.L.A. miniatures seems to be their occasional reinforcement of the Armenian position in their controversies over how the sacraments are to be administered. Thus the use of undiluted wine is alluded to in the Crucifixion (*page 561*) and the practice of communion by commixture is illustrated in Christ's Apparition by the Sea of Galilee (*page 570*). In other words it is the interpretation of the passage in a polemical context that suggests the development of the iconography; the liturgical aspect is part of the exegetical development of the subject.

[32] Athanase Renoux, *Le codex arménien Jérusalem 121. Introduction* and *Édition comparée du texte,* PO 35 and 36 (1969 and 1971).

[33] *Čašocʻ Girkʻ* (Jerusalem, 1873).

[34] Krikor H. Maksoudian, "Armenian Saints," *Dictionary of the Middle Ages,* I, 517–21.

CHAPTER SIX

The Iconography of the Life of Christ

1. The Genealogy of Christ (*Pages 28–35*)

The text illustrations of the U.C.L.A. Gospel begin with a series of forty-four figures, each enthroned beside the mention of his role in the human lineage of Christ (Matt. 1:1–17). Covering eight full pages, this series, which begins and ends with the figure of Christ himself, constitutes the richest treatment of the Genealogy in medieval manuscript art, whether in the East or the West. This unusual phenomenon fits into a special development of the subject in Armenian art, and its rationale is to be found in the peculiar importance of genealogies, both biblical and historical, in Armenia.

Brilliantly robed in tunics and cloaks that alternate vermillion and azurite, the ancestors assume uniform frontal poses; holding scrolls of authority in the left hand they gesture with the right to direct the viewer's gaze to their descendants, or make a sign of greeting with an open palm. Although Matthew mentions five of Christ's female ancestors, only the forefathers are shown, with the exception of the Virgin Mary. The figure of the Virgin is an exception in another way as well, for while the other ancestors are unmistakably the work of the Second Painter, the Virgin seems to have been repainted by T'oros Taronec'i. The smooth handling of drapery and the large, prominent features of hands, nose, and eyes is replaced in the Virgin with a streaky painting of drapery and tiny delicate features. Evidently here, as in the Annunciation (*page 305*), T'oros was anxious that the painting of the Virgin should be consistent throughout the manuscript.

The images are exactly coordinated with the text, arranged in two columns. Kings in the series are sharply distinguished by a regal chlamys, shoes, and a crown, as opposed to the halo on nonroyal ancestors (*pages 28–30 and 33*). The crowns of gold are all different, ornamented with pearls and precious stones; the pointed finials of some bear a resemblance to Western crowns, but the basic domed shape of most of them derives from the Byzantine *kamelaukion*, which is developed by the artist in a fanciful way.[1] It is worth noting that on *page 33* Salathiel is appropriately shown crownless because of his captivity in Babylon, while his son Zorobabel resumes the crown as restored king of Israel (cf. Ezra 3:2; Matt. 1:11–12). The following ten figures, not listed as royal in the Old Testament, are again left crownless; this effort at biblical accuracy is a recurrent trait of the U.C.L.A. Gospel. The kings also have another trait that sets them apart, namely, their long hair, falling in large curls on either shoulder. The luxurious hair that painters of Ełegis and Noravank' always attribute to Christ must be read as a royal attribute.

Byzantine art rarely illustrates the texts of Christ's genealogy, but Paris, B.N. gr. 74, presents little clusters of ancestors, unnamed and grouped symmetrically around the more prominent figures in the genealogy, such as Jacob or Judah.[2] This grouping of ancestors can be compared to the three groups of thirteen ancestors who stand around portraits of Abraham, David, and Jechoniah at the opening of the Lorsch Gospel.[3] However, these summary groupings

[1] Lord Twining, *European Regalia* (London, 1967), 37–40; Elizabeth Piltz, *Kamelaukion et mitra: Insignes byzantins impériaux et ecclésiastiques* (Uppsala, 1977). For the Armenian antecedents of the U.C.L.A. crowns, see the crowns of the Vehap'aṙ Gospel (fig. 469a) and the crown of the one remaining magus in the Nativity in the Homiliary of Muš, Erevan, Mat. 7729, Der Nersessian, *Armenian Art*, pl. 163.

[2] Henri Omont, *Évangiles avec peintures byzantines du XIe siècle* (Paris, 1908). Byzantine church decoration occasionally includes a set of Christ's ancestors, as in the famous narthex domes of Christos tēs Chōras in Constantinople. However, as Underwood has shown, these do not illustrate the text of Matthew but represent instead an expanded list of sixty-six "ancestors" including some who have no biblical claim to such status, such as Daniel and his companions. Underwood traced the list of ancestors to Christopher of Mytilene, who in the eleventh century introduced it into the synaxarion for the "Feast of Ancestors" on the Sunday before Christmas. This feast does not exist in the Armenian tradition. Paul A. Underwood, *The Kariye Djami*, 4 vols. (New York-Princeton, 1966–75), I, 52.

[3] Bucharest, National Library, Codex aureus, fol. 27. Cf. G. Schiller, *Iconography of Christian Art* (Greenwich, Conn., 1969), I, pl. 17.

of figures bear no resemblance to the Armenian development of the subject.

In Armenian art the Genealogy of Christ is a theme of major importance, introduced in the Gospel of Gagik of Kars in the mid-eleventh century, which illustrate both the Matthaean and the Lukan genealogy; but the miniatures, which were found in the bottom margins, were excised and their format is unknown (see Table 8). In the Cilician period artists explored three different formats for handling this subject, one borrowed from the West and the other two apparently Armenian developments.[4] The Western format, namely, a Tree of Jesse, proved to be the least successful in terms of accommodating the subject, for the tree was originally developed not to illustrate the genealogies of the Gospel but the text of Isaiah 11:1; the tree starts from David's father, Jesse, whereas Matthew's genealogy starts from Abraham and Luke's goes all the way back to Adam.[5] A second Cilician format arranged bust figures of the ancestors in medallions over the full page. T'oros Ṙoslin turned to this solution in his lavishly illustrated Gospel in Baltimore (fig. 35a), and the Armenian frieze gospel uses a variation of this design (fig. 35b). Der Nersessian has pointed to a possible Western source for this format in the Bohemian Vyšehrad Gospels of 1085–86; but the latter is unique in Western art, and its format mixes lozenges and circles.[6] Closer in format are the group portraits of the twelve minor prophets in the Byzantine Bible of Niketas.[7] But whatever its possible sources, the exploitation of this format as a vehicle for illustrating the Genealogy is an especially Armenian phenomenon.

The third format is the simplest and the most satisfying for the literal rendering of the text, and that is the individual portrait format used in the U.C.L.A. Gospel. Each ancestor is shown in the text alongside the mention of his name. This solution was adopted in another manuscript of T'oros Ṙoslin, Washington, Freer 32.18, in which bust medallions of the ancestors are used (fig. 35c). The U.C.L.A. Gospel is the only known example in which all the ancestors appear as full-length enthroned figures. A generation later the painter Awag, heir of the Glajor traditions, shows them in more lively poses, gesturing to one another; most sit in oriental fashion on the ground, but Judah is enthroned and Ezron is shown as a warrior (fig. 35d). The individual portrait system continued in use to the end of Armenian manuscript illumination.[8]

In discussing the iconography of the U.C.L.A. Gospel it is important to distinguish those interpretations that might be called the common heritage of Christianity from those interpretations that are peculiar to the Armenian tradition of exegesis. For while the treatment of a given subject in Armenian art often reflects the common Christian understanding of that subject, it often also embodies nuances that are special to the East Christian or Armenian outlook. Both may be entirely relevant.

In the common Christian acceptance of Matt. 1:1–17 two theological themes are set forth: the incarnation and the royal ancestry of Christ. Both of these themes are also the property of the Armenian exegetical tradition, and are firmly enunciated in the iconography. Chrysostom in explaining the text of Matthew turns first of all to the mystery of the incarnation.

> It is far beyond all thought to hear that God the Unspeakable, the Unutterable, the Incomprehensible, and he that is equal to the Father, has passed through a virgin's womb, and has vouchsafed to be born of a woman, and to have Abraham and David for forefathers. . . . . . The birth was twofold, both made like unto us, and also surpassing ours. For to be born of a woman indeed was our lot, but "to be born not of blood, nor of the will of the flesh, nor of man," but of the Holy Ghost, was to proclaim beforehand the birth surpassing us, the birth to come which He was about to give us of the Spirit.[9]

[4] Sirarpie Der Nersessian, "Western Iconographic Themes in Armenian Manuscripts," *Études,* I, 611–30. For published Cilician examples of the Tree of Jesse, see the following: Jerusalem, St. James 2568, the Second Prince Vasak Gospel (1268–84), Azaryan, *Kilikyan Manrankarč'ut'yun,* pl. 98; Erevan, Mat. 7651, fol. 10, Dournovo, *Haykakan Manrankarč'ut'yun,* pl. 51; Erevan, Mat. 9422, Gospel (late 13th century), Azaryan, *Kilikyan Manrankarč'ut'yun,* pl. x; Vienna, Mekhitarist 278, fol. 14, Buschhausen, *Die illuminierten armenischen Handschriften,* pl. 30, fig. 70.

[5] Arthur Watson, *The Early Iconography of the Tree of Jesse,* (Oxford, 1934).

[6] Der Nersessian, *Arm. Mss. Walters,* 26–27. For other Western examples of the Genealogy, see Adelheid Heimann, "A Twelfth-Century Manuscript from Winchcomb," *Journal of the Warburg and Courtauld Institutes* 28 (1965), 87–94.

[7] Hans Belting, *Die Bibel des Niketas* (Wiesbaden, 1979), figs. 7–8.

[8] For other published examples of the single-portrait system, see: Erevan, Mat. 7639, Gospel from New Julfa (1610), Dournovo, *Haykakan Manrankarč'ut'yun* (1967) pl. 74; Vienna, Mekhitarist 295, fol. 187, H. and H. Buschhausen, *Die illuminierten armenischen Handschriften,* pl. 72, fig. 216.

[9] Chrysostom, "In Matt. Hom. II," chaps. 2–3. *NPNF* x, pp. 9–10. This is repeated, in part verbatim, in the Armenian commentary of Nersēs Šnorhali, *Meknut'iwn,* 23–24; J. Cappelletti, *Sancti Nersetis Opera* (Venice, 1883), 41–42.

Christ had two births, first as the Son of the Father from all eternity, and second as Son of the Virgin Mary in time. It is this double birth to which one must appeal to explain the double appearance of Christ in the U.C.L.A. Genealogy. At the start he is represented ahead of Abraham in superhuman scale, seated on a grand throne (*page 28*), illustrating in a very literal sense Christ's own proclamation of his eternal nature when he declared, "Before Abraham was, I am" (John 8:58). The representation of Christ as beardless identifies him as the "Emmanuel," the eternal and unaging Son of God.[10] At the end of the Genealogy he appears again in smaller scale in the company of his human family with Mary and Joseph seated on a lowly seat (*page 35*).

The royalty of Christ's ancestry is the second theme of exegesis on the Genealogy, and since it is spelled out in the very first verse it could hardly be overlooked—"Jesus Christ, the Son of David" (Matt. 1:1).[11] The painter's interest in the attributes of royalty, both in Christ and his ancestors, has already been noted.

Beyond these two common themes of exegesis, however, the Syro-Armenian tradition adds to the ancestors another theological burden, namely, Christ's inheritance of priesthood and prophecy. As Murray has pointed out, the Syrian tradition in this respect departs from "mainstream" Christianity.[12] The common tradition viewed Christ's priesthood as spiritual and as standing outside of the Levitical line, like the priesthood of the maverick Melchizedek (Heb. 7:17); the Syrian tradition, on the contrary, saw Christ as heir of the Levitical priestly tradition. Various arguments were proposed to bolster the Syrian view.[13] According to Ephraem Syrus, Melchizedek was Noah's son Shem, and the priestly tradition went all the way back to Adam; at the other end of the line the Blessed Virgin was somehow connected with the tribe of Levi, since her cousin Elizabeth was of the priestly family. The priesthood of Levi, then, was inherited by John the Baptist and was formally conferred on Christ at his Baptism so that it might be transmitted to the Apostles, and by them to the Church. As Murray describes it, salvation became "a family affair."

This interpretation enters the Armenian tradition in *The Teaching of Saint Gregory:*

> Moses made the silver horn of his anointing from which were anointed the priests, prophets, and kings. Thence proceeded in order the unction in succession according to the command of the authority of the commandment, which proceeded in order by seniority. The mystery was preserved in the seed of Abraham, because they passed on the tradition to each other until John, priest, prophet, and baptist. And coming to him, it remained on him as on an heir. For it came to him from the first forefathers, the kings, prophets, and anointed priests, as to a keeper of a tradition. And he gave the priesthood, the anointing, the prophecy, and the kingship to our Lord Jesus Christ.[14]

The traditions of priest, prophet and king are not separate, but one inheritance.

This idea seems to remain current in Armenia throughout the Middle Ages. In the *Commentary on Matthew* by Nersēs Šnorhali, attention is drawn to points of contact between the Davidic and Levitical lines in Christ's ancestry. Since in other respects the *Commentary* is pure Chrysostom on the subject of the Genealogy, these points have special significance. The sister of Naason (Matt. 1:4), he believes, was Aaron's wife, and the daughter of Joram (Matt. 1:8) was married to a priest. Hence, Nersēs concludes, the ancestry of Christ was really mixed, royal and sacerdotal.[15]

The special importance attached to the ancestry of Christ in the Syro-Armenian tradition of exegesis must account for the special popularity of this theme in Armenian illuminated manuscripts. Christ's claim to the spiritual traditions which he was to pass on to his Church has to be founded in tangible family connections. At the same time, this theological position had a sociological counterpart in the *naxarar* structure of Armenian society. Armenian society was feudal in nature, in the sense that class was inherited; hence an extraordinary importance was attached to ancestry in medieval Armenia. For example, the *History* of Movsēs Xorenacʿi includes a Jewish genealogy for the Bagratuni family by way of Šambat Bagarat;[16] the Iberian branch of the same family founded their claim to rule on descent from David;[17] and Tʿovma Arcruni traced the Arcruni line back to Senecherim.[18] Priesthood, too, was largely inherited. The

[10] E. Lucchesi-Palli, "Christus-Emmanuel," *Lexikon der christlichen Ikonographie,* I, 390–92.

[11] Cf. Chrysostom, ed. Prevost, II, 6–8; Nersēs Šnorhali, *Meknutʿiwn,* 23–24; Cappelletti, *Opera,* 42–43.

[12] Murray, *Symbols,* 179.

[13] Murray, *Symbols,* 178–82; Louis Leloir, *Doctrines et méthodes de S. Ephrem,* 27–28.

[14] Thomson, *Teaching of St. Gregory,* chap. 433, p. 96.

[15] Nersēs Šnorhali, *Meknutʿiwn* on Matt. 1:14 and 1:18, 26–27; Cappelletti, *Opera,* 46–48.

[16] Movsēs Xorenacʿi, *History of the Armenians,* ed. R. Thomson (Cambridge, Mass., 1979), 132–33. See also Thomson's "Introduction," p. 40.

[17] Cyril Toumanoff, *Studies in Christian Caucasian History* (Washington, D.C., 1963), 306 ff. and 330–34.

[18] Tʿovma Arcruni, *History of the House of the Artsrunikʿ,* I, chaps. 1–11, 67–142.

families of the Grigorids and the Ałbianids claimed priesthood as their special prerogative.[19] The Byzantine council of Troullo went out of its way to condemn the Armenian custom in 692, but without effect.[20]

The solemn sequence of ancestors, therefore, is peculiarly Armenian in its implications. The authenticity of Christ's lineage guarantees his right to inherit the fullness of the ancient traditions as king, priest, and prophet; and this inheritance he will pass on intact to his Church. The ecclesiological theme of the continuity of the Church with ancient Israel will appear again and again in the iconography of the U.C.L.A. Gospel. The importance of the Genealogy in the U.C.L.A. Gospel is heightened by its role in the overall program. Having expanded the series of ancestors to eight pages the artists felt free to omit all illustration of the birth of Christ. Since the Genealogy concludes with Joseph, Mary, and Christ it effectively includes the mystery of Christ's birth presented emblematically.

2. The Beheading of John the Baptist (*Page 92*)

The loss of the miniature of the Baptism that once faced page 41 has interrupted the continuity of program in the first miniatures of the U.C.L.A. Gospel. It was at his Baptism, according to the East Christian understanding of these events, that Christ received the inheritance of the authentic traditions of priesthood, prophecy and kingship—the theme announced in the Genealogy. John the Baptist stood as middle man between the two testaments, a prophet and priest of the Old Testament who anointed his divine successor in the New. In this light the progression from Genealogy to Baptism to Beheading has a certain logic, bringing into greater prominence the role of John the Baptist. The absence of a liturgical justification for this selection of subjects makes the theological continuity of these subjects all the more cogent. It should be pointed out that in Armenian liturgy the Feast of the Decapitation takes its reading from Mark 6:14–29, instead of from the passage in Matthew 14:1–12 that is illustrated here.[1] After representing the Baptist's role, the U.C.L.A. Gospel then draws attention, in the miniatures that follow, to ecclesiological considerations, that is, to the continuity of the inheritance passed on to the church.

The illustration of Herod's banquet and the consequent execution of John has a long history, starting with the sixth-century Sinopensis Gospel, but the iconography admits of considerable variety.[2] The banquet is the element that is most standardized, with Herod seated at the left of a sigma table around which the banqueters gather, as in Walters 539 (fig. 92b). Other parts of the story—Salome's dance, the execution, the presentation of John's head, and his burial—may be added to this nucleus or singled out for separate illustration. The miniature in the U.C.L.A. Gospel offers a particularly brutal realization of the gruesome event in an iconography that departs in many ways from the traditional.

The composition reads clockwise from the bottom. In the foreground at the bottom is a sigma banquet table of porphyry on which are placed a wide golden plate with a low foot and a pitcher. Around the table are seated four banqueters, who wear a headdress of white striped material, which marks them as Jews in the manuscript.[3] On either side of the four banqueters, joining them at the table, are two ugly little creatures with bird-like bodies and black hairy heads. These are labeled "Beliar Šun" on the left, and "Sadayēl." The banqueters turn to the left and draw our attention to Herod, who sits on a faldstool at table and yet is also somewhat above and behind the banqueters, enframed by a domed niche. He is dressed in a purple sakkos with a vermilion chlamys over his shoulders, and he wears a heavy three-pointed crown. Before him kneels Salome making her plea, "Give me the head of John the Baptist here on a platter" (Matt. 14:8). Above to the right, in a separate panel, the actual beheading takes place. John, wearing a shirt of hair illogically painted blue and a yellow cloak, sits or squats, while a soldier in short red tunic vigorously grasps him by the beard and lays a sword to his neck. Blood spurts from his wound. The last scene of the drama is shown below to the right, where the executioner now presents to Salome the head of John on the same low-footed plate that had stood on the table moments before.

The miniature can be distinguished from traditional iconography by what it omits as much as by what it shows, for the dance of Salome, which prompted Herod's promise of anything she should

[19] Nicholas Adontz, *Armenia in the Period of Justinian: The Political Conditions Based on the Naxarar System*, trans. N. Garsoïan (Lisbon, 1970), 286–88.

[20] J. D. Mansi, *Sacrorum Consiliorum Nova et Amplissima Collectio* (Florence, 1759 ff.), II, 957–59.

[1] *Čašocʿ Girkʿ*, 290.

[2] Klaus Wessel, "Johannes Baptistes," *RBK*, III, 616–47.

[3] White material striped with black and red constitutes the typical Jewish headdress on *pages 126, 171, 252, 259*. In Byzantine art this headdress is often reserved for the Pharisees. Cf. O. Demus, *The Mosaics of San Marco in Venice* (Chicago, 1984), I, 1, 119 and I, 2, pl. 39.

ask (Matt. 14:6–7), is omitted. In Byzantine and Western renditions the dance is almost never omitted, and often it is the chief focus of the iconography. It develops at times into a dance of many veils or a sword dance. In the Vehapʿaṙ Gospel Salome dances in a great wide-sleeved garment with a bird in her headdress (fig. 92a).[4] The Armenian frieze Gospel, Erevan, Mat. 7651 shows her dancing with some sort of castanets in her hand (fig. 92c). The banquet, too, is often further developed. In Paris, B.N. gr. 74 a grape arbor arches over the banquet table and to one side a servant attends to a large vessel that looks like a samovar.[5] All such festive associations of the event have been banished from the miniature.

The non-biblical appearance of the two demons at Herod's banquet is unprecedented, and sets the tone for the whole miniature. The theme of diabolical possession runs through all of the East Christian sources on the Beheading of John. Chrysostom, who on one occasion is reported to have compared his own adversary, Empress Eudoxia, to Herodias "demanding the head of John,"[6] writes one of his most passionate homilies on the Beheading.[7] He is shocked at the spectacle of a birthday party turned into an execution, and the concatenation of immoral behavior—from evil companionship to dancing, drinking, adultery and finally murder—give wide scope to his indignation. "O diabolical revel! O satanic spectacle!" he exclaims, "For a murder more impious than all murders was perpetrated, and he that was worthy to be crowned and publicly honored, was slain in the midst, and the trophy of devils was set on the table."[8] When Salome begged for the head of John the devil pleaded with her and she herself "became altogether the devil's."[9] Ephraem Syrus implies something more sinister, namely that the plot itself began with Satan. As Satan had found that he could overcome Adam by means of his wife, so he could overcome Herod through his.[10]

The diabolical counterplot to the divine plan of redemption is spelled out in greater detail in the Armenian literature that grew up around the *Gospel of Nicodemus*. Satan, discussing his plans with the Master of Hell, reveals his at times confused part in John's death: "I entered into a beautiful woman a confidant of my works and during the meal I stirred her up against him, and she had him beheaded and gave the head to her daughter on a charger, and she played with it as with an apple."[11] Thus there existed in East Christian sources a tradition linking the death of the Baptist to a vast satanic conspiracy. This tradition was familiar to Yovhannēs Erznkacʿi in the fourteenth century. Satan plotted the banquet from the beginning;[12] he "wholly swallowed up" Salome in her perverse request;[13] and "he who conquered Adam through the rib, the same conquered Herod by the one with whom he fornicated."[14]

But the iconography of the U.C.L.A. Gospel goes a step beyond the exegetical material by showing two demons and identifying them as Beliar Šun, that is "Dog Beliar," and Sadayēl. Both are synonyms for Satan, who undergoes many metamorphoses in medieval Armenia. Beliar (or Belial) is synonymous with Satan in Paul's expression: "What fellowship has light with darkness? What accord has Christ with Belial?" (2 Cor. 6:14–15). In the twelfth-century Armenian apocalyptic *Sermo de Antichristo,* Beliar appears at times as a kind of twin colleague of Satan who helps establish the antichrist in Jerusalem;[15] in other passages he is identified as the evil dragon (*višap*). It is predicted that the antichrist will be destroyed on Epiphany, the same day on which Christ had trampled on the dragon Beliar in the Jordan.[16] This connection has something to do with the iconography, for in Tʿoros Taronecʿi's next surviving commission, the Gospel of Esayi Nčʿecʿi of 1307, the demon trampled by Christ in his baptism takes the form of a little black creature with hairy head and bird-shaped body, very similar to the demons of our miniature.[17] The doubling of demons in this miniature may refer to

[4] This miniature has suffered a great deal of damage, apparently purposeful. The great cloud over Salome's left shoulder is a stain.

[5] Bibliothèque Nationale gr. 74, fols. 28v and 75v.

[6] Socrates, *Historia Ecclesiastica,* VIII, chap. 20, *PG* 67, col. 1568; Sozomen, *Church History,* 8, 20.

[7] Chrysostom, "In Matt. Hom. 48," chaps. 4–5, *NPNF* x, pp. 298–300.

[8] Chrysostom, "In Matt. Hom. 48," chap. 4, *NPNF* x, p. 298.

[9] Chrysostom, "In Matt. Hom. 48," chap. 5, *NPNF* x, p. 299.

[10] Ephraem, *Commentaire,* book 11, chap. 28, p. 114.

[11] S. Der Nersessian, "An Armenian Version of the Homilies on the Harrowing of Hell," *Études,* I, 441; also found in another Armenian version of the same, eadem, "A Homily on the Raising of Lazarus and the Harrowing of Hell," *Études,* I, 462.

[12] Yovhannēs Erznkacʿi, *Meknutʿiwn* on Matt. 14:6, 319.

[13] Yovhannēs Erznkacʿi, *Meknutʿiwn* on Matt. 14:8, p. 320.

[14] Yovhannēs Erznkacʿi, *Meknutʿiwn* on Matt. 14:10, p. 321.

[15] Giuseppe Frasson, ed. and trans., *Pseudo-Epiphanii Sermo de Antichristo,* Bibliotheca Armeniaca 2 (Venice, 1976), 103, 141.

[16] Frasson, *Pseudo-Epiphanii,* 154–56. Beliar is also called *višap* on page 146.

[17] Venice, San Lazzaro 1917 (A.D. 1307), fol. 21v. See S. Der Nersessian, *Manuscrits,* fig. 105.

the demoniac possession of the two principals in the scene, Herod and Salome.

Other aspects of the iconography are also unusual. Salome's petition before Herod is rarely illustrated, and never does she appear kneeling. In Florence, Laurentiana VI, 23, fol. 29, Salome pirouettes before Herod, and he sits wearing a large turban.[18] Herod's place before a lofty domed niche, his size, and the focused attention of the guests bring him into greater prominence. He presides over and dominates the entire proceeding, and this seems to be a purposeful reworking of the subject. It is worth noting that in the *Commentary* of Yovhannēs Erznkacʿi Herod's role also underwent some revision. In the Gospel Herod appears as the reluctant collaborator in his consort's desire for revenge, for when Salome asked for John's head, "the king was sorry; but because of his oaths and his guests he commanded it to be given" (Matt. 14:9); accordingly, the Baltimore manuscript shows Herod weeping (fig. 92b). Erznkacʿi, however, proposes that the king's sorrow was only feigned. Departing from the exegesis of his mentor Chrysostom, Erznkacʿi takes his cue from Matt. 14:5, where it was said that Herod wanted to put John to death earlier but had feared the public reaction. Erznkacʿi attributes all the initiative to Herod: possessed by the devil through lust, he contrived everything; he knew Salome would dance and that he would respond with his oath; and he had prompted Herodias ahead of time to instruct her daughter to ask for John's execution.[19] Perhaps it is this kind of reading of the events that lies behind the prominence of Herod in the miniature.

The violence of the actual scene of execution contrasts sharply with standard Byzantine decapitations, in which the condemned kneels with bowed head while the executioner brings down his sword from behind.[20] The barbaric frontal assault on the prophet, his arms raised in pain and his eyes wild with dread, has no precedent in Byzantium or the West. Three parallels can be found, however, all within the ambience of the U.C.L.A. manuscript. In the southeast chapel at the church of Hagia Sophia in Trebizond (ca. 1250), the murder of Zacharias, the father of the Baptist, is shown in precisely the same frontal fashion as in our miniature, while in two manuscripts by Awag the executioner lays the sword to one side of John's neck while pulling his beard out in front.[21] One wonders if this new iconography of execution reflects actual practice, perhaps among the Mongols, or is simply the artist's way of characterizing the execution as brutal murder.

The last moment of the story in the miniature of the U.C.L.A. Gospel shows Salome delicately holding a napkin in one hand and receiving with the other the plate containing the oversized head of the Baptist. The revolting idea of serving the head on a dinner dish exercised an enormous fascination on the Christian imagination. "If we shudder at hearing these things," asks Chrysostom, "what must we suppose of the effect of that sight at the time? What of the feeling of those who sat with (Herod) at meat, on seeing blood dropping from a newly severed head in the midst of the revel?"[22] The head on the dish acquired a kind of symbolic importance even in the earliest representations of the subject. In the sixth-century Sinopensis the executioner presents an enormous oversized head to Salome,[23] and in the fragmentary Alexandrian *World Chronicle* the head on the dish was represented emblematically by itself, apart from the narrative.[24] It is this moment of the presentation of the head that was chosen for illustration in the Vehapʿaṙ Gospel (Erevan, Mat. 10780): Salome, dressed in a fantastic dancing costume, including a bird perched on her head, is about to receive the head from a soldier, who presents it on a footed dish as in the U.C.L.A. miniature (fig. 92a).

Ephraem saw a symbolic implication in the subject already in the fourth century: "Behold the head, which was placed like a lamp upon a dish, has been lighted for all generations of generations, and it accuses its murderers of adultery. This is the mouth which they silenced lest it speak any more, and the preaching of its silence has grown and blazed forth more forcefully than its voice."[25] The passage is repeated virtually verbatim by Yovhannēs Erznkacʿi. Commenting on the phrase "and (the head) was

[18] Velmans, *Le Tetraévangile*, fig. 58.

[19] Yovhannēs Erznkacʿi, *Meknutʿiwn* on Matt. 14:6–7, pp. 319–20.

[20] For Byzantine decapitations see the innumerable examples in *Il Menologio de Basilio II, Codices Vaticani* (Turin, 1907).

[21] David Talbot Rice, *The Church of Haghia Sophia at Trebizond* (Edinburgh, 1968), fig. 59. Awag's manuscripts are unpublished: Erevan, Mat. 212, fol. 52; Erevan, Mat. 6320, fol. 404v.

[22] Chrysostom, "In Matt. Hom. 48," chap. 6, *NPNF* x, p. 300.

[23] A. Muñoz, *Il Codice purpureo di Rossano*, pl. A, I.

[24] Moscow, Museum of Fine Arts, The Alexandrian World Chronicle, cf. A. Baur and J. Strzygowski, *Eine alexandrische Weltchronik*, Denkschriften der Kaiserlichen Akademie der Wissenschaften in Wien, phil.-hist. Klasse 5 (Vienna, 1905). For the history of this motif in Western art, see Hella Arndt and Renate Kroos, "Zur Ikonographie der Johannesschussel," *Aachner Kunstblätter* 38 (1946), 243–328.

[25] Ephraem, *Commentaire*, bk. 11, chap. 28, pp. 114–15.

given to the girl" (Matt. 14:11), he says further, "There was given the reason of the damnable brazenness and of the presuming shamelessness, which like a lamp was placed upon a plate, and gave light to all peoples, and put to shame the adultery of his murderers for times to come."[26] Going beyond the Gospel narrative, Erznkac'i narrates that Herodias brought the head home with her, and it lit up the house like a fire and caused her death.[27] The fatal effects of the head of John the Baptist for Herodias are also described by the contemporary Armenian poet Yovhannēs T'lkuranc'i in his work "On the Decapitation of John the Baptist."[28]

3. The Petition of the Canaanite (*Page 99*)

Christ's cure of the possessed daughter of the Canaanite woman takes him into Gentile territory in the region of Tyre and Sidon (Matt. 15:21–28). In his compulsion for completeness the painter of the Byzantine frieze Gospel, Florence, Laurentiana Plut. VI, 23, shows four distinct moments in the story: (1) the daughter in bed (Matt. 15:22); (2) a dining scene with dogs under the table (Matt. 15:26–27); (3) the Canaanite woman with arms raised in prayer (Matt. 15:22); and (4) the Canaanite prostrate at Christ's feet (Matt. 15:25).[1] From this extended narrative the Armenian frieze Gospel chose only the second moment to illustrate, that is the metaphor of the dog at the table (fig. 99b). The U.C.L.A. Gospel, however, chose another moment. The woman stands at the left before a conventional city-scape meant to represent her country of Tyre and Sidon, and she lifts her hands to call upon Christ over the heads of his disciples. "But he did not answer her a word. And his disciples came and begged him, saying, 'Send her away, for she is crying after us.' He answered, 'I was sent only to the lost sheep of the house of Israel'" (Matt. 15:23–24). Since the woman falls on her knees for her subsequent exchanges with Christ, it is clear that the illumination in the U.C.L.A. Gospel is concerned with this initial encounter between the two, and the illumination is located directly after this text. The illuminator has graphically caught the disciples' awkward situation between the persistent woman and their stubborn master. They gesture to him as they intercede on her behalf, and he turns to give his first reply.

This particular composition does not seem to have been part of the Byzantine or Western iconographic repertoire.[2] The composition derives rather from that used in the Vehap'aṙ Gospel (fig. 99a). The latter reverses the composition in Syrian fashion. Eight disciples of reduced scale gesture in unison toward Christ on the left, while he and the woman, in larger scale, converse over their heads. The discrepancy of scale is less prominent in the U.C.L.A. Gospel, but the grouping of figures is otherwise very close. In the Vehap'aṙ Gospel two extra disciples stand outside the group behind Christ, and this gives the composition a more horizontal format. Yet it was precisely such composition that the artist of the U.C.L.A. Gospel was evidently copying, for while adapting it to the vertical format he was unwilling to omit the two extra disciples and he therefore incongruously squeezed two additional faces into the group of eight, peering over the shoulders of the front row. The emphasis on Christ's encounter with the woman led Awag to omit the disciples entirely in his version of the subject thirty years later (fig. 99c).

The full-page format given the Petition of the Canaanite makes this seemingly unimportant incident an important subject in the U.C.L.A. Gospel. This special prominence finds its explanation in the Armenian exegesis of the event. Two principal themes run through East Christian commentaries on the Petition of the Canaanite Woman. The first might be called the moral lesson of the event, which is a lesson of humility, faith, and perseverance. This theme is so clear in the text of the Gospel itself that it escaped none of the commentators. Chrysostom enlarged it, adding to it, somewhat impertinently, a discourse on one of his favorite themes—what he calls "the art of almsgiving."[3]

There is another theme, however, which is more fundamental than these moral lessons. That is an ecclesiological theme, and this would seem to be the principal motive behind the iconography. The theme is first spelled out by Ephraem Syrus, who takes a

[26] Yovhannēs Erznkac'i, *Meknut'iwn* on Matt. 14:11, p. 321.

[27] Yovhannēs Erznkac'i, *Meknut'iwn* on Matt. 14:11, pp. 321–22.

[28] James R. Russell, *Yovhannēs T'lkuranc'i and the Medieval Armenian Lyric Tradition,* bachelor thesis, Faculty of Oriental Studies, Oxford, 1977, 90–92.

[1] Velmans, *Le Tétraévangile,* fig. 69.

[2] In the West this subject is one of three scenes from the story in the eleventh-century Gospel of Henry III, but the differences are more significant than the similarities. Only two disciples are shown, none of their gestures match those of the U.C.L.A. Gospel, and the woman is bent over, perhaps through some confusion with the cure of the bent woman in Luke 13:10–17. Escorial, Real Biblioteca, Cod. Vetrinas 17, fol. 39v; Schiller, *Iconography of Christian Art,* I, pl. 546.

[3] Chrysostom, "In Matt. Hom. 52," *NPNF* x, pp. 321–26.

"recognition" as his point of departure. According to Ephraem, Christ is the second "Jesus" to visit the Canaanites; the first was Joshua, at whose appearance an unclean spirit entered the Canaanites and incited them to take up arms against him (cf. Num. 13–14). But when the second Jesus came they recognized him as having the same features and acknowledged him as savior. Thereupon the unclean spirit left them and entered instead into Israel.[4]

This providential reversal of the roles of Jew and Gentile is of course a persistent theme in Christian ecclesiology, starting with St. Paul (cf. Rom. 9–11; Gal. 1–6). The Canaanite woman came to be a symbol of this mystery among East Christian exegetes. Chrysostom understands this as the meaning intended in Christ's allusion to Israel as "children" and to Gentiles as "dogs." But in a manner uncharacteristic of his moralizing mode Chrysostom cites a strictly allegorical interpretation of the event: "Some also taking it as an allegory say that when Christ came out of Judea, then the church ventured to approach him, coming out herself also from her own coasts. For it is said, 'Forget thine own people and thy father's house' (Ps. 45:10). For both Christ went out of his borders, and the woman out of her borders, and so it became possible for them to fall in with each other."[5] That such an exegesis is still current in fourteenth-century Glajor is attested by Yovhannēs Erznkacʿi, who enlarges on Chrysostom's allegory. To the exegete of Glajor the meeting of Christ with the Canaanite involves not just an excursion from Judea but the fundamental purpose of his incarnation.

> There were some who interpreted it in another way in saying that since the Word came from the Father and entered the world, in like manner also the Church of the Gentiles went out of its regions and took courage to come and approach him. Wherefore (the psalmist) says, "Forget your people and your father's house; the king desires your beauty" (Ps. 45:10). For if she were to remain in her own region she could not cry out before the Lord and seek mercy. Thus the Gentiles glorified God on account of his mercy, for their offspring that was cruelly possessed, having been made mad in the sacrifice of demons, obtained mercy through the coming of the Word.[6]

In the light of this exegetical tradition the representation in the U.C.L.A. Gospel takes on special significance. Narrative details, such as the daughter's illness, are omitted, as is the manifestation of the woman's humility in falling at Christ's feet. Instead it is the moment of the encounter that has been singled out. The woman, symbol of the Church of the Gentiles, has recognized her savior and calls out for deliverance. Leaving the idolatry of Tyre and Sidon, she will become the mystical spouse of the Word.[7]

4. Peter Receives the Keys (*Page 103*)

The image of Peter hardly requires extensive analysis. The facial type of the apostle with short grey hair and beard was already nearly a thousand years old when the Glajor Gospel was painted, and his attribute of the keys was a motif of equal antiquity.[1] The simplicity of the image is its most striking characteristic; Peter alone, against a plain blue background, is made to serve as illustration of Christ's conferral of authority in Matt. 16:13–20. In Armenia there was a tradition of illustrating this passage with the static, emblematic figure of the Apostle, rather than narratively.[2] In the Vehapʿaṙ Gospel Peter is represented seated, cross-legged in oriental fashion, clasping a book with both hands, enframed by a church (fig. 103a). The Zeytun Gospel by Tʿoros Roslin (1256) shows a bust of St. Peter enshrined in a diminutive Armenian church (fig. 103b), and this iconography is picked up in Vienna, Mekhitarist 278, later in the century.[3] The U.C.L.A. miniature stands within this tradition, though the church has been dropped from the image.

Given the presence of Latin missionaries in Armenia, one might be tempted by the possibility that this Petrine iconography reflects Roman insistence on

[4] Ephraem explains: "When Jesus came, by the true faith of the Canaanites he threw the unclean spirit out of the girl, who herself is the image of the Canaanite people. And they through the name of Jesus abandoned the polytheism of idols. But if you look at Israelites today you will find that all the wrath and viciousness and anger and hatred and envy of the Gentiles has taken possession of them." Ephraem Syrus, *Commentaire*, bk. 13, chap. 14, pp. 121–22.

[5] Chrysostom, "In Matt. Hom. 52," chap. 1, *NPNF* x, p. 321.

[6] Yovhannēs Erznkacʿi, *Meknutʿiwn* on Matt. 15:22, p. 337.

[7] The eighth-century theologian Grigoris Aršaruni in his discussion of Joshua identifies the "prince of Tyre and Sidon" as Satan himself. L. M. Froidevaux, *Grigoris Aršarouni, Commentaire du Lectionnaire* (Venice, 1975), 21, 66.

[1] H. Leclercq, "Pierre," *DACL* 14, 935–71.

[2] For the narrative mode of representing the subject see the Florence frieze Gospel, Laurentiana, Plut. VI,23, fol. 33v. Velmans, *Le Tétraévangile*, fig. 74.

[3] Istanbul, Armenian Patriarchate, Zeytun Gospel, described in Der Nersessian, *Études*, 560; Vienna, Mekhitarist 278, fol. 58v, described in Buschhausen, *Die illuminierten armenischen Handschriften*, 48.

the primacy of the pope. (It should be noted that Peter appears in over half of the narrative scenes of the U.C.L.A. Gospel, making him the most repeated figure after Christ.) However, Der Nersessian cites the resistance of the Armenian catholicos Constantine to the doctrine of papal supremacy in correspondence of 1248 and 1263.[4] Moreover, the Armenian interest in Peter in the Vehapʿaṙ Gospel antedates the Roman issue. This suggests one look instead to the special importance of Peter in the Armenian church, which must underlie the U.C.L.A. iconography.

In the Armenian liturgy the text of Matt. 16:14–19 is used frequently, and is taken as a basic ecclesiological statement applying both to the Christian church at large and to the church in Armenia. It occurs as the Gospel reading of Mass on three different occasions in the church calendar: the Third Sunday after Easter, which is called Universal Sunday; the Feast of the Holy Church; and the Feast of the Glory of Ējmiacin, commemorating the founding of that church.[5] The text is also read in the ceremony of consecrating every church.[6]

In Syro-Armenian exegesis the conferral of authority on Peter is directly connected with the theme enunciated in the Genealogy, that is the continuity of the priesthood of the church with that of the Old Testament. Murray has explored the Syriac sources dealing with the two basic images involved in this episode, namely the keys and the rock.[7] According to Ephraem Syrus the "keys of priesthood and prophecy" were held by the last priests of the Old Law, Simeon (of Luke 2:25 ff) and John the Baptist; the transmission of the keys to Christ and then to Peter marked the passing of the tradition from the Jews to the Gentiles. "The keys, therefore, which he (i.e., Christ) received from Simeon the priest he gave to 'Simeon' the Apostle, so that even if the Nation would not 'listen to' the former Simeon, the Nations should 'listen to' the other 'Simeon.' But since John was also a treasurer, of baptism, to him also came the Lord of stewardship, to receive from him the keys of the House of Absolution."[8] The authority that Christ received from the Levitical line was passed on to Peter, on whom was built the church, the "House of Absolution." The recipient of this authority, Ephraem understood, was not Peter alone, but the Apostles and the bishops of the church in their plurality.[9]

On the other hand the metaphor of rock contained in Simon's new name, Peter, was especially rich in associations in Syriac, according to Murray; for the same word could mean stones, whether small or large, rocks, cliffs, or precious stones.[10] According to Ephraem, Peter is the rock of foundation on which will be built a tower to heaven that will replace the old tower of Babel, which served to divide nations. It is a foundation that will resist all floods and a stone on which Satan will stumble.[11]

The same thought patterns underlie the commentary on the text of Matt. 16:13–19 in *The Teaching of Saint Gregory:*

> He made him (i.e., Peter) the rock of establishment of all the churches. And the apostles became the foundations, and received the grace of priesthood and prophecy and apostleship and knowledge of the heavenly mystery which came in the seed of Abraham, which John, the keeper of the tradition of the inheritance, gave to the Lord, and the Lord gave to the apostles. And he gave the keys of the kingdom into their hands. . . . So John gave the priesthood and the power and the prophecy and the kingship to our Saviour Christ: and Christ gave them to the apostles, and the apostles to the children of the church.[12]

Peter, then, is the crucial link between the priesthood of the Old Testament and that of the New. A relic of the saint was kept in Lambron, according to Ališan, and when Ošin established himself there in 1073 he built a chapel for the relic and dedicated Lambron and the entire province to St. Peter.[13]

5. The Transfiguration (*Page 106*)

The Transfiguration constituted one of the most popular subjects of Christian art. In Byzantium it constituted one of the so-called "festival" scenes, and it had a fairly rigid iconography. Although in the Cilician period the Armenian iconography of the subject generally conformed to the Byzantine, earlier Ar-

[4] Der Nersessian, *Arm. Mss. Freer,* 50–51.
[5] *Čašocʿ Girkʿ,* nos. 112, 223, and 255.
[6] Tiran Nersoyan, *Order of Blessing of the Foundation of a Church,* with translation by Mesrob Semerjian (New York, 1953), 76.
[7] Murray, *Symbols,* 182–87, 205–38.
[8] Ibid., 182–87, citing Ephraem's homily "On Our Lord," chaps. 54–55 (CSCO 270, Syr. 116, p. 51).
[9] Murray, *Symbols,* 184.
[10] Murray, *Symbols,* 205–6.
[11] Ephraem Syrus, *Commentaire,* pp. 185–86.
[12] *Teaching of St. Gregory,* chaps. 467–68 (ed. Thomson, pp. 105–6).
[13] Łewond Ališan, *Sissouan ou Arméno-Cilicie. Description géographique et historique* (Venice, 1899), 80.

menia preserved a certain amount of iconographic independence, which is all the more remarkable considering the central importance of the subject. The U.C.L.A. Gospel presents an unusually cogent statement of Armenian iconography. The understanding of the subject here must be sought in its theological implications rather than in the liturgy, for Matthew's account of the Transfiguration in 17:1–8 is never used in the Armenian liturgy; instead, the feast of the Transfiguration takes its text from Luke 9:27–36.[1]

The standard Byzantine iconography of the Transfiguration presents a white-clad Christ in a mandorla blessing with his right hand and holding a scroll in his left, as in the Queen Keṙan Gospel (fig. 106a).[2] To either side on the mountain, or sometimes on separate little peaks, stand the youthful Moses, on the viewer's right, and Elijah wearing sheepskin on the left. Below, the three privileged apostles react to the vision in various ways: Peter, generally on the left, rises on one knee gesturing toward the vision; John falls on his face; and James turns away in amazement. This iconography remained fairly constant in Byzantine art with few variations; in the Palaeologan period a new sense of drama was added by shattering the mandorla into prismatic shapes and making apostles fall headlong from the mountain. The U.C.L.A. Gospel departs from the Byzantine scheme in several notable details: Moses and Elijah are reversed; the apostles all fall on the ground, only Peter lifting his head; a pair of trees spring up from the mountain behind Christ; a dove spreads its wings over the mandorla; and the hand of God appears from a segment of heaven above. This combination of variants poses a curious problem for the art historian, for if one traces the visual sources of the motifs singly, they lead in many different directions and it is impossible to reconstruct a clear picture of how the present iconography emerged. Yet if one pursues the meaning of motifs they all converge and find their explanations in a fairly unified Armenian interpretation of the subject.

One might begin with the least important detail, the reversal of Moses and Elijah. In contrast to the standard Byzantine iconography, Moses stands on Christ's right in our miniature. The theological implications are not enormous, but this arrangement may reflect an Early Christian iconography that for some reason was abandoned. Some of the earliest Byzantine manuscripts of the Macedonian period place Moses on Christ's right[3] and this is common in the frescoes of Cappadocia.[4] The Armenian frieze Gospel also chose to place Moses on Christ's right, even though its Byzantine model was the other way (fig. 106d).[5] Logically this is the more correct arrangement, insofar as Moses is the senior of the two and the lawgiver of Israel. Yovhannēs Erznkacʿi seems to have understood this propriety. Among the many meanings Erznkacʿi finds in the presence of Moses and Elijah is an answer (by anticipation) of the petition of the Zebedees (illustrated in the U.C.L.A. Gospel on *page 122*). "The sons of Zebedee requested glory, one of them (to be) on the right and one on the left; and he said 'It is not for me to give to those to whom it has been given by my Father.' Because of this Moses appeared on the right and Elijah on the left, that they might see that it is necessary first to share in the sufferings, as they had done, and after in the glory."[6]

Trees seem unlikely on a mountaintop and uncalled for by the text of the Gospel. They occur only occasionally in Byzantine versions of the scene, such as the Paris Gregory,[7] where they are clearly palm trees with clusters of dates, or in some eleventh-century lectionaries.[8] In the frescoed churches of Cappadocia, however, more often than not the Transfiguration includes trees,[9] and in Armenian art trees also figure frequently.[10] Particularly interesting is the independent iconographic tradition of Armenia, in which the subject is developed asymmetrically, with Moses and Elijah standing to one side of Christ and the apostles prostrate on the other (fig. 106b).[11]

[1] *Čašocʿ Girkʿ*, 198.

[2] On the iconography of the Transfiguration, see Millet, *Iconographie*, 216–31 and Schiller, *Iconography of Christian Art*, I, 145–52.

[3] Paris, B.N. gr. 510, fol. 75, H. Omont, *Miniatures des plus anciens manuscrits grecs de la Bibliothèque Nationale* (Paris, 1929), pl. 28; Moscow, History Museum, ms. 129D, fol. 88v, M. B. Ščepkina, *Miniatjura Khludovskoj Psaltyri* (Moscow, 1977), 88v.

[4] M. Restle, *Byzantine Wall Painting in Asia Minor*, trans. I. R. Gibbons (Greenwich, Conn., 1967), II, pls. 175, 204, 231; III, pl. 50.

[5] Velmans, *Le Tétraévangile*, fig. 76.

[6] Yovhannēs Erznkacʿi, *Meknutʿiwn* on Matt. 17:3, p. 361.

[7] Paris, B.N. gr. 510, fol. 75, Omont, *Miniatures*, pl. 28.

[8] Athos, Iviron 1, fol. 296v, S. M. Pelikanidis et al., *The Treasures of Mount Athos, Illuminated Manuscripts*, trans. P. Sherrard (Athens, 1974–75), 2, fig. 5; Athos, Rossikon 2, fol. 252v.

[9] Restle, *Byzantine Wall Painting*, II, pls. 13, 30, 53, 175, 231, and III, pl. 303.

[10] For examples see the following: Erevan, Mat. 7736, Mułni Gospel, of the 11th century, in Izmailova, *Arm. miniatjura XI veka*, fig. 100; Washington, Freer 50.5, fol. 100, Der Nersessian, *Arm. Mss. Freer*, fig. 14; Baltimore, Walters 539, of 1262, fol. 163, Der Nersessian, *Arm. Mss. Walters*, pl. 64.

[11] Four examples of this iconography are known, all in Erevan: (1) Mat. 6201 (A.D. 1038), fol. 6, Izmailova, *Arm.*

Trees—one, two, or three—always accompany this iconography and one of them is sometimes heavily laden with fruit and labeled "The Tree," meaning the Tree of Life in the Garden of Eden. This may sound as though the artist is confused about the location, but Yovhannēs Erznkacʿi offers an explanation. The identity of the mountain in the story, he points out, is the subject of considerable speculation, some claiming it was Mt. Sion, others Sinai, and others Thabor. But, he goes on, "Some say—with whom I too am in agreement—the high mountain is Paradise because it is higher than the world, equal with the luminous hosts, surrounded alone by Cherubim, and separated by fiery sword from the nature of terrestrial beings. For the vision was as proof of the Resurrection, and it is nothing else than the establishment of the first glory of the Resurrection; hence he showed to the apostles, by bringing them there, the mystery of the Resurrection."[12] The connection is so obvious to Erznkacʿi that he does not have to supply the steps. The Resurrection is the reestablishment of man in the state of his first glory; but the Transfiguration is a vision of the Resurrection; therefore the proper location of the Transfiguration must be Paradise.

This kind of exegesis is a world apart from the sober moralizing of John Chrysostom. True to his Antiochene education, Chrysostom limits his theological speculation on the Transfiguration to what is most directly asserted by the Gospel text, namely, the divine sonship of Christ. "This is my beloved Son, with whom I am well pleased," said the voice from the cloud (Matt. 17:5). "Not because he begat him only, does he love him," comments Chrysostom, "but because he is also equal to him in all respects, and of one mind with him."[13] Beyond this the event is interpreted as a strengthening of the apostles for the trial of Christ's passion, and both the apostles and the prophets are seen as examples of zeal and devotion.[14]

By contrast, the Syrian and Armenian commentators tend instead to see each Gospel event in the largest possible dimensions of "salvation-history," as if everything were simultaneous in the divine perspective. The time machine of modern science fiction was a reality to the East Christian world view. Both past and future are telescoped in the vision of the Transfiguration, so that the believer should see here Christ's coming Resurrection and the restoration of Adam to his primitive Paradise. When the fabric of time becomes so fragile, themes of recognition and identification become correspondingly more important. Hence in the Canaanite's Petition, Jesus was Joshua returned, and he was identified as such by the already converted Gentiles. Recognitions figure in the present subject as well. Christ appears now in glory so that when he shall return after his Resurrection he will be recognized by the apostles as truly the same and not some phantasm.[15] At the same time, the recognitions work in the reverse direction: Moses and Elijah stand beside Christ to witness that he is the very same Lord whom they had seen face to face, one in the vision of the burning bush, the other in the whispering breeze.[16]

Most important for the interpretation of the U.C.L.A. miniature is the unusual insertion of the hand of God and the dove. Symbol of God the Father, the hand is never used in Byzantine Transfigurations, and is rare in Western art in this connection.[17] In Armenia, however, in the early fourteenth century, painters frequently included the hand of God (figs. 106c–e). The dove, on the other hand, is quite unprecedented. The unusualness of the iconography makes the tracing of the motifs to hypothetical sources particularly unfruitful, but it also makes the added layers of meaning seem all the more deliberate.

On one level the addition of the hand and the dove can be read as making a trinitarian statement. Neither Chrysostom nor Ephraem look for such implications in the Transfiguration, but Yovhannēs Erznkacʿi sees the mystery of the Trinity behind Peter's words, "Lord, it is well that we are here; if you wish, I will make three booths here, one for you and one for Moses and one for Elijah" (Matt. 17:4.). According to Erznkacʿi, Peter recognized the Trinity in the Vision—the Father manifest by his voice, the Son by his Transfiguration, and the Spirit by the protecting

miniatjura XI veka, fig. 25; (2) Mat. 4814 (1294), fol. 2, L. Zakʿaryan, pl. 7; (3) Mat. 4806 (1306), fol. 7, ibid., pl. 8; (4) Mat. 10780, fol. 44v, Izmailova, "Vehapaṙi Avetaranə," fig. on page 46.

[12] Yovhannēs Erznkacʿi, *Meknutʿiwn* on Matt. 17:1, p. 358.

[13] Chrysostom, "In Matt. Hom. 56," chap. 5, *NPNF* x, p. 348.

[14] Ibid., chap. 2–7, pp. 345–49.

[15] Ephraem, *Commentaire*, bk. 13, chap. 6, p. 136; Yovhannēs Erznkacʿi, *Meknutʿiwn* on Matt. 17:2, p. 359.

[16] Ephraem, *Commentaire*, bk. 13, chap. 8, p. 137; Yovhannēs Erznkacʿi, *Meknutʿiwn* on Matt. 17:3, p. 360. This theme of the recognition is found as well in the *Teaching of St. Gregory*, in which we learn that the authentic image of the Lord was revealed to Adam so that his descendants would recognize him in his successive manifestations. *Teaching of St. Gregory*, chaps. 264, 328, 330 (ed. Thomson, pp. 43, 64, 65). Further discussion of this theme in Mathews, "The Genesis Frescoes of Ałtʿamar," 245–57.

[17] In Western developments of the Transfiguration, the hand of God occurs in the apse mosaic of S. Apollinare in Classe and occasionally in Ottonian art. Schiller, *Iconography*, I, figs. 405, 416.

cloud.[18] Chrysostom had taken the cloud rather as the standard symbol of the Father from its Old Testament precedents,[19] and this symbolism is developed in the Armenian liturgy as well.[20] Erznkacʿi repeats Chrysostom's exegesis on this point but adds his own. The luminous cloud, he says, means the Holy Spirit, which is the true light that enlightens every man coming into this world.[21] The way the dove spreads its wings to embrace the mandorla in our miniature may be intended by the iconographer as a way of identifying the mandorla as the cloud and as the Holy Spirit.

Yet another layer of meaning may be uncovered, for as strange as this iconography is for the Transfiguration, the hand and the dove are standard in representations of the Baptism, and one may assume that the missing U.C.L.A. miniature of the Baptism included them.[22] It is important to note that the Father's message is identical on the two occasions. At the Baptism, when John saw the dove of the Spirit descend on Christ, the Father proclaimed, "This is my beloved Son with whom I am well pleased" (Matt. 3:17). The very same words are repeated at the Transfiguration, with the addition: "Listen to him" (Matt. 17:5). Commenting on the latter, Yovhannēs Erznkacʿi interprets the words as a correction to Peter, who had not received the message when it was delivered at the Jordan but had tried to oppose Christ's plan for man's redemption.[23] The repetition of the same message must have seemed to the artist to require a repetition of the same iconography.

The iconography must be linked to a third subject in the U.C.L.A. Gospel, namely, Christ Reading in the Synagogue of Nazareth (*page 327*), in which the dove is seen descending on Christ as he reads from Isaiah the text, "The spirit of the Lord is upon me because he has anointed me to preach good news to the poor" (Luke 4:21). In view of Christ's subsequent announcement, "Today this scripture has been fulfilled in your hearing," (Luke 4:21) the iconographer felt called upon to illustrate the fulfillment of the prophecy and show the dove descending on Christ before his listeners.

This triple representation of the Holy Spirit hovering over Christ is entirely unprecedented and cannot be without purpose. The U.C.L.A. Gospel's concern with these three passages must be connected with the survival in Armenia of one of the earliest christological positions, a position which Harnack named "adoptionism." In this view, according to Harnack, "Jesus is regarded as the man whom God has elected for his own, the one in whom the Deity or the Spirit of God dwelt, and who, after being tested, was adopted by God and endowed with full dominion."[24] In authentic adoptionism, developed by the theologians of Antioch before the first ecumenical councils framed the issue in Greek philosophical terms, Christ was not seen as divine from his birth but was divinized through his anointing by the Holy Spirit at his Baptism. Accordingly, the three passages under discussion were of critical interest to this theology. Although the adoptionist position came to be identified with Nestorianism and was condemned in Orthodox circles, in Armenia an adoptionist Christology remained alive throughout the Middle Ages within the sect of the Paulicians, also referred to as the Tʿondrakecʿikʿ. In her exhaustive analysis of the Armenian sources concerning this movement, Garsoïan has been able to trace the continuity of Paulicianism with Syrian adoptionism and its survival, in some mitigated form, down to the nineteenth century.[25] The classic statement of Paulician doctrine is found in the *Key of Truth,* a document tentatively dated around the seventh to the ninth centuries: "But the (created) man Jesus knew his Father, and by the inspiration of the Holy Spirit came to St. John in all gentleness and humility to be baptized by him. And at the same time he was crowned by the almighty Father, who said: 'Yonder is my well-loved son in whom I am well pleased.' . . . Forasmuch as the (created) man Jesus became very faithful to his Father, for this reason, the Father bestowed upon him a name of praise which is above every name."[26] Or, in another section one reads: "So then it was in the season of his maturity that he received baptism; then it was that he received authority, received the high priesthood, received the

[18] Yovhannēs Erznkacʿi, *Meknutʿiwn* on Matt. 17:14, p. 363.

[19] Chrysostom, "In Matt. Hom. 56," chap. 5, *NPNF* x, p. 348.

[20] Yovhannēs Erznkacʿi, *Meknutʿiwn* on Matt. 17:5, p. 364.

[21] Ibid.

[22] Schiller, *Iconography of Christian Art,* I, 127–43, figs. 346–88.

[23] Yovhannēs Erznkacʿi, *Meknutʿiwn* on Matt. 17:5, p. 365.

[24] Adolf von Harnack, *Lehrbuch der Dogmengeschichte,* 5th ed. (Tübingen, 1931–32), I, 21.

[25] Nina G. Garsoïan, *The Paulician Heresy: A Study of the Origin and Development of Paulicianism in Armenia and the Eastern Provinces of the Byzantine Empire* (The Hague, 1967). On the early stages of this development, see also Gabriele Winkler, "Eine bemerkenswerte Stelle im armenischen Glaubensbekenntnis: Credimus et in Spiritum Sanctum qui descendit in Jordanem proclamavit missum," *Oriens Christianus* 63 (1979), 130–620.

[26] *Banali Čšmartutʿean (The Key of Truth),* ed. and trans. F. C. Conybeare (Oxford, 1898), chaps. 79–80, pp. 11–12; quoted in Garsoïan, *The Paulician Heresy,* 152. On the date of the *Key of Truth,* see Garsoïan, ibid., 108.

kingdom and the office of chief shepherd. . . . Nay more, it was then he became chief of beings heavenly and earthly, then he became the light of the world, then he became the way, the truth and the life."[27]

Repeated condemnations of this position, such as that by the last king of Ani, Gagik II (1042–45), testify to the continued popularity of this belief,[28] but the question is how seriously such notions were being entertained by the painters of the U.C.L.A. Gospel.

Remarkably enough, there is further strong evidence of adoptionist leanings in the program of the manuscript. It is worth noting that those subjects that would serve to correct an adoptionist interpretation by insisting on Christ's divinity already in his infancy—namely, the Nativity and the Adoration of the Magi—are subjects that have been omitted from the U.C.L.A. Gospel. Significantly, they were omitted as well in the program model of the manuscript, the Vehapʿaṙ Gospel, in the early eleventh century. In view of the known orthodoxy of the vardapets of Glajor, it would be difficult to imagine that the Paulician position was being seriously entertained in the monastery. Yet the unsettled conditions of Armenia under Mongol rule led Armenians from many different parts of the country to seek refuge in Glajor, and among these displaced persons there may well have been Paulicians. Perhaps one should see this iconography as evidence of survival and conservatism rather than a deliberate and conscious effort to promote a heterodox position. In Armenia theology seems to have grown by a process of addition rather than a dialectic of rejection, so that archaic elements end up coexisting with later formulae with which they are logically inconsistent. Other manuscripts of Glajor have no hesitation about including the Nativity and the Adoration of the Magi, and the peculiar iconography of this Transfiguration does not reappear.

6. The Cure of the Epileptic (*Page 108*)

The next four scenes of the U.C.L.A. Gospel follow very closely the iconography of the Vehapʿaṙ Gospel. For the Cure of the Epileptic the scribe left the bottom third of the page free, providing space for a low horizontal miniature. At the left Christ, seated against a panel of gold, addresses the father of the epileptic; the latter kneels at the right and points his index finger towards his son. The boy is shown falling in wild frenzy, his limbs flailing in all directions.

[27] *Banali Čšmartutʿean* chap. 6, p. 75; Garsoïan, *The Paulician Heresy,* 153.

[28] Garsoïan, *The Paulician Heresy,* 159.

He wears white pyjamas with a chain around his waist, a reference to their inability to restrain him from throwing himself into fire and water (Matt. 17:15).[1] The miniature is marred by a diagonal scratch and a fold.

That this composition comes from the tradition of the Vehapʿaṙ Gospel needs little proof (fig. 108a). Christ has been seated to fit the low format of the miniature, but the other two figures are virtually identical in pose. The connection is strengthened by the absence of close parallels in Byzantine and Western art. In the West, contrary to the Gospel text, it is the son who kneels before Christ and begs for deliverance; the devil is shown clutching the boy by the neck.[2] In Byzantine art the father sometimes leads the son to Christ and sometimes stands and looks on as he does in the Armenian frieze Gospel (fig. 108b).[3] The dress of the boy in white pyjamas also appears in the Rockefeller McCormick New Testament, Chicago 2400/965.[4]

The commentators draw several lessons from the Cure of the Epileptic, chiefly concerned with faith.[5] The fact that Christ's disciples were unable to cast out the epileptic's devil is attributed to their lack of faith; faith, Christ explains, is so potent that a measure of faith as small as a mustard seed can move a mountain (Matt. 17:20). But our miniature focuses rather on Christ's exchange with the epileptic's father, which is bypassed in Byzantine iconography. Christ's reaction to the father's plea is an emotion-charged rebuke: "O faithless and perverse generation, how long am I to be with you?" (Matt. 17:17). This Chrysostom and Erznkacʿi interpret in an anti-Semitic sense as condemning the perverse Jews in general for their failure to believe Christ.[6] At the same time, Christ's impatience with them is interpreted as his longing for

[1] The Rockefeller McCormick New Testament and Leningrad State Library 105 show the Gadarene demoniac in white pyjamas. Cf. E. J. Goodspeed and H. R. Willoughby, *The Rockefeller McCormick New Testament* (Chicago, 1932), I, fol. 42, and III, pl. 39.

[2] See London, B.M. Harley 1526–27, II, fol. 32v. A. de Laborde, *La Bible Moralisée,* 3, pl. 503.

[3] For further Byzantine examples see Athos, Iviron 5, fol. 177v, Pelikanidis, *Treasures of Mount Athos,* 2, fig. 35; Florence, Laurentiana Plut. VI 23, fols. 35v, 80v, 125v, Velmans, *Le Tétraévangile,* figs. 78, 157, 216. The father kneels in Ṙoslin's Washington, Freer, 32.18; Der Nersessian, *Arm. Mss. Freer,* fig. 84.

[4] Goodspeed and Willoughby, *The Rockefeller McCormick New Testament,* I, fols. 19v and 42. See discussion in Annemarie Weyl Carr, *The Rockefeller McCormick New Testament.*

[5] Chrysostom, "In Matt. Hom. 57," chaps. 3–4, *NPNF* x, pp. 354–56; Yovhannēs Erznkacʿi, *Meknutʿiwn* on Matt. 17:14–21, pp. 370–73.

[6] Chrysostom, "In Matt. Hom. 57," chap. 3, *NPNF* x, p. 354; Yovhannēs Erznkacʿi, *Meknutʿiwn* on Matt. 17:17, p. 372.

his passion. "When he said, 'How long shall I be with you,' he indicated again death to be welcomed to him, and an object of desire, and his departure longed for, and that not crucifixion but being with them is grievous."[7] Hence the miniature, while carrying an instruction in the virtue of faith, also carries a premonition of Christ's fateful conflict with the Jews, which was to result in his own death.

7. The Blessing of the Children (*Page 117*)

Both the iconography and the exegesis of this subject depart significantly from the Gospel text. The touching lesson of the children is told in three simple verses. "Then the children were brought to him that he might lay his hands on them and pray. The disciples rebuked the people; but Jesus said, 'Let the children come to me, and do not hinder them; for to such belongs the kingdom of heaven.' And he laid his hands on them and went away" (Matt. 19:13–15). The lesson is plain, and Chrysostom explains it with little embellishment: "Teaching (the disciples) to be lowly, and to trample under foot worldly pride, He receives them. . . . This is the limit to true wisdom: to be simple with understanding; this is angelic life; yes, for the soul of a little child is pure from all the passions."[1] Surprisingly, this is not the lesson that the U.C.L.A. Gospel would have one draw from the incident.

In medieval art the Blessing of the Children is shown in a variety of ways.[2] Sometimes the composition reads from side to side and sometimes it is centrally organized, with Christ standing, or even enthroned, in the center.[3] The parents are often shown carrying and pushing forward their children toward Christ, as in the charming miniature in the Gospel in Baltimore (fig. 117b). In the Florence Gospel the disciples are shown trying to restrain the children, though this is not reflected in the Armenian frieze Gospel, where the parents are in front of the disciples (fig. 117c).[4] But contrary to the text of the Gospel, and contrary to the iconographic traditions of the scene elsewhere, the U.C.L.A. Gospel shows the disciples presenting the children. Peter seems to push the second of the two children forward in a composition that repeats very closely the corresponding miniature of the Vehapʿaṙ Gospel (fig. 117a). In the latter a certain ecclesiastical character is given to the scene by dressing two apostles in stoles. A similar note is struck in the U.C.L.A. Gospel by showing both Peter and, unexpectedly, the first of the children, tonsured.

The cutting or shaving of all or part of a man's hair was from early Christian times a sign of dedication to the Lord, whether in the monastic state or in the ranks of the clergy.[5] One of the first references to the custom is the mention of the tonsure of St. Euthymius when he was ordained lector in Melitene in Lesser Armenia in 379. But Christian piety traced the origins of the custom back to St. Peter, whose hair was cut in derision by his captors, according to a text in Sophronius of Jerusalem. Hence in medieval art Peter is often shown tonsured, and in the U.C.L.A. Gospel he has a tonsure in seven of the scenes.[6] But to explain the tonsure of the child, as well as the reversal of roles whereby the apostles present the children to Christ, we must appeal to the exegesis of Yovhannēs Erznkacʿi.

The fact that Christ received the children provides a lesson in meekness, according to Erznkacʿi; but the fact that he laid his hands on them to bless them indicates that he was thereby ordaining the next generation of priests.

> He gave the grace of priesthood and prophecy by the laying-on of hands, by which he called them to his discipleship; for as Elijah put his mantle on Elisha and left him everything and he followed him, so also those children, having been strengthened by the hands of the lord and having arrived at the age of maturity, became preachers of the gospel, and apostles of the savior, and even became martyrs for him; one of them was Ignatius, the God-bearing, who like sacred grain was ground by the teeth of beasts and he was found to be the holy bread of God.[7]

[7] Chrysostom, "In Matt. Hom. 57," chap. 3, *NPNF* x, p. 354.

[1] Chrysostom, "In Matt. Hom. 62," chap. 4, *NPNF* x, p. 385.

[2] Schiller, *Iconography of Christian Art,* I, 157; J. Siebert, "Kindersegnung Jesu," *Lexikon der christlichen Ikonographie,* II, 514.

[3] For the central composition see Paris, B.N. gr. 74, fols. 38, 85, 148, Omont, *Évangiles byzantins,* pls. 32, 75, 128; London, B.L. Add. 39627,1, fols. 57 and 113v, B. D. Filov, *Les miniatures de l'évangile du roi Jean Alexandre à Londres* (Sofia, 1934), pls. 26, 54.

[4] Florence, Laurentiana, Plut. VI 23, fols. 39, 82, 147, Velmans, *Le Tétraévangile,* figs. 84, 159, 246.

[5] H. Leclercq, "Tonsure," *DACL* 15, 2, 2429–43. For the tradition of tonsure in Armenia, see Otto F. A. Meinardus, "The Use of the Tonsura and Razura by the Armenian Clergy during the Safawid Dynasty," *REArm,* n. s. 12 (1977), 365–69.

[6] See miniatures on *pages 99, 216, 336, 438, 453, 570.*

[7] Yovhannēs Erznkacʿi, *Meknutʿiwn* on Matt. 19:15, p. 406.

The reference is to the famous bishop and martyr, St. Ignatius of Antioch (ca. 35–107), who expressed a passionate longing for martyrdom: "Suffer me to become food for the wild beasts, through whose instrumentality it will be granted me to attain God. I am the wheat of God, and let me be ground by the teeth of the wild beasts, that I may be found pure bread of Christ."[8] It is by the imposition of hands, Erznkacʿi goes on to say, that the church itself is constituted, whether in the ranks of the laity, deaconate, or priesthood, for the imposition of hands confers the grace of the Holy Spirit.[9] Christ in the miniature, then, is not bestowing a simple blessing, but is ordaining priests to secure the continuity of his work in the church. To Armenians, moreover, Ignatius of Antioch had a special importance, for it was he, according to the abbot of Glajor, Esayi, who added to the Trisagion hymn the controversial clause, "Who was crucified for us."[10] The miniature, therefore, contains an implied guarantee of the apostolic authenticity of Armenian traditions in the face of their challenge by the Latins.

8. The Petition of the Mother of James and John (*Page 122*)

The ecclesiological themes enunciated in the preceding miniatures are further developed in the present subject. The request of Zebedee's wife on behalf of her sons, James and John, raises the question of authority in the church: "Command that these two sons of mine may sit, one at your right hand and one at your left, in your kingdom" (Matt. 20:21). Christ's response distinguishes his kingdom from the political states of the present world in which lords vie one another for positions of authority. "Whoever would be great among you must be your servant, and whoever would be first among you must be your slave; even as the Son of man came not to be served but to serve, and to give his life as a ransom for many" (Matt. 20:27–28).

Simple though it be, there are a number of ways of representing this subject. In some representations the apostles' mother is omitted, as she is indeed in the parallel narrative of Mark (10:35–45).[1] There also exists a curious tradition in which the sons of Zebedee's wife are mistaken for children; this occurs in the West and is picked up in Armenia by Awag, who shows them carrying scepters (fig. 122d).[2] However, the usual Byzantine tradition shows Christ seated to one side while the apostles' mother and her sons approach, all standing. This is the iconography that Erevan, Mat. 7651 copies from the Byzantine frieze Gospel, Florence, Laur. Plut. VI, 23 (fig. 122c).[3] The Vehapʿaṙ Gospel, on the other hand, shows the mother kneeling before a standing Christ (fig. 122a), and this is the way the figures are shown in the famous Cilician manuscript, Washington, Freer 32.18 (fig. 122b) as well as in the U.C.L.A. Gospel. The change in postures points to a greater interest in a literal fidelity to the text, since Matthew refers to the mother as kneeling; but it also points to the existence of an independent Armenian tradition of representing the subject. Judging from the frequency with which the theme is illustrated in Armenian manuscripts, it must have had a special importance in Armenia.[4]

Chrysostom in his commentary on this passage does not take the subject further than the obvious lesson in humility and the necessity of suffering.[5] However, in the commentaries of Ephraem Syrus and Yovhannēs Erznkacʿi the subject is used rather as a lesson in collegial harmony in the church.[6] The petition of James and John springs from naïveté: having been shown the throne of Christ in his Transfiguration they wanted places of honor near to Christ. Elsewhere Ephraem even blesses their ambition: "That body (of the brethren) was composed of disciples, And the sons of Zebedee were its eyes. Blessed both

[8] Ignatius of Antioch, *Epistle to the Romans*, chap. 4 (*ANF*, I, 75).

[9] Yovhannēs Erznkacʿi, *Meknutʿiwn* on Matt. 19:15, pp. 406–7.

[10] See above, p. 30.

[1] See the illustrations of Mark's narrative in the strip narrative Gospels: Paris, B.N. gr. 74, fol. 86v, Omont, *Évangiles*, pl. 76; Florence, Laur. Plut. VI,23, fol. 84, Velmans, *Le Tétraévangile*, fig. 161.

[2] This appears to be the Gospel of Otto in the Cathedral Treasure of Aachen, S. Beissel, *Die Bilder der Handschrift des Kaisers Otto im Münster zu Aachen* (Aachen, 1886), pl. 11; it reappears a little later than the Armenian example of Awag in the Breviary of Jeanne d'Evreux, Chantilly, Musée Condé, ms. 1887, fol. 285v, V. Leroquais, *Les bréviaires manuscrits des bibliothèques publiques de France*, 5 vols. (Paris, 1934), pl. 38.

[3] Velmans, *Le Tétraévangile*, fig. 88. Another Byzantine instance of this iconography occurs in Athens, Byzantine Museum, ms. 820.

[4] In addition to the examples already cited, further occurrences could be found in Erevan, Mat. 7651, at Mark 10:35, unpublished; and in Vienna, Mekhitarist 278, fol. 69; Buschhausen, *Die illuminierten armenischen Handschriften*, fig. 85.

[5] Chrysostom, "In Matt. Hom. 65," chaps. 2–6, *NPNF* x, pp. 398–403.

[6] Ephraem Syrus, *Commentaire*, bk. 10, chap. 1, pp. 93–94; 14, chaps. 18–19, pp. 155–57; Yovhannēs Erznkacʿi, *Meknutʿiwn* on Matt. 20:20–28, pp. 425–29.

of them, who asked their Master for thrones, having seen his throne."[7] Erznkacʿi explains that they thought they deserved places of honor because they were closely related to Christ. Their mother was named Salome and she was the sister of the Blessed Virgin Mary.[8] The two brothers represent the twofold nature of the church, which ethnically is made up of Jews and Gentiles and hierarchically is made up of clergy and laity.[9] Both of the exegetes contrast the petition of James and John with that of Peter when he said, "Lo, we have left everything and followed you. What then shall we have?" (Matt. 19:27). Because Peter asked on behalf of all of the apostles Christ answered by promising them thrones over the twelve tribes of Israel and the inheritance of eternal life; because James and John asked just for themselves their petition was denied as being too corporeal.[10] In this view, then, the miniature would stand as a counsel to the clergy against personal and familial ambition, a counsel all the more appropriate in Armenia, where orders tended to be hereditary.

9. The Cure of the Blind in Jericho (*Page 124*)

The U.C.L.A. Gospel gives special prominence to the miracles in which Christ restores sight to the blind, devoting four miniatures to the subject (see *pages 235, 250, and 509*). This cure (Matt. 20:29–34) must be studied along with the Cure of Blind Bartimaeus on *page 250* (Mark 10:46–53). The texts involved are two variants of the same story, sharing such details as the locale, the initial rebuke of the blind by the crowd, the persistence of the blind, and their promptness to follow Christ after their cure. Yovhannēs Erznkacʿi identifies the two accounts; the fact that Matthew mentions two but Mark just one blind man named Bartimaeus, he explains by supposing that Bartimaeus was the one who spoke out.[1] Both in Matthew and Mark the story immediately precedes the account of Christ's Entry into Jerusalem, and in the U.C.L.A. Gospel the two miniatures precede by a single folio the two presentations of the Entry. Liturgically, too, the accounts of the cure are immediately linked to the celebration of Palm Sunday (called in Armenian "Całkazardi Kiwrakē," or "Flower Sunday"); the Markan text forms part of the Gospel reading for Mass, while the text in Matthew is read later in the day under the rubric "*i gerezmansn*" or "at the tomb."[2]

In format the two miniatures are very similar; in this one Christ and his disciples stand to the left and the two blind men sit on the right, each having a purse over one shoulder. The background distinguishes Christ's world with a panel of gold from the world of the blind men, a city-scape. Rough parallels exist in the Florence Gospel, both for the composition of Christ addressing the blind and for Christ sending a discipline to fetch the blind.[3]

Two kinds of meaning can be distinguished in the exegetes' treatment of this subject, moral and allegorical. The perseverance of the blind has set an example to imitate. "These then let us also emulate," says Chrysostom. "Though God defer the gift, though there be many withdrawing us, let us not desist from asking. . . . Not poverty, not blindness, not their being unheard, not their being rebuked by the multitude, not anything else, impeded their exceeding earnestness. Such is the nature of a fervent and toiling soul."[4] Ephraem and Yovhannēs Erznkacʿi draw similar morals from the miracle.[5] Erznkacʿi, however, also finds large allegorical meanings in the event based on its occurrence in Jericho as Christ set out for Jerusalem. According to Erznkacʿi, Jericho and Jerusalem are opposed as earth and heaven; "Bartimaeus" is interpreted as "Son of a blind man," which is interpreted as characterizing all the children of Adam who are blind sons of blind fathers. The gates of Jericho are the portals of death, passing through which Christ has illuminated both Gentile and Jew, that is, the two blind men.[6]

10. The Entry into Jerusalem and the Cleansing of the Temple (*Page 126*)

Christ's Entry into Jerusalem is illustrated twice in the U.C.L.A. Gospel, here and in Mark on *page 252*.

[7] Ephraem Syrus, Hymns on Virginity, 15, 7 (CSCO 223, Script. Syr. 94, 53), using the translation provided by R. Murray, *Symbols*, 92.

[8] Yovhannēs Erznkacʿi, *Meknutʿiwn* on Matt. 20:20, p. 425.

[9] Ibid., on Matt. 20:21, p. 426.

[10] Ibid., on Matt. 20:23, 427–28; Ephraem Syrus, *Commentaire*, bk. 15, chap. 18, pp. 155–56.

[1] Yovhannēs Erznkacʿi, *Meknutʿiwn* on Matt. 20:30, p. 430.

[2] *Čašocʿ Girkʿ*, 90.

[3] Florence, Laurentiana, Plut. VI,23, fols. 18v, 84v, and 148v; Velmans, *Le Tétraévangile*, figs. 31, 162, and 248.

[4] Chrysostom, "In Matt. Hom. 66," chap. 1, *NPNF* x, p. 404.

[5] Ephraem, *Commentaire*, bk. 15, chap. 22, p. 13; Yovhannēs Erznkacʿi, *Meknutʿiwn* on Matt. 20:30, pp. 430–31.

[6] Yovhannēs Erznkacʿi, *Meknutʿiwn* on Matt. 20:30, pp. 430–31.

This doubling of the iconography is unusual but not unparalleled. In the Vehapʿaṙ Gospel, the source of this program, the subject is also illustrated twice, but differently: at Matt. 21:7 Christ rides toward Jerusalem seated on the ass (fig. 126b), but at Mark 11:5 the disciples are shown fetching the ass. The Gospel of King Gagik also repeated the iconography of Christ's Entry into Jerusalem: the Entry itself was shown in Matthew, Mark, and John while the Fetching of the Ass was shown in Mark (in two stages) and in Luke (see Table 8). Curiously enough, in the Cilician period the Armenian frieze Gospel departs from its Byzantine model to return to the program of the Vehapʿaṙ Gospel with the Entry in Matthew and the Fetching of the Ass in Mark; moreover the iconography of the Entry follows the Vehapʿaṙ Gospel in reversing the composition in Syrian fashion (figs. 126b and 126d). In the U.C.L.A. Gospel both miniatures of the Entry were executed on leaves that are integral to their respective gatherings, hence the duplication of iconography was planned in the scribal stage of the manuscript.

In the execution of the manuscript the second occurrence of the theme was illustrated first, by the Second Painter. When the Fourth Painter, and then Tʿoros Taronecʿi, executed the miniature on *page 126* they followed in several details the model of *page 252:* the drawing of the ass and the pose of Christ; the way the boy lays out the two tunics on the street; the gestures of the two Jews who greet Christ's entry; and the representation of the temple as a little baldachino with a pointed dome resting on three columns above a tipped-up tower base. But the artists avoided simple duplication of the iconography by introducing a large panel in the upper right to show the sequel of Christ's entry, namely the Cleansing of the Temple (Matt. 21:12–13). This required a radical dislocation in the composition of the Entry: the city gate that Christ is about to enter has disappeared and the temple toward which he tends is now above and behind him; the consequent compression of the scene results in a reduction of the number of disciples and an elimination of the children climbing the trees. Finally, in a most unusual departure, the artists have shown the foal walking alongside the ass in such a way that while Christ sits on the ass his feet rest on the foal as on a footstool.

Insofar as the present iconography is copied from that on *page 252,* the discussion of sources will be postponed to the treatment of that miniature. Here it is our purpose to discuss instead the problems of interpreting the iconography of *page 126,* much of which will naturally apply to the later miniature as well.

Although the Entry into Jerusalem has generated considerable literature, little attention has been given to understanding the theme in its medieval context.[1] Modern art historical scholarship has interpreted the Entry into Jerusalem as a Christian borrowing of the Roman iconography of imperial "adventus."[2] Although this has been repeated often enough to become dogma, it is never observed how very little of the "adventus" iconography enters into the standard Byzantine representation of the Entry. Neither victory figures, nor personifications of subject cities, nor horses, nor chariots, nor armor, nor any of the trappings of the emperor's parade figure in the Entry into Jerusalem. Christ is indeed entering a city gate, but he wears his usual civilian dress and rides upon a rustic beast of burden. Most important, he rides sidesaddle, a pose used in early Byzantine art for women and the disabled.[3] No emperor would ever ride sidesaddle on an ass, but for a philosopher or teacher this mode of travel might be quite appropriate.

If there is any reflection of imperial iconography in the scene it lies rather in parody than imitation. This is how Matthew seems to have understood the event, for the prophecy of Zechariah that he cites makes a special point of emphasizing that the messianic triumph of Jerusalem will be realized through trust in the Lord rather than reliance on any military means.[4] Though art historians may want to connect the overall composition of man-on-a-beast-entering-city with the adventus composition, this is a connection without significance to the medieval observer.

To Chrysostom, ever the panegyrist of Christ's humility, the Entry offered a most congenial theme.

[1] For bibliography see E. Lucchesi-Palli, "Einzug in Jerusalem," *Lexikon der christliche Ikonographie,* I, 593–97, and Schiller, *Iconography of Christian Art,* II, 18–23.

[2] A. Grabar, *L'empereur dans l'art byzantin* (Strasburg, 1936), 234–36; restated in summary in idem, *Christian Iconography: A Study of Its Origins* (Princeton, 1968), 44–45. This thesis is carried to bizarre extremes in E. H. Kantorowicz, "The King's Advent and the Enigmatic Panels in the Doors of Santa Sabina," *Art Bulletin* 26 (1944), 207–31.

[3] For women riding sidesaddle see Hans Gerstinger, *Die Wiener Genesis* (Vienna, 1931), 23; for the disabled, see the scene of the Good Samaritan in the Rossano Gospel, Antonio Muñoz, *Il Codice Purpureo di Rossano,* pl. 12.

[4] To quote the prophecy in context: "Then I (i.e., the Lord) will encamp at my house as a guard, so that none shall march to and fro; no oppressor shall again overrun them, for now I see with my own eyes. Rejoice greatly, O daughter of Zion! Shout aloud, O daughter of Jerusalem! Lo, your king comes to you; triumphant and victorious is he, humble in riding on an ass, on a colt the foal of an ass. I will cut off the chariot from Ephraim and the war horse from Jerusalem; and the battle bow shall be cut off, and he shall command peace to the nations; his domination shall be from sea to sea, and from the River to the ends of the earth" (Zech. 9:9–10).

Christ, he points out, was born of a poor woman in a shed, he chose ordinary men for his disciples, he sat on the grass to eat, he possessed no home and he clothed himself in what was cheap.[5] He contrasts Christ's behavior with that of the princes of this world; Christ makes his advent, he says, "not driving chariots, like the rest of the kings, not demanding tributes, not thrusting men off, and leading about guards, but displaying his great meekness even hereby. Ask then the Jew, what king came to Jerusalem borne on an ass? Nay, he could not mention but this alone."[6]

This lesson was not lost on Erznkacʿi, who comments at length on Zechariah's use of the term "king" in this connection. The kingdom, he points out, is salvation, which was promised first to the Jews; but this "king" comes not on horses, stallions and chariots, but meek and seated on an ass and a foal.[7] Allegorical meanings were also attached to Christ's means of transport, as will be seen below.

According to Grabar, the palm branch is one of the motifs of imperial adventus that was borrowed in the iconography of the Entry.[8] But in ancient art the palm is widely used in the triumphs of gods and athletes, and has no specifically imperial connotation. Erznkacʿi was well aware of these other meanings in the motif. Going beyond his sources in Chrysostom and Ephraem, he tells us that the branches were broken from the trees to show that it was springtime in a spiritual as well as a physical sense, for in Christ life itself was riding in triumph over death and hell, and the curse of Adam that brought forth thistles from the earth was being removed (Gen. 3:18).[9] In the tenth-century frescoes of Ałtʿamar Christ carries a budding flower in his left hand in the Entry into Jerusalem (fig. 126a). In ancient times, Erznkacʿi continues, branches were offered to idols as a token of worship—a custom attested in Agatʿangełos' account of the trial of St. Gregory;[10] now they are offered to the true Lord, who has abolished idolatry. The branches strewn before Christ were of two kinds, according to Erznkacʿi: palm branches, which because of their height and sweet fruit symbolized the exalted and sweet teaching of Christ; and olive branches, which stand for the oil of forgiveness.[11]

The miniature of the Entry on *page 126* introduces the extraordinary motif of Christ riding simultaneously on both the ass and the foal. This seems to be a new invention in our manuscript. In Early Christian sarcophagi there are, indeed, instances where the foal walks so closely beside its mother that it snuggles under Christ's foot.[12] In these instances, however, Christ sits astride the ass so that both feet cannot rest on the foal. Later medieval use of the theme clearly shows the foal following the ass.[13] The only other representations of Christ riding on the two beasts at once are in manuscripts that depend on the U.C.L.A. Gospel for their iconography: Erevan, Mat. 6289, executed by Tʿoros Taronecʿi in 1323 (fig. 126f), and Erevan, 6230 executed by Tʿoros' disciple Awag (fig. 126g).

However strange it may seem to seat Christ on the two beasts simultaneously, it should be noticed that this is what Matthew actually says. While the other three evangelists say that the disciples fetched an ass or a colt and that Christ sat on *it,* in the singular, according to Matthew they were directed to bring both, and "they brought the ass and the colt, and put their garments on them, and he sat thereon" (literally the Greek and Armenian texts say "he sat on *them*" (Matt. 21:7).[14] We have noted elsewhere the artists' interest in literal representation of the text, even when it runs counter to known iconographic traditions; but generally there is a reason for insisting on such literalness.

In general the two animals were usually taken as symbolic of the Jews and the Gentiles. According to Chrysostom, the colt represents the unclean new nation, the church of the Gentiles; Christ sat on the colt, and its mother, the Jewish people, would follow out of emulation, according to Paul's prophecy that Israel was to be saved after the Gentiles (Rom. 11:25–26).[15]

[5] Chrysostom, "In Matt. Hom. 66," chap. 2, *NPNF* x, pp. 405–6.

[6] Ibid., p. 406. By contrast see later Byzantine commentaries that develop an "enthroning" image in Christ on the ass; Henry Maguire, *Art and Eloquence in Byzantium,* 68–74.

[7] Yovhannēs Erznkacʿi, *Meknutʿiwn* on Matt. 21:4–5, pp. 439–40.

[8] Grabar, *L'empereur dans l'art Byzantin,* 234–36.

[9] Yovhannēs Erznkacʿi, *Meknutʿiwn* on Matt. 21:8, pp. 443–44.

[10] Agatʿangełos, *History of the Armenians,* chap. 49 (ed. Thomson, p. 63).

[11] Yovhannēs Erznkacʿi, *Meknutʿiwn* on Matt. 21:8, p. 444.

[12] F. W. Deichmann, G. Bovini, and H. Brandenburg, *Repertorium der christlichen-antiken Sarkophage* (Wiesbaden, 1967), nos. 14 and 21. For a Romanesque survival of this motif, see the Avila Bible in Madrid, Walter Cahn, *Romanesque Bible Illumination* (Ithaca, N.Y., 1982), fig. 166.

[13] Munich Staatsbibl. Clm. 4452, Cim. 57, Pericope of Henry II, fol. 78, cf. G. Leiginger, *Miniaturen aus Handschriften der Kgl. Hof- und Staatsbibliothek in München* (Munich, 1912–28), V, pl. 16.

[14] Matthew got involved in this awkwardness by trying to make his account too literal a fulfillment of the prophecy of Zech. 9:9; the prophet's expression uses the figure of hendiadys, the same animal being an ass and the foal of an ass.

[15] Chrysostom, "In Matt. Hom. 66," chap. 2, *NPNF* x, p. 406.

This interpretation becomes a permanent part of the exegetical tradition and is alluded to in Nersēs Šnorhali's *Yisous Ordi;*[16] but while this explains the presence of the two animals it does not explain that literal sense of Matt. 21:7, since it has Christ sitting on only the colt.

When Erznkacʿi, in his verse-by-verse commentary, examines this passage he notices how Matthew's text differs from the other evangelists, and he tries to find compromises that will save the conflicting versions. The fact that Erznkacʿi makes a *crux interpretum* out of this phrase is itself significant, but more striking is the fact that the first solution offered amounts to a description of the iconography: "But how he sat upon the two must be examined, for they were not four but only two. What can we say of this? Some say that he sat on the ass, and the colt followed after and rubbed against the feet of the Savior, for which reason evidently Mark and Luke say they fetched only the colt."[17] Erznkacʿi does not at this point pursue the picture of the colt at the Savior's feet but offers another alternative: "It seems to me," he remarks, "that he sat first on the ass as far as the gate of Jerusalem, and thence after getting off the ass he sat on the foal."[18] The untried foal, he continues, submitted meekly because Christ as the second Adam has undone the sin that caused animals to revolt against man. He then identifies the two beasts as the Jews and Gentiles, following Chrysostom. This satisfies the literal text of the verse without making Christ ride simultaneously on two animals.

At the close of his discussion of this crux, however, Erznkacʿi finally offers an interpretation that both satisfies the literal text and requires that Christ sit on the ass and the foal, as in the U.C.L.A. miniature. "According to an allegory of a sort, the ass and foal are the soul and body—one instructed, that is the spirit, because of its reason, and the other cultivated, that is the body, because of its indocility—on which the Word sat unifying them by his own person."[19] The ass and the foal stand, then, for the harmony of the body and soul in the human nature of Christ. The Divine Word came to dwell in the two of them, creating the new hypostatic union of the God-Man. Thus the humble beasts of burden in the Entry carry a theological message of the most orthodox nature concerning the Incarnation, for the Word did not assume a human body, as some heretics had proposed, but took on both body and soul of human nature.

The supplementary panel showing the Cleansing of the Temple shows clear evidence of the part Tʿoros Taronecʿi played in finishing the work of his predecessors. The faces of Christ and of the last merchant were executed by the Fourth Painter in his swarthy manner and the remaining faces were done by Tʿoros in his more bland manner; the earlier painter had also sketched in four more hands, which Tʿoros overpainted by adding the shadows and highlights to the garments. It would seem too that Tʿoros was responsible for the mistaken insertion of the arcs of four haloes over the crowd of merchants; this makes the image ambiguous, opening the possibility that the crowd should be read as a procession of disciples with Christ following. That this was not the original intention seems clear, however, from the hunched-over pose of the eight figures who press to flee Christ, two of them looking back anxiously. Further, since there is no passage in the Gospel text that might explain a "procession" interpretation, one must connect this scene with the Cleansing of the Temple in Matt. 21:12–13. The temple location is indicated by a pair of marble columns framing the panel. Christ has taken a couple of palm branches for his whip, although for his previous purge of the temple, in John 2:15, he made a whip of cord.

It is the text of John that inspired the Byzantine iconography of this subject with such details as the whip of cord, the sheep and cattle involved in Christ's debate with the priests, all of which are lacking in Matthew's simpler account.[20] But the overturning of the tables, which is mentioned in all versions of the event and is generally part of the Byzantine iconography, is omitted in the U.C.L.A. Gospel; the simple massing of figures is closer to some Western manuscripts, such as the thirteenth-century Hamilton Psalter, though it would be difficult to argue for a dependence.[21]

Erznkacʿi follows Chrysostom in maintaining that John and the Synoptics spoke of two different occasions in their descriptions of the Cleansing of the

[16] "You were seated on the ass and the foal as types of the Jewish people and the unclean Gentiles, the latter made wise, the former indocile. Like them purify me and come to rest on me with your Spirit. As you sit on the cherubim take your place in my soul making of it a heavenly throne." Nersēs Šnorhali, *Yisous Ordi,* chaps. 674–75 (ed. Isaak Kechichian, p. 171).

[17] Yovhannēs Erznkacʿi, *Meknutʿiwn* on Matt. 21:7, p. 442.

[18] Ibid.

[19] Ibid., p. 443.

[20] The Byzantine tradition starts with the Rossano Gospel; for further examples and discussion see Schiller, *Iconography of Christian Art.* II, 23–24.

[21] Berlin Kgl. Kupferstichkab. 78.A.5., fol. 59.

Temple.[22] The lesson he attaches to the event is both the practical moral lesson of the evils of greed and the larger lesson of the direction in which salvation history was moving. Driving the Jews out of the temple was Christ's way of declaring the old worship of the temple empty and finished. In his subsequent Passion he would establish the new and eternal worship of the Father.

11. The Last Supper (*Page 156*)

In breaking the bread and offering the cup at the Last Supper, Christ was both anticipating his death and leaving to his followers the sacrament that would constitute the central act of Christian worship. The implications of this event are therefore so vast as to touch virtually every aspect of Christian thought. The vastness of the possibilities, however, emphasizes the limitations of any image of the event; every image, in effect, makes a choice of those aspects of the event that are to be developed. On the most fundamental level this choice involves decisions on which passages of the Gospel account to illustrate.

The narrative of the Last Supper in Matthew breaks in half, the first section dealing with Christ's prediction of his betrayal (Matt. 26:20–25), and the second with his celebration of the eucharistic meal (Matt. 26:26–30). In the miniature of the U.C.L.A. Gospel the artist chose to represent narratively the moment of the prediction by the gestures of Christ and Judas; at the same time he represents the Eucharist symbolically in the lamb, the bread, and the wine.

The supper takes place at the traditional sigma table of the Hellenistic world, at which Christ "reclined" according to the Greek text of Matt. 26:20; the reclining posture of the guests seems to have been abandoned in favor of sitting, a change that takes place in Byzantine art starting in the ninth century.[1] Yet Christ's couch has been retained, and, in disregard for spatial necessities, it overlaps the table.[2] In the etiquette of the ancient banquet the place of honor was at the right corner of the sigma table, a position directly opposite the host and at his right, and in Byzantine art this position is often reserved for Peter. This is the arrangement found in the King Gagik and Queen Keṙan Gospels (figs. 156a and 156c). In the Glajor miniature, however, a dark-haired apostle is shown here and Peter instead is found second from Christ's left. In this arrangement our iconography clearly depends on the Gospel of John, which is the only account that gives an intimation of the seating arrangement. When Christ had predicted an unnamed betrayer, John narrates, "One of his disciples, whom Jesus loved, was lying close to the breast of Jesus; so Simon Peter beckoned to him and said, 'Tell us who it is of whom he speaks'" (John 13:23–24). In this account, then, Peter would be next to John, who was next to Christ as in the miniature. The sign of the betrayer, however, is represented not according to John's account—"It is he to whom I shall give this morsel when I have dipped it" (John 13:26)—but according to Matthew's—"He who has dipped his hand in the dish with me, will betray me" (Matt. 13:23). Judas, his face shown in sinister profile, reaches across to dip in the common bowl. The miniature, therefore, has combined two Gospel versions of the prediction of the betrayer, a combination that is not uncommon in Byzantine art.[3]

Besides the choices the artist faced in the Gospel accounts of the Last Supper, he also had choices to make in the repertoire of symbols available for interpreting the subject. Millet tried to establish a distinction between a "Byzantine" and an "Oriental" way of handling the iconography on the basis of the position of Judas.[4] However, the variations he indicated have little geographical significance. For example, the circular table, which Millet wanted to assign to Syria, appears in Western iconography as well as in Armenia, while the rectangular table, which he assigns to the West, is common in Cappadocia and Armenia as well.[5] The breakdown of these distinctions seems

[22] Yovhannēs Erznkacʿi, *Meknutʿiwn* on Matt. 21:12–13, pp. 447–48.

[1] Moscow State Historical Museum, Khludov Psalter, fol. 40v; cf. M. B. Ščepkina, *Miniatjura Khludovskoj Psaltyri*, p. 40v. On the iconography of the Last Supper in general, see Millet, *Iconographie*, 286–309; K. Wessel, *Abendmahl und Apostelkommunion* (Recklinghausen, 1964); Schiller, *Iconography of Christian Art*, II, 24–41.

[2] Christ's couch begins to take on a mandorla shape in Laur. Plut. VI,23, fol. 53v; Velmans, *Le Tétraévangile*, fig. 110.

[3] See examples in Wessel, *Abendmahl*, passim.

[4] Millet, *Iconographie*, 286–309.

[5] For Western examples of the circular table, see Schiller, *Iconography of Christian Art*, II, figs. 73, 74, 75, 78, 79, 84, 85, 89, 91; for Armenian examples see Erevan, Mat. 2742, (Tʿargmančʿacʿ Gospel of 1232), fol. 140, Dournovo, *Haykakan Manrankarčʿutʿyun*, fig. 26; Erevan, Mat. 316, (Gospel of 14th century), L. Zakaryan, *Iz Istorii Vaspurakanskoj Miniatjur* (Erevan, 1980), fig. 42; for the rectangular table in Cappadocia, see Restle, *Byzantine Wall Painting*, 2, pls. 179, 235; 3, pl. 506; for Armenian examples see Erevan, Mat. 6201, (Gospel of 1038), fol. 7, Izmailova, *Arm. miniatjura XI veka*, fig. 27; Erevan, Mat. 4806, (Gospel by Yovsian, of

to indicate that the repertoire of variables for such a popular subject as the Last Supper was very widely shared. This does not mean that all nuances of iconography have been lost in indiscriminate interchange, but that in reading iconography, the large geographical areas are less significant than the careful interpretation of specific motifs in individual works of art.

The U.C.L.A. Gospel isolates that moment in the narrative in which John, leaning on Christ's breast, passes on Peter's inquiry as to the identity of the traitor. Chrysostom and Erznkac'i are in agreement in seeing in this event a sign of Christ's foreknowledge of his passion and therefore a proof of the freedom with which he embraced his death.[6] But their chief fascination with this moment is in the dramatic confrontation of the traitor's malice with the kindness of the Savior. Chrysostom sees the vagueness of Christ's words—"one of you will betray me" (Matt. 26:21)—as an effort to conceal Judas' identity, that he might have the opportunity to reconsider and repent.[7] Erznkac'i carries the Lord's mercy a step further, for he says that the sign of the betrayer was made known only to John so as to give Judas ample opportunity to repent, for had he revealed his identity to the apostles at large they would have turned on Judas as Peter turned on the servant of the high priest.[8] In this interpretation the intimacy of Christ and John in our miniature takes on a special significance; only the disciple "whom Jesus loved" fully appreciates the mystery of good and evil that is unfolding at the supper. In this connection one wonders whether the unusual iconography of John may have some importance. Unlike his representation in other narrative scenes in the U.C.L.A. Gospel, John is here shown as an old man with white hair and beard.[9] Since John was reputed to have outlived the other apostles[10] he is usually imagined to have been one of the youngest in the group; here, by a peculiar telescoping of time observable elsewhere in East Christian exegesis, John is represented in appearance as the ancient evangelist of Patmos, the one who preserved longest the personal remembrance of Christ.

In contrast to Western iconography, Byzantine representations of the Last Supper generally omit the Eucharist, since that subject is developed in another image, namely, the Communion of the Apostles.[11] At the same time, by a very curious twist in iconography, Byzantine art generally also omits the Passover meal and shows instead a symbol of Christ, the fish, on the table.[12] It is almost unknown that Byzantine art should include the paschal lamb at the Last Supper; in nearby Cappadocia, for example, there is not a single instance.[13] The precedents for the lamb in the U.C.L.A. Gospel would have to be found in Syrian manuscripts, in which it is the more usual, and in other Armenian manuscripts, in which it occurs often from the eleventh century on (fig. 156a-c).[14]

The importance of eucharistic symbolism in the miniature is clearly connected to its place in the program of the manuscript. The Last Supper is the first addition of the U.C.L.A. Gospel to the program of the Vehap'aṙ Gospel after the Genealogy. The decision to illustrate the Last Supper here, rather than with the account in one of the other evangelists, may have been prompted by the use of this reading, Matt. 26:17–30, as the Gospel for Mass on Holy Thursday, the feast commemorating the institution of the Eucharist.[15]

1306), fol. 11v, H. Hakopyan, *Haykakan Manrankarč'ut'yun Vaspurakan* (Erevan, 1978), fig. 16; Vienna, Mekhitarist 242, (Gospel, ca. 1330), fol. 65v. Buschhausen, *Die illuminierten armenischen Handschriften*, fig. 39.

[6] Chrysostom, "In Matt. Hom. 81," chap. 2, *NPNF* x, p. 486; Yovhannēs Erznkac'i, *Meknut'iwn* on Matt. 26:24, p. 556.

[7] Chrysostom, "In Matt. Hom. 81," chap. 1, *NPNF* x, p. 486.

[8] Yovhannēs Erznkac'i, *Meknut'iwn* on Matt. 26:23, p. 555.

[9] An aged apostle, white-haired but balding, sits beside Christ in the Rossano Gospel, fol. 4, but since he does not lean on Christ, Schiller's identification of him as John is doubtful; Schiller, *Iconography of Christian Art*, II, 31. The only unquestionable parallel to our aged John on the breast of Christ is in a Carolingian manuscript in Prague, Metropolitan Chapter, Bibl. Hs. Cim. 2, fol. 185v; which has nothing in common with the U.C.L.A. iconography. Ibid., II, fig. 82.

[10] John's longevity is hinted at already in his Gospel, John 21:21–23. Irenaeus says that he lived in Ephesus until the reign of Trajan. *Contra Haereses* II, chap. 22, para. 5, PG 7, col. 785.

[11] This is generally called the "Liturgical Eucharist"; cf. Schiller, *Iconography of Christian Art*, II, 28–30.

[12] On the origins of this iconography, see F. J. Dölger, *Ichthys: Das Fischsymbol in frühchristlicher Zeit* (Münster, 1943), V. For examples of this motif, see Millet, *Iconographie*, 286–309, or Wessel, *Abendmahl*, passim.

[13] See instances of Last Supper in Restle, *Byzantine Wall Painting*, II, pls. 51, 107, 179, 235, 272; III, pls. 313, 506.

[14] The lamb appears in the following manuscripts: London, Brit. Lib. Syr. Add. 7170, fol. 139v; London, Brit. Lib. Syr. Add. 7169, fol. 11v; Rome, Vat. Syr. 559, fol. 128; cf. Leroy, *Mss. syriaques*, figs. 88.3, 119.1, and 88.4. The lamb shows up in later Cilician and Vaspurakan manuscripts: Washington, Freer 32.18, page 169, Der Nersessian, *Arm. Mss. Freer*, fig. 98; Erevan, Mat. 4806 (Gospel by Yovsian of 1306), fol. 11v, cf. Hakopyan, *Haykakan Manrankarč'ut'yun Vaspurakan*, fig. 16.

[15] *Čašoc' Girk'*, 94.

The first question posed by Chrysostom and Erznkacʿi in commenting on the eucharistic meal is why the sacrament should have been instituted at the Passover. Christ meant to show: "both that he is the lawgiver of the Old Testament, and that the things therein foreshadowed these things. Therefore, I say, where the type is, there he puts the truth. . . . For if the type was a deliverance from such bondage, how much more will the truth set free the world, and will he be delivered up for the benefit of our race. Wherefore, I would add, neither did he appoint the sacrament before this, but when henceforth the rites of the law were to cease. And thus the very chief of the feasts he brings to an end, removing them to another most awful table."[16]

The lamb on the table refers both to the historical celebration of the Passover and to what it typifies, namely, Christ's sacrifice on the cross. Two eucharistic chalices are shown on either side of the lamb, representing the new sacrament replacing the old. Moreover, within the two chalices the artist has represented morsels of bread in the wine, illustrating the Armenian (and Byzantine) manner of communion by intinction.

In addition to its Old Testament reference, the institution of the Eucharist looks forward to the Crucifixion, and this is already contained in Christ's words, "This is my blood of the covenant, which is poured out for many for the forgiveness of sins" (Matt. 26:29). But it would be difficult to overemphasize the vividness with which the Eastern Fathers identified the Eucharist with Christ's actual death. To Chrysostom the identification was so real that he could use the Last Supper as a refutation of Marcionite and Manichean denials of the reality of Christ's physical suffering.[17] To Syrian and Armenian commentators, however, Christ is already dead from the moment of instituting the Eucharist. According to Ephraem, "From the moment in which he broke his body for his disciples and gave his body to his apostles, one counts the three days in which he was reckoned to be in the number of the dead, like Adam; for after eating of the tree (Adam) lived many years, but since he had transgressed the command he was counted in the number of the dead. . . . Since (Christ) gave his body to be eaten in the mystery of his death, he entered into their belly as into the earth."[18] This is a most unusual position in Patristic literature, but Ephraem in no way shrinks from its logical consequence, namely, that Christ has effectively killed himself in the Eucharist. "Even though the people killed him, he killed himself with his own hands. Those insane people on Golgotha crucified a man whose own hands had already killed him. If he had not killed himself in the mystery, they would not have killed him in reality. The day before, he killed himself in figure; and then the day after, they killed him."[19] Ephraem's exegesis concerning the counting of Christ's three days among the dead is quoted practically verbatim in Yovhannēs Erznkacʿi.[20]

The reality of this identification of the Eucharist with Christ's death adds another dimension to the presence of the lamb on the table. It is not only the Passover lamb but the Lamb of God. As Nersēs Šnorhali expressed it in his hymn for Good Friday: "In fulfillment of the law of Moses given on Sinai, he ate the prescribed lamb and the azyma with bitter herb, cancelling the old in the new and the shadow in the reality, being himself, in place of the lamb, the Lamb offered to God. In place of the azyma, the unleavened bread, he gave his own heavenly body, the virginal, pure, and incorruptible body, and in place of the blood of the lamb of the Old Testament, he gave to us his blood in a second testament, and in exchange for the bitterest herb he offered divine life."[21] A loaf of azyma lies before each apostle, with the lamb in the center; the body and blood of Christ in the chalices replaces them. Beside these, invading the space of the table, the artist has placed the physical body of Christ on his mandorla-like couch. Christ offers himself in place of the paschal meal as the Lamb of the New Testament.

12. The Agony in the Garden (*Page 160*)

With the present subject the U.C.L.A. Gospel returns to the precedent of the Vehapʿaṙ Gospel (fig. 160a), which remains the programmatic norm for the following six miniatures of the Passion as well. The miniature of the Agony in the Garden shows two mo-

[16] Chrysostom, "In Matt. Hom. 81," chap. 1, *NPNF* x, p. 491; see comparable passage in Yovhannēs Erznkacʿi, *Meknutʿiwn* on Matt. 26:26, pp. 557–58.

[17] Chrysostom, "In Matt. Hom. 81," chaps. 1–2, *NPNF* x, p. 492.

[18] Ephraem, *Commentaire*, bk. 19, chap. 4, p. 194; Aphraat expresses the same opinion: *Aphraatis Sapientis Persae Demonstrationes*, Patrologia Syriaca, I, Dem. 12, chaps. 6–8, pp. 515–26.

[19] Ephraem, *Hymn 48*, *Hymnes de Saint Ephrem*, PO 30 (1961), 225.

[20] Yovhannēs Erznkacʿi, *Meknutʿiwn* on Matt. 26:26, p. 558.

[21] Nersēs Šnorhali, *Inni Sacri*, 43–44.

ments in the Gospel narrative. Above, Christ prays, "My Father, if it is possible, let this cup pass from me; nevertheless, not as I will, but as thou wilt" (Matt. 26:39); three times Christ went apart from the disciples and prayed thus in the same terms, and the imagery does not try to distinguish among the three prayers. Then in the scene below, his reproach to the disciples is similarly repeated in the Gospel: "he came to the disciples and found them sleeping; and he said to Peter, 'So, could you not watch with me one hour? Watch and pray that you may not enter into temptation; the spirit indeed is willing, but the flesh is weak'" (Matt. 26:40–41).

It is generally observed that in Western versions, consistent with traditions of prayer in the Roman church, Christ usually kneels upright, while in Byzantine art he makes proskynesis.[1] Yet the Gospel of King Gagik (fig. 160b) shows Christ kneeling, as does the Vehap'aṙ Gospel (fig. 160a). In the U.C.L.A. Gospel, Christ makes proskynesis with his face to the ground, and before him the Hand of God emerges from a segment of heaven. The apparently unnecessary repetition of the segment of heaven in the upper left also occurs in Byzantine examples.[2] Below, under the dramatic diagonal of the descending mountain, Christ addresses the apostles, all of whom sleep except the first, John, who begins to open his eyes. In the West Christ usually addresses only the three apostles—Peter, James, and John—whom he had taken apart from the others in the garden of Gethsemane (Matt. 26:37); the U.C.L.A. miniature follows Byzantine art in showing Christ addressing all the apostles.[3] By oversight the artist in the U.C.L.A. Gospel has shown only ten apostles; but he has singled out Peter, James, and John in the front row. Although the apostles are strewn on the hillside in a variety of poses in Byzantine art, as they are in the Armenian frieze Gospel (fig. 160c), in the U.C.L.A. miniature they sit up in keeping with Christ's instruction to them, "Sit here, while I go yonder and pray" (Matt. 26:37).

The fact that there is nothing anomalous in this version of the Agony in the Garden does not mean that Armenian thinking on this subject was entirely conventional, but only that it required nothing distinctive for its visual expression. The prospect of Christ suffering in the garden, like the other episodes of his passion, prompts the exegete to reflect on the full humanity of the incarnate Word. Ephraem comments, "Because he had assumed the flesh he also put on its weakness, and in hunger he ate, and in labor he was tired, and by sleep he was shown to be weak, and when the time of his death was upon him it was necessary that he endure the urgency of the flesh, for the terror of death took hold of him, that his nature be disclosed—that he was a son of Adam over whom 'death reigned' according to the apostle's saying."[4] Chrysostom sums it up in a word, "See by how many things he shows the reality of the Incarnation: by what he speaks, by what he suffers."[5]

But while the reality of the Incarnation was universally acknowledged by Christians, the nature of this union of human and divine was the theme of immense theological inquiry. Commenting on the verse "the spirit indeed is willing, but the flesh is weak," (Matt. 26:41) Yovhannēs Erznkac'i perceives a parallel between the unity of soul and body in man and the unity of divine and human in Christ. The Agony in the Garden thus becomes a revelation of the Armenian Monophysite position: "Through this we confess that Christ exists of a nature not-come-into-being and one come-into-being, but we do not dare to distinguish after his unity lest we bring in thoughts of two sons and two persons, although we keep unconfused in particular natures, in order that his natures be not confused and his unity be not divided."[6] Armenian Monophysitism, in contrast to that of Alexandria, addressed itself rather against Nestorianism than against Chalcedon, and therefore spoke of two natures fused into a unity in the Incarnation.[7] But while the Armenian formulation of this position was enough to permanently sever the church from Byzantium it rarely manifests itself in iconography, given the abstruse character of the debate.[8]

Ephraem's reference to Christ as "Son of Adam"

[1] Schiller, *Iconography of Christian Art*, II, 48–51, figs. 10–11, 141–57.

[2] Parma, Bibliotheca palatina, ms. 5, fol. 90; cf. Schiller, *Iconography of Christian Art*, fig. 148.

[3] For example see Paris, B.N. gr. 923, Sacra Parallela of the 9th century, fol. 163, Kurt Weitzmann, *The Miniatures of the Sacra Parallela, Parisinus Graecus 923*, Studies in Manuscript Illumination 8 (Princeton, 1979), fig. 472; Florence, Laur. Plut, VI,23, Gospel, fol. 54v, Velmans, *Le Tétraévangile*, fig. 111; London, Brit. Lib. Egerton 1139, (Psalter of the 12th century), fol. 7; Buchthal, *Miniature Painting*, pl. 7a.

[4] Ephraem, *Commentaire*, bk. 20, chap. 4, pp. 202–3.

[5] Chrysostom, "In Matt. Hom. 83," chap. 1, *NPNF* x, p. 497.

[6] Yovhannēs Erznkac'i, *Meknut'iwn* on Matt. 26:41, p. 570.

[7] Karekin Sarkissian, *The Council of Chalcedon and the Armenian Church* (New York, 1957).

[8] For an unusual iconographic reference to Monophysitism, see Mathews, "The Annunciation at the Well," 343–56.

alludes to another distinctively East Christian preoccupation in Gospel exegesis. Syrian and Armenian exegetes see the life of Christ in the largest dimensions of salvation history; each event in the process of man's redemption is an undoing of the fall. Accordingly, Ephraem explains, Christ sweated "that he might cure the languishing Adam. He persisted in prayer in this garden that he might lead him back again into the other garden."[9] The first Adam by resisting the will of God delivered himself into the jaws of the adversary; "not as I will, but as thou wilt," says the second Adam, reestablishing the will of the creator in his creature and dissolving the hold of death over him.[10] One must see the Agony in the Garden as a first skirmish in the heroic and superhuman struggle of Christ with the adversary.

13. The Betrayal (*Page 162*)

In the accounts of the treachery of Judas and the arrest of Christ there are some slight variations from Gospel to Gospel, and the pictorial tradition tends to harmonize these by combining the information from the four accounts (Matt. 26:47–56; Mark 14:43–52; Luke 22:47–53; John 18:1–12). Thus John, who omits to mention the kiss, identifies Peter as the apostle who assaulted the servant of the high priest, and names the servant as Malchus (John 18:10); Luke alone adds the detail that Christ immediately healed the servant's wound (Luke 22:51). There are then two focuses of action in the representation of the subject, Judas' kiss and Peter's attack on the servant.

Byzantine manuscripts generally show Judas kissing Christ in the center, encircled by a mob carrying weapons. Peter's assault, more often than not, is not integrated into this group but is shown as a separate action located either to one side of, or in front of the crowd surrounding Christ.[1] By contrast the U.C.L.A. Gospel miniature shows two confronted crowds, the apostles to the left and the hostile mob with soldiers on the right. Peter lunges across from the apostles' sides to slash at one of the soldiers. At the same time, Christ is already raising his hand in blessing to heal the wound Peter has inflicted. The background is meant to suggest Jerusalem, whence the mob has come to arrest Christ. The soldiers carry round shields, a detail to be discussed in the context of the Crucifixion.

Millet tried to distinguish a Hellenistic from an oriental version of the Betrayal on the basis of Judas' position, whether left or right.[2] As in other instances, Millet's division seems to have been based on insufficient data; if one looks at a wide assortment of instances—Latin, Greek, Armenian, and Syrian—Judas' position has no relationship to the geographical origins of the iconography. On the other hand, the neat opposition of the crowd of apostles to the crowd of Christ's adversaries seems to follow geographical lines fairly clearly: it is both an Armenian feature and a Western one. In the West this confrontation is found in the mosaics of S. Apollinare Nuovo in Ravenna, and it reappears in manuscripts of the eleventh century to remain a standard throughout the Gothic period.[3] In Armenia it appears in the Vehap'aṙ Gospel in the eleventh century (fig. 162a) and remains in circulation through the Cilician period (fig. 162b). Whether this coincidence points to an interchange between Armenia and the West in the eleventh century or to earlier sources that they both had in common is not clear.

It is clear, however, that the composition of the U.C.L.A. miniature, both in the separation of apostles and mob and in Peter's position, derives from a tradition that has been available in Armenia since the eleventh century, for it differs from the composition of the Vehap'aṙ Gospel only in its adaptation to the full-page vertical format (fig. 162a). Christ's blessing gesture also occurs in the Vehap'aṙ Gospel. This can be found both in Byzantine and in Western sources, sometimes directed specifically toward Malchus and sometimes generally toward Christ's adversaries.[4] In the U.C.L.A. Gospel Christ is blessing Malchus.

[9] Ephraem, *Commentaire*, bk. 20, chap. 11, p. 206.

[10] Ibid., chaps. 8–9, pp. 204–5. See parallel in Yovhannēs Erznkac'i, *Meknut'iwn* on Matt. 26:39, p. 568.

[1] On the iconography of the Betrayal, see Millet, *Iconographie*, 326–44; Schiller, *Iconography of Christian Art*, II, 51–56. Typical of the Byzantine scheme is Paris, Bibliothèque Nationale gr. 74, fols. 55, 96v, and 202v, in which Peter's assault is shown off to one side. Cf. Omont, *Évangiles*, figs. 46, 84, 172.

[2] Millet, *Iconographie*, 326–28. For a recent appraisal of Millet's thesis, see Ann Derbes, *Byzantine Art and the Dugento*, 20–27.

[3] For S. Apollinare Nuovo, see Schiller, *Iconography of Christian Art*, II, fig. 158; for Romanesque examples of this, see Brussels, Bibl. Royale, Ms. 9428 (Lectionary, 11th century), fol. 86; Copenhagen, Köng. Bibl. Ms. Thott. 143, 2 (Psalter, 12th century), fol. 14; cf. *Greek and Latin Illuminated Manuscripts in Danish Collections* (Copenhagen, 1921), pl. 54.

[4] For example at Karanlık Kilise in Cappadocia, Christ directs his blessing toward Malchus, but in nearby Kiliclar

The presence of the apostles at Christ's betrayal is an integral part of the Gospel account and it is difficult to explain why Byzantine iconography generally omits them. As the traitor approached, Christ roused his slumbering apostles and bade them accompany him to meet Judas. "Behold, the hour is at hand, and the Son of man is betrayed into the hands of sinners. Rise, let us be going; see, my betrayer is at hand" (Matt. 26:45–46). Not until after the arrest is it said: "then all the disciples forsook him and fled" (Matt. 26:56). As Chrysostom remarked, they witness the willingness with which Christ accepted his passion.[5]

The contrast between Judas' kiss of treachery and Jesus' gesture of benediction heightens the antithesis that the exegetes found between Christ's meekness and the viciousness of his captors. "Oh! what depravity had the traitor's soul received," exclaimed Chrysostom. "For with what kind of eyes did he then look at his master? With what mouth did he kiss him? . . . He was emboldened by his master's gentleness, which more than all was sufficient to shame him, and to deprive him of all excuse for that he was betraying one so meek."[6] Such was the madness of the Jews, he continues, that on the very night in which they had eaten the paschal lamb they came like raging animals to carry off Christ.[7] A further association with the paschal lamb may be found in Peter's attack on Malchus, for his sword, according to Chrysostom and Erznkac'i, was a table knife from the Passover.[8] Indeed, in this miniature it looks much more like a knife than a sword. A meek lamb led to the slaughter, Christ forbids the violence by which Peter tries to prevent his capture; instead he heals the servant's wound.

14. Peter's Denial (*Page 166*)

Taken captive, Christ was first led to trial before the Jewish court presided over by the high priest Caiaphas (John inserts a hearing before Annas as well: John 18:12–27). It is while this religious trial of Christ is taking place that Peter three times denies knowledge of his master, and this poignant tale of the apostle's personal failure took on an importance in the Christian imagination far beyond its place in the trial itself. The evangelists differ slightly in details of the narrative (Matt. 26:69–75; Mark 14:66–72; Luke 22:54–62; John 18:15–27), but they all agree that Peter denied Christ first when he was questioned by a maid servant; John adds that she kept the door (John 18:16). All except Matthew mention that Peter had gone into the courtyard of the high priest and was warming himself at a fire, and they all noted that it was the crowing of the cock that reminded Peter of his master's prediction earlier that evening.

Peter's Denial is frequently illustrated in Armenian art. In Gospels that lack intratextual illustration the passage of Peter's Denial is often marked by a cock in the margin.[1] In Gospels with narrative scenes Peter's Denial is often repeated from one Gospel to the next with variations in iconography. Ṙoslin's two great narrative gospels from Hṙomkla each illustrate the event three times, as does Awag in Erevan, Mat. 212.[2]

In the U.C.L.A. Gospel the Denial is illustrated both in Matthew and in Luke (*page 438*), and in this it follows the program of the Vehap'aṙ Gospel. The present miniature reads from right to left: first the maidservant in a doorway accusing Peter; then Peter by himself crumpled up in grief with the cock crowing overhead. In the history of this imagery the simple elements of the maid in the door, Peter at the fire, the cock, and Peter in tears are scrambled countless times in various combinations.[3] The closest precedents for this miniature, however, are to be found in Syrian and Armenian sources. The tripartite composition, reading from right to left, is very similar to that of Vat. Syr. 559, though dress and specific poses vary.[4] Closer to the U.C.L.A. version, in the speaking gestures of Peter and the maid, and in the placement of the cock above, is the miniature of the Vehap'aṙ Gospel (fig. 166a).

The fact that it is the maid who is always shown

Kilise Malchus is omitted and Christ blesses his adversaries; Restle, *Byzantine Wall Painting*, II, pls. 236 and 271.

[5] Chrysostom, "In Matt. Hom. 83," chap. 2, *NPNF* x, p. 498.

[6] Ibid. See similar passage in Yovhannēs Erznkac'i, *Meknut'iwn* on Matt. 26:47, p. 572.

[7] Chrysostom, "In Matt. Hom. 84," chap. 1, *NPNF* x, p. 499; Yovhannēs Erznkac'i, *Meknut'iwn* on Matt. 26:51, p. 573.

[8] Chrysostom, "In Matt. Hom. 84," chap. 1, *NPNF* x, p. 502; Yovhannēs Erznkac'i, *Meknut'iwn* on Matt. 26:51, p. 574.

[1] For example, see Washington, Freer 56.11, fol. 232, Der Nersessian, *Arm. Mss. Freer*, fig. 183; Baltimore, Walters 539, fols. 193, 393, Der Nersessian, *Arm. Mss. Walters*, figs. 102, 134.

[2] Baltimore, Walters 539, fols. 119, 305, 392, Der Nersessian, *Arm. Mss. Walters*, figs. 82, 119, 133; Washington, Freer 32.18, pages 180, 314, 515, 516, Der Nersessian, *Arm. Mss. Freer*, figs. 102, 128, 160, 161. Awag illustrates the subject three times in Erevan, Mat. 212 (1340), fols. 88, 144 and 228.

[3] Schiller, *Iconography of Christian Art*, II, 58–60.

[4] Guillaume de Jerphanion, *Les miniatures du manuscrit syriaque no. 559 de la bibliothèque vaticane* (Rome, 1940), pl. XVIII.

accusing Peter, though in the text other bystanders also charged him, is the key to the meaning of the imagery. For in the eyes of the exegetes, Peter's disgrace was all the more shameful because he had denied his master at the question of "a miserable mean girl," as Chrysostom expressed it.[5] Although Christ had named him the "rock," even a girl could move him, Erznkacʿi observed.[6] The image shows Peter, the "rock," crumbling before the girl's interrogation. A different aspect of the subject is developed in the later miniature of Peter's Denial and Christ before the High Priest (*page 438*).

[5] Chrysostom, "In Matt. Hom. 85," chap. 1, *NPNF* x, p. 507.

[6] Yovhannēs Erznkacʿi, *Meknutʿiwn* on Matt. 26:69–70, p. 581.

15. The Message from Pilate's Wife (*Page 169*)

The story of Christ's trial before Pilate is told in the U.C.L.A. Gospel in two miniatures, one (*page 171*) showing the final moment of judgment, and the other, our present subject, showing a seemingly trivial incident in the deliberations. Only Matthew mentions this incident in a single enigmatic verse: "While (Pilate) was sitting on the judgement seat, his wife sent word for him, 'Have nothing to do with that righteous man, for I have suffered much over him today in a dream'" (Matt. 27:19). The evangelist does not mention what effect, if any, this had on Pilate. The apocryphal *Acts of Pilate,* a popular work available in an Armenian translation, fills this lacuna: "Pilate, summoning the Jews, says to them: You know that my wife is a worshipper of God, and prefers to adhere to the Jewish religion along with you. They say to him: Yes, we know. Pilate says to them: Behold, my wife has sent to me, saying, Have nothing to do with this just man, for many things have I suffered on account of him this night. And the Jews answering, say unto Pilate: Did we not tell thee that he was a sorcerer? Behold, he has sent a dream to thy wife."[1]

The U.C.L.A. miniature shows Pilate seated on a faldstool, the *sella curulis* of a Roman judge, beneath an arch, set against the plain white of the parchment. A messenger in pointed cap delivers a scroll while behind and below him a mob of Jews, many in sinister profile, eagerly watch the proceedings. The nearly full-page format gives the impression of being an enlargement of a miniature of smaller scale. The subject is rather unusual, and its realization here seems to be peculiarly Armenian. In Byzantine art this verse of Matthew does not seem to have been illustrated, while in Western iconography the message is delivered not in writing but orally. In the mosaic of S. Apollinare Nuovo in Ravenna, Kirschbaum and Schiller identify the figure whispering in Pilate's ear as his wife's messenger, and a similar figure appears occasionally in Gothic painting.[2] Elsewhere in the West, Pilate's wife delivers the message in person, setting aside the literal text of the Gospel.[3] In only a single known instance does a messenger deliver a written note to Pilate, and that in a scheme rather different from the U.C.L.A. iconography and considerably later than its first appearance in Armenian art.[4]

The U.C.L.A. iconography stems from the Vehapʿaṙ Gospel, although the format has been reversed right to left (fig. 169a). The servant, wearing a short tunic, boots and pointed cap, delivers a scroll to Pilate, who sits in profile; the figures are labeled "Pilate" and "the letter carrier from his wife," and the letter itself carries a minute inscription of the first words of her message, "Have nothing to do" (Matt. 27:19). In the Cilician period Ṙoslin illustrated Pilate's wife in bed sending the messenger (in Washington, Freer 32.18; fig. 169b). A little later than the U.C.L.A. Gospel the composition reappears in the work of Awag, only now the messenger has unfurled the scroll and reads to the procurator (fig. 169c).

Estimates of Pilate's character have ranged widely over the centuries, from a view that made him a weak and venal villain to the view that saw him as an innocent collaborator in man's salvation. In the Coptic and Ethiopic churches he is even celebrated as a saint, along with his wife Procla, and he is said to have been martyred for the faith in Rome.[5] Chrysostom, how-

[1] *Acts of Pilate,* chap. 2, *ANF,* VIII, 417. For the Armenian translation see F. C. Conybeare, *Studia Biblica et Patristica,* IV (Oxford, 1896), 59–132.

[2] F. W. Deichmann, *Frühchristliche Bauten und Mosaiken von Ravenna* (Baden-Baden, 1958), pl. 200; Kirschbaum, "Pilatus," *Lexikon der christlichen Ikonographie,* III, 436–39; Schiller, *Iconography of Christian Art,* II, 64, and figs. 208 and 215.

[3] For examples from the frescoes of S. Angelo in Formis and from a German altarpiece of Utrecht, see Schiller, *Iconography of Christian Art,* II, figs. 210 and 222. In Monreale, Pilate's wife sends a messenger without a scroll; see O. Demus, *Mosaics of Norman Sicily* (London, 1950), 287, pl. 68.

[4] In the thirteenth-century Bible Moralisée, a messenger with a pouch on his hip kneels before Pilate, who in turn places one hand on Christ's shoulder. London, British Library, Harley ms. 156–27, vol. 2, fol. 56, cf. A. de Laborde, *Bible Moralisée,* III, pl. 527.

[5] O. V. Volkoff, "Un saint oublié: Ponce Pilate," *Bulletin de la Société d'archéologie copte* 20 (1969–70), 167–75.

ever, judged him "unmanly and weak"; for, although he tried to contrive ways to release Christ, he gave in to the wicked scheme of the priests.[6] The dream of his wife, then, was meant to make more manifest Christ's innocence and recall Pilate from his course of action. For Yovhannēs Erznkacʿi, however, the matter is a little more complicated, and he therefore looks to allegory for a way out of the difficulty.

> There are some who say that this dream was from devils, for they saw that his death was to be the salvation of the world and they endeavored to prevent it; but others say it was from angels, so that they might show the innocence of Jesus and that the human origin of the cause of his death might be condemned. But I think the woman is a symbol of the sincere congregation of the Jews who were not interested in his death, and the dream is this life which passes like a dream, and the suffering of her torments are those which the Romans spared the Jews because of the blood of the Son of God.[7]

The report that Pilate's wife was a Jew is found in the *Acts of Pilate* cited above. Pilate's wife has thus become a symbol of that segment of the Jewish people which, unlike the mob before Pilate, did not take responsibility for Christ's death and escaped the destruction of Jerusalem by conversion, protected by the blood of the lamb. As we will see in the next miniature, the subject of the Jews' guilt or innocence is a special preoccupation in our manuscript.

16. Pilate Washes His Hands and the Self-Curse of the Jews (*Page 171*)

When Pilate's stratagem of offering the crowd a choice between Christ and Barabbas failed to dispose of the case before him, he simply let the crowd have its way. "He took water and washed his hands before the crowd, saying, 'I am innocent of this man's blood; see to it yourselves.' And all the people answered, 'His blood be on us and on our children!'" (Matt. 27: 24–25).

In the Glajor Gospel the artist presents a rather unusual rendition of this event. Framed in an arch, Pilate sits on a faldstool and leans forward to wash his hands; contrary to the standard manner of representing this action, the servant does not hold a basin beneath his hands but has placed a footed basin on a little stand before him.[1] Christ stands meekly before him, his hands evidently bound, but no soldier holds him and no attendants surround Pilate as they generally do. The servant's manner of pouring as well as his pose and dress are close replicas of these features in the corresponding miniature of the Vehapʿaṙ Gospel (fig. 171a). The inscriptions on the latter read "Pilate," "Servant," "The washing of hands." But the U.C.L.A. Gospel departs from the eleventh-century manuscript by adding a most graphic illustration of the self-curse of the Jews. Three bearded men with typical Jewish headdress place one hand on their own heads and the other on the heads of their children. This iconography seems without parallel in Byzantium, and its migration from the West to Greater Armenia can be traced via Cilicia. In a Bible Moralisée of the thirteenth century a single figure in the crowd of Jews puts his hand on his head and one other lays a hand on a child.[2] The motif is picked up in the Armenian frieze Gospel, in which tiny children gather under one of their parent's hands as they call down God's wrath on themselves (fig. 171b). Yet rare as it is, this self-curse of the Jews seems to have been of some importance in Armenia in the early fourteenth century, for Awag represents the subject twice with only slight variations on the motif used in the U.C.L.A. Gospel (figs. 171d and 171e).[3] Moreover, in the U.C.L.A. Gospel the development of the sparse nucleus of Pilate washing his hands by the addition of the self-curse clearly shifts the attention to the latter.

The blatant anti-Semitism of this subject receives a curious treatment in the exegetes. Bothered by the notion that the parents' sin should be visited upon their progeny—a principle rejected by Christ in John 9:2–3—they proposed that the curse was actually ineffective. In a passage quoted virtually verbatim in Yovhannēs Erznkacʿi, Chrysostom begins with amazement at the clamor of the Jews:

> See here too their great madness. For passion and wicked desire are like this. They suffer not men to see anything of what is right. For be it that you curse yourselves; why do you draw down the curse upon your children also? Nevertheless, though they acted with so much mad-

[6] Chrysostom, "In Matt. Hom. 86," chap. 1, *NPNF* x, p. 512.

[7] Yovhannēs Erznkacʿi, *Meknutʿiwn* on Matt. 27:19, p. 588.

[1] Schiller, *Iconography of Christian Art,* II, 63–66, figs. 204–10.

[2] Paris, Bibliothèque Nationale, ms. lat. 11560 (Bible Moralisée, 13th century), fol. 41v. Cf. A. de Laborde, *La Bible Moralisée,* II, pl. 265.

[3] Erevan, Mat. 212 (Awag, 1337–40), fol. 91.

ness, both against themselves, and against their children, the lover of man so far from confirming their sentence upon their children, confirmed it not even on them, but from the one and from the other received those that repented, and counts them worthy of good things beyond number. For indeed even Paul was of them, and the thousands that believed in Jerusalem; for, "thou seest, it is said, brother, how many thousands of Jews there are which believe" (Acts 21:20). And if some continued in their sin, to themselves let them impute their punishment.[4]

The last line is the most significant. According to Chrysostom and Erznkacʻi it is not the behavior of their forefathers at Christ's trial that curses contemporary Jews, but rather their continued unrepentance. To those who should embrace Christianity, like Pilate's wife in the preceding miniature, forgiveness would be always available. The "reasonableness" of such anti-Semitism must have made it all the more potent.

17. The Mocking of Christ (*Page 172*)

After Pilate had delivered Christ up to be crucified the soldiers gave him a mock royal reception before leading him away to his execution. "The soldiers of the governor took Jesus into the praetorium, and they gathered the whole battalion before him. And they stripped him and put a scarlet robe upon him, and plaiting a crown of thorns they put it on his head, and put a reed in his right hand. And kneeling before him they mocked him, saying, 'Hail, King of the Jews!' And they spat upon him, and took the reed and struck him on the head" (Matt. 27:27–30).

It is in the West, particularly northern Europe, that this subject has its greatest development.[1] For Byzantine sensibilities, however, the outrage was evidently too offensive, for the subject does not appear in Byzantine art, not even in the dense frieze Gospels.[2] On the other hand, Armenians seem to have had a special interest in the subject; it was illustrated in the Vehapʻaṙ Gospel (fig. 172a) and appeared no less than three times in the Gospel of King Gagik of Kars (see Table 8). In the Tʻoros Ṙoslin manuscripts in Baltimore and Washington, Christ is shown frontally in the center, either seated or standing, and the scoffers approach on either side to strike or spit on him (fig. 172b). This iconography Der Nersessian has traced to Western prototypes.[3] In the Armenian frieze Gospel (which twice adds the subject to the program of its model) Christ is surrounded by musicians and tumblers in an extravagant development of the scene (fig. 172c).[4]

The iconography of the U.C.L.A. Gospel miniature, however, depends not on such prototypes but on the tradition of the Vehapʻaṙ Gospel (fig. 172a). In both miniatures the composition is presented in an unusual frieze format.[5] Three soldiers are shown to the right, two kneeling and one standing, wearing pointed hats and making identical gestures. Christ sits in the U.C.L.A. miniature instead of standing, but this is simply an accommodation to the low horizontal format of the miniature. In both miniatures Christ carries a reed with a kind of tasseled end, and, most extraordinary, in the U.C.L.A. Gospel he wears a crown of cacti. In Western art his crown is generally a plaited circlet of some sort of thorny branches; in a uniquely Near Eastern interpretation the Fourth Painter has made the crown a pile of cacti; its shape was originally more angular but its corners have been rounded off by subsequent overpainting in white. A similar crown, though more domical in shape, is used a generation later by Awag (figs. 172d and 171e).

In John Chrysostom's *Commentary* the humiliation of Christ is intended to teach Christians humility. "He vouchsafed to stoop so much for us as actually to suffer these things, and to teach us all virtue. . . . For when thou seest Him, both by gestures and by deeds mocked and worshipped with so much derision, and beaten and suffering the utmost insults, though thou be very stone, thou wilt become softer than any wax, and wilt cast out of thy soul all haughtiness."[6]

In the Syro-Armenian view of the event, by contrast, it is not the example as much as the efficacy of Christ's suffering that is important. As Christ's suffering in the garden (*page 160*) was meant to cure

[4] Chrysostom, "In Matt. Hom. 86," chap. 2, *NPNF* x, p. 513. For comparable passage see Yovhannēs Erznkacʻi, *Meknutʻiwn* on Matt. 27:25, p. 590.

[1] Schiller, *Iconography of Christian Art*, II, 69–73, figs. 235–55; E. Lucchesi-Palli and R. Hausherr, "Dornenkrönung," *Lexikon der christlichen Ikonographie*, I, 513–16.

[2] Paris, Bibliothèque Nationale, gr. 74, cf. Omont, *Évangiles;* Florence, Bibliotheca Laurentiana, ms. Plut. VI,23, cf. Velmans, *Le Tétraévangile.*

[3] Der Nersessian, *Arm. Mss. Walters,* 18.

[4] Washington, Freer Gallery of Art, ms. 32.18, 319, and 516. Der Nersessian, *Arm. Mss. Freer,* figs. 125 and 160.

[5] This composition is unknown among the Byzantine and Western examples reviewed in Derbes, *Byzantine Art and the Dugento,* 89–128.

[6] Chrysostom, "In Matt. Hom. 87," chap. 1, *NPNF* x, p. 516.

Adam's suffering and restore him to the garden of paradise, so each new suffering in Christ's passion is seen as effective in the reversal of the damage done in the fall of man. Commenting on the crown of thorns, Ephraem Syrus writes, "The crown of thorns with which they insulted him was turned against them to their own derision, for good, so that by him the enemy (i.e., the devil) might be damned, for in wearing the crown he bore off the curse of the first Adam: 'Thorns and thistles it shall bring forth to you'" (Gen. 3:18).[7] Erznkacʿi echoes the same sentiment; further he explains that Christ endured the derisive jokes of his enemies so that we might be spared from becoming the devil's plaything. In the weakness of Christ was his power most manifest.[8]

All of the implements of Christ's suffering, moreover, have some symbolic meaning in Yovhannēs Erznkacʿi. His scarlet robe signifies the red of the sacrament, which is his blood poured out for the salvation of the world; or, if one follows John's reading here, it is purple because it is the chlamys of royalty.[9] The reed is a rod of judgment and a priestly staff, and it symbolizes Christ, on whom all the world leaned as on a staff.[10]

18. The Way of the Cross (*Page 173*)

Although in the West medieval piety expanded the Way of the Cross to truly epic proportions both in art and devotional literature, Byzantium treated the subject with the utmost restraint.[1] The standard Byzantine representation shows soldiers leading Christ by a rope while Simon of Cyrene carries the cross, either before or behind. This restraint accords perfectly with the laconic simplicity of the synoptic account. Matthew tells the story in two verses. "When they had mocked him, they stripped him of the robe, and put his own clothes on him, and led him away to crucify him. As they went out, they came upon a man of Cyrene, Simon by name; this man they compelled to carry his cross" (Matt. 27:31–32. Cf. Mark 15:20–21; Luke 23:26–31).

In the U.C.L.A. Gospel both verses of Matthew are illustrated. On the left Christ is seen returning the royal red cloak of his mocking to a soldier, and on the right Simon carries the cross. Both elements, as well as their combination, are unusual. The illustration of Christ removing his royal robe is unknown in Byzantine art and extremely rare in the West. Moreover the two known Western versions of this subject differ from the U.C.L.A. version by showing Christ in the process of taking the garment off over his head.[2] The U.C.L.A. representation of Christ handing over the cloak was the inspiration for Awag's painting of the subject, though Awag has reversed the composition (fig. 173b).

The carrying of the cross is also unusual. In the West the representation of Christ carrying his own cross, as told in John's gospel, gradually supplants Simon's carrying of the cross, starting in Romanesque times (John 19:16–17). Armenian iconography, following Byzantine, prefers to show Simon carrying the cross. This preference is manifest in the Gospel of King Gagik, which illustrated the subject in Mark and Luke, and remains standard in the Cilician period as well (see the frieze Gospel, for example, in fig. 172c). But while in Byzantine art Simon always carries the cross freely,[3] in the U.C.L.A miniature a soldier carrying an axe grabs Simon by the shoulder and "compels" him to carry the cross, according to the literal text of Mt. 27:32. This detail is copied very closely out of the Vehapʿaṙ Gospel; the soldier with axe and pointed hat grabs Simon by the shoulder, and Simon has the same hunched-over pose as he hefts the cross (fig. 173a). The inscriptions in the Vehapʿaṙ Gospel identify the soldier as "servant," along with "Simon of Cyrene."

Chrysostom comments neither on the putting aside of the cloak nor on the carrying of the cross. But Erznkacʿi in commenting on the mocking of Christ had pointed to the royal associations of his robe, and in connection with Matt. 27:31 he remarks that Christ's executioners had to strip off his royal garment lest they seem to be crucifying their king.[4]

[7] Ephraem Syrus, *Commentaire,* bk. 20, chap. 17, p. 209.
[8] Yovhannēs Erznkacʿi, *Meknutʿiwn* on Matt. 27:29, p. 592.
[9] Ibid., on Matt. 27:28, p. 591.
[10] Ibid., on Matt. 27:29, p. 591. See similar sentiments in Ephraem Syrus, *Commentaire,* bk. 20, chap. 17, p. 209.
[1] Millet, *Iconographie,* 362–79; Schiller, *Iconography of Christian Art,* II, 78–82, figs. 281–96; H. Laag and G. Jászai, "Kreuztragung Jesu," *Lexikon der christlichen Ikonographie,* II, 649–52.

[2] Cambridge, Library of St. John's College, K.21 (Miscellany of 14th century) fol. 51v; London, British Library, Harley 1526 (Bible Moralisée of 13th century), fol. 58. Cf. A. de Laborde, *Bible Moralisée,* III, pl. 529.
[3] For example, see Florence, Laurentiana, VI,23, fol. 58, Velmans, *Le Tétraévangile,* fig. 119.
[4] Yovhannēs Erznkacʿi, *Meknutʿiwn* on Matt. 27:31, p. 592.

Simon of Cyrene represents the Gentiles.[5] In this interpretation Erznkacʿi echoes sources from Early Christian times. Ephraem Syrus writes: "It was well that the Jews of their own volition gave the wood of the cross to the Gentiles, since in their insubordination they rejected his coming, who carried all blessings. In repudiating him they cast him upon the rival gentiles. They cast him aside out of rivalry, and to stir up their rivalry he was accepted by (the Gentiles), and he (in turn) accepted them, that through those who accepted him he might stimulate to rivalry those who repudiated him."[6]

The cross is identified with Christ, and Simon's acceptance of it is the Gentile acceptance of Christ. In this light the two halves of the iconography in the scene become complementary. On the one side the Jews are rejecting Christ and stripping him of his kingship, and on the other the Gentiles are embracing him.

19. The Women at the Tomb (*Page 179*)

The iconography of the Women at the Tomb has usually been discussed in terms of a broad East-West division. Millet formulated this geographic distinction on the basis of the number of women who come to the tomb, two being characteristic of Eastern art, three of Western.[1] This division he attributed to the separate versions of the story in Matthew and Mark, since the former mentions two, the latter three women; and the difference in liturgy, insofar as the Byzantine liturgy used Matthew, the Latin Mark for the Easter reading.[2] The Armenian material might be viewed as reinforcing this liturgical connection, while contradicting the geographical division, for the Armenian liturgy uses Mark for Easter,[3] and as a rule Armenian iconography, as in the U.C.L.A. Gospel, represents three women at the tomb.[4] Indeed, one of the earliest Armenian illustrations of the subject, the Gospel of King Gagik, shows four women (fig. 179a). But the preference for three women was the norm, in manuscripts of both Greater Armenia and Cilicia (figs. 179b–d). The Armenian frieze Gospel offers interesting witness to this preference, for while its model, Florence, Laurentiana VI,23, has two women, it includes three (fig. 179d). A simple counting of the women, however, does not do justice to the complexity of the subject. The third woman has a special importance in Armenia, where she is identified as the Blessed Virgin Mary, and other elements in the iconography also deserve comment.

To begin with, if one looks at all the elements of the scene it becomes evident that the U.C.L.A. version, like most renditions of the subject, is a composite narrative; that is, it incorporates elements taken from more than one Gospel account of the resurrection. The Gospels themselves, moreover, are quite irreconcilable as far as their narrative details of the event are concerned (Matt. 28:1–10; Mark 16:1–8; Luke 24:1–11; John 20:1–18). Matthew and Mark speak of one angel, Luke and John of two; and while Matthew and John place the encounter with the angels outside the tomb, Mark and Luke put it within the tomb. In the U.C.L.A. version, then, the single angel seated outside might agree with Matthew's text. The three women, however, might agree either with Mark or with Luke, who also names three. The linens carefully folded in the tomb, which are a prominent feature in the U.C.L.A. version, are explained only through John's account; finally the soldiers, who for fear of the angel "trembled and became as dead men" (Matt. 28:4) are mentioned only in Matthew. Unfortunately for Millet's thesis, then, the preference for one or another Gospel account does not succeed in explaining the imagery.

Apart from the third woman there are really no surprises in our iconography of the Women at the Tomb. The development of this iconography has been traced by Kartsonis in the period after

---

[5] Ibid. on Matt. 27:32, p. 592–93.

[6] Ephraem Syrus, *Commentaire*, bk. 20, chap. 20, p. 211.

[1] Millet, *Iconographie*, 517–40.

[2] Schiller, *Ikonographie der christlichen Kunst*, III, 18; J. Myslivec and G. Jászai, "Frauen am Grab," *Lexikon der christlichen Ikonographie*, II, 54–62.

[3] *Čašocʿ Girkʿ*, 97.

[4] In Armenian art the earliest example of three women at the tomb is found in Erevan, Mat. 6201 (of 1038); Dournovo, *Haykakan Manrankarčʿutʿyun*, pl. 8. Other manuscripts with the three women are Erevan, Mat. 2743 (of 1232), ibid., pl. 27; Jerusalem, St. James 2568 (of 1260–70), Azaryan, *Kilikyan Manrankarčʿutʿyunə*, pl. 104; Erevan, Mat. 979 (of 1286), Dournovo, *Haykakan Manrankarčʿutʿyun*, pl. 41; Erevan, Mat. 4818 (of 1316) and Erevan, Mat. 316 (of the fourteenth century), Zakaryan, *Vaspurakanskoj Min.*, pls. 14 and 39. Two women at the tomb can be found in the following manuscripts: Venice, San Lazzaro 141 (eleventh century) fol. 77, Janashian, *Armenian Miniature Paintings*, pl. 48d; Jerusalem, St. James 1796 (twelfth century), fol. 88v, Narkiss and Stone, *Jerusalem*, fig. 60; Washington, Freer ms. 32.18 (of ca. 1270), page 195; Der Nersessian, *Arm. Mss. Freer*, fig. 107; Baltimore, Walters 539 (of 1262), fol. 128, Der Nersessian, *Arm. Mss. Walters*, fig. 85.

Iconoclasm[5] and by the fourteenth century it had long been standard. Close parallel compositions abound in Byzantine art. Often the differences are restricted to such details as the shape of the vessels carried by the women, the contouring of the landscape, or the number of the soldiers. The thirteenth century Athos, Iviron ms. 5 and the fourteenth century Paris, Bibliothèque Nationale ms. 54 come very close, though the space in the composition is not as compressed as in the U.C.L.A. miniature.[6] The guards in these two manuscripts even carry pointed kite-shaped shields, as in the U.C.L.A. Gospel; this is an authentic medieval shield type, the point being designed for planting in the ground.

The fact that a standard iconographic formula is used for the Women at the Tomb in the U.C.L.A. Gospel does not mean that the formula is used without understanding; nor does it mean that the intention behind the formula is standard and without distinctive Armenian features. Liturgically the importance of the Women at the Tomb in Armenia does not depend so much on the reading of this narrative on Easter as it does on its reading every Sunday at Matins. This hour is a weekly commemoration of the women, and each week the Gospel reading is taken in turn from a different evangelist.[7] Although Sunday is everywhere a commemoration of the resurrection, this development of matins as the Office of the Myrophores (Paštōn Iwłabericʿ) is a unique Armenian observance.

The theme is then taken up musically at the start of Mass on Sundays, in the melody and the ode that precede the introit.[8] These two hymns sketch the themes of the women's encounter with the angel. To cite the ode:

The keepers did shake for fear,
For out of the new, virgin sepulchre,
Christ did arise, Christ did awake
Out of the virgin tomb, out of the tomb of light.

By the holy stone sat the marvelous one and cried aloud,
And the oil-bearing women announced joyfully:
Christ did arise, Christ did awake,
Out of the new tomb, out of the virgin tomb.[9]

Since Christ rose without disturbing the tomb—it was the angel who rolled back the stone—his resurrection is parallel to his virgin birth. Thus the symbolism of the event runs ahead of the simple Gospel accounts and requires that the Blessed Virgin herself be one of the women. It is she, therefore, who is pictured in the melody as conversing with the angel:

Mary called to the gardener:
"Didst thou remove my first-born, my love?"
"That fowl is risen, the wakeful being,"
The seraph did trumpet to the mother and those with her,
"The Savior of the world, Christ, is risen!
And he hath delivered mankind from death."[10]

Since Christ's earthly career began with an angel's salutation to Mary, it was inconceivable to an Armenian that she should not be present at the angelic annunciation that marked its conclusion.

The fact that the Gospels are silent on this point presents Yovhannēs Erznkacʿi with a major crux interpretum, for she, he says, was the one "most worthy to be named."[11] He reviews seven possible identifications for the Marys mentioned by the evangelists and is forced to conclude that the Virgin Mary is not one of them. Nevertheless he concludes on the basis of the tradition in hymns and in exegesis that the three women were the blessed Virgin Mary, Mary Magdalen, and Mary of Cleophas.[12] The fact that one of the three is understood to be the Virgin Mary is attested by frequent inscriptions of her name in Armenian miniatures of the subject.[13] This tradition has a history in iconography stretching back to the sixth-century Rabbula Gospel and the mosaics of S. Sergius of Gaza.[14] In the U.C.L.A. Gospel Tʿoros Taronecʿi,

[5] Anna Kartsonis, *Anastasis: The Making of an Image* (Princeton, 1986).

[6] Omont, *Miniatures*, pl. 94, fig. 12; S. M. Pelikanidis et al., *The Treasures of Mount Athos*, II, fig. 17.

[7] *Breviarium armenorum sive dispositio communium armeniacae ecclesiae precum*, trans. Isaac Kiudius and Joannis Mantagunensis (Venice, 1909), 90–112, esp. 102–3; *The Book of Hours of the Common Prayers of the Armenian Apostolic Orthodox Church*, trans. Tiran Nersoyan, 3–16 and 52–53.

[8] *Divine Liturgy of the Armenian Apostolic Orthodox Church together with the Directorium of Lessons and Practices*, trans. Tiran Nersoyan, 4th ed. (New York, 1970), 86–87.

[9] Ibid., 87.

[10] Ibid., 87.

[11] Yovhannēs Erznkacʿi, *Meknutʿiwn* on Matt. 28:1, pp. 609–10.

[12] Ibid., p. 610.

[13] For example, see the inscription in the miniatures of the Women at the Tomb in Erevan 316 and 4818, Zakaryan, *Vaspurakanskoj Min.*, pls. 39 and 14; or in New York, Metropolitan Museum of Art, ms. 57.185.3, Alice Taylor, "Vaspurakan Manuscript Illumination and Eleventh Century Sources," in *Medieval Armenian Culture*, University of Pennsylvania Armenian Texts and Studies 6 (1984), 306–14.

[14] Carlo Cecchelli, Giuseppe Furlani, and Mario Salmi, *The Rabbula Gospels, Facsimile Edition of the Miniatures of the Syriac Manuscript Plut. I, 56 in the Medicaean-Laurentian Library* (Olten, 1959), 70. For the Justinianic mosaics of Gaza see Choricius, *Laudatio Marciani*, 1, 76, in Cyril Mango, *The*

in keeping with his interest in having a homogeneous image of the Blessed Virgin in the manuscript, has repainted the face of the third woman as Mary.[15] Her expression of grief can be compared to that of Jairus' wife on *page 218*.

Other elements of the iconography are also significant. The stone that covered the tomb, which is a speckled green marble, was, according to Yovhannēs Erznkacʿi, the stone that served Jacob as a pillow (Gen. 28:10–22). Jacob anointed it and set it as a monument, naming it the House of God and the Gate of Heaven, for while it became a stone of scandal to the incredulous it was the gate of heaven to believers.[16] The soldiers who were placed at the tomb by the Pharisees and afterwards accepted a bribe from the priests to spread the story that the disciples had robbed the body (Matt. 27:62–66, 28:11–15), are also interpreted as witnesses to the resurrection. According to *The Teaching of Saint Gregory*, "the guards came stricken and dejected into the city, and related to the priests and disciples, especially to the excited crowd which had gathered, revealing it to many in the city."[17] The linens carefully folded in the tomb are the refutation of the priests' version of the events. As Chrysostom explains, "The linen clothes lying are a sign of the resurrection, for if anyone had stolen the body they would not have stripped it, nor taken the trouble to remove the napkin and roll it up; especially since the myrrh is an adhesive that sticks the clothes to the body. From this Peter and John believed in the resurrection."[18]

20. The Call of Peter and Andrew (*Page 193*)

The U.C.L.A. Gospel illustrates the Call of the Apostles in the two parallel stages as narrated in Mark 1:16–20. First Christ encounters Simon and Andrew fishing and calls them to follow him, which they do; then a little farther on he finds James and John working on their nets with their father and calls them. The two miniatures are very similar, and it would be hard to make a distinction in the message they carry; rather, the repetition is meant to reinforce their impact. In the first miniature Christ stands on a panel of earth shown in horizontal stripes alongside a cursory panel of city-scape (possibly Capernaum of Mark 1:21). In a boat with high gunwales Simon and Andrew bend at their toil and Christ makes his usual gesture of speech. The artist has decorated the boat with a pair of red-cross banners of Crusader origin; this importation first appears in Armenia in the Crucifixion of Ṙoslin's Malatia Gospel of 1268.[1]

Aside from the banner and the city, the imagery is not much different from other renditions of the scene. The same basic compositions appear in the eleventh-century frieze Gospel in Florence.[2] The Byzantine image however shows the boat floating on a mound of water rather than on a horizontal strip; this detail links the U.C.L.A. image more closely with the representation in the eleventh-century Armenian Vehapʿaṙ Gospel (fig 194a). The manner of dividing sea from land in blocks and showing the land in horizontal bands is also close to the frescoes of the Tokalı Kilise in Cappadocia.[3]

For Chrysostom there are two qualities to be extolled in the behavior of the apostles in this story: their promptness to follow Christ, and the poverty and lowliness of their vocation. "So exceedingly great was their poverty," he observes, not without exaggeration, "that they were mending what was worn out, not being able to buy others."[4] Elsewhere he explains that the apostles were illiterate, for, conversing with fishmongers and cooks, they were hardly in a better state than irrational animals.[5] Nersēs Šnorhali also remarks on the apostles' readiness to follow Christ, but all denigration of their profession is significantly missing.[6] Instead he develops another line of interpretation that is uniquely Armenian in that it depends on the Armenian text of the Gospel. When Christ bids the apostles to follow him he promises

Art of the Byzantine Empire, 313–1453, Sources and Documents Englewood Cliffs, N.J., 1972), 68.

[15] Taronecʿi also repainted the Virgin in the Genealogy (*page 35*) and the Annunciation (*page 305*).

[16] Yovhannēs Erznkacʿi, *Meknutʿiwn* on Matt. 27:60, p. 606.

[17] *Teaching of St. Gregory*, chap. 485, (ed. Thomson, p. 111).

[18] Chrysostom, "In Jn. Hom. 85," chap. 4, *NPNF* xiv, pp. 320–21. This argument is repeated in Chrysostom's "In Matt. Hom. 90," chap. 2, *NPNF* x, pp. 530–32.

[1] Korkhmazyan, *Armenian Miniatures of the 13th and 14th Centuries*, pl. 102.

[2] Florence, Laur. Plut. VI,23, fol. 9. Cf. Velmans, *Le Tétraévangile* (Paris, 1971), fig. 18. See brief discussions of the iconography of this subject in Millet, *Iconographie*, 566–67; Schiller, *Iconography of Christian Art*, I, 155–56.

[3] Restle, *Byzantine Wall Painting*, II, fig. 103.

[4] Chrysostom, "In Matt. Hom. 14," chap. 3, *NPNF* x, p. 88.

[5] Chrysostom, "In Jn. Hom. 2," chap. 1, *NPNF* xiv, p. 4.

[6] Nersēs Šnorhali, *Meknutʿiwn* on Matt. 4:18–22, pp. 82–84.

them, "I will make you become fishers of men" (Mark 1:17 and Matt. 4:19). The Armenian text, however, reads, "I will make you become hunters of men." This involves a play on words, since in Armenian a "fisher" is etymologically a "fish-hunter."[7] At the same time, the classification of apostles with hunters also reflects the special esteem in which hunting was held in ancient Armenia and Iran, where hunting was a special royal activity.[8] Accordingly Nersēs Šnorhali asks why the Lord had chosen his ancient prophets from among shepherds but chose the apostles from among hunters.[9] Shepherds, he explains, look after domestic animals as the prophets looked after the Jews, but hunters go after wild animals as the apostles were sent after the Gentiles. Thus was fulfilled the prophecy of Jeremiah, "I will send many hunters, and they shall hunt them from every mountain" (Jer. 16:16). This is a theme that Nersēs alluded to in his commentary on the canon tables (see below, p. 175). To the Armenian it is not the lowliness of the apostles but the loftiness of their calling that is significant.

21. The Call of James and John (*Page 194*)

The call of the second pair of disciples differs from the first only in that James and John, besides abandoning their employment, also left behind their father Zebedee. The Fourth Painter shows this second calling in a composition similar to the one on the preceding page, except that here the new disciples Peter and John are shown accompanying Christ, and Zebedee is shown in the boat, in grey hair and beard. The Vehapʿaṙ Gospel had omitted these extra figures in this scene (fig. 194a); Awag includes Zebedee but omits Peter and Andrew (194b). The miniature reinforces the message of the preceding miniature.

22. The Cure of the Leper (*Page 197*)

During his tour of the towns of Galilee, one of which appears as background in the U.C.L.A. miniature, Christ had occasion to cure a leper (Mark 1:40–45). The leper, covered with sores and clad only in a loincloth, kneels before Christ. While four apostles stand witness behind him, Christ reaches out with his right hand and touches the leper's head with two fingers. "Moved with pity, he stretched out his hand and touched him, and said to him, 'I will; be clean'" (Mark 1:41).

Simple as it is, the iconography of the cure of the leper is noteworthy. There are three moments in the story that suggest themselves for illustration: the leper's petition, the cure, and the leper's subsequent visit to the priests to be certified as clean. In the history of the iconography it is the first and last moments that are generally illustrated; and even if the cure is shown, Christ is rarely shown touching the leper.[1] The cure of the leper in Erevan, Mat. 7651 is a good example of the Byzantine iconography in this respect, since in this scene it copies very closely its Byzantine model (fig. 197c). In the left half of the frieze the leper kneels at the feet of Christ, who blesses from a distance; in the center the cleansed leper presents himself to a seated priest (on the right Christ teaches in Capernaum).

The iconography of the Glajor Gospel follows that of the Vehapʿaṙ Gospel, though the composition is reversed and the attendant figures are missing (197a). The leper in loincloth kneels and Christ reaches out to touch his head. This interest in Christ's physical contact shows up in three other East Christian manuscripts. In the twelfth century, Christ puts out his hand to touch the shoulder of a standing leper in Venice, San Lazzaro 888/159 (fig. 197b). The two great Syriac lectionaries of the thirteenth century, Vatican syr. 559 and London, British Library add. 7170, also show Christ touching the head of the kneeling leper, now with three attendant apostles.[2]

In the exegetical tradition the three separate moments of the story carry three separate lessons. The leper's petition teaches faith and humility in prayer, the cure manifests Christ's divinity, and the visit to the priest manifests Christ's attitude toward the Mosaic law. The U.C.L.A. Gospel elects the central moment of the transfer of power through the touch of Christ. Chrysostom, Ephraem, and Yovhannēs Erznkacʿi all point to the contrast between Christ's cure of the leper and Elisha's cure of the leprous Naaman, for the prophet did not so much as set eyes on the leper but just gave instructions for his bathing in the Jor-

[7] *Jknors* (fisher) = *jugn* (fish) + *orsord* (hunter). A similar play takes place in Syriac, in which *sayyādā* means both "fisher" and "hunter." Cf. R. Murray, *Symbols*, 176–78.

[8] Cf. Prudence Harper, *The Royal Hunter: Art of the Sasanian Empire* (New York, 1978).

[9] Nersēs Šnorhali, *Meknutʿiwn* on Matt. 4:20–22, pp. 83–84.

[1] Schiller, *Iconography of Christian Art*, II, 175. Carr remarks on how rarely Byzantine art shows Christ touching the leper (*The Rockefeller McCormick New Testament*, 199).

[2] Leroy, *Mss. syriaques*, album, pl. 82, 3–4.

dan.[3] Since the disease was contagious there was a real danger that the prophet would contract it. By contrast, Chrysostom remarks, "the Lord, to signify that he heals not as a servant, but as absolute master, does also touch. For his hand became not unclean from the leprosy but the leprous body was rendered clean by his holy hand."[4]

[3] Chrysostom, "In Matt. Hom. 25," chap. 2, *NPNF* x, p. 173; Ephraem, *Commentaire*, bk. 12, chap. 21, p. 125; Yovhannēs Erznkacʻi, *Meknutʻiwn* on Matt. 8:3, p. 187.

[4] Chrysostom, "In Matt. Hom. 25," chap. 2, *NPNF*, x, p. 173.

23. The First Storm at Sea (*Page 211*)

According to the evangelists, Christ twice miraculously calmed a storm at sea. On the first occasion he was already on ship, but asleep, when the storm arose (Matt. 8:23–27; Mark 4:35–41; Luke 8:22–25), but on the second, the disciples had taken ship without him, and he reached them in the middle of the storm walking on the sea (Matt. 14:22–23; Mark 6:45–52; John 6:15–21). Both miracles are illustrated in the U.C.L.A. Gospel, and both are illustrated in Mark's account, which is where they appear in the Vehapʻaṙ Gospel. The iconography of the two scenes is also extremely close to the eleventh-century prototype and markedly different from that of Byzantine or Western art.

There are two common ways of representing the First Storm at Sea.[1] One way represents two moments of the story side by side in the same ship. At one end of the ship Peter is seen waking Christ from his slumber, while at the other end Christ leans forward from the ship to subdue the raging storm.[2] This is the iconography followed by the Byzantine and Armenian frieze Gospels (fig. 211c).[3] Byzantine art more commonly uses another composition that omits the first moment and shows Christ already awake in the middle of the ship; on either side disciples witness with admiration as he makes a commanding gesture at the sea.[4] The U.C.L.A. Gospel represents a third option, omitting the stilling of the sea and showing the concerted effort of the disciples to awaken Christ. The disciples all stand in the ship, and in unison they reach forward, each one further than the last, to touch Christ. The disciple actually touching Christ is not Peter but one of the younger disciples, probably John. The same composition is found in the Vehapʻaṙ Gospel; only two disciples are shown, but they both reach forward to wake Christ, and the one in front is a young beardless man (fig. 211a). Tʻoros Ṙoslin illustrates the same moment in his Washington Gospel (fig. 211b). Though these differences may seem arbitrary, this iconography is in fact closer to the Gospel text than the Western versions of the subject, for the text does not attribute the action to Peter but to the disciples in the plural: "*They* woke him and (*they*) said to him: Teacher, do you not care if *we* perish?" (Mark 4:38, emphasis added).

Another unusual detail also links this miniature both to the Vehapʻaṙ Gospel and to a literal reading of the text. In Mark, but not in the parallel passages in Matthew or Luke, one reads that Christ was at the stern of the ship "asleep on the cushion" (Mark 4:38). This item of iconography seems to have gone unnoticed elsewhere, but it has been represented in the Vehapʻaṙ Gospel and in the U.C.L.A. Gospel. In both Christ sleeps on a kind of mattress, which is visible beneath his feet; in the U.C.L.A. Gospel it is purple. Other features also link the two representations. The ship extends the full width of the miniature and is framed above in a kind of canopy shape. At bow and stern banners fly; these are green with red tassels in the Vehapʻaṙ Gospel, but the U.C.L.A. Gospel makes them into crusader pennants carrying red crosses on a white field.[5] In addition the U.C.L.A. Gospel, besides augmenting the number of disciples, also adds a panel of gold behind Christ to distinguish his world from the troubled state of the disciples, who stand against the white parchment.

The miracle itself, in which Christ by a simple command, "Peace! Be still!" (Mark 4:40), quiets the winds and the waves, is obviously a demonstration of the divinity of Christ. According to Ephraem, by his power over the storm Christ shows that he is the Son of the Creator.[6] His power, Chrysostom says, is greater than that of Moses, who had to pray and use a rod to part the Red Sea.[7] Yovhannēs Erznkacʻi makes the same point, comparing Christ's mastery over the forces of nature to that of the Creator who

[1] Schiller, *Iconography of Christian Art*, I, 168–69; W. Kemp and R. Lauer, "Sturm auf dem Meer," *Lexikon der christlichen Ikonographie*, IV, 219–22.

[2] See also the Ottonian examples from the Codex Egberti, Trier Stadtbibl. ms. 24, and the Gospel of Otto II/III, Aachen Cathedral Treasury, in Schiller, *Iconography of Christian Art*, I, figs. 494–95.

[3] Florence, Laurentiana VI,23, fol. 70; Velmans, *Le Tétraévangile*, fig. 139.

[4] Paris, B.N. gr. 52; Schiller, *Iconography of Christian Art*, I, fig. 492.

[5] See the Call of Peter and Andrew, above pp. 117–18.

[6] Ephraem, *Commentaire*, bk. 6, chap. 25, p. 64.

[7] Chrysostom, "In Matt. Hom. 28," chap. 1, *NPNF* x, p. 190.

made the seas with a word and brought forth the flood of Noah's time.[8] Yet this dramatic demonstration of Christ's power is not the subject of the miniature; instead one finds Christ asleep.

The sleep of Christ, like other manifestations of weakness, confronts the theologian with the mystery of the two natures in Christ. The pillow is symbolic in this respect. Chrysostom says that he slept on a pillow to signify "his freedom from pride, and to teach us hereby a high degree of austerity;"[9] Yovhannēs Erznkacʿi says he slept on a pillow "so that he might declare his true humanity and show his humility and make the same an example for us."[10] His sleeping, the exegetes both explain, was a test to the disciples, for the greater their alarm at the storm the greater would be their impression of the miracle. But it was also a lesson on the nature of his unseen power. As Erznkacʿi puts it, Christ slept so that "they might perceive through his sleeping the awakening of the sea and by his rising might perceive the slumber of the sea, and thus understand his power that does not sleep."[11] The disciples in their lack of faith reached forth to awaken him, for they did not understand that Christ could sleep and command at the same time.[12] Although he slept, his divinity did not sleep, Ephraem remarked.[13]

This is not to deny the possibility that other meanings were also associated with this imagery. An allegorical interpretation of the storm-tossed ship as the soul beset by the vicissitudes of the present life is developed both in Gregory Narekacʿi and Yovhannēs Erznkacʿi.[14] But the first level of meaning is the more specific level that is spelled out in the image, the mystery of the divine power of Christ, which remains ever vigilant, even when his human nature sleeps.

24. The Woman with Hemorrhage and the Petition of Jairus (*Page 216*)

This miniature marks the point at which Tʿoros Taronecʿi took charge of the manuscript; as explained above, he began with a mistake. The scribe had provided a full blank page for this subject on page 214, which Tʿoros overlooked; having painted this subject where the following subject belonged, he had to add a leaf at *page 218*. The Gospel account (Mark 5:21–34, Matt. 9:18–22; Luke 8:40–48) places Christ's encounter with the woman with hemorrhage after Jairus' petition, when he was already following Jairus to his home. For some unknown reason the Armenian frieze Gospel and its Byzantine model place Christ's encounter with the woman before Jairus' petition (fig. 216c), but Tʿoros has followed the Vehapʿaṙ Gospel in depicting the woman's cure as simultaneous with Jairus' plea (fig. 216a). The crowd mentioned in the text is represented by four disciples behind Christ and a pair of men behind Jairus. Jairus is set against a panel of solid blue and is shown on his knees; the woman is bent over even further, touching the hem of his garment.

The healing of the woman with hemorrhage has a long iconographic history but very little development. The subject is fairly common in the Early Christian period, whether in catacomb art or on portable objects, on which it had an obvious apotropaic value.[1] Eusebius tells of a sculpture group of the subject at Caesarea Philippi,[2] and by the sixth century it had entered monumental wall decoration. Generally, Christ is shown noticing the woman who reaches out to touch him, though occasionally, perhaps by some confusion with the *Noli me tangere* iconography, he is shown trying to escape the woman's touch (fig. 216b). When the image is combined, however, with the representation of Jairus making supplication, Christ is shown listening to Jairus and ignoring the woman. This is the way the subject is handled in the Sacra Parallela, Paris, B.N. gr. 74, as well as in the thirteenth-century Syriac manuscripts, London, B.L. add. 7170 and Vatican Syr. 559.[3] Byzantine art, however, does not show the woman prostrate.[4] Tʿoros Taronecʿi's rendition of the subject differs from these in showing Jairus kneeling.

The Cure of the Woman with Hemorrhage, like the Cure of the Leper, involves Christ's contact with someone who was in the eyes of the law unclean. As in the Cure of the Leper, it is pointed out by the exegetes that, far from becoming impure from her

8 Yovhannēs Erznkacʿi, *Meknutʿiwn*, p. 197.
9 Chrysostom, "In Matt. Hom. 28," chap. 1, *NPNF* x, p. 190.
10 Yovhannēs Erznkacʿi, *Meknutʿiwn*, p. 196.
11 Ibid.
12 Ibid., pp. 196–97.
13 Ephraem, *Commentaire*, bk. 6, chap. 25, p. 63.
14 Gregory Narekacʿi, *Le Livre de prières*, trans. Isaac Kéchichian, SC 78 (Paris, 1961), prayer no. 25, pp. 154–59.

1 H. Leclercq, "Hémorroïsse," *DACL* 6, 2200–2209; Schiller, *Iconography of Christian Art*, I, 178–79.
2 Eusebius, *Historia Ecclesiastica*, VII, chap. 18 (PG 20, col. 680).
3 Millet, *Iconographie*, 583–85; London, B.L. add. 7170, fol. 83v and Vatican Syr. 559, fol. 73v are reproduced in Leroy, *Mss. syriaques*, pl. 83, 3–4.
4 Carr, *The Rockefeller McCormick New Testament*, 201.

touch, Christ purified her. As Ephraem Syrus observed, "If fire purges unclean things without itself becoming dirtied, how much more would the power of his divinity cleanse without being made unclean?"[5] Ephraem, indeed, finds this particular miracle extremely significant, for he devotes an entire chapter to its interpretation. The whole economy of salvation is involved in the event. The healing of the woman's unclean womb is demonstration against those who doubted that he truly came from the womb. "Indeed our Lord himself knew that he came from the womb, and he knew those who did not believe he came from the womb; for this reason he sent forth his power into her womb that through her unclean (womb) they might believe in his coming from the holy womb."[6] This underscores the purpose of the Incarnation: "He assumed flesh from men that men might have access to his divinity, and he revealed his divinity that they despise not his humanity."[7] This larger dimension of the miracle is found in Yovhannēs Erznkacʿi as well, for he sees the woman as a symbol of Adam's nature weighted down by matter.[8]

Our miniature, however, shows not only the woman bending to receive Christ's beneficent power, but Jairus simultaneously making his plea. The balancing of the two figures on either side of Christ suggests the contrast that is drawn between them in the exegesis. To Chrysostom the woman is superior to Jairus, though he was leader in the synagogue. "She detained (Christ) not, she took no hold of him, but touched him only with the end of her fingers, and though she came later, she first went away healed. (Jairus) indeed was bringing the physician along to his house, but for her a mere touch sufficed. For though she was bound by her affliction, yet her faith had given her wings."[9] For this reason Christ turned to her and said "Daughter, your faith has made you well" (Mark 5:34).

25. The Raising of the Daughter of Jairus (*Page 218*)

According to the scribe's layout, this miniature belonged in the half-page space on *page 216*, but due to Tʿoros' error a full page had to be added here to accommodate the subject. This accounts for the disproportionate architectural background that has been enlarged to fill the page. Around Jairus' daughter Tʿoros has grouped Christ and three apostles on one side and the parents on the other. Mark and Luke both mention that when Christ had rebuked the precipitate mourners, he took with him only Peter, James, and John and the girl's parents to witness her restoration to life (Mark 5:35–43, Luke 8:49–56; cf. Matt. 9:23–26).

Although the Raising of the Daughter of Jairus is itself a far more striking miracle, it is far less often represented than the Cure of the Woman with Hemorrhage.[1] The standard Byzantine composition of this scene was familiar in Cilicia a generation earlier. The Armenian frieze Gospel (fig. 218b) and Ṙoslin's Gospel in Baltimore (fig. 218c) both include it (although the latter has made the parents into two women).

While the iconography of the U.C.L.A. miniature is related to such compositions, certain features link it unmistakably to its model in the Vehapʿaṙ Gospel (fig. 218a). This is especially remarkable in that the U.C.L.A. Gospel has broken with the program of the Vehapʿaṙ Gospel in this scene, for the latter had illustrated the subject in Luke rather than in Mark. In the first place, Jairus' wife is shown kneeling, a detail not mentioned in the Gospel. In the second place, the bed of Jairus' daughter is excessively low; indeed the way the far side of the bed is indicated and the omission of all blankets and pillows make the bed look very much like a sarcophagus. Finally, and most significantly, Christ leans on a staff. In the Vehapʿaṙ Gospel this appears like the vardapet's T-shaped staff, but since it shows up nowhere else in the manuscript, its inclusion in this scene requires some explanation. As often, the unusual detail is the most telling.

The chief lesson Chrysostom draws from this subject is the courage with which Christians should face death. Christ's words, "She is not dead but sleeping," (Matt. 9:24; Mark 6:39; Luke 8:52) emphasize the fact that Christ has overcome death, death itself becoming no more than a sleep.[2] The Armenian exegete, however, takes this line of reasoning a step further, making the miracle, by synecdoche, a symbol of the whole work of mankind's salvation. To Yovhannēs Erznkacʿi the daughter of Jairus is a type of Eve, for

[5] Ephraem Syrus, *Commentaire*, bk. 7, chap. 8, p. 68.
[6] Ibid., chap. 15, p. 72.
[7] Ibid., chap. 17, p. 72.
[8] Yovhannēs Erznkacʿi, *Meknutʿiwn* on Matt. 9:20, p. 213.
[9] Chrysostom, "In Matt. Hom. 31," chap. 2, *NPNF* x, p. 207; similar sentiments can be found in Yovhannēs Erznkacʿi, *Meknutʿiwn* on Matt. 9:22–24, pp. 213–14.

[1] H. Leclerq, "Jaïre, La fille de," *DACL* 7, 2121–23; Schiller, *Iconography of Christian Art*, I, 179–80.
[2] Chrysostom, "In Matt. Hom. 31," chaps. 3–4, *NPNF* x, pp. 207–8.

Eve was in some sense a daughter to Adam, having been born from his side.[3] Referring to the central mystery of salvation he says that "(Christ) because of his patience went and placed his body over Adam and Eve by means of his death, whereby he established eternal life, as he said. 'I have come that you may have life' (John 10:10), and 'I am the resurrection and the life'" (John 11:25).[4] The Raising of the Daughter of Jairus thus becomes a raising of Eve, accomplished in Christ's death and descent into hell. It is this line of interpretation that seems to explain the otherwise anomalous details of Christ's staff and the tomb-like bed. In the iconography of the raising of Adam and Eve, that is in the Anastasis, Christ often leans on a staff topped with a cross, which he uses as a weapon against Satan, whom he tramples underfoot.[5] This is the formula followed in the frescoes of Ałt'amar.[6] Bearing down on his staff he reaches over to pull Adam from Hades. The iconography of the raising of Jairus' daughter has been assimilated to the iconography of the Anastasis because of the exegetical parallel between the two events. The raising of the girl is the raising of Eve, with whom all her children are being restored to life.

26. The Second Storm at Sea (*Page 227*)

On the occasion of the Second Storm at Sea the apostles were even more terrified than the first time, says Chrysostom, for this time they were alone, without Christ.[1] The history of the illustration of this subject starts in the third century, in the frescoes of Dura Europos, and it enjoys fairly wide use in the Early Christian period in catacombs, baptisteries, church decoration, and small portable objects.[2] The development of the iconography follows generally the narrative of Matthew, in which after the apostles have recognized Christ walking on the water Peter climbs out of the boat to walk to him; when his faith fails and he starts to sink, the Lord reaches out to save him from the waves (Matt. 14:22–23). It is this moment in the story that is illustrated in Dura Europos and other Early Christian examples, and medieval art both in Byzantium and the West follows suit. Those instances that depart from this rule illustrate instead the last moment of the story, by showing Christ climbing into the boat,[3] for both Matthew and Mark say that when Christ came on board the storm ceased (Matt. 14:32; Mark 6:51).

Breaking with this tradition the U.C.L.A. Gospel illustrates Mark's account, in which Peter's story is missing (Mark 6:45–52), and chooses the very first moment of the story, the apparition of Christ walking on the water. The same choice was made earlier in the Vehap'aṙ Gospel, in which the iconography is extremely close to that of the U.C.L.A. Gospel (fig. 211a). The compositions are reversed, as frequently happens with the Vehap'aṙ Gospel, but the same elements make up the two miniatures. Christ walks on the sea, his hand extended in speech; the disciples are grouped in the boat in two files, one above the other; and the boat's sail overhead forms a kind of canopy with banners flying fore and aft. In the U.C.L.A. Gospel these banners carry the Crusaders' red cross, as in the miniatures on *pages 193 and 211*.

The Cilician tradition was familiar with illustrations both of the rescue of Peter and of the apparition of Christ (figs. 227b and c), and Ṙoslin twice chose the former.[4] Hence, a real choice is involved in the preference expressed by the U.C.L.A. Gospel. Later, Awag shows the apparition of Christ even in illustrating the Matthaean story (fig. 227d). The two themes have contrasting messages. Peter's deliverance from the sea may carry with it baptismal associations of salvation through water, as the use of the subject in baptisteries indicates.[5] More commonly, however, the subject carries the obvious lesson of the text, that is, deliverance from danger through faith in Jesus. This is the theme of Chrysostom's exegesis of the passage,[6]

[3] Yovhannēs Erznkac'i, *Meknut'iwn* on Matt. 9:19, p. 212.

[4] Ibid.

[5] See S. Angelo in Formis or Daphni; Schiller, *Ikonographie der christlichen Kunst,* III, figs. 104 and 111. Kartsonis, *Anastasis: The Making of an Image,* passim. On the cross as weapon see Margaret E. Frazer, "Hades Stabbed by the Cross of Christ," *Metropolitan Museum of Art Journal* 9 (1974), 153–61.

[6] Der Nersessian, *Aght'amar,* fig. 65.

[1] Chrysostom, "In Matt. Hom. 50," chap. 1, *NPNF* x, p. 310.

[2] R. Lauer and W. Kemp, "Rettung Petri aus dem Meer," *Lexikon der christlichen Iconographie,* III, 546–49, Schiller, *Iconography of Christian Art,* I, 167–68. Schiller neglects the Early Christian development of the iconography.

[3] For example, see the eleventh-century Golden Gospel of Henry III (Schiller, *Iconography of Christian Art,* I, pl. 490), or the thirteenth-century Pamplona Bible (F. Bucher, *The Pamplona Bible* [New Haven, 1970], pl. 441.

[4] Der Nersessian, *Arm. Mss. Freer,* fig. 80; eadem, *Arm. Mss. Walters,* 73.

[5] Lauer and Kemp (see above, note 2) refer to Tertullian, *De Baptismate,* chap. 121, as the source of this, but while Tertullian mentions this opinion he disassociates himself from this interpretation. See PL 1, col. 245.

[6] Chrysostom, "In Matt. Hom. 50," chaps. 1–5, *NPNF* x, pp. 310–14.

and this must explain the use of the subject on gems and ampullae as a kind of talisman for the traveler.[7]

On the other hand, the story of Christ walking on the water, the choice made in the U.C.L.A. miniature, is a locus classicus for the debate on the corporeality of Christ's body. Indeed, it raised this question for the apostles themselves, for their first terrified reaction was to exclaim, "It is a ghost!" (Matt. 14:26). In the early centuries Nestorius, Pope Leo, and Severus of Antioch all made use of the passage, each in defense of his own Christology.[8] This too is the theme of Erznkacʿi's commentary on the passage. His interpretation follows in the main the order and development of Chrysostom's, but it expands this by the insertion of theological reflections on the reality of Christ's body. "While (the disciples) sat in the boat battered by the winds from the sea, they were doubly dismayed by the appearance of the Lord, for they thought it a phantasm before their eyes; and since they knew for certain concerning him that he had put on the weight of a body for which it is hard to walk on the waters, it was through no foolishness that they were terrified at seeing a body walk on the waves of the sea; moreover, he did not declare himself until they raised the cry, 'Who are you?' "[9]

According to Erznkacʿi, it is this realization that Christ's body is not just shadow or appearance that prompted Peter to climb out of the boat. "Peter understood that (Christ) said, 'It is I,' on account of the body, and (Peter) said (to himself), 'If that is the way, I have a body and may also go over the waters and know that you are with the same body that I have known you to walk in.' "[10] He climbed out of the boat, then, to prove by physical contact that Christ's body was of exactly the same nature, *homoousios*, as his own.

But neither of these additions is a new invention of Erznkacʿi; they are both from Ephraem Syrus' commentary.[11] In the fourth century, Ephraem was using this argument to refute the Docetism of Marcion, and one is surprised that the issue was still of real interest in the fourteenth. But Garsoïan has shown that a docetist Christology remained alive in medieval Armenia in Paulician circles.[12] Denying the reality of Christ's body one also denied the possibility of his suffering, and hence the accomplishment of redemption. In the eighth century the catholicos John of Ōjun (d. 728) struggled with Docetists and wrote an important treatise "Against the Phantasmiasts."[13] The insistence that the Word had not taken on just the appearance of a body but a true body capable of reacting as a human body, capable of suffering and dying, remained an important ingredient in Armenian Christology. Perhaps it was his own personal appreciation of this doctrine that led Tʿoros Taronecʿi to place his inscription on this miniature rather than some other.

27. The Cure of the Blind Man at Bethsaida (*Page 235*)

Although Christ curing the blind is a common subject in Christian art, representations of this particular cure in Mark 8:27–34 are very rare. Of the dozens of examples of cures of the blind cited by Leclercq and Schiller not one is recognizable as this specific incident in the gospel.[1] There are two noteworthy circumstances that differentiate this incident from others: first, Christ does not cure the blind man where he finds him but takes him by the hand and leads him outside the village of Bethsaida; secondly, the cure takes place in two stages of application of spittle to his eyes, and after the first stage the blind man reports that he has trouble telling men from trees.

Outside of the strip-narrative Gospels the subject does not seem to have been represented in Byzantine art, and in Paris, BN. gr. 74, none of the individuating circumstances of the miracle is represented.[2] In the Florence Gospel five stages of the story are shown: Christ meets the blind man, leads him by the hand, twice touches his eyes, and leaves him cured.[3] In Armenian art one can point to at least five instances of the theme. In the eleventh century it occurred in the Gospel of King Gagik of Kars; in the thirteenth century Ṙoslin shows the blind man partially cured and gesticulating wildly at a nearby tree (fig. 235b); and the Armenian frieze Gospel reduced

[7] *DACL* 6, fig. 5085, and 14, 968–71.

[8] See the discussion by Jaroslav Pelikan with citations: *The Christian Tradition. A History of the Development of Doctrine* (Chicago, 1971), I, 245.

[9] Yovhannēs Erznkacʿi, *Meknutʿiwn* on Matt. 14:26, pp. 327–28.

[10] Ibid., on Matt. 14:28, p. 328.

[11] Ephraem Syrus, *Commentaire*, bk. 12, chaps. 7–8, pp. 117–18.

[12] Nina G. Garsoïan, *The Paulician Heresy*, 94, 170.

[13] *Joannis Philosophi Catholici Armenorum Ozniensis Oratio Contra Phantasticos*, ed. and trans. I. Baptista Aucher (Venice, 1816).

[1] H. Leclercq, "Aveugles, miracles des," *DACL* 1, 3230–34; Schiller, *Iconography of Christian Art* I, 170–73.

[2] Paris, B.N. gr. 74, fol. 81, H. Omont, *Évangiles*, I, pl. 73.

[3] Florence, Laur. Plut. VI,23, fol. 78v; cf. Velmans, *Le Tétraévangile*, fig. 154.

the five stages of the Florence model to two, Christ encountering the blind man and Christ anointing his eyes (fig. 235a). After the U.C.L.A. Gospel the theme was picked up again by Awag, in Erevan, Mat. 212. The U.C.L.A. miniature is closer to the frieze Gospel than to Ṙoslin's, but the elements that comprise the scene could as easily be taken from the earlier Cure of the Blind in Jericho (*page 124*). Against the backdrop of the village of Bethsaida Christ is shown leading the blind man by the hand and anointing his eyes with spittle. The blind man wears a purse on a strap as did the blind man of Jericho.

Since this particular cure is narrated only in Mark, the Matthaean commentaries are of little use in its interpretation. Perhaps the miniature ought to be linked to the Cure of the Man Born Blind (*page 509*), in which Christ also made clay; the clay recalls the Lord's work in creating man (see below). The work of redemption is often spoken of as a new creation.

28. The Cure of Blind Bartimaeus (*Page 250*)

The story of the cure of Bartimaeus (Mark 10:46–53) is a variant of the Cure of the Blind in Jericho (*page 124*). Here only one blind beggar is mentioned and Jesus instructs his disciples to fetch him before restoring his sight. Tʿoros Taronecʿi has divided his miniature in half: Christ and Peter stand to the left against a background of gold over green, while on the right, against an ultramarine background, a young disciple takes the hand of the seated beggar. The beggar has a purse over one shoulder, and a hat is slipping off his head. The separation of Christ from the apostle fetching the blind man echoes the separation of the figures in the Vehapʿaṙ Gospel, where two lines of text intervene between them (fig. 250a). Neither of the Cilician examples of this subject give such prominence to this particular action in the story (figs. 250b and 250c).

The interpretation of this miniature has already been discussed in connection with the miniature on *page 124*.

29. The Entry into Jerusalem (*Page 252*)

Of the two miniatures of the Entry into Jerusalem, this one was executed first and served as model in part for the other (*page 126*). Since the interpretation of the subject was discussed in that connection, it remains to consider the sources of the iconography here.

In discussing the iconography of the Entry some fifty years ago, Millet distinguished a picturesque tradition from a severe tradition, calling the former Hellenistic and the latter Byzantine.[1] The picturesque tradition tended to multiply children in a variety of active poses; trees adorn the landscape and figures wave from the windows of the city. The severe tradition, on the other hand, tended to give sharper focus to the main action by eliminating secondary details; this tendency to simplification can be followed in the classic Middle Byzantine mosaics of Greece. These two traditions are not as neatly separable as Millet would have liked, and the opposition between "Hellenistic" and "Byzantine" is misleading, because both iconographic options were available to the Byzantine artist.

Nevertheless, one might say that within this range of possibilities the present miniature, by the Second Painter, shows a special interest in the picturesque. Behind Christ one sees the Mount of Olives, from which Christ began his journey, while two graceful trees arch over his head. Two children scramble in one of the trees and throw down branches, which can be seen falling around Christ—an unusual detail. In the foreground one child spreads tunics among fallen branches while another offers a branch to the ass to eat. Although there are no figures waving from the battlements of the city, the development of the temple as an onion-domed baldachino on tipped-up city walls containing a stone altar is far more explicit than most architectural representations. Millet thought he detected a special Cappadocian interest in the children and the trees, but this is a strong feature in Armenian and Syrian art as well. It appears in the tenth-century frescoes of Ałtʿamar (fig. 126a) and is common in eleventh-century Armenian illumination.[2] In the thirteenth century both Syrian and Armenian representations consistently show one, and more often two, prominent trees with children clambering in them and branches falling.[3]

[1] Millet, *Iconographie,* 255–84.

[2] Izmailova, *Arm. miniatjura XI veka,* figs. 35, 38, 43, 102.

[3] For example see the Gospel of Hałbat of 1211, Erevan, Mat. 6288, fol. 16v, Der Nersessian, *Armenian Art,* fig. 165; Istanbul, Galata Arm. Church, 35, Der Nersessian, *Études,* II, fig. 242; Baltimore, Walters, 539, fol. 174, Der Nersessian, *Arm. Mss. Walters,* fig. 97. For Syrian examples, see Leroy, *Mss. syriaques,* pls. 66 and 81a.

However, a very specific source can be cited for the U.C.L.A. composition in the Homiliary of Muš executed at Awagvankʿ on the Euphrates in 1202 (fig. 126c). The unusual architecture is identical with the tipped-up city walls revealing an altar beneath an onion-domed baldachino; the crenellations of the city walls and the wide square portal are also the same. The same three elders appear before the gate. The U.C.L.A. miniature has compressed the space into a vertical format, bringing Christ closer to the city and displacing the extra tree to the space behind Christ; but the tree before Christ splits in two exactly as that in the Muš manuscript and the children are seen in the same poses in the same places. The composition of Christ and the ass is also very similar.

While such details may be said to ally the present miniature with picturesque traditions, the total effect of the painting is solemn and monumental rather than "picturesque," if that term implies diverting or entertaining. By increasing the scale of the figures relative to the dimensions of the frame and reducing the total number of figures the artist has given the miniature a focus and intensity no less compelling than that of the classic Middle Byzantine representations of the subject. The reduction of the welcoming crowd to three powerfully drawn elders gives a special dignity to the event. At the same time the fact that one of the three elders turns his face in profile adds a threatening note, for in the U.C.L.A. Gospel the profile is consistently used with sinister implications to represent Judas and the adversaries of Christ.[4]

30. The Lesson of the Withered Fig Tree (*Page 255*)

Although the episode is rare in medieval art of the West, the story of Christ cursing the fig tree has a long and continuous history in Byzantine manuscripts, starting with the sixth-century Sinopensis manuscript.[1] In Armenian art the subject is fairly common, and it often happens that when a manuscript is not provided with intratextual miniatures the passages in Matthew and Mark that tell the story are marked with a fig tree in the margin. Tʿoros Taronecʿi has done this, for example, in his Hartford manuscript (fig. 255d), and Cilician examples are common.[2] In the U.C.L.A. Gospel the subject is given special attention by combining both methods of illustration; in Matthew's Gospel the text on page 128 is marked with a tree in the margin, and in Mark the beginning of the story is marked with a marginal tree on page 253, while the conclusion is illustrated with our intratextual miniature on *page 255*. This placement means that this miniature, unlike most miniatures of the subject, does not illustrate Christ cursing the fig tree (Mark 11:12–14), but the lesson that is drawn from the fig tree the following day, when Peter notices that the tree has already withered (Mark 11:20–25). Again the U.C.L.A. Gospel follows the program of the Vehapʿaṙ Gospel; the latter interrupts the text for the miniature after verse twenty and ours interrupts the text after verse twenty-one. A Lake Van miniature also focuses on this second moment in the story, for the label, "the fig tree withered to its roots," is taken from Mark 11:20 (fig. 255b).

This difference in emphasis accounts for the principal differences in this miniature from the standard version of the subject. Usually Christ is shown advancing ahead of the disciples, with his hand raised in malediction against the tree. The Glajor composition clearly derives from the tradition of the Vehapʿaṙ Gospel, with Peter in front asking about the tree; even the difference in scale between Peter and Christ is preserved (fig. 255a). To fill out the horizontal format of the composition three more disciples are added behind Christ, and the whole scene is given a

[4] See Judas in the Last Supper, *page 156,* or the soldiers in the passion scenes on *pages 162, 172, 173, 179, 441,* or Christ's Jewish adversaries on *pages 169 and 522.* On *page 162* Judas was represented in three-quarter view, but a later user of the book was offended by this and scratched out one eye.

[1] Paris, Bibliothèque Nationale suppl. gr. 1286, fol. 30v (Omont, *Miniatures,* pl. B). For the further history of the subject in Greek manuscripts, see the following seven manuscripts: Paris, B.N. gr. 510, fol. 310v (Omont, *Miniatures,* pl. XLV); Paris, B.N. suppl. gr. 27, fol. 96 (Omont, *Miniatures,* pl. C); Florence, Laur. Plut. VI,23, fols. 43 and 85 (Velmans, *Le Tétraévangile,* figs. 94 and 164); Paris, B.N. gr. 74, fols. 42 and 88v (Omont, *Évangiles,* I, pls. 36 and 78); Paris, B.N. gr. 115, fol. 95 (André Grabar, *Miniatures byzantines de la Bibliothèque Nationale* [Paris, 1939], fig. 31); London, British Library add. 39627, fols. 62 and 118 (Bogdan Filov, *Les miniatures de l'évangile,* pls. 28 and 56); Leningrad, Public Library gr. 105, fol. 93 (H. R. Willoughby, *The Four Gospels of Karahissar,* vol. II, *The Cycle of Text Illustrations* [Chicago, 1936], pl. LV). The bibliography on this subject is very scant and pays little or no attention to the Byzantine iconography, Cf. H. Leclercq, "Figuier stérile," *DACL* 5, 1593–94; Oswald Goetz, *Der Feigenbaum in der religiösen Kunst des Abendlandes* [Berlin, 1965], 68–70; G. Seib and G. Jászai, "Feigenbaum," *Lexikon der christlichen Kunst,* II, 22–24.

[2] See Baltimore, Walters 539, fol. 175, Der Nersessian, *Arm. Mss. Walters,* fig. 98; Washington, Freer 32.18, page 130, Der Nersessian, *Arm. Mss. Freer,* figs. 130–31.

mountainous background appropriate to the story (Mark 11:23). Only once in Byzantine art does one find an illustration of this second moment, which ought to be called the Lesson of the Withered Fig Tree, and that is in the Florence frieze Gospel, in which Christ stands to one side of the withered tree and explains its lesson to Peter and a pair of his colleagues, who stand on the other side.[3]

The lesson of this miracle is clearly focused by Christ's explanation, though exegetes were quick to find further ramifications in the story. "Have faith in God," Jesus urged. "Truly, I say to you, whoever says to this mountain, 'Be taken up and cast into the sea,' and does not doubt in his heart, but believes that what he says will come to pass, it will be done for him. Therefore I tell you, whatever you ask in prayer, believe that you have received it, and it will be yours" (Mark 11:22–24).

The fig tree was sometimes interpreted as a symbol of fruitless men in general,[4] or of the Jews in particular.[5] Ephraem Syrus, however, strenuously resists all attempts at turning the story into allegory. The time was ripe for the Jews to produce good works, he argued, but it was not the season for the fig tree to produce fruit; therefore the tree is not a metaphor for the Jews. Rather the fig tree was intended as a bold manifestation of the power of Christ's divinity as he approached his passion and death.[6] Yovhannēs Erznkacʿi, whose discussion of this subject is largely dependent on Ephraem, says that this was done to strengthen the disciples so they should not waver in faith at his Crucifixion.[7]

Another symbolic interpretation rejected by Ephraem would have the fig tree represent sin and the mountain the devil himself; Ephraem insists that the mountain was the real mountain on which the fig tree grew, and Christ mentioned it to emphasize the power of his word.[8] It should be pointed out in this connection that the Glajor Gospel is unusual in showing the mountain from which the fig tree grew.

Further presages of the passion of Christ are found in other details of the narrative. The fact that Christ was hungry is an assurance of the real corporeality of his body, which Erznkacʿi interprets as further refutation of the Phantasmiasts.[9] The fact that Christ chose a fig tree through which to manifest his power reminds the exegetes that it was with fig leaves that Adam covered himself when his sin stripped him of his primitive glory. Restoring Adam to his glory, Christ now stripped him of his robe of sin.[10]

[3] Velmans, *Le Tétraévangile,* fig. 164.

[4] *Teaching of St. Gregory,* chaps. 653–54 (ed. Thomson, p. 162).

[5] Nersēs Šnorhali, *Yisous Ordi,* 676, (trans. I. Kéchichian [Paris, 1973], p. 171).

[6] Ephraem Syrus, *Commentaire,* bk. 16, chaps. 1–5, pp. 159–61.

[7] Yovhannēs Erznkacʿi, *Meknutʿiwn* on Matt. 21:21–27, pp. 452–53.

[8] Ephraem Syrus, *Commentaire,* bk. 16, chaps. 6–7, pp. 161–62.

[9] *Meknutʿiwn* on Matt. 21:18, p. 450. See his discussion of this subject in connection with the Second Storm at Sea, *page 227.*

[10] Ephraem Syrus, *Commentaire,* bk. 16, chap. 10, p. 163; Yovhannēs Erznkacʿi, *Meknutʿiwn* on Matt. 21:19, p. 452. This theme also appears in a source attributed to Theophilus; see Der Nersessian, *Études,* 478.

31. The Question of Tribute to Caesar (*Page 259*)

The program of the U.C.L.A. Gospel attaches a certain importance to questions of money. The issue was touched upon in the Cleansing of the Temple (*page 126*), but it is addressed more directly in the present miniature and in the two following, which concern the lesson of the Widow's Mite (*page 263*) and the problem of the expensive oil in the Anointing of Christ at Bethany (*page 269*). The use of money is discussed further in connection with the Parable of the Cunning Steward (*page 403*). Doubtless the economic pressures imposed by Mongol rule gave these issues a special relevance in the early fourteenth century.

The story of the tribute money is told in virtually identical terms in the three synoptics (Matt. 22:15–22; Mark 12:13–17; Luke 20:20–26), as a plot of the Pharisees and the Herodeans to catch Christ in a dilemma: either he was a lax Jew or a disloyal citizen. Christ avoids the dilemma by asking for a denarius; pointing out Caesar's image and inscription on the coin he says, "Render to Caesar the things that are Caesar's, and to God the things that are God's."

Representations of this subject are so few in the Middle Ages that modern dictionaries of iconography have missed them entirely.[1] In the Byzantine frieze Gospels the subject is shown in two different ways. In Florence, Laur. Plut. VI,23, the passage is illustrated in each of the synoptics simply by Christ standing and disputing with the Jews who stand to one side.[2] In Paris, B.N. gr. 74, however, Matthew's

[1] Both Schiller and Laske maintain that the subject is unknown before the sixteenth century. Schiller, *Iconography of Christian Art,* I, 157; K. Laske, "Zinsgroschen," *Lexikon der christlichen Ikonographie,* IV, 571–72.

[2] Florence, Laur. Plut. VI,23, fols. 45v, 87, 153, Velmans, *Le Tétraévangile,* figs. 100, 167, 254.

account is illustrated with an enthroned, frontal Christ to whom the Jews, on one side, offer a coin, while the disciples look on from the other.[3] The Armenian versions of the subject do not seem to copy either of these. Even Erevan, Mat. 7651, which is ostensibly copying the Florence manuscript, comes up with a very different composition, in which two Jews are seated at a desk as if they are tax collectors, and one of them holds a great oversized coin bearing a fleur-de-lis (fig. 259b). But the U.C.L.A. Gospel and the Vehapʿaṙ Gospel (fig. 259a), as well as a manuscript by Awag a generation later (fig 259c), all show Christ holding the coin, following literally the text of Mark that they are illustrating, "Bring me a coin and let me look at it" (Mark 12:15). In the U.C.L.A. miniature the coin is a gold disk, large enough to carry an image, but left plain by the artist.[4] Our composition repeats that of the Vehapʿaṙ Gospel in the relative sizes and the gestures of Christ and his two questioners. The two Jews on the right wear tunics and striped headdresses, and the second carries something of cloth in his hand, which may be intended as the purse from which he produced the coin.

The political implications of the difficult question of tribute money are observed by all the commentators, and they admire the wisdom of Christ's response.[5] Chrysostom remarks that the skill of his answer ought to have been enough to convert them. "For indeed he gave them proof of his Godhead by revealing the secrets of their hearts, and with gentleness did he silence them."[6] Beyond this, however, Yovhannēs Erznkacʿi enlarges on the lesson for Christian conduct found in the passage.[7] If the believer must render to Caesar what is stamped with his image, then he must render to God what is stamped with his, namely, himself. This debt can be paid only through faith and good works. But Christ does not excuse one from obligations to his earthly rulers; as man is made of soul and body, so Erznkacʿi concludes he has two kinds of masters: God and earthly kings. Rendering what was due to their Mongol overlords must have been a difficult lesson for the subjugated Armenians to practice.

[3] Paris, B.N. gr. 74, fol. 44, Omont, *Évangiles,* I, pl. 36.

[4] The denarius was generally silver, but a gold denarius was not unknown, worth ten times the silver coin. Cf. Albert R. Frey, *Dictionary of Numismatic Names* (New York, 1947), s. v.

[5] Ephraem Syrus, *Commentaire,* bk. 16, chap. 21, p. 169; Chrysostom, "In Matt. Hom. 70," chaps. 1–2, *NPNF* x, pp. 426–27; Yovhannēs Erznkacʿi, *Meknutʿiwn* on Matt. 22:16–22, pp. 472–74.

[6] Chrysostom, "In Matt. Hom. 70," chap. 2, *NPNF* x, p. 427.

[7] Yovhannēs Erznkacʿi, *Meknutʿiwn* on Matt. 22:19–21, p. 474.

32. The Widow's Mite (*Page 263*)

In this miniature Christ converses with a pair of apostles while he gestures to a woman approaching the treasury. Wearing a French *couvrechef* with *quimple,* a fashion popular in Cilicia,[1] and a light tan dress that is tattered around the edges, the widow is about to deposit a small white coin into a vessel that is already full of much larger coins. The vessel is a kind of basin resting on a square, paneled wooden table; a blue-domed building stands in the background. In the two examples of this subject in Early Christian art the treasury is represented simply as a box with four legs,[2] but in Middle Byzantine art the temple of the Jews is interpreted as a Christian church and the treasury is often shown as an altar, complete with altarcloth, ciborium, and even liturgical vessels.[3] The blue dome in the background of the U.C.L.A. miniature seems to be a reminiscence of the ciborium in Byzantine miniatures of the subject, but the basin on the stand is rather an unusual form of a treasury. This subject is missing in the Vehapʿaṙ Gospel and the U.C.L.A. composition resembles, in overall lines if not in specific detail, Ṙoslin's image in the Washington Gospel (fig. 263b).

The widow's coins, *lepta* in Greek, were the smallest minted copper coins, valued at one-eighth of an *as.*[4] Erevan, Mat. 7651, in a detail not found in the Greek model, dramatizes the difference between the widow's meager offering and others' contributions; while she deposits two coins a gentleman approaches behind her with a whole bushel of coins (fig. 263a).[5]

[1] Camille Enlart, *Manuel d'archéologie française depuis le temps mérovingien jusqu'à la renaissance* (Paris, 1916), III, 178–85. See the use of French fashions in Washington, Freer 32.18, Der Nersessian, *Arm. Mss. Freer,* figs. 99, 160, 168, 171. Nersēs of Lambron observed in 1198 how the court of Sis had rejected the dress of their ancestors in favor of Frankish dress. *Recueil des historiens des croisades, Documents arméniens,* I (Paris, 1896), 597–98.

[2] See the five-part ivory diptych in the Cathedral Treasury, Milan, and mosaics of S. Apollinare Nuovo, Ravenna, in Schiller, *Iconography of Christian Art,* I, pls. 423 and 434. See also V. Osteneck, "Witwe, Scherflein der," *Lexikon,* IV, 534.

[3] For example, see Paris, B.N. gr. 923, fol. 301v, K. Weitzmann, *The Miniatures of the Sacra Parallela,* fig. 449; Paris, B.N. gr. 74, fols. 91v and 154, H. Omont, *Évangiles,* pls. 79 and 131.

[4] Albert R. Frey, *Dictionary of Numismatic Names,* s.v.

[5] Cf. Florence, Laur. Plut. VI,23, fols. 88v and 154v, T. Velmans, *Le Tétraévangile,* figs. 171 and 256.

Some such contrast seems called for by the text of the Gospel: "And he called his disciples to him and said to them, 'Truly, I say to you, this poor widow has put in more than all those who are contributing to the treasury. For they all contribute out of their abundance; but she out of her poverty has put in everything she had, her whole living" (Mark 12:43–44; cf. Luke 21:3–4). The history of exegesis has yet to explain the development of this subject in Armenia. It should be pointed out, though, that Yovhan Mandakuni in the fifth century cites the widow's contribution in his sermons both to show that the poor man's offering is as acceptable as the rich man's, and contrariwise, that a small theft for which one has not done penance is a serious offense.[6]

33. The Anointing of Christ at Bethany (*Page 269*)

All four evangelists tell of a woman anointing Christ, and the reconciliation of the differing accounts has always posed a problem for the commentators (Matt. 26:6–13; Mark 14:3–9; Luke 7:36–50; John 12:1–8). The versions in Matthew and Mark are virtually identical, while John presents some slight variations on the story. In these three the event takes place at supper in Bethany (at the house of Simon the leper, according to Matthew and Mark), and the disciples protest the extravagance of the gesture, suggesting that the oil could have been sold and the money given to the poor. Christ responds by commending the woman's good deed as a preparation for his burial. But while Matthew and Mark say she anointed Christ's head, John says she anointed his feet and he identifies the woman as Mary, the sister of Martha and Lazarus. The account in Luke, on the other hand, is set at the house of a Pharisee named Simon, and the lesson Christ draws from the action is explained in his parable of the two debtors; in Luke the woman anoints Christ's feet.

Chrysostom, and with him Greek exegetes in general, distinguished the Mary of John's account from the anonymous woman of the other evangelists, but the commentator from Glajor, Yovhannēs Erznkacʿi, like most Latin exegetes, maintained it was one and the same woman in all four accounts, namely Mary Magdalen.[1] This woman, Erznkacʿi proposes, undertook to anoint Christ three times: first, upon her conversion from a life of sin, as told in Luke; then, at Bethany shortly before his passion, as told in the other three evangelists; finally, after his death, when she came to the tomb with the other women to anoint him, only to discover him risen. Erznkacʿi finds a progression in the three events, from anointing Christ's feet to anointing his head, to anointing his entire body. Significantly, all three of these anointings are illustrated in the U.C.L.A. Gospel, providing an important subset within the overall program (see *pages 179 and 351*). The recurrence of themes like this established continuity in the program.

The confusion of the four accounts in the Gospel soon led to a confusion of the iconography in Byzantine art.[2] The preferred Byzantine way of rendering the subject showed Christ reclining on a couch at a sigma table while the woman anoints his feet, and this was used to illustrate both the Anointing of Christ at Bethany and the Anointing of Christ at the House of the Pharisee. Byzantine art almost never shows the anointing of Christ on the head. In Armenian art, however, the two anointings are more carefully distinguished. The Vehapʿaṙ Gospel illustrates the anointing in Mark with the profile view of Christ seated upright in a high-backed chair while the woman, approaching from behind, pours her ointment on his head (fig. 269a). This simple composition may have had some impact on Cilician representations of the subject, where a rare occurrence of a Byzantine anointing on the head was familiar in the frieze Gospel Florence, Laurentiana VI,23.[3] While Tʿoros Ṙoslin followed this Byzantine version fairly closely in his Washington ms., Freer 32.18 (fig. 269b), Sargis Picak revised the Florence composition in the Armenian frieze Gospel by making Christ sit upright; the sigma table has disappeared and Christ addresses three standing disciples (fig. 269c). The result is rather close to the composition of the U.C.L.A. Gospel, except that Tʿoros Taronecʿi emphasized the high-backed chair, derived from the Vehapʿaṙ Gospel, while in the frieze Gospel the chair disappears

[6] Yovhan Mandakuni, *Discourse on Almsgiving*, 5, and *Discourse on Penance*, 5, in Simon Weber, *Ausgewählte Schriften der armenischen Kirchenväter* (Munich, 1927), II, 88, 168.

[1] Chrysostom, "In Matt. Hom. 80," chap. 1, *NPNF* x, p. 480; Yovhannēs Erznkacʿi, *Meknutʿiwn* on Matt. 26:6, p. 547; on the two traditions of exegesis on this point, see Magdalen Larow, *The Iconography of Mary Magdalen: The Western Tradition until 1300*, diss., New York University, 1982, 1–10.

[2] Schiller, *Iconography of Christian Art*, I, 157–58; Goodspeed and Willoughby, *The Rockefeller McCormick New Testament*, III, 129–31, 178–81.

[3] Velmans, *Le Tétraévangile*, figs. 109 and 174.

into the architectural background. Christ sits against a panel of gold within a summary architectural setting; two disciples stand before him and the gesture of the first might be taken to express his protest against the woman's action. The woman pours a little white flask over Christ's head. A generation later Awag again pared the composition down to the two principal participants, but placed the woman in front of the seated Christ (269d).[4]

In the Armenian iconographic tradition, therefore, the fact that Christ was anointed on the head assumed a special importance, which it generally lost in the Byzantine tradition. Christ's acceptance of the woman's anointing follows two lines of argument: first he tells his disciples that they will always have the poor and can always do good to them (Mark 14:7); then he explains the prophetic meaning of her action as an anointing in preparation for his burial (Mark 14:8). Both arguments figure in the Armenian exegesis of the passage. On the first, Chrysostom, who is constantly advocating charity to the poor, sees an important practical application, comparing the woman's anointing to the offering of gifts to the church, a charity which, he allows, may at times take precedence over charity to the poor: "If you should see any one provide sacred vessels and offer them, and loving to labor upon any other ornament of the church, about its walls or floor, do not command what has been made to be sold, or overthrown, lest you spoil his zeal. But if, before he had provided them, he were to tell you of it, command it to be given to the poor."[5] This norm for almsgiving to the church is repeated in Yovhannēs Erznkacʿi as well.[6]

The foreshadowing of Christ's passion and death is a theme of relatively less importance for Chrysostom and of greater importance for Erznkacʿi. Chrysostom remarks that Christ's foresight of his passion is a sign of the freedom with which he accepted suffering and death, and this disclosure to his disciples is meant to console and strengthen them in the trials to come.[7] Erznkacʿi repeats these reflections but develops the theme further in another direction. As remarked above, the Glajor exegete understood this anointing as the second in a series that led from Mary Magdalen's conversion to her discovery of the risen Christ. More than a foreshadowing, her gesture in the present context is a dramatic prefiguration of Christ's death. The sweet-smelling oil is the divinity of Christ; the alabaster flask is the body of Christ; Mary's breaking of the bottle is Christ's death.[8] Hence, as frequently in the Syro-Armenian tradition of exegesis, the single Gospel incident contains, by synecdoche, the whole work of redemption. This work, however, is not over and done with in Christ's death but continues in the church; although his body, like the flask, can be broken, the oil cannot. When Christ tells the disciples, "You will always have the poor with you, . . . but you will not always have me" (Mark 14:7), what he means is that they will not see him, but in his divinity he will always remain with them.[9] For the anointing on the head is a sacrament (*xorhurd*), and it is by the sacraments of anointing that Christ remains present in his church.[10] Thus both of the arguments that develop out of the narrative of the Anointing of Christ at Bethany contain ecclesiological themes implicit in them, according to Armenian exegesis.

34. The Preparation for Passover (*Page 271*)

Against a brilliant architectural backdrop Tʿoros Taronecʿi has composed the simple scene of the encounter of two apostles with the man carrying a jar. This seemingly minor incident is related in Mark and Luke in almost identical terms (Mark 14:12–16 and Luke 22:7–11), except that Luke adds the information that the two apostles were Peter and John, a detail which agrees with the iconography of this miniature. Matthew abbreviates the account, omitting the watercarrier altogether (Matt. 26:17–19). According to Mark, Christ instructed the two, "Go into the city, and a man carrying a jar of water will meet you; follow him, and wherever he enters, say to the householder, 'The Teacher says, Where is my guest room where I am to eat the passover with my disciples?' And he will show you a large upper room furnished and ready; there prepare for us" (Mark 14:13–15). In our miniature the door prominent between the man with the jar and the apostles is meant to represent the entrance to the house, and the two windows above indicate the upper room.

[4] Awag uses this composition again, in illustrating the anointing in Mark, in Erevan, Matenadaran 212, fol. 139, unpublished.

[5] Chrysostom, "In Matt. Hom. 80," chap. 2, *NPNF* x, p. 482.

[6] Yovhannēs Erznkacʿi, *Meknutʿiwn* on Matt. 26:11, pp. 548–49.

[7] Chrysostom, "In Matt. Hom. 80," chap. 1–2, *NPNF* x, pp. 480–81.

[8] Yovhannēs Erznkacʿi, *Meknutʿiwn* on Matt. 26:12, p. 549.

[9] Ibid., on Matt. 26:11, pp. 548–49.

[10] Ibid., on Matt. 26:6–7, p. 547.

As simple as it may be, the miniature raises interesting questions by reason of the unusualness of this subject. In Byzantium only the prolific frieze Gospel in Florence shows this subject; in three vignettes one sees the apostles sent, encountering the man with the jar, and conversing with the owner of the house.[1] The Armenian copy of this frieze Gospel reverses the direction of the action and omits the last vignette (fig. 271b). In the West the subject appears only in the Bible Moralisée,[2] which, according to Evans is the source for Ṙoslin's composition in his Washington Gospel, with its curious twisting figure (fig. 271c).[3] The composition in the U.C.L.A. Gospel is simpler and more straightforward and depends rather on its model, the Vehapʿaṙ Gospel (fig. 271a). The two apostles stand in a row and make the same stereotypical gesture toward the man they encounter. In the Vehapʿaṙr Gospel the latter carries a wineskin, for which there is no justification in the text but which figures in the exegesis of the passage. (The inscriptions in the Vehapϙʿraṙ Gospel identify the figures as John, James, and "the man who carries the dregs.") Tʿoros Taronecʿi has given the man a jug and has added architecture to indicate the house with the upper room. Other, simpler examples of the subject can be found in Washington, Freer 134 of 1263,[4] in Awag's Gospel in Erevan (fig. 271d), and in Vienna, Mekhitarist Congregation 243 of ca. 1330.[5]

Chrysostom offers two explanations of the significance of this incident.[6] In the first place, the fact that the apostles had to look for a place to celebrate the Passover underscores the fact that neither Christ nor they had a home of their own. The poverty of Christ, as seen earlier, is a favorite theme of Chrysostom. Beyond this moral lesson, the fact that Christ predicts the apostles' encounter with the anonymous watercarrier indicates, to Chrysostom, Christ's complete control of the situation. Christ's words to the master of the house: "My time is at hand," show us, according to Chrysostom, that Christ approaches his passion with complete awareness of what lies before him and with perfect freedom. The man with the jar is a prophetic sign similar to the sign of the man with a wineskin, which was given to Saul (1 Sam. 10:3). In the Old Testament prototype the prophet Samuel, after anointing Saul king of Israel, gave him a series of signs that would lead him to a wild band of prophets, in whose company Saul was to be miraculously transformed. Against this background, Chrysostom sees the meeting with the watercarrier as an ominous portent pointing to the terrible divine plan that lay ahead of Christ. The iconography of the Vehapʿaṙ Gospel testifies to the currency of this exegesis in the eleventh century.

In the fourteenth century Yovhannēs Erznkacʿi recapitulates Chrysostom's interpretation of the story but expands it with his own explanation, and as often, what he adds is more important than what he repeats. To Erznkacʿi the preparation for the Passover is a preparation for the Eucharist, and this not in a dry dogmatic sense but in an intimate anagogical sense, that is, applying to the pedagogy of the soul. Like the obedient apostles, the Christian is urged to prepare his soul to receive with purity the Body of Christ.[7] The fact that this happened on "the first day of Unleavened Bread" (Mark 14:12) recalls the smearing of the blood of the lamb on the doorposts of the Jews in Egypt on the same day, and this in turn admonishes one to attend to the doorposts of his mind by which he is to receive the Virgin-born Body of Christ.[8] The man carrying the jar is a symbol of the priest and the water he carries is either the water of baptism or tears of repentance, both of which are the necessary preparation of the soul for the Eucharist.[9] Finally, the upper room itself has an anagogical meaning as representing the elevated and transformed soul; for, "those who are baptized and lifted up from the earth receive the spirit here; in them the Father and the Son and the Spirit take up their abode."[10] At the same time, Erznkacʿi continues, the upper room is a sign of the church as the eschatological heavenly Jerusalem. "The upper room is prophetic of the mystery of the church, for it is higher and heavenly, and in it (Christ) with life-giving hands distributed and distributes his holy Body and Blood for the salvation of the world and its spiritual adornment. Up until that (last) day his disciples prepare the same sacrament of the abundantly saving Lamb, for the glory of the Father and his Spirit. Amen."[11] The upper room is, therefore, both the vehicle of the

[1] Florence, Bibl. Laur., ms. Plut. VI,23, fol. 91v, Velmans, *Le Tétraévangile*, fig. 175.

[2] London, British Library, ms. Harley 1527, de Laborde, *Bible Moralisée*, pl. 519; also New York, Pierpont Morgan Library, ms. M.521.

[3] Helen C. Evans, *Armenian Manuscript Illumination.*

[4] Der Nersessian, *Arm Mss. Freer*, fig. 246.

[5] Buschhausen, *Die illuminierten armenischen Handschriften*, 34–35.

[6] Chrysostom, "In Matt. Hom. 81," chap. 1, *NPNF* x, p. 485.

[7] Yovhannēs Erznkacʿi, *Meknutʿiwn* on Matt. 26:17, p. 552.

[8] Ibid.

[9] Ibid., on Matt. 26:18, p. 553.

[10] Ibid., on Matt. 26:19, p. 553.

[11] Ibid., on Matt. 26:29, pp. 553–54.

soul's salvation and the saved soul itself. The upper room has further importance in two later miniatures in our manuscript, that of the Washing of the Feet (*page 532*) and that of the Promise of the Holy Spirit (*page 538*). Finally, the owner of the upper room is identified by Erznkacʿi as Joseph of Arimathea, a detail that will have special significance in connection with that disciple's role in the Descent from the Cross (*page 286*).[12]

35. Christ Ascending the Cross (*Page 283*)

This miniature forms a pair with the following one of the Descent from the Cross (*page 286*). Painted full-page on successive folios by Tʿoros Taronecʿi, they were consciously designed as a kind of diptych of matching compositions, dominated by the great cross set against the backdrop of the walls of Jerusalem. This pairing of the subjects, which was planned by the scribe, represents a certain departure from the eleventh-century program of the Vehapʿaṙ Gospel, for while the earlier manuscript does illustrate Christ Ascending the Cross (fig. 283a)—an important first in iconography—the removal of Christ from the cross is represented by Joseph of Arimathea requesting the body from Pilate. Awag's Gospel in Erevan follows the U.C.L.A. Gospel in showing both the Ascent and Descent in Mark, but the Ascent is assigned only quarter-page format. Hence, in Armenian manuscripts the balanced pairing of the two subjects is peculiar to the U.C.L.A. Gospel.[1]

Insofar as the Gospel does not describe how Christ was affixed to the cross, this subject is commonly called an extrabiblical subject. It does not occur in the Byzantine frieze Gospels or the Western *Bibles Moralisées*. Its introduction in Western and Byzantine art in the thirteenth and fourteenth centuries has generated an extensive literature.[2] Current consensus places the initiative for this iconography in the West, possibly in Franciscan circles, where a rich devotional literature sought to supply vivid detail for every moment of the passion and death of Christ. Our discovery of the subject in the early eleventh-century Vehapʿaṙ Gospel points toward an iconographic tradition of greater antiquity that requires a revision of the accepted belief. Armenian exegesis, moreover, offers a new line of interpretation for the subject.

In its Western use, which is almost exclusively Italian, Christ Ascending the Cross commonly has a strong Marian interest. Sometimes the Blessed Virgin is shown to one side clasping her hands in anguish or swooning, but in other instances she actively tries to prevent Christ's ascent, throwing one arm around him and warding off the soldiers with the other.[3] In the Byzantine development of the subject the Virgin recedes into the background, as at Staro Nagoričino, or she is entirely omitted, as at Čučer.[4] One, two, or three ladders may be used to get Christ onto the Cross, and the soldiers sometimes pull him up from above or force him from behind to mount the ladder, while a crowd of Jews urges the executioners on.

The U.C.L.A. miniature represents a fusion of the older Armenian version of the subject with current Byzantine and Western models. The subject has been pared down to Christ and the soldiers, the Virgin and crowds omitted. The strong and well-conceived figure of Christ grasps the crossbar of the cross with one hand and the upright with the other as he climbs the ladder. He turns an arresting gaze on the viewer, as he does in only one other miniature, the frontal seated Christ on *page 35*. The number of soldiers has been reduced from the four of the Vehapʿaṙ Gospel to three (omitting the soldier holding the flask of wine), and the figures have been disposed symmetrically on the two ladders. The soldier at the top of the ladder on the right, with a hammer in his belt, and the soldier urging Christ on from below are clearly borrowed from the Vehapʿaṙ Gospel. However, parallels for the third soldier, who carries nails, now much flaked, in his right hand, should be sought in contemporary manuscripts in the West.[5] As in the Vehapʿaṙ Gospel, the U.C.L.A. miniature indicates the place of the Crucifixion on mount Calvary as a rocky summit hollowed out underneath. This should be interpreted in conjunction with the representations of the cross on *pages 286 and 561*, both of which show the rocky peak of Calvary containing the skull of

[12] Ibid., p. 553.

[1] Another example of this kind of pairing of miniatures will be encountered below in the Annunciation and Visitation (*pages 305 and 312*).

[2] Millet, *Iconographie*, 380–95; Schiller, *Iconography of Christian Art*, II, 82–83, 87–88; M. Boskovits, "Kreuzbesteigung," *Lexikon*, II, 602–5; Derbes, *Byzantine Art and the Dugento*, 174–88.

[3] Schiller, *Iconography of Christian Art*, II, pl. 304; or see two examples by Guido da Siena and a follower of his in J. Stubblebine, *Guido da Siena* (Princeton, 1964), figs. 26 and 59.

[4] Gabriel Millet, *La peinture du moyen âge en Yougoslavie* (Paris, 1962), III, pls. 91.1 and 44.1, respectively.

[5] Cf. New York, Pierpont Morgan 643, fol. 22, Henry Yates Thompson, *Illustrations from One Hundred Manuscripts in the Library of Henry Yates Thompson* (London, 1908), 2, pl. 7.

Adam. While Byzantine art is somewhat inconsistent in showing the skull of Adam, and the majority of Western examples omit it, it is almost always present in Armenian Crucifixions. In the U.C.L.A. miniature, the cave of Golgotha is intended as the burial place of Adam, and in the Vehapʿaṙ Gospel the skull of the first man is shown within the cave. The Vehapʿaṙ Gospel, however, does not include the walls of Jerusalem. This detail can be found in contemporary Byzantine frescoes, such as those of the church of Curtea de Arges, in Valachia, which also pairs images of the Ascent and Descent; yet these Byzantine examples have little else in common with the U.C.L.A. images.[6]

In marked contrast to the violence and brutality to which he is subjected in other images, in the U.C.L.A. Gospel Christ ascends the ladder with perfect dignity and poise. Awag follows Tʿoros in this respect, showing Christ freely ascending the cross, though he departs in other respects (fig. 283b). As we will see in examining the Crucifixion (*page 561*), the freedom and strength of Christ in his death is one of the chief themes of Armenian reflection on the subject.

The iconographic traditions of the miniature are complex, but it is clear that while Tʿoros Taronecʿi is in contact with sources from outside Armenia he is also in contact with native sources of great antiquity. The Armenian literary sources shed some light on the thinking that lay behind this iconography in Armenia. It is worth noting that when Agatʿangełos refers to the Crucifixion it is in terms of Christ actively climbing onto the cross: "The son of God too became in the flesh an image of man, in the likeness of human images, mounting the elevated cross as if climbing a high summit."[7] The Gospel of Nicodemus, on the other hand, describes Christ as being forced to go up.[8] More interesting is the imagery of the fourteenth-century commentator. Yovhannēs Erznkacʿi, in commenting on Christ's arrival at Golgotha in Matt. 27:33, refers both to Adam's burial and to a ladder—the ladder of Jacob's vision—both of which belong to Golgotha. The whole passage is full of imagery of paradise restored.

> Here is where they used to cut off the heads of condemned men, for (Christ) too was thought by them to be one (condemned); in addition by providence he came upon the place where the ancients said was the grave of the first man, in order that he might heal the decapitated man. For as by his birth he released the curses of Eve in Bethlehem, so in his death on the place called Golgotha he released those of Adam. Again (Golgotha) means that the cross was raised in the highest of the mountains according to the prophecy of Micah (Micah 4:1), which is what skull means, which was raised higher than the worship of all idols by becoming the house of the God of Jacob, where Israel poured out oil on the rock at his vision of the ladder (Gen. 28:18–19); for this reason mountains of sweetness were produced and hills were bathed in milk, that is, the prophets and apostles (preached) the divine teaching of the cross by keeping milk and honey under their tongues, and by nourishing with the solid food and milk of disciples.[9]

In memory of his vision of the ladder reaching to heaven Jacob had named the site the "House of God" and the "Gate of Heaven" (Gen. 28:12–17). It is to this site that Christ is led by God's providence, that by ascending the cross and descending—in imitation of the angels ascending and descending Jacob's ladder—he might open the real Gate of Heaven. For here by his death on the spot where Adam was buried he undid the curse of Adam's transgression. The tradition that identifies Golgotha as the place of Adam's burial first appears in Origen[10] and turns up often thereafter in Armenian and other sources. The further identification of the site as Jacob's Bethel seems to be a special Armenian tradition, and Erznkacʿi mentioned it before in connection with the Women at the Tomb (*page 179*). The subject of Christ Ascending the Cross, therefore, seems to have had its origins in East Christian art (the sources of the Vehapʿaṙ Gospel are still obscure), where the subject was interpreted as an extension of Jacob's vision: ascending and descending the ladder of the cross he has opened Paradise to believers. The identification of the ladder of Jacob with the cross had also been proposed by earlier Syrian authors, Eustathius of Antioch in the fourth century and Moses Bar Kepha in the tenth.[11]

[6] Oreste Tafrali, *Monuments byzantins de Curtéa de Arges*, text vol. and album (Paris, 1931), album pl. LXXXI.

[7] Agatʿangełos, *History of the Armenians*, chap. 83 (trans. Thomson, pp. 92–93).

[8] *The Gospel of Nicodemus*, second Greek version, chap. 10, *ANF*, VIII, 430.

[9] Yovhannēs Erznkacʿi, *Meknutʿiwn* on Matt. 27:33, p. 593.

[10] Origen, *Comment. in Matt.* 126 (PG 13, cols. 1776–77).

[11] F. Cavallera, *S. Eustathii Antiocheni in Lazarum Fragmenta* (Paris, 1905), 70. Moses Bar Kepha: "The ladder which Jacob saw going up to heaven typified the cross," from *A Discourse in Separate Chapters for the Feast of the Cross*, chap. 13, 7, trans. Sidney H. Griffith, unpublished.

36. The Descent from the Cross (*Page 286*)

The Descent from the Cross, or the Deposition, first appeared in Byzantine art shortly after Iconoclasm, in the famous Paris Gregory manuscript of 880–83, and by the tenth century it had already developed along two somewhat different compositional lines, depending on whether one or both hands of Christ had been freed from the cross.[1] By the eleventh century both types of composition had already made their appearance in Armenia. In the wooden relief of 1031 in the Ējmiacin Cathedral Treasury, Christ's freed right hand falls across Joseph of Arimathea's back, while Nicodemus struggles to remove the nail from the left.[2] The fragmentary condition of the relief allows some doubt concerning the complete composition, but the relief does not seem to have included figures either of the Blessed Virgin or of St. John, which are standard in Byzantine versions of the iconography. This is all the more remarkable in that the legend that is associated with this relief attributes its miraculous manufacture to St. John's desire to offer the Virgin a memorial of her grief. However, in a contemporary manuscript of the Melitene group the full complement of figures appears (fig. 286a).[3] Both hands have been loosed from the cross and fall into the affectionate grasp of the Blessed Virgin and of St. John. Joseph on a ladder supports the torso of Christ while Nicodemus works to free his feet.

Painters of the Cilician kingdom were familiar with both versions and variants on them. T'oros Roslin employed the first composition in his Washington Gospel (fig. 286b) and a rather effective variant on the second composition in his Baltimore manuscript (fig. 286c). In the latter, instead of showing the veneration of the wounded hands of Christ, he has shown Joseph and Mary starting to transport the body of Christ towards the tomb.[4] The painters of Siwnik' inherited this imagery from Cilicia (figs. 286e and 286f). The specific source of the U.C.L.A. miniature is found in the splendid and somewhat baroque lectionary of the year 1286 in Erevan (fig. 286d).[5] The inclusion of subsidiary scenes of Joseph before Pilate and the Burial of Christ complicate the picture, but in both images John has been omitted, Joseph takes the same stretching stride toward Christ, and Nicodemus has the same very awkward pose as he stands on the same stool. Nicodemus was sketched differently in the underdrawing, with his face turned the opposite direction; perhaps it was problems such as this that led T'oros to seek out established models for this miniature. At the same time T'oros is rather free with his source; the Blessed Virgin does not embrace Christ's hand but lifts her mantle to her face in tears, in a manner similar to that in the very first appearance of the Descent from the Cross, in the Paris Gregory manuscript. The angels, too, are shown weeping, a theme that first appears in Italian art in the late thirteenth century.[6] A further Italian borrowing is evidenced by the use of a single nail to fix Christ's feet.[7]

With respect to his sources, then, T'oros Taronec'i has been curiously eclectic in the Descent from the Cross, and this may explain some of the inconsistencies in the painting. While in the model the insertion of the tomb of Christ occasioned the omission of John, in the U.C.L.A. miniature it makes for an unbalanced composition. Taronec'i also had problems

[1] Paris, Bibliothèque Nationale, ms. gr. 510 (880–86), fol. 30v (cf. Schiller, *Iconography of Christian Art,* II, fig. 548). The first type, with one hand free, Millet called the "Byzantine" type, the second he traced to Tavşanlı Kilise in Cappadocia (Millet, *Iconographie,* 467–88). But the second type is also common in art works from Constantinople, and its appearance in Western art from Carolingian and Ottonian times points to Constantinople as the source of its diffusion rather than Cappadocia. Both types, therefore, have equal right to be called "Byzantine." Y. Nagatsuka has recently tried to revive Millet's typological approach. In a purely formal discussion that omits every least allusion to the content of the theme, he has sorted over 400 instances of the Descent from the Cross into twenty "types" and numerous "subtypes." Unfortunately the critical question of when a change in motifs constitutes a new "type" is never addressed, an omission that vitiates the entire treatment. Yasushi Nagatsuka, *Descente de la Croix, son développement iconographique des origines jusqu'à la fin du XIVe siècle* (Tokyo, 1979).

For recent and more balanced discussions, see Émile Mâle, *L'art religieux du XIIe siècle en France,* 5th ed. (Paris, 1953), 101–4; M. Boskovits and G. Jászai, "Kreuzabnahme," *Lexikon der christlichen Ikonographie,* II, 590–95; Schiller, *Iconography of Christian Art,* II, 164–68; Elizabeth C. Parker, *The Descent from the Cross: Its Relation to the Extra-Liturgical "Depositio" Drama* (New York, 1978); Derbes, *Byzantine Art and the Dugento,* 199–247.

[2] See the discussion of his relief in Der Nersessian, *Études,* 410; for illustration see Der Nersessian, *Armenian Art,* fig. 81.

[3] For discussions of this manuscript, see Narkiss and Stone, *Jerusalem,* 36–40 and 148; Izmailova, *Arm. miniatjura XI veka,* 65–76.

[4] See also Jerusalem, St. James 1956 (T'oros Roslin, 1265), fol. 171, Narkiss and Stone, *Jerusalem,* fig. 70; and Erevan, Mat., 10675 (of 1268), fol. 98, Korkhmazyan, *Armenian Manuscripts of the 13th and 14th Centuries,* pl. 96.

[5] See the brief discussion of this manuscript in Korkhmazyan, *Armenian Miniatures of the 13th and 14th Centuries,* with pls. 112 and 113.

[6] Schiller, *Iconography of Christian Art,* II, figs. 508–10, 576, 600.

[7] H. Neumann, "Dreinagelkruzifix," *Lexikon der christlichen Ikonographie,* I, 552–53.

in handling the Blessed Virgin. Having decided to leave the hand of Christ free he had to place the Virgin lower down in the composition, giving her very squat proportions. The real accomplishment of Taronecʿi's Descent from the Cross lies rather in its central theme of Joseph cradling in his hands the displayed body of Christ. The torso has been turned toward the viewer to show it in best advantage and Joseph supports the body from behind with his left arm so as to conceal none of it. The decision to let Christ's right hand fall free may be motivated by a similar intention.

In the Gospel versions of the event, Mark's account is virtually identical with the other synoptics', except that he remarks Pilate's surprise at Joseph's petition and his inquiry to make sure of Christ's death (Mark 15:42–47; cf. Matt. 27:57–61, Luke 23:50–54). John introduces Nicodemus to the story (John 19:38–42), and in art he is assigned the task of removing the nails. However, Joseph of Arimathea is the principal agent in recovering Christ's body from the cross, and this physical closeness to Christ suggested a kind of priestly role for Joseph, which is developed in the exegetical sources. According to Yovhannēs Erznkacʿi, "This Joseph indeed formerly kept hidden, but now with great daring he took courage after the death of Christ; he had not been an obscure person or a foreigner of unknown origin, but was from great and distinguished stock from the city of Arimathea, whence Samuel was, and he came and dwelt in Jerusalem in order that he might become a servant of the mystery, for indeed he looked forward to the kingdom of God."[8] Erznkacʿi identifies Arimathea with Ramathaim (or Ramah), the seat of the priestly family of Samuel (I Sam. 1:1 and 19). The "mystery" referred to is the sacrament of the Eucharist. As noted in the Preparation for the Passover, the upper room wherein the Eucharist was instituted belonged, according to Erznkacʿi, to Joseph of Arimathea.[9] As he played a part in the preparation for the Eucharist, so he now plays a part in its completion, receiving with reverence the body of Christ. Ephraem Syrus sees a parallel between the role of this second Joseph and that of Joseph the spouse of the Virgin: as in his nativity in the cave the Lord entrusted himself to the earlier Joseph, so here he entrusted his body to the second Joseph, to be placed in the tomb by his just servant.[10] Esayi Nčʿecʿi attributes another role to Joseph of Arimathea, making him the author of the Trisagion.[11] The liturgical analogy is complete; as the deacons carry forward the bread to the chant of the Trisagion, Joseph carries the body of Christ.

[8] Yovhannēs Erznkacʿi, *Meknutʿiwn* on Matt. 27:57, p. 605. Compare this to the simpler explanation in Chrysostom, "In Matt. Hom. 88," chap. 1, *NPNF* x, p. 522.

[9] Yovhannēs Erznkacʿi, *Meknutʿiwn* on Matt. 26:18, p. 553.

[10] Ephraem Syrus, *Commentaire*, bk. 21, chap. 20, p. 232.

[11] See above, p. 30.

37. The Annunciation (*Page 305*)

The Annunciation, one of the more impressive miniatures in the U.C.L.A. Gospel, must be studied in association with the following miniature of the Visitation on *page 312*. The two were obviously conceived as a pair or kind of diptych, assigned full-page format on conjugate leaves of the same sheet with the reverse left blank, an unusual procedure in this manuscript (see discussion of codicology above, p. 35). The pair offers an interesting sidelight upon the artists' working methods, for after the Second Painter had executed the Annunciation he left the Visitation blank. Faced with the task of completing the manuscript, Tʿoros Taronecʿi composed a Visitation that matched in its general rhythm of composition and its narrow, decorated borders the earlier painting of the Annunciation. When he finished, however, he evidently sensed a certain incongruity in that the protagonist of the two scenes, the Blessed Virgin, had very different features. Accordingly, he proceeded to repaint the face of the Virgin of the Annunciation in his own fashion. He did his best to integrate the face with the rest of the figure by adding modeling lines in black to the Virgin's veil and decorating her halo with his usual pearl and jewel outline. Finally, noticing that the Second Painter had omitted the dove of the Holy Spirit, Tʿoros made up the omission with a sketchy white dove painted over gold ground above the Virgin's house, which is now much flaked. The dove is very like Tʿoros' dove with Christ in the Synagogue, *page 327*. In addition to these indications of intentional matching of Annunciation and Visitation, the two miniatures revealed a common dependence on apocryphal sources.

Approaching from the left, clad in azurite tunic, magenta mantle, and vermilion pearl-studded shoes, the angel Gabriel extends his right hand in greeting toward the Virgin. His clenched left hand was meant to carry the customary staff, but both artists neglected this detail. Tʿoros' contemporary Awag is guilty of the same omission in his handsome Jerusalem Gospel.[1] Gabriel's wings are displayed, one above and one behind him, and the architectural background is

[1] Jerusalem, St. James 1941, fol. 2v, unpublished.

crowned with a gable and an onion-domed cupola. On the right, the Virgin, wearing a mantle of magenta and an azurite dress with a rich gold brocade pattern, stands before a golden seat with a vermilion cushion. She answers the angel's message by raising her right hand, palm outward, in a gesture of protestation; in her left she holds a spindle wound with vermilion yarn. Behind her stands her house with a tiled, pitched roof, while the dove with outspread wings sends down rays of light on her head. Between Mary and the angel stands a hexagonal stone well, from the lip of which a stream of water flows down into a two-handled water pitcher. Behind the well grows a sinuous tree, green in both trunk and leaf. Two branches along the trunk have been pruned back, but it flourishes anew at the top. Overhead the dove with outspread wings sends down rays of light on the Virgin.

The bare essentials of the scene are simply the angel and the Virgin, and Byzantine art, with its leaning toward classic elegance, often reduces the entire subject to these two figures.[2] By contrast, the U.C.L.A. Annunciation is heavily laden with narrative and symbolic elements: the yarn, the well, the pitcher, the tree, and the dove. Each of these elements taken separately has a long and episodic history that it is beyond our scope to trace. It is sufficient to examine the more proximate sources of the imagery in Armenian and Syrian art. All the ingredients of the U.C.L.A. Annunciation, except for the pitcher, can be found together in the famous Queen Keṙan Gospel of 1272 (fig. 305a). Though the Virgin sits and attends to her spinning with both hands, in other respects the imagery is very close. The inclusion of the well is far more common in Armenian and Syrian art than it is in Byzantine. The imagery of the Queen Keṙan Gospel, minus the tree, was used in the illuminated Syrian lectionaries in the British Library and the Vatican fifty years earlier.[3] When the Annunciation at the Well is picked up in Siwnikʿ in this period a special interest in the pitcher or vessel is added. The U.C.L.A. miniature seems to be the earliest expression of this interest, and in 1307 Tʿoros Taronecʿi repeated this iconography verbatim in the Venice Gospel (fig. 305b). In his subsequent Annunciations of 1318, 1321, and 1323, however, he introduces the curious motif of a two-spigot fountain and shows the Virgin's pitcher either above or beside the urn (figs. 305c–e). Kirakos picks up this theme in his manuscript of 1330 (fig. 305f).

The story of the Annunciation at the Well has its origins in the *Protoevangelium* of James in the mid-second century.[4] Espoused to Joseph, and occupied with the task of spinning the purple and scarlet for the temple veil, the Blessed Virgin had taken a pitcher to draw water, when suddenly she heard the disembodied voice of the angel greeting her. Seeing no one, she returned to her house, where she resumed spinning; thereupon the angel appeared to her in visible form and completed the message he had come to relate, in the terms familiar in Luke's account. Probably originally composed in Greek, the *Protoevangelium* enjoyed wide popularity in Syriac and Armenian translations as well. In Armenian, moreover, the whole story was also rewritten in a much amplified version, called the *Armenian Infancy Gospel*, the history of which has been traced by P. Peeters.[5] Already available in Armenia in the sixth century, the document was condemned in 590 and lapsed into oblivion for a while. In the tenth century, however, it was reworked and the language "modernized," after which it gained quasi-official recognition in the Armenian church and was, according to Peeters, widely used in the twelfth and thirteenth centuries.

All of the elements of the iconography have their foundation in these two apocryphal accounts. Yet it is not enough to have located the literary source; one must also ask the meaning of the motifs both in the imagery and in the literature. In the imagery of the Annunciation in general, the most common apocryphal element is certainly the spindle with yarn, though this motif is noticeably more common in Armenian art than it is in Byzantine.[6] While the imagery helps to convey the story of the Apocrypha, the motif carries more than mere narrative color. In the ancient world spinning was the occupation of the noble woman and a sign of her devotion to domestic duties. On Greek and Roman funerary reliefs the faithful

[2] For example, see the mosaic at Daphni, Otto Demus, *Byzantine Mosaic Decoration* (London, 1948), pl. 4. On the Annunciation in general, see Schiller, *Iconography of Christian Art*, I, 33–52; J. H. Emminghaus, "Verkündigung an Maria," *Lexikon der christlichen Ikonographie*, IV, 422–37.

[3] British Library ms. syr. 7170 (1216–20), and Vat. syr. 559 (1219–20), Leroy *Mss. syriaques*, pls. 73, 3 and 73, 4. See also Gospel of Deir es-Zaʿfaran (1250), ibid., pl. 127, 1.

[4] O. Cullmann, "Protoevangelium of James," in Edgar Hennecke and Wilhelm Schneemelcher, *New Testament Apocrypha*, trans. R. M. Wilson (Philadelphia, 1963), 370–74 for introductory material; 380 for the narrative of the Annunciation.

[5] Paul Peeters, *Évangiles apocryphes*, II, *L'évangile de l'enfance* (Paris, 1914), cf. i–lix for introductory material, 69–286 for the text.

[6] For example, it occurs in scarcely a third of the representations of the Annunciation in Cappadocia, while it shows up in eighty percent of the Armenian representations according to this author's count. Cf. M. Restle, *Byzantine Wall Painting*, passim.

wife is shown repeatedly with distaff, spindle, and basket.[7] It was important, therefore, that Mary, when receiving this strange visitor in the absence of her spouse, should be represented spinning both in the literary apocryphal account and in the visual imagery of the subject, to give assurance of her noble and upright character.

So too with the well and the tree. These may be regarded as narrative details and perhaps even as topographical features of where the event took place. Their earliest occurrence is on an Early Christian ampulla from Palestine on which the Virgin, pitcher in hand, kneels beside a stream beneath a spreading palm tree.[8] The ampulla is inscribed: "A blessing of the Mother of God of the Rock of (B)oudiam," which seems to refer to a specific place of pilgrimage.[9] The tree is of fairly frequent occurrence in Armenian Annunciations; it shows up in an eleventh-century Gospel in Venice and in several Cilician manuscripts.[10] But as with the spinning, more than mere storytelling seems to be involved in these details. As in the Ascension, the palm tree here is an apt metaphor for Paradise, the garden from which man was expelled through the first Eve's sin and to which man is readmitted through the virtue of the second Eve. This theme is commonplace in patristic authors, whether Byzantine or Armenian. To Gregory Narekacʿi, Mary is herself the "living Paradise of delight, the tree of immortal life," images that are repeated in the writings of Nersēs Šnorhali.[11] The hymn sung on the feast of the Annunciation greets the Blessed Virgin as Paradise: "O thou living Eden, soil of the immortal plant, the verdant place of the flower born of the bosom of the Father."[12]

The well, too, is more than a narrative detail; strictly speaking it is not called for in the story, since the Apocrypha tell of a double annunciation and the angel does not make himself visible at the well but in the Virgin's house. That something more is involved here than storytelling becomes clear in the development of the two-spigot fountain, which must be taken as a metaphor of Armenian Monophysitism. The metaphor of mixing, used by theologians to explain the manner of the union of the two natures in Christ, is graphically portrayed by two streams of water falling into a single basin.[13] The U.C.L.A. Annunciation, however, shows the water pouring in a single stream into the vessel below. Both well and vessel are common metaphors of the Blessed Virgin in the hymns of the Armenian church, which refer to her as the "fountain of living water" and the "golden pitcher."[14]

That Tʿoros Taronecʿi took special care to add the dove of the Holy Spirit with wings spread over the head of the Virgin may indicate a special consciousness of the importance of the Holy Spirit in this mystery. It is worth noticing that the words of the angel, "The Holy Spirit will come upon you and the power of the Most High will overshadow you," (Luke 1:35) have a special place in the Armenian liturgy. At the conclusion of the prothesis ceremony in which the bread and wine are prepared for the Eucharist, this verse is repeated three times, a custom not known in Byzantium.[15] The account of the Annunciation is one of the most frequently read lections in the Armenian liturgy, figuring both in the Epiphany celebrations and in feasts of the Mother of God.[16]

38. The Visitation (*Page 312*)

Mary's meeting with Elizabeth evoked the *Magnificat,* in which she extolled the special mercy of the Lord in her regard: "My soul magnifies the Lord, and

[7] For some examples from the eastern part of the Roman Empire, see M. A. R. Colledge, *The Art of Palmyra* (London, 1976), figs. 63, 64, 68, 74, 76, 83, and 85. See discussion of Annunciation iconography in Mathews, "The Early Armenian Iconographic Program of the Ējmiacin Gospel," *East of Byzantium: Syria and Armenia in the Formative Period,* ed. N. G. Garsoïan et al. (Washington, D.C., 1982), 204–5.

[8] A. Grabar, *Ampoules de Terre Sainte* (Paris, 1958), 31 and pl. 31. The Greek term *pēgē* in the Protoevangelium can mean either "well" or "spring," so that either way of representing it is equally faithful to the text.

[9] Jacqueline Lafontaine-Dosogne, "Iconography of the Cycle of the Life of the Virgin," in Underwood, *The Kariye Djami,* IV, 189.

[10] Venice 141/102, Janashian, *Armenian Miniature Paintings,* pl. L; Jerusalem, St. James 2568, fol. 154, unpublished; Jerusalem 2568, Azaryan, *Kilikyan Manrankarčʿutʿyunə,* fig. 99; Erevan, Mat. 9422, Dournovo, *Haykakan Manrankarčʿutʿyun,* pl. 48.

[11] See collection of quotes in K. Algermissen, *Lexikon der Marienkunde* (Regensburg, 1967), I, 361–62, with citation of Gregory Narekacʿi from his hymn to the Mother of God (Venice, 1840), 213; from Nersēs Šnorhali, "Sermon on the Assumption" (Venice, 1830), 489. Schiller also takes the tree in the Annunciation as a paradise motif: *Iconography of Christian Art,* I, 40. Maguire has found spring symbolism in Byzantine Annunciations, *Art and Eloquence in Byzantium,* 42–52.

[12] *Divine Liturgy of the Armenian Apostolic Orthodox Church,* trans. Nersoyan, 91.

[13] Mathews, "The Annunciation at the Well," 343–56.

[14] *Šarakan Hogewor Ergocʿ* (Jerusalem, 1936): fountain, 28, 36, 193; pitcher, 23, 674, 891.

[15] *Divine Liturgy of the Armenian Apostolic Orthodox Church,* trans. Nersoyan, 18.

[16] See Table 9.

my spirit rejoices in God my Savior, for he has regarded the low estate of his handmaiden. For behold, henceforth all generations will call me blessed" (Luke 1:46–48). The Visitation, therefore, announces an important Marian theme, and in the Armenian liturgy it is used on the chief feasts of the Mother of God (see Table 9). At the same time, the subject carries another less obvious but also important theme, for when Mary and Elizabeth met, the unborn Jesus and John the Baptist also met. "When Elizabeth heard the greeting of Mary, the babe leaped in her womb" (Luke 1:41). It is this second theme, the Precursor's first salutation of his Lord, which the U.C.L.A. Visitation seems especially intended to highlight.[1]

The standard Byzantine iconography of the Visitation consists simply of Mary and Elizabeth embracing.[2] In the U.C.L.A. miniature two flanking figures have been added, a grey-haired, long-bearded old man sitting in a domestic architectural frame on the right, and a young woman following the Blessed Virgin on the left. The identity of the two figures again refers to apocryphal accounts of the infancy of Christ.

In the sixth-century mosaic of the Visitation in the church of Poreč a young woman, apparently a domestic of Elizabeth's household, stands in the doorway of the house in back of Elizabeth, where she pulls aside the door curtain and watches the event with surprise.[3] This iconography occasionally occurs in the Middle Byzantine Period; in Cappadocia, for example, it can be found at the Old Tokalı Kilise and the Soğanlı church of St. Barbara.[4] A similar attendant is shown in the 1041 Gospel in Jerusalem (fig. 312a). The woman here, however, accompanies Mary, not Elizabeth. Companions for the Virgin might seem at first to be a western feature, insofar as a tradition of such figures can be traced from Carolingian times down to Giotto's Arena Chapel.[5] However, in Armenia the Mułni Gospel of the mid-eleventh century already shows a pair of companions for the Blessed Virgin (fig. 312b).

Companions of the Blessed Virgin are not mentioned by Luke, but according to the Gospel of Pseudo-Matthew, St. Joseph, on the occasion of his espousal to Mary, insisted that she be assigned five virgins as guarantee of her continued chastity.[6] These five kept her company in Joseph's house, each spinning material for the veil of the temple, and after Mary's conception they bore witness to the fact that she had seen no man. Like the Virgin's spinning in the Annunciation, her companion here is meant as a sign of the chastity and upright behavior of Mary.

Male companions are far less common in the Visitation. A pair of men appeared in the lost Visitation panel of the throne of Maximianus in Ravenna, whom Cecchelli identified as Joseph and Zachariah.[7] The figure's long grey hair leaves no doubt that this is Zachariah in the U.C.L.A. Gospel; T'oros' characterization of St. Joseph consistently shows a younger, round-faced man with short-cropped beard and hair.[8] Like the inclusion of the Virgin's companion, the representation of Zachariah is prompted by theological more than historical thinking. As the maiden witnesses to the perpetual virginity of the pregnant Mary, so Zachariah, now divinely struck dumb until the birth of his son, witnesses to the miraculous nature of Elizabeth's conception. Such a role might be inferred from the Gospel account (Luke 1:8–26). In the apocrypha, however, Zachariah is transformed into one of the major actors of the life of Christ. According to the *Protoevangelium* of James, Zachariah was more than a simple priest, he was the High Priest and it was he who had to find a celibate spouse for the Virgin Mary.[9] The early Armenian miniatures of the Ējmiacin Gospel clothed Zachariah as High Priest, alluding to the Syro-Armenian tradition that Christ's priesthood was transmitted directly from the line of Old Testament priests that finished with Za-

[1] Two Cilician instances of the Visitation actually show the unborn infants within their mothers: Jerusalem, St. James, 2568, fol. 155, and Erevan, Mat. 979, fol. 40. Cf. Der Nersessian, "Le Lit de Salomon," *Études*, 52.

[2] H. Leclercq, "Visitation," *DACL* 15, 3130–33; M. Lechner, "Heimsuchung Mariens," *Lexikon der christlichen Ikonographie*, II, 229–35; Schiller, *Iconography of Christian Art*, I, 55–56.

[3] Schiller, *Iconography of Christian Art*, I, fig. 131.

[4] Restle, *Byzantine Wall Painting*, II, pl. 64, and III, pl. 437.

[5] Schiller, *Iconography of Christian Art*, I, 55.

[6] "Gospel of Pseudo-Matthew," chap. 8, *ANF*, VIII, 372; G. Millet cites the same text in this connection: *Iconographie*, 90–91. The *Armenian Infancy Gospel* follows the *Gospel of James* in assuming that Mary dwelt alone in Joseph's house: P. Peeters, *Évangiles apocryphes*, II, 88. Evidently both accounts were familiar in Armenia, inspiring a not totally consistent iconography of the Virgin's life.

[7] Carlo Cecchelli, *La cattedra di Massimiano* (Rome, n.d.), 182.

[8] See Venice, San Lazzaro 1917, Gospel of 1307, fols. 18v and 159, Der Nersessian, *Manuscrits*, figs. 103, 104; Jerusalem, St. James 2360, Gospel of 1321, fol. 155v, unpublished; Erevan, Mat. 6289, Gospel of 1323, fols. 15v and 148, Emma Korkhmazyan, *T'oros Taronac'i* (Erevan, 1984), pl. unnumbered; Erevan, Mat. 206, Gospel of 1318, fol. 443, ibid.

[9] *Protoevangelium*, chap. 8 (Hennecke and Schneemelcher, *New Testament Apocrypha*, I, 378–79).

chariah and John the Baptist.[10] The *Armenian Infancy Gospel* enlarged on Zachariah's close connections with the infancy events: Zachariah assigned Mary her employment of spinning for the veil of the temple; after her conception he forecast the salvation that would arise from her; when Joseph was accused of having violated Mary's virginity he presided over the trial-by-poison that proved their innocence; finally, during the Massacre of the Innocents he laid down his life in the sanctuary rather than reveal the whereabouts of his newborn son John.[11] As implied in the Genealogy, it was important that Christ's priesthood should be a family affair, like the hereditary priesthood of the Armenian clergy.

39. Christ Reading in the Synagogue (*Page 327*)

After the illustration of the Marian themes that look forward to the birth of Christ, the program of the U.C.L.A. Gospel omits all subjects of the birth and infancy and instead moves directly to the opening of Christ's public life. The omission is significant and requires some explanation. The subject of Christ Reading in the Synagogue is not common in Byzantine art and the manner of rendering it in the U.C.L.A. Gospel is out of the ordinary. Most interesting is the appearance of the dove of the Holy Spirit descending on Christ, a motif that has a special Armenian history and reiterates a theme that was analyzed earlier in connection with the Transfiguration.

According to Luke, directly after his trials in the desert Christ started teaching in the synagogues in Galilee, to considerable public acclaim (4:14–30). The story of his teaching in the synagogue of Nazareth has three parts: (1) his standing to read from the book of Isaiah; (2) his explanation of the text, for which he sat according to synagogue custom; and (3) the wrathful reaction of his listeners who tried to throw him from a cliff. All three parts are illustrated in Byzantine art, but there is sometimes confusion as to exactly what action in the narrative is being illustrated. Thus the problematic Brescia casket shows Christ standing and unfolding a scroll in the center of six listeners who sit around him, while the Menologion of Basil II shows Christ standing with a codex, encircled by standing auditors.[1] Curiously enough, however, in neither of these images is Christ actually shown reading; rather he opens the book or scroll to show it to his listeners. Other representations seem intended to illustrate the second part of the story, but for an as yet unexplained reason they illustrate the seemingly insignificant action of returning the book: "And he closed the book, and gave it back to the attendant, and sat down" (Luke 4:20).[2] Christ is shown in the act of reading only in the Rockefeller McCormick New Testament in Chicago and a related manuscript in Berlin.[3]

None of these provide the antecedent for the U.C.L.A. composition. In this miniature Christ turns to the right and holds a codex on a folding reading stand, the *grakal,* the portable lectern traditional in the Armenian church.[4] The composition has been developed from that of the Vehapʻaṙ Gospel, in which Christ assumes exactly the same pose before the *grakal;* in the Vehapʻaṙ Gospel Christ wears a stole, and the attendant before him carries a liturgical cloth in one hand and an unidentified object, perhaps a censer, in the other (fig. 327a). In the U.C.L.A. Gospel the attendant is shown at the top of the crowd but with empty, outstretched hands. A crowd of eight men is shown looking up attentively at Christ, while above Christ's head, against a ground of gold, the dove is seen descending with spread wings. The iconography is decisive in its choice of the moment when Christ "opened the book and found the place where it was written, 'The Spirit of the Lord is upon me, because he has anointed me to preach good news to the poor'" (Luke 4:17–18).

The choice of this moment in the story seems to have been important in the Armenian tradition. It was illustrated in the Gospel of King Gagik and the Vehapʻaṙ Gospel in the eleventh century, and in the twelfth century, in a Venice manuscript, the initial that opens the passage at Luke 4:14 carries a medal-

[10] R. Murray, *Symbols,* 178–82; Mathews, "The Early Armenian Iconographic Program of the Ējmiacin Gospel."

[11] *Armenian Infancy Gospel,* chaps. IV, 8, V, 13, VII, 3–9, XIV, 1–8, trans. Peeters, in *Évangiles apocryphes, II,* 89, 101, 114–19, 157–61. Esayi Tayecʻi, *Ankanon Girkʻ Nor Ktakaranacʻ: Tʻangaran Haykakan Hin ew Nor Prupṭʻeancʻ* (Venice, 1898), II, pp. 13–14, 22, 31–34, 57–59.

[1] F. W. Volbach, *Early Christian Art* (London, 1961), 86. *Il menologio di Basilio II,* Codices e Vaticanis selecti 8 (Turin, 1907), pl. 1.

[2] See the lectionary Leningrad, Public Library 21, fol. 11v, Weitzmann, *Roll and Codex,* pl. 191; and the lectionary New York, Pierpont Morgan 639, fol. 294, Dorothy E. Miner, ed., *Studies in Art and Literature for Belle da Costa Greene* (Princeton, 1954), fig. 319.

[3] Goodspeed and Willoughby, *The Rockefeller McCormick New Testament,* I, pl. fol. 62v, and III, pl. 58.

[4] Malachia Ormanian, *A Dictionary of the Armenian Church,* trans. Bedros Norehad (New York, 1984), 69.

lion of Christ carried on the wings of a dove.[5] In the Zeytʿun Gospel, Ṙoslin marks the same letter by a standing figure of Christ with the dove sitting on his halo, and the scroll that Christ reads is inscribed, "The Spirit of the Lord is upon me" (fig. 327b). The Armenian frieze Gospel also makes a significant choice at this point in its illustration, for its model, Florence, Laurentiana VI,23, shows Christ sitting and returning the book to the attendant and then being expelled from Nazareth, but the Armenian painter substituted Christ standing and reading (fig. 327c).[6] Finally, the Awag Gospel in Erevan, which copies much of the program of the U.C.L.A. Gospel, again shows Christ reading at the *grakal* (fig. 327d).

The U.C.L.A. Gospel, as remarked above (p. 97), illustrated three times the descent of the Holy Spirit upon Christ—in the Baptism, the Transfiguration, and the present scene—the three classic "adoptionist" texts. The absence of any infancy scenes strengthens the adoptionist tone of the program. Christ appears abruptly in these three epiphany scenes, as if the Father's adoption of the adult Christ was what made him Son of God. Yet, strong as this implication seems, it would be difficult to accuse the Armenians of fourteenth-century Siwnikʿ of adoptionism; certainly Esayi Nčʿecʿi's Christology gives no evidence of it. Moreover, the commentary of Cyril of Alexandria, one of the mainstays of Armenian exegesis, made of this passage a special vehicle for explaining the Trinitarian mystery.

For Cyril of Alexandria the descent of the dove naturally raised the question of why Christ, *already* in full possession of the divinity, should have needed the addition of the Spirit. Cyril affirmed that, "the Son was anointed in no other way than by having become according to the flesh such as we are, and taken our nature. For being at once God and man, he both gives the Spirit to the creation in his divine nature, and receives it from God the Father in his human nature; while it is he who sanctifies the whole creation, both as having shone forth from the Holy Father, and as bestowing the Spirit, which he himself pours forth, as that which is his own, both upon the powers above and upon those who recognized his appearing."[7] In a very vivid turn of speech, Cyril makes Christ himself explain the mystery: "The Spirit which by nature is in me by the sameness of our substance and deity, also descended upon me from without."[8] It was not for himself that Christ received the Spirit, Cyril continues, but for mankind, which had lost the Spirit; in Christ all human nature was anointed and delivered from captivity.[9] The illustration of Christ Reading in the Synagogue, therefore, must be taken as a presentation in miniature of the whole mystery of God's entry into human history and his redemption of man. The fact that the U.C.L.A. program appears adoptionist should perhaps be laid to conservatism—a tendency to preserve old elements even when they are in conflict with current thinking.

[5] Venice, San Lazzaro 1635, fol. 164v, Der Nersessian, *Manuscrits,* fig. 57.
[6] Velmans, *Le Tétraévangile,* fig. 192.
[7] Cyril, *Commentary on St. Luke,* trans. R. M. Tonneau, CSCO 140 (1953), pp. 58–59.
[8] Ibid., p. 59.
[9] Ibid., p. 60.

40. The Cure of the Paralytic (*Page 336*)

The story of how a paralytic was carried to Christ and lowered through the roof of the house where he was teaching because of the density of the crowd is told in virtually identical terms in Mark and Luke, and in somewhat abbreviated form in Matthew (Matt. 9:1–8; Mark 2:1–12; Luke 5:17–26). Yovhannēs Erznkacʿi explains that it is one and the same miracle that is being described in the three accounts.[1] The history of the iconography goes back to the catacombs, where the last moment of the story is commonly illustrated, namely, the paralytic carrying his bed.[2] By the sixth century, however, the lowering of the paralytic from the roof had entered the repertoire, as at S. Apollinare Nuovo in Ravenna, and by the eighth century the two moments were illustrated together in the same composition in the frescoes of S. Saba, Rome.[3] In Middle Byzantine art the subject occurs frequently.[4] In monumental examples the paralytic carrying his bed is liable to be omitted, but in its use in running narrative programs both moments are commonly illustrated, as in the frieze Gospel Florence, Laurentiana, VI,23, in which the subject is represented three times.[5] Its derivative, Erevan, Mat. 7651, follows this example fairly closely (fig. 336c).[6]

[1] Yovhannēs Erznkacʿi, *Meknutʿiwn* on Matt. 9:2, p. 202.
[2] H. Leclercq, "Paralytique," *DACL* 13, 1615–26.
[3] Deichmann, *Frühchristliche Bauten und Mosaiken von Ravenna,* pl. 175; Underwood, *The Kariye Djami,* IV, [Underwood], fig. 31.
[4] See Paul A. Underwood, "Some Problems in Programs and Iconography of Ministry Cycles," *The Kariye Djami,* IV, 293–97.
[5] Velmans, *Le Tétraévangile,* figs. 27, 132, 198.
[6] Erevan, Mat. 7651, fols. 27v, 87, and 146v.

There are then no real surprises in the iconography used by the U.C.L.A. Gospel for the subject. Christ sits to the left with three disciples squeezed in behind him. Two awkwardly drawn men on the roof hold ropes, by which they have lowered down the sick man. A dense crowd watches on the right, some of them painted in the ugly livid manner that T'oros Taronec'i reserves for the adversaries of Christ. In front of them the paralytic, now cured, walks off with his bed over his back. The scene bears a striking resemblance to that of the Vehap'aṙ Gospel in its general composition and in the relationship of the two protagonists (fig. 336a).[7] The extra figures in the U.C.L.A. Gospel have been piled on top of one another without any adjustments in the composition.

However, while the iconography of the subject is standard, its choice within the context of the U.C.L.A. Gospel deserves to be examined. The importance of the Cure of the Paralytic in Armenian art should be noted. In the eleventh century the subject was illustrated three times in the Gospel of King Gagik, one of which miniatures survives (fig. 336b), and twice in the Vehap'aṙ Gospel (see Table 8). In Cilicia, besides its triple use in the Armenian frieze Gospel (fig. 336c), the subject was illustrated in Washington, Freer 56.11 of 1263 and in Ṙoslin's Freer Gospel.[8] And in Glajor, after the U.C.L.A. Gospel, Awag takes up the theme again in London, British Library Or. 5304 (fig. 336d).

The lesson of the Cure of the Paralytic is spelled out in the Gospel account, for before commanding the sick man to "rise, take up your bed and go home," Christ first pronounced his sins forgiven. The scribes and Pharisees protested this absolution, saying, "Who can forgive sins but God only?" The physical cure, then, is Christ's proof of his authority to forgive sins (Luke 5:17–26). Thus, according to Chrysostom's reading of the passage, Christ performed two miracles: the first was invisible, and the second confirmed the first and gave a sign "of his own Godhead and of his equality in honor with the Father."[9]

Yovhannēs Erznkac'i, the exegete of Glajor, follows Chrysostom verbatim in this christological argument, adding, however, his own soteriological consideration of the bodily cure of the paralytic. Renovating the health of the man's body, Christ demonstrated that he was the Creator who had infused man's body with life and who in his resurrection would renew the body and make it share the form of his divinity.[10] This is the Syrian mode of exegesis by symbolic synecdoche: the cure of the paralytic stands for the cure of all mankind. The Lord came in his humanity to cure mankind bodily. Erznkac'i continues, "He who took a body did not reject manhood and called himself 'the Son of man' on account of Adam and the Virgin, also because by donning all humanity he would cleanse all humanity."[11]

There is also an important ecclesiological dimension to the Cure of the Paralytic, which would have been familiar to Armenian scriptural scholars through Cyril of Alexandria, in that Christ's authority to forgive sins was one of the principal sacraments of the Church. When Christ prefaced his cure of the paralytic with the intention "that you may know that the Son of man has authority on earth to forgive sins" (Luke 5:24), he is referring, Cyril says, to us: "For he forgives sins as being the incarnate God, the Lord of the law, and we too have received from him this splendid and most admirable grace. For he has crowned man's nature with this great honor also, having said to the holy apostles, 'Truly, I say to you, whatever you bind on earth shall be bound in heaven, and whatever you loose on earth shall be loosed in heaven' (Mt. 18:18)."[12] The sacramental implication of the story was widely recognized, and was cited in the Apostolic Constitutions.[13] In view of the broad pattern of ecclesiological concerns in the program of the U.C.L.A. Gospel it is quite likely that this motivated the choice of the present miniature. The Cure of the Paralytic is an affirmation of the continued authority of the church to forgive sin. Esayi Nč'ec'i urged the faithful to confess their sins every week.[14] Forgiveness of sins is the theme of the following miniature as well.

41. The Anointing of Christ at Simon's House (*Page 351*)

The anointing of Christ's feet at the house of Simon the Pharisee (Luke 7:36–50) is, according to Yovhannēs Erznkac'i, the first of three anointings by Mary Magdalen, all of which are illustrated in the U.C.L.A. Gospel, constituting a kind of subset in the

[7] The inscription in the Vehap'aṙ Gospel reads, "Rise, take up your bed and go" (Luke 5:24).

[8] Der Nersessian, *Arm. Mss. Freer*, figs. 69 and 223.

[9] Chrysostom, "In Matt. Hom. 29," chap. 2, *NPNF* x, p. 196.

[10] Yovhannēs Erznkac'i, *Meknut'iwn* on Matt. 9:7, pp. 204–5.

[11] Ibid., on Matt. 9:6, p. 204.

[12] Cyril of Alexandria, *Commentary on St. Luke* (trans. Tonneau), 84.

[13] *Apostolic Constitutions*, 2, 20, *ANF*, VII, p. 405.

[14] See above, p. 30.

program (see above, p. 128). This particular anointing marked the sinner's conversion from her former way of life, and thus it continues the theme of forgiveness announced in the preceding miniature.

While Byzantine art commonly confuses this scene with the Anointing of Christ at Bethany, Armenian art tends to distinguish the two occasions.[1] T'oros Taronec'i's painting of this subject shows Christ seated in profile pose on a backless chair with Mary on her knees before him. Christ's pose, with one hand raised in speech and Mary's attitude, with her loose hair falling into the basin and the footed basin itself—entirely uncalled-for in the narrative of the incident—all derive from the Vehap'aṙ Gospel (fig. 351a). Around this nucleus the composition has been filled out with the usual architectural background, including a panel of gold to mark Christ's place, and the figures of Simon and two disciples. Simon the Pharisee has a long grey beard and wears a long red tunic; the disciples are given coarse, ugly features, perhaps because the artist confused them with Christ's enemies (see above, pp. 47–48). The dinner table, standard in other representations of the subject, has been omitted, although Taronec'i had room for it. As in the Anointing of Christ at Bethany (*page 269*), the artist prefers to show Christ sitting up rather than reclining in the Byzantine fashion, and this preference can be noted in other Armenian paintings of the subject, such as Venice, San Lazzaro 888/159, Baltimore, Walters 539, and the Armenian frieze Gospel (figs. 351b–d).[2] The instance of the Armenian frieze Gospel, Erevan, Mat. 7651, is especially noteworthy because its model, Florence, Laurentiana VI,23, shows Christ reclining on a couch.[3]

Seeing what was happening, the Pharisee concluded that certainly Christ was no prophet, or he would have known what sort of woman was handling his feet (Luke 7:39). Reading his thoughts, Christ offered the parable of the two debtors whose unequal debts were canceled; he who is forgiven more will love more. To the woman Christ said, "Your sins are forgiven." There are, therefore, two washings taking place, as Ephraem Syrus remarked: she washes his feet, but he washes her of her sins.[4] The lesson has a universal applicability for the Christian. According to Cyril of Alexandria:

> (Christ) taught the Pharisee, and all who were assembled there, that the Word being God, "came into the world in our likeness, not to condemn the world, but that the world might be saved by him" (John 3:17). He came that he might forgive the debtors much and little, and show mercy upon small and great, that there might be no one whatsoever who did not participate in his goodness. . . .
>
> The woman who was guilty of many impurities, and deserving of blame for most disgraceful deeds, was justified, that we also may have confidence that Christ certainly will have mercy upon us, when he sees us hastening to him, and endeavoring to escape from the pitfalls of wickedness. Let us too stand before him; let us shed the tears of repentance; let us anoint him with ointment; for the tears of him that repents are a sweet savor to God.[5]

While the Cure of the Paralytic emphasizes the power of Christ and his church to forgive sins, this incident seems to emphasize the required disposition of the repentant sinner. As Christ says, inverting his own parable, "Her sins, which are many, are forgiven, because she loved much" (Luke 7:47). Der Nersessian has published the summary of a sermon existing in Armenian, though attributed to Theophilus of Alexandria, which consists of a psychological examination of the repentant woman through a series of imagined soliloquies as she worked up her courage to make the dramatic gesture of washing and anointing Christ's feet.[6]

42. The Parable of the Cunning Steward (*Page 403*)

The miniature of the Parable of the Cunning Steward is found on the recto of a single leaf, the verso of which was blank. As mentioned in the discussion of the codicology (above, p. 36), this leaf was misbound in the very first binding of the codex, having been placed between the present pages 424–25. The text of those two pages is Luke 20:21–38, which includes two questions put to Christ, the question of paying tribute to Caesar, and the problem posed by the resurrection in the case of a woman with multiple hus-

[1] Schiller, *Iconography of Christian Art,* I, 157–58; Goodspeed and Willoughby, *The Rockefeller McCormick New Testament,* III, 129–31, 178–81.

[2] To these could be added Washington, Freer, 56.11, fol. 133v, Der Nersessian, *Arm. Mss. Freer,* fig. 243, and Erevan, Mat. 212, fol. 179v, unpublished.

[3] Velmans, *Le Tétraévangile,* fig. 206.

[4] Ephraem, *Commentaire,* bk. 10, chaps. 8–10, pp. 98–99.

[5] Cyril of Alexandria, *Commentary on St. Luke* (trans. Tonneau), 158–60.

[6] S. Der Nersessian, "Armenian Homilies Attributed to Theophilus," *Études,* 478–79.

bands. It is clear that the iconography of the present miniature has nothing to do with either of these subjects, and this was recognized by an early user of the book, who wrote in the upper margin, "This is the rich man and his steward and it is not in its proper place." By this view the miniature belongs with the text of Luke 16:1–9, which is divided between pages 402 and 405. That this is the correct location of the miniature is proven by its correspondence with the illustration of this passage in the Vehapʿaṙ Gospel (fig. 403a-b).

According to the parable, a rich man found one of his stewards wasting his property and decided to dismiss him. Before giving up his office, however, the cunning steward decided to ingratiate himself with his master's debtors by writing off portions of their debts. "He said to the first, 'How much do you owe my master?' He said, 'A hundred measures of oil.' And he said to him, 'Take your bill, and sit down quickly and write fifty'" (Luke 16:6). It is at this point that the Vehapʿaṙ Gospel breaks the column of text to insert the figure of the debtor sitting and writing (fig. 403a). The text continues, "Then he said to another, 'And how much do you owe?' He said, 'A hundred measures of wheat.' He said to him, 'Take your bill, and write eighty'" (Luke 16:7). Here the text is interrupted again, now with the steward seated on a high-backed chair instructing the second debtor, who sits on a lower chair and writes (fig. 403b). The only other known Armenian illustration of this passage is found in the Armenian frieze Gospel, Erevan, Mat. 7651, in which the steward stands and instructs one of the seated debtors to revise his bill (fig. 403c). As often, this represents a departure from the model, Florence, Laurentiana VI,23, which shows the master seated and reproving the steward and then the steward standing and speaking with a debtor who also stands.[1]

Tʿoros Taronecʿi develops the iconography on two registers. On the lower register, in a composition that echoes very closely the second episode in the Vehapʿaṙ Gospel, the steward sits on a high-backed chair and instructs the two debtors, on lower chairs, to revise their bills. On the upper register Taronecʿi shows the steward appearing before his master, a composition with some similarity to that of Laurentiana VI,23. In the U.C.L.A. Gospel, however, the master sits in profile pose and he has been transformed into Christ. Moreover, the steward and the debtors are all given haloes.

In the absence of Armenian exegetical material that might explain the importance of this subject, one can rely only on the iconography itself and the text of Sacred Scripture. To the modern reader the conclusion of the parable comes as a surprise if not a shock, for the master, instead of reproving his dishonesty commends the shrewdness of the steward. The moral of the parable concerns the proper use of money: "Make friends for yourselves by means of unrighteous mammon, so that when it fails they may receive you into the eternal habitations" (Luke 16:9). Money is part of the unrighteous and transitory world that the Christian finds around him; if he uses it properly, however, by giving alms, for example, he wins a welcome reception in the world to come. This is a theme enunciated earlier, in Luke 12:33: "Sell your possessions, and give alms; provide yourselves with purses that do not grow old, with a treasure in the heavens that does not fail, where no thief approaches and no moth destroys."[2] For this reason Tʿoros Taronecʿi has canonized all the participants in the scene; they typify just Christians purchasing rewards in heaven with the proper use of their money on earth. Money is an important theme in the U.C.L.A. Gospel, whether it be in the Question of Tribute to Caesar (*page 259*), the Widow's Mite (*page 263*), or in incidental mentions of alms to the poor or to the church, as in the Anointing of Christ at Bethany (*page 269*). At a time when Mongol overlordship was impoverishing every institution outside of the church the careful use of money must have been a very real preoccupation. The tax-exempt status of monasteries made them a tax shelter for whatever money was invested in them.

43. Peter's Denial and Christ before Caiaphas (*Page 438*)

The subject of Christ before Caiaphas is not uncommon in medieval art in general, but its focus is different from that of the present miniature. Either it shows Christ's persecutors making accusation or it shows Caiaphas dramatically rending his robes as he declares Christ guilty of blasphemy, as narrated in Matt. 26:57–68.[1] In the U.C.L.A. Gospel, on the other hand, Christ's accusers are absent and Caiaphas makes only a vague gesture toward Christ. Illustrating the text of Luke 22:54–62, this miniature is chiefly concerned with Peter. In two registers, it reads from the bottom up: first, Peter denying Christ to the maidservant in the presence of soldier witnesses on

[1] Velmans, *Le Tétraévangile*, fig. 242.

[2] See the parallel in Matt. 6:19–20.

[1] Schiller, *Iconography of Christian Art*, II, 58–60.

either side; then, Christ before Caiaphas turning and looking over his shoulder at Peter, who raises his hand to his face in grief. While Caiaphas sits on a kind of Roman faldstool, his pose, with one leg drawn up, is that of an Islamic judge.[2] Though the trial scene is shown in larger scale under a triple arch, all attention is directed toward Christ's glance at Peter. Luke in fact says nothing of what transpired in Christ's appearance before Caiaphas, but he alone of the evangelists narrates that when the cock crowed, "the Lord turned and looked at Peter," and it was this glance that reminded Peter of the Lord's prediction (Luke 22:61).

This detail of the narrative is unknown in Byzantine and Western iconography, but it has a long history in Armenia. In the Vehapʿaṙ Gospel in the early eleventh century it appears in reverse, with Caiaphas on his faldstool on the left and Peter hunched over in grief on the right (fig. 438a). Christ makes the same turn to look at Peter. In the Cilician period the theme is taken up by Tʿoros Ṙoslin, who conveys a more vivid sense of the spatial setting. Christ, within the palace of the high priest, looks back over the heads of a crowd of soldiers to see Peter seated in the courtyard outside; Peter has looked up and his eyes meet Christ's (fig. 438b). After the U.C.L.A. Gospel, the painter Awag twice illustrated the subject, each time with new variations. In his London manuscript Awag has imagined Christ being led away to prison by a guard; crossing the courtyard he glances back at Peter (fig. 438c). In Erevan Mat. 212 Christ is bound before Caiaphas and a guard, and he again looks over his shoulder.[3] The U.C.L.A. miniature also shows Christ with his hands together as if bound, a detail mentioned in John 18:22, but the ropes are not visible. In each of these occurrences the miniature is immediately associated with its proper text in Luke.

The lesson of Peter's Denial was already examined in connection with the earlier illustration of this subject on *page 166*. Although Chrysostom's and Yovhannēs Erznkacʿi's commentaries deal expressly with Matthew, they both mention Luke's detail of Christ looking at Peter. This demonstrates, for Chrysostom, that Peter "not only denied (Christ), but was not even brought to remembrance from within, and this though the cock had crowed; but he needed a further remembrance from his master, and his look was to him instead of a voice: so exceedingly was he full of fear."[4] This personal contact between Christ and Peter, however, was to be the remedy for Peter's sin, and this miniature should be viewed as pendant to the very last miniature in the U.C.L.A. Gospel, Christ's Apparition by the Sea of Tiberias on *page 570*, in which Christ exacts a threefold confession of love from Peter. Ephraem Syrus pointed to the antithesis between the two moments, both taking place over a fire of coals: "The chief of the disciples was tormented and tried, that he might become a doctor to those who were wounded. Lest sinners be ashamed to do penance, (Christ) who is above all sin encouraged them through Simon the sinner to come to him. By night Simon denied (him), but by day he confessed him over the coals. The earth was witness when he denied (him), and when he confessed him both sea and dry land stood witness according to their nature."[5] Peter's triple denial of weakness, Erznkacʿi adds, was healed by his triple confession of love.[6] The disgrace of the first apostle is therefore a lesson in hope for all future disciples who weaken in their following of Christ.

44. Christ before Herod (*Page 441*)

This iconographic subject is unusual, and it remains rather enigmatic in the absence of published exegetical sources touching on it. Luke alone tells how Pilate, upon hearing the priests' accusation that Christ was stirring up the people of Galilee, sent Christ to Herod Antipas, tetrarch of Galilee (Luke 23:6–12). Herod had been interested in seeing Christ and questioned him at length in the presence of his accusers. Christ, however, refused to say a word, so Herod and his soldiers resorted to mocking him before returning him to Pilate.

Christ before Herod occurs very rarely in medieval art in the West or in the Byzantine sphere.[1] It was represented in the Byzantine frieze Gospel in Florence, in three figures—a soldier, Christ, and Herod—but the Armenian copy omits the subject.[2] It does occur four times in Armenia, however, in closely related miniatures. In the Vehapʿaṙ Gospel (fig. 441a)

[2] See the examples in the thirteenth-century Hariri manuscripts in Paris, B.N. arab. 6094, B.N. arab. 3465, B.N. arab. 5847, in Hugo Buchthal, *Art of the Mediterranean World, A.D. 100 to 1400* (Washington, D.C., 1983), figs. 5, 22, 24, 26, 30.

[3] Erevan, Mat. 212, fol. 228v, unpublished.

[4] Chrysostom, "In Matt. Hom. 85," chap. 1, *NPNF* x, p. 507. This is repeated in Yovhannēs Erznkacʿi, *Meknutʿiwn* on Matt. 26:75, pp. 582–83.

[5] Ephrem Syrus, *Commentaire,* bk. 20, chap. 14, p. 207.

[6] Yovhannēs Erznkacʿi, *Meknutʿiwn* on Matt. 26:75, pp. 582–83.

[1] Schiller, *Iconography of Christian Art,* II, 65; Derbes, *Byzantine Art and the Dugento,* 69–75.

[2] Velmans, *Le Tétraévangile,* fig. 262; Erevan, Mat. 7651, fol. 200, unpublished.

Herod sits on the right on a high-backed chair, wearing a two-tiered crown surmounted by a kind of cross or fleur-de-lis ornament. Christ appears in the center, inappropriately making a gesture of speech in answer to Herod's gesture, and behind him stand his accusers, labeled "the high priests," wearing outlandish three-pointed headdresses. In Roslin's Freer manuscript the same grouping of figures appears against an elegant interior setting (fig. 441b).[3] The U.C.L.A. miniature resembles Roslin's in that Christ is clothed in white; but it seems nevertheless to depend on the Vehapʿaṙ Gospel. The miniature is inserted in the text at exactly the same word (the last word of Luke 23:12), and while Taronecʿi has transformed the two high priests into five soldiers, incongruously he has given the first two the strange three-pointed headdress of the Vehapʿaṙ high priests. They have ugly, livid faces. Herod is now gorgeously arrayed in a red tunic trimmed in gold and a huge crown, and he sits on a pedestal before a pair of porphyry columns and a background of rich ultramarine. Christ's hands are held together as if restrained, though no rope appears. Awag copies Tʿoros Taronecʿi's composition in Erevan, Mat. 212, reducing the soldiers to two (fig. 441c).

In the West the trial before Herod is sometimes paired with the trial before Pilate—a pairing reflecting the Jew-and-Gentile constitution of the church. But the U.C.L.A. miniature is missing such a pendant. The fact that Tʿoros Taronecʿi has clothed Christ in white and has changed the priests into soldiers draws attention to the mocking rather than to the charges being brought against Christ or to Herod's interrogation of him. The miniature therefore is probably to be assigned some of the implications of the earlier representation of the Mocking of Christ on *page 172*.

45. The Apparition on the Way to Emmaus (*Page 448*)

According to Luke 24:13–35, on Easter Sunday two of the disciples, one of them named Cleopas, were on their way to the town of Emmaus when Jesus joined them, without their recognizing him. The disciples told him of their confusion over reports of the empty tomb, and he answered, "O foolish men, and slow of heart to believe all that the prophets have spoken! Was it not necessary that the Christ should suffer these things and enter into his glory?" (Luke 24:25–26). Drawing near the village, the three stopped for supper, where the disciples recognized their Lord in the breaking of the bread.

In the U.C.L.A. Gospel, Christ, clad in a pilgrim's tunic of haircloth, enters from the left with a panel of gold marking his presence. Ahead of him the two disciples carry knapsacks on staffs over their shoulders. In the background one sees a mountainous landscape and a suggestion of the village of Emmaus. Representations of this subject are fairly common, especially in the West, and offer some measure of the special character of the Armenian iconography.[1] The knapsacks are unknown in Western and Byzantine art; since the three were travelers, and the disciples mistook Christ for a "visitor to Jerusalem" (Luke 24:18), medieval art in the West often shows them with scrip and staff, the way Christ is represented in the Second Prince Vasak Gospel, Jerusalem, St. James, 2568 (fig. 448b). The provision of the disciples with knapsacks clearly comes from the eleventh-century Armenian model, the Vehapʿaṙ Gospel (fig. 448a). A third instance of this motif can be found in Awag's Gospel, Erevan, Mat. 212 (fig. 448c). In all three Armenian instances Christ strides behind the two disciples and is represented in larger scale than them. While the general composition and the motif of the knapsacks is traceable to an Armenian source, Tʿoros Taronecʿi departed sharply from the Vehapʿaṙ Gospel in showing Christ dressed as a penitent pilgrim. This is a Western detail that first appears in the Albani Psalter in the twelfth century, where Christ wears a cloak of haircloth.[2] A "visitor to Jerusalem" in the Middle Ages was equated with a pilgrim and therefore was dressed like one.

The fact that the first episode of the Emmaus story is shown, namely, the encounter on the way, rather than the meal, calls the reader's attention to the lessons Christ taught in his instruction of the disciples. According to Cyril of Alexandria, Christ "brings forward Moses and the prophets, interpreting their hidden meaning, and making plain to the worthy what to the unworthy was obscure, so settling in them that ancient and hereditary faith taught them by the sa-

[3] This miniature is misidentified in Der Nersessian as "Jesus before Pilate." Der Nersessian, *Arm. Mss. Freer,* fig. 159. The correct identification has been made by Helen C. Evans, *Armenian Manuscript Illumination.*

[1] G. Schiller, *Ikonographie der christlichen Kunst,* III, 99–104. H. Feldbusch, "Emmaus," *Lexikon der christlichen Ikonographie,* I, 622–26; Mâle, *L'art religieux du XIIe siècle en France,* 137–39.

[2] G. Schiller, *Ikonographie der christlichen Kunst,* III, figs. 311–12.

cred books. . . . In their due place servants were sent to make ready for the presence of the Master, by bringing in beforehand prophecy as the necessary preparative for faith, that, like some royal treasure, what had been foretold might in due season be brought forward from the concealment of its former obscurity."[3] The disciples are made trustees of the hidden meanings of Sacred Scripture, which they are to explain to the church. This understanding of the event may be connected with the identity of the two disciples to whom Christ speaks, a detail of iconography that might go unnoticed were it not for the Vehap'aṙ Gospel. For in that miniature (fig. 448a) the disciples are labeled "Cleopas" and "Paul." T'oros Taronec'i dropped the labels, as he does throughout the manuscript, yet the figure on the right, with receding hairline and pointed beard, is the type of Paul, as can be confirmed from his appearance in the very next miniature, the Ascension on *page 453*. Historically, of course, Paul should not be present in either of these scenes, for his first encounter with Christ was his vision in Acts 9:1–19, and speculation on the identity of the second disciple usually settled on one Simon, following Origen and Cyril of Alexandria, or on Luke himself, the author of the story, according to Latin authors.[4] The introduction of Paul into the iconography of the Apparition on the Way to Emmaus is certainly deliberate, and must point to a special role assigned Paul in the transmission of divine revelation. A similar interest in the transmission of revelation was observed in Peter Receives the Keys (*page 103*) and the Blessing of the Children (*page 117*).

46. The Ascension (*Page 453*)

The Ascension is one of the two signed miniatures of T'oros Taronec'i in the U.C.L.A. Gospel. The development of Taronec'i's competence from this to later paintings of the subject has already been noticed: the problem of too many left hands in the group of apostles on the left he resolved in the Venice manuscript of 1307 (fig. 453c), in which the figures acquire greater assurance; in a still later version, Erevan, Mat. 206, the groupings of figures are loosened up and the angels wheel about the sky in wild abandon (fig. 453d).

[3] Cyril of Alexandria, *Commentary on St. Luke* (trans. Tonneau), 726–27.

[4] Ibid., 726; Origen, *Commentarium in Joannem*, 1, chap. 8 (PG 14, col. 34).

The final episode in the Gospel according to St. Luke is described with the utmost simplicity. "Then (Christ) led them out as far as Bethany, and lifting up his hands he blessed them. While he blessed them, he parted from them, and was carried up into heaven" (Luke 24:50–51). For the iconography of the Ascension artists had recourse to the fuller description of the event in Acts 1:6–11. In that account are recorded Christ's last words to his disciples, in which he promised them, "You shall receive power when the Holy Spirit has come upon you; and you shall be my witnesses in Jerusalem and in all Judea and Samaria and to the end of the earth." Thereupon he was lifted up, out of their sight, and two angels appeared standing by the apostles and telling them, "This Jesus, who was taken up from you into heaven, will come in the same way as you saw him go into heaven." Despite the brevity of its treatment in Luke this is a common place for the illustration of the Ascension in Armenian manuscripts. It was located here in the program of the Gospel of King Gagik (see Table 8) and in Roslin's Gospels in Baltimore (fig. 453a) and Washington.[1] The Armenian frieze Gospel, Erevan, Mat. 7651, also concludes Luke with an Ascension, even though its model, Florence, Laurentiana, VI,23, lacks this subject (fig. 453b).[2]

The Ascension is one of the most often illustrated events of the life of Christ, and frequency of illustration led to its standardization. There are few surprises in the Ascension of the U.C.L.A. Gospel; the enthroned Christ in mandorla, the angels that encircle him, the twelve apostles gesturing in astonishment, the Virgin in orans pose, and the pair of white-clad angels addressing the apostles, all these elements were introduced in the sixth century and were repeated countless times in the interval. The development of this iconography has been described a number of times, its origins traced to an iconographic formula that was given currency in Palestine through its use on pilgrims' ampullae.[3] The greater freedom allowed in the West in reworking the scene has no impact on the U.C.L.A. miniature. Still, one or two peculiarities in Taronec'i's handling of the scene

[1] Der Nersessian, *Arm. Mss. Freer*, fig. 166.

[2] Erevan, Mat. 7651, fol. 207v; cf. Velmans, *Le Tétraévangile*, fig. 266.

[3] H. Leclercq, "Ascension dans l'Art," *DACL* 1, 2926–34; Ernest T. DeWald, "The Iconography of the Ascension," *AJA* 19 (1915), 277–319; S. Helena Gutberlet, *Die Himmelfahrt Christi in der bildenden Kunst von den Anfängen bis ins hohe Mittelalter* (Strassburg, 1935); A. A. Schmid, "Himmelfahrt Christi," *Lexikon der christlichen Ikonographie*, II, 268–76; G. Schiller, *Ikonographie der christlichen Kunst*, III, 144–64.

should be noted, and however standard the iconography, its meaning in the present context must be reviewed.

At the top of the painting the blue mandorla breaks through the border and starts into the margin; this graphic way of representing the ascending motion of Christ was employed a generation earlier by T'oros Roslin in his Baltimore Gospel (fig. 453a). The mandorla itself is painted in concentric zones in shades of ultramarine with flashes of light radiating out from the center. Although the encircling angels owe something to the classical motif of victories supporting a shield, or *imago clipeata*, the mandorla itself containing the figure of Christ cannot be suitably interpreted by this derivation.[4] In Roman art the *imago clipeata* is always a bust portrait, and therefore it reads clearly as an image of an image. The figure of Christ, however, is a standing, full-length figure; it is clearly not "painted" on the mandorla but moves freely in front of it and often overlaps its edge, as here with his blessing hand. The mandorla is not a shield but a circle of light borrowed from Buddhism, where it had been in use at least since the second century.[5] In the U.C.L.A. miniature the rays of light and the gradations of blue within the mandorla testify to the painter's awareness of the light symbolism he was employing. Ascending to his rightful place in heaven, Christ is the source of all light. The throne or the arc of heaven on which Christ sits has been omitted by Taronec'i, a problem that persists in his later versions of the Ascension as well (figs. 453c–d).

Around the mandorla, against a sky of gold, four angels fly. The number of angels varies in Ascension iconography without important implications, but the tetramorphs that appear in the Rabbula Gospel and connect that Ascension to Ezekiel's vision have no part in the standard Byzantine iconography of the scene.[6] One ought also to distinguish these angels from the two standing on the ground below, mentioned in Acts 1:10–11. These clearly belong to the realm of heaven, where they must be seen as welcoming Christ triumphant into his kingdom. They figure in this connection in the Midday Hymn of the Armenian liturgy of the Ascension: "He ascended this day with divine power in the Father's chariot, being ministered unto by the angelic choirs. . . . The heavenly authorities were amazed and with awful voices cried aloud one to another: Who is this king of glory that comes in the body and with marvellous power? Lift up your gates, O ye princes, and the king of glory shall come in."[7]

The fact that it is Christ's physical human body that ascended into heaven is also emphasized in the liturgy and is the chief thrust of exegetical commentary on the scene. The Melody for the feast of the Ascension announces, "This day the firstborn of the Father, the only-begotten Son, soars into heaven in the form of Adam."[8] The Ode for the day expands on this theme: "And arising into heaven and going up on the wings of winds, Thou didst ascend in the body with which thou didst die and rise again. . . . And our human nature, which the Evil One made fit for hades, Thou didst lift higher than the nature of the fiery spirits."[9] This is the lesson that Cyril of Alexandria also insists on in his commentary on the passage: "Having blessed them, and gone a little in advance, He was carried up unto heaven, that he might share the Father's throne even with the flesh that was united unto Him. And this new pathway the Word made for us when He appeared in human form: and hereafter in due time He will come again in the glory of His Father with the angels, and will take us up to be with him." The beginning and end of human history are thus tied together in the Ascension; in Adam's body Christ mounts to heaven to pave the way for the ascension of the rest of mankind. God became man, in the classic formula of Christian theology, in order that man might become God.

On the earthly zone below, Taronec'i has represented a mountainous landscape with his usual formula of tan and magenta crags with white highlights. The apostles stand in a double file clasping books in front of them. The books are missing in Byzantine precedents and are common in Western iconography; but they occur in Early Christian examples from Palestine and Egypt, and start to appear in Armenian art in the Cilician period (fig. 453a).[10] Perhaps the books allude to the teaching mission of the apostles, a point strengthened by the nonhistorical presence of Paul. Taronec'i seems not to have taken Paul for granted in this context, since he does not include him in his Venice Ascension of 1307, and in Erevan, Mat.

[4] A. Grabar espoused the clipeate origins of the mandorla in an often cited but seldom criticized article: "Imago clipeata chrétienne," *L'art de la fin de l'antiquité et du moyen âge,* I (Paris, 1968), 607–13.

[5] For a fuller discussion of the origins of the mandorla with appropriate bibliography see Mathews, "Iconographic Program of the Ējmiacin Gospel," 205–9.

[6] G. Schiller, *Ikonographie der christlichen Kunst,* III, 148, and fig. 459.

[7] *Divine Liturgy of the Armenian Apostolic Orthodox Church* (trans. Nersoyan, p. 104).

[8] Ibid., 103.

[9] Ibid., 103.

[10] G. Schiller, *Ikonographie der christlichen Kunst,* III, figs. 456, 461.

206 he shows only eleven apostles (figs. 453c–d). Paul's appearance here may be associated with his unexpected appearance in the Apparition on the Way to Emmaus (*page 448*), where his role is that of transmitter of the divine traditions.

The Blessed Virgin and Paul are standard in Byzantine representations of the Ascension. The nonhistorical presence of the Virgin should be connected with her equally nonhistorical presence in the Women at the Tomb (*page 179*). The identification of the Blessed Virgin as the Church and the mother of the faithful entered the Armenian tradition with Ephraem Syrus. The symbolism depends on Paul's identification of Christ as the second Adam (Rom. 5:12); Ephraem explains: "Just as by the condemnation of the one Adam all bodies died and must die, so by the victory of this one body of Christ, the whole Church found life and lives. But just as, because the bodies which themselves have sinned, themselves must also die, and the earth their mother was cursed, so because of this body, because it is itself the Church, which is not corrupted, its earth was blessed from the beginning. For the earth is the body of Mary, the temple which received the seed."[11] In typical Syrian fashion Ephraem has rolled it all into one. The Virgin is the earth from which Christ and the Church are born; through Christ's victory in his body the curse of the first Adam has been reversed and Mary, the earth, and all her progeny are blessed.[12] Read this way the imagery of the Ascension presents man's salvation in two stages, incorporation into the body of the Church below and ascension with the body of Christ above.

47. The Wedding Feast at Cana (*Page 469*)

Christ's first miracle, the changing of water into wine at the Wedding Feast of Cana (John 2:1–11), had a special importance in Armenian art, for the subject made a very direct appeal to the popular imagination. Genre details of local interest, colorful costumes, and figures celebrating or making music could be introduced without impropriety. Der Nersessian has demonstrated how in miniatures of the Xizan school of the fourteenth and fifteenth centuries the groom at Cana is dressed like the groom in an Armenian wedding of the day.[1] Closer to the Glajor Gospel, Awag in 1337 introduced a pair of female musicians to the scene, one with a flute, another with a drum.[2]

The miniature in the U.C.L.A. Gospel, however, makes little appeal to the imagery of everyday life. Perhaps the lions rampant in the spandrels above are meant to evoke the situation of some princely palace (but see the lions in the Crucifixion *page 561*). Beside this detail only the wedding crowns of the bride and groom refer to contemporary life. According to Armenian practice the bride and groom exchanged crosses on the occasion of their betrothal (the bride carries one such cross in the Hartford manuscript of T'oros Taronec'i [fig. 469d]), and at the wedding ceremony itself the priest blessed crowns and placed them on the heads of the couple.[3] But wedding crowns also figure in Byzantine ceremonial and Byzantine iconography. Still, it is significant that the most important use made of this passage in the Armenian liturgy is its use as the Gospel text for weddings.[4] This may in part explain the popularity of the subject in Armenian Gospel illumination.[5]

The standard Byzantine iconography of the Wedding Feast at Cana presents three successive moments in the narrative in a single unified composition.[6] The thirteenth-century Gospel, Mount Athos, Iviron, ms. 5, offers a good example.[7] The first moment is at the banquet table, where the Mother of God, noticing the failure of the wine, discreetly brings the matter into Christ's attention, standing and leaning over his shoulder to talk with him.[8] The second moment, the actual miracle, is shown to the far right; here Christ

[11] Ephraem, *Commentaire*, bk. 4, chap. 15, pp. 55–56; translation here cited from Murray, *Symbols*, 83–84.

[12] For the Blessed Virgin as the Church in Ephraem and other early Syrian writers, see Murray, *Symbols*, 142–50.

[1] Der Nersessian, *Arm. Mss. Walters*, 38.

[2] Erevan, Mat. 212, fol. 246, in Zakaryan, *Awag*, plate unnumbered.

[3] Frederick C. Conybeare, *Rituale Armenorum, Being the Administration of the Sacraments and the Breviary of the Armenian Church* (Oxford, 1905), 108–14.

[4] Ibid., 109. In the course of the regular church year the passage is read on the First Sunday or the Octave of the Nativity and on Friday of the second week after Easter. See Table 9.

[5] Often the subject is abbreviated in the margins of manuscripts, as in T'oros Taronec'i's Hartford manuscript (fig. 469d), or in his London manuscript, B.L. add. 15411, fol. 246, unpublished,

[6] On the Byzantine iconography of Cana, see H. Leclercq, "Cana, miracle de," *DACL* 2, 1802–19; Schiller, *Iconography of Christian Art*, I, 162–64; U. Nilgen, "Hochzeit zu Kana," *Lexikon der christlichen Ikonographie*, II, 299–305; Paul Underwood, "Some Problems in Program and Iconography of the Ministry Cycle," in *The Kariye Djami*, IV, 280–85.

[7] Pelikanidis, *The Treasures of Mount Athos*, II, pl. 38.

[8] The Mother of God is seated in the Rockefeller McCormick New Testament and occasional Cappadocian and Ottonian examples; Carr, *The Rockefeller McCormick New Testament*, 173.

appears a second time, supervising the pouring of water into six jars, where his blessing transforms it into wine. Finally the action returns to the banquet table, where the servant is shown offering a cup of the new wine to the chief steward. Clearly this is the basic compositional scheme that lies behind the Cana miniature in Washington, Freer, 32.18 (fig. 469b). The Armenian frieze Gospel has omitted the banquet altogether, departing from its model in the Florence frieze Gospel (fig. 469c).[9]

By contrast, the story in the U.C.L.A. Gospel unfolds in two superimposed scenes: the banquet above and the transformation of water into wine below. This division of the miracle into two registers has a long and consistent history in the East Christian art. It is used in Ałtʿamar in the early tenth century,[10] and again in the great Syrian lectionaries of the early thirteenth century.[11] Later in the century it is picked up in a Christian Arabic manuscript from Mardin in Mesopotamia.[12] In the fourteenth century it is the standard format for Cana scenes, whether in the two narrative Gospels of Awag from eastern Armenia,[13] or in the work of Zakʿaria Ałtʿamarcʿi from the region of Lake Van.[14] The presentation of narrative subjects beneath ornamental arches, often multi-lobed, is also common in Islamic miniatures.

Within this two-register format Tʿoros Taronecʿi has reworked the iconography of the changing of water into wine; in the upper register he followed very closely the composition of the Vehapʿaṙ Gospel, but switched Christ and the chief steward at either end of the table (fig. 469a).[15] The first moment in the Byzantine version, namely, the conversation between Christ and his mother, has been omitted. Mary gestures toward the groom and steward, who are just discovering the miracle; the steward has just passed the cup to the groom after observing, "You have kept the good wine until now" (John 2:10). At the other end of the table Christ holds in two hands an enormous, conical glass beaker full of red wine. The upper register, therefore, is made to represent the moment after the miracle rather than the moment before. In the lower register the miracle itself has also been revised, by omitting Christ from the work of transforming water into wine. This is closer to the plain Gospel narrative than the Byzantine iconography, for John implies that the miracle took place in the pouring, simply by following Christ's directions. This is exactly how Tʿoros portrays the event: while the disciples stand by with cups ready a servant pours a stream of blue water into the last of the six jugs, but one can see that already the water in the other jugs has turned to red wine.

These revisions of iconography are not without purpose. Byzantine art had an interest in illustrating the conversation between Christ and his mother, for Chrysostom had found a very useful moral lesson in the incident. Insofar as Christ at first rebuffed his mother, Chrysostom concludes that mere physical kinship is of no value for salvation; the Christian must place his trust not in the distinction of his birth but in the merits of his good works.[16] Tʿoros instead has stripped away this family interest of the subject in order to reinterpret the banquet of Cana as a prototype of the Eucharist. The great beaker held by Christ is significant in this respect. It should be noted that in the Vehapʿaṙ Gospel, Christ does not hold a cup but gestures down, pointing toward where the six jugs should have been represented below the table (fig. 469a). Curiously enough, medieval art never shows Christ actually eating or drinking, even though there are several places in the Gospel where he ate and drank. The only context in which Christ is shown with a cup is the Eucharist—whether the Last Supper or the Communion of the Apostles—in which Christ offers the cup to his apostles. The rectangular altar-like shape of the table reinforces the eucharistic connection, and Tʿoros has added, right in the center of the composition, a great, oversized chalice full of red wine. The chalice floats against the neutral ground of the white parchment and the apostles and attendants seem to direct their attention toward it, rather than toward the miracle.

Although scholars allege that Cana is a common type of the Eucharist,[17] Byzantine exegetes generally did not take it that way. Lessons in sobriety, Christian joy, and the sacredness of marriage are extracted from the text, but connections with the Eucharist are

[9] Velmans, *Le Tétraévangile,* fig. 271.

[10] Der Nersessian, *Aghtʿamar,* pl. 67.

[11] London, British Library, add. 7170, fol. 67, and Vatican, ms. syr. 559, fol. 57v, Leroy, *Mss. syriaques,* pl. 82, 1 and 2.

[12] Florence, Laur. Orient. 387, fol. 36v, David Diringer, *The Illuminated Book, Its History and Production,* 2nd ed. (London, 1967), pl. III, 8, a.

[13] British Library, ms. orient. 5304, fol. 58, unpublished, and Erevan, Mat. 212, fol. 256; Zakaryan, *Awag,* plate unnumbered.

[14] Erevan, Mat. 5347, and 10527, Hakopyan, *Haykakan Manrankarčʿutʿyun Vaspurakan,* pls. 37 and 38.

[15] The figures in the Vehapʿaṙ Gospel are labeled from left to right as follows: "The Chief Steward, The Virgin, The Bride, The Groom, Lord Jesus."

[16] Chrysostom, "In Jn. Hom. 22," chaps. 1–3, *NPNF* XIV, pp. 72–76.

[17] See Schiller and Nilgen in note 6 above.

not established.[18] Rather it is in the Christian East that this theme is developed, starting with Cyril of Jerusalem and Ephraem Syrus. Cyril cites the miracle as proof of Christ's powers of transubstantiation, for if he can change water into wine then he can change wine into his blood.[19] Ephraem, on the other hand, sees the miracle, paired with the multiplication of loaves, as part of Christ's plan to lead man gradually to the more spiritual gift, when he could offer his flesh and blood for food: "He gave these insignificant gifts gratis, that this might stir us up to go and receive without paying what is more excellent. The insignificant bread and wine that he gave were sweet to the mouth, but the gift of his body and blood was profitable to the mind. Through that which pleases the palate he excited us, that he might lead us to what vivifies the spirit. . . . In the first of his signs he made wine giving joy to the banqueters, in order to show that his blood would give joy to all generations of the Gentiles."[20] It is not surprising that such an interpretation should find its way into Armenia, where Cyril and Ephraem were among the most popular of Early Christian authors. Nersēs Šnorhali echoes this interpretation in the twelfth century, ascribing to the cup of Cana the saving power of the cup of the Eucharist.[21]

48. The Samaritan at the Well (*Page 480*)

Common in Early Christian art from the third century on, the Samaritan at the Well is usually represented in Byzantine art simply by the two figures of Christ and the woman in conversation, with the well between them.[1] Such, for example, is the composition in the Homilies of Gregory, Paris, B.N. gr. 510.[2] The story of Christ's encounter with the Samaritan woman and her compatriots, however, is capable of a variety of interpretations (John 4:1–42). A baptismal significance is sometimes attributed to the well by representing it as a four-lobed baptismal font, as in the mosaics of S. Marco, Venice.[3] Moreover, the thirteenth-century Syrian lectionaries point to a more basic christological symbolism by showing Christ superimposed on the well, his feet in the water:[4] the imagery identifies Christ with the water, as he explained to the woman, "Whoever drinks of the water that I shall give him will never thirst; the water that I shall give him will become in him a spring of water welling up to eternal life" (John 4:14) This is a theme to which Christ returned later, in his instruction at the Feast of Tabernacles (John 7:37).

On the other hand, in some instances Byzantine art develops the subject in a narrative fashion by showing more than one moment to the story. Thus at S. Marco, Venice, while Christ, with a pair of disciples behind him, converses with the Samaritan, a later moment in the narrative is shown further to the right, with the woman explaining to her townsfolk, "Come, see a man who told me all that I ever did. Can this be the Christ?" (John 4:29). This is the format followed by T'oros Ṙoslin in his Baltimore Gospel, Walters 539, though he has enriched the imagery with a representation of Sychar, the city of Samaria, in the background and a pair of puzzled disciples in the center (fig. 480b). The frieze Gospel, Florence, Laurentiana, VI,23, adds a vignette of still a third moment, that is, Christ instructing one of the Samaritans; for they invited him to stay with them for two days, "and many more believed because of his word" (John 4:41).[5] The Armenian copy of this, Erevan, Mat. 7651, eliminates this little epilogue to the story (fig. 480c).

In this context the miniature in the U.C.L.A. Gospel is unusual, for it has rolled several successive moments of the narrative into one. The core of the image depends on the Vehap'aṙ Gospel (fig. 480a): the gesture of the seated Christ, the pose of the woman holding the rope, and the long-necked vessel placed on the ground are all very similar. This element illustrates the early part of the story, when the woman came to draw water. The Vehap'aṙ Gospel has inscribed here Christ's first words to her, "Give me a drink" (John 4:7). Behind the woman Taronec'i has painted a gentleman with a pointed hat and a fur-

[18] In addition to Chrysostom, the following texts were searched in this connection: Eusebius *Demonstratio Evangelica* 9 (PG 43, cols. 761 ff.); Cyril of Alexandria, *In Ioannem* 2 (PG 73, 225 ff.); idem, *Scholia Vetera in Ioannem* (PG 106, 224 ff.); Theophylactus, *Enarratio in Evangelium Ioannis* 2 (PG 123, 1192 ff.); Euthymius Zigabenus, *Commentaria in Ioannem* 2 (PG 1148 ff.); Theodore Prodromos, *Tetrasticha in Novum Testamentum* (PG 133, 1204).

[19] Cyril of Jerusalem, *Catechesis Mystagogica* 4, 2 (PG 33, cols. 1097–99).

[20] Ephraem Syrus, *Commentaire,* 12, 1–2 (ed. Leloir, p. 115).

[21] Nersēs Šnorhali, *Yisous Ordi,* 349 (ed. and trans. Kéchichian, p. 108).

[1] H. Leclercq, "Samaritaine," *DACL* 15, 725–34; Schiller, *Iconography of Christian Art,* I, 159–60.

[2] Omont, *Manuscrits,* pl. 39.

[3] O. Demus, *The Mosaics of San Marco in Venice,* I, fig. 147.

[4] London, 7170, fol. 199 and Rome, Vat. syr. 559, fol. 183, Leroy, *Mss. syriaques,* pl. 96, 3–4.

[5] Velmans, *Le Tétraévangile,* fig. 275.

trimmed coat, elements of contemporary dress introduced into Armenia with the arrival of the Mongols. The prominence of this figure and his closeness to the woman identify him as her "husband." According to the Gospel, when Christ had promised to give her the water of eternal life he asked the woman to call her husband. She replied evasively, "I have no husband"; but Christ, knowing her secret, reinterpreted her remark, "You are right in saying, 'I have no husband'; for you have had five husbands, and he whom you now have is not your husband; this you said truly" (John 4:17–18). His ability to read her heart convinced the woman that Christ was a prophet. She therefore asked whether God ought to be worshipped on Mount Gerizim, sacred to the Samaritans, or in Jerusalem. Christ's answer put the nature of religion on a more universal basis: "The hour is coming, and now is, when the true worshippers will worship the Father in spirit and truth" (John 4:23).

Meanwhile the apostles, who had left Christ in search of food, returned and were puzzled to see him talking with a woman. Three disciples are shown in a second plane above a kind of architectural screen behind the well. The meaning of this architectural element is not clear, but the Vehapʿaṙ Gospel also shows a curious rectangle above the well (fig. 480a), and the two Syrian lectionaries show other kinds of architectural framings behind the well. Also obscure is the object carried by the first of the disciples, which looks like the top of a basket but seems to have been left unfinished by the painter. The underdrawing in red shows a curve continuing the line of the disciple's right arm, as if he were supposed to be cradling the basket. The lower, slightly domed curve may have been part of the background. The Gospel, however, clarifies the imagery, for the disciples returned carrying the food they had sought and they presented it to Christ saying, "Rabbi, eat." Christ replied allegorically, "My food is to do the will of him who sent me, and to accomplish his work. Do you not say, 'There are yet four months, then comes the harvest'? I tell you, lift up your eyes, and see how the fields are already white for harvest" (John 4:31–35). The fields waiting for harvest, of course, were mankind waiting to be converted; hence Christ stayed in Sychar to preach to the Samaritans. The painting shows a city door open and three men emerging: "They went out of the city and were coming to him" (John 4:30). The miniature focuses on Christ's work of conversion.

This iconography is quite unusual, and it is regrettable that contemporary Gospel commentaries that might explain it are lacking. The commentary of Ephraem Syrus, however, enjoyed a continued popularity in Armenia, and Ephraem, in keeping with the message of the iconography, makes two points in discussing the Samaritan at the well.[6] First he notices the gradualness of the conversion process: Christ led the woman by steps, first to see himself as a man thirsting, then as a Jew, then as a prophet, and finally as Christ the Lord; and after the woman was converted gradually the whole town followed. Secondly Ephraem notices the universality of the mission of Christ. Rejecting the exclusive claims of true worship on this or that mountain he looks forward to a spiritual worship to which the whole world will be invited. The miniature therefore departs from the usual imagery of this subject in order to express this aspiration for the universal success of Christ's mission; perhaps the Mongol dress of the Samaritan's "husband" implies the expectation that they too should be won over to true worship.

49. The Cure of the Paralytic at the Pool (*Page 484*)

Like the preceding subject, this miniature also involves water. Christ stands against a gold background and makes an awkward blessing gesture over a cylindrical well. Beyond this pool lies the paralytic, imploring Christ's help with his outstretched hands; his misshapen legs vividly convey his helplessness, and his thin pointed beard and wispy moustache give a distinctly Asiatic impression to his face. He reclines on a low-footed pallet. Behind him three smaller figures with pained expressions and distorted limbs approach the pool. In the background five arches and a kind of tower define the "five porticoes" of the pool mentioned by John.

According to the evangelist (John 5:1–18), a multitude of invalids gathered around the pool, for an angel of the Lord would visit the water from time to time and whoever entered the water first would be cured. The paralytic whom Christ singled out for cure could never get to the water as quickly as the others to benefit from the angel's miracle. "Jesus said to him, 'Rise, take up your pallet, and walk.' And at once the man was healed, and he took up his pallet and walked. Now that day was the sabbath" (John 5:8–9). To the Jews' criticism of Christ's violation of the sabbath rest he answered, " 'My Father is working still, and I am working.' This was why the Jews sought all the more to kill him, because he not only broke the sabbath but also called God his own Father, making himself equal with God" (John 5:17–18).

[6] Ephraem, *Commentaire*, bk. 12, chaps. 16–20, pp. 122–24.

The nucleus of this miniature derives from the corresponding miniature in the Vehapʿaṙ Gospel (fig. 484a); it has been reversed right to left, a change suggested by the shape of the available space, but Christ's gesture remains the same, and the paralytic with misshapen legs and imploring gesture lies on the same sort of low-footed pallet.[1] Byzantine art commonly shows a high and quite substantial bed.[2] To this nucleus Taronecʿi has added details from the more or less standard Byzantine iconography of the subject. A cylindrical well with three invalids approaching, and a screen of five arches (supported, as they ought to be, on columns) appear in nearly this arrangement in the fourteenth-century frescoes of Ravanica in Serbia.[3]

The use of this subject on Early Christian sarcophagi was apparently motivated by an implicit resurrection symbolism.[4] This was suggested by Christ's own words in his subsequent explanation of his relationship to the Father, "As the Father raises the dead and gives them life, so also the Son gives life to whom he will" (John 5:21). The subject is also capable of a baptismal interpretation; Chrysostom saw the miraculous power of the pool as a figure of the baptism that Christ was to give, possessing much greater power.[5] This is the interpretation intended in the eleventh-century lectionary, Athos, Dionysiou 578, in which the angel is shown descending over a quatrefoil baptismal font, but the cure of the paralytic is omitted.[6] The Armenian frieze Gospel also shows a baptismal font, cruciform in shape, enclosed in a structure that might be read as a baptistery (fig. 484b).

The U.C.L.A. miniature, however, shows a cylindrical pool, and the cure of the paralytic, according to the Gospel, takes place outside of the pool. Attention, therefore, is focused on the work of Christ, which Christ himself equates with the work of the Father. As Ephraem Syrus says regarding Christ's words on this occasion, "If created works and things cannot be constrained on the sabbath, such as angels, heavenly bodies, dew, rain, springs and rivers, how much more their creator."[7] The miracle does not demonstrate that man is lord of the sabbath, but rather that Christ is God who legislated the sabbath and therefore is not bound by the law.[8] At the same time, Christ's conflict with the Jews adds a sinister overtone to the miracle. When first questioned by the Jews, the paralytic was unable to identify Jesus as the one who had told him to violate the sabbath; but when he learned who he was the paralytic returned to the Jews with this information (John 5:12–15). Although John says nothing of his intentions, Gregory of Narek interprets this as a malicious betrayal of Christ and adds that the cured paralytic subsequently took part in Christ's passion, joining those who struck Christ.[9] This particular miracle, then, is seen by Gregory of Narek as a demonstration of the extraordinary beneficence of Christ, that he should cure one who, he foresaw, would persecute him. Perhaps the Mongol features given to the paralytic in Taronecʿi's painting are intended to suggest this sinister aspect of the subject.

[1] The inscription in the Vehapʿaṙ Gospel reads "The Paralytic."

[2] Schiller, *Iconography of Christian Art*, I, figs. 497–99; Underwood, "Some Problems in Programs," *The Kariye Djami*, IV, figs. 27–30.

[3] Underwood, "Some Problems in Programs," *The Kariye Djami*, IV, fig. 28.

[4] H. Leclercq, "Piscine Probatique," *DACL* 14, 1126–27.

[5] Chrysostom, "In Jn. Hom. 36," chap. 1, *NPNF* xiv, p. 126; Schiller, *Iconography of Christian Art*, I, 169–70.

[6] Athos, Dionysiou 578, fol. 17v, Pelikanidis, *The Treasures of Mount Athos*, I, fig. 202.

[7] Ephraem, *Commentaire*, bk. 13, chap. 4, p. 129.

[8] Ibid., p. 131.

[9] Gregory Narekacʿi, *Le Livre des prières*, chap. 58 (trans. Kéchichian, p. 311).

50. The Cure of the Man Born Blind (*Page 509*)

Although Taronecʿi was responsible for finishing the faces in this miniature, the rest is the work of the Second Painter, and it is the only miniature by his hand that is less than full page. It is evidence, therefore, of his intention to paint all the narrative miniatures, regardless of their size, before he was interrupted in his work. It is also important evidence for his dependence on the Vehapʿaṙ Gospel in formulating his composition. The background he reduces to three broad bands of color—gold, red, and green—against which three disciples stand in a row behind the considerably larger figure of Christ. Christ holds a ball of mud in his left hand and applies some of it with his right to the closed eyes of the blind man. The blind man kneels before him. Simple as it is, the image stands apart from the usual ways of handling this subject and makes an important statement.

This is the fourth miniature in the U.C.L.A. Gospel illustrating the cure of a blind man (*pages 124, 235, 250*). John's story resembles that in Mark 8:27–34 insofar as it involves the use of clay and takes place in stages. First Christ made clay and applied it to the man's eyes; then he sent the man to wash in the pool of Siloam, where he gained sight (John 9:1–12). Like the Cure of the Paralytic at the Pool, this miracle was performed on the sabbath, and this provokes the Pharisees to investigate the incident (John 9:13–41). Accordingly, Byzantine art, from the Rossano Gospel through the middle Byzantine period, illustrates two stages in the miracle: Christ touching the eyes of the blind man and the blind man washing his eyes in the pool.[1] The frieze Gospels draw the story out further, to five scenes in the Florence, Laurentiana VI, 23, and eight scenes in Paris, B.N. gr. 74.[2] The Cilician painters concentrate on the discussion of the miracle rather than on the cure itself. The Armenian frieze Gospel illustrates three moments in the story: Christ's first notice of the blind man, the Pharisees' interrogation of the man, and Christ's conversation with him, but the two stages of cure are omitted.[3] Ṙoslin also shows the Pharisees investigating the case, without showing the miracle.[4]

The U.C.L.A. miniature stands apart from the Byzantine tradition in that only the first stage of the miracle is shown. In that stage, moreover, the blind man's staff, ubiquitous in Byzantine representations, is missing and the blind man kneels before Christ instead of standing. In both these respects the miniature copies the Vehap'aṙ Gospel (fig. 509a). Not satisfied with merely two figures, however, the Second Painter added three apostles, identifiable as John, Peter, and James. The same three apostles in similar static poses appear in this scene in the Syrian lectionaries of the thirteenth century, although the blind man is there represented standing with a staff and purse.[5] But the most significant detail in the U.C.L.A. miniature is the ball of clay that Christ holds in his left hand, a piece of which he is applying to the blind man's eyes. According to John, "(Christ) spat on the ground and made clay of the spittle and anointed the man's eyes with the clay" (John 9:6); yet this detail is never illustrated in Byzantine or Western art. The Vehap'aṙ Gospel shows Christ touching the blind man's eyes without showing the clay, but a manucript of Sargis Picak, of 1331, includes the detail (fig. 509b).

It is unfortunate that no published Armenian source deals directly with the exegesis of this subject, but the frequency with which Armenian exegesis returns to the story of creation as the starting point for interpreting the Gospel makes it not unlikely that this is what is intended in the detail of the ball of clay, namely, an allusion to the creation of man out of clay in Genesis 2:7. This is the line of exegesis that is taken by Chrysostom in dealing with this passage. When Christ told his disciples that the man's blindness was not the result of sin but "that the glory of God should be manifest," Chrysostom says: "He spoke of himself, not of the Father; his (the Father's) glory was already manifest. For since they had heard that God made man, taking the dust of the earth, so also Christ made clay. To have said, 'I am he who took the dust of the earth, and made man,' would have seemed a hard thing to his hearers; but this when shown by actual working, no longer stood in their way. So that he by taking earth, and mixing it with spittle, showed forth his hidden glory; for no small glory was it that he should be deemed the architect of the creation."[6] Such an interpretation would account for the focus in our miniature on this single moment of the story and the detail of the clay. Christ's own words in introducing the miracle associate it with the Creator's works: "We must work the works of him who sent me, while it is day; night comes, when no one can work. As long as I am in the world, I am the light of the world" (John 9:4–5). As the Creator made light and separated light from darkness and made man from clay, so Christ made light where there had been darkness, making clay to cure the man's blindness. The making of the new man is parallel to the creation of the old. Further, Christ made the man born blind into a symbol of all mankind awaiting redemption, saying, "For judgment I came into this world, that those who do not see may see, and that those who see may become blind" (John 9:39).

51. The Raising of Lazarus (*Page* 522)

As early as the third century the Raising of Lazarus was represented in the catacombs, and in the fourth century Christians were embroidering it onto their

[1] H. Leclercq, "Aveugles, miracles des," *DACL* 1, 3230–34; Millet, *Iconographie*, 672–73, W. Jaeger, "Blindheilung," *Lexikon der christlichen Ikonographie*, I, 304–7; Schiller, *Iconography of Christian Art*, I, 171–73.

[2] Velmans, *Le Tétraévangile*, figs. 284–85; Bibliothèque Nationale, *Évangiles avec peintures byzantines du XIe siècle* (Paris, n.d.), II, 159–61.

[3] Erevan, Mat. 7651, fols. 235–235v, unpublished.

[4] Washington, Freer 32.18, pp. 607 and 610, Der Nersessian, *Arm. Mss. Freer*, figs. 172–73; Baltimore, Walters 539, fol. 358, Der Nersessian, *Arm. Mss. Walters*, fig. 127.

[5] Leroy, *Mss. syriaques*, pl. 84, 1, 2.

[6] Chrysostom, "In Jn. Hom. 56," chap. 2, *NPNF* xiv, p. 201. Chrysostom seems to have had an alternate reading of John 9:3, for the *textus receptus* does not say "that the *glory* of God should be made manifest," but "that the *works* of God might be made manifest in him."

garments.[1] In Byzantine art the iconography of the subject holds few surprises. The principal ingredients of the subject are already established in the sixth-century Rossano Gospel, in which one reads the story in a longitudinal composition from left to right: first, Christ speaking, with Mary and Martha prostrate at his feet; then a crowd of Jews, including a pair of young men gesturing wildly; and finally a figure holding his nose and leading Lazarus from the tomb wrapped in white winding cloth.[2] Middle Byzantine art tends to tighten this composition, often compressing it into vertical format, by eliminating the excited young men and by regrouping the other figures in foreground and background planes; a servant removing the tombstone is added in the lower right corner.[3] This Middle Byzantine scheme was clearly familiar in Cilicia (figs. 522b and c).

Although the U.C.L.A. Gospel continues to follow the program of the Vehapʿaṙ Gospel in its selection of subjects in John, the Second Painter here turns to the standard iconography instead of the schematic, four-figure version of the scene in the eleventh-century model.[4] The painter has further heightened the sense of drama of the composition. He has reduced the apostles to two—Peter and one younger member, presumably John—and has omitted the figure removing the tombstone, though the stone is still present. At the same time he has reduced the landscape to a bare minimum of stage props. The top of a mountain appears above the apostles, balancing the arch of Lazarus' tomb on the right, and the ground is a horizontal band. This simplification, far from producing a more sparse composition, results in a more tense scene, for the scale of all the figures has been greatly increased relative to the frame. This change in scale brings Christ into immediate contact with the crowd of Jews, one of whom confronts him face to face and makes a gesture of speech, countering Christ's call to Lazarus. This Jew, white-haired and bearded, is shown in profile, as is another behind him with dark hair and prominent nose; they represent the Jews as Christ's adversaries and they closely resemble the group of Jews in the Entry into Jerusalem, *page 252*.

This sense of confrontation between Christ and the Jews is the most unusual iconographic feature of the miniature. It has a precedent in a Cilician manuscript of 1260–70 (fig. 522b), which also shows a white-haired Jew addressing Christ in this position, and it has a sequel in Tʿoros Taronecʿi's Gospel of 1307, in which, as shown above, Tʿoros relied heavily on several of the miniatures of the Second Painter in the U.C.L.A. Gospel.[5] But in the U.C.L.A. Gospel this conflict receives special prominence, not only in this miniature but also in the two miniatures of the Entry into Jerusalem, and in the self-curse of the Jews at the trial (*pages 126, 252, 171*). The conflict of Christ with the Jews is a very integral part of John's narrative. When Christ announced to his disciples his intention to return to the vicinity of Jerusalem, they protested to him that the Jews had recently tried to stone him. John describes the crowd of Jews who witnessed the miracle as being of two minds, some sympathetic and some antagonistic. When he wept over Lazarus, some remarked, "See how much he loved him!" but others said, "He opened the eyes of the blind man, why could he not have done something to stop this man from dying?" (John 11:36–37). The division persisted even after the miracle, which, according to John, "caused many of the Jews who had come to visit Mary, and had seen what Jesus did, to put their faith in him. Some others, however, went to the Pharisees and reported what Jesus had done" (John 11:45–46).

Beyond Christ's confrontation with the Jews there is little unusual in the iconography of the Raising of Lazarus. Some details of dress in the miniature may strike one as strange, but they turn out to be minor variations holding no special meaning. Thus Lazarus, besides his winding cloth, wears a patterned cape or cloak over his shoulders joined in front. But this cloak is fairly common in the frescoes of Cappadocia[6] and it appears earlier in an Armenian Gospel book of the eleventh century (fig. 522a). The dress of the attendant who unwraps Lazarus may also appear unusual, but it consists of a tunic tucked up for free movement, as commonly done in the ancient world, and shoe straps that have been extended illogically up the thighs.[7]

[1] On the development of the iconography of the Raising of Lazarus, see Millet, *Iconographie*, 232–54; Robert Darmstaedter, *Die Auferweckung des Lazarus in der altchristlichen und byzantinischen Kunst* (Bern, 1955); Schiller, *Iconography of Christian Art*, I, 181–86. Asterius of Amasia mentions the subject on garments: Mango, *The Art of the Byzantine Empire, 313–1453*, 51.

[2] Schiller, *Iconography of Christian Art*, I, pl. 565.

[3] For example, see Monreale; Otto Demus, *The Mosaics of Norman Sicily*, fig. 67b.

[4] Erevan, Mat. 10780, fol. 243, unpublished.

[5] Venice, 1917, fol. 263v; Der Nersessian, *Manuscrits*, fig. 107.

[6] It can be found at the churches of Elmalı, Carıklı and Karanlık. Restle, *Byzantine Wall Painting*, II, figs. 176, 205, and 232.

[7] In Byzantine art the former detail can be found in Walters, ms. 531, fol. 173 (cf. Gary Vikan, *Illuminated Greek Manuscripts from American Collections* [Princeton, 1973], 158, fig. 76), and the latter in the frescoes of Pantanassa, Mistra (cf. G. Millet, *Monuments byzantins de Mistra: Matériaux pour*

The iconography, therefore, makes no special departure from the standard, apart from the confrontation between Christ and the Jews. East Christian exegesis of the subject, however, explores another, more profound level of meaning in the Raising of Lazarus, connecting it with the dispute over the union of the natures in Christ. By reason of its abstract theological character this discussion was not destined to make an impact on the iconography itself; yet it offered Armenians a substantially different way of reading the subject from that which was current in Byzantium or in the West. The same iconography, it must be recognized, can carry different meanings, which at times may depend more on who is reading it than on modifications in the visual language itself.

In the debate that followed the Council of Chalcedon, manifestations of the bodily weakness of Christ were a special focus of theological concern. To the orthodox the fact that Christ wept upon seeing Lazarus' tomb (John 11:35) was proof that he was fully *homoousios*, "of the same nature" as us. But the Monophysites were anxious to affirm that Christ was *homoousios* not with fallen, corruptible human nature, but only with the resurrected human nature. According to this line of reasoning, "even though Christ wept over Lazarus, it was his incorruptible and divine tear that raised him (Lazarus) from the dead."[8] In other words, the fact that his human tears were having their effect in the world of the dead proved that they were not tears of weakness but tears of extraordinary divine power. The Armenian redaction of Theophilus' homily on the Raising of Lazarus takes this argument to its logical conclusion, a conclusion that is explicitly and contentiously Monophysite. The author seizes not on the tears of Christ but on the voice of Christ calling Lazarus from the tomb as the most striking proof of the unity of Christ's two natures. The command, "Lazarus, come forth!" (John 11:43) spoken by Christ the man and heard by the human bystanders penetrated to the world beyond to summon Lazarus back from death to life. "He called as man, and raised as God. One was the voice of God and man, as he who called was man and God. It is not possible to divide the voice into two, nor can the two natures united in one voice be divided into two; neither in the passion, nor in death nor in the sepulchre."[9] While one might imagine that so pointed a doctrinal use of the miracle might have faded with the passage of time, it should be noticed that all three manuscripts in which this version of the homily has been found are dated to the fourteenth century.[10] The assault of the Unitores on Armenian separatism in the fourteenth century evoked a strong reaffirmation of exactly the traditional Armenian theological position.

At the same time it should be pointed out that beyond this particular Monophysite significance, the Raising of Lazarus also had enormous cosmic symbolism in the Christian East, as elsewhere. When Christ robbed Hades of Lazarus he announced the end of death's dominion over mankind. Ephraem sees all of nature in sympathy with this great process of rebirth: "Christ's tears, then, were like rain, Lazarus was as seed and his tomb as the earth. Christ broadcast his voice as thunder and death shook at its sound; like grain Lazarus came forth and worshipped the Lord who gave him life."[11] This powerful vernal metaphor is developed as well by Mambrē, the fifth-century Armenian theologian. The tears of Christ were the rainstorm of the mercy of the God-man passing over a planted field; as the appearance of a single sprout after the rain fills us with hope that all will sprout, so the resurrection of Lazarus is a pledge of the resurrection of all mankind.[12]

52. The Washing of the Feet (*Page 532*)

Christ's extraordinary lesson in humility and fraternal love is represented in the Glajor Gospel within a rich and unusual architectural frame. Below, a great vault of stone represents the lower story to create the setting of the scene in the upper chamber, as mentioned in Mark's and Luke's accounts of the Last Supper (Mark 14:15, Luke 22:12). Above, columns rise on either side to support multiple corbels spanned by a shouldered arch. In an interesting reversal of space, the spandrels of this arch show a view of the city of Jerusalem that lay outside the upper room: in a subdued monochrome are represented various blocks of architecture covered with tile roofs, and an occasional

l'étude de l'architecture et de la peinture en Grèce aux XIVe et XVe siècles [Paris, 1910], pl. 140).

[8] This Monophysite position is quoted by Anastasius Sinaiticus, *Hodēgos*, chap. 23 (PG 89, col. 301); Jaroslav Pelikan has commented on its use in this context, *The Christian Tradition*, I, 272.

[9] Der Nersessian, "A Homily on the Raising of Lazarus and the Harrowing of Hell," *Études*, 463.

[10] Ibid., 457.

[11] Ephraem, *Commentaire*, bk. 16, chap. 9, p. 179.

[12] Mambrē Vercanoł, "Homily on the Raising of Lazarus," chap. 14, in S. Weber, *Bibliothek der Kirchenväter*, 58, *Arm. Kirchenväter* 2 (1927), 20.

window. Within, a single lamp hangs from the arch, a detail common in Islamic representations of mosque interiors.[1]

Although parallels for the two-story setting of this subject are unknown,[2] the source of this scheme is obviously the imagery of Pentecost. Since the coming of the Holy Spirit was believed to have taken place in the same room in which the Last Supper had been celebrated (according to Acts 2:13), it was perfectly natural for the artist to borrow Pentecost imagery for this feature. What is significant is the artist's interest in specifying the location of the action. The symbolic importance of the upper chamber for Yovhannēs Erznkacʿi as a type of the soul or the church was examined in connection with the Preparation for Passover, *page 271*. This seems to reflect a long-standing Armenian line of thinking. Already in the eighth century Grigor Arcruni plays with the Armenian word for the upper room (*vernatun*) and takes it to refer to the "elevated" instruction that was imparted there.[3] The Washing of the Feet is a unique encapsulation of Christ's instruction.

The scene itself in the U.C.L.A. Gospel differs in two respects from the common Byzantine formula for the subject. In the first place, instead of showing the apostles in various poses of removing their sandals, as in the famous Middle Byzantine mosaics of Greece,[4] the artist has simply grouped them one behind the other, motionless, watching the dialogue between Christ and Peter. Although the Greek version is known in Armenia (fig. 532c), the simpler grouping of figures is common (figs. 532b and 532d); it also has parallels in Byzantine art.[5] In the second place, the dialogue itself is represented by a simple speaking gesture on Peter's part, as if to portray his protest against being served by his master. The more common gesture makes Peter put his hand to his head to portray his final response in the exchange: "Lord, not my feet only but also my hands and my head!" (John 13:9). The Glajor iconography picks an earlier moment in the encounter between Peter and Christ. "Then (Jesus) poured water into a basin, and began to wash the disciples' feet, and to wipe them with the towel with which he was girded. He came to Simon Peter; and Peter said to him, 'Lord, do you wash my feet?' Jesus answered him, 'What I am doing you do not know, but afterward you will understand.' Peter said to him, 'You shall never wash my feet.' Jesus answered him, 'If I do not wash you, you have no part in me'" (John 13:5–8). The miniature shows Peter still protesting before the eventual submission.

Peter's gesture of protest has a long history in iconography, with its origins in the earliest Gospel illuminations of the event, in the Codex Rossanensis and the St. Augustine Gospel of Cambridge.[6] In the course of medieval art this gesture remains common in the West, while in Byzantine art it is almost entirely supplanted by the hand-to-head gesture. Armenian art generally follows the Byzantine lead in this detail (fig. 532b-d), and in his two later representations of this subject Tʿoros Taronecʿi also uses the hand-to-head gesture.[7] The Glajor Gospel's preference for the earlier way of representing Peter clearly depends on the Vehapʿaṙ Gospel (fig. 532a). Christ's gesture and Peter's are exactly the same, and the type of low-footed basin and the unusual high-backed chair are also the same. Indeed, the change in scale between the two main protagonists and the smaller apostles permits one to see the Glajor Gospel as filling out the nucleus copied from the Vehapʿaṙ Gospel.

The interpretation of the iconography of the Washing of the Feet has been somewhat clouded by a work of vast erudition, in which Kantorowicz proposed that the event was literally regarded both in the East and the West as the baptism of the apostles.[8] Giess has already indicated the chief source of Kantorowicz' confusion in his failure to distinguish sufficiently among the various kinds of evidence he is citing, whether liturgical texts, commentaries on the liturgy, or exegesis of the Gospels.[9] One piece of evidence, critical to his argument, comes from Aphraat and deserves to be examined for its bearing on East

[1] Buchthal, *Art of the Mediterranean World,* figs. 11, 16, 55, and 56.

[2] On the iconography of the Washing of the Feet, see Millet, *Iconographie,* 310–25; Hildegard Giess, *Die Darstellung der Fusswaschung Christi in den Kunstwerken des 4.–12. Jahrhunderts* (Rome, 1962); "Fusswaschung," *Lexikon,* II, 69–72; Schiller, *Iconography of Christian Art,* II, 41–48.

[3] *Commentaire du Lectionnaire,* chap. 34 (trans. L. M. Froidevaux), p. 131.

[4] Ernst Diez and Otto Demus, *Byzantine Mosaics in Greece* (Cambridge, Mass., 1931), pl. 12 and fig. 94.

[5] For other Armenian examples, from Vaspurakan, see Erevan, Mat. 4870 by Zakʿaria Ałtʿamarcʿi (1385) and Mat. 6324 by Tʿuma (1428) in Hakopyan, *Vaspurakani Manrankarčʿutʿyunə,* pl. VIII and fig. 61; and from the work of Tʿoros Taronecʿi see Erevan, Mat. 206, fol. 506 (1318), Avetisyan, *Haykakan Manrankarčʿutʿyan Glajori Dprocʿə,* pl. 38; Venice, San Lazzaro 1917, fol. 271v (1307), Der Nersessian, *Manuscrits,* fig. 110. For Byzantine examples see Schiller, *Iconography of Christian Art,* II, figs. 122–25.

[6] Codex Rossanensis, fol. 3, and Cambridge, Corpus Christi College, 286, fol. 125, in Schiller, *Iconography of Christian Art,* II, fig. 69 and 119.

[7] See above, note 5.

[8] E. H. Kantorowicz, "The Baptism of the Apostles," *DOP* 9–10 (1956–57), 203–51.

[9] Giess, *Die Darstellung der Fusswaschung,* 88–92.

Christian exegesis.[10] In the passage from Aphraat, which Kantorowicz cites from the Latin translation, the Syrian father speaks of the new Passover, that is the Passion of Christ, as "a baptism to be baptized with" (Luke 12:50; cf. Mark 10:38–39). The Washing of the Feet is taken as a sign of this mystery, but it is not itself said to be the apostles' baptism. By having their feet washed the apostles are united to Christ in the "baptism" of his death as Israel entered into the antetypical Passover by passing through the Red Sea. This baptismal typology reappears in the last of six hymns that comprise the canon of hymns for the Armenian celebration of the Holy Thursday,[11] but in Armenia as elsewhere in the Christian world the principal direction of exegesis lies much closer to the explicit interpretation of Christ's actions in John's Gospel (John 13:1–16).

Having finished the menial task of washing the apostles' feet, Christ explained, "If I wash your feet—I who am Teacher and Lord—then you must wash each other's feet. What I did was to give you an example: as I have done, so you must do" (John 13:13–15). Giess, in her very balanced assessment of the iconography of the Washing of the Feet, has traced the course of patristic commentary on this theme in Latin and Greek down to the twelfth century.[12] The humility of Christ, the self-abasement of the Son of God, was the antidote to Adam's destructive pride and the cause of our salvation.[13] Armenian reflection on the theme followed a similar line.

As elsewhere in the Christian world, one of the principal vehicles for conveying the lesson of the Washing of the Feet was the liturgical reenactment of the event on Holy Thursday. Attested in the Byzantine liturgy in the tenth century, the rite was adopted in Armenia by the time of Nersēs Šnorhali (1102–73), who wrote the canon of hymns for the celebration.[14] This set of six hymns Nersēs united by a single theme, which he restates in various ways in five of them. The fact that, according to John's narrative, "(Jesus) rose from supper, laid aside his garments, and girded himself with a towel" (John 13:4) in order to wash his disciples' feet is seen by Nersēs as a vivid enactment of Paul's description of the Incarnation: "(He) emptied himself taking the form of a servant, being born in the likeness of men" (Phil. 2:7). It is this self-humiliation of the Lord that is the cause of human redemption. The hymn *Tēr Erknicʿ* is typical of the whole canon:

> O God, whose essence is eternal, today you have put on the garment of a slave of this earth, thus covering the nakedness of our first parent. Blessed be him who has come for the salvation of the human race.
>
> You who are exalted by the cherubim (of the color) of fire, today you voluntarily came to the elevated chamber of the mystery; you washed the disciples as an example for us. Blessed be him who has come for the salvation of the human race.
>
> You who with the Father are seated on the throne of glory, today you deigned to sit with your disciples, sharing your body and immaculate blood. Blessed be him who has come for the salvation of the human race.[15]

The humility of Christ is vividly expressed in the Vehapʿaṙ Gospel by showing Christ on his knees before Peter (fig. 532a). The drawing of Christ in the U.C.L.A. miniature is ambiguous, and may show Christ either kneeling or standing on a level below Peter. There is also some ambiguity in the drawing of Christ's garment, due doubtless to the fact that the miniature was begun by the Second Painter and finished by Tʿoros; but the artists were clearly attempt-

[10] Kantorowicz, "The Baptism of the Apostles," 211–12. Much of Kantorowicz' argument rests on this passage, of which he cites only the first sentence. William F. Macomber of St. John's University, Collegeville, Minnesota, has graciously offered the following literal translation with two cautions: first, that the meaning of the passage turns on one's interpretation of the Syriac word *raza,* which Parisot translates "sacramentum" but which can also carry the meanings of "type," "foreshadowing," or "mystery"; secondly, the meaning is further obscured by a lacuna in the text: "For Israel was baptized in the sea in that night of the Pasch in the day of redemption; and our Lord washed the feet of his disciples in the night of the Pasch, a type/sacrament of baptism. And, moreover, so that you may know, my dear, that until that night, at that time [lacuna] . . . our Redeemer gave the true baptism. For while he was still conversing with his disciples, (he conferred) that baptism as John says, 'Repent of your sins.' And in that night he showed them the mystery/type/sacrament of the baptism of salvation of his death, as the Apostle says, 'In baptism you were not only buried with him but also raised to life with him by the power of God.'" For the Syriac text and Latin translation, cf. *Aphraatis Sapientis Persae Demonstrationes,* trans. J. Parisot, *Patrologia Syriaca* I (1894), 527–30.

[11] A. Renoux, "Le triduum pascal dans le rite arménien et les hymnes de la grande semaine," *REArm,* n. s. 7 (1970), 96.

[12] See above, note 2.

[13] Giess, *Die Darstellung der Fusswaschung,* 19, quoting Augustine, *In Joann.* 55, 7 (PL 35, col. 1787).

[14] On the Greek rite of the Washing of the Feet, see L. Petrides, "Le lavement des pieds le jeudi-saint dans l'église grec," *Echos d'Orient* 3 (1899–1900), 321–26. On the Armenian rite see the texts in Conybeare, *Rituale Armenorum,* 204–20; Mesrob Ashjian, *The Great Week in the Armenian Tradition* (New York, 1978), 38–41; Renoux, "Le triduum pascal," 55–122. See also the study by A. Jaubert, "Une lecture du lavement des pieds au mardi-mercredi saint," *Le Muséon* 79 (1966), 257–86. Bibliography on the rite in the West can be found in Giess, *Die Darstellung der Fusswaschung.*

[15] Renoux, "Le triduum pascal," 96.

ing to show that Christ had changed garments for the humble task of washing feet.

53. The Promise of the Holy Spirit (*Page 538*)

This miniature marks the beginning of the reading in John in which Christ, at the Last Supper, promises to send the Holy Spirit. "I will pray the Father, and he will give you another Counselor, to be with you for ever, even the Spirit of truth, whom the world cannot receive, because it neither sees him nor knows him; you know him, for he dwells with you, and will be in you" (John 14:15–17). In the Byzantine frieze Gospels this passage is illustrated by stock images of Christ instructing his apostles,[1] but the U.C.L.A. Gospel leaps ahead in time to show the fulfillment of Christ's promise as narrated in Acts 2:1–13. Since in the Armenian liturgy the passage John 14:15–24 is the Gospel reading for Mass on Pentecost, the imagery of Pentecost is appropriate at this point.[2] T'oros Taronec'i continues to place Pentecost at this passage in his later manuscripts,[3] and Awag does the same in his Erevan, Mat. 212.[4] This practice is traceable to Cilicia, for in his Baltimore manuscript (1262) T'oros Ṙoslin also places a full-page illumination of Pentecost at John 14 (fig. 538a). The Vehap'aṙ Gospel omits the subject.[5]

We have already seen that for his later paintings of the Descent of the Holy Spirit T'oros Taronec'i relies heavily on the iconography of the present miniature. In Venice, San Lazzaro 1917 (fig. 538b) and in Erevan, Mat. 206 (1318) T'oros uses not only the general format but a number of very specific details: the literally tongue-shaped streams of fire that descend from the throne above; the peculiar wooden paneled benches on which the apostles sit; the gestures of some of the apostles; and the three figures below (both in pose and gesture), representing the nations of the earth.[6] The formation of this iconography holds few surprises, for in its major lines it conforms to iconography in use in Byzantium at the time.[7] As early as the ninth century, in the Paris Gregory manuscript, Byzantine art was employing a three-layered composition for Pentecost, with the Throne of God (or *Hetoimasia*) and dove in the top layer, the apostles seated in a semicircular synthronon in the middle, and the nations below listening to the preaching of the apostles (Acts 2:5–13).[8] This basic format appears in Armenian art in the eleventh century, in the Mułni Gospel.[9] Within this iconographic format the peculiarities of the U.C.L.A. miniature are of secondary importance; yet they are worth noting for the nuances they add to the basic message.

According to Acts 2:3, "there appeared to (the apostles) tongues as of fire, distributed and resting on each one of them." Curiously enough, the standard iconography of the subjects shows nothing resembling tongues; in Byzantine art the Descent of the Holy Spirit is visualized as rays of light, while in the West it commonly takes the form of flames, sometimes even a sea of fire.[10] The iconography of the U.C.L.A. Gospel is unusual in showing very literally twelve long, red tongues arching down from the Throne of God. This bold tongue image appeared earlier in Ṙoslin's Baltimore manuscript (fig. 538a),[11] but its source seems to be Syrian, for it is used in several Syrian manuscripts of the thirteenth century.[12] The motif obviously refers to the eloquence of the Holy Spirit.

In representing the apostles the artist introduces two interesting variations. Contrary to the Scriptural account, the iconography of Pentecost generally introduces Paul to make up for the defection of Judas and to restore the symmetry of the number twelve. In spite of the balanced number, however, the image often gives Peter a special importance by moving him into the center; this happens commonly in Western art and occasionally in Byzantine art, as in the Paris

[1] Florence, Bibl. Laur. VI,23, fol. 200v, Velmans, *Le Tétraévangile*, fig. 294.

[2] See Table 9.

[3] Venice, San Lazzaro, 1917 (1307), fol. 274v, Der Nersessian, *Manuscrits*, fig. 116; Erevan, Mat. 206 (1318), fol. 507, Avetisyan, *Haykakan Manrankarč'ut'yan Glajori Dproc'ə*, fig. 40; Erevan, Mat. 6289 (1323), fol. 264, unpublished.

[4] Erevan, Mat. 212 (1337–40), fol. 288, unpublished.

[5] Baltimore 539 (1262), fol. 379, Der Nersessian, *Arm. Mss. Walters*, fig. 131.

[6] See above, p. 74.

[7] Grabar, *L'art de la fin de l'antiquité et du moyen âge*, I, 615–27; Schiller, *Ikonographie der christlichen Kunst*, IV, 1, 11–38; S. Seeliger, "Pfingsten," *Lexikon der christlichen Ikonographie*, III, 415–23.

[8] Schiller, *Ikonographie der christlichen Kunst*, IV, 1, fig. 204.

[9] Erevan, Mat. 7736, fol. 21, Izmailova, *Arm. miniatjura XI veka*, pl. 106.

[10] Schiller, *Ikonographie der christlichen Kunst*, IV, 1, figs. 1–75.

[11] In her discussion of this iconography Der Nersessian takes no note of the form of the tongues; *Arm. Mss. Walters*, 21.

[12] Diarbakir, Tûma Huri Bechara Collection, bifolium from an evangelary, Leroy, *Mss. syriaques*, fig. 101, 3; Midyat, Syro-orthodox Episcopacy, Evangelary, fol. 257v, ibid., fig. 104, 1; Deir es-Za'faran, Evangelary, 371, ibid., fig. 134, 2; Mardin, Syro-orthodox Episcopacy, Evangelary, fol. 4v, ibid., fig. 139, 2.

Gregory.[13] The Second Painter, however, has gone out of his way to avoid such imbalance by seating the two preeminent apostles on the same cushion of green. Peter's only precedence is his placement to the right of the Throne of God. A clear parallel for this has not been found, but another peculiarity in representing the apostles has definite Syrian sources, and that is the wood-paneled benches. These occur commonly in Syrian representations of the Descent of the Holy Spirit in the thirteenth century, as in London, B.L. add. 7170;[14] and the same style of paneling can be found in contemporary Islamic representations of the mimber.[15]

In the lowest zone of the U.C.L.A. miniature the different nationalities are represented by three variously dressed men. The man in the center wears royal garb of tunic, chlamys, and crown; those on either side wear illogical combinations of baggy trousers and coat of mail (somewhat flaked in the left figure), and gathered tunic, with cloaks. The foreignness of these figures is further emphasized by their profile views. Although there are only three such figures here, it is worth noting that the Armenian artists show a strong interest in representing a diversity of foreign types at Pentecost, often including a dog-headed man in the group, as in Ṙoslin's miniature (fig. 538a).[16]

The Descent of the Holy Spirit is the preeminent ecclesiological theme. At his Ascension, Christ promised, "You shall receive power when the Holy Spirit has come upon you; and you shall be my witnesses in Jerusalem and in all Judea and Samaria and to the ends of the earth" (Acts 1:8). The Descent of the Holy Spirit gave the apostles the power to teach, and with it the gift of eloquence in foreign languages. They immediately began preaching to the Jews of all nations, who had gathered in Jerusalem for the feast-day (Acts 2:4–13). But while they speak in many languages, the twelve all give witness to the same revelation: the twelve tongues in the Glajor Gospel all proceed from the same divine source. Moreover, the principal revelation that they carry to the nations is that of the Trinity of the Godhead, symbolized by the Throne of God, on which rest the Gospel and Cross of the Word Incarnate, and the dove of the Holy Spirit. According to the explanation of Pentecost given in the Armenian catechism, *The Teaching of Saint Gregory:* "They (the apostles) prophesied the hidden mysteries, they suddenly spoke all tongues, they enabled all races to rise together to the kingdom. They received the revelations of visions, they related to all the dispensation of the ineffable Word, they revealed the mystery of the eternal marriage of the Son of God, that is the rising to adoption, and the rejoicing with the Father through the same Son and Spirit."[17] The entire final section of *The Teaching of Saint Gregory* is concerned with the revelation given through the Holy Spirit and broadcast by the apostles throughout the world.[18]

The same theme reappears in the liturgy of Pentecost, but with a new doctrinal precision. The chief vardapet of Glajor, Esayi Nčʻecʻi, took a Western position on the *filioque* dispute; the Midday Hymn of Pentecost, however, takes the Greek position: "The Holy Spirit, who is from the inoriginate eternal Being, and is inseparably consubstantial and jointly creator with the Son, this day divided tongues with fire unto the preachers, and brought the nations of men to the Light, by dividing manifold gifts unto them. Let us bless and worship him."[19] Beyond the Holy Spirit's role in the founding of the church, the hymn defines the procession of the Holy Spirit from the Father, the "inoriginate." The issue, however, has no direct bearing on the imagery under discussion.

54. The Crucifixion (*Page 561*)

In the U.C.L.A. Gospel no image better embodies the spirit of the Armenian faith than the miniature of the Crucifixion. Moreover, located almost at the end of the manuscript, and portraying the most central act of Christ's redeeming work, it stands as a powerful climax to the entire program. It must be counted as the masterpiece of the Second Painter's work in the book.

The more important a subject is, the more standardized its imagery; but the more standardized the imagery, the more critical are the nuances of an individual example that might indicate how the subject was received in a given situation. The figures that make up the U.C.L.A. Crucifixion were used repeatedly in the long history of this image; the question is what special implications ought to be attached to the

[13] Schiller, *Ikonographie der christlichen Kunst,* IV, 1, figs. 15, 19, 23, 26, 29, 61, and, for the Paris Gregory, fig. 7.

[14] For similar renderings of wood paneling, see London, syr. add. 7170, fol. 106, Leroy, *Mss. syriaques,* fig. 85, 1; Vat. syr. 559, fols. 150v and 181v, ibid., figs. 94, 2 and 97, 2; Deir es-Zaʻfaran, Evangelary, 338, ibid., fig. 135, 1.

[15] See Paris, B.N. arabe 6094, fols. 64 and 93, Buchthal, *Art of the Mediterranean World,* figs. 11 and 27.

[16] On the cynocephalus see Der Nersessian, *Arm. Mss. Walters,* 21.

[17] *Teaching of St. Gregory,* par. 672 (ed. Thomson, p. 167).

[18] Ibid., par. 661–715, (ed. Thomson, pp. 164–82).

[19] *Divine Liturgy,* trans. Nersoyan, 106.

way they are used here. Common as the subject was in the history of art, this image is quite unusual.

While a more economic version of the iconography, reduced to three figures, was popular in the monumental arts of the Middle Byzantine period, the more complete version of the U.C.L.A. image was always common in manuscripts and the minor arts.[1] Even in monumental painting, moreover, the complete version was the preferred iconography in nearby Cappadocia, where it was sometimes expanded with the addition of the two thieves.[2] The basic composition of the U.C.L.A. Crucifixion is well documented in Armenian art from the eleventh century on (fig. 561a). What distinguishes the U.C.L.A. Crucifixion from Byzantine representations is not the number of figures but their attitudes.[3]

A large cross that stretches almost to the four borders of the image is set against a plain gold ground, with no distracting elements of scenery. On this cross there hangs, or rather stands, the figure of Christ, for he is shown virtually upright with his head almost erect and his arms extended horizontally from a powerful chest.[4] This in itself sets the image apart from the general run of Byzantine Crucifixions, in which Christ is clearly suspended, limp in death. Instead, Christ here gives an unmistakable impression of strength and self-contained power. This upright pose of Christ is fairly standard in Greater Armenia. It appears in the work of Ignatios of Ani in 1236 (fig. 561b) and again in the work of Kirakos of Tabriz (fig. 561f). As might be expected, T'oros Taronec'i copies this pose in several of his subsequent works (figs. 561c and d). Elsewhere the upright Christ is not unknown, but it is quite archaic by the year 1300; its closest parallels are in the twelfth-century painted crosses of Tuscany or in the frescoes of S. Angelo in Formis.[5] Significantly, all of these Italian Crucifixions show Christ alive, his eyes open and staring at us. Though in the U.C.L.A. miniature Christ has closed his eyes in death, and his side has been pierced to prove his death, yet the body fails to fall limp.

From Christ's pierced side two very distinct jets of water and blood flow out in gravity-defying streams. This detail, too, is worth remarking, for Byzantine art shows the two streams flowing together rather than separately.

A hierarchy of size governs all the figures in the composition; after Christ, who is shown in more than life-size, come the Virgin and John, then the women and the centurion, then Christ's executioners. The prominent placement of Mary and John on either side of the cross alludes to the narrative found only in John 19:25–27, in which Christ, seeing the two of them standing nearby, committed his mother to John's care, and it is certainly significant that in the U.C.L.A. Gospel the Crucifixion is inserted directly after that passage in the text. But the attitudes of the two figures are also quite remarkable. The Mother of God holds one hand to her breast and points with the other toward her son; while Byzantine art usually shows her downcast in sorrow, the Second Painter has shown her gazing firmly at Christ. John, too, is most commonly shown downcast in Byzantine art, holding his hand to his head in grief or wiping his tears; in other examples, where he is not sorrowing he holds a book, making a gesture of speech as the evangelist who witnessed the event; here, on the contrary, he makes the unusual classical gesture of contemplation, putting a finger to his mouth, his head held back to behold his Lord.[6]

A similar attitude of contemplation characterizes the other figures in the composition. In other Crucifixions the centurion commonly makes a waving gesture of amazement, but here he echoes John's pose in staring at the miracle of Christ's death.[7] He is clad in chlamys and tunic and holds a circular shield bearing the image of a lion in a leafy surround; the lion is another significant detail for which no parallel seems to exist.[8] Of the two women who accompany the Vir-

[1] On the iconography of the Crucifixion in general see Millet, *Iconographie*, 396–460; E. Lucchesi Palli and G. Jászai, "Kreuzigung Christi," *Lexikon der christlichen Ikonographie*, II, 606–42; Schiller, *Iconography of Christian Art*, II, 88–164; for a recent discussion see Demus, *San Marco*, I, 202–4.

[2] In Cappadocia only Göreme 33 employs the reduced Middle Byzantine iconography. Restle, *Byzantine Wall Painting*, II, pl. 285. The full composition is augmented with the two thieves at Kokar Kilise and Pürenli Seki Kilise in Irhala, and at Bahatın Samanlığı Kilise in Belisırama. Ibid., III, pls. 476, 485, and 517.

[3] One might take the mosaic of San Marco in Venice as a fair representative of the Byzantine approach to the subject. Demus, *San Marco*, I, pl. 332.

[4] Illogically the artist has shown the suppedaneum on the back of the upright of the cross.

[5] I am indebted to Hugo Buchthal for suggesting this connection. For examples of the painted crosses see Schiller, *Iconography of Christian Art*, II, figs. 495–99; for S. Angelo in Formis see ibid., II, fig. 348.

[6] No exact parallel for this appears; very occasionally John holds his hand to his mouth as in the Pantokrator Psalter (Millet, *Iconographie*, fig. 462) or in the Tongeren ivory (Schiller, *Iconography of Christian Art*, II, fig. 377). On John's pose in the Crucifixion see Millet, *Iconographie*, 400–404.

[7] Millet noted that Crucifixion iconography generally represents a harmonizing of the accounts in Byzantine iconography. Millet, *Iconographie*, 423–34. Thus while the story of the piercing of Christ's side occurs only in John 19:34–37, the synoptics, but not John, mention the centurion who confessed his faith in Christ. Matt. 27:54; Mark 15:39; Luke 23:47.

[8] A lion was used as a royal emblem on the coinage of the Armenian kingdom of Cilicia in the thirteenth and four-

gin, one makes a hand-to-mouth gesture to convey surprise and the other, by exception, turns her head away from the scene.

More striking still, even Christ's executioners have paused in their grisly employment. In Byzantine art the lance bearer is generally shown in the act of piercing Christ's side and his companion raises the sponge toward his lips. In this miniature, on the other hand, they stand more like soldiers at attention, gazing at the victim between them. The lance bearer somewhat incongruously holds a sword, point down, in his left hand. Both have fallen victim to the revenge of some pious user of the book, who scratched out their faces.

This pervasive attitude of attention includes heaven as well, where the angels are riveted by the cosmic event taking place; rather than weeping or making eye contact with the spectator, as they frequently do, they extend their hands in a gesture of adoration and look at Christ.

Above the angels the sun and the moon turn toward the cross and seem to look at one another. The detail that the sun was darkened is mentioned in the synoptics, but pairing it with the red moon on the left was suggested not by the Gospels but by Peter's words in Acts 2:20 (quoting Joel 2:31): "The sun shall be turned into darkness and the moon into blood." In the U.C.L.A. Crucifixion the color of the moon matches the blood flowing from Christ's side. Curiously enough, the positions of the sun and the moon are reversed from their usual positions in Byzantine art. These heavenly bodies are common in Crucifixion iconography but in Armenian art they are almost invariable. For example, while the Byzantine frieze Gospel omits them, the Armenian copy, Mat. 7651, takes care to put them in (fig. 561e).[9]

The inscription fastened above Christ's head is also common, for all four evangelists mention the charge that was posted on the cross. But the wording of the charge differs slightly in each evangelist, and the U.C.L.A. miniature uses the text of Luke 23:38: "This is the king of the Jews."

All four evangelists identify the location of Christ's death as Golgotha, "the place of the skull" (Matt. 27:33; Mark 15:22; Luke 23:33; John 19:17); accordingly a skull is often shown beneath the cross of Christ. But while this motif is evidently optional in other traditions, in Armenian art it is almost universal. In the U.C.L.A. Gospel its size and prominence are unusual, but a comparable instance can be found in the frescoes of Ałtʿamar.[10]

The U.C.L.A. Crucifixion, therefore, seems to stand apart from the more usual Byzantine renditions of this subject in the powerful pose of Christ's body, which is the focus of everyone's attention, and in the treatment of certain details, such as the lion shield, the separate streams of blood and water, and the prominent skull of Adam. All of these differences carry important nuances that must be understood. First of all one must examine the representation of Christ and ask how the Armenians understood Christ's death.

The iconography of the Crucifixion has undergone a long and complex development, and the image, far from being mere narrative, has always been heavily freighted with theological content. This was clearly unavoidable, since the event stands at the very center of the mystery of salvation and the death of Christ obviously posed enormous theological problems to churchmen concerned with explaining how the God-Man could suffer and die. Only in recent years has scholarship begun to sort out the relationship of Crucifixion imagery to the evolution of Christian belief. Although Christ's death was sometimes described in the early Fathers as the withdrawal of the Word from the flesh, this formula was soon rejected as inadequate, since it implied that the Incarnation had been undone.[11] The protracted debate on the hypostatic union, starting with Arianism, forced theologians to be more precise. Two extremes had to be avoided in the discussion of Christ's death: one could not suppose that in Christ's passion God had actually suffered (the heresy of Theopaschism), but neither could one maintain that Christ had only appeared to suffer, as if his body were a phantasm (the position of Docetists or Aphthartodocetists). If Christ were to save humanity he had to have shared completely in human nature; according to orthodox theology, Christ's death, like any man's, consisted in the separation of his soul from his body; the Word, however was separated from neither. Even in Christ's death the body was united to the Divine Nature, which preserved it from corruption.

The first images to deal with this mystery, as in the Rabbula Gospel, show the crucified dressed in a long tunic with his side already pierced in death, but with

teenth centuries, though it generally carries a cross on its back. Paul Z. Bedoukian, *Coinage of Cilician Armenia;* idem, "Medieval Armenian Coins," *REArm,* n. s. 8 (1971), 365–431; idem, "The Single Lion Coronation Coins of Levon I," *JSAS* 2 (1985–86), 97–105.

[9] This image is a copy of Florence VI,23, fol. 208; cf. Velmans, *Le Tétraévangile,* fig. 297.

[10] Der Nersessian, *Aghtʿamar,* pl. 69.

[11] Athanasius uses this expression; see discussion by L. H. Grondijs, *Iconographie byzantine du Crucifié mort sur la croix,* Bibliotheca Byzantina Bruxellensis, I, 2nd ed. (Brussels, 1947), 7–14. This study must be used with caution; much of it is refuted by Grillmeier (see next note).

his eyes still wide open. Grillmeier has brilliantly demonstrated that this is really a metaphorical way of referring to the continued presence of the Divinity that "sleeps not" (Ps. 121:4) even in Christ's death.[12] Grillmeier cites in this connection the lion imagery of the *Physiologus*, according to which that noblest of beasts sleeps with his eyes open as a type of Christ, whose body slept in death while his divinity, at the right hand of the Father, remained ever watchful.

The earliest discussion of an actual image showing Christ dead on the cross has been found by Kartsonis in Anastasius Sinaites in the seventh century, in a context where the author is using the image didactically to refute the error of Theopaschism. Anastasius contended that only the body of Christ, and not his soul or his divinity, suffers and dies, and to prove this he appealed to an image of Christ's body dead on the cross.[13] When the first surviving examples of this new iconography appear after Iconoclasm, as in the Khludov Psalter, they have further anti-heretical uses. Martin has found an anti-Iconoclast argument in the imagery, in that a body that can be crucified is most clearly circumscribable, and Corrigan has found anti-Muslim and anti-Paulician arguments, since both of these groups had denied the reality of Christ's death.[14]

One might expect that being "Monophysite", the Armenian church would have a different use for representations of the Crucifixion. The difference is inherent in the special nature of the Armenian Monophysite position, which was arrived at, according to Sarkissian, as a consequence of their rejection of Nestorianism; the Orthodox position of the Council of Chalcedon seemed to them to have divided Christ into two separable natures, which in turn seemed like two persons.[15] On the subject of Christ's death, then, Armenian commentators are more concerned with affirming the unity of the divine and human natures than with the refutation of the above heresies. In fact, Armenian readiness to affirm the involvement of the Divinity in Christ's death has led to accusations of Theopaschitism.

The critical text in this regard is the Armenian version of the Trisagion hymn, sung three times over in solemn cadence during the First Entrance of the divine liturgy. Esayi Nčʿecʿi defended the text vigorously:

Holy (is) God,
holy and mighty,
holy and immortal,
who was crucified for us.
Have mercy on us![16]

Because of its everyday familiarity, and because controversy over the added fourth line made it a rallying cry for the cause of Armenian separatism, this hymn is certainly the most important text for interpreting the Armenian imagery of the Crucifixion. While Byzantine commentators took the three invocations of the hymn to be addressed to the three persons of the Trinity, the Armenians addressed the entire hymn to Christ alone. He who was crucified was the "holy God, holy and mighty, holy and immortal." *The Teaching of Saint Gregory* makes the statement even more openly Theopaschite; in a passage that makes the Tower of Babel an antetype of the cross, he says, "The tower is the cross on which hung the Son of God. The cross is on the earth and the body on it. But the Godhead who reaches above the heavens, beyond the infinite, limitless nature of the material creatures, *was contained and nailed to the wood of the cross,* filling and extended in both the material and immaterial spheres."[17]

An Armenian sermon published by Der Nersessian, however, spells out the Monophysite position, affirming that God could be crucified without actually suffering. "At the time of his passion the temple was destroyed, as he himself said, but one was the essence of the Godhead and the manhood; one son, perfect God and perfect man. The Godhead was not separated from the manhood, neither during the passion, nor in death, for it did not suffer, nor did it die. And that which was indivisible in the body on the cross, was also inseparable from the Father in heaven, and there neither suffering reached nor death. And I confess God who suffered and boldly say: God was crucified in his body and he was on the cherubic throne; God died in his body and was glorified with the Father; God was in the sepulchre and he was inseparable from the Father's bosom."[18] This is the spirit that animates both Armenian exegesis of the

[12] Alois Grillmeier, *Der Logos am Kreuz: Zur christologischen Symbolik der älteren Kreuzigungsdarstellung* (Munich, 1956), 81–96.

[13] Kartsonis, *The Anastasis,* 49–53.

[14] John R. Martin, "The Dead Christ on the Cross in Byzantine Art," *Late Classical and Medieval Studies in Honor of Albert Mathias Friend, Jr.,* ed. Kurt Weitzmann (Princeton, 1955), 189–96; Kathleen Corrigan, *The Ninth Century Byzantine Marginal Psalters,* diss., University of California, Los Angeles, 1984, 168–74.

[15] Sarkissian, *The Council of Chalcedon and the Armenian Church.*

[16] On the text of this hymn and its original meaning, see Juan Mateos, *La célébration de la parole dans la liturgie byzantine* (Rome, 1971), 98–106.

[17] *Teaching of St. Gregory,* chap. 629 (ed. Thomson, p. 155); emphasis added.

[18] Sirarpie Der Nersessian, "Homily on the Raising of Lazarus," *Études,* 463.

death of Christ and the U.C.L.A. representation of the Crucifixion. The exegetes talk of the death of Christ as a demonstration of the power of God rather than a proof of the full human weakness of Christ.

Starting with Chrysostom and Ephraem, those sourcebooks for Armenian exegesis, the Armenian tradition emphasizes three important signs of the power of God in Christ's death: the power of Christ's final shout from the cross, the miraculous response of nature in the earthquake and eclipse, and the miracle of the blood and water from his side. It is through this display of divine power that Christ triumphs over death.

The voice of Christ in the Raising of Lazarus became for Armenian exegetes an important sign of the inseparability of the natures of Christ; the words spoken with human tongue in this world carried with divine power into the world beyond the grave, awakening the dead. So too in his last moment on the cross, Chrysostom remarks, Christ died with a loud shout "that it might be shown that the act is done by power. . . . This cry rent the veil, and opened the tombs, and made the house desolate."[19] It was this loud manifestation of power, he says, that converted the centurion and many bystanders. But Ephraem, ever fascinated by the paradoxes of salvation, notes that while the dead heard Christ's voice and obeyed, the living (i.e., the Jews) refused to listen.[20] The fifth-century *Teaching of Saint Gregory* picks up this theme. "He came willingly to death, and as All-powerful, was forced by no one. Therefore He cried with a loud voice to fulfill the saying of the prophet: . . . 'The Lord will cry from Sion and raise his voice from Jerusalem' [Amos 1.2; Joel 3.16]. What man, when troubled in mind and near death, would raise a cry or shout? He would rather keep his mouth closed and remain speechless before dying. But the Creator of souls, Christ, willingly in his love coming to death, announced with a loud voice with awesome signs that even in death He was one in will and deed with the Father."[21]

This theme of Christ's last shout appealed strongly to the Armenian imagination and entered into the liturgy. The commemoration of the Resurrection in the weekly Sunday liturgy invokes the powerful image of Christ as lion on the cross:

I praise the voice of the lion
Who roared on the four-winged cross,
On the four-winged cross he roared,
His voice resounding in the Hades.[22]

In the U.C.L.A. image, the unusual device of the lion on the centurion's shield must be read in this context. The lion is symbolic of the divine power still present in the dead Christ. This imagery had its origin in the *Physiologus,* a work that enjoyed wide circulation in Armenia in translation.[23] The liturgy also likens the shout of Christ on the cross to Gabriel's trumpet, and this tradition was familiar to the Glajor exegete, Yovhannēs Erznkacʿi, who echoes Ephraem's paradox: the dead heard his shout, but the stupidity of the bystanders made them deaf.[24]

The miracles of nature that accompanied Christ's death further demonstrated his divine power. At Christ's suffering, according to Ephraem, all of nature suffered; the sun refused to give its light lest it look upon Christ while he remained on the cross.[25] The darkening of the sun, says Chrysostom, was even a greater miracle than if he should have descended from the cross as his scoffers required, for remaining on the cross he still had power over the sun; the three hours' darkness proved that this was no natural eclipse.[26] *The Teaching of Saint Gregory* expands on the theme. "The sun and moon became heralds at that time. For the sun protested by darkening its light, by revealing to all the Lord on the cross; and being unable to bear that vision, it became dark for it could not endure to see the indignities of the Lord. The moon also showed marvels, for in a likeness, as in a mirror, it showed to all creatures the blood in itself, above in the heights—the salvation of all lands which will receive with their minds this blood as their kingdom."[27] It is because they cannot endure to see the sufferings of Christ that the Second Painter has shown the sun and moon looking rather at one another than at Christ. Nersēs Šnorhali repeats this line of thought in his meditative hymn on the life of Christ.[28] Erznkacʿi approaches the subject with a

[19] Chrysostom, "In Matt. Hom. 88," 27:45 ff., *NPNF* x, p. 521.

[20] Ephraem, *Commentaire,* bk. 21, chap. 30, pp. 216–17.

[21] *Teaching of St. Gregory,* chaps. 477–78 (ed. Thomson, p. 109).

[22] *Divine Liturgy of the Armenian Apostolic Orthodox Church,* trans. Nersoyan, 86.

[23] Franciscus Sbordone is responsible for sorting out the various redactions of the text, *Physiologi graeci singulis variarum aetatum recensione codicibus fere omnibus tunc primum excussis collatisque* (Milan, 1936); Nikolai Marr has studied the Armenian tradition, *Fisiolog, Armianogrusinskij isvod* (St. Petersburg, 1904).

[24] *Divine Liturgy,* trans. Nersoyan, 112; Yovhannēs Erznkacʿi, *Meknutʿiwn* on Matt. 27:46, p. 599.

[25] Ephraem, *Commentaire,* bk. 21, chap. 5, p. 225.

[26] Chrysostom, "In Matt. Hom. 88," 27: 45 ff., *NPNF* x, p. 520.

[27] *Teaching of St. Gregory,* chap. 677 (ed. Thomson, p. 169); see also chaps. 473–77, (pp. 108–9).

[28] Nersēs Šnorhali, *Yisous Ordi,* chaps. 741–42 (trans. Kéchichian, 183–84).

more scientific mind, pointing out that the Passover moon cannot eclipse the sun, since a full moon is necessarily in the opposite sky; therefore, the celestial miracle consisted in the moon's unnatural hastening in its course and later returning to its place.[29]

The piercing of Christ's side presented a more difficult mystery for the commentators, and the interpretations of the Armenians and the Greeks become sharply divided on this point. The disagreement revolves around the ritual use of water in the eucharistic wine in the Byzantine rite and the use of pure wine in the Armenian. In preparing the elements in the Byzantine prothesis rite, the priest cuts the bread with a lance, reciting the words of John 19:34–35 on the piercing of Christ's side; he then pours water and wine into the chalice in a symbolic reenactment of the event.[30] A second admixture of water, now warm water, occurs just before Communion, and this is called the *zeon;* this is intended to symbolize the descent of the Holy Spirit.[31] Whatever their origins, these rites had become, by the sixth century, a source of acrimony between the Greek and Armenian churches. The Armenian patriarch Moses II Ełivardec'i (574–608) denounced the Greek practice, and the Greeks, at the Council in Trullo (692), condemned the Armenian practice.[32] The polemic on this subject is fairly regular; along with the disagreement over the celebration of Christmas, it was one of the principal obstacles to the union of the Armenian with the Greek church, and, in the fourteenth century, with the Latin.[33] The firm stance that Esayi Nč'ec'i took on this issue was mentioned earlier.

In the U.C.L.A. Crucifixion the painter's conscious effort to keep the streams of blood and water separate represents a deliberate rejection of this Byzantine interpretation. While the Byzantine church interpreted the blood and water flowing from Christ's side as typical of the eucharistic mixing of wine with water, Armenians saw in the blood and water the mystery of the birth of the church, the separate streams signifying the sacraments of baptism and the Eucharist. This seems in fact to be the older exegetical tradition. Chrysostom, otherwise so literal in his method, takes the water as the regeneration of baptism and the blood as the Eucharist.[34] The piercing of Christ's side reminded Ephraem of the removal of a rib from Adam's side; but while much trouble came out of Adam's side, from Christ's side came water to quench the fire of Adam's sin, and blood, which is the church.[35] Nersēs Šnorhali incorporates Chrysostom's interpretation in his poem *Yisous Ordi,*[36] and Yovhannēs Erznkac'i echoes Ephraem's exegesis of the event, adding his own poetic turn: "As woman was built of body and soul from the side of Adam, so from the side of the second Adam was built the church, which is cleansed by water and nourished by blood. . . . By the tearing of his side was breached the enclosure of the Garden that Seraphim closed, and through the blood of the savior we receive the kingdom of heaven which we irrigate with the water of the spirit that we had lost."[37]

The prominent skull in the U.C.L.A. image also refers to Adam. Chrysostom remarks, "Some say that Adam died there and lies there; and that in this place where death had reigned Jesus also set up the trophy."[38] The most fundamental statement of this mystery is Paul's formula: "As in Adam all die, so also in Christ shall all be made alive" (1 Cor. 15:22). As we have seen frequently in Armenian iconography and exegesis, the events of Christ's life must always be seen within the largest dimensions of the story of man's salvation.

55. Christ's Apparition at the Sea of Galilee (*Page 570*)

According to John, Christ's last apparition took place at the Sea of Galilee (or Tiberias) where Peter

[29] Yovhannēs Erznkac'i, *Meknut'iwn* on Matt. 27:45, p. 598. The medieval commentator could not have known that, according to modern astronomical computations, there was actually an eclipse of the moon on the 14th of Nisan (that is, 3 April) in the year 33. Dietrick E. Thomsen, "The Passover Computation," *Science News* 125 (21 Jan. 1984), 40.

[30] Casimir Kucharek, *The Byzantine-Slav Liturgy of St. John Chrysostom, Its Origin and Evolution* (Combermere, Ont., 1971), 260–78.

[31] Ibid., 682–88.

[32] See Grondijs, *L'iconographie byzantine du Crucifié mort sur la croix,* 67–70, 82–94. For Trullo, see Concilium Quinisextum, canon 32, Mansi, XI, 950.

[33] F. Conybeare published a tenth-century Armenian polemic on the date of Christmas which deals also with the eucharistic wine: "Dialogus de Christi die natali," *Zeitschrift für die neutestamentliche Wissenschaft* 5 (1904), 332. The Armenian liturgy departs from the Byzantine in its use of the imagery of Christ's piercing. In the prothesis ceremony, pouring wine alone into the chalice, the priest says, "In remembrance of the redeeming economy of our Lord God and Savior Jesus Christ; through the fountain of whose blood flowing from his side all creatures have been renewed and made immortal" (*Divine Liturgy,* trans. Nersoyan, 17).

[34] Chrysostom, "In Jn. Hom. 85," 19:16 ff, *NPNF* xiv, p. 319.

[35] Ephraem, *Commentaire,* bk. 21, chaps. 10–11, p. 227.

[36] Nersēs Šnorhali, *Yisous Ordi,* 749–50 (ed. Kéchichian, 185).

[37] Yovhannēs Erznkac'i, *Meknut'iwn* on Matt. 27:50, p. 601.

[38] Chrysostom, "In Jn. Hom. 85," 19:16 ff., *NPNF* xiv, p. 318.

had gone fishing along with six other disciples (John 21:1–19). After they had labored in vain the whole night, Jesus, unrecognized, appeared on the shore and instructed them to cast the net on the right side. The miraculous abundance of fish that then filled their net revealed the identity of the Lord. "When Simon Peter heard that it was the Lord, he put on his clothes, for he was stripped for work, and sprang into the sea. But the other disciples came in the boat, dragging the net full of fish. . . . When they got on land, they saw a charcoal fire there, with fish lying on it, and bread" (John 21:7–9). After the meal Christ three times questioned the apostle whom he had made his key-keeper, "Simon, son of John, do you love me?" (John 21:15–17). Each time, Peter's ardent profession of love is followed by the command from Christ, "Feed my sheep."

The concluding miniature in the U.C.L.A. Gospel recalls themes illustrated elsewhere in the manuscript. The representation of the disciples fishing recalls that the disciples were shown fishing when Christ first invited them to follow him (*pages 193 and 194*); Peter's triple profession of love recalls his triple denial, which was illustrated in both Matthew and Luke (*pages 166 and 438*); the miraculous meal recalls the miraculous meals of Cana and the Last Supper (*pages 156 and 469*); finally, and most unexpectedly, Peter's walking on the water recalls the miracle of Christ walking on the water in the Second Storm at Sea (*page 227*). The last miniature, therefore, presents us with a kind of reprise of themes encountered in some of the earlier miniatures. As frequently in the U.C.L.A. Gospel, however, the iconography of the miniature both expands and interprets the simple Gospel narrative.

Apart from some doubtful representations on sarcophagi,[1] Christ's apparition at the Sea of Galilee is unknown in Early Christian art. When it appears in the Middle Ages there are three very different ways of representing Peter.[2] In Byzantine art, Peter is always shown swimming to shore, which indeed is what the text implies, since it says literally, both in Greek and Armenian, that Peter "threw himself into the sea."[3] The Gospel text notwithstanding, Western art sometimes represents Peter not swimming but walking boldly across the surface of the water, as he is shown in this miniature. Schiller overstates her case when she asserts that this is the usual Western way of representing Peter, for in fact the more common Western iconography employs a third manner, showing Peter emerging halfway from the water, as if just finishing his swim; of her instances only the Egbert Evangelary (ca. 980) and the Bury St. Edmunds Evangelary (1020–40) show the unexplained iconography of Peter walking on the water.[4] In both of these examples Christ stands to one side on the shore and Peter stands before him on the water, as in the Glajor Gospel; yet other details differ in the two Western examples, for in the Egbert Evangelary Peter is shown dragging the net, and in the Bury St. Edmunds manuscript the net is omitted entirely. In the U.C.L.A. miniature the six disciples in the boat drag the net full of fish of different colors. T'oros' successor, Awag, repeats virtually the same composition in more compact form in Erevan 212 (fig. 570a). Other Armenian examples of this iconography are lacking.[5] The representation of Peter walking on the water as opposed to swimming has the effect of placing Peter and Christ in conversation with one another, alluding to the triple exchange between them.

Equally important in the iconography is the manner of representing the meal. While Western examples sometimes show the fish on a grill and sometimes even show the meal taking place at the table, the Armenian examples make a more abstract or symbolic statement. Awag places a fish and two loaves above Peter's head, against the gold background, while T'oros places the bread in a chalice beside the fish, against his abstract paneled background of magenta.

These adjustments in iconography take the reader beyond the text of the Gospel by interpreting its meaning. The fact that Peter now walks confidently on the water, whereas formerly he sank through lack of faith (Matt. 14:28–31) is the clearest way of indicating the change that has come over the apostle. Ephraem Syrus thus explains God's purpose in permitting the earlier weakness of Peter. "The first of the disciples was troubled and tried that he might become a doctor to those who were wounded. If trans-

[1] H. Leclerq discusses two such sarcophagi, "Pêche miraculeuse," *DACL* 13, 2875–77, fig. 10018; the second sarcophagus is illustrated in *DACL* 14, 969, fig. 10244.

[2] Schiller makes this distinction in *Ikonographie der christlichen Kunst,* III, 114–17. The Byzantine iconography is discussed briefly by Millet, who was working under the erroneous belief that the mosaics of the Holy Apostles in Constantinople described by Nicholas Mesarites belonged to the sixth century: *Iconographie,* 571–76. See also W. Medding, "Erscheinung des Auferstandenen am See Genesareth," *Lexikon der christliche Ikonographie,* I, 672–73.

[3] John 21:7: "ənkecʿ zinkʿn i covn."

[4] Schiller, *Ikonographie der christlichen Kunst,* III, figs. 371 and 332.

[5] The Cilician narrative Gospels omit this subject, with the exception of Erevan, Mat. 7651 (fols. 266 and 266v), which illustrates two unusual moments in the story: first, the disciples fishing and catching nothing (John 21:3); second, Christ's instructions after they have reached shore, when he said, "Bring some of the fish that you have caught" (John 21:10).

gressors should be ashamed to do penance, (the Lord) encourages them through Simon the transgressor to come to him who is above all transgressions. By night Simon denied (the Lord), but by day he confessed him. He denied him over the coals; he confessed him over the coals. When he denied him the earth was witness, and when he confessed him sea and dry land, each according to its nature, gave witness."[6] In the miniature the sea gives witness to Peter's confession both by yielding the miraculous catch of fish and by miraculously supporting the weight of Peter's body. It is a new Peter, to whom Christ can now entrust his church. According to Chrysostom, "He was the chosen one of the apostles, the mouth of the disciples, the leader of the band. . . . Jesus puts into his hands the chief authority among the brethren; and he brings not forward the denial, nor reproaches him with what had taken place, but says, 'If you love me, preside over thy brethren.'"[7] The importance of this ecclesiological theme was especially appreciated in Armenia, for in Armenian liturgy the passage John 21:15–19 was read as a "last Gospel" at the end of Mass from Easter to Pentecost, as if to reinforce the authority of the legitimate hierarchy.[8]

The meal that Christ prepared for the disciples also has special significance. Chrysostom says that whereas before his resurrection Christ had miraculously provided food by starting with loaves and fish that already existed, now he created the loaves and fish anew.[9] The iconography takes the miracle a step further, for the bread of the meal has been made the bread of the Eucharist. In contrast to the Latin rite, in which bread and wine are received separately in Communion, the Armenian rite prescribes Communion by commixture, that is, the bread is broken and dropped into the chalice.[10] This is pointedly illustrated by showing the broken fragments of bread immersed in the chalice of wine. The iconography, therefore, is not only identifying the meal on the shore of the Sea of Galilee as the Eucharist, but is asserting the apostolic origins of the Armenian way of administering the sacrament. This polemical interest in defending the Armenian rite is evidently directed against potential Latinizers, a preoccupation that has appeared elsewhere in the U.C.L.A. Gospel—in the Last Supper (*page 156*) and the Crucifixion (*page 561*).

The miniatures of the U.C.L.A. Gospel, therefore, end on a polemical or defensive note, perfectly understandable in the embattled climate of Glajor in the early years of the fourteenth century. T'oros Taronec'i evidently interpreted Christ's Apparition at the Sea of Galilee as a reaffirmation of the hierarchy and sacraments of the Armenian church. The repentant Peter, and by implication the authentic clergy who continue his work, is commissioned to "preside" over the flock and is allowed to share in the miraculous powers of Christ; and the meal by which Christ refreshes his disciples is the sacrament of his Body and Blood in the form in which this is administered in the Armenian church.

[6] Ephraem Syrus, *Commentaire*, bk. 20, chap. 14, p. 207.
[7] Chrysostom, "In Jn. Hom. 88," 1, *NPNF* xiv, p. 331.
[8] F. E. Brightman, *Liturgies Eastern and Western* (Oxford, 1896), 456.
[9] Chrysostom, "In Jn. Hom. 87," 2, *NPNF* xiv, p. 329.
[10] Brightman, *Liturgies Eastern and Western*, 449; *Divine Liturgy*, trans. Nersoyan, 48–49.

CHAPTER SEVEN

The Iconography of the Canon Tables

1. The U.C.L.A. Canon Tables and Their Place in the Tradition of Canon Table Decoration

The index system for the Gospels, invented by Eusebius of Caesarea in Palestine in the fourth century, quickly became an integral part of the standard edition of the four Gospels, in Greek and in all the languages into which they were translated. This index, arranged into the so-called canon tables, provided the serious reader with a key by which he could find his way through the overlapping material of the four different versions of the life of Christ. Whereas Tatian's attempt to harmonize the four Gospels in his *Diatessaron* mutilated the texts in order to make them fit together in a single continuous version, Eusebius' solution respected the integrity of each of the Gospels. He divided each of the Gospels into numbered sections, and then he sorted out the sections according to whether they occurred in all four Gospels, in only three or two, or were unique. It was then possible for him to arrange these numbers into a series of tables. The reader, starting with a given section in one of the evangelists, had only to consult the number of that section in Eusebius' index to find the parallel passages in the other Gospels.

According to Nordenfalk's fundamental study of the subject, the rectangular grids of numbers of the Eusebian canon tables were from the outset arranged on pages, within architectural frames consisting of columns supporting arches.[1] From the outset, too, beyond their practical use to the reader, the canon tables had some symbolic import. Nordenfalk observed that the number ten of Eusebius' tables does not mathematically exhaust all the possible comparisons among the four evangelists (the full number would be twelve), but the tables for the two shortest sets of comparisons were omitted, probably because of the symbolic importance of ten.[2] Eusebius pointed out that ten has a special relationship to four, the number of the Gospels, in that it is the total of the series one to four; furthermore he reflected that "the number ten, which contains the end of all numbers, and terminates them in itself, may truly be called a full and perfect number as comprehending every species and every measure of numbers, proportions, concords and harmonies."[3] Because of their importance, both practical and symbolic, canon tables became a subject for artistic embellishment throughout the Middle Ages. A wide repertoire of motifs was employed, whether drawn from the world of nature or invented by fancy. The interpretation of this imagery poses special problems.

Within the medieval development of canon table decoration the Armenian material occupies a special place. In the first place, as Nordenfalk has argued, the Armenian tradition presents us with examples of canon tables that stand closer to the fourth-century archetype than do other surviving manuscripts. In the second place, the Armenian tradition, especially during the Cilician period, developed the decoration of the tables with an unparalleled richness of symbolic motifs.[4] Finally, as we shall see, it is only within the Armenian tradition that a genre of literature developed that was concerned with the interpretation of the symbolic content of the tables. This literature provides a unique key to understanding the iconography of the canon tables.

The fourth-century Greek archetype from which Armenian canon tables derive has been reconstructed by Nordenfalk from surviving manuscripts of the sixth to the eleventh centuries. In the archetype, as in its closest copy in the Ējmiacin Gospel (Erevan, Mat. 2374), the recto and verso of the first folio contained the prologue, in which Eusebius explained the use of the tables. The ten tables themselves were

[1] Carl Nordenfalk, *Die spätantiken Kanontafeln*.

[2] Ibid., 47–48.

[3] Eusebius, *Laus Constantini*, chap. 6 (trans. A. C. McGiffert, *NPNF*, ser. 2, vol. I, pp. 587 and 589); Carl Nordenfalk, "The Beginning of Book Decoration," *Essays in Honor of Georg Swarzenski* (Chicago, 1951), 16.

[4] Hugo Buchthal has discussed the precedence of Armenian manuscripts over Byzantine in the development of canon table decoration in "Studies in Byzantine Illumination of the Thirteenth Century," *Jahrbuch der Berliner Museen* 25 (1983), 27–102.

then distributed over the next seven pages (fols. 2–5) and the entire set concluded with a *tempietto* (fol. 5v), which carried no textual material but seems to have had some symbolic meaning. Thus the original set occupied ten pages, though the ten index tables themselves were compressed onto seven of these pages. While this ten-page format was followed with minor adjustments by the earliest Greek manuscripts, another, longer format appeared in the tenth century, which virtually displaced the original model in Greek manuscript production. The longer format spread the index tables over ten full pages, which the two pages of the prologue brought to a total of twelve.[5] Meanwhile Latin and Syrian scriptoria developed even longer formats for their editions of the Gospels. Only in Armenia did the original ten-page total remain sacrosanct, despite internal changes within the set.

The canon table format that was established in the scriptoria of Cilicia and became normative for subsequent Armenian editions of the Gospels differed from the archetype in several significant respects. First, the set begins not on a recto but on a verso, so that the two pages of the Eusebian prologue face one another.[6] Second, because of the artists' preference for painting on the hair side of the parchment, two blank pages intervene between every pair of table pages—an expensive procedure unknown in Byzantium that doubled the amount of parchment needed to complete the set. Furthermore, the tables themselves were arranged in four pairs on eight pages, and the concluding *tempietto* was dropped.[7] It is this format that is followed in the U.C.L.A. Gospel, the iconography of which must now be investigated.

In general the decoration of the U.C.L.A. canon tables fits comfortably within the painting tradition developed in Cilicia in the twelfth and thirteenth centuries. Executed on a more expensive vellum than the rest of the codex—it is smoother, whiter, and more supple—the ten pages are arranged in pairs, with pairs of blank pages intervening. In overall layout the facing pages mirror one another, but in particulars they are constantly changing in subtle ways. If the columns are repeated, the capitals and bases change (*pages 16–17*); where the design of the headpiece is repeated, the decorative field within the headpiece changes pattern (*pages 8–9 or 20–21*); and when the patterns themselves remain constant, new color combinations are introduced (*pages 8–9 or 12–13*). The result is a diversity that invites endless exploration.

Byzantine and Armenian manuscripts of about the year 1000 seem to have introduced simultaneously the rectangular headpiece, where earlier manuscripts had used a free-standing arch. At the same time the tables of numbers were redisposed in two panels per page, framed by three columns. Both of these changes had the effect of strengthening the unity of the set, and it is this more homogeneous set that the Cilician artists worked with. Three areas of decoration must be considered in tracing the origins of the U.C.L.A. canon tables: the headpiece and its supporting columns; the flora or trees in the margins flanking the tables; and the fauna and cultic furnishing (chalices, vases, fountains, crosses, and candles), whether in the margins or on top of the architecture.

The five pairs of headpieces of the U.C.L.A. canon tables exhibit five different designs, which may be described by their most prominent features as follows: (1) a horseshoe arch containing a half-length figure (*pages 4–5*); (2) a triangular pediment (*pages 8–9*); (3) a cinquefoil arch with lions in the spandrels (*pages 12–13*); (4) a chevron-patterned arch intersected by five radiating bands (*pages 16–17*); and (5) a pair of mosaic arches, one inside the other (*pages 20–21*). These headpieces are supported by two columns except in the first pair of pages, where there are three. The columns show a variety of stylized leaves and blossoms in dense overall patterns that make them appear quite flat. The simplest columns are those of the first set, painted in monochrome red and green, while the richest are those of the last set, which are wider and more densely patterned than the others. Lion heads are used for the capitals on the first pair of pages, along with addorsed lions or birds for the bases. On the other pages the capitals and bases are designed around rosette or fleur-de-lis patterns, except for the bird capitals on *page 16*.

Almost all of these elements of canon page design can be found a generation earlier in the manuscripts of the scriptorium of T'oros Ṙoslin. The Queen Keṙan Gospel (Jerusalem, St. James 2563), executed in 1272, exhibits the same five headpiece designs in the same order, with the exception of the third set.[8] The flat, densely decorated columns of the canon tables begin to appear in Cilicia in the 1280s, as in the

[5] On the medieval development of Greek canon tables, see the recent article by Robert S. Nelson, "Theoktistos and Associates in Twelfth-Century Constantinople: An Illustrated New Testament of A.D. 1133," *J. Paul Getty Museum Journal* 15 (1987), 53–78.

[6] Der Nersessian, *Manuscrits,* 17.

[7] The eight-page format is common in Middle Byzantine manuscripts, though the intervening blank pages are unknown there.

[8] The canon tables of this ms. are not yet published; for discussion see Narkiss and Stone, *Jerusalem,* 63–64, 149, and Der Nersessian, *Armenian Art,* 144–48.

handsome example in Erevan, Mat. 9422.[9] Animated capitals and bases also have numerous precedents in Cilician manuscripts. The lion-headed capitals of *pages 4 and 5* can be compared to those of the Gospel of Constable Smbat, Erevan, Mat. 7644, of 1260–76,[10] while the addorsed birds of *pages 5 and 17* can be compared with those of T'oros Roslin's Gospel of 1260, Jerusalem, St. James, 251.[11] The cinquefoil arches with lions are the most contemporary design feature of the U.C.L.A. headpieces, introducing a motif that Armenian sculptors and architects had adopted from Islamic sources during the thirteenth century.[12]

To the right and left of each of the U.C.L.A. canon tables trees or other plants are represented springing up from the ground line. Some of these are too abstract to be securely identified with named species, but others are recognizable with a little detective work. The tree on *page 21* is unmistakably a date palm, with bunches of fruit hanging beneath the wide fronds. The heavy umbrella of foliage on the trees in the margins of *pages 4 and 5* is probably intended to suggest the olive, the shaggy crown of which, Nersēs Šnorhali remarks, remains always green (on *page 4* it is olive green, while on *page 5* it is blue). This identification can be confirmed by looking at Cilician prototypes, such as Washington, Freer, 44.17, of 1253, in which umbrella-shaped trees in the same position, flanking the Eusebian prologue, carry birds feeding on clusters of olives.[13] The trees of golden foliage in the outer margins of *pages 8 and 9* are also easier to recognize in their models than in their more generalized representations here. While the fruit here appear somewhat heart-shaped, they are identifiable as pomegranates in earlier manuscripts, where they appear with the same willowy branches in the same context of the second pair of tables.[14] The five-leaved trees on *pages 12 and 13* bear some resemblance to identifiable palm trees in earlier manuscripts, and the vine in the inner margins of *pages 20 and 21* may be intended as a grape vine. The three-leaved or three-petaled plants that appear in the outer margins of the fourth set of tables (*pages 16–17*) and on the inner margins of some others (*pages 3, 4, 8, 9*) provide very few botanical clues as to their identity, but both of the Armenian commentators to be discussed below include the lily along with the symbolic trees just examined. Since Armenian canon tables never show a realistic lily, one is probably justified in identifying this common three-petaled plant as the lily, parallel to the fleur-de-lis abstraction of that flower in the West.

A few of the birds on the U.C.L.A. canon tables are also too generalized to be identified, while a few others are too fantastic to exist at all. The birds with excessively long necks on *pages 20 and 21* could never negotiate in the real world, and the blue bird that swoops down to feed its young on *page 16* has green and red offspring—an unlikely phenomenon. Several species, however, are obvious. The long-legged and long-necked birds that stand on the top of *pages 4, 5, and 12,* or struggle with serpents on *page 21,* must be either herons or cranes (in spite of the red and green wings). There is no mistaking the peacocks on *pages 8, 9, 12, and 13,* shown with golden feathers in crest and tail. The black birds with white scapulars, perching on trees in the margins of *pages 9 and 12,* have the distinct markings of magpies, and their long-tailed cousins on *pages 8 and 12* may be freer renditions of the same. The birds on the top of *pages 8 and 9* have the profile and many of the body markings of the partridge, perhaps the chukar partridge of the Near East. The paired birds on the top of *page 13* make respectable doves; proud roosters cavort on the top of *pages 16 and 17;* and some members of the duck family drink at the lion-headed fountain on *page 20.* On the last two pages of the set, seated monkeys hold candlesticks. The monkey on *page 20* sits on the ground and his candle is extinguished, while that on *page 21* sits on a stool and holds a lighted candle. Finally, the very last page is surmounted by a foliate cross flanked by a pair of lions.

The identifiable species of fauna in the U.C.L.A. canon tables are very traditional. With the exception of the magpie, all of these species had appeared in the canon tables of the sixth-century Rabbula Gospel

[9] Korkhmazyan, *Armenian Miniatures of the 13th and 14th Centuries,* pls. 132–35.

[10] Ibid., 108–9.

[11] Narkiss and Stone, *Jerusalem,* pl. 61

[12] The cinquefoil headpiece is not known in Cilician canon tables; in Armenian architecture it can be found in the belltower of Hałbat (1245) or in the facade of the *gawit'* of Yovhannavank' (1250), while in sculpture it can be found in *xač'k'ars* of the thirteenth and beginning of the fourteenth century. See respectively: Step'an Mnac'akanyan and Adriano Alpago-Novello, *Hałbat,* Documenti di architettura armena 1 (Milan, 1974), pl. 34; Géza de Francovich, *Architettura medievale armena* (Rome, 1968), pl. 191; Levon Azarian and Armen Manoukian, *Khatchkar,* Documenti di architettura armena 2 (Milan, 1969), pls. 45, 46; Levon Azaryan, *Haykakan Xač'k'ar* (Erevan, 1973), pls. 89, 91, 94, 103, 107, 115. In Islamic art it occurs frequently in muqarnas. This development seems to be independent of the introduction of the cinquefoil in English gothic architecture. F. Bond, *An Introduction to English Church Architecture* (London, 1912), I, 455–61.

[13] Der Nersessian, *Arm. Mss. Freer,* figs. 33–34.

[14] Cf. Washington, Freer, 50.3 of the 12th century, Der Nersessian, *Arm. Mss. Freer,* figs. 11–12; Freer, 44.17, of 1253, ibid., figs. 39–40.

in Syria.[15] All of the same birds, minus the magpie and the rooster, reappear in the tenth-century Ēǰmiacin Gospel.[16] The magpie was introduced into the repertoire of birds by T'oros Ṙoslin, perhaps as a substitute for the crow or raven of earlier manuscripts, since they are of the same family and scavengers, and all are known for their ability to imitate human speech.[17]

2. The Armenian Commentators and Their Theory of Canon Table Symbolism

The U.C.L.A. canon tables in most of their symbolic decorations repeat the formulae of Cilician canon tables; although some motifs have lost in specificity, they would very likely have been recognized by one familiar with the tradition. The interpretation of such motifs, however, is another matter. The wide range of material—floral, faunal, liturgical, and abstract—spread over ten pages, seems to present a puzzle of enormous complexity to the iconographer. The problem is further complicated, moreover, by the indefinite variability of the set from one manuscript to the next. While some of the motifs can be found in the same order in earlier manuscripts, other manuscripts would present quite another order and quite a different selection of motifs. To the modern viewer this variability implies an arbitrariness that contravenes any serious symbolic intention.

Yet the seriousness of the artistic endeavor implies that more than mere decoration is involved. The selection of a finer parchment and the lavish use of twice as much parchment as necessary shows that a special importance was attached to these pages; the density of intricate ornament indicates the investment of far more man-hours of labor than any other part of the manuscript. Indeed, the canon tables are often ornamented when no other part of a Gospel is decorated. The consistent conformity of Armenian canon tables of the original ten-page count must be intentional, in view of the standard departures from ten in other traditions. Finally, the obvious symbolic import of such motifs as altars and chalices leads one to suppose that meaning was attached to other elements as well. The canon tables are a serious work of art that calls for a serious effort of understanding.

Scholarship on the iconography of the canon tables has generally had a retrospective orientation, concerned with origins and lost archetypes rather than with medieval developments. Within this framework, moreover, it has dealt only with special aspects of the subject. Nordenfalk addressed the problem of reconstructing the lost archetype that was formulated in the scriptorium of Eusebius of Caesarea, to which he attached a numerological symbolism.[18] The number ten, as discussed below, is an important ingredient in the symbolism, but obviously there is much that it does not explain. Moreover, the significance of the number ten was soon lost sight of in Byzantine, Syrian, and Latin scriptoria, in which the set was spread over twelve or more pages. In another study Nordenfalk has discussed the symbolism of tables ornamented with bust medallions of the twelve apostles, as in the sixth-century London, B.L. add. 5111.[19] But while this is one of the most ancient schemes of canon table decoration, it is also one of the rarest.

The other direction in which the iconography of the tables has been explored is the interpretation of the *tempietto* that concludes some of the earliest and most authentic sets of canon tables. This page of symbolic architecture without tables or text has challenged several art historians, but no consensus has emerged from their investigations. While Nordenfalk and Klemm associate the *tempietto* with the structure that Constantine erected over the tomb of Christ, Wessel thinks it alludes instead to the shrine of Bethlehem; Underwood finds baptistery associations in the *tempietto,* Bandmann takes it to be the Christian church in general, and Klauser sees it as a shrine for the Gospels.[20] These divergent readings of the *tempietto* are by no means mutually exclusive, and perhaps at different times some suggestions of all of them were intended. Still, this does not take one very far in understanding the medieval phenomenon of

[15] Carlo Cecchelli, Giuseppe Furlani, and Mario Salmi, *The Rabbula Gospels, Facsimile Edition of the Miniatures of the Syriac Manuscript Plut. I, 56 in the Medicean-Laurentian Library* (Olten, 1959), passim.

[16] F. Macler, *L'évangile arménien* (Paris, 1920), passim.

[17] See Baltimore, Walters, 539, fols. 4–6, Der Nersessian, *Arm. Mss. Walters,* figs. 46–48.

[18] Nordenfalk, *Die spätantiken Kanontafeln,* 47–48; idem, "The Beginning of Book Decoration," 16.

[19] Carl Nordenfalk, "The Apostolic Canon Tables," *Gazette des Beaux-Arts* 62 (1963), 17–34.

[20] Klaus Wessel has provided a useful review of the literature on this subject, "Kanontafeln," *RBK,* 3, 927–68; see also: Nordenfalk, *Die spätantiken Kanontafeln,* 109–16; E. Klemm, "Die Kanontafeln der armenischen Hs. Cod. 697 im Wiener Mechitaristenkloster," *Zeitschrift für Kunstgeschichte* 35 (1972), 69–99; Paul Underwood, "The Fountain of Life in Manuscripts of the Gospels," *DOP* 5 (1950), 41–115; G. Bandmann, "Beobachtungen zum Etschmiadzin-Evangeliar," *Tortulae,* Supplement zur Römische Quartalschrift (Rome, 1966), 11–29; T. Klauser, *Das Kiborium in der älteren christlichen Buchmalerei,* Nachrichten von der Akademie der Wissenschaften 7 (Göttingen, 1961).

canon table decoration, since the *tempietto* is only a single page that appears in only a handful of manuscripts, and, with the exception of out-of-the-way Ethiopia, it does not appear after the eleventh century.

None of these discussions attempts to deal with canon tables as a set, and none deals with the general problem posed by the Armenian development. The most serious inquiry into Armenian canon table symbolism is that undertaken by Der Nersessian in connection with her catalogues of Armenian manuscripts, particularly those of San Lazzaro, Venice, and the Freer Gallery, Washington.[21] Although in this context she limits herself to the discussion of the particular manuscripts at hand, Der Nersessian has introduced into the argument three Armenian commentaries on the canon tables, namely those by Stepʿanos Siwnecʿi, Nersēs Šnorhali, and Mikʿayēl of Sebastia. This adds a whole new dimension to the investigation, in that it opens up authentic contemporary sources on the subject that had previously not been tapped. Unfortunately, in the context of catalogue writing Der Nersessian did not feel called upon to examine the literature as a whole, but contented herself with citing it for the interpretation of individual motifs in the manuscripts under study. But the commentaries establish an important point of view from which to begin the general study of Armenian canon table iconography, and for this reason it has seemed important to supply a translation of the two medieval commentaries and to examine them in some detail.[22] The aesthetic they enunciate is quite different from that to which the Western scholar is accustomed, and it is not fair to cite them piecemeal, the way one might use a modern handbook of iconography, without trying to understand their scope and intention.

The first of the two documents is incomplete. The author is identified in some manuscripts as the eighth-century bishop Stepʿanos of Siwnikʿ. While confirmation of this attribution must await proper textual studies, Der Nersessian has observed some internal evidence that points to a date in the period of Stepʿanos Siwnecʿi. The range of birds discussed in the commentary, she notes, all appear in the canon tables of the Ējmiacin Gospel, which represents the oldest and most authentic canon table tradition in Armenia, and the peculiar triple spray of pomegranate—symbol of the sweet content of the New Law in the bitter rind of the Old—is found only in that manuscript.[23] In addition, it can be observed that the commentator evidently had before him a set of tables in which the arches stood free and were not yet enclosed in the rectangular headpieces that appear in the eleventh century, for he refers to "birds on top of the arches" and an altar "above the arches."[24] Furthermore, none of the other details mentioned by the author is inconsistent with early Armenian manuscript illumination. Finally, the author's interest in canon tables is entirely consistent with what is known of the career of Stepʿanos Siwnecʿi, who wrote a commentary on the Gospels and personally knew the great Byzantine commentator on ecclesiastical symbolism, the patriarch Germanos.[25]

The second document, which survives intact, is attributed to Nersēs Klayecʿi, surnamed Šnorhali or "the Graceful," and serves as the introduction to his *Commentary on the Gospel of St. Matthew.*[26] Nersēs, catholicos of Armenia (1163–73), was a theologian, poet, and hymnographer of considerable accomplishment, who entered into dialogue with the Byzantine emperor Manuel Comnenus on the possibility of union between the Greek and Armenian churches.[27] He attempted in his encyclical letters to define the Armenian position on the natures of Christ vis-à-vis the Greek, and a hint of this shows up in the *Commentary on the Ten Canon Tables* in the unusual formula "unconfused commingling," *xaṙnmamb anšpʿotʿeaw* that he uses to describe the incarnation.[28] Although the metaphor of "mixing" was one of the earliest expressions used to explain the union of the human and divine natures in Christ, the Greek church firmly rejected such language in the Chalcedonian formula "unmixed in two natures," *en duo physesin asynchytōs.* The Armenian church, however, retained the more ancient language, and in the Encyclical Letter with which he began his tenure as catholicos Nersēs confessed that "the incorporeal Word commingled (*xaṙni*) with the body, making it divine by the mixture (*xaṙnmamb*) but not undergoing any change or alter-

[21] Der Nersessian, *Manuscrits,* 58–61; *Arm. Mss. Freer,* 16–17, 100–101.

[22] See below, Appendix D.

[23] Der Nersessian, *Arm. Mss. Freer,* 17; cf. Stepʿanos Siwnecʿi, *Commentary,* 6 (Appendix D, below).

[24] Stepʿanos Siwnecʿi, *Commentary,* 4 and 6 (Appendix D, below).

[25] On Stepʿanos Siwnecʿi see Norayr Połarian, *Hay Grołner* (Jerusalem, 1971), 112–15.

[26] Nersēs Šnorhali and Yovhannēs Erznkacʿi, *Meknutʿiwn Surb Awetaranin or əst Mattʿēosi* (Constantinople, 1825), 5–12; see below, Appendix D. Der Nersessian remarks that some have attributed the commentary on the canon tables to Erznkacʿi without supplying references; the work fits better in the career of Nersēs, as explained. Der Nersessian, *Arm. Mss. Freer,* 16, note 51.

[27] Połarian, *Hay Grołner,* 233–39.

[28] *Commentary on the Ten Canon Tables,* chap. 2 (Appendix D, below).

ation in this union."[29] The expression "unconfused commingling" is patently a contradiction in terms (an "unmixed mixing"), which is being advanced by Nersēs Šnorhali with an ecumenical nod toward the Greek position.

It is clear that in writing his *Commentary on the Canon Tables* Nersēs had before him one or more earlier commentaries. In his conclusion he remarks, "These (are the teachings) of our learned fathers and brothers regarding the cause of wisdom and the foundation of the beginning of this (mighty) host of the Gospel, so that we may know that the first fathers did not portray the flowery ornaments of multicolored hue of the ten mystical Canon Tables in vain or without meaning." Nersēs evidently knew of a tradition of canon table commentary that he was enlarging and updating to suit the canon tables he saw in his own times. The earlier commentary of Step'anos Siwnec'i may well have been one such source familiar to him, for the two commentaries have several points in common. For example, concerning the first table, they both refer to four elements or parts and mention the angelic Thrones; concerning the second table both refer to black as a symbol of God's incomprehensibility and to the "middle priesthood" of angels; both mention an altar aflame in the third table; and both talk of red symbolizing the blood of Christ in the fifth table.[30] Yet on this level, that is, in the interpretation of specific symbolic motifs, it is surprising how often they diverge, whether in the location of a given motif or its meaning. They both say the horns of the altar mean Moses and Aaron, and the pomegranate represents the sweetness of the New Law in the bitter rind of the Old, but Step'anos associates these with the fifth table and Nersēs with the eighth and ninth.[31] Step'anos takes peacocks to represent the Jews, who were overfond of the externals of the Law, but Nersēs sees them as angels. Moreover, the same commentator can use the same symbol in different ways in different contexts, for Nersēs takes the date palm as a symbol of angels in one context and a symbol of Christ in another (chap. 8,14; cf. Step'anos, chap. 1, 5). This flexibility says something about the nature of this genre of literature. The commentary clearly does not consist in the accumulation of motifs, but rather in providing a frame of reference in which a great variety of motifs can be interpreted, and a method of approach to the material. The most important thing that the two commentaries share is that they both see the canon tables as representing the mystery of man's redemption from its source in the inaccessible divinity to its realization in the church on earth.

Insofar as Nersēs Šnorhali is more self-conscious in explaining his purpose, his commentary is the best key to understanding the rationale of canon table decoration. It is also important to observe the association of this document with Glajor through Yovhannēs Erznkac'i. Since the commentary is connected with Nersēs' unfinished commentary on the Gospel, and since the latter was taken up for completion by Erznkac'i, scribe and exegete of Glajor, it is safe to assume that it was known in Glajor. On the other hand, it should be noticed that no canon table set from Glajor, or for that matter from Cilicia either, seems to try expressly to follow the commentary. This is not the intention of the commentaries. Unlike the painters' manuals of the West, the commentaries are not prescriptive. They do not give the artist instructions; rather they instruct the viewer how to see the tables, in what frame of mind to approach them, or what to look for in them.[32]

In his opening paragraphs Nersēs tries to define how the devout viewer should approach the canon tables. What the Gospels teach, Nersēs begins, is that in spite of the fallen state in which man finds himself, he is "the image of God, and Paradise is his habitation, and the Tree of Life is the occasion of his immortality" (chap. 1). By the Tree of Life he means the cross. Man's origins are in Paradise, and it is the recollection of his original glory that leads man to desire the food immortal, which is Christ. Paradise in this sense embraces at once the beginning and the culmination of human history, that is the creation of Adam and redemption in Christ. The first and most encompassing symbolism of the canon tables is therefore paradisiac. For now the Garden of Paradise, he tells us, "is walled around, not by the terrifying fire and the flaming Seraphic sword, but by the luxurious floral pictures and colorful, splendid ornament in the form of the drawing of the canon tables" (chap. 3). Many of the paradisiac associations, therefore, that Underwood found in analyzing the *tempietto* page rightfully belong to the entire set of canon tables.[33]

[29] Nersēs Šnorhali, Encyclical Letter, as cited by Pascal Tékéyan, *Controverses christologiques en Arméno-Cilicie dans la seconde moitié du XIIe siècle (1165–1198)*, OCA 124 (Rome, 1939), 86, from the edition of Constantinople (1825), 177.

[30] Nersēs, *Commentary on the Ten Canon Tables*, chaps. 7–10; Step'anos Siwnec'i, *Commentary on the Ten Canon Tables*, chaps. 2–6.

[31] Nersēs, *Commentary on the Ten Canon Tables*, chaps. 13 and 14; Step'anos Siwnec'i, *Commentary on the Ten Canon Tables*, chap. 6.

[32] For this reason it is not really to the point to ask, as Der Nersessian does, whether a given artist could have read Nersēs' commentary. Der Nersessian, *Manuscrits*, 59–60.

[33] Underwood, "The Fountain of Life in Manuscripts of the Gospels," 41–115.

The luxurious character of the paradisiac ornament, however, suggests a further consideration to Nersēs, which is at the heart of his theory of canon tables. In an aesthetic thesis of great importance for the study of Armenian art, he proposes that the whole world of experience may be divided into two classes of objects, the necessary and the pleasurable or sensuous (chap. 3). Such a distinction, of course, is commonplace among Christian authors struggling with the problem of religious art; the distinction is always used, however, to denigrate the pleasurable or the sensuous. One might cite Hypatius of Ephesus for example: "For our part, we take no pleasure whatever in any sculpture or painting. However, we permit simple folk, inasmuch as they are less perfect, to learn such things in an introductory manner by means of sight, which is appropriate to their natural development, having found on many occasions that even the old and new ordinances of God may be brought down to the level of the weaker for the sake of their spiritual salvation."[34] Pope Gregory the Great offers the same sort of distinction when he advises that "what writing supplies to readers painting offers to uneducated viewers."[35] For Nersēs Šnorhali, however, the situation is exactly the reverse. The sensual pleasures of the canon tables are not designed for simple or uneducated folk but rather for "perfected" ones, that is for the initiate. Pleasures, he says, "which are not accounted important, are of great utility to perfected (ones), when by this manifest color, taste, smell, hearing and the rest we ascend to the spiritual and to the rational enjoyment (of) the good tidings of God, which eye has not seen and ear has not heard and which the heart of man has not recalled, which God (has) prepared for his loved ones" (chap. 3). Through the visual pleasures of the canon tables one is supposed to ascend to the spiritual enjoyment of the Gospels themselves. Nersēs returns to this theme at the end of his commentary, where he calls the flowery meadows of the canon tables an "evangelical preparation" that precedes the Gospel. Drawing an analogy with the encampment of the Israelites at Sinai when they were required to wash and purify themselves before being admitted to the awesome vision of the Lord, Nersēs calls the canon tables "baths of sight and hearing for those approaching the soaring peaks of God" (chap. 18). By washing his eyes in the beauty of these tables and by "circling with care in the tabernacle of this holy temple," the reader was to prepare himself for the greater vision to be had in reading the text that followed (chap. 18).

The image use that Nersēs had in mind for these ornamented pages was as a kind of instrument of contemplation: a visual aid to meditation, they were to prepare the soul by removing distractions. By focusing the viewer's attention on largely abstract forms and colors, the canon tables were meant to focus the powers of his soul on the central mysteries of Christian revelation.

Psychologically this is a most interesting role to assign the art work. Two premises lie behind such an approach, neither of which is commonplace in medieval art. The first premise is the frank acceptance of the sensuous as something good in itself and therefore worthy of the serious attention of the educated or the initiate. According to Nersēs, "God gave the lover of material things understanding of the heavenly" (chap. 4). Accepting this premise, the artist found himself free to explore the limits of his craft in intricacy of pattern and richness of color apart from the practical necessity of illustrating this or that subject. Colors are displayed both in their highest intensities and in the widest range of their mixed shades simply for their own beauty. The purpose of the mosaic rainbows and chevron arches is to show the sumptuous possibilities of the artist's palette.

The second premise is that the most profound meanings contained in the canon tables must be left hidden. This is the exact opposite of the symbolic systems of Western medieval art, which are didactic in intent and therefore depend on spelling out all meanings explicitly: saints, symbols, and personifications must all carry identifying attributes or be carefully labeled to make their lessons readable. But the more explicit the content, the more particular and limited it becomes. As instruments for contemplation, the Armenian canon tables were designed to be suggestive rather than explicit, with open-ended significance. To reinforce this intention Nersēs invents a pseudo-etymology for the Armenian word for canon table, *xoran*. Etymologically the word means "canopy," or "tent," but Nersēs derives it instead from the unrelated but similar sounding word *xorhrdakan*, which means "mystical," or "mysterious" (chap. 6).[36] Nersēs goes on to explain, "The mystery is not apparent to all, but (only) to a few, and (its) entirety (is known) to God." In other words, the canon tables are absolutely inexhaustible to the viewer who approaches them in faith.

[34] Mango, *Art of the Byzantine Empire, 312–1453*, 117.

[35] Pope Gregory, *Epistola XXII ad Serenum Massiliensem episcopum*, PL 77, col. 1128.

[36] See Nersēs' *Commentary on the Ten Canon Tables*, chap. 6, note by James Russell.

It is this open-ended character of Armenian canon tables that puts them in a class by themselves among medieval art works. The viewer must understand that the meaning is always going to elude him, always surpass what he has been able to explain. This attitude must be responsible for the enormous outpouring of artistic effort in decorating these pages. At the same time, this sense that the tables are absolutely brim-full of meaning is responsible for the development of the literature of commentary that offers suggestions on how to explore the symbolism of the tables.

3. Interpreting the U.C.L.A. Canon Tables

The boundless possibilities of meaning in the Armenian canon tables frustrate all efforts to impose system on their decoration. While Western iconographic complexes generally consist of a limited number of parts in fixed order, all adding up to a single whole (the Seven Sacraments or the Three Theological Virtues, for example), the Armenian canon tables have no such neat anatomy. The pious viewer is given license to construct the kinds of symbolism that correspond to his own devotional needs. This did not prevent the commentators, however, from offering suggestions on how to interpret specific symbolic aspects of the set. Such suggestions were not intended to circumscribe either the artist or the viewer; rather they were meant to provide examples of how to proceed with a given set of tables. It is clear from the specificity of their references that both Step'anos Siwnec'i and Nersēs Šnorhali had before their eyes one (or more) actual sets of canon tables; it is also clear from the immense variety of surviving sets that no sequence of symbols was ever regarded as fixed and canonical.

As noted above, the two commentators found a similar progression in the canon tables, in that they symbolize the gradual unfolding of the mysteries of human salvation from the Divinity residing in inaccessible glory to the accomplishment of man's redemption in the church. Nersēs Šnorhali worked this out in some detail. Central to his explanation of this symbolism is the host of associations connected to the Armenian word *xoran*. Etymologically the word means "tent" or "canopy," like the Greek *skēnē;* hence it designates a kind of dwelling in general. In particular in Old Testament usage it refers to the "ark," whether that of Noah or that of the covenant, and to the "tabernacle" or "temple." In discussions of the Christian church building, however, it enjoys a range of meaning beyond the parallel Greek term, for it can mean the "altar," the "sanctuary," the "ciborium" or the "dome."[37] Hence this development of canon table symbolism linked to the word *xoran* seems to be particularly Armenian. Each of the ten canon tables is interpreted as a dwelling for one of the great mysteries of salvation history, as follows:

1. The Blessed Trinity; Thrones, Seraphim and Cherubim
2. The Middle Priesthood of Angels
3. The Last Priesthood of Angels
4. The Garden of Paradise
5. The Ark of Noah
6. The Altar of Abraham
7. The Holy of Holies of Moses
8. The Outer Court of Moses' Tabernacle
9. Solomon's Temple
10. The Holy Catholic Church

By assigning the successive *xorans* these meanings, Nersēs created an overall structure in which the meaning of individual motifs might be interpreted. The structure itself, however, carries a theological burden.

In the first place, the sequence of ten mysteries points to the basic continuity of salvation history. As Nersēs explains it, the Creator made man in his own image, and although man sinned, still a "recollection of the good" was preserved in him (chap. 1). In the progeny of Adam this "good recollection" was handed down as a mystery, which the Gentiles did not understand until its original prototype, namely, Christ, should appear: "(He) filled the thirst of our longing, our Prototype, the image of the Father, in superabundance: not only by revealing himself to us as the one whom we had desired, but by making our wretched and abashed natures the communicants of his unparalleled divine glory, by forming body and members of the tangible Godhead, and by showing at the same time the desirable food immortal, which the Tree of Life brought forth as fruit for us" (chap. 2). The beginning and end of history are tied together: placed in the Garden of Paradise man learned to desire the fruit of the Tree of Life, which he would finally receive only when Christ appeared. This sense of the completeness and consistency of human history has been encountered in the Gospel iconography, a characteristic of the Syro-Armenian approach. Characteristic too is the sense that the thread that holds all this history together is a secret tradition, a

[37] Robert W. Thomson, "Architectural Symbolism in Classical Armenian Literature," *Journal of Theological Studies*, n.s. 30 (1979), 102–14.

hidden knowledge passed on from generation to generation from Adam to Christ; the tradition of canon table commentary is regarded by Nersēs as a similar kind of esoteric wisdom (chap. 17).

A certain neo-Platonic notion of revelation also underlies Nersēs' commentary on the canon tables. God himself resides in "inaccessible light" (chap. 5), and makes himself known by degrees. The nine choirs of angels, divided into three ranks of three, derives, of course, from Pseudo-Denis; Nersēs' language is authentically Dionysian in referring to the angels as priestly and in speaking of the lower priesthoods of angels learning from the higher (chap. 8).[38] The fullness of divine revelation is to be found only in the holy, catholic church: the tenth canon table "contains within itself the mystery of all (the others)" (chap. 6). By the church is meant not only the present assembly of the faithful, but the future church, the "new Jerusalem," in which "all the forever-changing churches (will) unite" (chap. 16), another reference to Nersēs Šnorhali's ecumenical consciousness. In the tenth canon, therefore, one is looking forward to the appearance of the sign of the Son of Man on the last day.

Number symbolism enters into this overall structure, though it is exploited far less than it might have been in view of its popularity with Armenian authors.[39] Ten is the most important number for the set and Nersēs calls it "a holy number and a gift of God" (chap. 5). According to Nersēs, the number ten was chosen by Eusebius by divine inspiration, for ten is the number of the commandments, the curtains of the temple (Exod. 36:8), the parts of the body and its senses, the Categories of Aristotle, the petitions of the Lord's Prayer, the articles of the Nicene Creed, and the ages of the world.[40] It is therefore a number of completeness. In the fourth table, which symbolizes the Garden of Paradise, the number four is appealed to as the number of the four elements of which the world is made (chap. 9). In the seventh canon table Nersēs finds (seven?) doves, symbolic of the gifts of the Holy Spirit (chap. 12), and the ninth reminds him that nine is three times the number of the synoptic evangelists, who described the earthly genealogy of Christ (chap. 14). Insofar as this number symbolism—and further possible variations of it—has little to do with any specific feature of the decoration (except that Nersēs counts four columns in the fourth table), it can be applied to any set of Armenian canon tables; it requires only that the set be tenfold, as Armenian sets always are.

Canon tables, however, are decorated with more concrete motifs, and for these the commentators offered more specific associations, linked more or less to the ten mysteries enumerated above. Colors naturally had strong powers of suggestion, and the two commentators show considerable agreement in their interpretation of them. Purple is the color of the "omnipotent kingdom" of the Divinity (chap. 7; cf. Step'anos, chap. 2); green suggests the "everlasting immortality" of angels (chap. 8); black is the color of the "incomprehensibility of God" (chap. 8; cf. Step'anos, chap. 3); blue refers to the sinfulness and shadowy character of life under the Old Law (chaps. 9, 13, 15; cf. Step'anos, chap. 3); and red means sacrifice, the wine of Melchisedek, and the Blood of Christ (chap. 10, 13, 15; cf. Step'anos, chaps. 3, 6). In the U.C.L.A. Gospel it may be significant that purple and green are used in the first two tables and blue in the fourth in the sequence described by Nersēs, in the columns that support the headpiece. Black, however, is not used, nor is there a perceptible progress from blue to red in the last four tables. There is, however, a greater brilliance and intensity of color in the last table, to symbolize the fullness of revelation in the church.

Four kinds of flora are mentioned by Nersēs, which were probably represented in pairs in the outer margins. When he found date palms in the tables of the angels he took them to refer to the lofty nature and sweet blessings of these heavenly creatures (chap. 8);[41] but when he found them in the ninth table they referred to Christ, sprung from the root of David as truth sprung from the earth (chap. 14; cf. Step'anos chap. 5). The olive tree has three associations for Nersēs: its greenness suggests the longevity of the patriarchs, the sourness of its fruit, the austerity of their lives, and its oil the illumination of their teaching (chap. 11). The lily also has multiple meanings: its colors of white, yellow, and red mean purity, patience, and manliness; the water lily signifies the patriarchs' ability to rise above the world around them; the desert lily stands for the ascetics of the desert (chap. 11). Finally, the pomegranate refers to the sweetness of the New Law within the bitter rind of the Old (chap. 14; cf. Step'anos, chap. 6). All four of these flora are

[38] Pseudo-Denis, the Areopagite, *De caelesti hierarchia*, PG 3, cols. 119–370.

[39] Robert W. Thomson, "Number Symbolism and Patristic Exegesis in Some Early Armenian Writers," *Handēs Amsorya* 90 (1976), 117–38.

[40] John of Ōjun lists the ten parts of the body as the mind, the eyes, ears, nostrils, mouth, and hands; cf. ibid., 131.

[41] The same symbolism is developed by Yovhannēs Erznkac'i in connection with the palm trees of Palm Sunday. See above, p. 103.

used in the U.C.L.A. Gospel, although the order is different: olive, pomegranate, date palms, lilies, date palms. Still the range of interpretations suggested by Nersēs shows how one ought to proceed with this material.

Nersēs offers an interpretation for six different species of birds in canon tables. Birds played an important role in Armenian art from the start. The forty birds surrounding an eagle in the sixth-century Armenian mosaic in Jerusalem have been convincingly interpreted by Evans as symbolic of the deceased flocking around Christ; precedents for this positive use of bird symbolism Evans found in Sasanian sources, in which birds are described as the special creation of Ohrmazd to purify the world of "noxious creatures."[42] Indeed the range of variety of birds in Armenian canon tables matches rather closely the range of birds in Sasanian art.[43] The symbolism of birds in canon tables developed from Near Eastern antecedents, whether in Sasanian Iran or Early Christian Armenia and Syria. Thus, according to Nersēs, the cock appearing in the ninth table "close to the morning of righteousness, proclaimed the apparition of the ineffable light" (chap. 14), that is, the advent of Christ; according to Step'anos, the gold feathers of the cock made it represent those who are purified and worthy of the Holy Spirit (chap. 6); it is "splendid and bold, commanding and awesome" (chap. 4). In Zoroastrianism the cock was the companion of Sroasha (angel defender of mankind), who proclaimed the arrival of day and called men to prayer; hence it symbolized true religion. Cocks appear in the seventh and eighth tables of the U.C.L.A. Gospel (*pages 16–17*), and later on in the scene of Peter's Repentance (*page 166*).[44] Scavenger birds, such as the crow or magpie, not mentioned in the two commentators, were valued in Zoroastrianism for their service in cleansing the land of waste.[45] Magpies show up in the third, fourth and fifth tables (*pages 8–12*).

Doves may stand for the gifts of the Holy Spirit (Nersēs, chap. 12), or for those who have received the gifts of the Holy Spirit (Nersēs chap. 13; Step'anos, chap. 5), a symbolism developed in early Christian Armenia by Agat'angelos.[46] Their appearance in the seventh and eighth tables of the U.C.L.A. Gospel would be especially appropriate, for Nersēs connects them with the inspiration of Bezalel and Oholiab, the artists of Moses' temple (*pages 16–17*). Both commentators associate the partridge with the "harlots" who by ruse came to have a role in Christ's lineage. Nersēs explains that "it is the way of partridges to steal eggs and make them its own, even as they (i.e., the three women) stole by cunning from the house of Abraham and his son the fruit of blessings, and became the fore-mothers of Christ" (chap. 13; cf. Step'anos, chap. 6). They occur on the third and fourth canon tables of the U.C.L.A. Gospel, where they seem to disagree with themes Nersēs assigned those tables. The notion that partridges hatched the eggs of other birds derives from the *Physiologus,* as Evans noticed.[47]

The tradition that made herons symbols of the apostles involved a peculiarity of the Armenian version of Scripture, for when Nersēs, alluding to Christ's call of the apostles, says that from being fishermen the apostles were made "hunters of men", the Armenian word for fishermen is in fact a "fish-hunter" (chap. 15).[48] Hence fishing birds were appropriate symbols of apostles. In the U.C.L.A. Gospel, however, they appear in a combative role struggling with black serpents, a role perhaps appropriate to the apostles (*page 21*), and eating some sort of fruit in the first pair of tables, a role hardly right for herons. The teal, a small freshwater duck, takes its spiritual meaning from its preference for fresh water; Nersēs calls them "sea-divers of the depths of God" that drink in the Holy Spirit to distribute it to all (chap. 15). In the ninth U.C.L.A. canon table they drink at a lion-headed fountain (*page 20*). Finally, peacocks with their gold feathers represent the purity of angelic spirits for Nersēs (chap. 8), but for Step'anos they represent the vain attention to externals of the Jews of the Old Testament (chap. 2). Perhaps something else is intended in the U.C.L.A. Gospel, in which they appear on four successive tables, the third to the sixth (*pages 9–13*).

All the birds in the U.C.L.A. canon tables, therefore, can be taken as positive and personal symbols within the unfolding of the mystery of human salvation. The pair of monkeys that figure in the last pair

[42] Helen C. Evans, "Nonclassical Sources for the Armenian Mosaic near the Damascus Gate in Jerusalem," *East of Byzantium: Syria and Armenia in the Formative Period,* ed. N. G. Garsoïan, et al. 217–221.

[43] See the exhibition catalogue of Sasanian art prepared by Prudence Harper (*The Royal Hunter*), in which the following birds appear: eagle (nos. 14, 62), cock (nos. 21, 58, 62), partridge (nos. 13, 49), guinea fowl (no. 20), herons or cranes (no. 59), peacock? (no. 26), and the mythical senmurv (nos. 34, 56).

[44] Harper, *The Royal Hunter,* 65.

[45] J. D. Moulton, *Early Zoroastrianism* (London, 1912), 399–400.

[46] Agat'angelos, *Teaching of St. Gregory,* chap. 605; cf. Evans, "Nonclassical Sources for the Armenian Mosaic," 218.

[47] Evans, "Nonclassical Sources for the Armenian Mosaic," 221; O. Seel, *Der Physiologus* (Zurich, 1960), 18–19.

[48] See above, p. 118.

of tables is a new introduction in the tradition and more difficult to interpret spiritually (*pages 20–21*).[49] The *Physiologus* identified the ape with the devil, an identification that affected the whole family of simians throughout the Middle Ages.[50] In Gothic art, however, this insidious characterization loses much of its force when apes and monkeys are called upon to play parodies of humans. In manuscript marginalia they appear miming the exploits and foibles of men, whether knights or nobles or clergy.[51] This more playful tradition may lie behind the introduction of monkeys into Armenian manuscripts. What is significant in their present use is less their character than their action, for on *page 20,* representing the Temple of Solomon, the monkey sits on the ground and holds a candle that has been extinguished, while on the facing page, symbolic of the Catholic Church, the monkey sits on a chair and his candle is lighted. The Church has replaced the Temple as the dwelling place of the Divinity.

Rampant lions appear twice in the U.C.L.A. canon tables: in the spandrels of the third pair of tables (*pages 12–13*) and in the upper margin of the very last page, where they flank a kind of foliate cross (*page 21*). These too represent a late introduction into Armenian canon table decoration, made under Western influence in Cilicia; they are not mentioned in either of the commentators. Scriptural use of the lion for Christ, the just man, or the devil would give the viewer ample room to find symbolism in its use in the canon tables (for example, see Rev. 5:5; Prov. 28:1; 1 Pet. 5:8).[52] In the U.C.L.A. Crucifixion the lion on the centurion's shield seems to allude to the ever watchful Divinity in Christ.[53]

All of these specific symbols admit of a great deal of variety in their employment and are capable of a range of interpretations. They ornament the tables and suggest to the viewer ways of expanding his reflections on the larger mysteries of salvation history. Only after one has purified one's eyes and mind by this contemplation is one ready to start the reading of the Gospel text.

[49] Monkeys occur occasionally in Greek manuscripts: a monkey with a candlestick shows up in Berlin, Staatsbibliothek Quarto 88, fol. 4r (Carr, *Byzantine Illumination, 1150–1250,* fiche 8, D2), and a chained monkey with a bowl of fruit appears in a margin of Athos, Dionysiou 4, fol. 6, of the 13th century (Pelikanidis, *Treasures of Mount Athos,* I, 49). In Armenian manuscripts a climbing monkey appears in the marginal ornament of Erevan, Mat. 979, fol. 295, of 1286 (Dournovo, *Haykakan Manrankarč'ut'yun,* pl. 43), but the Glajor Gospel seems to mark the first appearance of monkeys in Armenian canon tables.

[50] O. Seel, *Der Physiologus,* 36. H. W. Janson, *Apes and Ape Lore in the Middle Ages and the Renaissance* (London, 1952), 16.

[51] Janson, *Apes and Ape Lore,* 163–69.

[52] Lions appear elsewhere in the U.C.L.A. Gospel: with prey on the incipit page of Matthew (*page 27*); as the symbol of Mark (*pages 188–89*); rampant in the spandrels of the Wedding Feast at Cana (*page 469*); and as a shield device in the Betrayal (*page 162*) and Crucifixion (*page 561*).

[53] See above, p. 162.

CHAPTER EIGHT

The Iconography of the Evangelists' Portraits

Portraits of the four evangelists are by far the commonest subjects for illustration in medieval Gospel illumination.[1] Unfortunately, their repeated recurrence from manuscript to manuscript in a limited variety of poses and settings soon exhausts the patience of the modern art historian, and the vast field of evangelist portraits does not receive the full attention it deserves.[2] Yet the repetition of the subject is the clearest evidence of its extraordinary importance to medieval man; if the budget for making a Gospel book allowed any decoration at all, the evangelists were the first subject that had to be illustrated. It might almost seem that the artists had made the evangelists more important than their Gospels, insofar as illustrations of the narrative content are so exceptional in absolute percentages. The special prominence assigned the author portrait is certainly not a matter of chance, as if it were the result of a tradition that somehow grew spontaneously without inner reasons; so central a theme must have developed out of profound convictions about the nature of divine revelation and the authorship of the Gospels. It warrants more extensive investigation than it has received, but, as usual in the study of Christian iconography, more attention has been given to classifying the variety of types of iconography than to explaining their significance.

[1] Robert S. Nelson, *The Iconography of Preface and Miniature in the Byzantine Gospel Book* (New York, 1980), 3.

[2] In a now classic study Albert M. Friend sought to trace the proliferation of medieval evangelist portraits to two basic sets of Late Antique portrait groups; his attribution of these groups to Antioch and Ephesus should be questioned (A. Friend, "The Portraits of the Evangelists in Greek and Latin Manuscripts," *Art Studies* 5 [1927], 115–50, and 7 [1929], 3–29). Studies of individual manuscripts have sometimes dealt with sets of evangelist portraits, as Kurt Weitzmann, "The Constantinopolitan Lectionary, Morgan 639," *Studies in Art and Literature for Belle da Costa Greene*, ed. Dorothy Miner (Princeton, 1954), 358–73; Hugo Buchthal, "A Byzantine Miniature of the Fourth Evangelist and Its Relatives," *DOP* 15 (1961), 127–40. The broadest surveys of the material are the dictionary articles of Herbert Hunger and Klaus Wessel, "Evangelisten," *RBK* II, 452–507, and Ursula Nilgen, "Evangelisten und Evangelistensymbole," *Lexikon der christlichen Ikonographie*, I, 696–713.

The iconography of the U.C.L.A. evangelists constitutes a very fresh realization of the ancient theme that departs in many details from standard representations. Some elements are newly introduced and others are reworked in the present context. What is important is the degree to which the artist, the Second Painter, has achieved an intelligent statement of the theme in keeping with Armenian iconographic traditions.

The evangelist's portraits constitute a set of four double-page compositions: the four authors are pictured on versos, as is usual, facing the beginning of their books on the opposite rectos, and the two are linked compositionally and by the repetition of the evangelists' symbols (*pages 26, 27, 188, 189, 298, 299, 460, 461*). The paired pages must be studied together; the analysis of the iconography of the evangelists, therefore, must take into account several elements beside the evangelists themselves. On the evangelist's page both the author himself and the framing that encloses him, with its symbolic capitals and angel-filled spandrels, deserve attention. On the incipit page one must consider the initial letter formed of the evangelist symbol; the headpiece with the decoration in the margin above it; and the cross in the right-hand margin with its rich ornamental support. Though these different elements evolved separately, the Second Painter has assembled them here to make a coherent statement about the authors of the Gospels.

In their general types, the U.C.L.A. evangelists follow compositions that enjoyed wide popularity in Byzantine art. The first three can be placed in the categories that Hunger and Wessel developed: Matthew and Luke fall in the category of the "writing" evangelist, while Mark falls in that of the "posing" evangelist, consulting a book; Mark, however, has been made to write as he consults, which results in a certain awkwardness.[3] The portrait of John dictating to Prochorus is a less usual type in Byzantine art, which generally prefers the type of the seated "med-

[3] Hunger and Wessel, "Evangelisten," *RBK* II, 459–462.

itating" evangelist.[4] However, the alternative composition of John dictating is also used in Byzantium. The story that the fourth Gospel was dictated to Prochorus originated in the fifth-century Acts of John.[5]

While their figure types are common, the backgrounds of the Glajor evangelists set them apart from the standard Byzantine representations. The commonest Byzantine treatment is a plain gold ground; when architecture is introduced it usually derives from the antique "scenae frons."[6] To use a cluster of buildings showing peaked roofs and baldachinos is very uncommon in Byzantine art; to use such a background for John dictating to Prochorus is unknown. The usual setting for the latter is a mountainous landscape.

In Armenian art, however, these unusual features are common, if not standard. For his immediate models the Second Painter turned to a tradition familiar in thirteenth-century Siwnikʿ that placed the authors in arched frames. This tradition appears in the University of Tübingen, MA XIII, 1, and in Erevan, Mat. 7737 (fig. 298a).[7] Der Nersessian had pointed out the relationship of these manuscripts to Tʿoros Taronecʿi's Gospel of 1307, and the discovery of the U.C.L.A. Gospel allows one to be more precise about the line of transmission, for the Venice manuscript received the tradition by way of the U.C.L.A. Gospel.[8] The U.C.L.A. evangelists in turn were copied again, once in a manuscript in the Ēǰmiacin Patriarchal Treasury dated 1491, and again, in 1628, in a manuscript executed in New Julfa in the former Hazarian Collection (fig. 460i).[9]

The comparison of the U.C.L.A. Luke to the corresponding miniature in Mat. 7737 is instructive (*page 298*, fig. 298a). In reworking the portrait the Second Painter has placed the figure more nearly in the center, which crowded the evangelist's desk off to the right; he enlarged the architectural elements and enlivened the image with beasts—lions in his seat, a fish for a lectern, lion and ox heads in the baldachino—a strong link to the miraculous proliferation of creatures on the opposite incipit page. But the evangelist's pose is the same, as he holds the book on his left knee with his right, and the general handling of the clothes is similar, with a short-sleeved tunic and a circle of drapery on the right thigh. The seats and desks are also similar and the large simple massing of the architecture is the same.

Many of the same traits show up in the other portraits as well (*pages 26, 188, 460*). The figures are generally moved to the center of the page and enlarged in scale; desks in Matthew's and John's portraits are entirely eliminated; architecture is simplified and enlarged, and evangelist symbols are developed. St. Matthew's desk is crowded right off the page and replaced with a carpet.

In his book on prefatory miniatures in Byzantine Gospels, Nelson has advanced the thesis that the evangelists' portraits, and other prefatory illustrations, could be interpreted through the prefaces that are invariably added to Gospel manuscripts.[10] Although von Soden published the principal versions and most important variants of these prefaces, the text tradition of this material still has not been sorted out.[11] In the U.C.L.A. Gospel these prefaces are each comprised of four parts: (1) the *hypothesis* or summary of contents; (2) the *bios* or capsule biography of the evangelist; (3) a count of chapters, quotations and verses; and (4) the etymology of the evangelist's name (see Appendix B). The *hypotheses* and *bioi* closely parallel the common Greek version, with the exception of a shortening of John's life.[12] The Greek manuscripts also include the count of chapters, quotations, and verses, but the last element, the etymological meaning of the evangelist's name, is not known in the Greek tradition, but derives from an unknown Syrian source.[13]

What the prefaces say about the evangelists has some bearing on their appearance in the U.C.L.A. Gospel. The prefaces identify two of the evangelists, Matthew and John, as disciples of Christ himself, of the number of the twelve apostles, while the other two are described as belonging to the next generation, disciples of Peter and Paul who received their information from them. However unhistorical this may be to the modern form criticism of the Gospels,

[4] Buchthal, "A Byzantine Miniature of the Fourth Evangelist," 127–39.

[5] Ibid., 133; *Neutestamentliche Apocryphen,* ed. E. Hennecke (Tübingen, 1924), 174.

[6] Hunger and Wessel, "Evangelisten," 479–82.

[7] L. A. Dournovo and S. Der Nersessian, *Armenian Miniatures* (New York, 1961), 72–77; L. R. Azaryan, *Kilikyan Manrankarčʿutʿyunə,* pls. 2–7.

[8] Der Nersessian, *Manuscrits,* 121–22.

[9] One lone miniature from the Ēǰmiacin manuscript was published, without additional information, in *Ēǰmiacni Ganjer,* foreword by Sirarpie Der Nersessian (Ēǰmiacin, 1984), no page or plate numbers.

[10] Nelson, *The Iconography of Preface and Miniature.*

[11] Hermann Freiherr von Soden, *Die Schriften des Neuen Testaments in ihrer ältesten erreichbaren Textgestalt,* 2 vols. (Berlin, 1902), 294–327.

[12] Ibid., 297–98, 314–16.

[13] The derivations are not all clear, but *Marqos* in Syriac might suggest the Semitic base RQʿ, "firmament," hence "exalted"; and Yovhannēs has in its base HN, meaning "to be meek, pleasing," and hence "obedience." I am indebted to James Russell for these suggestions.

the tradition was current as early as the middle of the second century in the work of Papias of Hieropolis and was repeated by Eusebius; the point of the tradition was to find apostolic authority for all of the Gospels.[14] Accordingly, the visual tradition of the four portraits makes Matthew and John older men, with white hair and beards, and Mark and Luke younger, dark-haired men, and this tradition is continued in the U.C.L.A. Gospel.

Another iconographic detail reinforces this apostolic association in the prefaces, and that is the unusual architectural backgrounds. The clusters of buildings introduced behind the evangelists should be taken as abbreviated city-scapes, alluding to the places where the evangelists wrote. According to the U.C.L.A. prefaces, Matthew wrote his Gospel in Jerusalem, Mark in Alexandria, Luke in Antioch, and John in Ephesus. The insistence on placing John in a city rather than on the island of Patmos, as sometimes stated, should be connected with the desire to associate each evangelist with one of the great apostolic sees.[15]

The symbols that accompany the evangelists in the U.C.L.A. Gospel, whether on the evangelist's page or on the facing incipit, further expand the iconography of the evangelists' special authority. It must be noted that while the arches that frame the evangelists are part of the model of Erevan, Mat. 7737, the decoration of those arches, with evangelist symbols in the capitals and angels in the spandrels, is an innovation of the U.C.L.A. Gospel. Thirteenth-century manuscripts in Cilicia had indeed used evangelist symbols in the first letter of the incipit page and had fashioned birds and beasts into the capitals of their canon tables.[16] But to use the framing of the evangelists to double the symbols that are represented in the initials opposite is the Second Painter's invention. In this way he has made the capitals reinforce the symbolism of the initials and tied the two pages together. In three cases the capitals repeat in style and handling the symbol opposite: the innocent angel heads, the scowling lion heads, and the oxen curled as if trussed up for sacrifice on altars. In the portrait of St. John, however, a pair of six-winged Cherubim have been substituted for the eagle, the significance of which will be uncovered momentarily.

The spandrels too have been used to develop the iconography. In the spandrels of St. Matthew standing angels make gestures that might be interpreted as astonishment. In St. Mark the angels fly and put a finger to their lips to call for reverent silence; and the angel on the left carries a symbol of ecclesiastical authority, the T-shaped vardapet's staff. In St. Luke, flying angels make orans gestures toward the evangelist. In St. John, however, the angels are replaced with fields of eight-pointed stars (there are twenty-six stars, thirteen in each spandrel, which seems not to be significant in numerology).[17] The equivalence of stars and angels is little noticed in the language of iconography, but it is a theme of great antiquity. In Job 38:7 it is said that the morning stars "sang together" at the creation, and they are described as the "sons of God," language which is certainly not referring to inanimate lights in the heavens. In the representation of the tomb of Christ in the baptistery of Dura Europus, the angels who were seen to sit "one at the head and one at the feet" (John 20:12) are represented by stars at either end of the sarcophagus.[18] In accounts of the coming of the Magi, the guide of the Magi is sometimes said to be a star (as in Matt. 2:2) and sometimes an angel; the Armenian Infancy Gospel alleges that it was the angel Gabriel who summoned them to Bethlehem,[19] and the Arabic Infancy Gospel relates that on their return, "there appeared to them an angel in the form of that star which had before guided them on their journey."[20] The iconography of the Nativity and the Adoration of the Magi reflects this interchangeability of angel and star, showing at times one, at times the other.[21] The fields of stars surrounding the cross or Christ himself, then, should not be taken as astronomical representations but as symbolic language for the choirs of angels that surround Christ in his glory.[22] So, here in the span-

[14] Eusebius, *Historia Ecclesiastica*, 2, 15; 2, 22; 3, 23–24; 3, 39, 16; *Eusebius' History of the Church*, trans. G. A. Williamson (New York, 1966), 88–89, 97, 128–34, 152.

[15] The eleventh-century Mułni Gospel and its relatives also employ this architectural background for John. Tatiana Izmailova, *Haykakan Manrankarč'ut'yun: Hovannes Sandłkavanec'i* (Erevan, 1986), pls. 5, 14, 24.

[16] On the Western sources for this use of evangelist symbols, see Helen C. Evans, *Armenian Manuscript Illumination;* on birds and beasts in the capitals of the canon tables, see above, pp. 175–76.

[17] On Armenian number symbolism see Thomson, "Number Symbolism and Patristic Exegesis," 117–38.

[18] Grabar, *Christian Iconography*, pl. 44.

[19] *Armenian Infancy Gospel*, 5, 10 (in Peeters, *Évangiles apocryphes*, II, 97).

[20] *Arabic Gospel of the Infancy of the Saviour,* chap. 7, *ANF*, VIII, 406, Constantin von Tischendorf, *Evangelia Apocrypha* (Hildesheim, rpr. 1966), 184.

[21] Schiller, *Iconography of Christian Art*, I, figs. 152 ff.

[22] See, for example, the mosaic of S. Apollinare in Classe, Ravenna (Schiller, *Iconography of Christian Art*, I, fig. 405) or the Sinai icon of the Ancient of Days (Grabar, *Christian Iconography*, fig. 287). Most striking is the cupola mosaic of the Baptistery of S. Marco, Venice, Kirschbaum, *Lexikon der christlichen Ikonographie*, I, 638, fig. 11.

drels of St. John, the stars continue the iconography of the spandrels of the preceding evangelists; the multiplication of stars must be meant to imply the infinity of the angelic hosts.

The framing of St. John makes another allusion to the angelic choirs by substituting cherubim for the evangelist's symbol in the capital. This raises the problem of the meaning of the evangelists' symbols in general, which involves the iconography of the incipit pages as well.

Each of the four Gospels in the U.C.L.A. manuscript begins with a grand zoomorphic letter, in which the evangelist's symbol twists or gestures to assume the form of the letter. In each letter the figure carries a Gospel book; for St. Mark's symbol a pair of lions have been used. When Der Nersessian fifty years ago outlined the history of the Armenian zoomorphic letter, she embraced a general "oriental origin" for the phenomenon and found the earliest Armenian example in a manuscript from Sebaste, Erevan, Mat. 331, in the year 1066.[23] She has since observed that the incipit pages of Mat. 331 are subsequent additions to the manuscript;[24] they were probably painted in the 1270s in Cilicia. Accordingly, the introduction of the zoomorphic letter has been reexamined by Evans, who has linked its emergence, in Skevṙa in the 1170s, to similar letters in Benedictine manuscripts from Monte Cassino.[25] The founder of the scriptorium of Skevṙa, Nersēs Lambronacʿi, had a special interest in Benedictine monasticism and had Benedictine manuscripts translated into Armenian. The fact that the symbols are used in the "Jeromian" man-lion-ox-eagle order could also be seen as evidence of a Western borrowing; it is significant that Byzantine manuscripts used a number of different sequences for the symbols, and when in Palaeologan times the Jeromian sequence finally became standard in Byzantine art, it was part of a wider pattern of Western influence following the Crusades.[26] Yet the history of the evangelists' symbol in the initial letter in Armenia starts a century earlier, and the man-lion-ox-eagle ordering of the evangelists' symbols was familiar in Armenia even earlier.

The evolution of the evangelist symbol in the zoomorphic initial can be developed in two steps. The first consisted of adding to the initials the heads or forequarters of the four beasts, which can be observed in Ereven Mat. 3793 of 1053, and in the Mułni Gospel of the middle of the eleventh century, Erevan, Mat. 7736.[27] A second step is reached in Hṙomkla in 1166 when the artist of Erevan, Mat. 7347 introduces the full-fledged zoomorphic letter, the entire evangelist symbol posing in the form of the initial letter.[28] Since the evangelist symbols are known in this role in Western art from Carolingian and even pre-Carolingian times, there can be no question that the ultimate derivation was Western, and Evans seems correct in tracing a Benedictine path of transmission.[29] In all of the Armenian uses of the evangelist symbols, however, it should be noted that the order of the symbols remained the Jeromian order.

However, before the evangelists' symbols appeared in Armenian evangelist portraits the meaning of the symbols was already familiar in Armenia, and the order was the so-called Jeromian man-lion-ox-eagle order. In his exploration of the evangelist symbols in Byzantine Gospels, Nelson noted that Jerome seems to have taken his ordering of the four symbols from an earlier source in a biblical exegete whom he much admired, Epiphanius of Salamis.[30] In his wide-ranging introduction to biblical exegesis, which is entitled *On Weights and Measures*, composed in 392, Epiphanius explained the meaning of the four beasts. Because the work was early translated into Armenian and circulated widely, it should be regarded as the basic text on this subject for Armenian art; indeed, one can confirm its use in Siwnikʿ from its appearance in Venice, San Lazzaro 265, illustrated by Tʿoros Taronecʿi in 1317–18.[31] After explaining the special preeminence of the first four books of Scripture, namely, Genesis, Exodus, Leviticus, and Numbers, Epiphanius takes the occasion to enlarge on the special significance of the number four, and in this context he introduces the four beasts of Ezekiel.

> There are four rivers out of Eden, four quarters of the world, four seasons of the year, four watches in the night, four successive times for prayers in a day and (corresponding) periods, four *xestai* in the *stamnos* measure for the manna,

[23] Der Nersessian, *Manuscrits*, 41–43, 67–69.

[24] Der Nersessian, *Arm. Mss. Walters*, 29, n. 77.

[25] Helen C. Evans, "Cilician Figurative Letters and the West," *17th International Byzantine Congress, Abstracts of Short Papers* (Washington, D.C., 1986), 110–11; published in full in her dissertation, *Armenian Manuscript Illumination*.

[26] Nelson, *The Iconography of Preface and Miniature*, 15–53.

[27] Izmailova, *Arm. miniatjura XI veka*, pls. 57–63, and 89–96.

[28] See Evans, notes 16 and 25, above.

[29] Wilhelm Köhler, *Die karolingischen Miniaturen*, 4 vols. (Berlin, 1930–60); E. H. Zimmerman, *Vorkarolingische Miniaturen*, 4 vols. (Berlin, 1916).

[30] Nelson, *Iconography of Preface and Miniature*, 13, note 47.

[31] See below, Appendix C, no. 51. Armenian manuscripts attribute a great many works to Epiphanius, many of them apocryphal. I. Hausherr, "Spiritualité arménienne," 864.

> four spiritual creatures which were composed of four faces, which typify the coming of the Messiah. One had the face of a man, because the Messiah was born a man in Bethlehem, as Matthew teaches. One had the face of a lion, as Mark proclaims him coming up from the Jordan, a lion king, as also somewhere it is written: "The Lord has come up as a lion from the Jordan." One had the face of an ox, as Luke proclaims—not he alone, but also the other Evangelists—him who, at the appointed time of the ninth hour, like an ox in behalf of the world was offered up on the cross. One had the face of an eagle as John proclaims the Word who came from heaven and was made flesh and flew to heaven like an eagle after the resurrection with the Godhead.[32]

That there were four evangelists, no more no less, is of course an important issue in defining the canon of Sacred Scripture.[33] Apocryphal gospels must not be allowed the status of the four Gospels, and nothing in any of the four can be questioned. Four is therefore the number that guarantees authenticity. To Epiphanius it was a number that was predetermined in the divine plan from the foundation of the world. God decided on four evangelists, the way he decided on four rivers of Eden, four quarters of the earth or four winds: they are part of the cosmic order of the world. Hence the beasts that adorn the framing of the evangelists and the facing incipit pages should be seen as further guarantee of the authenticity of the evangelists' texts.

One can go a step further in interpreting this iconography, for in Christian exegesis Ezekiel's vision of the coming of the Messiah (Ezek. 1:4–28) was interpreted as a vision of the four evangelists. Epiphanius explains how each of the symbols represents the Messiah under a different aspect: the man signifies Christ's humanity, the lion his kingship, the ox his sacrifice, and the eagle the Word. The representation of Luke's oxen trussed up as if for sacrifice certainly alludes to this symbolic interpretation. In this way the four creatures are taken as prophetic signs and the writings of the four evangelists are authenticated by their correspondence to the Old Testament prophecies of Christ's coming.

At the same time, the four spiritual creatures—and with them the four evangelists whom they signify—are identified by Epiphanius as the cherubim, the highest rank of the angelic hosts. In this he also followed Ezekiel, who describes the four beasts as cherubim, wheeling about under the throne of the Lord (Ezek. 10:1–22). This level of symbolism is alluded to in the U.C.L.A. Gospel by the substitution of cherubim for the eagles in the framing capitals of St. John's portrait, and in insertion of venerating angels in the spandrels. The four evangelists are more than human; they rank immediately below the throne of God. This indeed is not an especially Armenian idea; the Byzantine liturgy and the Byzantine iconography of the beasts surrounding the throne of Christ made the same connections.[34] The creatures-cherubim-evangelists are assigned the worship of the Trinity in singing without intermission the "holy, holy, holy" of the celestial liturgy. The evangelists, then, must not be seen simply as sacred historians, writing what they have seen or heard of the life of Christ, but as quasi-angelic witnesses, who stand closest of the saints to the Divinity and, therefore, in the neo-Platonic transmission of revelation, are the first and fullest partakers in the mysteries that they pass on to their readers. It is the special accomplishment of the Second Painter that he could convey so much of this in his set of portrait-incipit pages.

Three further elements of iconography remain on the incipit pages: the headpiece, the motifs in the margin above the headpiece, and the cross-as-tree-of-life in the right-hand margin. In part this contains a reprise of the symbols of the evangelists. The cross on Mark's incipit page is carried on a fantastic interlace of birds, fish, men, and monkeys, which surround a column of the four evangelists' symbols, now in man-eagle-lion-ox order. Lions appear again above the headpiece of Matthew's incipit, now demonstrating their strength by pouncing on deer. The motifs above the other headpieces repeat birds already seen in the canon tables—aquatic birds or others—which should be interpreted in the same spirit. The luscious decoration of the headpieces and the crosses should also be taken as allusions to the paradisiac content of the canon tables—abstract decoration in which to bathe one's eyes before reading the text itself and symbols of Christ's advent. The crosses are especially eloquent in the richness of their variety. Like the tradition of *xačʿkʿars*, these crosses are a peculiarly Armenian development, marking the beginning of each Gospel with the sign of Christ. They are not known

[32] James Elmer Dean, *Epiphanius' Treatise on Weights and Measures, the Syriac Version* (Chicago, 1935), 52. The Greek original of this treatise being lost, Dean has translated the Syriac.

[33] R. M. Grant, "The New Testament Canon," *Cambridge History of the Bible*, ed. P. R. Ackroyd and C. F. Evans (Cambridge, 1970), 284–307.

[34] Guillaume de Jerphanion, "Les Noms des quatre animaux et le commentaire liturgique de Pseudo-Germain," in *La Voix des monuments: Notes et études d'archéologie chrétienne* (Paris, 1930), 250–59.

in Byzantine manuscripts, but they begin to appear in the eleventh century, growing out of fairly restrained interlace patterns, and gradually develop in complexity and size until they extend the height of the page.[35] Like the cross that appears on the last of the canon tables, it is the signal of the arrival of the plenitude of revelation in Christ, "the vessel of our salvation and the crown of the Church, the divine sign coming as the pride of the Christians and the terror of the faithless."[36]

[35] Among the earliest are those in Venice, San Lazzaro 141/102 and 888; Janashian, *Armenian Miniature Paintings*, pls. 49 and 51.

[36] Nersēs Šnorhali, *Commentary*, chap. 16 (Appendix D, below).

CHAPTER NINE

Conclusion

The disparate evidence surveyed in the preceding chapters suggests a simple conclusion, and that might be called the principal thesis of this book, namely, that there existed a distinctively Armenian way of illuminating the Gospel. This Armenian approach was less a formula of style—though the manner of painting is distinctive enough—than a frame of mind. A distinctively Iranian cultural background, a theological separateness studiously cultivated, a self-conscious literature of great richness, ancient Christian rituals jealously guarded for centuries—these involved distinct patterns of thought and behavior in Armenia that gave shape to Armenian art. Thus, in spite of centuries of intellectual and artistic interchange with Byzantine neighbors and Western proselytizers, Armenia developed an iconographic tradition of its own, which exhibited a remarkable durability. Of this the U.C.L.A. Gospel, at the opening of the fourteenth century, remains an important witness. This Armenian tradition is difficult to define in a word, for its Christian content is shared, in its broad lines, by the whole medieval world. Nevertheless, the emphases are different, and over and over again one finds familiar themes being used in an unfamiliar way. Having followed the long route of patiently reading the nuances of images and painstakingly searching for their intelligibility in the Armenian sources, one is in a position to summarize the main lines of the tradition as manifest in this material. The addition of all the nuanced readings of individual subjects yields not simply a random collection of eccentric components, but a consistent and coherent tradition. The tradition has clear, salient characteristics that constitute in some sense a logical whole.

In the evangelists' portraits the four holy authors are given two roles. Their representation in front of the holy cities of Jerusalem, Alexandria, Antioch, and Ephesus stresses their place as representatives of the ancient church traditions of those centers. One might call this their earthly ecclesiastical role. At the same time, the authors are accompanied by their beasts, which not only certify the authentic message of their books but also identify the evangelists with the cherubim, the highest rank of the angelic hosts. The divine message is mediated by these angelic seers.

The decoration of the canon tables manifests a spiritual aesthetic that is quite different from anything enunciated in Byzantium or the West. A frank materialism, that is, an acceptance of the physical world in itself for its pure sensuous beauty, underlies the Armenian approach to the canon tables. Nersēs Šnorhali epitomizes this attitude in his saying: "God gave the lover of material things understanding of the heavenly." The way of ascent is not necessarily a way of renunciation, the *via negativa* of Christian asceticism; a *via affirmativa* opens up an alternate route. The pleasurable things of the world of taste and sound and sight are, to the initiate, a means of understanding the things that are invisible. On this basis the canon table commentators developed an open-ended system of mystical meanings attached to the tables that invite the reader to discover the entire mystery of salvation in the rich but largely abstract decorations. The sequence of ten tables are ten dwellings, tents, or tabernacles in which the Divinity has revealed itself to mankind from the Creation of the World to the foundation of the Church, or the New Jerusalem.

There are interesting points of coincidence between the content attributed to this abstract art and that found in the narrative subjects of the book. In the Armenian approach to the canon tables, two kinds of themes predominate: soteriological and ecclesiological. Though the pious viewer is given free rein to enlarge on the subjects according to his own reflection on Scripture, the commentators suggest that the thread that holds the decoration together is the unfolding of God's plan of salvation in the church. Dionysian echoes resonate in this "plan," insofar as God's revelation of himself is shared through three successive ranks of nine choirs of angels, who are described as "priesthoods" of angels. In God's relationship to mankind, however, the Armenian view reflects a wider East Christian view, which saw revelation as a secret given in Paradise to Adam and preserved in a priesthood of which Adam was the first member.[1] In spite of his sin, Adam preserved the "recollection of the good," which he passed on to his seed until its original prototype, namely, Christ, should appear. The beginning and end of human history are tied together, and they are tied together by a tradition and a priesthood. Abraham and Melchisedek and Moses and Aaron are the personal links in this sacred tradition; the successive tabernacles, altars, and temples of the Old Testament are its material embodiment. Yet the tradition has its fulfillment only in the rejection of the Jews. The temple of Solomon must be replaced by the church of Christ; life under the Old Law is sinful and shadowy, the Jews are peacocks interested only in external display. In the New Jerusalem all the churches of the world will be united.

The abstract nature of canon table decoration does not permit one to spell out this theme more specifically; this is rather the burden of the individual narrative subjects in the Gospel, the analysis of which has been the chief concern of this study.

In the narrative iconography one must first note the general independence of the Armenian tradition from that of Western Europe and from that of Byzantium. Although a great deal of Western material was available and borrowed in far-off Siwnikʿ, as noticed by Der Nersessian and Korkhmazian,[2] it is surprising how little Western iconography appears in the U.C.L.A. Gospel. The clearest instances of borrowings are all minor details of peripheral importance, such as the tonsure of Peter (*page 103* and elsewhere), the Crusader banners on ships (*pages 211 and 227*), the widow's couvrechef (*page 263*), the pilgrim's garb of Christ (*page 448*). These demonstrate the artists' contact with Western manuscripts and perhaps indicate their interest in being fashionable or au courant; it is significant that all these examples belong to the category of dress or fashions. But it has not been possible to assign any meaningful iconographic intention to these minor alterations.

On the other hand, when the Armenian iconography has Western parallels in more significant motifs, they seem to have been arrived at separately in the two traditions, and the Armenian use of the motif is well justified by Armenian interpretations of the subject. Thus the third woman in the Women at the Tomb (*page 179*) is common in the art of the West, but it is also traditional in Armenian art and appeared already in the Syrian Rabbula Gospel in the sixth century. At the same time, Armenian commentary on the subject, quite independent of Western influence, always insisted on the importance of the third woman, the Mother of God, in this scene. Similarly, the Mocking of Christ (*page 172*) seems to have been developed quite independently in Armenia and the West; certainly no Western artist would think of crowning Christ with cacti. Since the story is found in three of the evangelists, it is hardly surprising that Western and Armenian artists both developed the subject; what is surprising is rather the Byzantine squeamishness that would not allow them to show Christ's humiliation.

The parallel appearance of Christ Ascending the Cross (*page 283*) in Armenia and the West must be taken as evidence of the impact of Eastern iconography on the West rather than the reverse. As an extrabiblical detail of iconography, the ladder of ascent is not likely to have been invented twice independently. But the early eleventh-century appearance of the subject in the Vehapʿaṙ Gospel antedates Western examples. Since so obscure a manuscript is not likely to have been copied in the West, one must suppose that the subject had a wider circulation in the Christian East than is now evident, and this somehow found its way to Western Europe. The fact that Syrian and Armenian exegetes had developed the symbolic connections between the cross and Jacob's ladder lends credence to this hypothesis.

More considerable than the occasional Western intrusions is the Byzantine component of the U.C.L.A. iconography. The basic program of the U.C.L.A. Gospel was taken from the ancient and venerable Vehapʿaṙ Gospel; of its fifty-six miniatures, forty-six are of subjects shared with the Vehapʿaṙ Gospel, and forty-three are at exactly the same place in the program. In thirty-four of the miniatures a substantial iconographic dependence on the Vehapʿaṙ Gospel has been demonstrated, in composition, specific gestures, or motifs. To the program of the Vehapʿaṙ Gospel, however, the U.C.L.A. Gospel added ten new subjects (see Table 8); it also enlarged many others to full-page format, a format not used in the narrative scenes of its model (see Table 1). Many of these changes can be accounted for as attempts to enrich the Vehapʿaṙ Gospel with the Byzantine "festival" set. The "festival" set is somewhat flexible, but the follow-

[1] This priesthood from Adam is witnessed in the Syrian *Book of the Cave of Treasures* and the *Armenian Infancy Gospel*. Cf. Ugo Monneret de Villard, *Le leggende orientalie sui magi evangelici*, Studi e Testi 163 (Vatican City, 1952); Esayi Tayecʿi, *Ankanon Girkʿ Nor Ktakaranacʿ: Tʿangaran Haykakan Hin ew Nor Dprutʿeancʿ*, II (Venice, 1898); Peeters, *Évangiles apocryphes, II: Évangile de l'enfance*.

[2] Der Nersessian, "Western Iconographic Themes in Armenian Manuscripts," *Études*, 611–30; Emma Korkhmazyan, "The Sources of the Old Testament Illustrations in the Bible Illuminated by Tʿoros Taronatsi (Matenadaran no. 206)," *Fourth International Symposium on Armenian Art: Theses of Reports* (Erevan, 1985), 209–10.

ing ten images in the U.C.L.A. Gospel may be said to represent the set: the Annunciation, the Transfiguration, the Raising of Lazarus, the Entry into Jerusalem, the Last Supper, the Crucifixion, the Descent from the Cross, the Women at the Tomb, the Ascension, the Promise of the Holy Spirit (and one might add the robbed Baptism). It might be questioned, however, whether such iconography needs to be seen as a "Byzantinization" of the Armenian program. In the first place, it is unclear which of these subjects, if any, were specifically Byzantine inventions—that is, were first introduced in Constantinople rather than Jerusalem, for example. Secondly, all of these subjects had been in circulation in Armenia and the Christian East since the tenth or eleventh centuries, if not earlier, and must have been regarded as an integral part of their artistic language. Most significant in this analysis of the subjects, however, is the degree to which the U.C.L.A. Gospel alters these compositions. Although in Middle Byzantine art these "festival" images reached a certain iconographic standardization, the U.C.L.A. Gospel seems intent on avoiding the standard. Indeed, not a single subject can be said to be an exact copy of the Byzantine standard.

A careful reading of the iconography alongside the Armenian sources has demonstrated in most instances that Armenian modifications of these standard subjects are not casual, but meaningful reworkings to allow the iconography to carry content that was important in Armenia. The content is sometimes tied to Armenian christological teaching, sometimes to the defense of the Armenian church and its ritual, sometimes to Armenian social and economic concerns. In most instances the peculiarity of the Armenian imagery can be best explained by appealing to exegetical sources. In this connection the *Commentary on the Gospel according to Matthew* by Yovhannēs Erznkac‘i is especially precious because of the author's demonstrable links to Esayi Nč‘ec‘i, the patron of the U.C.L.A. Gospel, and to T‘oros Taronec‘i, the last painter to work on it.

From the overwhelmingly scriptural and exegetical nature of the manuscript output of Glajor during the half-century of its flourishing one may conclude that the chief study of the monastery was biblical commentary. This indeed was Esayi Nč‘ec‘i's lifelong work.[3] The repeated connections of the iconography of the U.C.L.A. Gospel and its tradition to commentaries on the Gospels support the belief that manuscript illustration, at least in this tradition, must be seen as an extension of the process of commentary. Exegesis is the paradigm for the picture-language of Gospel illustration. The pictures serve not to decorate but to elucidate or interpret the text. This method of reading the images introduces a very rich-textured iconography, full of associations, allusions, subplots, symbolism, reminiscences, and anticipations, all of which get washed out if one rests content with the approach of literal reading, simply identifying figures and recounting stories.

If this seems an overly recondite and bookish approach to the imagery, it must be insisted that this is not a popular or folk art. It is the work of scholarly monks and priests for an audience of their peers. On the other hand, the exegesis of Yovhannēs Erznkac‘i—and by the same token that of the U.C.L.A. Gospel imagery—is by no means abstruse, speculative, or innovative, but stands squarely in the age-old Armenian tradition of exegesis starting with Chrysostom, Ephraem, and Gregory the Illuminator. A great deal more remains to be learned about Armenian exegesis, but the available evidence seems to indicate that the concepts involved here were accessible and in wide circulation in Armenia. The methods of interpretation were also very familiar. Elaborate allegories were avoided in favor of straightforward exempla for Christian living drawn out of an exact reading of the text; theological issues were argued from specific details of the narrative; and more profound lessons were drawn through what can be called mystical synecdoche. This latter method, first championed by Ephraem, allowed one to find in each event of the life of Christ a microcosm of his entire saving work for mankind, often looking back to the Creation and Fall and forward to the restoration of Paradise.

By these methods the illustrator-exegetes (for there is no better term for the creators of this iconography) developed several major themes in the U.C.L.A. Gospel. The largest theme is clearly the soteriological. The work of Christ is the restoration of mankind: greeting the Canaanite, he is Joshua returned to greet his bride the Church who, unlike Israel, reaches out to receive him (*page 99,* the Petition of the Canaanite); raising the daughter of Jairus, he restores Eve to eternal life (*page 218,* the Raising of the Daughter of Jairus); transfigured on the mountain, he transports his disciples back (or forward?) to Paradise reclaimed by his Resurrection (*page 106,* the Transfiguration); making clay to cure the blind man, Christ reveals his "hidden glory" as "architect of creation" (*page 509,* Cure of the Man Born Blind); suffering in the garden or crowned with thorns, he undoes the curse of sweat and thorns which Adam brought on mankind (*pages 160 and 172,* the Agony in the Garden and the Mocking of Christ); climbing the ladder of the cross, he answers Jacob's vision of

[3] See above, p. 24.

angels climbing to heaven to open the way for mankind (*page 283*, Christ Ascending the Cross); ascending into heaven, he is marking out with his flesh the "new pathway" of human ascent to God (*page 453*, the Ascension).

Christ is also depicted nine times in the U.C.L.A. Gospel as the Divine Physician, a major development of the soteriological theme. Four cures of the blind are illustrated (*pages 124, 235, 250, 509*), the paralytics at Capernaum and Bethesda are both shown (*pages 336 and 484*), as are the cures of the epileptic (*page 108*), the leper (*page 197*), and the woman with the hemorrhage (*page 216*). Christ the Physician is a prominent theme in Syrian exegesis, and Murray calls it Ephraem's favorite appellation for the savior.[4] His cures of the body are emblems of his more radical cure of all mankind.

Second in prominence to soteriological interpretations, and sometimes implied in them, are subjects that carry an ecclesiological content. This is, of course, entirely in keeping with the patronage of the manuscript; churchmen are by vocation committed to the interests of the church and arguments about the legitimacy of orders and the role of the church in the world are of great importance to them. The Genealogy of Christ (*page 28*) is interpreted as carrying Christ's inheritance of priesthood—source and prototype of hereditary priesthood in the Armenian church; the Blessing of the Children (*page 117*) is an ordination ceremony constituting the next generation of priests, so that "those children, having been strengthened by the hands of the Lord and having arrived at the age of maturity, became preachers of the gospel, and apostles of the savior, and even became martyrs for him"; the call of the apostles, illustrated twice in the U.C.L.A. Gospel (*pages 193–194*), underscores the vocation of the clergy as "hunters" of men, a vocation developed further in the Samaritan at the Well and the Promise of the Holy Spirit (*pages 480 and 538*). The latter shows the unusual Armenian iconography of literal tongues to illustrate the Spirit's gift of eloquence to the apostles.

Closely related to ecclesiological concerns is the anti-Semitism of the U.C.L.A. Gospel. Medieval man seems to have been incapable of conceptualizing the founding of the church except in terms of the rejection of Israel. This theme appears in many situations: in the Petition of the Canaanite, who represents the church of the Gentiles (*page 99*); in the Petition of the Mother of James and John, who may represent the Jews and the Gentiles (*page 122*); in the Way of the Cross, in which Simon accepts the Cross while the Jews reject Christ (*page 173*). In other miniatures the Jews are singled out by being represented with striped headdress: the Beheading of John the Baptist (*page 92*); the first Entry into Jerusalem (*page 126*); Pilate Washes His Hands (*page 171*); the Question of Tribute to Caesar (*page 259*). These last three illustrate situations of conflict between Christ and the Jews, and to them one might add the special sense of confrontation that the Second Painter has put into the second Entry into Jerusalem (*page 252*), and the Raising of Lazarus (*page 522*). But the subjects of Christ's betrayal by Judas and trial deal most explicitly with the issue: the Last Supper (*page 156*); the Betrayal (*page 162*); the Message from Pilate's Wife (*page 169*); and Pilate Washes his Hands and the Self-Curse of the Jews (*page 171*). Concerning the latter two, Yovhannēs Erznkacʿi tried to deal with the issue of Jewish guilt, absolving Pilate's Jewish wife for her belief in Christ while he condemned contemporary unconverted Jews for "continuing in their sin."

Ruled by Mongol overlords and surrounded by Islamic culture, Armenians in fourteenth-century Siwnikʿ must have felt themselves in an ever more precarious situation. But like Constantinople in its final years, Armenia rejected all pledges of help from the outside that might in any way compromise its integrity. Instead of looking abroad for a lifesaver, Armenia looked within and sought strength in its oldest and most genuine traditions. This is the way one must understand the fervor with which Esayi Nčʿecʿi and his collaborators rejected the advances of the Catholic Church and reasserted age-old Armenian doctrines. This is more than an automatic defense mechanism; it was a serious attempt to understand the logic of the old Armenian positions in contrast to the new teachings. Two major themes were the focus of this theological effort, Christology and the Sacraments.

In two miniatures, the Transfiguration and Christ in the Synagogue (*pages 106 and 327*), traces appear of the oldest level of Armenian christological thinking, namely, adoptionism. Since it does not yet appear in the writings of Glajor, one must assume this to be a kind of latent or subconscious element. Perhaps among the Armenians who from all sides sought the sanctuary of Glajor minorities of Paulicians or other heterodox groups were included. Easier to document at Glajor is concern with the Armenian doctrine of the two natures of Christ. This concern is echoed in the Entry into Jerusalem (*page 126*), in which Christ sits on the ass and the foal as the Divinity indwells his human body and soul. The affirmation of Christ's palpable humanity is made often in connection with his passion in Yovhannēs Erznkacʿi, but it appears in

[4] Murray, *Symbols*, 199–203.

striking form in connection with the miniature of the First Storm at Sea (*page 211*). It is an "apparition" of Christ which the apostles first mistake for a ghost, but which Peter will prove is a human, consubstantial with himself, by making physical contact with him. The Second Storm at Sea (*page 227*) illustrates the opposite side of the mystery; while his body sleeps, the Divinity in Christ is ever awake and watchful. In these respects, of course, Armenian Christology is perfectly "orthodox." The Monophysite character of the unity of natures in Christ was connected with the great mysteries of the Raising of Lazarus and the Crucifixion (*pages 522 and 561*). This last especially stands as a most eloquent statement of the Armenian point of view; even in death, the body of Christ cannot be separated from the Divinity.

Equally important in this last phase of Armenian culture was the defense of Armenian ritual. The ceremonies which had guaranteed their survival and prosperity would continue to sustain them. The miniatures of the Last Supper, the Wedding Feast at Cana, and Christ's Apparition by the Sea of Galilee all illustrate the Eucharist, and the last even illustrates the rite of Communion by immixture in defense of this Armenian practice against the propaganda of the Latins (*pages 156, 469, and 570*). The representation of the separate streams of blood and water in the Crucifixion (*page 561*) is intended to refute Greek insistence of mixing water in the eucharistic wine. At the same time, the powerful stance of the dead Christ on the Cross is a vivid proclamation of the Armenian version of the Trisagion Hymn from the celebration of the Eucharist: "Holy (is) God, holy and mighty, holy and immortal, who was crucified for us." Esayi Nč'ec'i exhorted the faithful to frequent participation in the Eucharist.[5] Christ Reading in the Synagogue (*page 327*) shows the manner of reading lessons at the *grakal* in an Armenian church. The necessity of confession and the right of the church to forgive sins is also urged in the U.C.L.A. imagery. This is naturally developed in the Paralytic at Capernaum and the Anointing at Simon's House (*pages 336 and 351*), in which Christ speaks directly of the forgiveness of sins. It is also prominent in the Petrine subjects: Peter Receives the Keys (*page 103*), Peter's Denial (*pages 166 and 438*), and Christ's Apparition by the Sea of Galilee (*page 570*).

Perhaps even miniatures dealing with questions of money and trade should be subsumed under church-related themes. The Cleansing of the Temple (*page 126*), the Question of Tribute to Caesar (*page 259*), the Widow's Mite (*page 263*), the Parable of the Cunning Steward (*page 403*), and the Samaritan at the Well (*page 480*) all seem to imply strong justifications of the financial support of the church. This may seem self-serving, coming from a clerical context; but since only church property was tax-exempt it may well have seemed that the church was the only vessel of salvation left, even in the business world.

[5] See above, p. 30.

APPENDIX A

Colophons and Inscriptions

transcribed and translated by Avedis K. Sanjian

Page 1. Remember Vaxa*n* [sic], the last owner of this (Gospel).

Page 24a. Remember the owner of this holy Gospel and say, "God have mercy." Amen!

Page 24b. Ostan, servant of God.

Page 24b. /// (I, Ostan?) wrote that I am a servant of the Holy Mother of God at Surb Karapet.

Page 25. By consent of the congregation of the church of Mec Xōǰencʿ, this holy Gospel was offered to the priest Yōvakim Abraham, so that he would pray for them all. By consent of the congregation, I, Yarutʿiwn Yakobian, testify to this. Shamsi 23, in the year 209 (= March 23, A.D. 1824).

Yarutʿiwn Yakobian
(seal)

Page 25. In the year 209, on Hamiray 20 (= December 6, A.D. 1824) /// I, *žamarar* (i.e., officiating priest) Yōvakim inscribed (this) concerning my children Barełēn; my daughter Mērxatʿun, who is age ///; my son Sarkʿis, 7 years old; Martiros, 5 years old; Galēstan, 2 years old.

Page 25. I offered this holy Gospel, the priceless divine treasure, to my beloved Mayiš Ostan for his enjoyment and for the enjoyment of his family, together with my fervent prayers that this shall always be a protector and deliverer from all evil, and protector against all temptations and unexpected evil hazards. Today is the first day of May, in the year 1901 of our Lord.

Archpriest Xačʿ(atur) Tēr
Martiros Tēr Yovakimian

Page 156. *Žamarar* (i.e., officiating priest) Ohanēs, son of the priest Yakob, in the year 104 (= A.D. 1719/20).

Page 1. Inscription at the top of blank page, in *bolorgir*: *Զվերջին ստացօղ սորին Վախանն յիշեցէք:*

Page 24a. Inscription in *bolorgir*: *Զըստացօղ սուրբ Աւետարանիս յիշեցէք և Աստուած ողորմի ասացէք. ամէն:*

Page 24b. Inscription in *notragir*: *Ոստանս ծառայ Աստուծոյ:*

Page 24b. Inscription in lower margin in crude *notragir*: /// (*Ոստանս*?) *գիրեցի թէ ես ձառայ սուրբ Աստուածածին ի սուրբ Կարապետիս:*

Page 25. Inscription in *notragir*: *Սուրբ Աւետարանս Մեծ Խօջէնց եկեղեցուն ժողովրդեանն գիտութեամբն ընծա(յ)եցին տէր Յօվակիմ Աբրահամին որ աղօթող լինի բոլորին: Ժողովրդեանն գիտութեամբն վկայեմ տէր Յարութիւն Յակոբեան. թիւն 209 շամսի* 23 (= *23 Մարտ, 1824*):

Կնիք՝ Յարութիւն Յակոբեանի

Page 25. Inscription in *notragir*: *Թիւն 209 Համիրայ Ի̅ (= Դեկտ. 6, 1824)* /// *ես ժամարար տէր Յովակիմս գրեցի որ իմ որդաց Բարեղէն, զդուստրս Մէրխաթուն, տարեքէն որ է* /// *իմ որդի Սարքիսէն Է̅ տարեքէն, Մարտիրոսին Ե̅ տարեքէն, Գալէստանէն Բ̅ տարեքէն:*

Page 25. Inscription in modern script: *Սոյն այս սուրբ Աւետարան, անգին գանձի աստուածային, ընծայեցի իմ սիրելի Մայիչ Ոստանի, ի վայելս իւր և իւրայնոց, հանդերձ իմ ջերմեռանդ հայցուածովք, զի լիցի սա միշտ պահապան և փրկիչ ամենայն չարեաց և պահպանող ամենայն փորձութեանց և անակնկալ չար դիպուածոց: Այսօր է մին Մայիսի 1901 թուին Տեառն:*

Խաչ (ատուր) Տէր Մարտիրոս Աւագ քահանայ
Տէր Յովակիմեան

Page 156. Inscription below the full-page miniature of the Last Supper, in *notragir*: *Ժամարար Ոհանէս որդի տէր Յակոբին. ՃԴ. ամին* (= *1719/20*).

Page 182. I beg you to remember in the Lord, O holy readers, the baroness Vaxax, the last owner of this holy Gospel, and may God remember you.

Page 227. O great master of mine, Esayi, remember this unworthy disciple of yours, T'oros.

Page 297. O holy readers, I beg you to remember in your prayers the baroness Vaxax, the last owner of this resplendent book, and may God remember you. Amen!

Page 453. I beseech you to remember in the Lord Jesus the unworthy painter T'oros, who labored later.

Page 459. O holy readers, I beg you to remember in your prayers the baroness Vaxax, the last owner of this (Gospel), and may God remember you. Amen and may it so be.

Page 575–577. Colophon of 1377.

[p. 575] Glory to the unity of rule and trinity of persons of the Father and the Son and the Holy Spirit, now and always and forever and ever. Amen! [p. 576] Those who would keep the eye of the mind pure and clear, with heavenly intent(?) toward the uncreated light and the vision of the intelligible, are totally unconcerned about things that are of this world and that lead by way of transitory and corruptible natures. Rather, they (look) entirely (to) the flame of love which the living fire has put in our rational nature, (and) they daily kindle their souls by inextinguishable fervor, and by providing gifts of spiritual things by which they are enlightened according to the saying of the prophet chastised by God, "the commandment of the Lord is pure, enlightening the eyes" (Psalm 18:9).

Now, as an example of the same, the strong-in-faith, Christ-loving and glorious queen, baroness Vaxax, daughter of the majestic and royal prince, baron Inanik, son of the honorable baron Biwrt'ēl, son of Ēlēkum, son of Tarsayič, pursues things divine. By the vision of her intelligent eyes she shines brilliantly and sublimely, and striving for divine love she constantly engages in spiritual matters. By reason of this, she considers all bodily possessions as transitory and as nothing; rather she has acquired only life-giving possessions; that is, the divine commandments and spiritual books, the evangelical message about God by our Savior and God. With very great desire and covetous longing, she later acquired [p. 577] this

Page 182. Inscription at the end of the Gospel of Matthew in *bolorgir*: *Զվերջին ստացող սուրբ Աւետարանիս զպարոն Վախախն. աղաչեմ յիշել ի Տէր, ով սուրբ ընթերցողք, և Աստուած զձեզ յիշէ:*

Page 227. Inscription inside the miniature of Christ Walking on the Sea, written in small *bolorgir* in red ink: *Ո՛վ մե՛ծ րաբունապետ իմ Եսայի՝ յիշեա զանարժան աշակերտս քո զԹորոս:*

Page 297. Inscription on the blank page following the Index and Preface to the Gospel of Luke, in *bolorgir*: *Զվերջին ստացող լուսագարդ մատենիս, զպարոն Վախախն. աղաչեմ յիշել յաղաւթս, ո՛վ սուրբ ընթերցողք, և Աստուած զձեզ յիշէ, ամէն:*

Page 453. Inscription below the miniature of the Ascension of Christ, written in small *bolorgir* in black ink: *Զանարժան նկարագրաւղ զԹորոս, որ յետոյ աշխատեցայ. աղաչեմ յիշել ի տէր Յիսուս:*

Page 459. Inscription following the Preface to the Gospel of John, in *bolorgir*: *Զվերջին ստացող սորայ զպարոն Վախախն՝ աղաչեմ յիշել յաղաւթս ձեր, ո՛վ սուրբ ընթերցողք, և Աստուած զձեզ յիշէ. ամէն և եղիցի:*

Pages 575-577. Principal colophon, written in *bolorgir*: *Փառք եզակի տէրութեանն և եռահիւսակ անձնաւորութեանն՝ հաւր և որդոյ և հոգոյն սրբոյ, այժմ և միշտ և յաւիտեան և յաւիտեանս յաւիտենից. ամէն:*

[p. 576] *Որք ըզմտաց աչս անաղօտ և վճիտ ունիցին, երկնանըկ* (ատ?) *դիտմամբ առ էականն լոյս և իմանալեացն տեսարան, նոցին ոչինչ է փոյթ բովանդակ բընաւին ինչ որ յաշխարհի և որ ընդ հոսանուտ և եղծանելի բնութեանս բերին: Այլ միանգամայն զհուր սիրոյն, զոր հուրն կենդանի արկ ի բանական բնութիւնս, աւրըստաւրէ արծարծեն յոգիս անշիջանելի բորբոքմամբ. հոգևորացն տուր և առութեամբ, որով և լուսաւորին ըստ բանի աստուածահայր* [*աստուածահար*] *մարգարէին որ ասէ, "պատուիրանք տեառն լոյս են և լոյս տան աչաց"* (*Սաղմ. ԺԸ*, 9):

Արդ՝ ըստ նոյն ապացուցի աստուածայնոց իրաց հետեւեալ մեծահաւատ և քրիստոսասէր դըշխոյն և գերափառ արքայուհին պարոն Վախախն, դուստր վեհափառ և արքայաշուք իշխանին պարոն Ինանիկին, որդոյ մեծապատիւ պարոնին Բիւրթէլին, որդոյ Էլէկումին, որդոյ Տարսայիճին: Եւ իմանալի աչաց տեսութեամբ պայծառապէս և գերաբնաբար արտափայլեալ և փափագմամբ աստուածային սիրոյն միշտ հոգով պարապեալ: Որոյ աղագաւ զամենայն մարմնական ստացուածս անցաւոր և ոչինչ համարեալ, այլ միայն ստացուած կենդանի ստացեալ, այսինքն է զպատուիրանս աստուածայինս և զհոգէշունչ մատեանս զաւետարանական աստուածախաւս քարոզութիւնս փրկչին մերոյ և Աստուծոյ: Յոյժ փափագանաւք և մեծատենչ ըղձմամբ

book concerning God, which is called the good tidings of the kingdom of heaven, through her just and honestly earned assets, in memory of her soul and for her personal protection, and for her husband, the Christ-loving and noble prince, the baron Arłutʿay, son of J̌um, son of Ēačʿi, son of Amir Hasan, son of the prince of princes Př̌oš, and for her children granted by God, Biwrtʿēl and Liparit, and for all of her blood relatives.

Accordingly, those of you who happen upon this in reading or copying, remember in your prayers the above-mentioned last acquirer of this (book), the baroness Vaxax and her mother, the baroness Xošakʿ, who in her great piety has passed on to Christ, and her father, the baron Inanik, and all of her blood relatives, whom we have mentioned above. And may those of you who should remember, be remembered by Christ on the eternal day and in the frightful judgment, when words shall cease and deeds shall reign.

This (Gospel) was written in Vayocʿ Jor, and the monastery which is called Glajor. Later, however, it was acquired by the baroness Vaxax, through her honestly earned means, in the year 826 of the Armenians (= A.D. 1377). May the Lord God permit her to enjoy it, as well as her children, until a ripe old age, generation after generation, and children after children, forever and ever. Amen!

Page 578. In this, the year 830 of the Armenian Era (= A.D. 1381), the devout prince baron Iwanē, son of the illustrious prince baron Biwrtʿēl, joined Christ for whom he had longed. May their memory be blessed. Amen!

Pages 578–580. Colophon of 1393–1404.

[p. 578] With the assistance and powerful reinforcement of the omnipotent God, the Father, and the Son, Jesus Christ, and the all-powerful true Spirit.

During the reign of King Gēorgi, at the time when the filthy and accursed Tʿimur plundered our lands, I, baron Martiros, son of Šahanša, and my wife, baroness Ładam, daughter of baron Arłutʿay, son of J̌um, grandson of the prince of princes Př̌oš, after much effort and expense rescued, through our honest means, this our holy ancestral Gospel, which had fallen captive into the hands of foreigners, and we now hold it as our steadfast hope and for a memorial for our souls, and for the eternal repose in Christ of our kind parents. In addition, (let it be) a rampart and guardian and a source of enjoyment for our God-granted children, baron Liparit and baron Dawitʿ and baron Šahin; may the Lord God permit them to enjoy it until a ripe old age.

Accordingly, those of you who happen on this God-inspired Gospel, remember in your prayers the above-mentioned baron Martiros and baroness Ładam, and their tender children /// [lacuna].

յետոյ ստացաւ [p. 577] զաստուածախաւս մատեանս՝ որ յորջորջի աւետաւոր երկնից արքայութեանն. ի յարդար և ի հալալ ընչից իւրոց. ի յիշատակ հոգոյ և ի պաշտպանութիւն անձին իւրոյ, և առն իւրոյ քրիստոսասէր և մեծազարմ իշխանին պարոն Արղութային, որդոյ Ջումին, որդոյ Էաչոյ, որդոյ Ամիր Հասանայ, որդոյ իշխանաց իշխանին Պռօշայ: Եւ աստուածատուր զաւակացն իւրոց Բիւրթէլին և Լիպարտին. և ամենայն արեան մերձաւորաց իւրոց:

Արդ՝ որք հանդիպիք սմայ, կարդալով կամ աւրինակելով, յիշեցէք յաղաւթս զվերոյ գրեալ վերջին ստացող սորայ զպարոն Վախախն և զմայրն իւր զպարոն Խոշաքն, զփոխեցեալն մեծաւ բարեպաշտութեամբ առ Քրիստոս, և զհայրն նորայ զպարոն Ինանիկն, և զայլ ամենայն արեան մերձաւորսն իւր, զորոյ վերոյ գրեցաք: Եւ յիշողքդ յիշեալ լիջիք ի Քրիստոսէ յաներեկ աւուրն և ի սոսկալի ատենին, յորժամ բանք սպառին և գործք թագաւորեն:

Գրեցաւ սայ ի Վայոց Ձոր, ի վանս որ կոչի Գլաձոր: Բայց յետոյ ստացաւ զսայ պարոն Վախախն ի հալալ արդեանց իւրոց: Ի թվին Հայոց ՊԻԶ (*826+551=1377*): Զոր Տէր Աստուած վայելել տացէ նմայ և որդոց իւրոց մինչև ի խորին ծերութիւնն ազգաց յազգս, և որդոց մինչև յորդիս, յաւիտեանս յաւիտենից. ամէն:

Page 578. Inscription in *bolorgir*: Ցայսմ ամի էր թվ. Հայոց ՊԼ (*830+551=1381*) վերափոխեցաւ առ ցանկալին իւր Քրիստոս բարեպաշտ իշխանն պարոն Իւանէ, որդի մեծաշուք իշխանին պարոն Բիւրթելին: Որոց յիշատակն աւրհնութեամբ եղիցի. Ամէն:

Pages 578-580. Colophon, in *bolorgir*: [p. 578] Աւգնականութեամբ և կարող զօրութեամբ ամենակալին Աստուծոյ հօր և որդոյն Յիսուսի Քրիստոսի և ամենազօր հոգւոյն ճշմարտի:

Յամս թագաւորութեանն Գէորգեայ, ի ժամանակին յորում պեղծն և անիծեալն Թէմուր աւար հարկանէր զաշխարհս: Ես պարոն Մարտիրոս, որդի Շահանշի, և կենակից իմ պարոն Ղադամ, դուստր պարոն Արղութային, որդոյ Ջումին, թոռն իշխանաց իշխանին Պռոշոյ, բազում աշխատանօք և ծախիւք, ի հալալ ընչից մերոց, ազատեցաք զմեր հայրենաւոր սուրբ Աւետարանս, զի անկեալ էր գերի ի ձեռս այլոց. և ունիմք զսայ այժմ յոյս հաստատուն և յիշատակ հոգոց մերոց, և ի Քրիստոս հանգուցեալ բարի ծնողաց մերոց մինչև յաւիտեան: Այլ և պարիսպ և պահապան և ի վայելումն աստուածապարգև զաւակաց մերոց, պարոն Լիպարտին և պարոն Դաւթին և պարոն Շահինին, զոր Տէր Աստուած վայելել տացէ մինչև ի խորին ծերութիւնն:

Արդ՝ որք հանդիպիք այսմ աստուածաշունչ սուրբ Աւետարանիս, յիշեցէք յաղօթս ձեր զվերոգրեալսն, զպարոն Մարտիրոսն և պարոն Ղադամն, և զնորաբողբոջ զաւ /// (folio missing).

[p. 579] By the will of God, the omnipotent Father, by the mercy of the only begotten Son, and by the grace of the Holy Spirit, we the servants of God, Martiros, and my pious and devout wife, the baroness Ładam, daughter of the illustrious prince Arłutʿay and princess Vaxax, have offered this ancestral, holy, and exquisite Gospel to holy Ayrivankʿ and Gełard, through the intercession and at the hands of Simēon Vardapet, for the hope and love of the immortal life and the kingdom of heaven, and for the remission of our sins, for the salvation of the soul and for the indelible memory of our loyal and pious mother Vaxax, and for the prosperity of our blooming and tender children Liparit, Dawitʿ, and Šahvēl.

The monks in this holy and God-pleasing community or the servants of God-pleasing Gełard, whether of our family or of others, holy bishops, holy vardapets, holy priests, or holy monks, henceforth and until the coming of Christ, shall continuously and always, with good intentions and thoughts, remember us before God, with holy masses, fervent prayers, and compassionate supplications, and by saying "God have mercy." In addition, on the feast of John the Evangelist, they shall offer mass for us, and after the mass they shall read this, our memorial from the sanctuary, and all the monks in unison shall proclaim God immaculate and uncreated and Christ the Son. We have offered all this most willingly, as attested by Simēon Vardapet, bishop Martiros, and the monks Eremiay and Karapet.

On the other hand, we the servants of God, Simēon Vardapet, bishop Martiros, and the priests Eremiay and Karapet, and the monks of Ayrivankʿ, the servants of the holy and God-piercing Gełard, have taken an oath before God and recorded thus: that no one from among our princes or foreign princes, be they laity or clergy, has the authority or permission to remove this Gospel from Ayrivankʿ by selling or dividing or stealing or confiscating it. And whoever dares and endeavors to remove it shall be judged by God and all the saints, and he shall receive the lot and portion of Cain and Judas and [p. 580] the crucifiers, and he shall forever suffer and be tortured even as Satan, and he shall be condemned and accursed by all mankind. Amen!

Moreover, falling on my face, I beg all you holy guardians of this divinely-speaking Gospel to remember devoutly before God this humble vardapet (i.e., Simēon), as well as the holy priests Eremiay and Mesrob, who labored hard with me to bring this Gospel from Georgia. And may God remember you in His bountiful mercy. Amen! May it so be.

[p. 579] Կամաւ ամենակալին Աստուծոյ Հաւր և ողորմութեամբ որդւոյն միածնի և շնորհաւք սուրբ Հոգւոյն, մեք ծառայքս Աստուծոյ Մարտիրոս և աստուածասէր և բարեպաշտ ամուսինս պարոն Ղադամ, դուստր մեծափառ իշխանացն Արղութին և Վախախին, վասն յուսոյ և սիրոյ անմահ կենացն և երկնից արքայութեանն և վասն թողութեան մեղաց մերոց, ընծայեցաք զհայրենատուր սուրբ և զպատուական Աւետարանս Այրեվանից և սուրբ Գեղարդեանն, միջնորդութեամբ և ձեռաւք Սիմէոն վարդապետին, վասն փրկութեան Հոգւոյ և անջինջ յիշատակի հաւատարիմ և բարեպաշտ մաւրն մերոյ Վախախին, և վասն արեւշատութեան ծաղծեալ և նորաբողբոջեալ զաւակաց մերոց, Լիպարտին, Դաւթին և Շահվէլին:

Եւ միաբանք որ ի սուրբ աստուածընկալ ուխտն կան և սպասաւորք աստուածընկալ Գեղարդեանն, թէ ի մեր ազգէ և թէ յայլոց ազգաց, սկսեալ յայսմհետէ մինչև ի գալուստն Քրիստոսի, սուրբ եպիսկոպոսք, սուրբ վարդապետք, սուրբ քահանայք և սուրբ կրաւնաւորք, հանապազ և միշտ զմեզ բարի կամաւք և մտաւք յիշատակեն առաջի Աստուծոյ սուրբ պատարագաւք և ջերմեռանդ աղաւթիւք և գորովալիր պաղատանաւք և Աստուած ողորմի ասելով: Եւ ի տաւնի Աւետարանչին Յովհաննու պատարագ մատուցանեն մեզ, և յետ պատարագին զմեր յիշատակարանս կարդան ի բեմն, և անբիծք և Աստուած անեղ և Քրիստոս որդի ասեն ամենայն միաբանքն ի մի բերան: Եւ մեք ամենայն յաւժարութեամբ տուաք վկայութեամբ Սիմէոն վարդապետիս և Մարտիրոս եպիսկոպոսիս և Երեմիայ և Կարապետ աբեղայիցս:

Դարձեալ՝ մեք ծառայքս Աստուծոյ, վարդապետս Սիմէոն և Մարտիրոս եպիսկոպոս և քահանայքս Երեմիայ և Կարապետ, և Այրավանաց միաբանքս, սպասաւորք սուրբ և աստուածամուխ Գեղարդեանն, այսպէս ուխտեցաք առաջի Աստուծոյ և արձանագրեցաք: Որ չունի ոք իշխանութիւն և հրաման ի մերոց իշխանաց և կամ յաւտարաց, յաշխարհականաց և կամ ի կարգաւորաց, որ զԱւետարանս ի յԱյրեվանից հանէ, ծախելով կամ բաշխելով կամ գողանալով կամ խլելով: Եւ որ ոք յանդգնի և հանել ջանայ, դատի յԱստուծոյ և յամենայն սրբոց, և մասն և բաժին զԿայենի և զՅուդայի և զխա[p. 580]չահանուացն առցէ և յաւիտեան ընդ սատանայի տանջի և չարչարի, և յամենայն մարդոյ նալաթ և անիծած լիցի. ամէն:

Այլ և յերեսս անկեալ աղաչեմ զամենեսեան զուրբ պատահողսդ աստուածախաւս Աւետարանիս՝ յիշել ջերմեռանդ սրտիւ առաջի Աստուծոյ, զիս զնուաստ վարդապետս, և զԵրեմիայ և զՄեսրոբ քահանայք սուրբք, որ ընդ իս աշխատեցան բազում, ի բերել զԱւետարանս ի Վրաստանէ: Եւ Աստուած զձեզ յիշէ յիւր առատ ողորմութիւնն. ամէն, եղիցի:

Page 579. Written in the year 1901.

Page 579. In the lower margin in crude *notragir*: Գրվեցավ թվին Ռ և Ջ և Ա.ում (= *1901*):

Page 580. I, *žamarar* (i.e., officiating priest) Yōvakim, the unworthy and sinful servant of Jesus Christ, wrote this. He who reads this (inscription), may he plentifully /// ask for the remission of the sins of this poor sinner. This was written in the year 1901. In the Lord God. Amen!

Page 580. This holy Gospel is 307 years old.

Page 580. Inscription in *notragir*: *Յիսուսի Քրիստոսի անարժան և մեղայոր ժամարար տէր Յօվակիմ գրեցի. օվ օր կարդայ մի լիայպէ(ս) բերանօվ /// նվաստիս մեղավորիս մեղացէն թողու(թիւն). գրվեցայվ թվ. Ռ և Ջ նաև Ա. ումն (= 1901), ի Տէր Աստուծոյ, ամէն:*

Page 580. In *bolorgir*: ԳՃ̅Է (*307*) *տարոյ է այս սուրբ Աւետարանս:*

APPENDIX B

The Gospel Prefaces

translated by Avedis K. Sanjian

Preface to the Gospel of Matthew

Page 22. This Gospel is inscribed "according to Matthew," since Matthew himself, disciple of the Lord, wrote this Gospel. He recounts for us the beginning, the birth in the flesh of the Savior, from the descent of David. For this reason he tallies up the enumeration down to Christ, forty-two generations. He also recounts in order the baptism by John, and the temptation on the mountain by demons, and the signs and extraordinary miracles wrought by the Savior, and the choice of the disciples, and concerning the plot of the betrayal and the consummation, for he was betrayed to Pilate and was crucified in the flesh, and his body was laid in the tomb, and the soldiers divided his garments. In the same manner (he recounts) the resurrection on the third day and the commission to the disciples that they make disciples of all nations and baptize them. He promised to be with them all days even to the consummation of the world.

Matthew wrote his Gospel in the city of Jerusalem in the Hebrew language eight years after the ascension of the Savior, at the request of the church of Jerusalem. It (the Gospel) has 355 chapters; 32 testimonies; 2,600 verses.

"Matthew" means "song of life."

Նախադրութիւն Մատթէոսի Աւետարանին

Աւետարանս որ ըստ Մատթէոսի գրեալ է։ Զի ինքն Մատթէոս աշակերտ Տեառն գրեաց զԱւետարանս զայս. և պատմէ մեզ զի սկըզբանն, զըստ մարմնոյ ծնունդ փրկչին, ի զաւակէ Դաւթի, վասնորոյ և զազգահամարն, ժողովէ մինչև ի Քրիստոս, ազգ քառասուն և երկուք։ Բերէ ըստ կարգի և զմըկըրտութիւնն Յովհաննու, և ի լերինն ի դիւաց զփորձութիւնն, և նշանս և արուեստս մեծամեծս ի փրկչէն եղեալ։ Եւ զընտրութիւն աշակերտացն։ Եւ վասն խորհրդոյ մատնութեանն, և զկատարածն, զի մատնեցաւ Պիղատոսի, և խաչեցաւ մարմնով, և մարմինն եդաւ ի գերեզմանի, և զինուորքն բաժանեցին զհանդերձս նորա։ Նոյն և զերեքաւուր յարութիւն, և զպատուէր աշակերտացն, աշակերտել զամենայն հեթանոսս և մկրտել զնոսա։ Պատուիրեաց լինել ընդ նոսա զամենայն աւուրս մինչև ի կատարած աշխարհի։

Մատթէոս գրեաց զԱւետարանն իւր յԵրուսաղէմ քաղաքի, ի լեզու եբրայեցի։ Զկնի ութ ամի համբառնալոյ փըրկչին, ի խնդրոյ եկեղեցոյն Երուսաղէմի։ Ունի գլուխս, յծե։ Վկայութիւնս, լբ։ Տունս, սո։

Մատթէոս թարգմանի երգ կենաց։

Preface to the Gospel of Mark

Page 186. This Gospel, which is "according to Mark," was written by Mark himself, the disciple of Peter and companion of Paul. He wrote this Gospel, and he begins saying "the beginning of the Gospel" with the witness of the prophet Isaiah. He also notes the temptation in the mountain, but does not say "temptations." He also recounts the calling of the disciples and the signs and miracles that he did; and the plot of betrayal and the consummations; and how he was betrayed to Pilate and was crucified in the flesh; and how the soldiers divided his garments; and how his body was laid in the tomb; and his resurrection on

Նախադրութիւն Մարկոսի Աւետարանին

Աւետարանս որ ըստ Մարկոսի, գրեալ է սոյն Մարկոս աշակերտ Պետրոսի և ընթացակից Պաւղոսի։ Գրեաց զԱւետարանս զայս, և դնէ սկիզբն և ասէ սկիզբն Աւետարանի ի Յովհաննու քարոզութենէն. և զմկրտութիւնն Յովհաննու և առնու վկայութիւն յԻսայայ մարգարէէ. նշանակէ և զփորձութիւնն ի լերինն, և ո՛չ ասէ զփորձանքն։ Եւ պատմէ և վասն ընտրութեան աշակերտացն և նշանս և արուեստս զոր արար. և զխորհուրդ մատնութեանն և զկատարածն։ Եւ որպէս մատնեցաւ Պիղատոսի և խաչեցաւ մարմնով. և զի՞ զինուորքն բաժանեցին զհանդերձս նորա. և զի՞ մարմինն

the third day; and the descent of the angel and his apparition to the women, who related the same to the disciples.

Mark wrote this Gospel by order of Peter the rock, in the city of Alexandria, in the Egyptian language, fifteen years after the Savior's ascension. It has 233 chapters; 15 testimonies; 1,600 verses.

"Mark" means "lofty bulwark" or "above the housetops."

եղաւ ի գերեզմանի. և յարեաւ երեքաւրեայ. և զիջանել Հրեշտակին և երևել կանանցն. և զնոյն պատմեցին աշակերտացն:

Մարկոս Հրամանաւ Պետրոսի վիմի գրեաց զԱւետարանս իւր յԱղեքսանդր քաղաքի, ի լեզու եգիպտացի. զկնի ժե ամի Համբառնալոյ փրկչին:

Ունի գլուխս, մլգ: Վկայութիւնս, ժե: Տունս, ռո:

Մարկոս՝ բարձր պատուար, կամ ի վերայ տանեացն:

Preface to the Gospel of Luke

Page 295. This Gospel, which is inscribed "according to Luke," Luke himself (wrote who) was a disciple of Peter, and was a companion of Paul who ordained him and testified concerning him. He wrote this Gospel; he began with the birth of John and what concerns it. He recounts also the incarnation of the Savior composing the genealogy in ascending order from Joseph to [p. 296] David, and from David to Adam. He also relates the baptism by John, and the temptation by Satan when on the mountain. (He recounts) also the calling of the disciples and the other seventy; he describes the many signs and miracles that happened; and the plot of betrayal and consummation, when he was betrayed to Pontius Pilate and was crucified in the flesh; (and) how the soldiers divided his garments, and one of the two thieves who were crucified confessed his repentance; and how his body was laid in the tomb, and how he rose on the third day, and thereafter ascended to heaven, witnessed by the angels.

A physician by profession, Luke became a disciple of the Savior, and is thought to have been called in the number of the seventy. He later became a disciple of Paul, for which exclaim: "Praise be to his Gospel!" He wrote his Gospel by order of Paul, in the city of Antioch, in the Syriac language, seventeen years after the Savior's ascension. It has 342 chapters; 17 testimonies; 2,800 verses.

"Luke" means "resurrection."

Նախադրութիւն Ղուկայ Աւետարանիս

Աւետարանս որ ըստ Ղուկայ գրեալ է, նոյնինքն Ղուկաս՝ աշակերտ էր Պետրոսի, և ձեռնադրեցաւ ընթացակից Պաւղոսի և վկայեցաւ ի նմանէ: Սա գրեաց զԱւետարանս զայս, սկիզբն առնէ ի ծննդենէն Յովհաննու և զոր ըստ նմին: Պատմէ և զմարմնանալ փրկչին ազգաթիւ առնէ և ելանէ ի Յովսեփայ ի Դաւիթ, և ի Դաւթայ մինչև յԱդամ: Պատմէ սա և զմկրտութիւնն Յովհաննու, և լինելով ի լեառնն զփորձելն ի սատանայէ: Եւ զընտրութիւն աշակերտացն և այլ եւթանասունս. եցոյց նշանս և արուեստս բազումս եղեալս, և զխորհուրդ մատնութեան և զկատարածն որ մատնեցաւ Պիղատոսի Պոնտացւոյ և խաչեցաւ մարմնով. զի՞ զինուորք բաժանեցին զՀանդերձս նորա: Եւ որք խաչեցան յերկուց աւազակացն մին ապաշխարեաց խոստովանութեամբ. և զի մարմին նորա եդաւ ի գերեզման. և յարեաւ յերրորդ աւուրն. և յետ այսորիկ Համբարձաւ յերկինս տեսանելով Հրեշտակացն:

Ղուկաս՝ արուեստիւ բժիշկ գոլով, սա աշակերտեցաւ փրկչին, և Համարեալ կոչեցաւ ի թիւս եւթանասնիցն: Իսկ յետոյ աշակերտեցաւ Պաւղոսի, վասն որոյ ասի՝ գովութիւն սորա յԱւետարանին: Սա Հրամանաւ Պաւղոսի գրեաց զԱւետարանս իւր յԱնտիոք քաղաքի ի լեզու ասորի, զկնին ժէ ամի Համբառնալոյ փրկչին: Ունի գլուխս, յխբ: Վկայութիւնս, ժէ: Տունս, սպ:

Ղուկաս՝ յարութիւն:

Preface to the Gospel of John

Page 458. The Gospel of John was written by John, who is the brother of James Zebedee and who lay on the breast of the Lord. He himself wrote this Gospel, and began with the divine Word. He also mentions his fleshly birth saying: "And the Word was made flesh." He also mentions the baptism by John and the calling of the disciples, as well as the signs and miracles that happened, and the consummation when he was betrayed to Pontius Pilate and was cru-

Նախադրութիւն Յովհաննու Աւետարանիս

Յովհաննու Աւետարանն գրեալ է Յովհաննու, որ եղբայր է Յակովբայ Զեբեդեայ, որ անկաւ ի վերայ լանջացն Տեառնն. նոյն սա՛ գրեաց զԱւետարանս զայս, և սկիզբն առնէ յաստուածական բանէն: Եւ զըստ մարմնոյ ծնունդն յիշատակէ յասելովն, և բանն մարմին եղև: Եւ յիշատակէ զմկրտութիւնն Յովհաննու և զընտրութիւն աշակերտացն, այլ և զնշանս և արուեստս զոր եղեն և զկատարածն որ

cified; whereupon the soldiers divided his garments and cast lots for his coat, and his body was laid in the tomb, and he rose on the third day and appeared to his disciples.

Page 459: John, who also (is called) the son of thunder, told us with thundering the heavenly (truths). Fifty-three years after the ascension of the Savior, he wrote his Gospel in the Greek language in the city of Ephesus, at the request of the church of Asia. There are 232 chapters; 15 testimonies; 1,800 verses.

Altogether, the four Gospels (consist of) 1,162 chapters; 79 testimonies; (and) 8,800 verses.

"John" (means) "obedience."

մատնեցաւ Պոնտացւոյ Պիղատոսի և խաչեցաւ, յորում և զինուորքն բաժանեցին զհանդերձս նորա և ի վերայ պատմուճանի նորա վիճակ արկին, և մարմին նորա եդաւ ի գերեզմանի և յարեաւ յերրորդ աւուր երևեցաւ աշակերտացն ինքն:

Յովհաննէս՝ որ և որդի որոտման, զվերինն որոտալով պատմեաց մեզ: Սա՝ զկնի ծգ ամի Համբառնալոյ փրկչին՝ գրեաց զԱւետարանս իւր յԵփեսոս քաղաքի, ի խնդրոյ եկեղեցւոյն Ասիայ ի լեզու յոյն: Եւ է գլուխս, մլբ: Վկայութիւնս, ժե: Տունս, ռպ:

Միանգամայն չորեքեան Աւետարանքս գլուխք, ռճկբ: Վկայութիւնք, հթ: Տունք, փպ:

Յովհաննէս՝ Հնազանդութիւն:

APPENDIX C

The Manuscripts Executed at Glajor

by Avedis K. Sanjian

The scope of the intellectual pursuits of the scholars of Glajor can be determined, to a considerable degree, by the extant manuscripts executed there. The task of compiling a list of the codices executed at Glajor was made difficult because of the diffusion of Armenian manuscript collections in libraries and museums scattered throughout the world. Consequently, we have had to rely principally upon available published catalogues of these collections. We are especially grateful to Ō. Eganyan for detailed descriptions he provided us of many of the manuscripts in the Matenadaran, Erevan.

Besides the data found in the catalogues of the major manuscript holdings at the Matenadaran in Erevan, the Armenian Patriarchate of Jerusalem, and the Mekhitarist monasteries at Venice and Vienna, partial references to Glajor codices are found in several sources: A. N. Avetisyan, *Haykakan Manrankarč'ut'yan Glajori Dproc'ə* [The Glajor School of Armenian Miniature Painting] (Erevan, 1971), 88–89; Łewond Ališan, *Sisakan* (Venice, 1893), 131–37; Garegin Yovsēp'ian, *Xałbakeank' kam Pr̄ošeank' Hayoc' Patmut'ean mēǰ* [The Xałbakians or Pr̄ošians in Armenian History], 2nd printing (Antilias, Lebanon, 1969), 251–96; and N. Covakan (= Norayr Połarian), "T'oros Taronec'i," *Sion* (monthly, Jerusalem), 9–10 (Sept.-Oct. 1970), 454–55. In the appendix (pp. 130–82) to his monographic study, *Glajori Hamalsaranə* [The University of Glajor] (Erevan, 1983), Ašot Abrahamyan reproduced the texts of fifty-six colophons of manuscripts that were either written at or contain references to Glajor. Our examination of these colophons, however, shows that twelve of them (that is, his nos. 4, 7, 9, 19, 20, 24, 27, 45, 46, 52, 53, 54) have no connection whatsoever with Glajor; hence only forty-four of these codices can be identified as having been executed at Glajor. Two other works also purport to provide exhaustive lists of manuscripts executed at Ałberc'/Glajor. The first of these is in the appendix (pp. 367–416) to L. G. Xač'eryan's monographic study, *Esayi Nč'ec'i ew Glajori Hamalsaranə, 1280–1340* [Esayi Nč'ec'i and the University of Glajor, 1280–1340] (Los Angeles, 1988), which provides brief descriptions and texts of the colophons of seventy-two manuscripts. We have determined, however, that fourteen of these codices (nos. 1, 6, 11, 13, 15, 23, 24, 26, 28, 37, 38, 54, 59, 64) were in fact not written at Ałberc'/Glajor, and that five of the remainder (nos. 22/66, 31/33, 34/72, 46/71, 56/57) have actually been listed twice. Moreover, in her article "Glajori Hamalsaranum Ǝndorinakvac jer̄agrer" [The Manuscripts Executed at Glajor], *Ēǰmiacin* 11–12 (1984), pp. 56–59), A. H. Łazarosyan has a list of fifty-one manuscripts, of which twelve (nos. 2, 7, 9, 10, 13, 20 23, 26, 32, 33, 50, 51) were definitely not written at Ałberc'/Glajor. We have also benefited greatly from H. Ačar̄ian's five-volume *Hayoc' Anjnanunneri Bar̄aran* [Dictionary of Armenian Personal Names] (Erevan, 1942–62), which contains considerable information about many individuals associated with Glajor, including data on scholars, scribes, artists, and sponsors of manuscripts. What follows, then, is the most comprehensive, though not necessarily complete, list to date of the manuscripts written and/or illustrated at Glajor during its roughly sixty-year existence. It should be pointed out that fifty of the total of sixty-nine manuscripts listed below are expressly attributed by their colophons to Glajor or Ałberc'; the other twenty codices are attributed to Glajor because the persons involved in their production were at Glajor. Fifty-nine of the manuscripts have precise dates of execution; the dates of some of the others have been determined on palaeographic or other grounds. The list that follows is given by alphabetical order of cities and numerical order within a given collection.

List of Manuscripts Executed at Glajor

1. Aleppo, Forty Martyrs, 110 (72): *Tałaran* (Book of Hymns).

13th–14th century; exact date unknown, due to a tear in the colophon. Written and illustrated at Glajor by T'oros (Taronec'i). See Artavazd Surméyan, *Catalogue des manuscrits arméniens se trouvant à Alep à l'Église des Quarante Martyrs, ainsi qu'auprès des particuliers,* I

(Jerusalem, 1935), pp. 187–89; N. Covakan, "T'oros Taronec'i," 454.

2. Erevan, Mat. 49: *The Works of Dionysius the Areopagite,* translated by Step'anos Siwnec'i.
A.D. 1282. Written at Glajor by the scribe Step'anos Krōnawor for Nersēs Hřetor (Mšec'i). Corrections in the text made by Esayi Nč'ec'i, as indicated in inscription on fol. 296. See brief description in Eganyan, *C'uc'ak Matenadarani,* I, col. 237; and the text of the colophon in Ašot Abrahamyan, *Glajori Hamalsaranə,* no. 2, pp. 130–31, and Xač'eryan, *Esayi Nč'ec'i,* no. 4, p. 370.

3. Erevan, Mat. 167: *The Works of Dionysius the Areopagite,* translated by Step'anos Siwnec'i. *Commentary on Isaiah,* by Esayi Nč'ec'i.
Late 13th century; exact date unknown. Written from an exemplar found at the monastery of Hałbat, by the scribe Yovhannēs Hořomiayrec'i for Esayi (Nč'ec'i), evidently at Glajor. See Eganyan, *C'uc'ak,* I, col. 263; and text of colophon in Abrahamyan, *Glajor,* no. 3, 131, and Xač'eryan, *Esayi Nč'ec'i,* no. 68, p. 414.

4. Erevan, Mat. 206: Holy Bible.
A.D. 1318. Written by the scribes Step'anos, Kiwrakē, and Yovhannēs Erznkac'i (Corcorec'i), and illustrated by T'oros Taronec'i for Esayi Nč'ec'i, evidently at Glajor. The codex is known as "Esayi Nč'ec'i's Bible." See Eganyan, *C'uc'ak,* I, col. 272; Abrahamyan, *Glajor,* no. 37, pp. 166–67; Xač'eryan, *Esayi Nč'ec'i,* no. 48, pp. 400–401.

5. Erevan, Mat. 353: Holy Bible.
A.D. 1317. Written evidently at Glajor, by the scribes Kirakos Vardapet, Karapet, Movsēs, Yovhannēs Sarkawag, and Tirac'u, for the scribe Kirakos Vardapet himself, and illustrated by T'oros (Taronec'i). See Eganyan, *C'uc'ak,* I, cols. 304–5; Abrahamyan, *Glajor,* no. 33, pp. 162–63; Xač'eryan, *Esayi Nč'ec'i,* no. 42, pp. 395–96.

6. Erevan, Mat. 437: Miscellany.
Early 14th century; exact date unknown. Written evidently at Glajor by Esayi (Nč'ec'i), Sargis, and Simon, for Esayi Vardapet (probably Nč'ec'i himself).

(1) On the writings of Gregory of Narek
(2) Yohan Orotnec'i, *Commentary on John*
(3) Treatises of Gregory Nazianzenus
(4) Philo Judaeus
(5) On the destruction of Ilion
(6) Gregory of Nyssa, *On the Beatitudes*
(7) A treatise of Basil of Caesarea
(8) A treatise of Gregory Nazianzenus
(9) A treatise of Philo
(10) An introduction to Philo the Philosopher
(11) A commentary on David's *Definitions of Philosophy*
(12) David the Invincible, *On Grammar*
(13) John the Philosopher, *On Triangles*
(14) Gregory's commentaries on the works of Evagrius
(15) A commentary on David's *Definitions of Philosophy*
(16) Catholicos Nersēs Šnorhali, *Commentary on David's "Definitions of Philosophy"*
(17) A commentary on Philo's *On Providence*
(18) Plato, *Timaeus*
(19) The works of Dionysius the Areopagite
(20) The fables of Olympianus
(21) Catholicos Yakob, *Commentary on Basil*
(22) A commentary on Philo's *On Providence*
(23) A commentary on Gregory Nazianzenus
(24) The Names of Cities (this is an 18th-century addition)

See Eganyan, *C'uc'ak,* I, col. 320; Abrahamyan, *Glajor,* no. 6, pp. 133–34; Xač'eryan, *Esayi Nč'ec'i,* no. 5, pp. 370–71.

7. Erevan, Mat. 560: Thomas Aquinas, *Book of the Seven Sacraments* (i.e., Aquinas' *Commentary on Book IV of the Sentences of Peter Lombard*).
A.D. 1325. Written at Glajor by the scribe T'oros for Sargis Vardapet. Yovhannēs Erznkac'i (Corcorec'i) claims that he translated this work by order of the Pope (John XXII) from the Latin original at the monastery of Corcor in 1321, with the help of the Latin missionary Archbishop Bartholomew (of Maragha). See Eganyan, *C'uc'ak,* I, col. 348; Abrahamyan, *Glajor,* no. 39, p. 168; M. A. van den Oudenrijn, "Uniteurs et Dominicains d'Arménie," 95–96; Xač'eryan, *Esayi Nč'ec'i,* no. 50, pp. 402–3.

8. Erevan, Mat. 749: Gregory of Nyssa, *On the Beatitudes* and *On the Pater Noster.*
Early 14th century; exact date unknown. Written evidently at Glajor by the scribe Vardan (pupil of Esayi Nč'ec'i). See Eganyan, *C'uc'ak,* I, col. 402; Abrahamyan, *Glajor,* no. 16, p. 144; Xač'eryan, *Esayi Nč'ec'i,* no. 67, pp. 413–14.

9. Erevan, Mat. 844: Miscellany.
A.D. 1325. Written evidently at Glajor. The names of the scribe and sponsor are unknown.

(1) Nemesius of Emesa, *On the Nature of Man*
(2) Gregory of Nyssa, *On the Creation of Man* (i.e., *De hominis opificio*)
(3) Gregory of Nyssa, *On Virginity*

Ō. Eganyan suggests that the date of execution of the manuscript has been erroneously interpreted. He claims that the date 74 is not according to the Great Armenian Era but the Lesser Armenian Era (that is,

74 + 1084 = 1158). See also Eganyan, *C'uc'ak,* I, col. 424.

10. Erevan, Mat. 1094: Vardan Arewelc'i, *Commentary on the Pentateuch.*
Early 14th century; exact date unknown. Written at Glajor by the scribe Yohanēs for Nersēs Vardapet. See Eganyan, *C'uc'ak,* I, col. 473.

11. Erevan, Mat. 1097: Miscellany.
A.D. 1280. Written by the scribes Luser and Esayi (Nč'ec'i) for Nersēs Vardapet (Mšec'i), evidently at Glajor.

(1) Epiphanius of Salamis, *On 22 Creations, 22 Patriarchs, 22 Alphabets, and 22 Old Testament Books*
(2) An introduction to Kings
(3) Ephraem Syrus, *Commentaries on Samuel, Kings, Joshua, and Judges*
(4) Ełišē Vardapet, *Commentary on Joshua and Judges*
(5) Eznik Vardapet Kołbac'i, *Refutation of the Sects*
(6) A commentary on Judges

See Eganyan, *C'uc'ak,* I, col. 474; Abrahamyan, *Glajor,* no. 1, p. 130; Xač'eryan, *Esayi Nč'ec'i,* no. 3, p. 369.

12. Erevan, Mat. 1141: Miscellany.
A.D. 1335. Written at Glajor by the scribe Grigor for the priest Sargis.

(1) Nersēs Lambronac'i, *Commentaries on Proverbs, Ecclesiastes,* and the *Song of Solomon*
(2) Vardan Arewelc'i, *Commentary on the Song of Songs,* written at the behest of Kirakos Vardapet
(3) Grigor Narekac'i, *Commentary on the Song of Songs,* written at the behest of King Gurgēn of Anjewac'ik'

See Eganyan, *C'uc'ak,* I, col. 486; Abrahamyan, *Glajor,* no. 50, pp. 179–80; Xač'eryan, *Esayi Nč'ec'i,* no. 65, pp. 412–13.

13. Erevan, Mat. 1275: Esayi Nč'ec'i, *Commentary on Ezekiel.*
A.D. 1322. Written probably at Glajor by the scribes Asil Dpir (Sarkawag) and Yohanēs for Yovhannēs Vardapet. See Eganyan, *C'uc'ak,* I, col. 515.

14. Erevan, Mat. 1363: Miscellany.
A.D. 1292. Written at Glajor by the scribe Yovasap' for Esayi (Nč'ec'i).

(1) John Chrysostom, *Commentary on the Acts of the Apostles*
(2) Vardan Arewelc'i, *Commentary on the Ten Commandments*
(3) Grigor Kesarac'i, *Epistle to Catholicos Melk'isēt'*

See Eganyan, *C'uc'ak,* I, col. 535; Abrahamyan, *Glajor,* no. 14, pp. 141–42; Xač'eryan, *Esayi Nč'ec'i,* no. 14, p. 377.

15. Erevan, Mat. 1379: John Chrysostom, *Commentary on the Fourteen Epistles of Paul.*
A.D. 1334. Written at Glajor by the scribes T'oros and Manuēl for Kirakos Vardapet, and illustrated probably by the scribe Manuēl. See Eganyan, *C'uc'ak,* I, col. 538.

16. Erevan, Mat. 1409: Miscellany.
A.D. 1298. Written at Ałberc' (= Glajor) by the scribe Mkrtič' Bǰnec'i for an unknown sponsor.

(1) A collection of commentaries on the seven Catholic Epistles
(2) Andrew of Cappadocia and Aretas of Caesarea, *Commentaries on Revelation*
(3) Nersēs Lambronac'i, *Commentary on John*
(4) Nersēs Šnorhali, *Commentary on David the Invincible's Encomium "Exalt the Lord"*
(5) Tēr Bartholomeos, *Prologue to the Book of Sermons* (Frankish Bishop of Maragha), translated into Armenian; also a sermon on the penthesis

See Eganyan, *C'uc'ak,* I, col. 545; Abrahamyan, *Glajor,* no. 15, pp. 142–44; Xač'eryan, *Esayi Nč'ec'i,* no. 17, pp. 378–79.

17. Erevan, Mat. 1419: Miscellany.
A.D. 1318. Written at Glajor by the scribe Ep'rem for Martiros Vardapet.

(1) Andrew of Cappadocia, *Commentary on Revelation*
(2) Nersēs Lambronac'i, *Commentary on John*
(3) The works of Evagrius Ponticus
(4) Vardan Arewelc'i's compilation of *Commentaries on the Song of Songs,* at the behest of Kirakos Vardapet

See Eganyan, *C'uc'ak,* I, col. 547; Abrahamyan, *Glajor,* no. 38, pp. 167–68; Xač'eryan, *Esayi Nč'ec'i,* no. 49, pp. 401–2.

18. Erevan, Mat. 1422: Miscellany.
A.D. 1284. Written evidently at Glajor by Esayi (Nč'ec'i) for Archbishop Grigor of the canton of Sararad.

(1) Andrew of Cappadocia, *Commentary on Revelation*
(2) Nersēs Lambronac'i, *Commentary on John*

See Eganyan, *C'uc'ak,* I, col. 548; Abrahamyan, *Glajor,* no. 8, pp. 136–37; Xač'eryan, *Esayi Nč'ec'i,* no. 8, p. 373.

19. Erevan, Mat. 1460: Miscellany.
A.D. 1311. Written evidently at Glajor by the scribe Kiwrion (or Kerion) for an unknown sponsor.

(1) Nersēs Šnorhali, *Commentary on David the Invincible's Encomium "Exalt the Lord"*
(2) A commentary on the Epistles of Paul
(3) Nersēs Lambronacʻi, *Commentary on "He was with His brethren"*
(4) Vardan Arewelcʻi and Grigor Narekacʻi, *Commentaries on the Song of Songs*
(5) Questions by Juvenal and responses by Movsēs (Kʻertʻoł) and Dawitʻ

See Eganyan, *Cʻucʻak,* I, cols. 556–57; Abrahamyan, *Glajor,* no. 29, p. 157; Xačʻeryan, *Esayi Nčʻecʻi,* no. 35, pp. 390–91.

20. Erevan, Mat. 1657: Miscellany.
Early 14th century; exact date unknown. Written evidently at Glajor by the scribes Grigor Vardapet Erznkacʻi and Barseł Erēcʻ for an unknown sponsor.

(1) Basil, *Homilies on the Hexaemeron*
(2) Gregory of Nyssa, *Against Eunomius and His Followers*

See Eganyan, *Cʻucʻak,* I, col. 602; Xačʻeryan, *Esayi Nčʻecʻi,* no. 43, pp. 396–97.

21. Erevan, Mat. 1681: Miscellany.
Early 14th century; exact date unknown. Written evidently at Glajor by the scribe Kiwrakos for Esayi (Nčʻecʻi).

(1) "Girkʻ Pitoyicʻ" (Book of Rhetoric), an Armenian version of Aphthonius' *Elements of Rhetoric,* attributed to Movsēs Xorenacʻi
(2) Movsēs Kʻertʻoł, *Admonition to His Pupil Theodorus To Be Well Instructed in Rhetoric*
(3) David the Invincible, *Definitions of Philosophy*
(4) Various definitions
(5) Philosophical sayings
(6) Six essential things for judges
(7) Anania Širakacʻi, *On Weights and Measures*
(8) Philosophical definitions
(9) Key to astronomers

See Eganyan, *Cʻucʻak,* I, col. 607; Abrahamyan, *Glajor,* no. 55, p. 182; Xačʻeryan, *Esayi Nčʻecʻi,* no. 69, pp. 414–15.

22. Erevan, Mat. 1751: Miscellany.
Early 14th century; exact date unknown. Written probably at Glajor by the scribe Tiratur for an unknown sponsor.

(1) David the Invincible, *Definitions of Philosophy*
(2) Porphyry, *Introduction to Aristotle's "Categories"*
(3) David the Invincible, *Commentary on Porphyry's "Introduction"*
(4) Nersēs Šnorhali, *Commentary on David the Invincible's "Definitions of Philosophy"*
(5) Commentaries on Aristotle's *Categories,* and *De Interpretatione*
(6) Pseudo-Aristotle, *Virtues and Vices*
(7) The names of philosophers
(8) Išawx, *Book on Nature*
(9) *Girkʻ Ēakacʻ,* that is, Aristotle's *Organon*
(10) Dawitʻ Harkʻacʻi on Aristotle

See Eganyan, *Cʻucʻakʻ,* I, cols. 628–29; Abrahamyan, *Glajor,* no. 56, p. 182; Xačʻeryan, *Esayi Nčʻecʻi,* no. 34, p. 390 and no. 72, pp. 415–16.

23. Erevan, Mat. 2187: Book of Homilies.
A.D. 1346. Written at Glajor by Tʻoros (Taronecʻi) for Martiros Sanahnecʻi. The codex contains homilies by Vanakan Vardapet, Tiratur Vardapet, Kirakos Vardapet, Yovhannēs Siwnecʻi, Esayi Nčʻecʻi, and Yovhannēs Erznkacʻi. See Eganyan, *Cʻucʻak,* I, col. 741.

24. Erevan, Mat. 2520: Miscellany.
A.D. 1306. Written at Glajor by the scribe Yovhannēs Erznkacʻi for himself.

(1) Stepʻanos Siwnecʻi, *Commentary on John*
(2) Nana the Syrian, *Commentary on John*
(3) Andrew of Cappadocia, *Commentary on Revelation*

See Eganyan, *Cʻucʻak,* I, col. 817; Abrahamyan, *Glajor,* no. 22, p. 151; Xačʻeryan, *Esayi Nčʻecʻi,* no. 27, p. 386.

25. Erevan, Mat. 3393: Four Gospels.
A.D. 1309. Written at Glajor by the scribe Tiratur Kilikecʻi for an unknown sponsor. See Eganyan, *Cʻucʻak,* I, col. 1002; Abrahamyan, *Glajor,* no. 25, p. 156; Xačʻeryan, *Esayi Nčʻecʻi,* no. 31, p. 389.

26. Erevan, Mat. 3463: Miscellany.
Early 14th century; exact date unknown. Written probably at Glajor by the scribe Kiwrion.

(1) Nemesius of Emesa, *On the Nature of Man*
(2) Gregory of Nyssa, *On the Creation of Man* (i.e., *De hominis opificio*)
(3) Gregory of Nyssa, *On Virginity*

See Eganyan, *Cʻucʻak,* I, cols. 1017–18; Abrahamyan, *Glajor,* no. 28, p. 157; Xačʻeryan, *Esayi Nčʻecʻi,* no. 36, p. 391.

27. Erevan, Mat. 3606: Miscellany.
A.D. 1303. Written by the scribe-priest Tʻadēos at the monastery of Nṙnōnicʻ and the scribe Mxitʻar Vardapet at Glajor, for Yovhannēs Vardapet (Varžapet).

(1) Nersēs Lambronac'i, *Commentary on the Twelve Minor Prophets*
(2) Vardan Arewelc'i, *Commentary on Daniel* (based on the commentaries of Ephraem, Hippolytus, and Step'anos)

See Eganyan, *C'uc'ak,* I, col. 1049; Abrahamyan, *Glajor,* nos. 21 and 51, pp. 150–51, 180–81; Xač'eryan, *Esayi Nč'ec'i,* no. 22, pp. 383–84.

28. Erevan, Mat. 5566: Esayi Nč'ec'i, *Commentary on Ezekiel.*
A.D. 1303. Written at Glajor. Other details not available. See Eganyan, *C'uc'ak,* II, col. 135; Abrahamyan, *Glajor,* no. 18, pp. 147–48; Xač'eryan, *Esayi Nč'ec'i,* no. 21, pp. 382–83.

29. Erevan, Mat. 6289; Four Gospels.
A.D. 1323. Written at Glajor by an unknown scribe for Esayi (Nč'ec'i), and illustrated by T'oros Taronec'i. See Eganyan, *C'uc'ak,* II, col. 288; Abrahamyan, *Glajor,* no. 42, pp. 170–72; Xač'eryan, *Esayi Nč'ec'i,* no. 55, pp. 405–6.

30. Erevan, Mat. 6348: Four Gospels.
Early 14th century; exact date unknown. Written probably at Glajor by an unknown scribe, and illustrated by T'oros (Taronec'i). See Eganyan, *C'uc'ak,* II, col. 300.

31. Erevan, Mat. 6558: Miscellany.
A.D. 1302. Written at Glajor and the monastery of T'ełeneac' by the scribes Yovhannēs Erznkac'i (at Glajor), Vardan Kilikec'i (at Glajor), and Mkrtič' Rabuni (at T'ełeneac'), for Esayi (Nč'ec'i).

(1) Nersēs Lambronac'i, *Commentary on the Psalms*
(2) Samuel Anec'i, *The Life of Bishop Nersēs (Lambronac'i)*
(3) Grigor Skewṙac'i, *Encomium of Nersēs Lambronac'i*
(4) Nersēs Šnorhali, *Encomium of the Archangels Michael and Gabriel*
(5) Nersēs Šnorhali, *Encomium of the Holy Archangels* (in verse)

See Eganyan, *C'uc'ak,* II, col. 344; Abrahamyan, *Glajor,* no. 17, pp. 145–47; Xač'eryan, *Esayi Nč'ec'i,* no. 20, pp. 380–82.

32. Erevan, Mat. 6897: Miscellany.
A.D. 1317. Written probably at Glajor by the scribes Karapet Vardapet and Kiwrakē, and illustrated by T'oros for an unknown sponsor.

(1) Dionysius Thrax, *Ars Grammatica*
(2) Esayi Nč'ec'i, *Commentary on Grammar*
(3) Dawit' Nerginac'i, *Introduction to the "Definitions of Philosophy"*
(4) Porphyry, *Introduction to Aristotle's "Categories"*
(5) David the Invincible, *Commentary on Porphyry's "Introduction"*
(6) David the Invincible, *Commentary on Aristotle's "Categories"*
(7) Aristotle, *De Interpretatione,* and David the Invincible, *Commentary on Aristotle's "De Interpretatione"*
(8) Pseudo-Aristotle, *On the Cosmos*
(9) Pseudo-Aristotle, *Virtues and Vices*
(10) Grigor Magistros, *Four Letters* (written in verse)
(11) Questions by Juvenal and responses by Movsēs K'ert'oł and David the Philosopher
(12) David the Philosopher, *Girk' Ēakac'* [Book of Beings]
(13) Dawit' Hark'ac'i, *Observations on Aristotle*
(14) The names of gems
(15) Philosophical aphorisms
(16) Eznik, *Refutation of the Sects* (excerpts)
(17) On the miracles performed in Jerusalem
(18) Philosophical definitions
(19) Movsēs K'ert'oł, *Commentary on Aristotle's "Categories"*
(20) Egypt's ten scourges
(21) Tree of essence and philosophy
(22) Yovhannēs Sarkawag Imastasēr, excerpt from his mathematical work
(23) Three texts in Georgian script: (a) the numerical significance of the Georgian alphabet; (b) the Georgian alphabet; (c) Homily on Christ
(24) On the planets
(25) Six things that are essential for judges
(26) Anania Širakac'i, *On the Course of the Sun and on Measures*
(27) Miscellaneous definitions
(28) An excerpt from *Explication of Ecclesiastical Orders*
(29) Movsēs Xorenac'i, *Book of Rhetoric*

See Eganyan, *C'uc'ak,* II, cols. 416–17; Abrahamyan, *Glajor,* no. 34, p. 163; Xač'eryan, *Esayi Nč'ec'i,* no. 44, p. 397.

33. Erevan, Mat. 7650: Four Gospels.
A.D. 1329. Written at Glajor by the scribes Grigor Erēc' and Awag Dpir for Aslan, and illustrated by Awag Dpir. See Eganyan, *C'uc'ak,* II, col. 579.

34. Erevan, Mat. 7842: Four Gospels.
A.D. 1313. Written at Glajor by the scribe Pōłos Vardapet and illustrated probably by Momik for an unknown sponsor. See Eganyan, *C'uc'ak,* II, col. 621; Abrahamyan, *Glajor,* no. 30, pp. 157–58; Xač'eryan, *Esayi Nč'ec'i,* no. 39, p. 392.

35. Erevan, Mat. 8936: Four Gospels.
A.D. 1317. Written probably at Glajor by the scribe Yovsēp and illustrated by T'oros (Taronec'i) for an unknown sponsor. See Eganyan, *C'uc'ak,* II, col. 840.

36. Erevan, Mat. 9150: Colophon of a Gospel.
A.D. 1314. Eight folios, written at Glajor by the scribe Pōłos Vardapet for bishop Step'anos (Tarsayič). The colophon belonged to a codex once found at the monastery of Ganjasar. See Eganyan, *C'uc'ak*, II, col. 881; Abrahamyan, *Glajor*, no. 31, pp. 158–60; Xač'eryan, *Esayi Nč'ec'i*, no. 41, pp. 394–95.

37. Erevan, Mat. 9222c: Colophon of a Collection of Philosophical Works.
A.D. 1334. Codex written at Glajor by the scribe Yunan for himself. Only the colophon has survived. See Xač'ikyan, *XIV dari*, 261; Abrahamyan, *Glajor*, no. 48, pp. 178–79; Xač'eryan, *Esayi Nč'ec'i*, no. 62, p. 411.

38. Hartford, Connecticut, Case Memorial Library of the Hartford Seminary Foundation, 3: Four Gospels.
A.D. 1307–31. Begun at Noravank' by the scribes Momik and Pawłos Vardapet for Ovanē Ōrpēli. Completed by the scribe Yohanēs/Yovhannēs, and illustrated by T'oros (Taronec'i) at Glajor, and bound, in 1331, for Archbishop Step'anos-Tarsayič Ōrbēlian. See Der Nersessian, "An Illustrated Armenian Gospel of the XIVth century," *Études*, I, 631–34; Sanjian, *Catalogue*, 81–89; Xač'eryan, *Esayi Nč'ec'i*, no. 30, pp. 388–89.

39. Jerusalem, St. James, 365: Gēorg of Skewṙa, *Commentary on Isaiah*.
Written in 1299 in Cilicia by the scribe Vardan for Archbishop Kostandin, and sent by Kostandin of Caesarea to Esayi Nč'ec'i in Glajor, where the portrait of Esayi on p. 2 was painted. See Połarian, *Jerusalem Catalogue*, II, 269–71; Narkiss and Stone, *Jerusalem*, 76–77, 151; Xač'eryan, *Esayi Nč'ec'i*, no. 19, p. 380.

40. Jerusalem, St. James, 540: Holy Bible (fragmentary).
A.D. 1291–98? Written at Glajor by the scribe Yovhannēs for Karapet Vardapet Tospec'i. See Połarian, *Jerusalem Catalogue*, II, 557–61; Xač'eryan, *Esayi Nč'ec'i*, no. 16, p. 377.

41. Jerusalem, St. James, 1309: Collection of Philosophical Works.
A.D. 1312. Written probably at Glajor for Vardan Vardapet (Barjrberdc'i?). Part I of the codex written by the scribe Margarē and Part II by Xapar or Grigor Sarkawag.

(1) Porphyry, *Introduction to Aristotle's "Categories"*
(2) Dawit' Nerginac'i, *Commentary on Porphyry's "Introduction"*
(3) Aristotle, *Categories*, and Dawit' Nerginac'i, *Commentary on Aristotle's "Categories"*
(4) Aristotle, *On Interpretation*, and David the Philosopher, *Commentary on Aristotle's "On Interpretation"*

See Połarian, *Jerusalem Catalogue*, IV, 549–50; Abrahamyan, *Glajor*, no. 26, p. 156; Xač'eryan, *Esayi Nč'ec'i*, no. 32, pp. 389–90.

42. Jerusalem, St. James, 1414: Gregory Nazianzenus, *Orations*.
A.D. 1321. Written at Glajor. The names of the scribe and sponsor are unknown. See Połarian, *Jerusalem Catalogue*, V, 71–73.

43. Jerusalem, St. James, 1709: Miscellany.
A.D. 1298. Written at Glajor by the scribe Vardan Vardapet Kilikec'i for himself.

(1) Dionysius the Areopagite, *On the Heavenly Hierarchies*, translated by Step'anos Siwnec'i
(2) David the Invincible, *Definitions of Philosophy*

See Połarian, *Jerusalem Catalogue*, VI, 15–18; Xač'eryan, *Esayi Nč'ec'i*, no. 10, pp. 374–75.

44. Jerusalem, St. James, 2360: Four Gospels.
A.D. 1321. Written and illustrated at Glajor by T'oros (Taronec'i) for Princess Vaxax. See Połarian, *Jerusalem Catalogue*, VII, 510–14; N. Covakan, "T'oros Taronec'i," 454.

45. London, B.L. add. 15411: Four Gospels.
A.D. 1321. Written at Glajor by the scribe Kiwreł (who also calls himself Kerion) and illustrated by T'oros (probably Taronec'i), for Martiros Vardapet. See F. C. Conybeare, *Catalogue*, 22–24; Abrahamyan, *Glajor*, no. 40, pp. 168–69; Xač'eryan, *Esayi Nč'ec'i*, no. 51, p. 403.

46. Los Angeles, U.C.L.A., 1: Four Gospels.
Completed ca. 1305. The scribe and first two illuminators evidently worked elsewhere (very likely at Noravank'), but the rest of the miniatures were completed at Glajor by T'oros Taronec'i and others. Although the original colophon is missing, the inscription on page 227 indicates that the manuscript was intended for the Vardapet Esayi (Nč'ec'i).

47. New Julfa, All-Savior Monastery, 166; Gregory of Nyssa, *On the Structure of Man*.
A.D. 1318. Written at Glajor, by an unknown scribe, for Yakob (T'agorc'i). See L. G. Minasian, *C'uc'ak Jeṙagrac' Nor-Julayi S. Amenap'rkč'ean Vanac' T'angarani*, II, 174–77; Abrahamyan, *Glajor*, no. 36, pp. 164–65; Xač'eryan, *Esayi Nč'ec'i*, no. 47, pp. 399–400.

48. New Julfa, All-Savior Monastery, 373: Collection of Commentaries.
Two separate manuscripts bound together. First codex written in A.D. 1621 at an unknown location, by the scribe Awetik' for the priest Step'anos. This manuscript (fols. 5a–267a) contains Grigor Tat'ewac'i's *Commentaries on Matthew and John*. The second

codex (fols. 276a–386a) was written in A.D. 1284 at the monastery of Ałberc' (= Glajor) by the scribe Matt'ēos K'ahanay for an unknown sponsor.

(1) Nersēs Lambronac'i, *Commentary on Revelation*
(2) Nersēs Lambronac'i, *Commentary on the Death of John*

See Smbat Tēr-Awetisian, *C'uc'ak Hayerēn Jeṙagrac' Nor Jułayi Amenap'rkič' Vank'i,* I, 567–69.

49. Tabriz, Church of Surb Astuacacin, 1: Four Gospels.
A.D. 1311. Written, probably at Glajor, by the priest Cer for himself, and illustrated by T'oros (Taronec'i). See Hrač'eay Ačaṙian, *C'uc'ak Hayerēn Jeṙagrac' T'awrizi,* 70–74.

50. Venice, San Lazzaro, 12 (1007): Holy Bible.
A.D. 1332. Written at Glajor, by the scribes Dawit' and Ep'rem, and illustrated by T'oros (Taronec'i), for Nersēs Vardapet. See Barseł Sargisian, *Mayr C'uc'ak Hayerēn Jeṙagrac' Matenadaranin Mxit'areanc' i Venetik,* I, 117–28; Abrahamyan, *Glajor,* no. 47, pp. 177–78; Xač'eryan, *Esayi Nč'ec'i,* no. 61, pp. 410–11.

51. Venice, San Lazzaro, 265 (1108): *Oskep'orik.*
A.D. 1317–18. Written at Glajor by the scribe Sargis Abełay and illustrated by T'oros Taronec'i, for Grigoris and his wife Mamaxat'un.

(1) Gregory of Nyssa, *Treatise on the Nine Beatitudes*
(2) Gregory of Nyssa, *Treatise on the Lord's Prayer*
(3) The names of God, untitled text containing 1,060 appellations
(4) Vardan Vardapet, *The Lives of the Holy Fathers*
(5) Evagrius, *Spiritual Admonitions*
(6) Eusebius of Caesarea (more likely by Severianus of Emesa), *Treatise on Alexander*
(7) Pseudo-Epiphanius, *On Blue Devils*
(8) Catholicos Yakob I (1268–86), encyclical letter (concerning Nersēs Šnorhali's encyclical letter)
(9) Nersēs Šnorhali, encyclical letter
(10) Anania Vardapet, *Admonition to the Priests*
(11) Vardan Vardapet, *Admonition to All Christians from the Canons of the Apostles, Church Fathers, and Divines*
(12) Canonical writings (divided into 31 sections)
(13) Canonical admonitions pertaining to priests and monks
(14) Questions and responses (on seventy-one sundry subjects)
(15) Questions by Juvenal and responses by Movsēs K'ert'oł and David the Philosopher. (Probably related to the *Girk' Ēakac',* "Book of Beings")
(16) Nersēs the Catholicos of the Armenians, *The Confession of Faith of the Armenians*
(17) Epiphanius, *On Weights and Measures*
(18) The life and writings of Evagrius
(19) Nersēs Šnorhali, *On Instruction to Women* (an excerpt from his encyclical letter)
(20) Commentary on the verse "Sell your possessions, and give alms" (Luke 12:33)
(21) Five anonymous fables
(22) Thirty-five fables attributed to Olympianus
(23) Useful philosophical sayings
(24) Fables from the Prophecy of Jeremiah (probably from the work *De Vitis Prophetarum,* which is full of fables concerning the prophets and disciples, spuriously attributed to Epiphanius)
(25) On the signs of Jerusalem
(26) Testimonies concerning the birth and baptism of the Lord (from the writings of a large number of Armenian and non-Armenian church fathers)
(27) A prayer by John Chrysostom: "I know a holy man who, while praying, said nothing more than 'I thank you Lord, for all your goodness . . .'"
(28) A dialogue between Basil of Caesarea and the heretic Apollinarius
(29) Genealogical tables
(30) Homily by Yohanēs Vardapet Pluz: "God created man as soul and flesh, and fashioned him in His own image and likeness . . ."

See Sargisian, *Mayr C'uc'ak,* II, cols. 847–60; Xač'eryan, *Esayi Nč'ec'i,* no. 45, pp. 398–99.

52. Venice, San Lazzaro, 1917: Holy Bible (known as the "Bible of Esayi Nč'ec'i").
A.D. 1307. Written at Glajor by the scribe Pōłos and illustrated by T'oros Taronec'i for Esayi Vardapet (Nč'ec'i) and Dawit' Vardapet. See Sirarpie Der Nersessian, *Manuscrits,* 112–36; H. K'iwrtian, "T'oros Taronec'i," 218–19; N. Covakan, "T'oros Taronec'i," 454; A. Avetisyan, "Glajori Dproc'i mec Manrankarič' T'oros Taronec'in," 64–70; Abrahamyan, *Glajor,* no. 23, pp. 152–53; Xač'eryan, *Esayi Nč'ec'i,* no. 29, pp. 387–88.

53. Vienna, Mekhitarist Congregation, 353: Collection of Philosophical Works.
A.D. 1325. Written probably at Glajor, by an unknown scribe, for Esayi Nč'ec'i.

(1) David the Invincible, *Definitions of Philosophy*
(2) David the Invincible, *Encomium of the Holy Cross*
(3) Dionysius the Areopagite, *Letter to Bishop Titus*
(4) Porphyry, *Introduction to Aristotle's "Categories"*
(5) Dawit' Nerginac'i, *Commentary on Porphyry's "Introduction to Aristotle's 'Categories'"*
(6) Aristotle, *Categories,* and David the Invincible, *Commentary on Aristotle's "Categories"*

See Yakobos Tašian, *C'uc'ak Hayerēn Jeragrac' Matenadaranin Mxit'areanc' i Vienna,* I, 806–7; Abrahamyan, *Glajor,* no. 43, p. 172; Xač'eryan, *Esayi Nč'ec'i,* nos. 56–57, pp. 406–7.

54. Vienna, Mekhitarist Congregation, 382: Miscellany.
A.D. 1284. Written at the monastery of Ałberc' (= Glajor) by the scribe Matt'ē (also Matt'ēos) K'ahanay for himself.

(1) The story of the assumption of the Virgin Mary
(2) Sahak Arcruni, *The Epistle to Movsēs Vardapet Xorenac'i*
(3) Movsēs Xorenac'i, *Response to the Epistle of Sahak*
(4) Nersēs, *Commentary on the Prayers in the Gospel of John,* written at the request of his teacher Step'anos Vardapet

See Tašian, *C'uc'ak Hayerēn Jeragrac,* I, 833–35; Xač'eryan, *Esayi Nč'ec'i,* no. 9, pp. 373–74.

Present Locations Unknown
(listed in chronological order)

55. Nersēs Lambronac'i's *Commentary on Revelation and on the Death of John.*
A.D. 1283. Written at Glajor by the scribe Matt'ēos Vardapet Kilikec'i for Nersēs Vardapet Mšec'i. See Ališan, *Sisakan,* 131.

56. Commentary on the Epistles.
A.D. 1291. Written at Ałberc'/Glajor by the scribe Yohanēs for an unknown sponsor. See Ališan, *Sisakan,* 131; idem, *Hayapatum,* 525; Abrahamyan, *Glajor,* no. 13, p. 141; Xač'eryan, *Esayi Nč'ec'i,* no. 12, p. 376.

57. *Girk' Pitoyic'* (Handbook of Rhetoric).
A.D. 1298. Written at Glajor by the scribe Yohannēs for an unknown sponsor. See Ališan, *Sisakan,* 133; Xač'eryan, *Esayi Nč'ec'i,* no. 18, pp. 379–80.

58. Four Gospels.
A.D. 1304. Written at Glajor by the scribe Oskan Vardapet for an unknown sponsor. See Ališan, *Sisakan,* 134; Garegin Sruanjteanc', *T'oros Ałbar,* II, 375; Abrahamyan, *Glajor,* no. 49, p. 179; Xač'eryan, *Esayi Nč'ec'i,* no. 25, p. 385.

59. *Girk' Lucmanc'* (Book of Explications).
A.D. 1314. Written at Glajor by the scribe Grigoris C'ałmanec'i for an unknown sponsor. See Ališan, *Sisakan,* 137; Xač'eryan, *Esayi Nč'ec'i,* no. 40, pp. 392–94.

60. *Definitions of Philosophy* by David the Invincible.
A.D. 1314. Written at Glajor by the scribe Mxit'ar Eznkayec'i and illustrated by T'oros (Taronec'i) for Grigoris C'ałmanec'i. See Ališan, *Sisakan,* 135, 138; Ališan, *Hayapatum,* III, 113–14; Abrahamyan, *Glajor,* no. 32, pp. 160–62.

61. *The Epistles of Nersēs Šnorhali,* Compiled by Sargis.
A.D. 1317. Written at Glajor. The names of the scribe and sponsor are unknown. See Ališan, *Sisakan,* 133 and 136.

62. Miscellany.
A.D. 1317. Written at Glajor by the scribe Sargis Abełay for an unknown sponsor.

(1) The works of Gregory of Nyssa
(2) The epistles of Klayec'i (Nersēs Šnorhali)

See Ališan, *Sisakan,* 133.

63. Gregory of Nyssa, *On the Structure of Man (De Hominis Opificio).*
A.D. 1318. Written at Glajor by the scribe Yakob T'agorc'i for an unknown sponsor. See Ališan, *Sisakan,* 133.

64. *The Lives of Evagrius the Hermit and of Nileus.*
A.D. 1319. Written at Glajor; the names of the scribe and sponsor are unknown. See Sruanjteanc', *T'oros Ałbar,* II, 386, which lists this codex among those found at the monastery of Barjrahayeac' Surb Astuacacin in Arłni.

65. David the Invincible, *Definitions of Philosophy.*
A.D. 1320–21. Written at Glajor by the scribe Nersēs for Vardan. See Sahak A. Muratian and Nazarēt' P. Martirosian, *C'uc'ak Jeragrac' Mšoy S. Arak'eloc'-T'argmanč'ac' Vank'i ew Šrjakayic',* 22–23; Abrahamyan, *Glajor,* no. 41, pp. 169–70; Xač'eryan, *Esayi Nč'ec'i,* no. 52, p. 404.

66. Holy Bible.
A.D. 1327–28. Written at Glajor by the scribe Dawit' Getkec'i and illustrated by T'oros (Taronec'i) for Arak'el Vardapet Hałbatec'i. The codex once belonged to the monastery of Surb Karapet at Amrdol in Bałēš (= Bitlis). See Yovsēp'ian, *Xałbakeank',* 274–75, 350–51; N. Covakan, "T'oros Taronec'i," 455; Abrahamyan, *Glajor,* no. 44, pp. 172–74; Xač'eryan, *Esayi Nč'ec'i,* no. 58, pp. 407–9.

67. Four Gospels.
A.D. 1330. Written at Glajor by an unknown scribe and illustrated by T'oros (Taronec'i), for an unknown sponsor. See Łewond P'irłalemian, *Nšxark' Patmut'ean Hayoc',* no. 86, cited in Yovsēp'ian, *Xałbakeank',* 275.

68. Four Gospels.
A.D. 1334. Written at Glajor by the scribe Pōłos Vardapet Aknerc'i for the priest Grigor. See *Luys,* 1905, p. 367, cited by N. Covakan, "Akanc' Anapat kam Akneroy Vank'," *Sion* 7–8 (July-Aug. 1948), 229.

69. Four Gospels.
A.D. 1334. Written at Glajor by the scribe Oskan Vardapet for an unknown sponsor. See Sruanjteanc', *T'oros Ałbar,* II, 375; Xač'eryan, *Esayi Nč'ec'i,* no. 63, pp. 411–12.

APPENDIX D

Two Interpretations of the Ten Canon Tables

translated by James R. Russell

1. An Interpretation Attributed to Step'anos Siwnec'i

1. Worthy of great admiration is the mighty magnificence of the words beautifully and usefully adorned,[1] for with lofty speech these varicolored houses of the ten canons, adorned with pictures, with multi-storied canopies, with different colors, and with paints of varying hues, announce the prophecy of the four evangelists, describing properly the participation [*metałp'*, an allusion to the incarnation] of the celestial body; thus paired and linked together the varied readings are set down which are the words of the testimony about Jesus. Thus (in) the delineations with paints, beginning from the first canon until the tenth, columns and capitals are painted in the color of red blood, which indicate to us the incarnation and the cross.

2. Now the first Canon Table [*xoran*] is painted in four colors of ink, and it has the mystery of the four parts of the Canon Table. The purple columns (represent) the existent establishment of the thrones of the outer elements. The birds on top of the arches are peacocks (which) concern the (people of) the Old Law (who were) outside the church, with splendid bodily adornments (but) not speaking in the new church.

3. Now the second Canon Table is of similar honor to this one, adorned with four colors, for it has the black color inside, which demonstrates true existence, too difficult for the seers to see, and above it is the red in the form of an arch on account of the blood of sacrificial offerings sent up in petition to God. And sky-blue is painted in the middle [with corporeal ways of acting ordaining the spiritual, and the gold-colored][2] arch has the meaning of the priesthood standing in the middle. And the red, the color of wine, is on account of Melchizedek's bringing forth the mysteries in the type of Christ. And the black of the upper story (which) extends generally over all like a cloud cover [*ambawk'* sic! (*amp* 'cloud')] has the meaning of the arrival of God's economy.

4. And the third, with similar colors, on the arrival of the mystery of the revelation of God, takes its beginning from the canon before, expressing the three faces [i.e., persons] of the revelation of a united God; and above the arches of this is the altar with blazing fire. And above, it (is covered) by columns as by a veil, for so is covered the mystery of Christ; and the birds are roosters looking at the reason of the economy of the Canon Table and the cross, just as roosters in the hencoops are splendid and bold, commanding and awesome.[3]

5. And then the fourth, by concordant history in four colors, shows the face of the churches (which are) united in their thoughts but with various arches, having the cross in these arches. And there are two birds in the form of doves looking in them as if they were not really doves but likenesses of doves, namely those who have received the Holy Spirit and have become receptacles of the Holy Spirit; and on the outside they are a light shade of black because they had been foreshadowed by the transient Old Law (which anticipated) a purification by the red blood of Christ. Similarly also the altar is shaded but the flame is made bright, indicating that (fire) which Christ casts. And the horns of the arches above the capitals are paired with each other, red and blue, anchored with five parts each next to the five judges, which means the five tablets of the law [i.e., the Pentateuch]; and date palms (are) growing up from below because from this earth the truth sprouted up and ap-

[1] The publication of this text by Garegin Sruanjteanc' (*T'oros Ałbar* [Constantinople, 1884], 191–94), was not available to us; we have used instead the text published by Sirarpie Der Nersessian from a twelfth-century manuscript in Washington, Freer 50.3, fols. 3–6v (*Arm. Mss. Freer,* 103–4. It should be noted that Classical Armenian often omits essential verbs and other parts of speech; where the clarity of the text would otherwise be impaired we have restored or added such words in parentheses. Where commentary is required, or where emendations or figurative translations are needed to make sense of the text, remarks are made in square brackets or in notes.

[2] Lacuna in the text, supplied by S. Der Nersessian.

[3] The reference is most likely to the Armenian version of Prov. 30:31, *ak'ałał or šrǰi sigalov i mēǰ mareac'* 'the cock, which strolls pridefully amongst the hens' = LXX, *alektōr emperipatōn thēleiais eupsychos.*

proached the higher orders becoming green in righteousness, as it is written. And the two birds with red beaks and red breasts, like the servants of the first Canon Table, (are shown thus) because even though in body they were separate from the new mysteries, still with their voices and with their mouths they convey the same mystery.

6. And the fifth Canon Table has the same meaning but the shadow is gone and the red becomes brighter and the lily blossoms, because the cross has come near and the oracles approached the resurrection, announcing the salvation of the gentiles through the blood of Christ. But there is still a mask over it, for it still means the prophetic mysteries, on account of which there are only three, namely, the prophetic, the regal, and the sacerdotal. So there are three pomegranate branches spreading out in one bunch, bearing a symbol of the new by the old, in the Canon Table and the testament, insofar as the bitter-tasting peel (of the pomegranate) conceals within the sweetness of the fruit.[4] And the horns are close to the top of the table and symbolize Moses and Aaron, as we know in another canon. And the partridges[5] represent the prostitutes Mar and Rahab. The fish-hunting birds have the voice of these hunting in the waters, excited at the sight of the prophets and looking at the feet of the evangelists. And the roosters with golden feathers are thus adorned because they (represent those who) are worthy of the Spirit. First they purify their own souls.

7. And the sixth[6] and the seventh have the black waning and the red enriched. Priesthood entered underneath the arch.

8. And the eighth and the ninth and the tenth are like one another and are adorned with the old and the new for the cross and the crucified one, for the apostles, and for the fulfillment of the prophets in him.

2. An Interpretation by Nersēs Klayecʿi (Šnorhali), d. 1173

1. The spiritual books and the inspired teachings of wisdom preach the venerable holy Trinity, the eternal being. (They preach) eternal good, and the abiding and remaining of the works of the Creator, for which he provides in the good, (which are) all existing things (created) of nothing. (They proclaim) that we, rational creatures, through our self-governing appetites are separated from the good; they display the same Creator as merciful and kind to man by reason of His own virtues, (to those) who wish to become whole through renewed recollection of the good, as it is in this (that is by) see(ing) the faith of these words. For although our nature is turned toward death and corruption through lack of counsel, in animal ignominy, yet the Beneficent One has not hidden from this (man) the honor of his noble lineage or the cause of his life, (but has) said that man is the image of God, and paradise is his habitation, and the Tree of Life is the occasion of his immortality, planted by the hands of God. For keeping this recollection in mind, (man) may sometime ask for the prototype and the food of life and the place of pleasure, and (so) may (re)turn to his proper glory. But some other has He extinguished from glory, (who) has as his leader his own willful perdition, which opened a myriad of paths of confusion before him, until he is found to have multiplied evil, being the enemy of his own salvation; (these evils) it is not easy to enumerate, but none of the learned hearers is ignorant (of them).

2. However, the good recollection, planted by the original good, has not entirely dried up the root, nor has the lightning flash of God's graces been extinguished from our nature after centuries upon centuries, amongst noble men, the progeny of Adam, until the abysses of the Lord's mercy were opened and the time of revelation of the mystery arrived, which had been hidden from the nations, and (he) became the intercessor of our nature, the Creator of nature, the only begotten Son having taken this nature by an unconfused commingling. And in the way of nature he came for our salvation, which is the fulfillment of the will of the Father and the Holy Spirit. (He) filled the thirst of our longing, our Prototype, the image of the Father, in superabundance: not only by revealing himself to us as the one whom we had desired, but (also) by making our wretched and abashed natures the communicants of his unparalleled divine glory, by forming body and members of the tangible Godhead, and by showing at the same time the desirable food immortal, which the Tree brought forth as fruit for us. (This) is the history of the salvation of God's glory, which this book of good tidings encompasses, which is before us for interpretation.

3. The Garden (is) understood as having erected at (its) center the Tree of Life, for from the house of the Lord that water is caused to spring which flows in life everlasting; it is this which is walled around, not by the terrifying fire and the flaming Seraphic sword, but by the luxurious floral pictures and colorful, splendid ornament in the form of the drawing of the Canon Table. But also (there are) shaped the crea-

[4] In Armenia, as in neighboring Iran and in other places, the pomegranate with its many seeds symbolizes immortality. The legendary heroes of the epic of Sasun, for instance, regularly imbibe *nṙan gini* 'pomegranate wine.'

[5] *Kakʿaw* 'partridge' is also the name of a lewd dance of ancient Armenia which was condemned by the early fathers of the Armenian church.

[6] The abbreviation of the entries for the sixth through the tenth canon tables seems to indicate that a great deal of the text has been lost and that a later author tried to make good the loss with these few lines.

tions of certain plants; and little birds and the ordering of tables and columns and flowers possess within themselves profound mysteries, unrevealed meanings, and hidden ingenuities which are not to be passed by in vain, for all that is in the world may be divided into two parts: important (things), and pleasures. The important (things) are (the) necessary, such as light, air, and earth, and the bread from it, and the springs of the waters without which (things) cannot exist. And pleasures are (those) luxurious and soft things, such as wine, fruit, spices, (fine) cookery, bright colors, and sounds pleasing to the ear, which are the luxuries of the senses: pleasure and repose. But even (those things) which are not accounted important are of great utility to perfected (ones), when by this manifest color, taste, smell, hearing and the rest we ascend to the spiritual, and to the rational enjoyment (of) the good tidings of God which eye has not seen and ear has not heard and which the heart of man has not recalled, which God (has) prepared for his loved ones.

4. As God taught Israel by the marvelous ornament of the tabernacle [*xoran*] and temple, (so) he gave the lover of material things understanding of the heavenly by beguiling (him) with earthly treasures, as he commanded the rich youth to exchange the corporeal for the spiritual: "Go," he said, "and sell all that you have here, and place your treasure in heaven." Observing this, the compilers and founders of the Gospel illustrated (it) with luxurious herbs and multicolored flowers and various inventions, as a foretelling of earthly and heavenly things and a service to the virtues, and through these the text before us gives us to understand also what the spiritual pleasures and imperishable beauties are.

5. And (this) is the explanation of the ten Canon Tables [*xoranacʻ*]. First is that which is written: one Carpianos in midland [i.e., Upper] Egypt asked of Eusebius, the ecclesiastical philosopher, "Confirm for us unerringly the correspondence of the Gospels; where the four assent, and where the three, and in what place the two, and where they speak alone and individually. And list the number of their verses, lest they be stolen by heretics, and also so that we may with facility separate each without confusion." And Eusebius fulfilled the request of Carpianos, writing in ten canons the reliable knowledge of them, as the blessed Euthalius (had done for) the letters of the Apostles and the Acts together with the Epistles [*katʻułikēiwkʻn*], against the followers of Sabinos and other heretics.[7] And by a mystery he saw ten, which is a holy number and a gift of God, according to the ten sayings of the Law, and according to the hall(s) [*srahi*] of the tabernacle, and according to the ten parts of the creatures, and the senses of the body and the powers of the spirit which are in us. But if one wishes, the honor of the decade increases: in the Categories, and in the ten sayings of the Lord's prayer, and in the Nicaean Creed, and in all other things. And this is a particularly marvelous understanding, for the mystery of the Gospel, which was hidden in the divine (in time) without beginning, was revealed in the tenth (age?) [emending *tasnerrordi* to *tasnerordi*], visibly built at the completion of time. And it is so. The first Canon Table is where the Divinity himself is said to repose: in inaccessible light.

6. And the second and third Canon Tables are where the middle and last priesthoods of the incorporeal ones are said to be. The fourth (is) the garden. The fifth (is) the ark of Noah. The sixth (is) the tabernacle of Abraham. The seventh and the eighth (are) of Moses: the Holy of Holies and the outer tabernacle. The ninth (is) the most perfect and full of truth, the holy and Catholic Church, which contains within itself the mystery [or meaning, Arm. *xorhurd*] of all (the others). And they are called *xoran*s [Canon Tables, lit. 'canopy, tent'] because they are all *xorhrdakan* ['mystical'].[8] And the mystery is not apparent to all, but (only) to a few, and (its) entirety (is known) only to God. Now, in these Canon Tables there are four shades of color: red, green, black, blue, and a particular purple [*cirani*] apart from these four. And there are four trees in them: the date palm, olive, lily, and pomegranate, and another date palm again. And they have in them five birds: the peacock twice, the dove, the partridge, the cock, and the heron. There is also a sixth found in the same Gospels, the teal [*mrtmunkʻ*].

7. Now the first Canon Table is singly and entirely purple, fashioned (in) three (parts), which symbolizes the fixedness of the existent throne of God outside the four elements. The Canon Table (is) ineffable, where alone by itself the Holy Trinity revolves as one, leaving outside (itself) all creations; accordingly, the color purple indicates the omnipotent kingdom, inexhaustible and unending. This Canon Table is said to be encircled by the first curtain. However, three ranks: (the angels) of the throne, the Seraphim and the Cherubim, according to their ability immediately enjoy the spectacle of his glory.

8. And the second and third Canon Tables are painted in green and black (symbolic of) the incomprehensibility of God, which is hidden from them; for by means of the church through the incarnation [lit. 'becoming human,' Arm. *mardełutʻiwn*] of the Son, he announced manifold wisdom. There are three arches because the personality of the Trinity was known to them, (as they had) learnt the Trisagion from the Seraphim. And in these Canon Tables there

[7] Euthalius is the author credited with certain prefatory material for Acts and the Pauline letters.

[8] *Xorhrdakan*, adj. of *xorh-urd*, derives from a base that means 'to think' and is not connected etymologically with *xoran*, which is derived by Ghilain from Pth. *xwaran* 'tent.'

are date palms and peacocks. The trees indicate (the angels' lofty) height in nature and their place in glory; and the fruit (indicates) the sweetest pronouncement of blessing. And the gold-feathered and gilt-tailed peacock symbolizes their pure, fine and unblemished nature.

9. And the fourth Canon Table typifies the Garden (of Paradise), for it stands on four columns as an allegory of the tangible elements of which (it) is a mixture. And it is blue and black in color, for the radiance of Adam and his sons disappeared; the garment of skins allegorizes (this). (He) was screened from the glory of God and from the Garden which he had first enjoyed. There is also the form of an altar [lit. 'table,' Arm. *sełan*] in each of the Canon Tables. In the second and third Canon Tables (it is) shown aflame [i.e., with a flame burning on it] to symbolize the intelligible food of the corporeal ones and the rational offering [*patarag*] which they make to God. And in other Canon Tables in murky shape a Cross appears palely beneath the canopies, which demonstrates the mystery of Christ, who came secretly in the first times, descending from God amongst the angels, and from them the mystery of intellect (was given) to Adam and his progeny.

10. And red additionally (is used) for the fifth Canon Table, for by the ark of Noah and the tabernacle of Abraham the mystery of the blood of Christ was glorified (with) the righteousness of the church, which is the faith.

11. And the altar rose up together with the cross in the sixth Canon Table over the canopies, for it was made known by Abraham through the plant of the thicket and the ram [*sabekay tnkovn ew xoyiwn*], according to which it (is) said: "Abraham saw and was happy."[9] And the multicolored aspect of the columns symbolizes the priesthood of Melchizedek in the hypostasis [*dēms*] of Christ. And in these Canon Tables are olive trees and the lily flower; the olive indicates the longevity of the Patriarchs for the counsel of their kin, for they were their unwritten law. And since they kept unwilted the flower of virtue, as the olive (keeps) its splendid, shaggy crown, the sour taste (of the olive) allegorized (both) their austere virtue and their thick locks, from which the meaning of intelligence derives. As the fuel of light (comes) from the fruit of the olive, (the light) by which things pleasing to God become visible, so (it is) with the light of righteousness through Noah, Abraham, Isaac, Jacob, and Joseph. And the lily has three aspects: whiteness, yellowness, and redness. The white symbolizes purity and simplicity; the yellow, their patience; and the red, the labor of deeds accomplished in manliness. There is a kind of lily that grows in the sea and rises above the water, as the Patriarchs rose above the sea of this world through faith and works. And there is (a kind of lily that grows) in waste and desert lands and blossoms with the rain, even as the Gentiles by natural wisdom alone were pleasing to God, like Cornelius [cf. Acts 10] and many others. And again there is (a lily) that flowers beneath the flaming sun when others wilt, like the ranks of the dwellers in deserts [i.e., ascetics], (who) through the heat of the flame of the love of Christ made visible diverse proofs [*handēss*]; hence in laxity and luxury we wither.

12. And the seventh Canon Table (is) apparent, which exemplifies the splendor of the tabernacles [*xoranac'n*] of Moses; accordingly, the columns [restoring *siwnk'*] are blue and spiraled, and adorned with five parts, describing the law, which is divided into two pentads and was a staff (of support) to the people, so that they might not fall easily into error through transgression of the commandments. And here beneath the arches blue is increased and red is lessened, for they were tenebrous and prophesiers [i.e., merely tenebrous foreshadowing] of truth. And the paucity of red (is) because the sacrifices of animals could but slightly cleanse the people. Now, it is the tabernacle which unifies, as the first (was) in the glory of divinity; and as the Garden, which had Adam for only a short time. And again, the flood of the waters parted man (from it) on this side, having Noah as the beginning. And the other (tabernacles) are in pairs, as those of the angels, of Noah, and of Abraham, and (so also were) the Mosaic (ones), the Holy of Holies by which Moses and a few others were worthy, in the manner of Christ our savior. And the outer tabernacle is the one which is the entrance of the common people, and those who worshipped the Lord by it had as an example the lives of those (who lived) until the time of the building of the temple, beginning with Moses. In the seventh Canon Table the birds are red-beaked doves, who shelter in their shadow the disciples of the Holy Spirit, who filled Bezalel the architect of the tabernacle and Eliav [= Oholiab] and in it [i.e., once it was built], through Moses, Joshua, and the elders.

13. And in the eighth Canon Table the partridges are a sign of whorish and foreign women: Tamar, Rahab, and Ruth. For the partridge (is) fond of copulation; and again it is the way of the partridge to steal eggs and make them its own, even as they [i.e., the three women] stole by cunning from the house of Abraham and his son the fruit of blessings and became the foremothers of Christ. And some see in the doves on the table Moses and his like, to whom God spoke as a friend, and Joshua and David, who looked upon the mystery of the incarnation of Christ. As Moses says: "O prophet, the Lord your God will arise for you from your brothers like me." [cf. Deut.

[9] In the Armenian text of Gen. 22:13, the ram is not 'caught,' as in the Hebrew and LXX, but *kaxec'aw*, 'hung' from the bush. It is shown in manuscript illustrations actually dangling in the air at the scene of the sacrifice of Isaac. Hence the sense of 'rising up' in the commentary is particularly Armenian.

18:15]. And the two horns of the altar they speak of as Moses and Aaron, who were the powers of the people, which butt against their opponents.

14. And the ninth Canon Table signifies the temple; accordingly it is richly colored, for the black and blue (have) waned and the red has waxed brilliant. For the advent of the Emmanuel has come close, and the sons of the prophets elevate the theology of the Son of God. Accordingly, the birds (are) cocks: They symbolize the same as those who, close to the morning of righteousness, proclaimed the apparition of the ineffable light, trampling death underfoot, saying, "Death, where is your victory?" Hence many, emboldened, scorned the transitory and were crowned with the death of the righteous, like the manly Maccabean witnesses prophesying the death of Christ; wherefore the altar, barren and without stores, shows their time, when by Antiochus they were forbidden to bring offerings to the altar according to the Law [cf. 1 Macc. 1:45]. And here the trees (are) pomegranates, which symbolize the words of the prophets, who as though with rinds by allegories concealed the good tidings of sweetness to the Gentiles, feeding to the Jews the bitterness of warnings, which reached them (as) the thorny roughness of woes and captivities, (whilst) filling the stores of the church of the Gentiles with the goodness of rational fruit. So it is here that the date-palm (is seen) sprouting on high from below, which announces to us (that tree) of David; truth sprouted from the earth and righteousness was made manifest from heaven. And thus the secret of the ninth Canon Table, which is thrice here, symbolizes for us the three synoptic [or 'concordant,' Arm. *hamabarbaṙ*] evangelists: Matthew, Mark, and Luke, who in agreement with each other wrote down the place and time of the incarnation of Christ, showing his genealogy according to the body; for the first stage will be (that) of the ascent of the faithful and their understanding of the ineffable and the timeless. Who will relate his timeless genealogy? As by the hand of Joshua (he) gave good tidings of the land of fountains of milk and honey, (so he) displayed to the unperfected people Jesus Christ and the higher realm.[10]

15. And the ten(th) Canon Table, which stands facing the ninth, affirms the stability and perfection of the holy church, which fulfilled the inadequacies of the Law, and, in truth, of the tenebrous things, in whose midst John [the Baptist] was the morning star of the sun of righteousness, the fulfillment of the Prophets and the beginning of the Apostles. Wherefore opposite the cocks are the herons, which reveal the meaning of the Apostles, (who were) fishermen. They by the command of the Lord became hunters of men, hunting the faithful of the Gospel from death into life; some of them indeed were turned toward the cocks, for the Apostles were interpreters of the Prophets, and half are (opposite) each other, since they were the preachers of a single religion; while others (face) the altar, since they take that which they preach from the first fountain. And the teals standing close by signify the evangelists in perfection: they became the penetrating sea-divers of the depths of God, and drank of the abundant rivulets of the Holy Spirit, and, flying to all by the wings of the same and gathering the same life-giving water, they scattered the dew of healing over the dry and sickened souls of men, for health and the irrigation of immortality. And by their red feet they verify (the words) of the Prophets: "The feet of the evangelists [*awetaranč'ac'n*] are beautiful" [cf. Isa. 52:7]. And by their mouths (they signify) the fire-colored [*hragunakn*] mystery wherewith they were intoxicated and evangelized in the same manner, for the purification of the souls of Christians. And since the necks of some of the herons are intertwined and (those) of the teals are figured toward each other, they show the unity and intimacy of the Old and New Testaments. And since the tenth Canon Table is most ornamented and resplendent and brilliant, with rosy red paint, blue is entirely exhausted, for the ancient darkness of sin and ignorance, of lamentation and sadness, is past, and all has become new, bedaubed with the blood of Christ. Accordingly (he) came and stood at the head of the upper arch, for the mystery of God was completed, and the preaching of the cross possesses the entire universe, and the Crucified One (preached) divine wisdom to all the earth in the glory of the Father and of the Holy Spirit.

16. And this ten(th) Canon Table has again the mystery of the highest tabernacle, which will become manifest at the fulfillment of eternity, at the perfection of the sensible world and (at) the inauguration of shapeless and formless heavenly good tidings, at which everything will attain perfection and the new Jerusalem will descend from heaven in ineffable ornament and splendor, according to the Apocalypse of St. John. All the forever changing churches unite and become one in it, and in splendidly adorned beauty (the church) is wedded to Christ, to receive him in the marriage chamber of glory [*yaṙagast p'aṙac'*]. At the perfection, (Christ) will give dominion into the hands of God and the Father, (and) will frustrate the dominions and powers of the demons and the conquerors empowered by them, who will be placed beneath his feet for the defeat of death, the last enemy. For all things are subject to him, the willing and the unwilling, the lofty and the base, the right and the left, hell and the kingdom, and from him they will take recompense according to their deserts, from the righteous judge, immortally and for boundless eternity. And then he will receive understanding of ineffable things, to be with God in every year. And with respect

[10] Here, the intention seems to be the explanation of ineffable things through familiar ones.

to this in the ten(th) Canon Table the splendidly adorned cross appears with shining rays, for on the last day we of faith set our eyes on the clouds to see (them) suffused with beams of light: the vessel of our salvation and the crown of the church, the divine sign coming as the pride of the Christians and the terror of the faithless, for the complete destruction of the demons through merciless and unending torment.

17. These (are the teachings) of our learned fathers and brothers regarding the cause of wisdom and the foundation of the beginning of this (mighty) host of the Gospel, so that we may know that the first fathers did not portray the flowery sculptures of multicolored hue of the ten mystical Canon Tables in vain or without meaning. But they, guided by pleasure in rational beauty, fashioned these, seeing them with spiritually trained wisdom, and recast them before the eyes of rational beings as apparent displays (painted) with visible materials. As Paul says: "If invisible things are of God, they are seen by the perception of visible things," [cf. Rom. 1:20] in which may we be enlightened to the things of the mind, hidden from sight, through these Canon Tables. Gathering flowers from the meadows of manifold virtues for the fashioning of woven crowns of imperishable glory, circling with care in the tabernacle of this holy temple with unblemished steps (leaving no imprint of) dust, with evangelical preparation here at the pedestal of this preface to the Gospel, assisted even as the nation of Israel about Mount Sinai, adorned with ablutions sprinkled about (them), they became worthy of the apparition of God, [cf. Exod. 19:10–11] particularly as this mountain standing close, inhabited by God, seeks modesty above (all else). For that one demanded but three days of legal spouses (that they) be pure and purify their visible garments and bodies. But the Lord commands disciples of this Gospel to (wear) a single garment, without bronze in (their) belt(s), and without knapsacks or shoes. (And he commanded them) not to fornicate with their eyes, nor to call their brothers moron [*moros*] or fool; nor to be owing before Gehenna and judgment; nor to oppose the one who opposes us; and to present the other (cheek) to him who slaps our right cheek; and to give also the outer garment to him who strips off the inner; and for the one compelling us to walk a mile under guard, to walk after him another two; and in the road of this life not to give greeting to transient pleasures; and if we have erred in something, to render account in this world before the judgment of the great day; and to forgive seventy-seven (times them) that they sin against us, and other such words of counsel and exhortation wherewith teems the encampment of the Gospel. (They) are cleansing baths of the sight and hearing for those approaching the soaring peaks of God, which (we) will succeed (in climbing), at the base of the introduction to the Gospel. Let us therefore enter in the manner of Moses, into the mists of unknown multitudes, into the depths of the writing of this Gospel, bearing with us the tablets of our hearts. For in the prayers of our fathers and brothers God will inscribe in efficacious (letters) the power of this Gospel which stands before us, which he assigned to us (in) ten Canon Tables with the impress, instead of the ten commandments which are on the divine tablets, for the enjoyment of your hearts and of upright ways (of living), (and) as gifts, the donations of offerings of rational (oblations), (that we may) take (them) with our weak arms in the incapacious platters of our minds and of our words, mediocre in conception, as a sweet fragrance for you and for your salvation and liberation from debt. May the Holy Spirit, guide and sustainer of all, make us and you worthy of this, by your and our benefactor, alive and dead, worthy (indeed) of the portion of the righteous, for the glory and praise of the Divine, to extol and to thank (him) now and forever. Amen.

Bibliography

Abrahamyan, Ašot. "Glajor, Erkrord At'ēnk' Pancali" [Glajor: The Glorious Second Athens]. *Garun* (monthly, Erevan), 9 (1978), 76–84.

———. "Glajori Hamalsarani Tełə ev Himnadrut'yan Taret'ivə [The Location and Date of Founding of the University of Glajor]. *Patma-Banasirakan Handes* (quarterly, Erevan), 1 (1982), 159–76.

———. *Glajori Hamalsaranə* [The University of Glajor]. Erevan, 1983.

Ačaṙian, Hrač'eay. *C'uc'ak Hayerēn Jeṙagrac' T'awrizi* [Catalogue of the Armenian Manuscripts in Tabriz]. Vienna, 1910.

———. *Hayoc' Anjnanunneri Baṙaran* [Dictionary of Armenian Personal Names]. 5 vols. Erevan, 1942–62; repr. Beirut, 1972.

Ackroy, P. R., and C. F. Evans, eds. *The Cambridge History of the Bible*. Cambridge, 1969 ff.

Adontz, Nicolas. *Denys de Thrace et les commentateurs arméniens*. Traduit du russe. Louvain, 1970.

———. *Armenia in the Period of Justinian: The Political Conditions Based on the Naxarar System*. Translated by Nina G. Garsoïan. Lisbon, 1970.

Agathangełos. *History of the Armenians*. Translation and commentary by Robert W. Thomson. Albany, N.Y., 1976.

Algermissen, K. *Lexikon der Marienkunde*. Regensburg, 1967.

Ališan, Łewond. *Ayrarat*. Venice, 1890.

———. *Sisakan*. Venice, 1893.

———. *Hayapatum*. 3 vols. Venice, 1901–2.

———. *Sissouan ou Arméno-Cilicie. Description géographique et historique*. Venice, 1899.

Allen, W. E. D. *A History of the Georgian People*. London, 1932.

Alpōyačian, Aršak. *Patmut'iwn Hay Dproc'i* [History of Armenian Education]. Cairo, 1946.

American Society for Testing and Materials. *X-ray Powder File*. Rev. ed. Philadelphia, 1960.

Anasyan, H. S. *Haykakan Matenagitut'yun, V–XVIII dd.* [Armenian Bibliology, V–XVIII Centuries]. 2 vols. Erevan, 1959–76.

Ant'abyan, P'. "Ardyok' Hay Aṙajin Hamalsaranə Glajorn ē" [Is Glajor the First Armenian University?]. *Banber Erevani Hamalsarani* (quarterly, Erevan), 2 (1974), 192–205.

———. "Ašxarhac'uyc' Vardanay Vardapeti" [The Ašxarhac'uyc' of Vardan Vardapet]. *Patma-Banasirakan Handes* 3 (1984), 87–102.

Aphraat. *Aphraatis Sapientis Persae Demonstrationes*. Translated by J. Parisot. *Patrologia Syriaca* I (1894).

Aṙak'el Siwnec'i. *Yałags K'erakanut'ean Hamaṙawt Lucmunk'* [On Grammar: Concise Explication]. Critical text with an introduction by L. G. Xač'eryan. Los Angeles, 1982.

Aṙak'elyan, B. "Kazmeri zardarman arvestə miǰnadaryan Hayastanum." *Banber Matenadarani* 4 (1958).

Arevšatyan, S. S., and A. S. Mat'evosyan. *Glajori Hamalsaranə Miǰnadaryan Hayastani Lusavorut'yan Kentron* [The University of Glajor: A Center of Medieval Armenia's Enlightenment]. Erevan, 1984.

Arndt, Hella, and Renate Kroos. "Zur Ikonographie der Johannesschussel." *Aachner Kunstblätter* 38 (1946), 243–328.

Arpee, Leon. *A History of Armenian Christianity*. New York, 1946.

Ashjian, Mesrob. *The Great Week in the Armenian Tradition*. New York, 1978.

Ašxarhac'uyc' Vardanay Vardapeti. Critical text with an introduction by Hayk Pērpērian. Paris, 1960.

Avetisyan, A. "Glajori Dproc'i Mec Manrankarič' T'oros Taronac'in" [T'oros Taronac'i: The Great Miniaturist of the School of Glajor]. *Ēǰmiacin* (monthly, Erevan), 7–8 (1957), 64–70.

———. "Glajori Hamalsaranə" [The University of Glajor]. *Ēǰmiacin* 4–5 (1956), 82–92.

———. *Haykakan Manrankarč'ut'yan Glajori Dproc'ə* [The Glajor School of Armenian Miniature Painting]. Erevan, 1971.

Azaryan, L. R. *Kilikyan Manrankarč'ut'yunə XII–XIII dd.* Erevan, 1964.

———. *Haykakan Xač'kar*. Erevan, 1973.

Azaryan, L. Ṙ., and Armen Manoukian. *Khatchkar*, Documenti di architetura armena 2. Milan, 1969.

Babayan, L. H. *Hayastani Soc'yal-Tntesakan K'ałak'akanut'yunə XIII–XIV darerum* [The Social-Economic Policies in Armenia in the XIII–XIV Centuries]. Erevan, 1964.

Banali Čšmartut'ean [The Key of Truth]. Edited and translated by F. C. Conybeare. Oxford, 1898.

Bandmann, G. "Beobachtungen zum Etschmiadzin-Evangeliar," *Tortulae,* Supplement zur *Römische Quartalschrift.* Rome, 1966.

Bar Kepha, Moses. "The Ladder Which Jacob Saw Going up to Heaven Typified the Cross," *A Discourse in Separate Chapters for the Feast of the Cross.* Translated by Sidney H. Griffith. Unpublished.

Baronian, Sukias, and F. C. Conybeare. *Catalogue of the Armenian Manuscripts in the Bodleian Library.* Oxford, 1918.

Barxudaryan, S. G. *Divan Hay Vimagrut'yan.* Vol. III: Vayoc' Jor, Ełegnajori ev Azizbekovi Šrǰanner [Corpus of Armenian Inscriptions]; Vol. III: Vayoc' Jor, the Regions of Ełegnajor and Azizbekov. Erevan, 1967.

Baur, A., and J. Strzygowski. "Eine alexandrinische Weltchronik," *Denkschriften der kaiserlichen Akademie der Wissenschaften in Wien, phil.-hist. Klasse* 5. Vienna, 1905.

Bedoukian, Paul Z. *Coinage of Cilician Armenia.* American Numismatic Society, Numismatic Notes and Monographs 14. New York, 1962.

———. "Medieval Armenian Coins." *REArm* 8 (1971), 365–431.

———. "The Single Lion Coronation Coins of Levon I." *JSAS* 2 (1985–86), 97–105.

Beissel, S. *Die Bilder der Handschrift des Kaisers Otto im Münster zu Aachen.* Aachen, 1886.

Belting, Hans. *Die Bibel des Niketas.* Wiesbaden, 1979.

Bibliothèque Nationale. *Évangiles avec peintures byzantines du XIe siècle.* 2 vols. Paris, n.d.

Bond, F. *An Introduction to English Church Architecture.* London, 1912.

Book of Hours of the Common Prayers of the Armenian Church together with the Directorium of Lessons and Practices. Translated by Tiran Nersoyan. Evanston, Ill., 1964.

Boyle, A. "Indjū." *Encyclopedia of Islam,* new ed., vol. III, fasc. 59–60. Leiden, 1971.

Branner, Robert. *Manuscript Painting in Paris during the Reign of St. Louis.* Berkeley, 1977.

Breviarium armenorum sive dispositio communium armeniacae ecclesiae precum. Translated by Isaac Kiudius and Joannis Mantagunensis. Venice, 1909.

Brightman, F. E. *Liturgies Eastern and Western.* Oxford, 1896.

Bucher, François. *The Pamplona Bible.* New Haven, 1970.

Buchthal, Hugo. *Art of the Mediterranean World, A.D. 100 to 1400.* Washington, D.C., 1983.

———. *Miniature Painting in the Latin Kingdom of Jerusalem.* Oxford, 1957.

———. "A Byzantine Miniature of the Fourth Evangelist and Its Relatives," *DOP* 15 (1961), 127–40.

———. "Studies in Byzantine Illumination of the Thirteenth Century." *Jahrbuch der Berliner Museen* 25 (1983), 27–102.

Burney, Charles, and D. M. Lang. *The Peoples of the Hills.* London, 1971.

Buschhausen, Heide and Helmut. *Die illuminierten armenischen Handschriften der Mechitaristen Congregation in Wien.* Vienna, 1976.

———. *Armenische Handschriften der Mechitaristen-Congregation in Wien: Katalog zur Sonderausstellung in der Österreichischen Nationalbibliothek.* Vienna, 1981.

Busse, Adolfus. *Davidis Prolegomena et in Porphyrii Isagogen Commentarium.* Berlin, 1904.

Cabelli, Diane E., and Thomas F. Mathews. "The Palette of Khatchatur of Khizan." *Journal of the Walters Art Gallery* 40 (1982), 37–40.

———. "Pigments in Armenian Manuscripts of the Tenth and Eleventh Centuries." *REArm,* n.s. 18 (1984), 33–47.

Cabelli, Diane E., M. Virginia Orna, and Thomas F. Mathews. "Analysis of Medieval Pigments from Cilician Armenia." *Archaeological Chemistry* 3, Advances in Chemistry series 205. Washington, D.C., 1984, 243–54.

Cabrol, Fernand, and Henri Leclercq, eds. *Dictionnaire d'Archéologie Chrétienne et de Liturgie.* Paris, 1910 ff.

Cahn, Walter. *Romanesque Bible Illumination.* Ithaca, N.Y., 1982.

Cambridge History of the Bible. Edited by P. R. Ackroyd and C. F. Evans. Cambridge, 1970.

Č'amč'ian, Mik'ayēl. *Patmut'iwn Hayoc'* [History of Armenia]. 3 vols. Venice, 1786.

Cappelletti, J. *Sancti Nersetis Opera.* Venice, 1883.

Carr, Annemarie Weyl. *The Rockefeller McCormick New Testament: Studies toward the Reattribution of Chicago University Library, ms. 965.* Ph.D. dissertation. University of Michigan, 1973.

———. *Byzantine Illumination 1150–1250: The Study of a Provincial Tradition.* Chicago, 1987.

Carswell, John. *New Julfa: The Armenian Churches and Other Buildings.* Oxford, 1968.

Čašoc' Girk'. Jerusalem, 1873.

The Catholic Encyclopedia. New York, 1909.

Cavallera, F., ed. *S. Eustathii Antiocheni in Lazarum Fragmenta.* Paris, 1905.

Cecchelli, Carlo, Giuseppe Furlani, and Mario Salmi. *The Rabbula Gospels. Facsimile Edition of the Miniatures of the Syriac Manuscript Plut. I, 56 in the Medicaean-Laurentian Library.* Olten, 1959.

———. *La cattedra di Massimiano.* Rome, n.d.

Colledge, M. A. R. *The Art of Palmyra.* London, 1976.

Conybeare, Frederick C. *A Catalogue of the Armenian Manuscripts in the British Museum.* London, 1913.

———. *Studia Biblica et Patristica.* Vol. IV. Oxford, 1896.

———. *Rituale Armenorum, Being the Administration of the Sacraments and the Breviary of the Armenian Church.* Oxford, 1905.

———. "Dialogus de Christi die natali." *Zeitschrift für die neutestamentliche Wissenschaft* 5 (1904), 332 ff.

Corrie, Rebecca. "The Conradin Bible: Since 'Since DeRicci.'" *Journal of the Walters Art Gallery* 40 (1982), 13–24.

Corrigan, Kathleen. *The Ninth Century Byzantine Marginal Psalters.* Ph.D. dissertation, University of California, Los Angeles, 1984.

Covakan, N. [= Norayr Połarian]. "Akancʿ Anapat kam Akneroy Vankʿ." *Sion* 7–8 (1948), 229.

Cyril of Alexandria. *Commentary on Saint Luke.* Translated by R. M. Tonneau. CSCO 140 (1953).

———. *In Joannem.* PG 73–74.

Cyril of Jerusalem. *Catechesis Mystagogica.* PG 33, cols. 1065–1128.

Daniélou, Jean. *From Shadow to Reality. Studies in the Biblical Typology of the Fathers.* London, 1960.

Darmstaedter, Robert. *Die Auferweckung des Lazarus in der altchristlichen und byzantinischen Kunst.* Bern, 1955.

Davitʿ Anhałtʿ. *Erker* [David the Invincible: Works]. Translation, introduction, and annotations by S. S. Arevšatyan. Erevan, 1980.

Dawitʿ Anyałtʿ. *Erkasirutʿiwnkʿ Pʿilisopʿayakankʿ* [David the Invincible: Philophical Works]. Critical texts and introduction by S. S. Arevšatyan. Erevan, 1980.

Dean, James Elmer. *Epiphanius' Treatise on Weights and Measures, the Syriac Version.* Chicago, 1935.

Dédéyan, Gérard, ed. *Histoire des Arméniens.* Toulouse, 1982.

Definitions and Divisions of Philosophy by David the Invincible Philosopher. Translated by Bridget Kendall and Robert W. Thomson. University of Pennsylvania, Armenian Texts and Studies 5. Chico, Calif., 1983.

Deichmann, Friedrich W., G. Bovini, and H. Brandenburg. *Repertorium der christlichen-antiken Sarkophage.* Wiesbaden, 1967.

———. *Frühchristliche Bauten und Mosaiken von Ravenna.* Baden-Baden, 1958.

De Morgan, Jacques. *Histoire du peuple arménien.* Paris, 1919.

Demus, Otto. *The Mosaics of San Marco in Venice.* Chicago, 1984.

———. *Byzantine Mosaic Decoration.* London, 1948.

———. *The Mosaics of Norman Sicily.* London, 1950.

Derbes, Ann. *Byzantine Art and the Dugento: Iconographic Sources of the Passion Scenes in Italian Painted Crosses.* Ph.D. dissertation, University of Virginia, 1980.

Der Nersessian, Sirarpie. *Manuscrits arméniens illustrés des XIIe, XIIIe et XIVe siècles de la Bibliothèque des pères Mekhitharistes de Venise.* Paris, 1937.

———. *Armenia and the Byzantine Empire: A Brief Study of Armenian Art and Civilization.* Cambridge, Mass., 1947.

———. *Armenian Manuscripts in the Freer Gallery of Art.* Freer Gallery of Art, Oriental Studies 6. Washington, D.C., 1963.

———. *Aghtʿamar, Church of the Holy Cross.* Harvard Armenian Texts and Studies 1. Cambridge, Mass., 1965.

———. "The Kingdom of Cilician Armenia." In *A History of the Crusades,* ed. K. M. Setton, vol. II, 630–59. Madison, Wisc., 1969; repr. in Der Nersessian, *Études,* 329–52.

———. *Armenian Manuscripts in the Walters Art Gallery.* Baltimore, 1973.

———. *Études byzantines et arméniennes.* 2 vols. Louvain, 1973.

———. *Armenian Art.* London, 1978.

———. "L'Évangile du Matenadaran no. 10.525 de l'an 1306: Contribution à l'étude de la miniature en Siwnikʿ au XIVe siècle." *REArm,* n.s. 16 (1982), 327–43.

———. "Évangile du roi Gagik de Kars: Jérusalem, no. 2556." *REArm,* n.s. 18 (1984), 85–107.

——— (foreword). *Ējmiacni Ganjer* [The Treasures of Ējmiacin], 1984.

Der Nersessian, Sirarpie, and Arpag Mekhitarian. *Armenian Miniatures from Isfahan.* Brussels, 1986.

Devreesse, Robert. "Chaines exégétiques grecques." *Dictionnaire de la Bible, Supplément.* Vol. I, pp. 1084–1233. Paris, 1928.

DeWald, Ernest T. "The Iconography of the Ascension." *AJA* 19 (1915), 227–319.

Diez, Ernst, and Otto Demus. *Byzantine Mosaics in Greece.* Cambridge, Mass., 1931.

Dionysius the Pseudo-Areopagite. *The Ecclesiastical Hierarchy.* Translated and annotated by Thomas L. Campbell. Lanham, Md.-New York-London, 1981.

Diringer, David. *The Illuminated Book. Its History and Production.* London, 1967.

Divine Liturgy of the Armenian Apostolic Orthodox Church. Translated by Bishop Tiran Nersoyan. New York, 1950.

Divine Liturgy of the Armenian Apostolic Orthodox Church together with the Directorium of Lessons and Practices. Translated by Tiran Nersoyan, 4th edition. New York, 1970.

Dölger, F. J. *Ichthys. Das Fischsymbol in frühchristlicher Zeit.* Münster, 1943.

Dournovo, Lydia A. *Miniatures arméniens.* Paris, 1960.

———. *Armenian Miniatures.* New York, 1961.

———. *Haykakan Manrankarčʿutʿyun.* Edited by R. G. Drampyan. Erevan, 1967.

Dulaurier, Édouard. *Recherches sur la chronologie arménienne technique et historique.* Paris, 1859.

Eganyan, Ō., et al. *Cʻucʻak Jeṙagracʻ Maštocʻi Anvan Matenadarani.* 2 vols. Erevan, 1965–70.

Enlart, Camille. *Manuel d'archéologie française depuis le temps mérovingien jusqu'à la renaissance.* Paris, 1916.

Ephraem Syrus. "Commentaire de l'évangile concordant." Translated by Louis Leloir. CSCO 137–38, Scriptores Armeniaci 1–2. Louvain, 1953–54.

———. "Commentaire de l'évangile concordant, texte syriaque." Translated by Louis Leloir. Chester Beatty Monographs 8. Dublin, 1963.

———. *Doctrines et méthodes de S. Ephraem d'après son commentaire de l'évangile concordant.* CSCO 220, Subsidia 18. Louvain, 1961.

———. *Hymns on Virginity.* CSCO 223, Scriptores Syri 94.

———. *Hymnes de Saint Ephrem.* PO 30 (1961), 225.

Esayi Nčʻecʻi. *Verlucutʻiwn Kʻerakanutʻean* [Commentary on Grammar]. Critical text with annotations by L. G. Xačʻeryan. Erevan, 1966.

Esayi Tayecʻi. *Ankanon Girkʻ Nor Ktakaranacʻ: Tʻangaran Haykakan Hin ew Nor Dprutʻeancʻ.* Venice, 1898.

Eusebius. *Historia Ecclesiastica.* PG 20, cols. 9–909.

———. *Demonstratio Evangelica.* PG 22, cols. 9–794.

Evans, Helen C. "Nonclassical Sources for the Armenian Mosaic near the Damascus Gate in Jerusalem." In *East of Byzantium: Syria and Armenia in the Formative Period,* edited by Nina Garsoïan et al. (Washington, 1982), 217–21.

———. "Canon Tables as an Indication of Teacher-Pupil Relationships in the Career of Tʻoros Roslin." In *Medieval Armenian Culture,* ed. T. Samuelian and M. Stone, 272–90. University of Pennsylvania Armenian Texts and Studies 6. Chico, Calif., 1983.

———. "Cilician Figurative Letters and the West." *17th International Byzantine Congress. Abstracts of Short Papers.* Washington, D.C., 1986, 110–11.

———. *Armenian Manuscript Illumination at the Patriarchate in Hṙomkla and the West.* Ph.D. dissertation, Institute of Fine Arts, New York University, 1990.

Filov, B. D. *Les miniatures de l'évangile du roi Jean Alexandre à Londres.* Sofia, 1934.

Folda, Jaroslav. *Crusader Manuscript Illumination at Saint-Jean d'Acre, 1275–1291.* Princeton, 1976.

Francovich, Géza de. *Archittetura medievale armena.* Rome, 1968.

Frasson, Giuseppe, ed. and trans. *Pseudo-Epiphani Sermo de Antichristo.* Bibliotheca Armeniaca 2. Venice, 1976.

Frazer, Margaret E. "Hades Stabbed by the Cross of Christ." *Metropolitan Museum of Art Journal* 9 (1974), 153–61.

Frey, Albert R. *Dictionary of Numismatic Names.* New York, 1947.

Friend, Albert M. "The Portraits of the Evangelists in Greek and Latin Manuscripts." *Art Studies* 5 (1927), 115–50, 7 (1929), 3–29.

Froidevaux, L. M. *Grigoris Aršarouni. Commentaire du Lectionnaire.* Venice, 1975.

Galanos, Kłemēs. *Miabanutʻiwn Hayocʻ Surb Ekełecʻwoyn ənd Meci Ekełecʻwoyn Hṙovmay* [Union of the Holy Church of the Armenians with the Great Holy Church of Rome]. Vol. I. Rome, 1650.

Garsoïan, Nina G. *The Paulician Heresy: A Study of the Origin and Development of Paulicianism in Armenia and the Eastern Provinces of the Byzantine Empire.* The Hague, 1967.

———. *Armenia between Byzantium and the Sasanians.* London, 1985.

———. "L'indépendance retrouvée: Royaume du Nord et royaume du Sud (IXe–XIe siècles)." In *Histoire des Arméniens,* ed. Gérard Dédéyan, 215–68. Toulouse, 1982.

Garsoïan, Nina G., et al., eds. *East of Byzantium: Syria and Armenia in the Formative Period.* Washington, D.C., 1982.

Gerstinger, Hans. *Die Wiener Genesis.* Vienna, 1931.

Giess, Hildegard. *Die Darstellung der Fusswaschung Christi in den Kunstwerken des 4.–12. Jahrhunderts.* Rome, 1962.

Gilanents, Sarkis. *The Chronicles of Petros di Sarkis Gilanents.* Translated by C. O. Minasian. Lisbon, 1959.

Girkʻ or Kocʻi Yaysmawurkʻ [Book Called Menologium]. Constantinople, 1730.

Girkʻ Pitoyicʻ. Published by Y. Zōhrapian. Venice, 1796; repr. 1843.

Goetz, Oswald. *Der Feigenbaum in der religiösen Kunst des Abendlandes.* Berlin, 1965.

Goodspeed, Edgar J., and Harold R. Willoughby. *The Rockefeller McCormick New Testament.* Chicago, 1932.

Grabar, André. *L'empereur dans l'art byzantin.* Paris, 1936.

———. *Miniatures byzantines de la Bibliothèque Nationale.* Paris, 1939.

———. *Ampoules de Terre Sainte.* Paris, 1958.

———. *Christian Iconography: A Study of Its Origins.* Princeton, 1968.

———. "Imago clipeata chrétienne." *L'art de la fin de l'antiquité et du moyen âge.* Paris, 1968.

Grape, Wolfgang. *Grenzprobleme der byzantinischen Malerei.* Dissertation, University of Vienna, 1973.

Gratzl, Emil. *Islamische Bucheinbände des 14. bis 19. Jahrhunderts.* Leipzig, 1924.

———. "Lacquer Bindings of the 16th to the 19th Centuries." In *Survey of Persian Art.* London, 1938.

Greek and Latin Illuminated Manuscripts in Danish Collections. Copenhagen, 1921.

Grigoryan, G. M. *Syunik'i Vanakan Kalvacatirut'yunə IX–XIII Darerum* [Monastic Landownership in Siwnik' in the IX–XIII Centuries]. Erevan, 1973.

———. *Syunik'ə Ōrbelyanneri Ōrok', XIII–XV Darer* [Siwnik' under the Ōrbēlians, XIII–XV Centuries]. Erevan, 1981.

Grillmeier, Alois. *Der Logos am Kreuz: Zur christologischen Symbolik der älteren Kreuzigungsdarstellung.* Munich, 1956.

Grondijs, L. H. *Iconographie byzantine du Crucifié mort sur la croix.* Bibliotheca Byzantina Bruxellensis 1, 2nd ed. Brussels, 1947.

Gutberlet, Helena. *Die Himmelfahrt Christi in der bildenden Kunst von den Anfängen bis ins hohe Mittelalter.* Strasbourg, 1935.

Hakobyan, T'. X., and S. T. Melik'-Baxšyan. *Step'anos Ōrbelyan.* Erevan, 1960.

Hakobyan, Vazgen, and Ašot Hovhannisyan. *XVII Dari Hayeren Jeṙagreri Hišatakaranner, 1621–1640* [Colophons of Armenian Manuscripts of the Seventeenth Century, 1621–1640]. Vol. II. Erevan, 1978.

Hakopyan, Hravard. *Vaspurakani Manrankarč'ut'yunə.* Erevan, 1976.

Harnack, Adolf von. *Lehrbuch der Dogmengeschichte.* 5th ed. Tübingen, 1931–32.

Harper, Prudence. *The Royal Hunter: Art of the Sassanian Empire.* New York, 1978.

Hausherr, Irénée. "Spiritualité arménienne," *Dictionnaire de Spiritualité,* I. Paris, 1932, 862–67.

Hausscherr, Reiner. *Bible Moralisée: Faksimile-Ausgabe in Originalformat des Codex Vindobonensis 2554 der Österreichischen Nationalbibliothek.* 2 vols. Graz, 1973.

Hay Mšakuyt'i Nšanavor Gorcič'nerə, V–XVIII Darer [Famous Figures of Armenian Culture, V–XVIII Centuries]. Erevan, 1976.

Hay Žołovrdi Patmut'yun [History of the Armenian People]. Publication of the Armenian S.S.R. Academy of Sciences. Vol. III, Erevan, 1976; vol. IV, Erevan, 1972.

Haykakan Sovetakan Hanragitaran [Soviet Armenian Encyclopaedia]. Vols. I–IX. Erevan, 1974–83.

Hedfords, H., ed. *Compositiones ad Tingenda Musiva.* Uppsala, 1932.

Heimann, Adelheid. "A Twelfth-Century Manuscript from Winchcomb." *Journal of the Warburg and Courtauld Institutes* 28 (1965), 87–94.

Hofenk-de Graaff, J. H. *Natural Dyestuffs for Textile Materials: Origin, Chemical Constitution, Identification.* Brussels, 1967.

Hôtel Drouot. *Art d'Iran, Art d'Orient.* Paris, 20 November 1974. Lot 117.

Ideler, L. *Lehrbuch der Chronologie.* Berlin, 1831.

Ignatius of Antioch. *Epistle to the Romans. ANF,* vol. I.

Ilg, Albert. *De Coloribus et Artibus Romanorum.* Vienna, 1873. Also in Merrifield, M. P. *Original Treatises on the Arts of Painting.* New York, 1967, 166–257.

———. *Heraclius, von den Farben und Künsten der Römer.* Vienna, 1873.

———. *Theophilus Presbyter Schedula Diversarum Artium.* Vienna, 1874.

Il Menologio di Basilio II. Codices e Vaticanis Selecti 8. Turin, 1907.

Irenaeus. *Contra Haereses.* PG 7, cols. 437–1224.

Irigoin, Jean. "Pour une étude des centres de copie byzantins." *Scriptorium* 12 (1958), 208–27; 13 (1959), 177–209.

Issaverdenz, J. *Rites et cérémonies de l'église arménienne.* Venice, 1876.

Izmailova, Tatiana A. "Le cycle des fêtes du tétraévangile de Mougna: Maténadaran, no. 7736." *REArm,* n.s. 6 (1969), 105–39.

———. "Les racines prébyzantines dans les miniatures arméniennes: Les canons du tétraévangile de Mougna." In *Armeniaca: Mélanges d'études arméniennes,* pp. 28–41. Venice, 1969.

———. *Armianskaya Miniatjura XI Veka.* Moscow, 1979.

———. "Quelques miniatures de l'évangile du Catholicos (Vehapar)." *Fourth International Symposium on Armenian Art: Theses of Reports,* pp. 171–73. Erevan, 1985.

———. *Haykakan Manrankarč'ut'yun: Hovannes Sandłkavanec'i.* Erevan, 1986.

J̌ahukyan, G. "Davt'i K'erakanakan ašxatut'yan norahayt ambołjakan jeṙagir tek'stə," *Banber Matenadarani* 3 (1956), 242–64.

Janashian, Mesrop. *Armenian Miniature Paintings of the Monastic Library at San Lazzaro.* Translated by Bernard Grebanier. Venice, n.d.

Janson, H. W. *Apes and Ape Lore in the Middle Ages and the Renaissance.* London, 1952.

Jaubert, A. "Une lecture du lavement des pieds au mardi-mercredi saint." *Le Muséon* 79 (1966), 257–86.

Jerphanion, Guillaume de. *Les miniatures du manuscrit syriaque no. 559 de la bibliothèque vaticane.* Rome, 1940.

———. "Les noms des quatre animaux et le commentaire liturgique de Pseudo-Germain." In *La voix des monuments: Notes et études d'archéologie chrétienne.* Paris, 1930.

Joannis Philosophi Catholici Armenorum Ozniensis Oratio

Contra Phantasticos. Edited and translated by I. Baptista Aucher. Venice, 1816.

John Chrysostom. "Homilies on the Gospel of St. Matthew." Translated by George Prevost. *Nicene and Post-Nicene Fathers,* ser. 1. New York, 1888.

———. "Homilies on the Gospel of St. John," Translated by Philip Schaff. *Nicene and Post-Nicene Fathers,* ser. 1, vol. XIV. New York, 1889.

Kantorowicz, E. H. "The King's Advent and the Enigmatic Panels in the Doors of Santa Sabina." *Art Bulletin* 26 (1944), 207–31.

———. "The Baptism of the Apostles." *DOP* 9–10 (1956–57), 203–51.

Kartsonis, Anna. *Anastasis: The Making of an Image.* Princeton, 1986.

Kassardjian, K. *L'Église apostolique arménienne et sa doctrine.* Paris, 1943.

K'asuni, Ełia. *Patmut'iwn Hin Hay Dastiarakut'ean* [History of Education in Ancient Armenia]. Beirut, 1959.

Khorenats'i, Moses. *History of the Armenians.* Translation and commentary by Robert W. Thomson. Cambridge, Mass., 1978.

Kirakos Ganjakec'i. *Patmut'yun Hayoc'* [History of Armenia]. Edited by K. A. Melik'-Ōhanǰanyan. Erevan, 1961.

———. *Kirakos Gandzaketsi. Istoria Armenii.* Translated from classical Armenian with notes and commentary by L. A. Khanlarian. Pamiatniki pis'mennósti Vostoka 53. Moscow, 1976.

Kirschbaum, Engelbert, and Wolfgang Braunfels, eds. *Lexikon der christlichen Ikonographie.* 8 vols. Freiburg, 1968–76.

K'iwrtian, Y. "J̌ułayec'i Xōǰay Nazar ew Anor Gerdastanə" [Xōǰay Nazar and His Family]. *Hayrenik'* (monthly, Boston) 4 (1943), 72–82; 5 (1943), 63–73; 6 (1943), 69–87.

———. "T'oros Taronac'i." *Bazmavep* (monthly, Venice) 7–8 (1947), 218–19.

Klauser, Theodor. *Das Kiborium in der älteren christlichen Buchmalerei.* Nachrichten von der Akademie der Wissenschaften 7. Göttingen, 1961.

Klemm, E. "Die Kanontafeln der armenischen Hs. Cod. 697 im Wiener Mechitaristenkloster." *Zeitschrift für Kunstgeschichte* 35 (1972), 69–99.

"K'nnakan Tełekagir P'rof. N. Adonc'i" [Professor Adontz' Evaluative Report]. *Sion* 12 (1936), 368–69.

Köhler, Wilhelm. *Die karolingischen Miniaturen.* 4 vols. Berlin, 1930–60.

Korkhmazyan, Emma, Irina Drampyan, and Hravard Hakopyan. *Armenian Miniatures of the 13th and 14th Centuries from the Matenadaran Collection, Yerevan.* Leningrad, 1984.

———. *T'oros Taronac'i.* Erevan, 1984.

———. "The Sources of the Old Testament Illustrations in the Bible Illuminated by T'oros Taronatsi (Matenadaran no. 206)." *Fourth International Symposium on Armenian Art: Theses of Reports.* Erevan, 1985, 209–10; full publication in press.

Kucharek, Casimir. *The Byzantine-Slav Liturgy of St. John Chrysostom. Its Origin and its Evolution.* Combermere, Ont., 1971.

Laborde, Alexandre de. *La Bible Moralisée conservée à Oxford, Paris et Londres.* 5 vols. Paris, 1911–27.

Lalayan, Eruand. "Šarur-Daralageazi Gawaṙ. I Masn, Vayoc'-Jor kam Daralageaz" [The Canton of Šarur-Daralageaz. Part I: Vayoc'-Jor or Daralageaz]. *Azgagrakan Handēs.* Vol. XII. Tiflis, 1904–5.

Łaribyan, Igit. "Glajori Hamalsarani Hnagitakan Pełumnerə" [The Archaeological Excavations at the University of Glajor]. *Banber Erevani Hamalsarani* 2 (1971), 251–60.

———. *Glajor: Tełagrut'yunə, Pełumnerə, Vimakan Arjanagrut'yunnerə* [Glajor: Its Location, Excavations, and Epigraphic Inscriptions]. Erevan, Publication of the State University, 1983.

Larrow, Magdalen. *The Iconography of Mary Magdalen: The Western Tradition until 1300.* Ph.D. dissertation, New York University, 1982.

Łazarosyan, A. H. "Glajori Hamalsaranum Əndorinakvac Jeṙagrer" [The Manuscripts Executed at Glajor]. *Ēǰmiacin* 11–12 (1984).

Leiginger, G. *Miniaturen aus Handschriften des Kgl. Hof- und Staatsbibliothek in München.* Munich, 1912–28.

Leloir, Louis. "Doctrines et méthodes de S. Ephraem d'après son commentaire de l'évangile concordant." CSCO 220, Subsidia 18 (Louvain, 1961).

Leroquais, Victor. *Les bréviaires manuscrits des bibliothèques publiques de France,* 5 vols. and atlas. Paris, 1934.

Leroy, Jules. *Les manuscrits syriaques à peintures conservés dans les bibliothèques d'Europe et d'Orient.* Paris, 1964.

Leroy, Julien. *Les types de reglure des manuscrits grecs.* Institut de recherche d'histoire des textes: bibliographies, colloques, travaux préparatoires, Centre National de la Recherche Scientifique. Paris, n.d.

Lockhart, Laurence. *The Fall of the Safavī Dynasty and the Afghan Occupation of Persia.* Cambridge, 1958.

Lubac, Henri de. *L'exégèse médiévale. Les quatre sens de l'écriture.* 4 vols. Paris, 1959–64.

Lucchesi-Palli, E. "Christus-Emmanuel." *Lexikon der christlichen Ikonographie* I, 390–91.

Maas, A. J. "Exegesis." *The Catholic Encyclopedia,* vol. V, cols. 692–706. New York, 1909.

Macler, Frédéric. *L'évangile arménien. Edition phototy-*

pique du manuscrit 229 de la Bibliothèque d'Etchmiadzin. Paris, 1920.

Madoyan, A. "Davitʿ Anhałtʿ ev Nersēs Šnorhali." In *Davitʿ Anhałtʿ, Hodvacneri Żołovacu* [David the Invincible: A Collection of Articles]. Erevan, 1980, 123–42.

Maguire, Henry. *Art and Eloquence in Byzantium*. Princeton, 1981.

Maksoudian, Krikor H. "Armenian Saints." *Dictionary of the Middle Ages*. Vol. I, 517–21.

Mâle, Émile. *L'art religieux du XIIe siècle en France*. Paris, 1910 (and subsequent editions).

———. *L'art religieux du XIIIe siècle en France*. Paris, 1922.

Mango, Cyril. *The Art of the Byzantine Empire, 313–1453. Sources and Documents*. Englewood Cliffs, N.J., 1972.

Mansi, J. D. *Sacrorum conciliorum nova et amplissima collectio*. Florence, 1759 ff.

Manvelichvili, Alexandre. *Histoire de Géorgie*. Paris, 1951.

Marr, Nikolai. *Fisiolog, Armianogrusinskij isvod*. St. Petersburg, 1904.

Martin, John R. "The Dead Christ on the Cross in Byzantine Art." In *Late Classical and Medieval Studies in Honor of Albert Mathias Friend, Jr.* Edited by Kurt Weitzmann. Princeton, 1955.

Maškeworcʿi, Barseł Čon. *Meknutʿiwn srboy Awetaranin or əst Markosi*. Constantinople, 1826.

Maštocʿ Jeṙnadrutʿean [Ritual of Ordination]. Vałaršapat, 1876.

Mateos, Juan. *La célébration de la parole dans la liturgie byzantine*. Rome, 1971.

Matʿevosyan, Artašes. "Hiravi, Erb ev Orteł ē Himnadrvel Glajori Hamalsaranə" [Indeed, Where and When was the University of Glajor Founded?]. *Garun* 7 (1980), 55–59.

———. "Vehapʿaṙi Avetaranə," *Ējmiacin* 5 (1978).

Mathews, Thomas F. "The Annunciation at the Well: A Metaphor of Armenian Monophysitism." In *Medieval Armenian Culture*, University of Pennsylvania Armenian Texts and Studies 6. Edited by T. Samuelian and M. Stone. Chico, Calif., 1984, 343–56.

———. "The Genesis Frescoes of Ałtʿamar." *REArm* 16 (1982) 245–57.

———. "The Early Armenian Iconographic Program of the Ējmiacin Gospel." In *East of Byzantium: Syria and Armenia in the Formative Period*. Edited by N. G. Garsoïan et al. Washington, D.C., 1982, 199–205.

———. "A Pigment Analysis of Medieval Armenian Manuscripts." *XVI Internationaler Byzantinistenkongress = Jahrbuch der Österreichischen Byzantinistik* 31 (1981), section 3.2, 1–4.

———. "Gospel Iconography in Greater Armenia." *Fourth International Symposium on Armenian Art*. Erevan, in press.

McCrone, W. C., and J. G. Delly. *The Particle Atlas*. 2nd ed., 6 vols. Ann Arbor, 1974–78.

McCrone, W. C., L. B. McCrone, and J. G. Delly. *Polarized Light Microscopy*. Ann Arbor, 1978.

Mécérian, J. *Histoire et institutions de l'Église arménienne*. Beirut, 1965.

Meinardus, Otto F. A. "The Use of the Tonsura and Rzura by the Armenian Clergy during the Safavid Dynasty." *REArm*, n.s. 12 (1977) 365–69.

Millet, Gabriel. *Recherches sur l'iconographie de l'évangile aux XIVe, XVe, et XVIe siècles d'après les monuments de Mistra, de la Macédoine et du Mont Athos*. Paris, 1916.

———. *Monuments byzantins de Mistra. Materiaux pour l'étude de l'architecture et de la peinture en Grèce aux XIVe et XVe siècles*. Paris, 1910.

———. *La peinture du moyen âge en Yougoslavie*. Paris, 1962.

Minasian, L. G. *Cʿucʿak Jeṙagracʿ Nor-Jułayi S. Amenapʿrkčʿean Vanacʿ Tʿangarani* [Catalogue of the Manuscripts in the Museum of the Monastery of All-Savior in New Julfa]. Vol. II. Vienna, 1972.

Miner, Dorothy E., ed. *Studies in Art and Literature for Belle da Costa Greene*. Princeton, 1954.

Mnacʿakanyan, Stepʿan, and Adriano Alpago-Novello. *Hałbat*. Documenti di architettura armena 1. Milan, 1974.

Monneret de Villard, Ugo. *Le Leggende orientale sui magi evangelici*. Vatican City, 1952.

Moulton, J. D. *Early Zoroastrianism*. London, 1912.

Movsisyan, A. X. *Urvagcer Hay Dprocʿi ev Mankavaržutʿyan Patmutʿyan, X–XV Darer* [Outlines for the History of Armenian Education and Pedagogy, X–XV Centuries]. Erevan, 1958.

Muether, H. E., N. L. Balazs, and M. J. Cotter. "Neutron Activation Analysis of Manuscripts." *College Art Association Abstracts* (New Orleans, 1980), 133.

Muether, H. E., N. L. Balazs, W. Voelkle, and M. J. Cotter. "Neutron Autoradiography and the Spanish Forger." *MASCA Journal* 1, 4 (June 1980), 112–13.

Muñoz, Antonio. *Il Codice Purpureo di Rossano e il frammento sinopense*. Rome, 1907.

The Munsell Book of Color, Neighboring Hues Edition, Matte Finish Collection. Baltimore, 1976.

Muratian, Sahak A., and Nazarētʿ P. Martirosian. *Cʿucʿak Jeṙagracʿ Mšoy S. Aṙakʿelocʿ-Tʿargmančʿacʿ Vankʿi ew Šrǰakayicʿ* [Catalogue of the Manuscripts at the Monastery of the Holy Apostles/Translators in Muš and Its Environs]. Published by A. Galayčian. Jerusalem, 1967.

Murray, Robert. *Symbols of Church and Kingdom. A Study in Early Syriac Tradition*. Cambridge, 1975.

Mxitʿar Goš. *Girkʿ Datastani* [Book of Laws]. Edited by Xosrov Tʿorosyan. Erevan, 1975.

Nagatsuka, Yasushi. *Descent de la Croix. Son développement iconographique des origines jusqu'à la fin du XIVe siècle.* Tokyo, 1979.

Narekac'i, Gregory. *Le livre de prières.* Translated by Isaac Kéchichian. SC 78. Paris, 1961.

Narkiss, Bezalel, and Michael E. Stone. *Armenian Art Treasures of Jerusalem.* Jerusalem, 1979.

Nelson, Robert S. *The Iconography of Preface and Miniature in the Byzantine Gospel Book.* New York, 1980.

———. "An Icon at Mt. Sinai and Christian Painting in Muslim Egypt during the Thirteenth and Fourteenth Centuries." *Art Bulletin* 65 (1983), 201–18.

———. "Theoktistos and Associates in Twelfth-Century Constantinople: An Illustrated New Testament of A.D. 1133." *J. Paul Getty Museum Journal* 15 (1987), 53–78.

Nersēs Šnorhali. *Commentary on the Ten Canon Tables* (see above, Appendix D).

Nersēs Šnorhali and Yovhannēs Erznkac'i. *Meknut'iwn Surb Awetaranin or əst Matt'ēosi.* Constantinople, 1825.

———. *Inni Sacri.* Translated by Mesrobio Gianascian. Venice, 1973.

———. *Yisous Ordi* [Jesus fils unique du père]. Translated by Isaac Kéchichian. SC 203. Paris, 1973.

Nersessian, V. *Armenian Illuminated Gospel-Books.* London, 1987.

Nersoyan, Tiran. *Order of Blessing of the Foundation of a Church.* Translated by Mesrob Semerjian. New York, 1953.

New Testament Apocrypha. Edited by Edgar Hennecke and Wilhelm Schneemelcher, translated by R. M. Wilson. Philadelphia, 1963.

Nordenfalk, Carl. *Die spätantiken Kanontafeln. Kunstgeschichtliche Studien über die eusebianische Evangelien-konkordanz in den vier ersten Jahrhunderten ihrer Geschichte.* Göteborg, 1938.

———. "The Beginning of Book Decoration." In *Essays in Honor of Georg Swarzenski.* Chicago, 1951, 9–20.

———. "The Apostolic Canon Tables." *Gazette des Beaux-Arts* 62 (1963), 17–34.

Nšanian, Mesrop. "The Portrait of King Gagik of Kars." *Ararat* (August 1911), 683–87.

Omont, Henri. *Évangiles avec peintures byzantines du XIe siècle.* Paris, 1908.

———. *Miniatures des plus anciens manuscrits grecs de la Bibliothèque Nationale.* Paris, 1929.

Ōrbēlian, Step'anos. *Hakačaṙut'iwn əndem Erkabnakac'* [Disputation against the Dyophysites]. Constantinople, 1758.

———. *Patmut'iwn Nahangin Sisakan* [History of the Province of Sisakan]. Published by K. V. Šahnazareanc'. 2 vols. Paris, 1859.

———. *Histoire de la Siounie par Stéphanos Orbélian.* Traduite de l'arménien par M. Brosset. 2 vols. St. Petersburg, 1864–66.

———. *Patmut'iwn Nahangin Sisakan* [History of the Province of Sisakan]. Tiflis, 1910.

———. *Žamanakagrut'iwn* [Chronicle]. Edited by A. Abrahamyan. Erevan, 1942.

Origen. *Commentarium in Joannem.* PG 14, cols. 21–330.

Ormanian, M. *The Church of Armenia.* Translated by G. Marcar Gregory, edited by Terenig Poladian. London, 1955.

———. *Azgapatum* [National History]. Vol. II, second printing; Beirut, 1960.

———. *Cisakan Baṙaran* [Liturgical Dictionary]. Antilias, Lebanon, 1979.

———. *A Dictionary of the Armenian Church.* Translated by Bedros Norehad. New York, 1984.

Orna, Mary Virginia, and Thomas F. Mathews. "Pigment Analysis of the Glajor Gospel Book of U.C.L.A." *Studies in Conservation* 26 (1981), 57–72.

———. "Uncovering the Secrets of Medieval Artists." *Analytical Chemistry* 60 (1 Jan. 1988), 47A–56A.

Orna, Mary Virginia, Patricia L. Lang, J. E. Katon, Thomas F. Mathews, and Robert S. Nelson. "Applications of Infrared Microspectroscopy to Art Historical Questions about Medieval Manuscripts," *Archaeological Chemistry* 4 (1989), 265–88.

Ortiz de Urbina, Ignatius. *Patrologia Syriaca.* 2nd ed. Rome, 1965.

Oskian, Hamazasp. *Mayr C'uc'ak Hayerēn Jeṙagrac' Mxit'arean Matenadaranin i Vienna* [Grand Catalogue of the Armenian Manuscripts in the Mekhitarist Library at Vienna]. Vol. II. Vienna, 1963.

Oudenrijn, M. A. van den. "La lettre encyclique de Jean de Qrhnay dans la 'Conciliatio' de Galanus." *Neue Zeitschrift für Missionwissenschaft* (Beckenried, Switzerland) 1 (1947), 25–39.

———. "Yovhannēs K'ṙnec'ii əndhanrakan T'ułt'ə Kalanosi 'Conciliatio' in Mēǰ" [Yovhannēs K'ṙnec'i's Encyclical Letter in Galanos' 'Conciliatio']. Translated by Gnēl Čērēčian. In *Hask Hayagitakan Taregirk'.* Vol. II. Antilias, Lebanon, 1949–50, 199–208.

———. "Uniteurs et Dominicains d'Armenie." *OC,* ser. 4, 40 (1956), 94–112; 42 (1958), 110–33; 43 (1959), 110–19; 45 (1961), 95–108; 46 (1962), 99–116.

———. *Lingua Haicane Scriptores, Ordinis Praedicatorum Congregationis Fratres Unitorum.* Bern, 1960.

Outtier, Bernard. "Le cycle d'Adam à Ałt'amar et la version arménienne du commentaire du S. Ephrem sur la Genèse." *REArm,* n.s. 18 (1984), 589–92.

Parker, Elizabeth. *The Descent from the Cross. Its Relation to the Extra-liturgical "Depositio" Drama.* New York, 1978.
Parker, John. *The Works of Dionysius the Areopagite.* Two parts. Merrick, N.Y., 1897–99; repr. 1976.
Peeters, Paul. *Les Évangiles apocryphes, II: L'Évangile de l'enfance.* Paris, 1914.
Pelikan, Jaroslav. *The Christian Tradition. A History of the Development of Doctrine.* 5 vols. Chicago, 1971–89.
Pelikanidis, S. M., et al. *The Treasures of Mount Athos. Illuminated Manuscripts.* Translated by Philip Sherrard. Athens, 1974–75.
Petrides, L. "Le lavement des pieds le jeudi-saint dans l'église grecque." *Echos d'Orient* 3 (1899–1900), 321–26.
Petrosyan, Eznik. "Avetarani Mijnadaryan Haykakan Meknut'yunner" [Medieval Armenian Interpretations of the Gospels]. *Ejmiacin* 1 (1982), 35–41.
Piltz, Elizabeth. *Kamelaukion et Mitra: Insignes byzantins impériaux et ecclésiastiques.* Uppsala, 1977.
Pivazyan, Ē. "Darjyal Glajori Dproc'i Hamalsaranakan Bnuyt'i Masin [Again, On the Question of the Nature of the School of Glajor as a University]. *Banber Erevani Hamalsarani* 3 (1975), 154–69.
Plesters, Joyce. "Ultramarine Blue: Natural and Artificial." *Studies in Conservation* 11 (1966), 62–91.
Połarian, Norayr. *Mayr C'uc'ak Jeṙagrac' Srboc' Yakobeanc'* [Grand Catalogue of St. James Manuscripts]. 9 vols. Jerusalem, 1966–79.
———. *Hay Grołner* [Armenian Authors]. Jerusalem, 1971.
———. "T'oros Taronac'i." *Sion* (monthly, Jerusalem), 9–10 (1970), 454–55.

Recueil des historiens des croisades. Documents arméniens. Paris, 1896.
Regemorter, Berthe van. "La reliure arménienne." *Bazmavep* 8–10 (1953), 200–204.
Renoux, Athanase. "Le codex arménien Jérusalem 121. Introduction et édition comparée du texte." PO 35 (1969), 36 (1971).
———. "Le triduum pascal dans le rite arménien et les hymnes de la grande semaine." *REArm* 7 (1970), 55–122.
Restle, Marcell. *Byzantine Wall Painting in Asia Minor.* Translated by I. R. Gibbons. Greenwich, Conn., 1967.
Richter-Bernburg, Lutz. *Persian Medical Manuscripts at the University of California, Los Angeles: A Descriptive Catalogue.* Malibu, California, 1978.
Roosen-Runge, H. *Farbgebung und Technik frühmittelalterlicher Buchmalerei.* Munich, 1967.
Roosen-Runge, H., and A. E. A. Warner. "The Pigments and Medium of the Lindisfarne Gospels." In *Codex Lindisfarnensis,* vol. 2. Basel, 1960, 263–72.
Russell, James R. *Yovhannēs T'lkuranc'i and the Medieval Armenian Lyric Tradition.* Bachelor's thesis, Faculty of Oriental Studies, Oxford, 1977.

Saint-Martin, M. J. *Mémoires historiques et géographiques sur l'Arménie, suivis du texte arménien de l'Histoire des Princes Orpélians par Étienne Orpélian, archevêque de Siounie, et de Géographies attribuées à Moyse de Khoren et au docteur Vartan, avec plusieurs autres pièces relatives à l'histoire d'Arménie, le tout accompagné d'une traduction française et de notes explicatives.* 2 vols. Paris, 1818–19.
Salmaslian, A. *Bibliographie de l'Arménie.* Erevan, 1969.
Samuēli K'ahanayi Anec'woy Hawak'munk' i Groc' Patmagrac' [The Priest Samuel Anec'i's Collection from Historical Works]. Edited by Aršak Tēr-Mik'ēlian. Vałaršapat, 1893.
Sanjian, Avedis K. *Colophons of Armenian Manuscripts, 1301–1480: A Source for Middle Eastern History.* Cambridge, Mass., 1969.
———. *A Catalogue of Medieval Armenian Manuscripts in the United States.* University of California Pubs., Near Eastern Studies 16. Berkeley, Calif., 1976.
Sarafian, Kevork A. *History of Education in Armenia.* Los Angeles, Calif., 1930.
Šarakan Hogewor Ergoc'. Jerusalem, 1936.
Sargisian, Barseł. *Mayr C'uc'ak Hayerēn Jeṙagrac' Matenadaranin Mxit'areanc' i Venetik* [Grand Catalogue of the Armenian Manuscripts in the Mekhitarist Library at Venice]. Vols. I–II. Venice, 1914–24.
Sarkissian, Karekin. *The Council of Chalcedon and the Armenian Church.* New York, 1957.
Sbordone, Franciscus. *Physiologi graeci singulis variarum aetatum recensione codicibus fere omnibus tunc primum excussis collatisque.* Milan, 1936.
Sčepkina, M. B. *Miniatjura Khudovskoj Psaltyri.* Moscow, 1977.
Schiller, Gertrud. *Ikonographie der christlichen Kunst.* 4 vols., 2nd ed. Gütersloh, 1969.
———. *Iconography of Christian Art.* 2 vols. Translated by Janet Seligman. Greenwich, Conn., 1969.
Seel, O. *Der Physiologus.* Zurich, 1960.
Sewleṙnec'i, Ignatios. *Meknut'iwn Srboy Awetaranin or əst Łukasi.* Constantinople, 1824.
Siwrmēian, Artawazd. *C'uc'ak Hayerēn Jeṙagrac' S. K'aṙasun Mankunk' Ekełec'woy ew Masnaworac'* [Catalogue des manuscrits arméniens se trouvant à Alep à l'Église des Quarante Martyrs, ainsi qu'auprès des particuliers]. Vol. I. Jerusalem, 1935.
Smalley, Beryl. *The Study of the Bible in the Middle Ages.* 2nd ed. Oxford, 1952.
Smith, Cyril Stanley, and J. G. Hawthorne, eds. and

trans. *Mappae Clavicula: A Little Key to the World of Medieval Techniques.* Philadelphia, 1974.

Socrates. *Historia Ecclesiastica.* PG 67, cols. 1033–1630.

Soden, Hermann, Freiherr von. *Die Schriften des Neuen Testaments in ihrer ältesten erreichbaren Textgestalt.* 2 vols. Berlin, 1902.

Sotheby Parke Bernet, Inc. *Catalogue of Fine Oriental Miniatures, Manuscripts and Printed Books.* London, 28 April 1981.

Spicq, P. C. *Esquisse d'une histoire de l'exégèse latine au moyen âge.* Bibliothèque Thomiste 26. Paris, 1944.

Srapyan, Armenuhi. "Hovhannes Erznkac'i (Corcorec'i)." *Haykakan Sovetakan Hanragitaran.* Vol. 6, 558–59. Erevan, 1980.

Sruanjteanc', Garegin. *T'oros Ałbar.* Vol. II. Constantinople, 1884.

Step'anos Siwnec'i. *Commentary on the Ten Canon Tables* (see above, Appendix D).

Stepanyan, N. *Dekorativnoe Iskusstvo Srednevekovoi Armenii.* Erevan, 1971.

Striker, C. L. "Work at the Kalenderhane Camii in Istanbul: Preliminary Reports." *DOP* 22 (1968), 185–93; 25 (1971), 251–58.

Stubblebine, James. *Guido da Siena.* Princeton, 1964.

Tafrali, Oreste. *Monuments byzantins de Curtéa de Arges.* Paris, 1931.

Talbot Rice, David. *The Church of Hagia Sophia at Trebizond.* Edinburgh, 1968.

Tašian, Yakovbos. *C'uc'ak Hayerēn Jeragrac' Matenadaranin Mxit'areanc' i Vienna* [Catalogue of the Armenian Manuscripts at the Mekhitarist Library in Vienna]. Vol. I. Vienna, 1895.

Taylor, Alice. "Vaspurakan Manuscript Illumination and Eleventh Century Sources." In *Medieval Armenian Culture,* University of Pennsylvania Texts and Studies 6 (1984), 306–14.

The Teaching of Saint Gregory: An Early Armenian Catechism. Translation and commentary by Robert W. Thomson. Harvard Armenian Texts and Studies 3. Cambridge, Mass., 1970.

Tékéyan, Pascal. *Controverses christologiques en Arméno-Cilicie dans la seconde moitié du XIIe siècle (1165–98).* OCA 124. Rome, 1939.

Tēr-Awetisian, Smbat. *C'uc'ak Hayerēn Jeragrac' Nor Jułayi Amenap'rkič' Vank'i* [Catalogue of the Armenian Manuscripts in the All-Savior Monastery at New Julfa]. Vol. I. Vienna, 1970.

Tēr-Ghwondyan, Aram. *The Arab Emirates in Bagratid Armenia.* Translated by N. G. Garsoïan. Lisbon, 1976.

Tēr-Mik'ēlian, A. *Die armenische Kirche in ihren Beziehungen zur byzantinischen, vom IV. bis XIII. Jahrhundert.* Leipzig, 1892.

———. "Mijin Dareri Kat'ołikosneri Jgtumnerə Ekełec'akan Xałałut'ean Hamar" [The Endeavors of Catholicoses of the Middle Ages for Ecclesiastical Harmony]. *Ararat* (Vałaršapat) 2 (1893), 129–45.

Tēr Yovhaneanc', Yarut'iwn. *Patmut'iwn Nor Jułayu or Yaspahan* [History of New Julfa in Isfahan]. 2 vols. New Julfa, 1880.

Theodore Prodromos. *Tetrasticha: Epigrammata in Novum Testamentum.* PG 133, cols. 1175–1220.

Theophylactus. *Ennaratio in Evangelium Ioannis.* PG 123, cols. 1127–1348.

Thierry, Jean-Michel. *Les arts arméniens.* Paris, 1987.

Thierry, Nicole. "Le cycle de la création et la faute d'Adam à Ałt'amar." *REArm,* n.s. 17 (1983), 289–329.

———. "Les peintures d'Ałt'amar (915–21), le cycle de la passion et de la résurrection," in press.

Thierry, N., and Thierry, M. "Peintures murales de caractère occidental en Arménie: Église Saint-Pierre et Saint-Paul de Tatev (début du Xme siècle)." *Byzantion,* n.s. 38 (1968), 180–242.

Thompson, Henry Yates. *Illustrations from One Hundred Manuscripts in the Library of Henry Yates Thompson.* London, 1908.

Thomsen, Dietrick E. "The Passover Computation." *Science News* 125 (Jan. 21, 1984), 40.

Thomson, Robert W. "The Fathers in Early Armenian Literature." *Studia Patristica* 12.1 (Berlin, 1975), 457–70.

———. "Number Symbolism and Patristic Exegesis in Some Early Armenian Writers." *Handes Amsorya* 90 (1976), 117–38.

———. "Architectural Symbolism in Classical Armenian Literature." *Journal of Theological Studies* 30 (1979), 102–4.

Tischendorf, Constantin von. *Evangelia Apocrypha.* Hildesheim, repr. 1966.

Toumanoff, Cyril. *Studies in Christian Caucasian History.* Washington, D.C., 1963.

———. "Armenia and Georgia." *CMH* IV, pt. 1 (1966), 593–638.

———. *Manuel de généalogie et de chronologie pour l'histoire de la Caucasie chrétienne* (Arménie-Géorgie-Albanie). Rome, 1976.

Tournebize, F. *Histoire politique et religieuse de l'Arménie . . . jusqu'à la mort du leur dernier roi (l'an 1393).* Paris, 1910.

T'ovma Arcruni. *History of the House of the Artsrunik'.* Translated with a commentary by Robert W. Thomson. Detroit, 1985.

T'ovma Mecop'ec'i. *Patmut'iwn Lank-T'amuray ew Yajordac'* [History of Tamurlane and His Successors]. Paris, 1860.

T'umanyan, B. E. *Hay Astłagitut'yan Patmut'yun* [History of Astronomy in Armenia]. Vol. I. Erevan, 1964.

Twining, Lord. *European Regalia.* London, 1967.

Ulubabyan, B. A. *Xač'eni Isxanut'yunə X–XVI Darerum*

[The Principality of Xač'en in the X–XVI Centuries]. Erevan, 1975.
Underwood, Paul A. *The Kariye Djami.* 4 vols. New York-Princeton, 1966–75.
———. "The Fountain of Life in Manuscripts of the Gospels." *DOP* 5 (1950) 41–115.

Vardan Arewelc'i. *Meknut'iwn K'erakani* [Commentary on Grammar]. Edited by L. G. Xač'eryan. Erevan, 1972.
Velmans, Tania. *Le Tétraévangile de la Laurentienne, Florence, Laur. VI. 23.* Paris, 1971.
Vikan, Gary, ed. *Illuminated Greek Manuscripts from American Collections.* Princeton, 1973.
Volbach, F. W. *Early Christian Art.* London, 1961.
Volkoff, O. V. "Un saint oublié: Ponce Pilate." *Bulletin de la Societé d'archéologie copte* 20 (1969–70), 167–75.

Watson, Arthur. *The Early Iconography of the Tree of Jesse.* Oxford, 1934.
Weber, S. *Die katholische Kirche in Armenien.* Freiburg, 1903.
———. *Ausgewählte Schriften der armenischen Kirchenväter.* Munich, 1927.
Weitzmann, Kurt. *Illustrations in Roll and Codex: A Study of the Origin and Method of Text Illustration.* 2nd printing with addenda. Princeton, 1970.
———. *Studies in Classical and Byzantine Manuscript Illumination.* Edited by Herbert Kessler. Chicago, 1971.
———. *The Miniatures of the Sacra Parallela, Parisinus Graecus 923.* Studies in Manuscript Illumination 8. Princeton, 1979.
———. *Studies in the Arts at Sinai.* Princeton, 1982.
———. "Crusader Icons and Maniera Greca." In *Byzanz und der Westen: Studien zur Kunst des europaïschen Mittelalters,* edited by I. Hutter. Sitzungsberichte der Österreichischen Akademie der Wissenschaften, phil.-hist. Klasse 432. Vienna, 1984.
———. "The Constantinopolitan Lectionary, Morgan 639." In *Studies in Art and Literature for Belle da Costa Greene,* edited by Dorothy Miner. Princeton, 1954, 358–73.
Wessel, Klaus, and Marcell Restle. *Reallexikon zur byzantinischen Kunst.* Stuttgart, 1963 ff.
———. *Abendmahl und Apostelkommunion.* Recklinghausen, 1964.
Williamson, G. A. *Eusebius' History of the Church.* New York, 1966.
Willoughby, Harold R. *The Four Gospels of Karahissar.* Chicago, 1936.
Winkler, Gabriele. "Eine bemerkenswerte Stelle im armenischen Glaubensbekenntnis: Credimus et in Sanctum Spiritum qui descendit in Jordanem proclamavit missum." *Oriens Christianus* 63 (1979) 130–62.
———. *Das armenische Initiationsrituale.* OCA 217. Rome, 1982.

Xač'eryan, L. G. "Matenagrakan Tełekut'yunnerə Glajori Hamalsarani Masin" [The Literary Sources concerning the University of Glajor]. *Patma-Banasirakan Handes* 4 (1965), 193–200.
———. *Esayi Nč'ec'i, Verlucut'iwn K'erakanut'ean.* Erevan, 1966.
———. *Glajori Hamalsaranə Hay Mankavaržakan Mtk'i Zargac'man Mēǰ, XIII–XIV dd.* [The University of Glajor and the Development of Armenian Pedagogy in the XIII–XIV Centuries]. Erevan, 1973.
———. "Glajori Hamalsaranakan Bnuyt'ə ev Oč' t'e Nra Aṙaǰnekut'yan Harc'ə" [The Question of Glajor as a University and Not Its Primacy]. *Banber Erevani Hamalsarani* 3 (1975), 135–53.
———. *Esayi Nč'ec'i ew Glajori Hamalsaranə, 1280–1340* [Esayi Nč'ec'i and the University of Glajor, 1280–1340]. Los Angeles, 1988.
Xač'ikyan, Levon. "Glajori Hamalsaranə ev Nra Saneri Avartakan Atenaxosut'yunnerə" [The University of Glajor and the Valedictory Orations of Its Pupils]. In *Erevani Petakan Hamalsarani Gitakan Ašxatut'yunner* (Erevan State University Scientific Works), vol. III (1946), 423–50.
———. *XIV Dari Hayeren Jeṙagreri Hišatakaranner* [Colophons of Armenian Manuscripts of the XIVth Century]. Erevan, 1950.
———. "Artazi Haykakan Išxanut'yunə ev Corcori Dproc'ə" [The Armenian Principality of Artaz and the School of Corcor]. *Banber Matenadarani* 11 (1973), 125–210.
Xosrov Anjewac'i. *Žamakargut'ean Meknut'iwn* [Commentary on the Canonical Hours]. Constantinople, 1730–37.

Yovhannēs Erznkac'i. *Hawak'umn Meknut'ean K'erakani* [Collection of Commentaries on Grammar]. Edited by L. G. Xač'eryan. Los Angeles, Calif., 1983.
Yovhannēs Erznkac'i and Nersēs Šnorhali. *Meknut'iwn Surb Awetaranin or əst Matt'ēosi* [Commentary on the Holy Gospel of Matthew]. Constantinople, 1825.
Yovhannēs K'ṙnec'i. *Yałags K'erakanin* [On Grammar]. Edited by L. S. Avagyan. Erevan, 1977.
Yovsēp'ian, Garegin. "Esayi Nč'ec'i's Commentary on Ezekiel." *Ararat.* Vałaršapat, 1917.
———. "Jagavanic' Žołovə" [The Council of Jagavan]. *Šołakat.* Vałaršapat, 1913.
———. "Tarsayič Ōrbēliani ew Mina Xat'uni Serundə" [The Descendants of Tarsayič Ōrbēlian and Mina Xat'un]. *Hask Hayagitakan Taregirk'* 1 (1948), 1–28.
———. *Xałbakeank' kam Pṙošeank' Hayoc' Patmut'ean*

Mēǰ [The Xałbakians or Pṙošians in Armenian History]. Second printing in single volume. Antilias, Beirut, 1969.

Zakaryan, Lilith. *Awag*. Erevan, 1984.
———. *Iz Istorii Vaspurakanskoj Miniatjur.* Erevan, 1980.
Zarbhanalian, Garegin. *Matenadaran Haykakan T'argmanut'eanc', 4–13 dd.* [Catalogue of Early Armenian Translations, 4th–13th Centuries]. Venice, 1889.
———. *Patmut'iwn Hayerēn Dprut'ean, Nor Matenagrut'iwn* [Armenian Literary History: Modern Literature]. Venice, 1905.
———. *Patmut'iwn Hay Hin Dprut'ean, IV–XIII Dar* [Histoire littéraire de l'Arménie ancienne, siècles IV–XIII]. Venice, 1932.
Zenker, Jules T. *Dictionnaire Turc-Arabe-Persan.* Leipzig, 1866–76.
Zimmerman, E. H. *Vorkarolingischen Miniaturen.* 4 vols. Berlin, 1916.

Table 1

Table of the Five Painters

f = full-page miniature
x = miniature less than full-page
r = reworking of miniature

First Painter	Second Painter	Third Painter	Fourth Painter	T'oros Taronec'i	Page	
f					4	Canon Table, Eusebian Prologue, with Portrait of Eusebius
f					5	Canon Table, Eusebian Prologue, with Portrait of Carpianos
f					8	Canon Table One
f					9	Canon Table Two
f					12	Canon Tables Three and Four
f					13	Canon Table Five
f					16	Canon Tables Six and Seven
f					17	Canon Tables Eight and Nine
f					20	Canon Table Ten
f					21	Canon Table Ten
	f				26	Portrait of St. Matthew
	f				27	Incipit of the Gospel of Matthew
	f				28	The Genealogy of Christ (Abraham, Issac, Jacob)
	f				29	The Genealogy of Christ (Judah to Nahshon)
	f				30	The Genealogy of Christ (Salmon to Solomon)
	f				31	The Genealogy of Christ (Rehoboam to Ahaz)
	f				32	The Genealogy of Christ (Hezekiah to Joshiah)
	f				33	The Genealogy of Christ (Jechoniah to Eliakim)
	f				34	The Genealogy of Christ (Azor to Jacob)
	f			r	35	The Genealogy of Christ (Joseph, Mary, Christ)
		f		r	92	The Beheading of John the Baptist
		f			99	The Petition of the Canaanite
		x			103	Peter Receives the Keys
		f			106	The Transfiguration
		x			108	The Cure of the Epileptic
		x			117	The Blessing of the Children
		x			122	The Petition of the Mother of James and John
			x		124	The Cure of the Blind in Jericho
			f	r	126	The Entry into Jerusalem and the Cleansing of the Temple
	f				156	The Last Supper
			f		160	The Agony in the Garden
			f	r	162	The Betrayal
			x	r	166	Peter's Denial
			x	r	169	The Message from Pilate's Wife
			f	r	171	Pilate Washes His Hands
			x	r	172	The Mocking of Christ
			x	r	173	The Way of the Cross
			f	r	179	The Women at the Tomb
	f				188	Portrait of St. Mark
	f				189	Incipit of the Gospel of Mark
			x		193	The Call of Peter and Andrew
			x		194	The Call of James and John
			x		197	The Cure of the Leper

Table of the Five Painters, *continued*

f = full-page miniature
x = miniature less than full-page
r = reworking of miniature

First Painter	Second Painter	Third Painter	Fourth Painter	T'oros Taronec'i	Page	
			x		211	First Storm at Sea
				x	216	The Woman with Hemorrhage and the Petition of Jairus
				f	218	The Raising of Jairus' Daughter
				x	227	The Second Storm at Sea
				x	235	The Cure of the Blind Man at Bethsaida
				x	250	The Cure of Blind Bartimaeus
	f				252	The Entry into Jerusalem
				x	255	The Lesson of the Withered Fig Tree
				x	259	The Question of Tribute to Caesar
				x	263	The Widow's Mite
				x	269	The Anointing of Christ at Bethany
				x	271	The Preparation for Passover
				f	283	Christ Ascending the Cross
				f	286	Descent from the Cross
	f				298	Portrait of St. Luke
	f				299	Incipit of the Gospel of Luke
	f			r	305	The Annunciation
				f	312	The Visitation
				f	327	Christ Reading in the Synagogue
				f	336	The Cure of the Paralytic
				f	351	The Anointing of Christ at Simon's House
				f	403	The Parable of the Cunning Steward
				f	438	Peter's Denial and Christ before Caiaphas
				x	441	Christ before Herod
				x	448	The Apparition on the Way to Emmaus
				f	453	The Ascension
	f				460	Portrait of St. John
	f				461	Incipit of the Gospel of John
				f	469	The Wedding Feast at Cana
				x	480	The Samaritan at the Well
				x	484	The Cure of the Paralytic at the Pool
	x			r	509	The Cure of the Man Born Blind
	f				522	The Raising of Lazarus
	f			r	532	The Washing of the Feet
	f				538	The Promise of the Holy Spirit
	f				561	The Crucifixion
				f	570	Christ's Apparition at the Sea of Galilee

TABLE 2

Data from the Microscopical Examination and X-ray Diffraction Analysis of Some Representative Samples

Sample No.	Refractive Index (relative to "Aroclor")	Average Particle Size (μm)	Description	d-Values of Principal Lines (Å)	Identification
1.B.189(110,45)	<1.66	16	70% colorless matrix; med. to dark blue rounded crystals; transparent; isotropic	6.38, 3.80-3.62, 2.95-2.85, 2.65-2.60, 1.78	Ultramarine
2.B.189(165,70)	>1.66	20	50% colorless matrix; lt. blue crystal faces; pleochroic, anisotropic; anomalous green & yellow	5.15, 3.52, 2.52, 2.23	Azurite
2.R.561(100,75)	<1.66	4	85% colorless matrix; isotropic reddish-brown particles; + test for madder		Red lake pigment
3.R.92(110,170)	>1.66	8	Bright red anisotropic crystals	3.35, 2.86, 2.09, 1.98, 1.74, 1.67	Vermilion
5.G.312(65,70)	<1.66 (Blue) >1.66 (Yellow)	16	Mixture of dark blue rounded isotropic crystals with yellow highly absorbing anisotropic crystals	4.13, 3.98, 3.70, 3.36, 3.17, 2.98, 2.85, 2.69, 2.45	Orpiment + Ultramarine
5.O.453(85,45)	>1.66	8	Anisotropic orange particles; anomalous 1st order green	3.39-3.32, 3.18-3.12, 2.89-2.84, 2.02, 1.77-1.76, 1.58, 1.40	Minium
5.W.469(115,165)	>1.66	<4	Highly absorbing anisotropic particles	4.50, 4.29, 3.62, 3.30, 2.63, 2.47, 2.24, 2.11, 2.06, 1.70, 1.53	White Lead

Table 3

A Comparison of the d-Values of Sample 3.B.106(20,40) with Ultramarine

3.B.106(20,40) d (Å)	Ultramarine (ASTM #2-0325) d (Å)	Relative Intensity %
11.60		
6.18 (2)*	6.49	80
4.50	4.59	10
3.90		
3.77-3.65 (1)	3.74	100
2.99-2.86 (1)	2.91	100
2.64-2.60 (1)	2.65	100
2.27 (3)	2.29	40
2.12 (3)	2.16	60
1.96	1.95	10
1.84		
1.77 (2)	1.79	80
1.67	1.66	20
1.60 (3)	1.62	60
1.55 (3)	1.57	40
1.50 (4)	1.52	40
1.47 (4)	1.48	40
1.36 (3)	1.37	80
1.31 (5)	1.32	40
1.28 (5)	1.29	40
1.24 (3)	1.24	60

*Estimated relative intensities from the film. (1) indicates the most intense line.

Table 4

A Comparison of the d-Values of Sample 4.W.126(45,160) with White Lead

4.W.126(45,160) d (Å)	White Lead (ASTM #13-131) d (Å)	Relative Intensity %
4.48 (3)	4.47	60
4.22 (3)	4.25	60
3.58 (2)	3.61	90
3.27 (2)	3.29	90
2.85		
	2.71	20
2.61 (1)	2.62	100
2.49	2.49	30
	2.26	10
2.23 (3)	2.23	50
2.12	2.12	30
	2.10	20
2.05	2.05	30
1.89	1.88	20
1.85	1.86	30
1.70	1.69	40
	1.65	20
	1.61	30
1.59	1.58	10
1.48	1.49	20
1.30	1.31	30

Table 5

A Comparison of the d-Values of Sample 2.R.189(50,225) with Vermilion

2.R.189(50,225) d (Å)	Vermilion (ASTM #6-0256) d (Å)	Relative Intensity %
3.42-3.28 (1)	3.35	100
3.15 (2)	3.16	30
2.92-2.80 (1)	2.86	95
2.10-2.06 (2)	2.07	25
2.01	2.02	12
1.95 (2)	1.98	35
1.76	1.76	20
1.71 (2)	1.73	25
1.68 (2)	1.68	25
1.65		
1.43		
1.34	1.34	12
1.30	1.30	10
1.25		

Table 6

Pigments Listed by Hue and Artist as Used in the Glajor Gospel Book

Artist No.	1	2	3	4	5
Hue					
Black	Charcoal black	Charcoal black	Charcoal black	Charcoal black	Charcoal black
Blue	Ultramarine	Azurite	Ultramarine	Ultramarine	Ultramarine
Brown		Vermilion + Orpiment + Gypsum + Charcoal black	Vermilion + Orpiment + Gypsum + Charcoal black	Vermilion + Orpiment + Whiting + Charcoal black + Iron oxide hydrate	Vermilion + Orpiment + Gypsum
Flesh		Orpiment + Realgar	Orpiment + Realgar + Gamboge + Gypsum		Vermilion + Anhydrite + Gamboge
Gold		Gold	Gold	Gold	Gold
Green	Orpiment + Ultramarine	Orpiment + Azurite	Orpiment + Gamboge + Ultramarine	Orpiment + Ultramarine	Orpiment + Ultramarine + Vermilion + Anhydrite
Magenta	Red Lake + White Lead	Red Lake	Red Lake	Red Lake	Red Lake
Olive				Gamboge	
Orange			Orpiment + Minium		Minium
Purple			Red Lake + Ultramarine	Red Lake + Ultramarine	Red Lake + Ultramarine
Red	Vermilion	Vermilion; Red Lake	Vermilion	Vermilion	Vermilion
White	Calcined bone; Quartz		White Lead	White Lead	White Lead
Yellow	Orpiment	Orpiment	Realgar + Orpiment + Gamboge + Massicot	Gamboge	Orpiment + Massicot
Yellow-Brown		Realgar + Orpiment + Vermilion + Charcoal black	Gamboge	Vermilion + Gamboge + Gypsum	Vermilion + Gamboge

Table 7

The Palette of the Glajor Gospel Book

Pigment Name	Chemical Identification	Comments	Method of Identification*
Anhydrite	$CaSO_4$	Native anhydrous calcium sulfate	XRD
Azurite	$2CuCO_3 \cdot Cu(OH)_2$	Blue crystalline material	XRD, M
Calcined bone (bone white)	$Ca_3(PO_4)_2$	Made from animal bone ash	XRD, M
Charcoal black	Carbon plus mineral impurities	Known to be in use in the mid-East from ancient times	XRD, M
Gamboge	Mixture of garcinolic acids and resins	Yellow gum resin produced by trees of the genus *Garcinia;* widely used in MS painting	M
Gold	Au		XRD, XRF
Gypsum	$CaSO_4 \cdot 2H_2O$	Important raw material used in art	XRD, M
Iron oxide hydrate	FeO(OH)		XRD
Massicot	PbO	Ancient pigment	XRD
Minium	Pb_3O_4	Ancient pigment	XRD, M
Orpiment	As_2S_3	Naturally occurring in many places; ancient pigment	XRD, M
Realgar	As_2S_2	Ancient pigment; usually mixed with orpiment	XRD, M
Red Lake	Alizarin and related compounds	Derived from root of herbaceous perennial, *Rubia tinctorium*	M, MC
Ultramarine	Clathrate compound of sulfur in silicate mineral	Obtained from semiprecious stone, lapis lazuli	XRD, M
Vermilion	HgS	One of the most ancient of the synthetic pigments; also found as cinnabar ore	XRD, M
White Lead	$2PbCO_3 \cdot Pb(OH)_2$	Widely used in ancient times	XRD, M
Whiting (Chalk)	$CaCO_3$	In use in painting from ancient times	XRD

*Key: XRD = X-Ray Diffraction
XRF = X-Ray Fluorescence
M = Polarized Light Microscopy
MC = Microchemical Tests

Table 8

Table of Armenian Gospel Programs
inside back cover

TABLE 9

Table of Liturgical Uses

MATTHEW

PAGE	SUBJECT	PASSAGE	LITURGICAL USES
28–35	Genealogy of Christ	1:1–17 1:1–17	6 January, Nativity, Epiphany—Office 8 September, Birth of the Virgin—Mass
41	Baptism	3:1–17	6 January, Nativity, Epiphany—Blessing of Water
92	Beheading of John the Baptist	14:1–23	Thurs., 4th Week of Easter—Office
99	Petition of the Canaanite	*15:21–28 15:21–28	Fri., 5th Week of Easter—Mass Wed., 6th Week of Easter—Mass
103	Peter Receives the Keys	16:13–19 16:13–19 16:13–19	3rd Sun. of Easter or Universal Sunday—Mass Sat. before Assumption, Feast of the Ējmiacin Cathedral—Mass Wed. after Feast of the Holy Cross—Mass
106	Transfiguration	17:1–8	
108	Cure of the Epileptic	*17:14–20 17:14–20	Mon., 6th Week of Easter—Office Transfiguration or "Rosey" Sunday—Office
117	Blessing of the Children	19:13–26	Wed., 3rd Week after the Transfiguration—Mass
122	Petition of the Mother of James and John	20:17–28 20:17–28	Great Monday—Office Fri. after the Ascension—Office
124	Cure of the Blind in Jericho	*20:29–21:17	Palm or "Flower" Sunday—Mass
126	Entry into Jerusalem and the Cleansing of the Temple	*20:29–21:17	7th Sun. of Easter or Second "Flower" Sunday—Office
156	Last Supper	26:17–30	Holy or "Great" Thursday—Mass
160	Agony in the Garden	26:31–27:56	Good or "Great"—Friday
162	Betrayal		
166	Peter's Denial		
169	Message from Pilate's Wife		
171	Pilate Washes His Hands and the Self-Curse of the Jews		
172	Mocking of Christ		
173	Way of the Cross		
179	Women at the Tomb	*28:1–20	Holy or "Great" Saturday—Mass

*Gospel of Healing

MARK

PAGE	SUBJECT	PASSAGE	LITURGICAL USES
193	Call of Peter and Andrew	1:14–20	New Sunday or Sun. after Easter—Office
194	Call of James and John		
197	Cure of the Leper	*1:35–45 *1:35–45	Tue., 1st Week of Easter—Office Fri., 3rd Week after the Transfiguration—Mass
211	First Storm at Sea	4:35–40 4:35–5:20	3rd Sun. after Assumption—Mass Mon., 4th Week of Easter—Office
216	Woman with Hemorrhage and the Petition of Jairus	5:21–34	Tues., 4th Week of Easter—Office
218	Raising of the Daughter of Jairus		
227	Second Storm at Sea	6:45–52 6:45–56 6:45–56 6:45–56	Mon., 3rd Week after Pentecost—Mass Mon., 5th Week of Easter—Office Wed., 3rd Week after Assumption—Mass Mon., 4th Week of Holy Cross—Mass
235	Cure of the Blind Man at Bethsaida	8:10–26	Sat., 5th Week of Easter—Office
250	Cure of Blind Bartimaeus	*10:46–11:11 *10:46–11:11	Palm or "Flower" Sunday—Mass 7th Sun. of Easter or Second "Flower" Sunday—Office
252	Entry into Jerusalem	11:1–10	Palm or "Flower" Sunday—Mass
255	Lesson of the Withered Fig Tree	11:12–26	Mon., 7th Week of Easter—Office
259	Question of Tribute to Caesar	12:13–44	"Great" Tuesday—Office
263	Widow's Mite	12:35–44 12:35–44	Thurs., 7th Week of Easter—Office 5th Sunday of Holy Cross—Mass
269	Anointing of Christ at Bethany	14:1–11	"Great" Wednesday—Office
271	Preparation of the Passover	14:1–26 14:1–26	Sat., 7th Week of Easter—Office Holy or "Great" Thursday—Office
283	Ascending the Cross	15:20–37	7th Sun. of Easter or Second "Flower" Sunday—Office
286	Descent from the Cross	15:42–16:1	Easter Sunday—Office

*Gospel of Healing

LUKE

PAGE	SUBJECT	PASSAGE	LITURGICAL USES
305	Annunciation	1:26–38 1:26–38 1:26–38 1:26–38 1:26–38 1:26–38 1:26–38	6 January, Nativity, Epiphany—Office 3rd Day after the Nativity—Mass 7 April, Annunciation—Mass 5th Sun. after Pentecost / Finding of the Relic of the Virgin—Office Assumption of the Virgin—Mass Tues. of Assumption—Office 5 January, Candlelight of Nativity—Office
312	Visitation	1:39–80 1:39–56 1:39–56 1:39–56 1:39–56 1:39–56 1:39–56	6 January, Nativity, Epiphany—Office 5th Day after the Nativity—Mass Assumption—Office Mon. of Assumption—Office 3rd Sun. after Assumption—Office 21 November, Presentation of the Virgin at the Temple—Mass 9 December, Conception of the Virgin—Mass
327	Christ Reading in the Synagogue	4:14–23 4:14–23 4:14–23	Sat. after Pentecost—Mass Thurs. after Transfiguration / Feast of Isaiah Prophet—Mass 6th Sun. of Holy Cross—Mass
336	Cure of the Paralytic of Capernaum	*5:17–26 *5:17–26	Thurs., 2nd Week of Easter—Office Fri., 6th Week of Holy Cross—Mass
351	Anointing at Simon's House	7:36–50 7:36–50 7:36–48	"Great" Thursday—Office Wed., 3rd Week of Easter—Office Wed., 7th Week of Holy Cross—Mass
403	Parable of the Cunning Steward	20:9–18 20:9–19	2nd Day after Feast of Nativity—Office 7th Week of Easter—Office
438	Peter's Denial and Christ before Caiaphas	22:54–62	
441	Christ before Herod	23:6–12	
448	Apparition on the Way to Emmaus	24:13–35 24:13–35 24:13–35	Easter Sunday—Office Tues. of Easter Week—Mass Wed. of Easter Week—Office
453	Ascension	24:41–53	Ascension Thursday—Office

*Gospel of Healing

JOHN

PAGE	SUBJECT	PASSAGE	LITURGICAL USES
439	Wedding Feast at Cana	2:1–11 2:1–11	1st Sun. after Nativity—Mass Fri., 2nd Week of Easter—Mass
480	Samaritan at the Well	4:1–23 4:24–42	Wed., 3rd Week of Easter—Mass Thurs., 3rd Week of Easter—Mass
484	Cure of the Paralytic at the Pool	*5:1–18	Sat., 3rd Week of Easter—Mass
509	Cure of the Man Born Blind	*9:1–38	Wed., 5th Week of Easter—Mass
522	Raising of Lazarus	11:1–46 11:1–46 11:1–46 11:1–46 11:1–46 11:1–54	6th Day after Nativity—Mass Palm or "Flower" Sunday—Office Easter Sunday—Office Wed., 6th Week of Easter—Office Assumption Sunday—Office Sat. of Lazarus—Office
532	Washing of the Feet	13:1–11 13:1–15 13:12–15	"Great" Thursday—Office Thurs., 7th Week of Easter—Mass "Great" Thursday—Office
538	Promise of the Holy Spirit	14:15–24 14:15–24 14:15–24	Sun. of Descent of the Holy Spirit / Pentecost—Mass Sun. of Descent of the Holy Spirit / Pentecost—Office Pentecost Monday—Office
561	Crucifixion	19:16–22 19:16–22 19:16–22 19:16–22 19:16–22	Fri. after the feast of the Cross—Mass Easter Sunday—Office "Great" Friday—Office 5th Sun. after Easter / Apparition of the Holy Cross—Office Assumption Sunday—Office
570	Christ's Apparition at the Sea of Galilee	21:1–14 21:1–14 21:1–14 21:1–14 21:15–25 21:15–25 21:15–22	Fri. of Easter Week—Office Fri. of Easter Week—Mass Fri. of Easter Week—Office Sat. of Easter Week—Office Sat. of Easter Week—Office New Sunday / Sun. after Easter—Office Feast of SS. Peter and Paul—Office

*Gospel of Healing

General Index

Index of Biblical Citations

The Glajor Gospel

Color Plates

Page 17: Canon Tables Eight and Nine. By the First Painter.

Page 26: Portrait of St. Matthew. By the Second Painter.

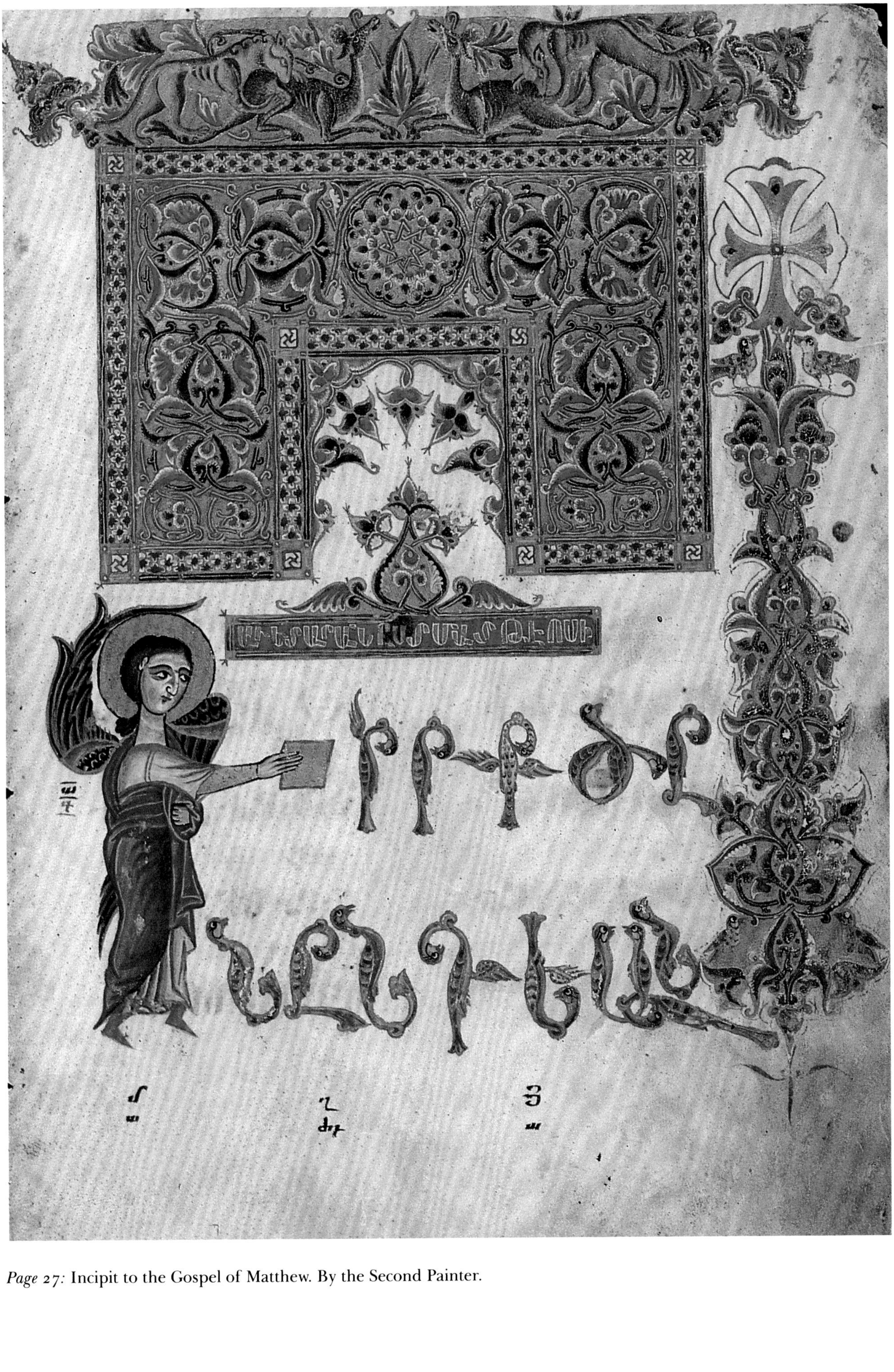

Page 27: Incipit to the Gospel of Matthew. By the Second Painter.

Page 30: The Genealogy of Christ (Salmon to Solomon). By the Second Painter.

Page 106: The Transfiguration. By the Third Painter.

Page 126: The Entry into Jerusalem and the Cleansing of the Temple.
By the Fourth Painter and T'oros Taronec'i.

Page 227: The Second Storm at Sea. By T῾oros Taronec῾i.

Page 250: The Cure of Blind Bartimaeus. By T῾oros Taronec῾i.

Page 305: The Annunciation. By the Second Painter and T'oros Taronec'i.

Page 327: Christ Reading in the Synagogue. By T'oros Taronec'i.

Page 453: The Ascension. By T'oros Taronec'i.

Page 561: The Crucifixion. By the Second Painter.

Page 4: Canon Table, Eusebian Prologue: Detail of Eusebius. By the First Painter.

Page 156: The Last Supper: Detail of Christ. By the Second Painter.

Page 188: Portrait of St. Mark: Detail of St. Mark. By the Second Painter.

Page 106: The Transfiguration: Detail of Christ. By the Third Painter.

Page 126: The Entry into Jerusalem: Detail of Christ, Peter and John. By the Fourth Painter.

Page 162: The Betrayal: Detail of Christ and Judas. By the Fourth Painter.

Page 227: The Second Storm at Sea: Detail of Christ. By Tʿoros Taronecʿi.

Page 453: The Ascension: Detail of Christ. By Tʿoros Taronecʿi.

Page 111: Detail of Heading Decoration at Matt. 18:10. By the First Painter.

Page 319: Detail of Heading Decoration at Luke 3:1. By the First Painter.

Page 299: Detail of Heading Decoration at Luke 1:1. By the Second Painter.

Page 514: Detail of Heading Decoration at John 10:11. By the Second Painter.

The Glajor Gospel

Black and White Illustrations

Front Cover of the U.C.L.A. Gospel (1824–25).

Front Doublure of the U.C.L.A. Gospel (1824–25).

Page 4: Canon Table, Eusebian Prologue, with Portrait of Eusebius. By the First Painter.

Page 5: Canon Table, Eusebian Prologue, with Portrait of Carpianos. By the First Painter.

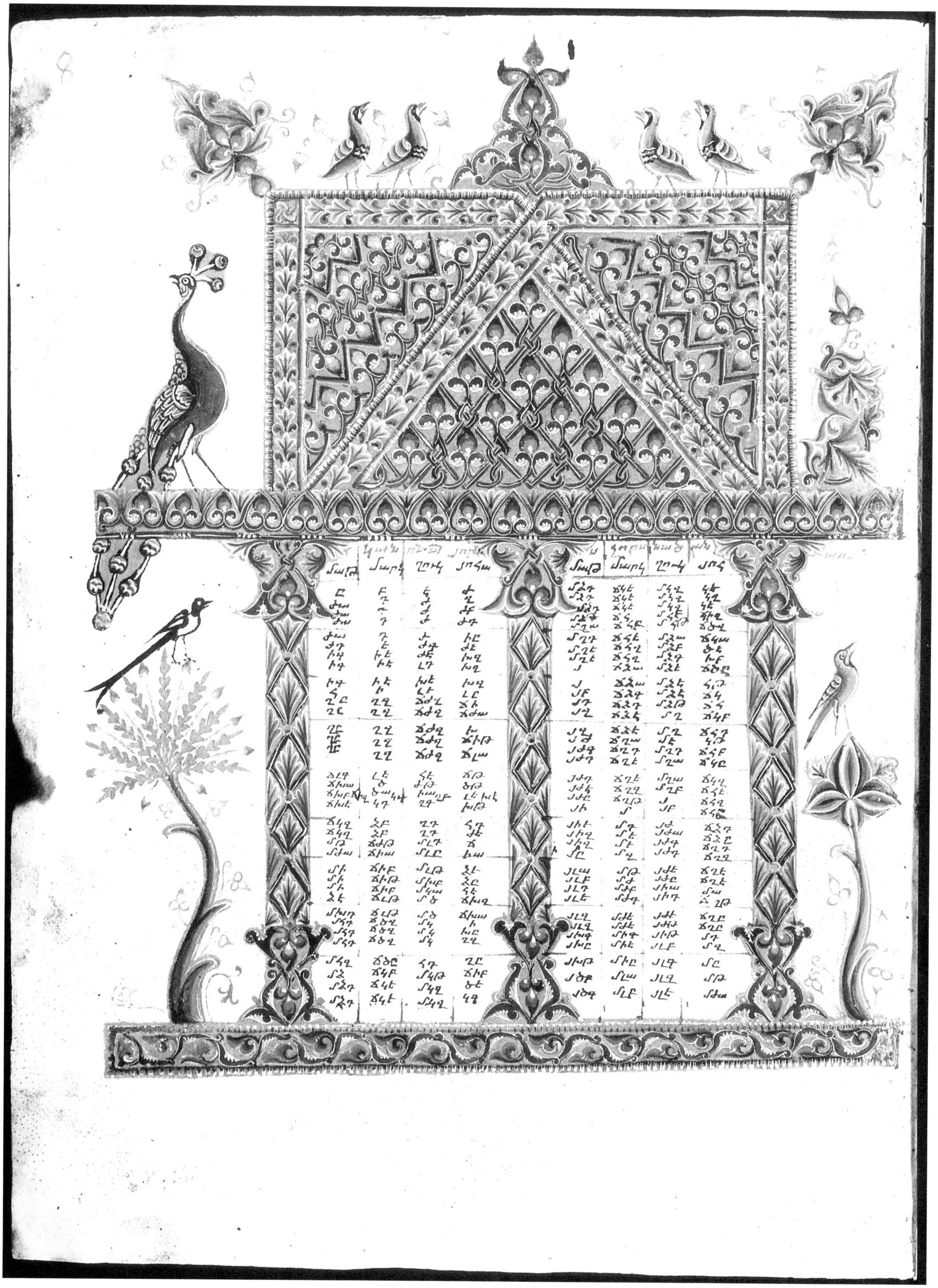

Page 8: Canon Table One. By the First Painter.

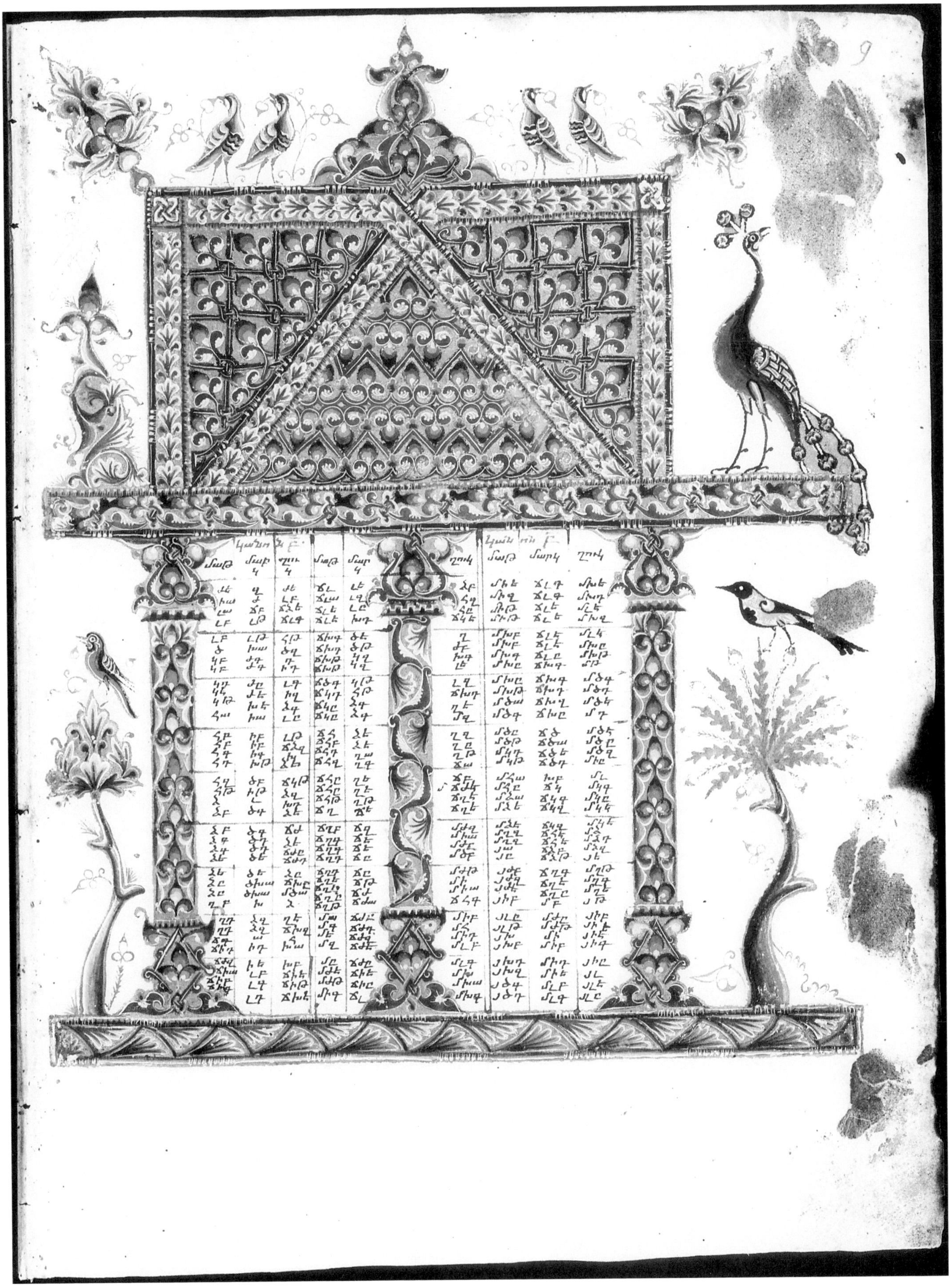

Page 9: Canon Table Two. By the First Painter.

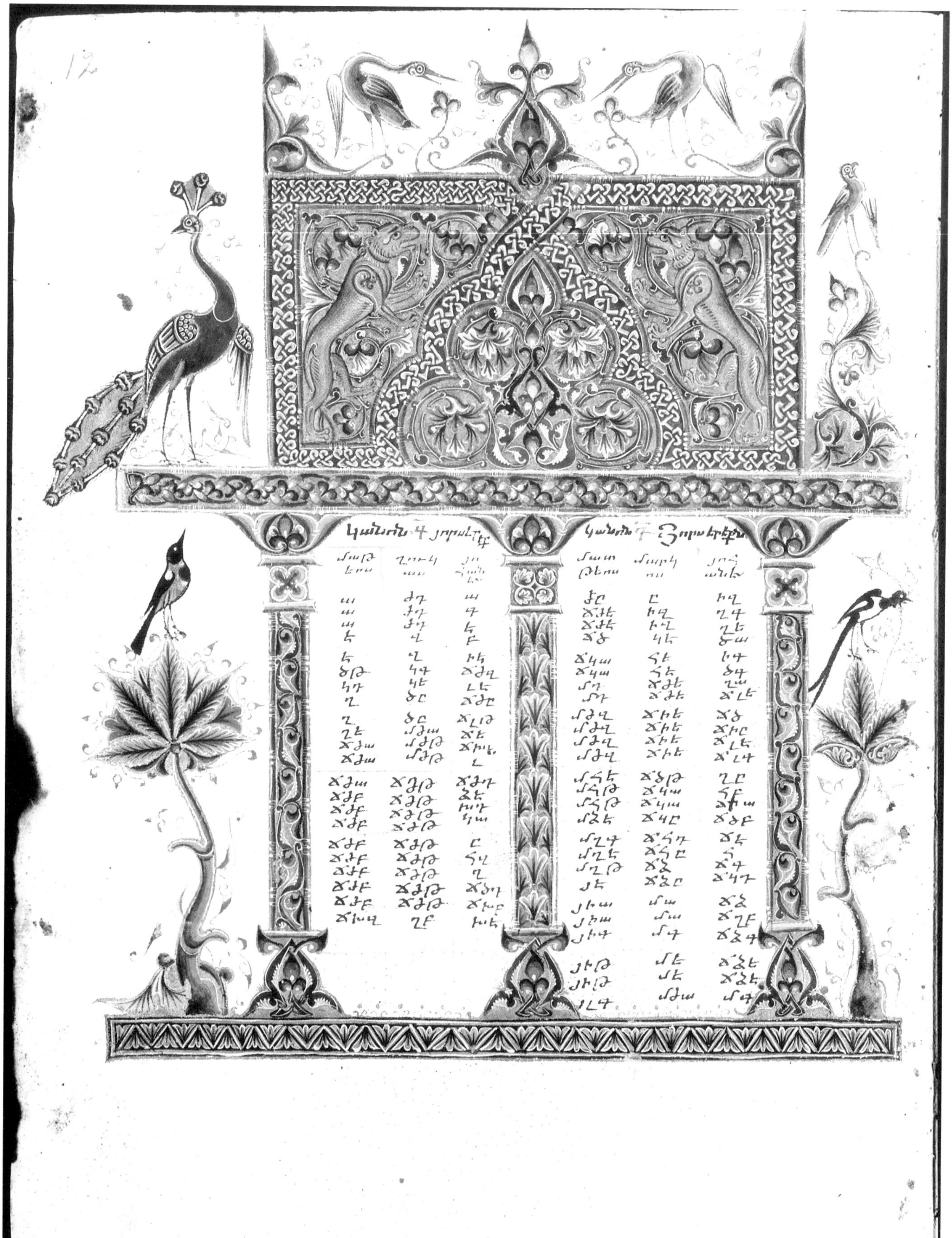

Page 12: Canon Tables Three and Four. By the First Painter.

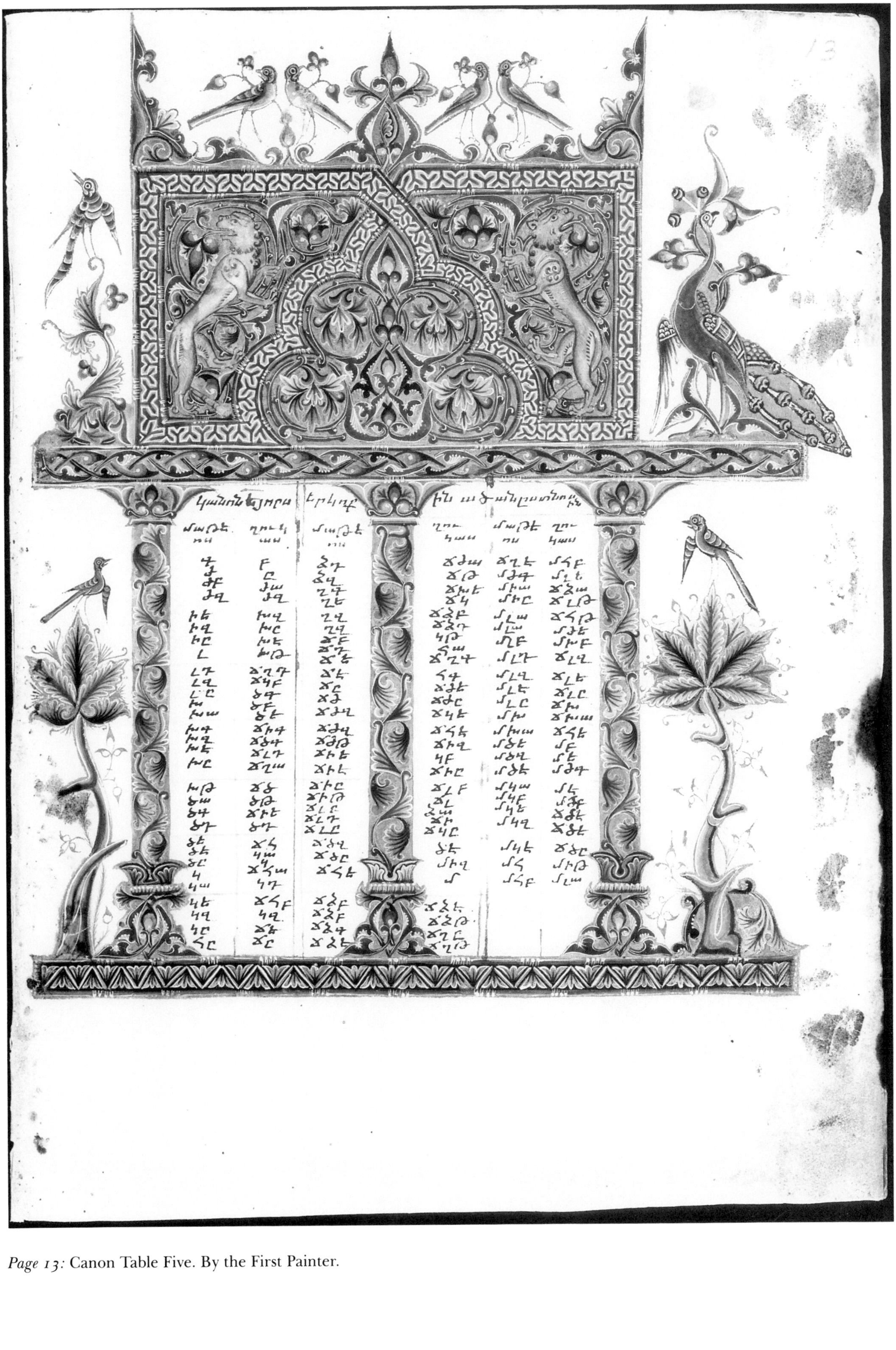

Page 13: Canon Table Five. By the First Painter.

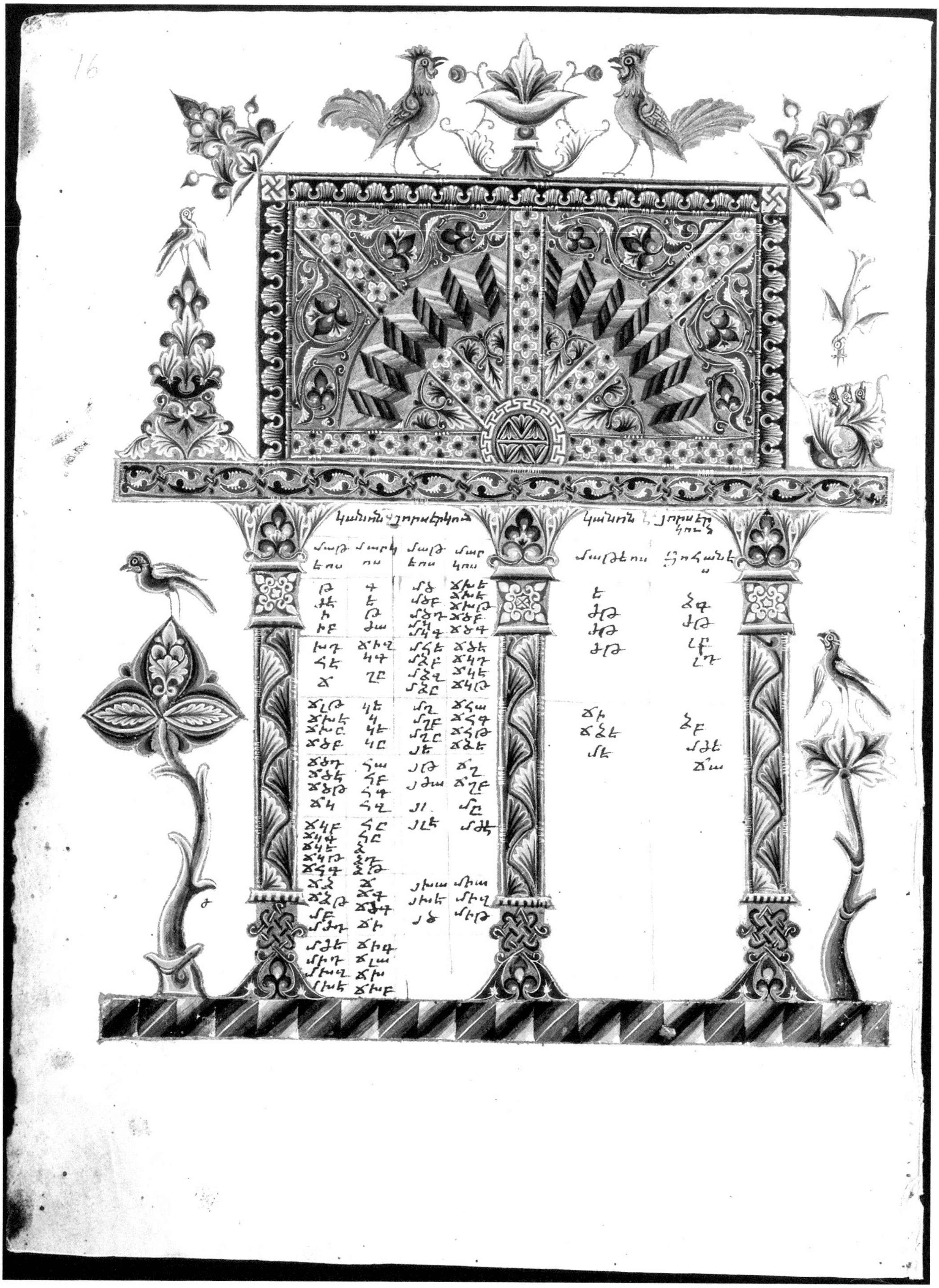

Page 16: Canon Tables Six and Seven. By the First Painter.

Page 17: Canon Tables Eight and Nine. By the First Painter.

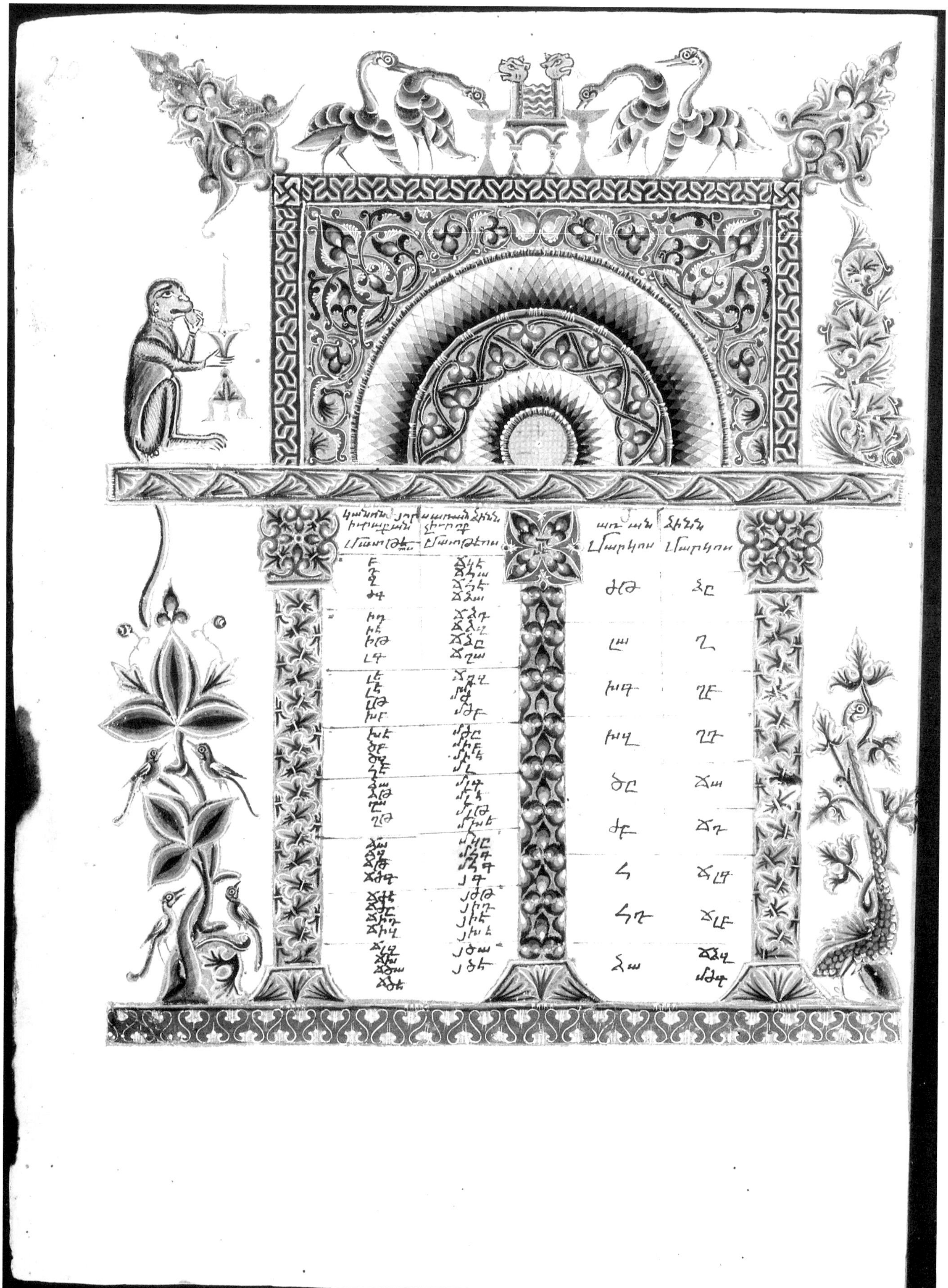

Page 20: Canon Table Ten. By the First Painter.

Page 21: Canon Table Ten. By the First Painter.

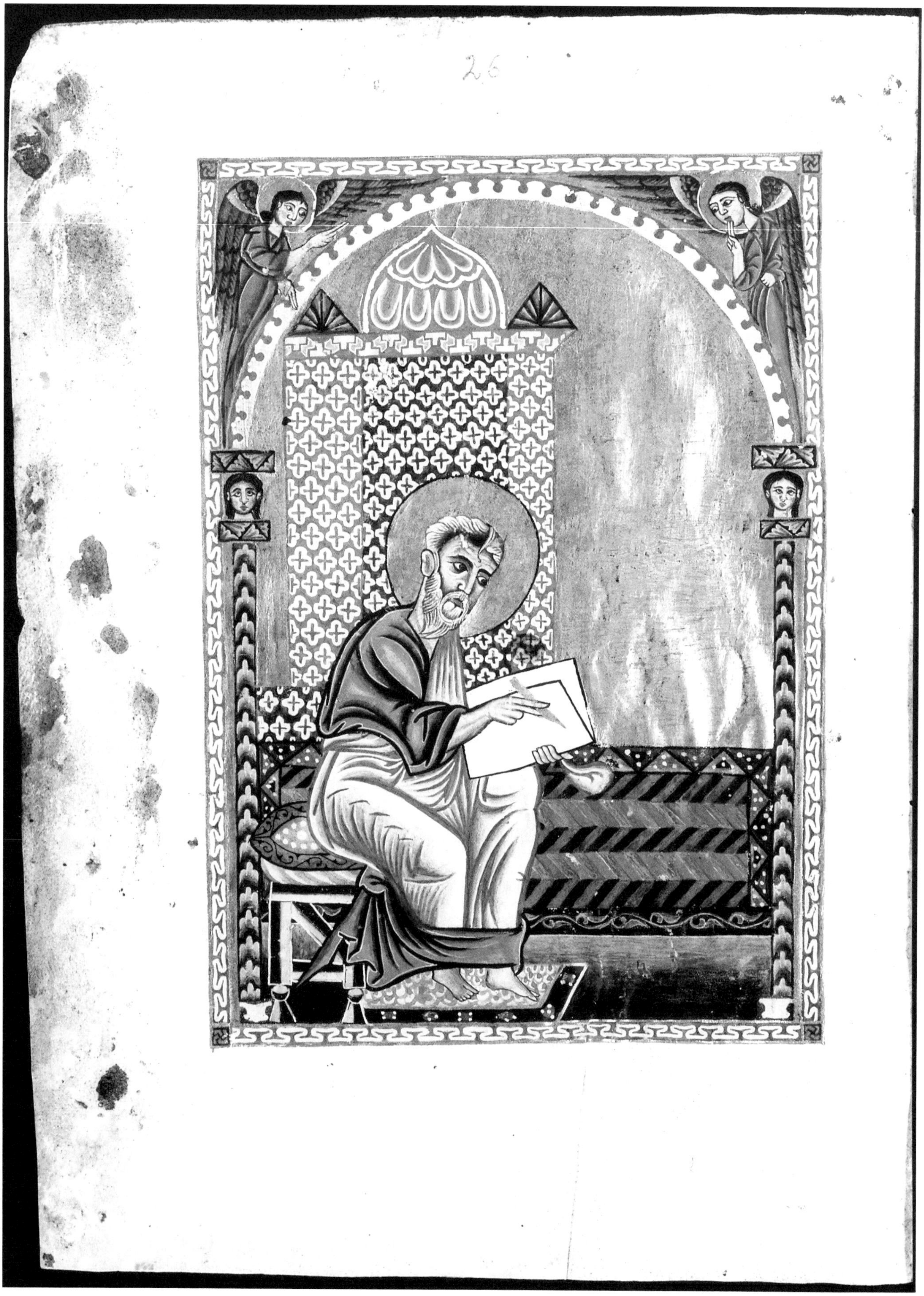

Page 26: Portrait of St. Matthew. By the Second Painter.

Page 27: Incipit to the Gospel of Matthew. By the Second Painter.

Page 28: The Genealogy of Christ (Abraham, Isaac, Jacob). By the Second Painter.

Page 29: The Genealogy of Christ (Judah to Nahshon). By the Second Painter.

Page 30: The Genealogy of Christ (Salmon to Solomon). By the Second Painter.

Page 31: The Genealogy of Christ (Rehoboam to Ahaz). By the Second Painter.

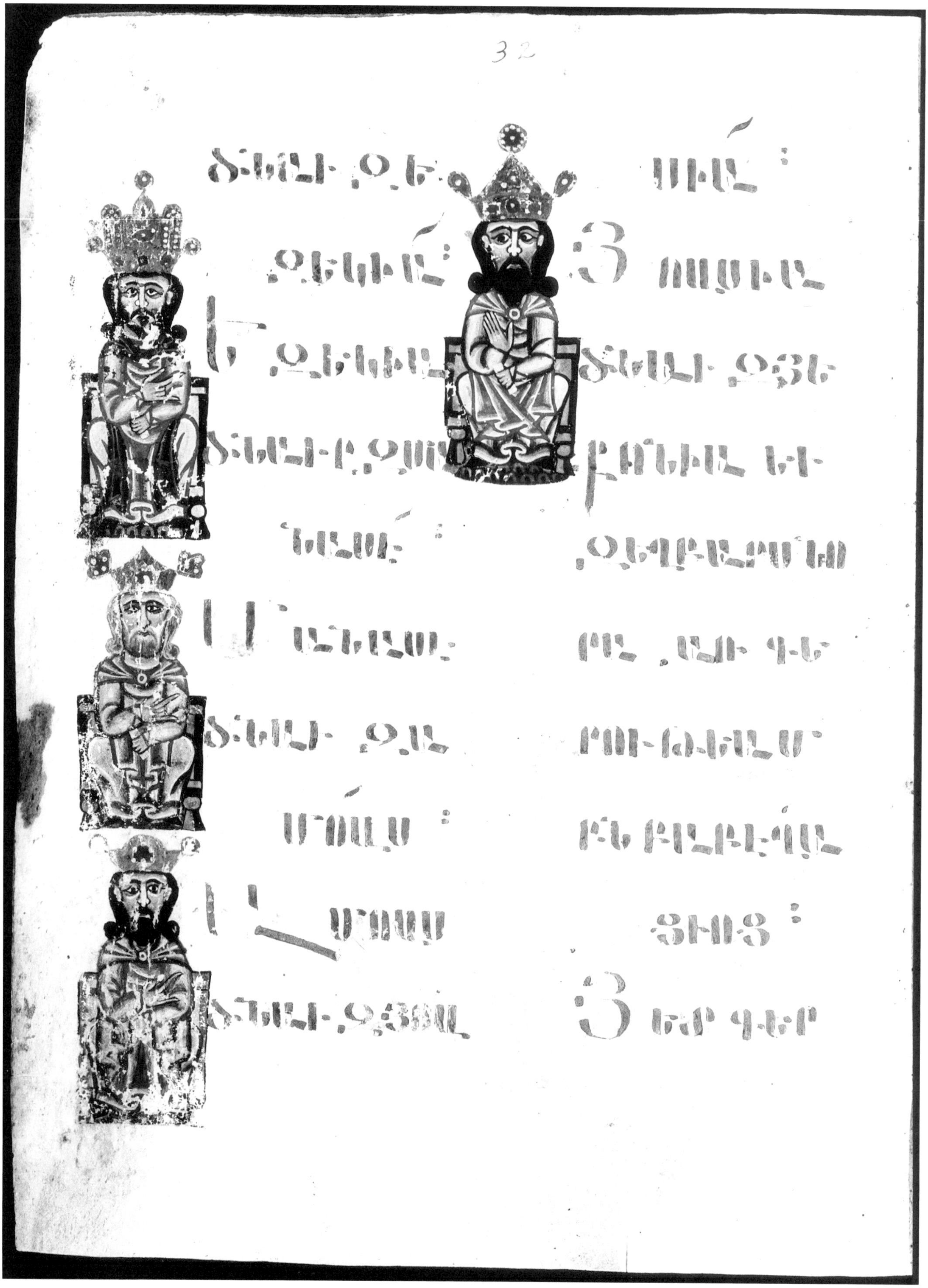

Page 32: The Genealogy of Christ (Hezekiah to Joshiah). By the Second Painter.

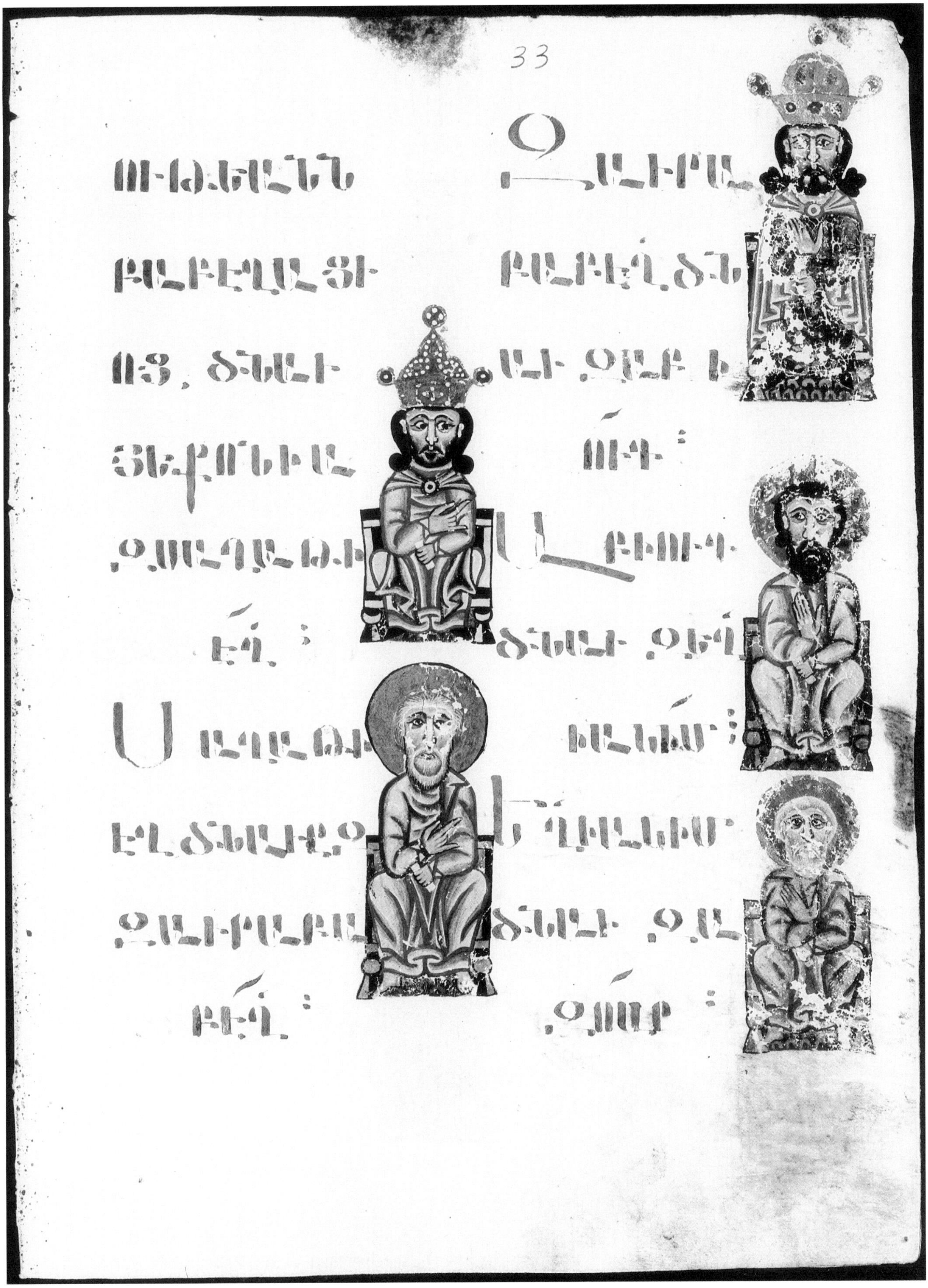

Page 33: The Genealogy of Christ (Jechoniah to Eliakim). By the Second Painter.

Page 34: The Genealogy of Christ (Azor to Jacob). By the Second Painter.

Page 35: The Genealogy of Christ (Joseph, Mary, Christ). By the Second Painter and T'oros Taronec'i.

Page 92: The Beheading of John the Baptist. By the Third Painter and T'oros Taronec'i.

Page 99: The Petition of the Canaanite. By the Third Painter.

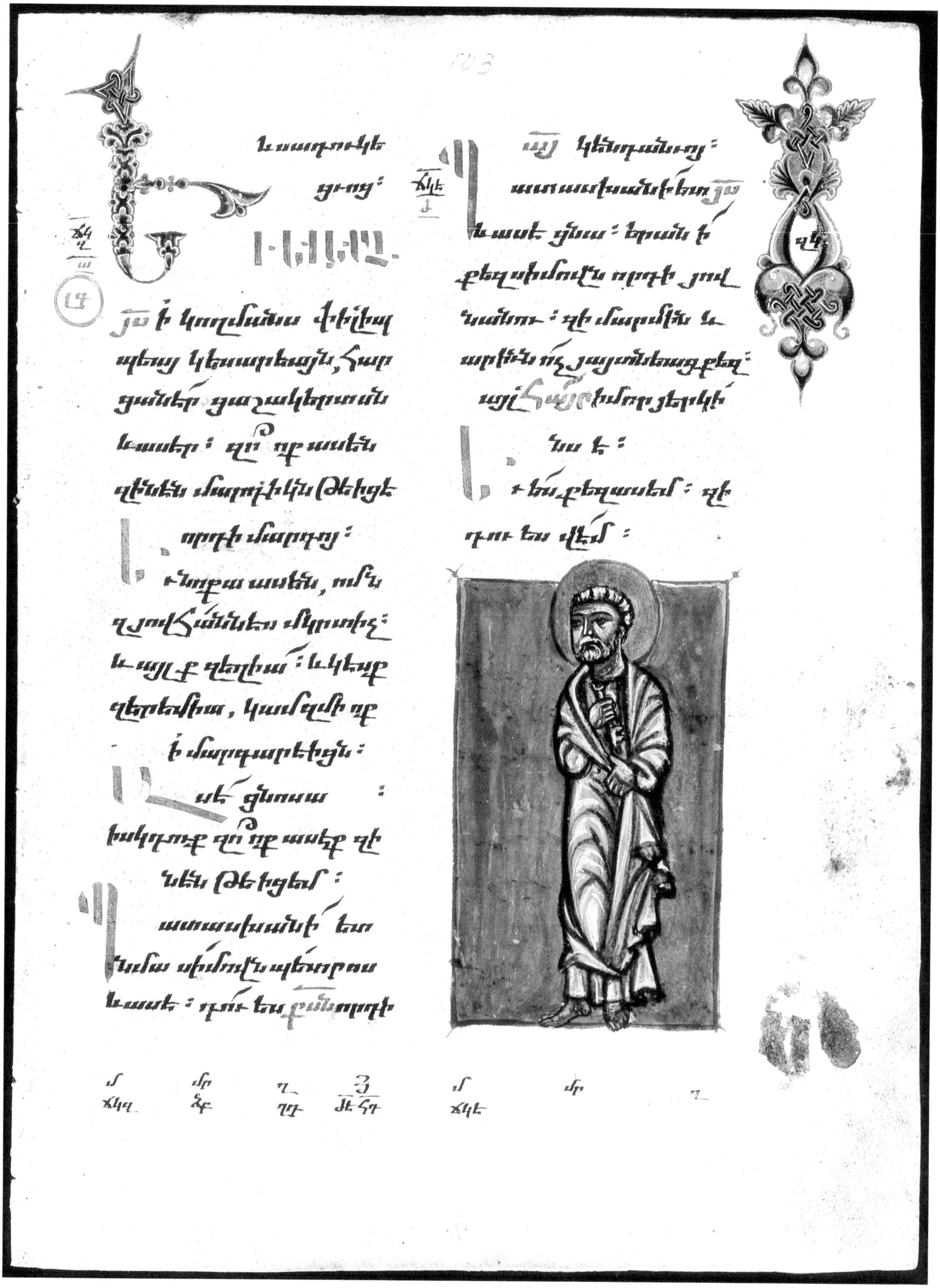

Page 103: Peter Receives the Keys. By the Third Painter.

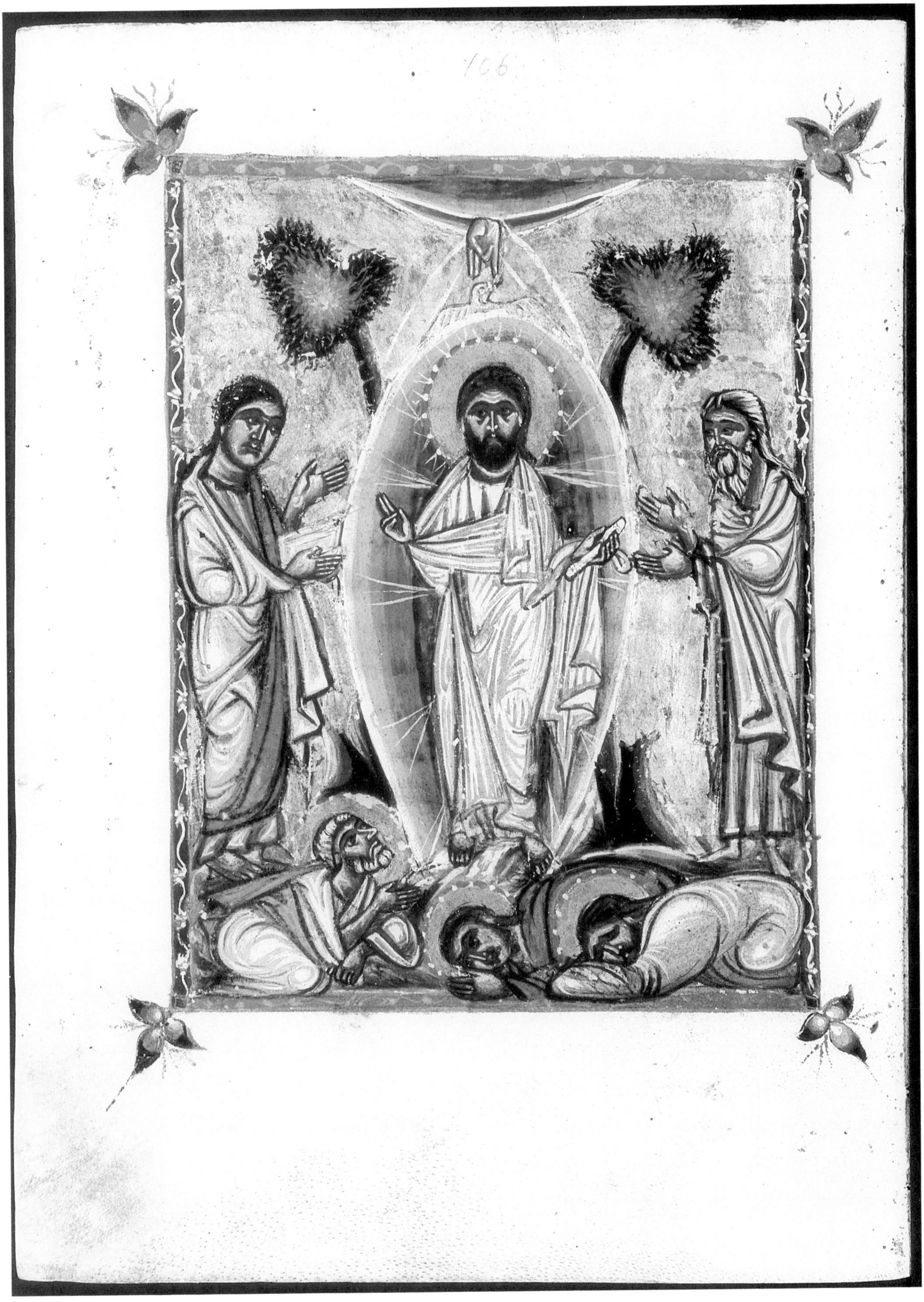

Page 106: The Transfiguration. By the Third Painter.

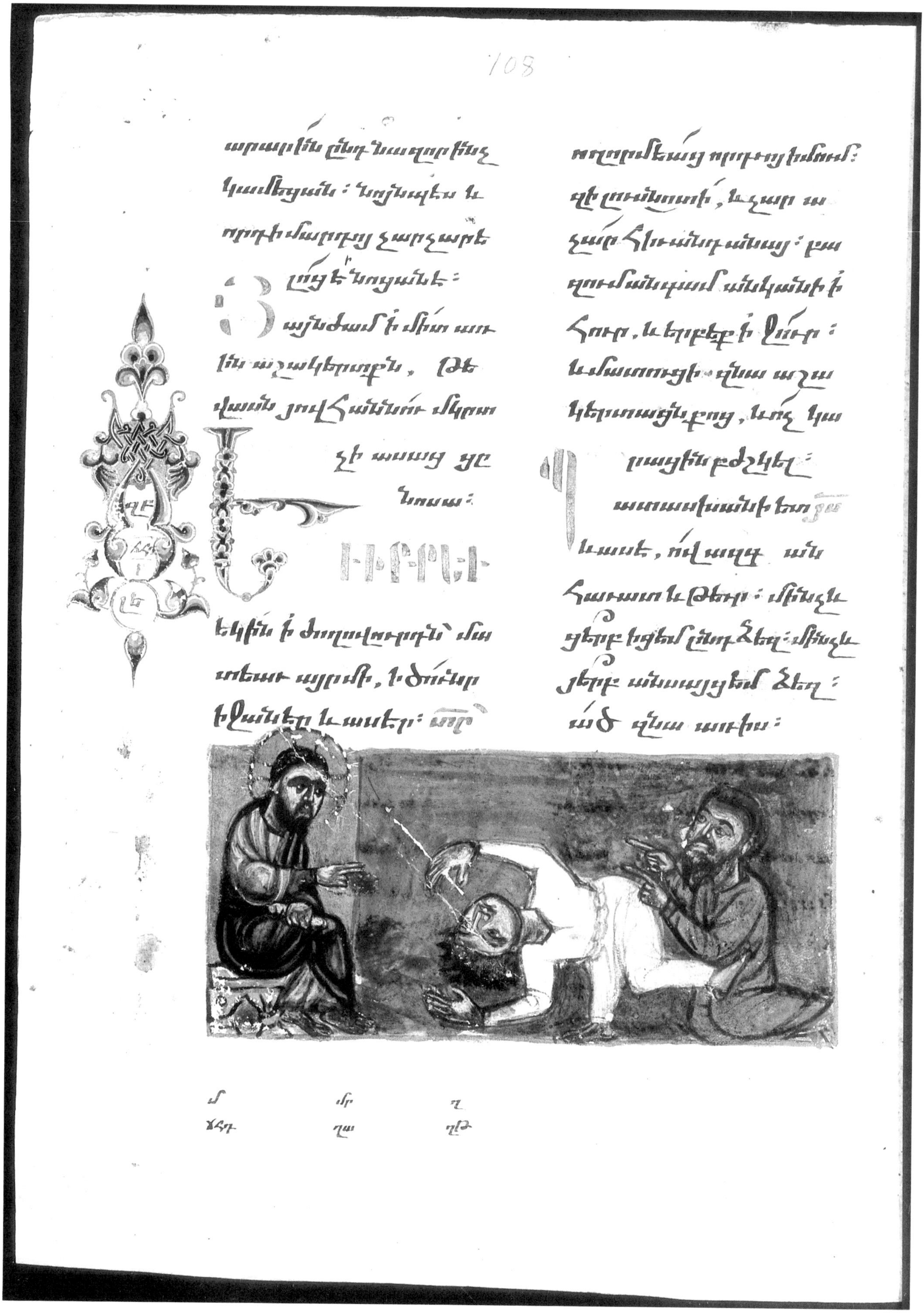

Page 108: The Cure of the Epileptic. By the Third Painter.

Page 117: The Blessing of the Children. By the Third Painter.

Page 122: The Petition of the Mother of James and John. By the Third Painter.

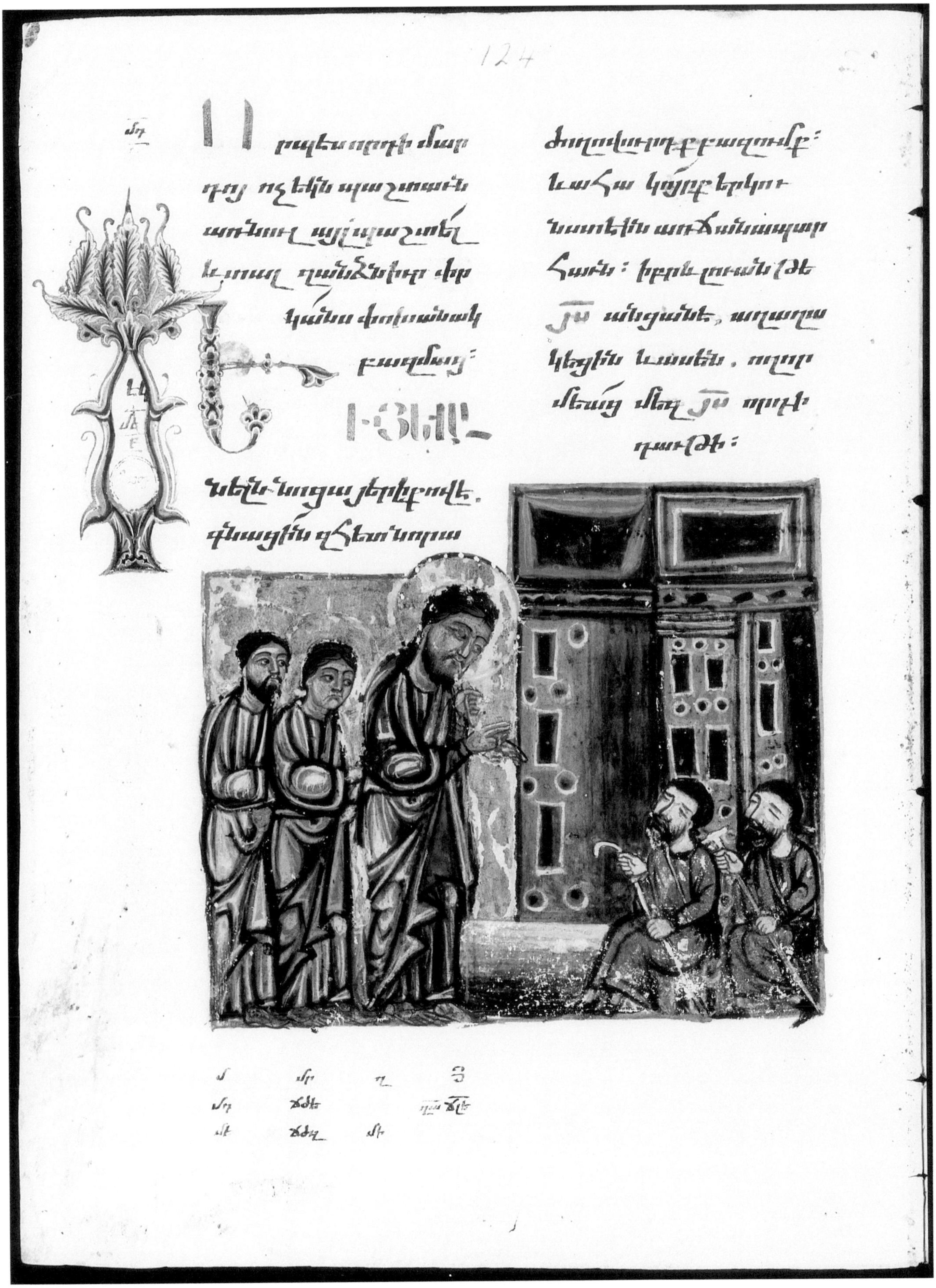

Page 124: The Cure of the Blind in Jericho. By the Fourth Painter.

Page 126: The Entry into Jerusalem and the Cleansing of the Temple. By the Fourth Painter and T'oros Taronec'i.

Page 156: The Last Supper. By the Second Painter.

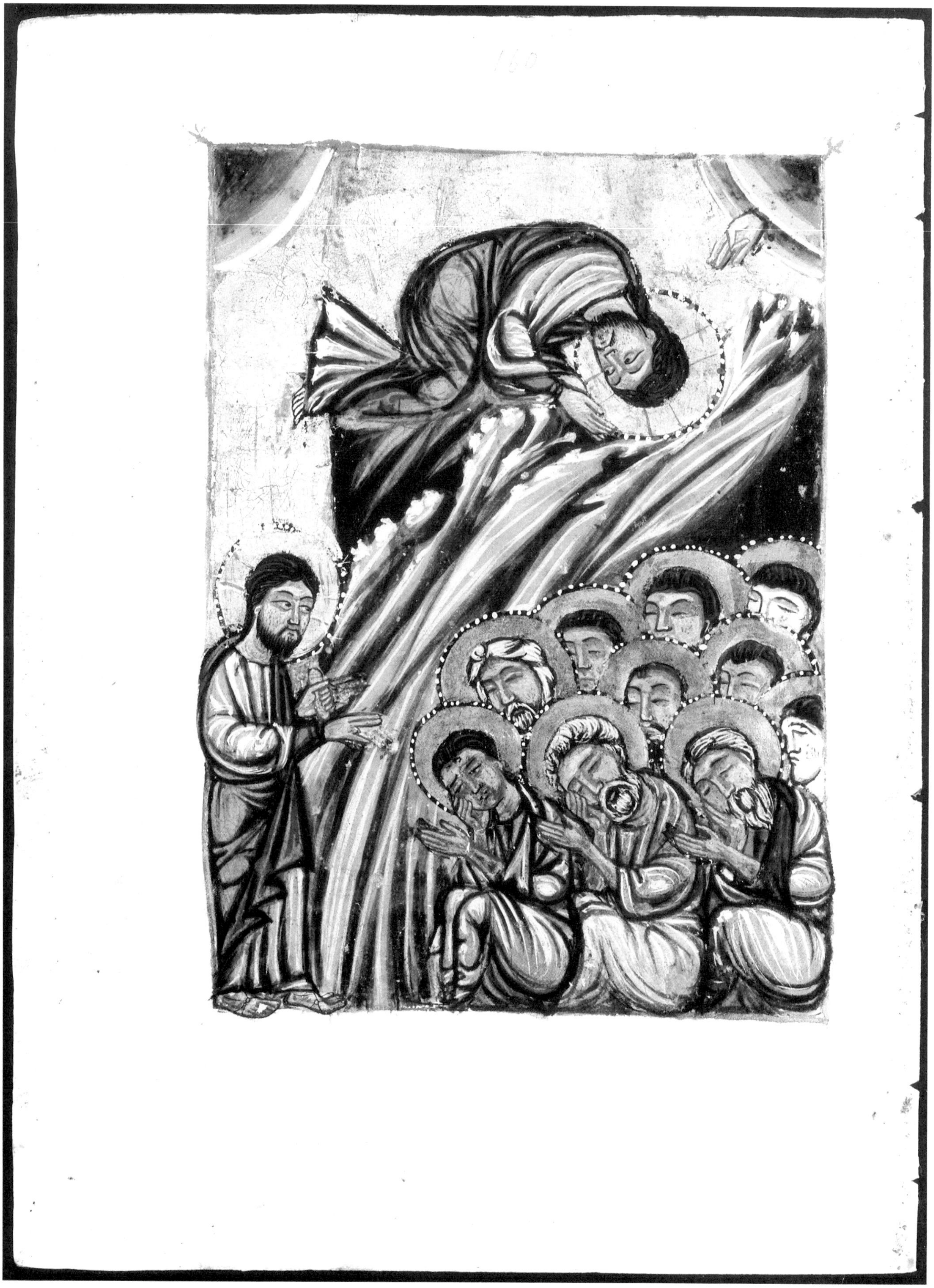

Page 160: The Agony in the Garden. By the Fourth Painter.

Page 162: The Betrayal. By the Fourth Painter and T'oros Taronec'i.

Page 166: Peter's Denial. By the Fourth Painter and T'oros Taronec'i.

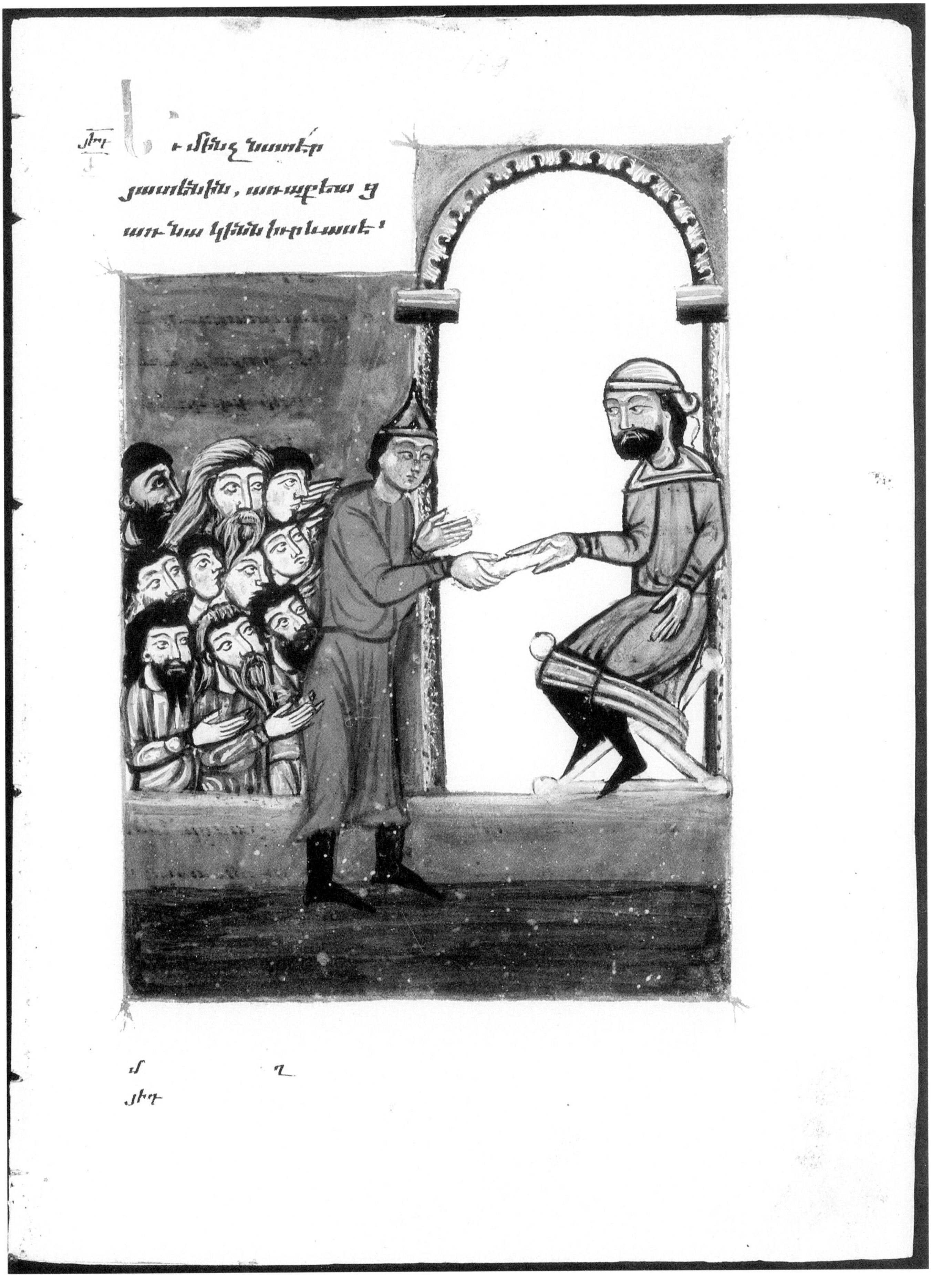

Page 169: The Message from Pilate's Wife. By the Fourth Painter and Tʿoros Taronecʿi.

Page 171: Pilate Washes His Hands. By the Fourth Painter and Tʿoros Taronecʿi.

Page 172: The Mocking of Christ. By the Fourth Painter and T'oros Taronec'i.

Page 173: The Way of the Cross. By the Fourth Painter and T'oros Taronec'i.

Page 179: The Women at the Tomb. By the Fourth Painter and T'oros Taronec'i.

Page 188: Portrait of St. Mark. By the Second Painter.

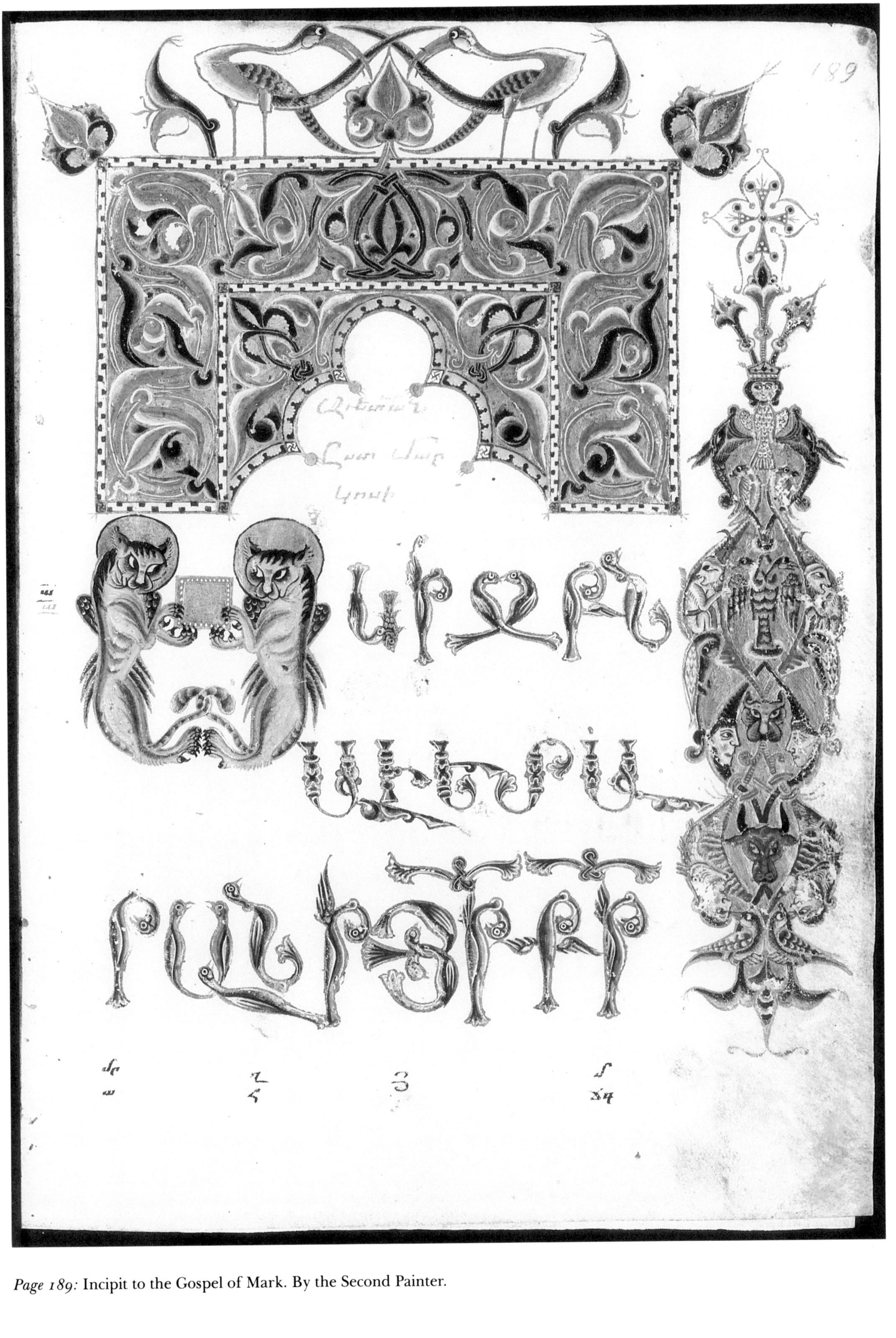

Page 189: Incipit to the Gospel of Mark. By the Second Painter.

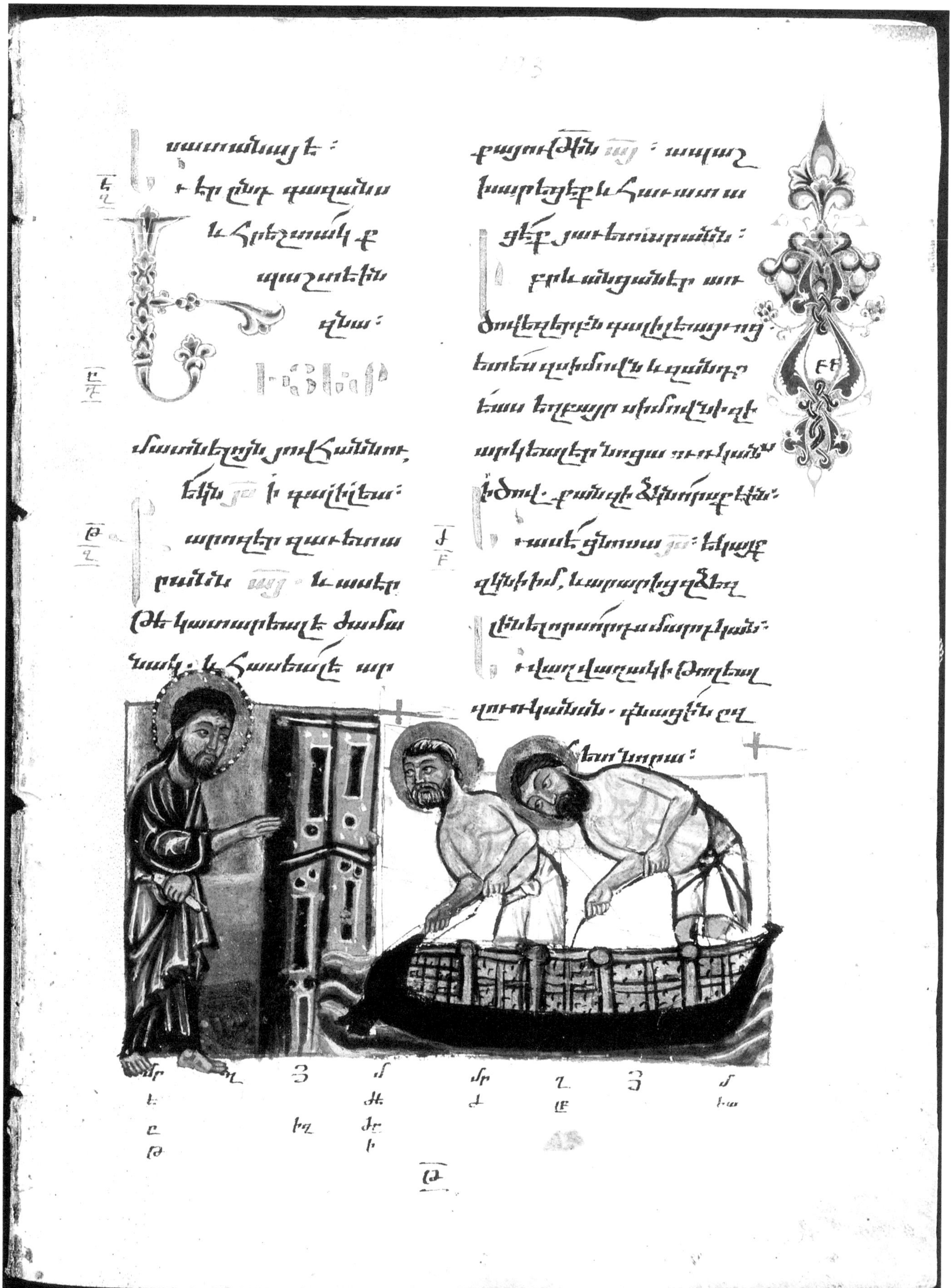

Page 193: The Call of Peter and Andrew. By the Fourth Painter.

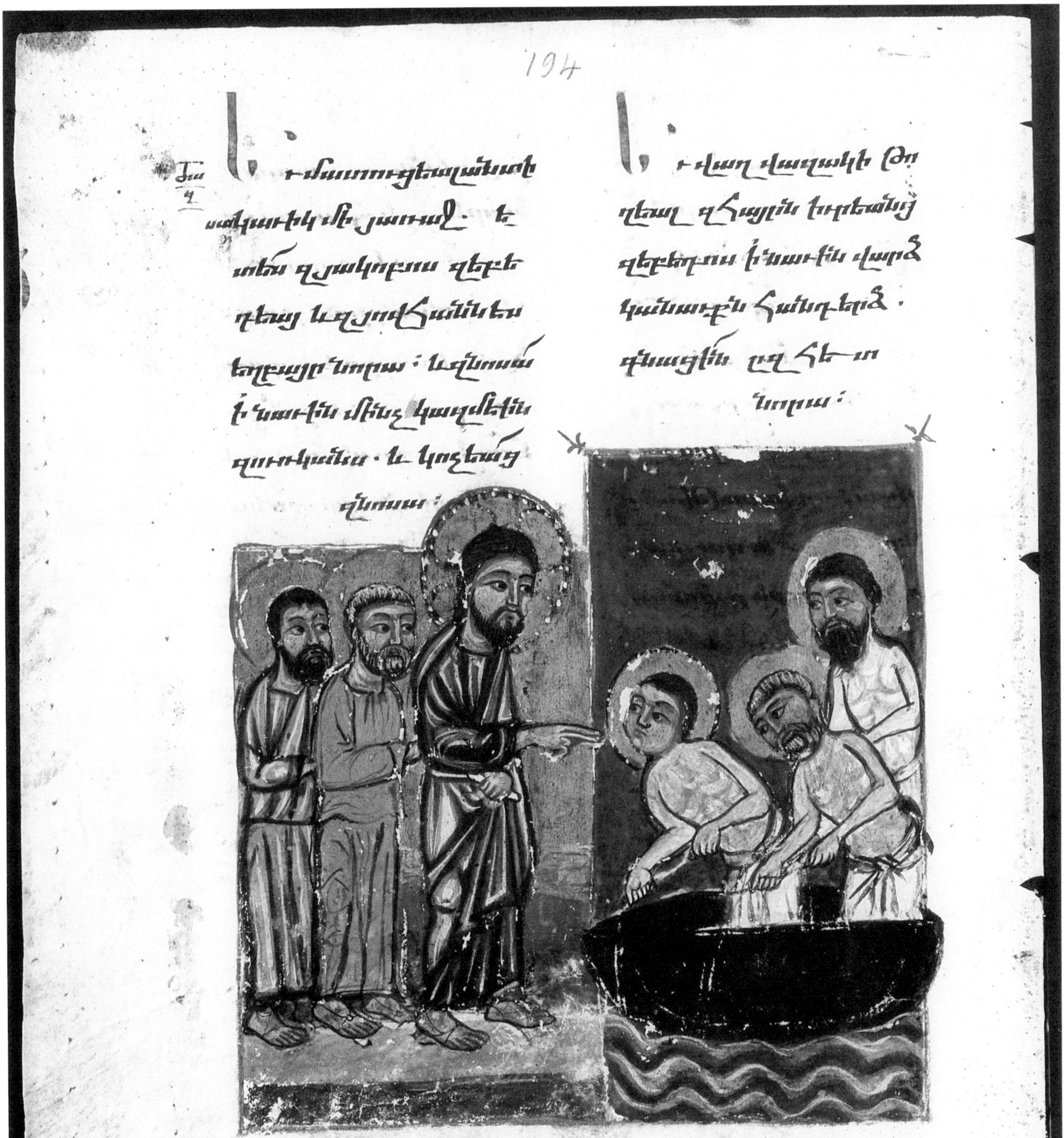

Page 194: The Call of James and John. By the Fourth Painter.

Page 197: The Cure of the Leper. By the Fourth Painter.

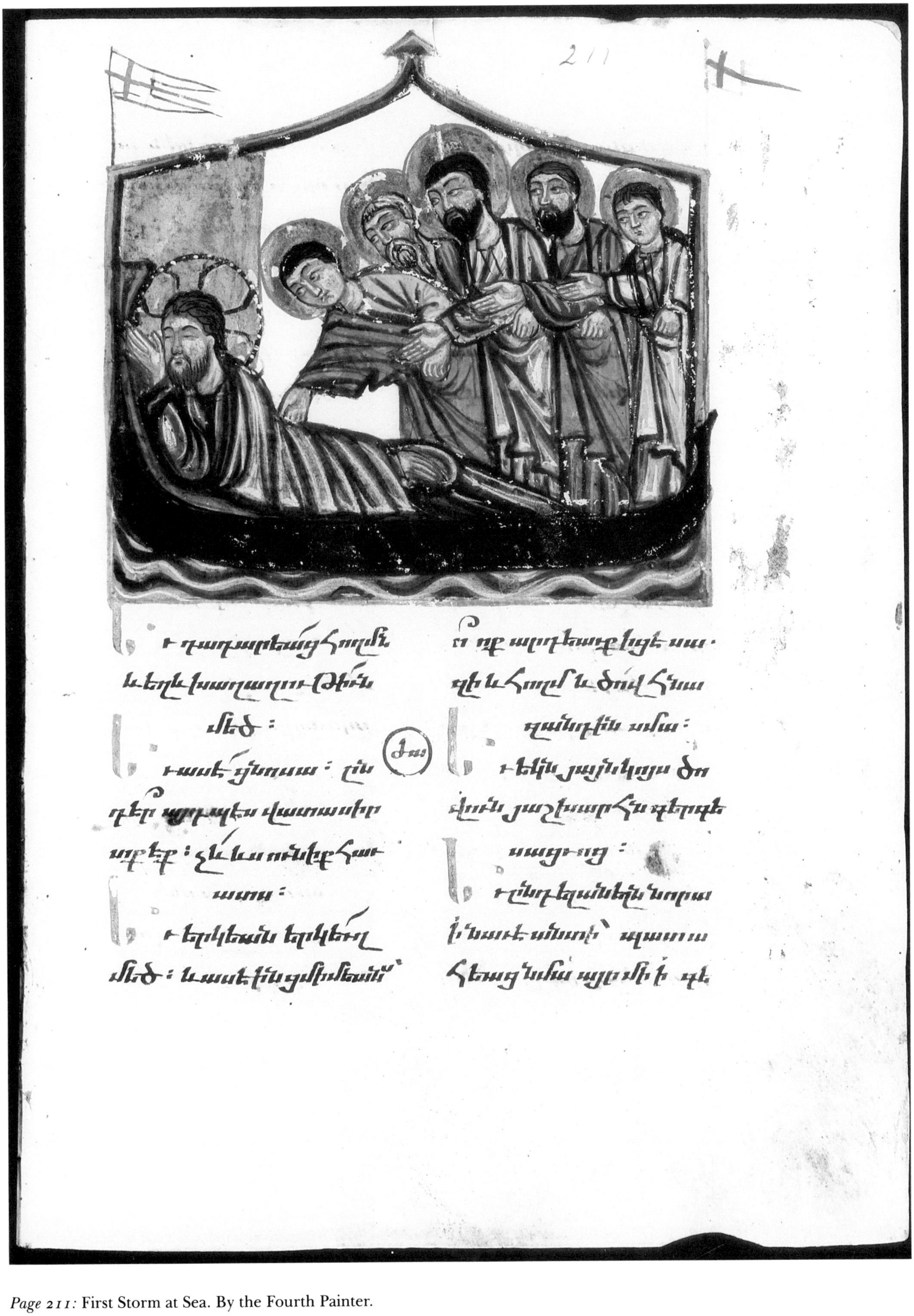

Page 211: First Storm at Sea. By the Fourth Painter.

Page 216: The Woman with Hemorrhage and the Petition of Jairus. By Tʿoros Taronecʿi.

Page 218: The Raising of Jairus' Daughter. By T'oros Taronec'i.

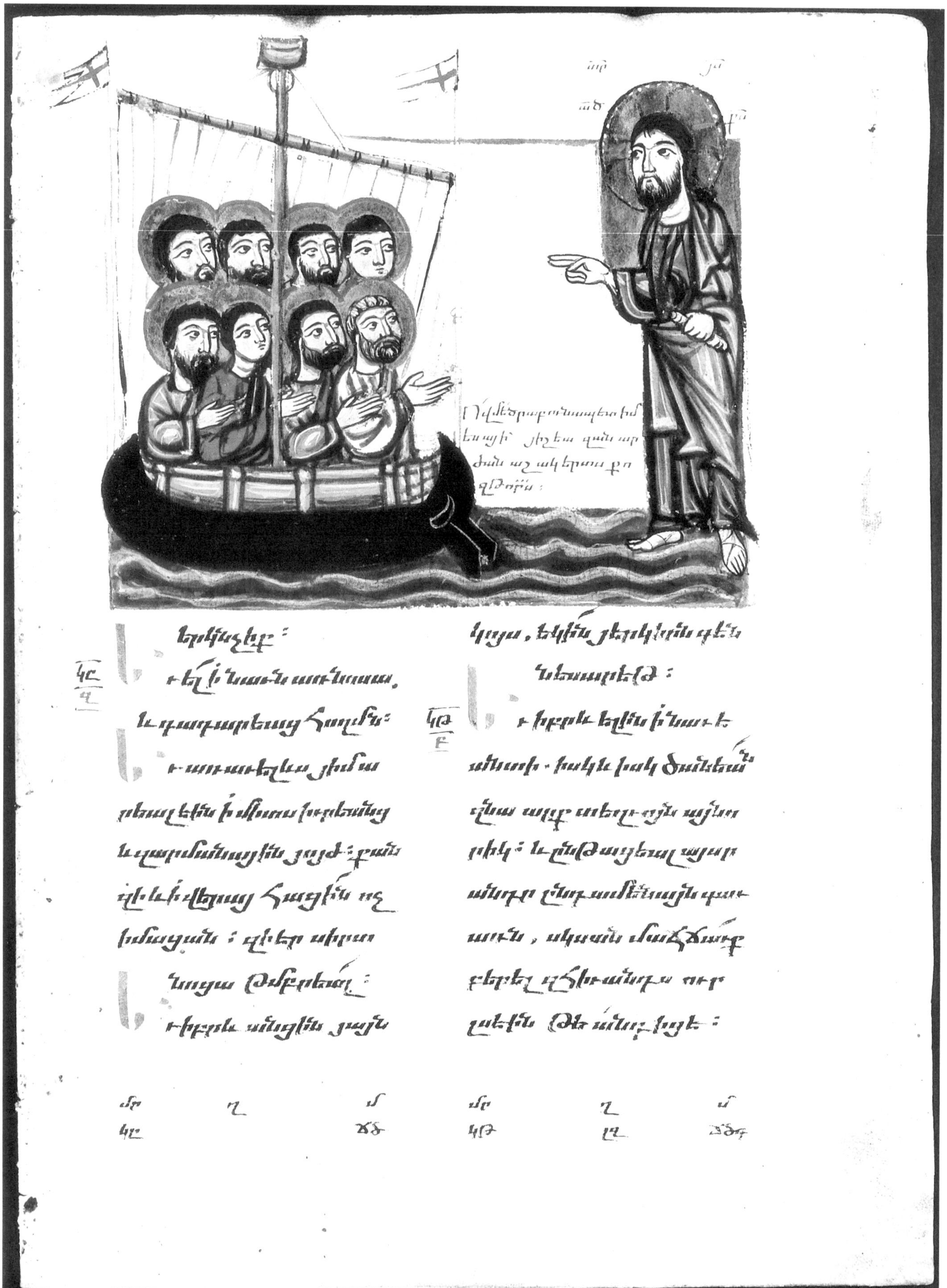

Page 227: The Second Storm at Sea. By Tʻoros Taronecʻi.

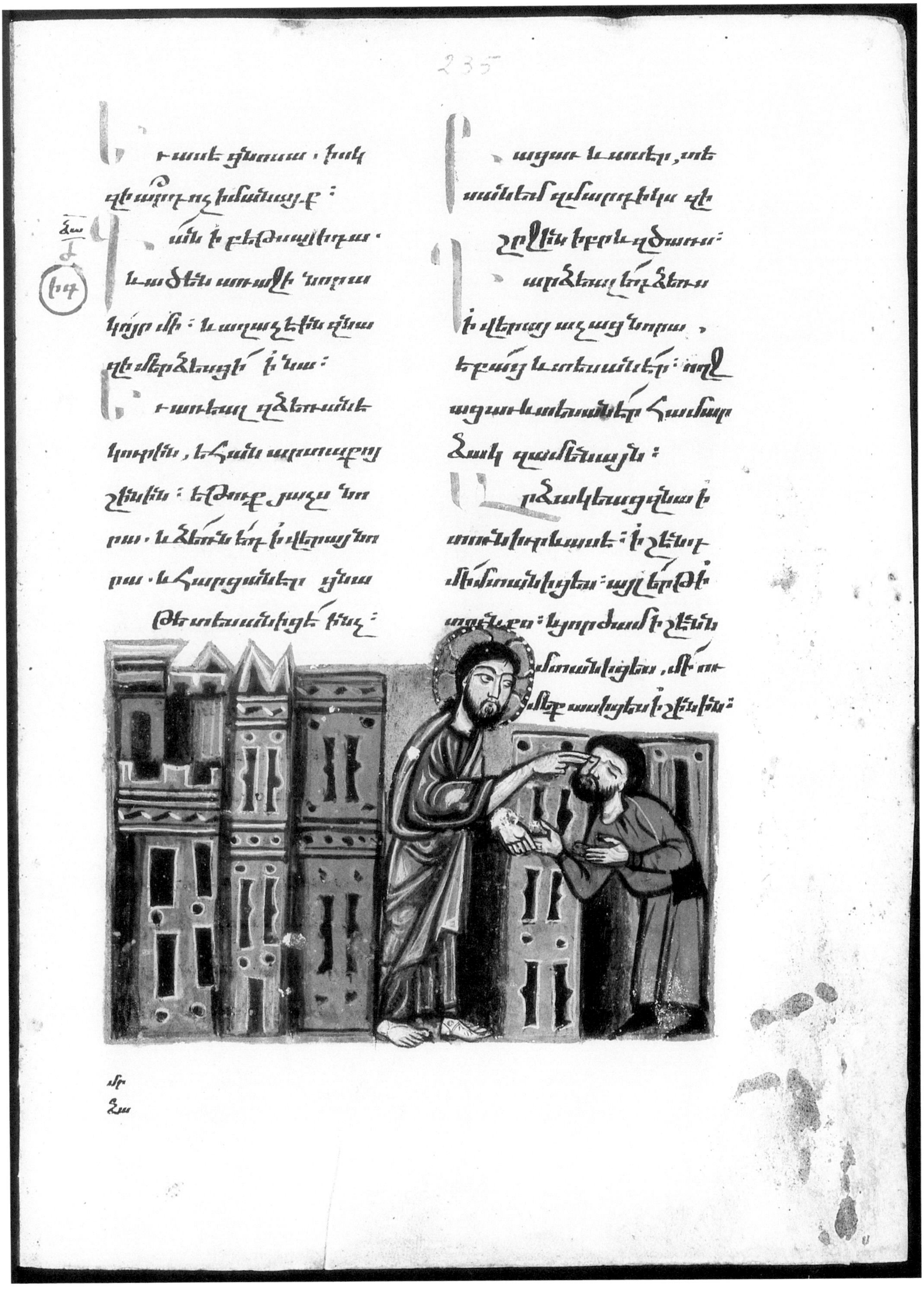

Page 235: The Cure of the Blind Man at Bethsaida. By T'oros Taronec'i.

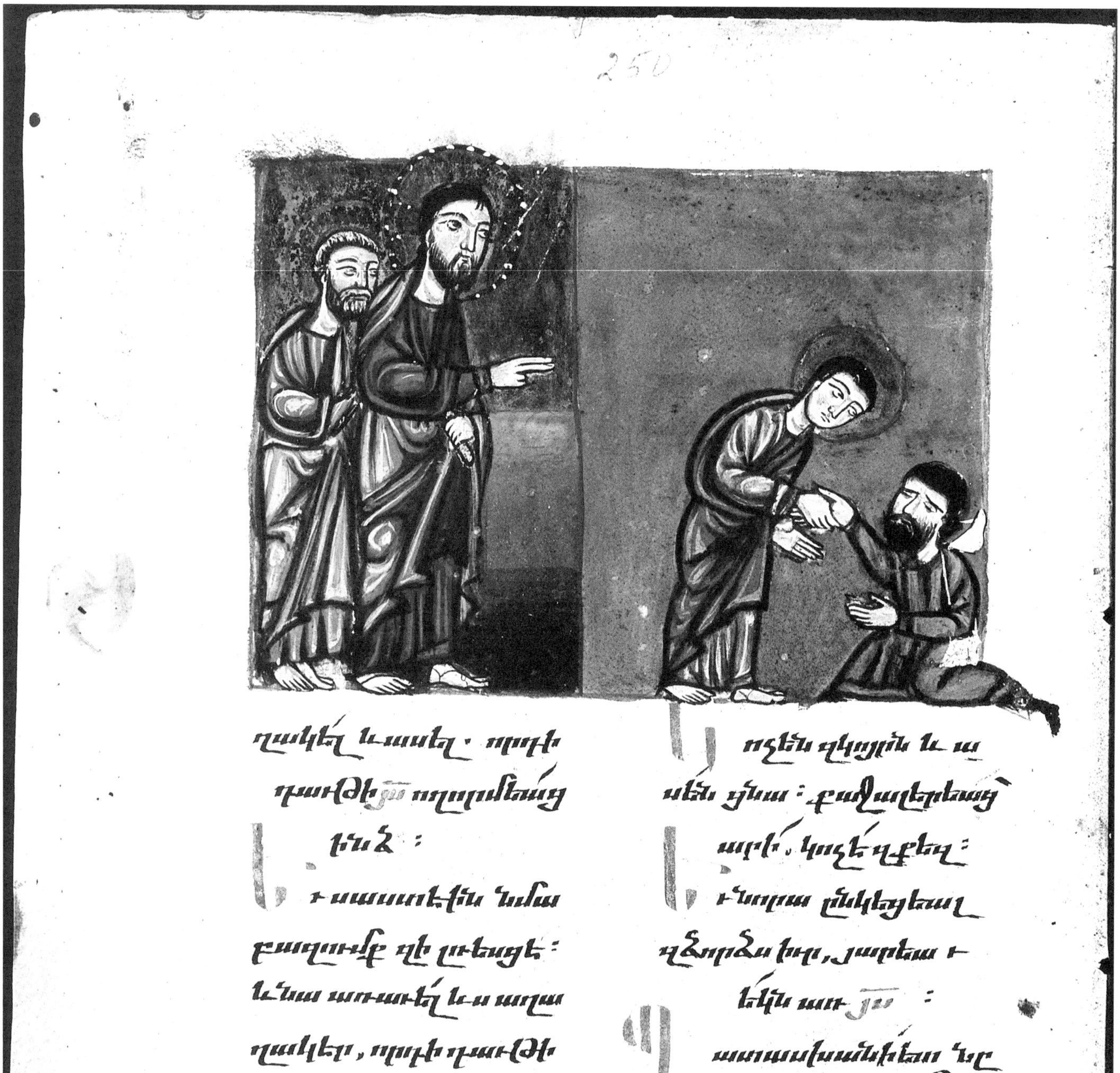

Page 250: The Cure of Blind Bartimaeus. By T'oros Taronec'i.

Page 252: The Entry into Jerusalem. By the Second Painter.

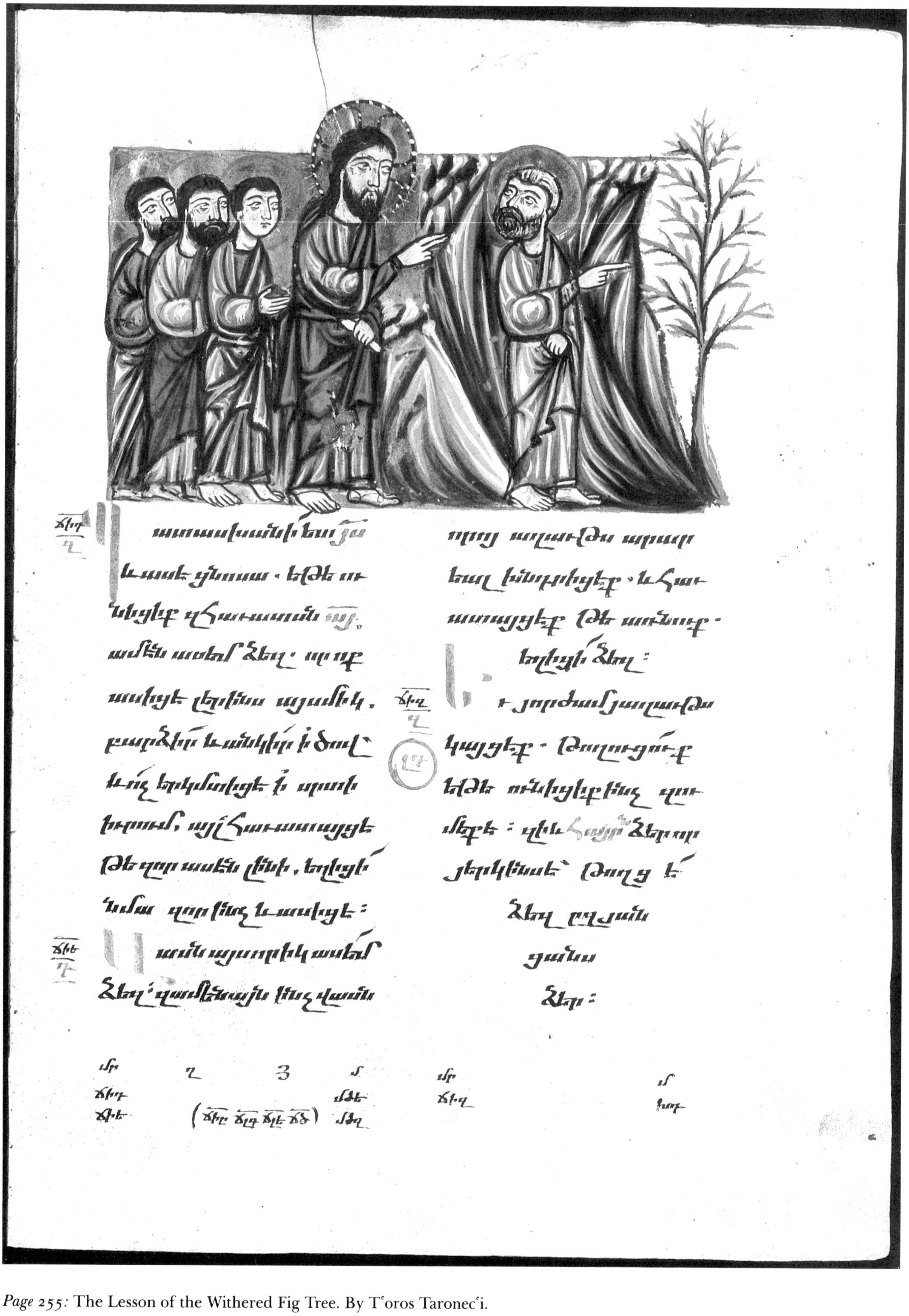

Page 255: The Lesson of the Withered Fig Tree. By T'oros Taronec'i.

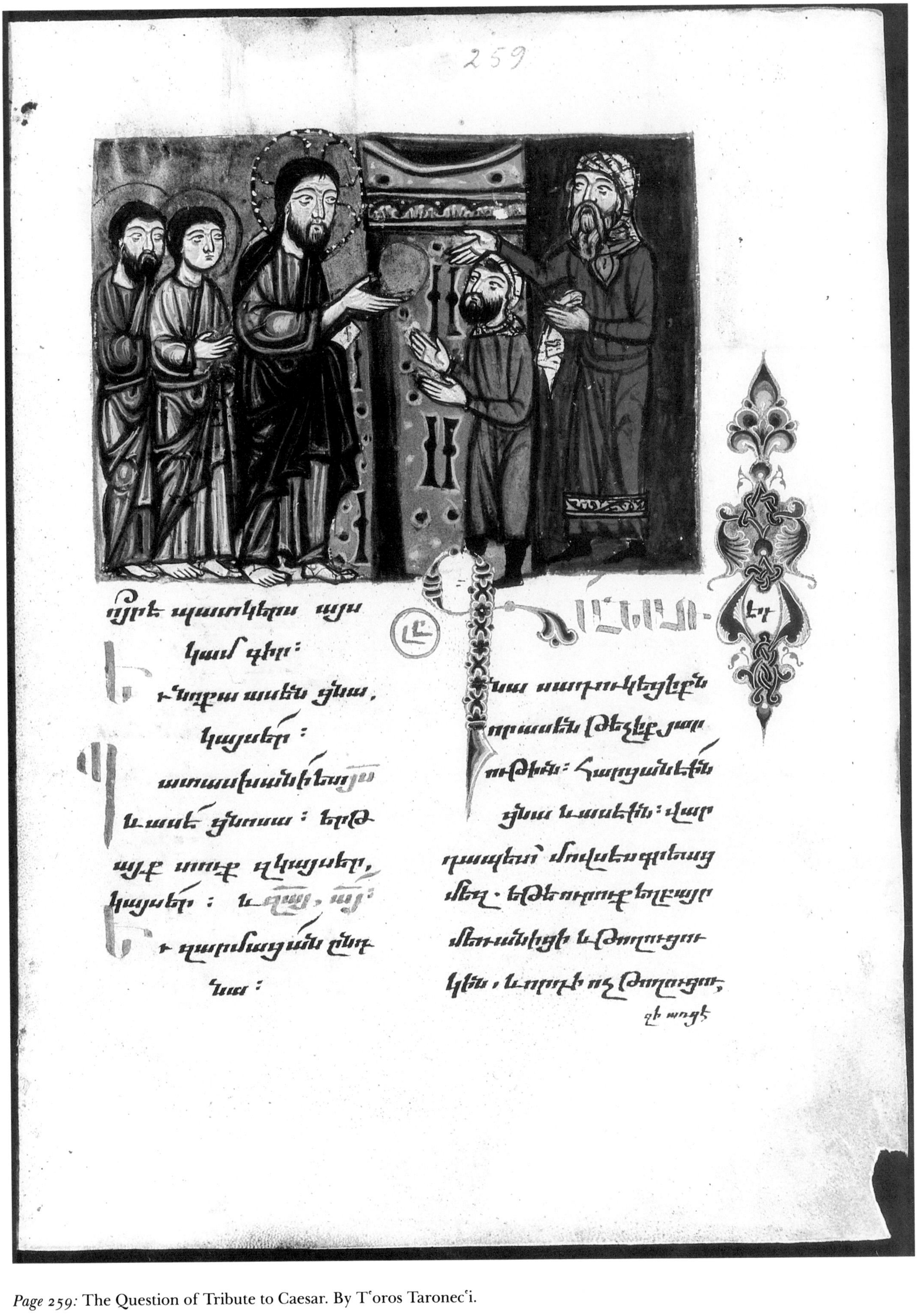

Page 259: The Question of Tribute to Caesar. By T'oros Taronec'i.

Page 263: The Widow's Mite. By T'oros Taronec'i.

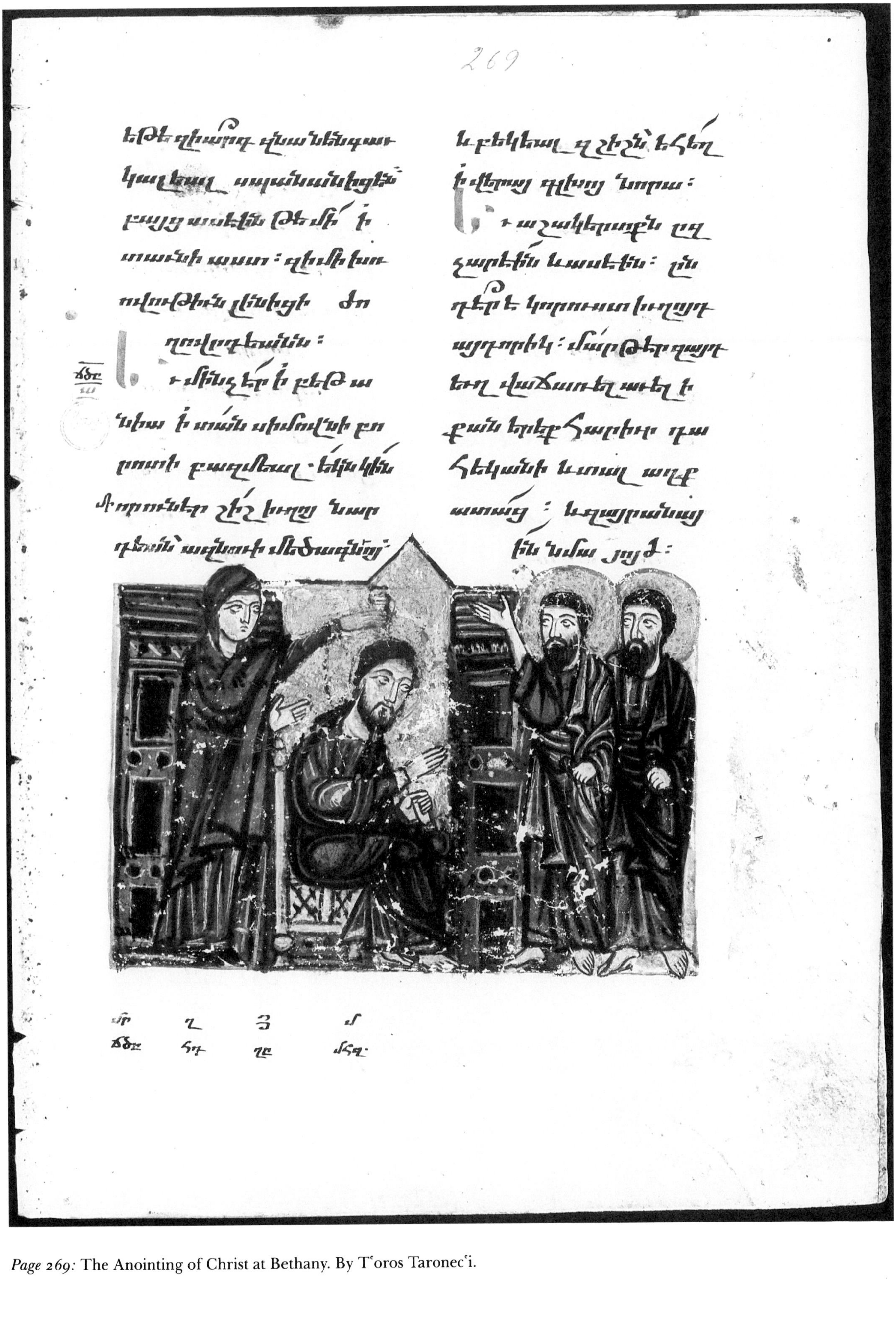

Page 269: The Anointing of Christ at Bethany. By Tʿoros Taronecʿi.

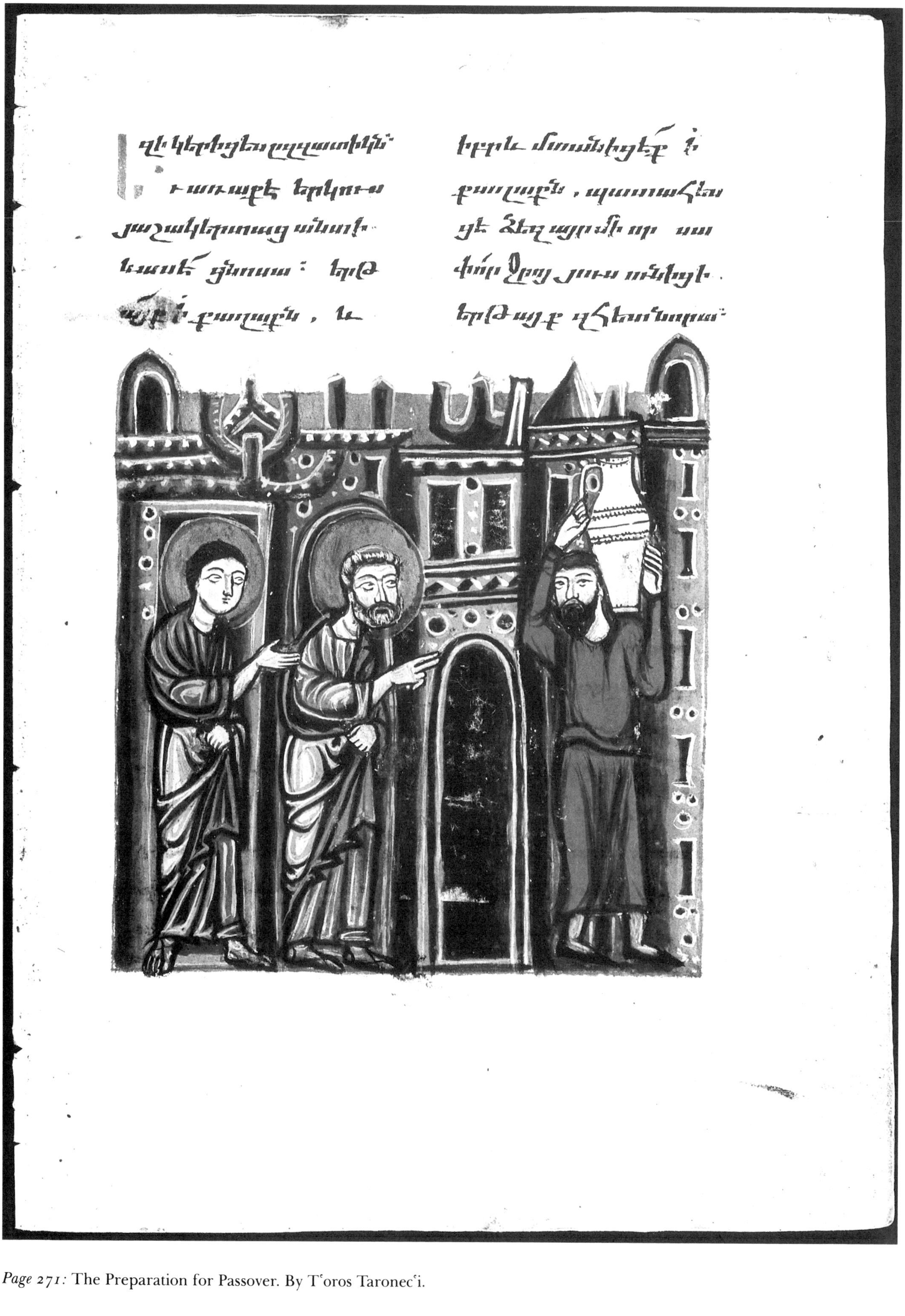

Page 271: The Preparation for Passover. By T'oros Taronec'i.

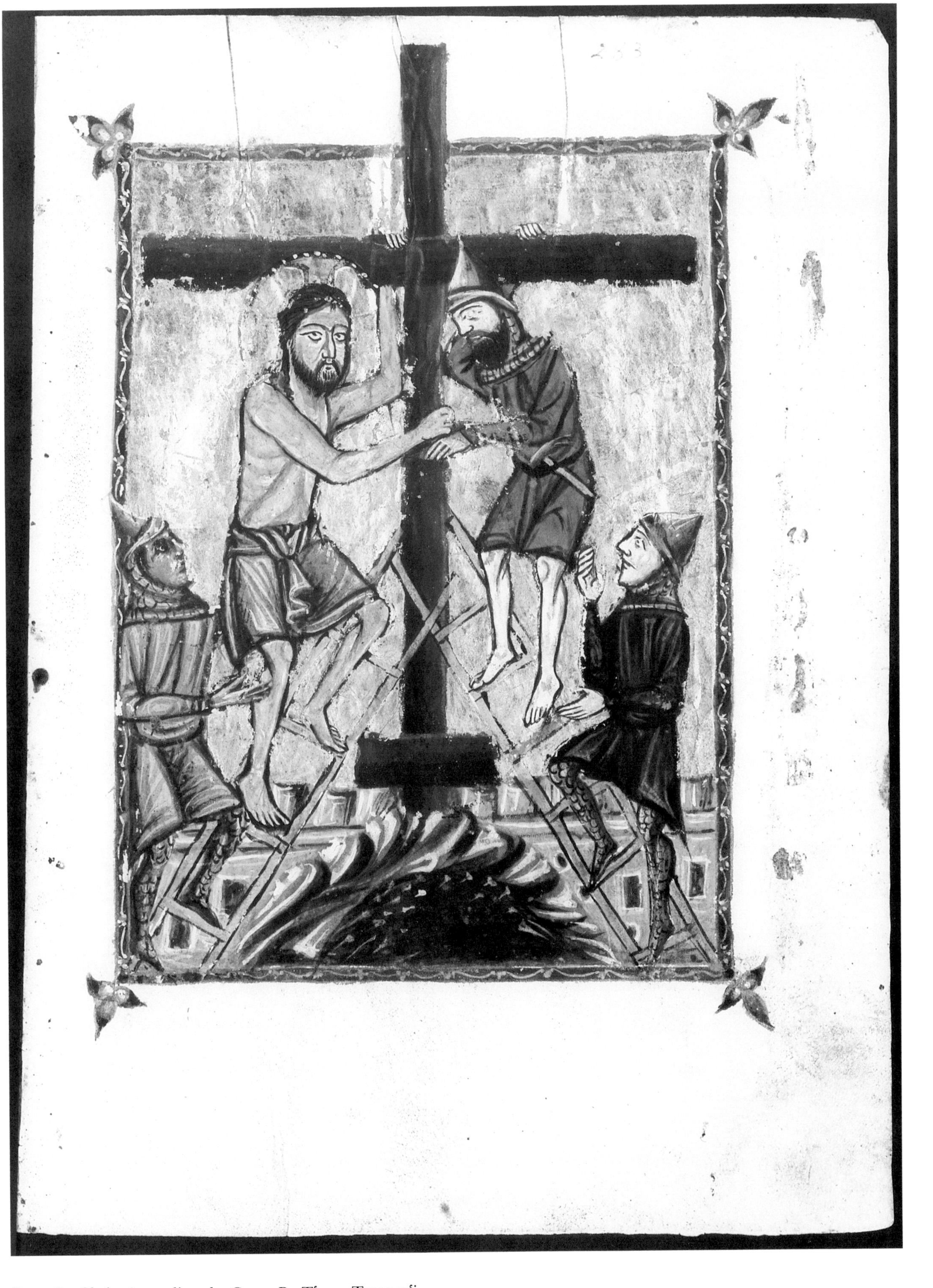

Page 283: Christ Ascending the Cross. By Tʿoros Taronecʿi.

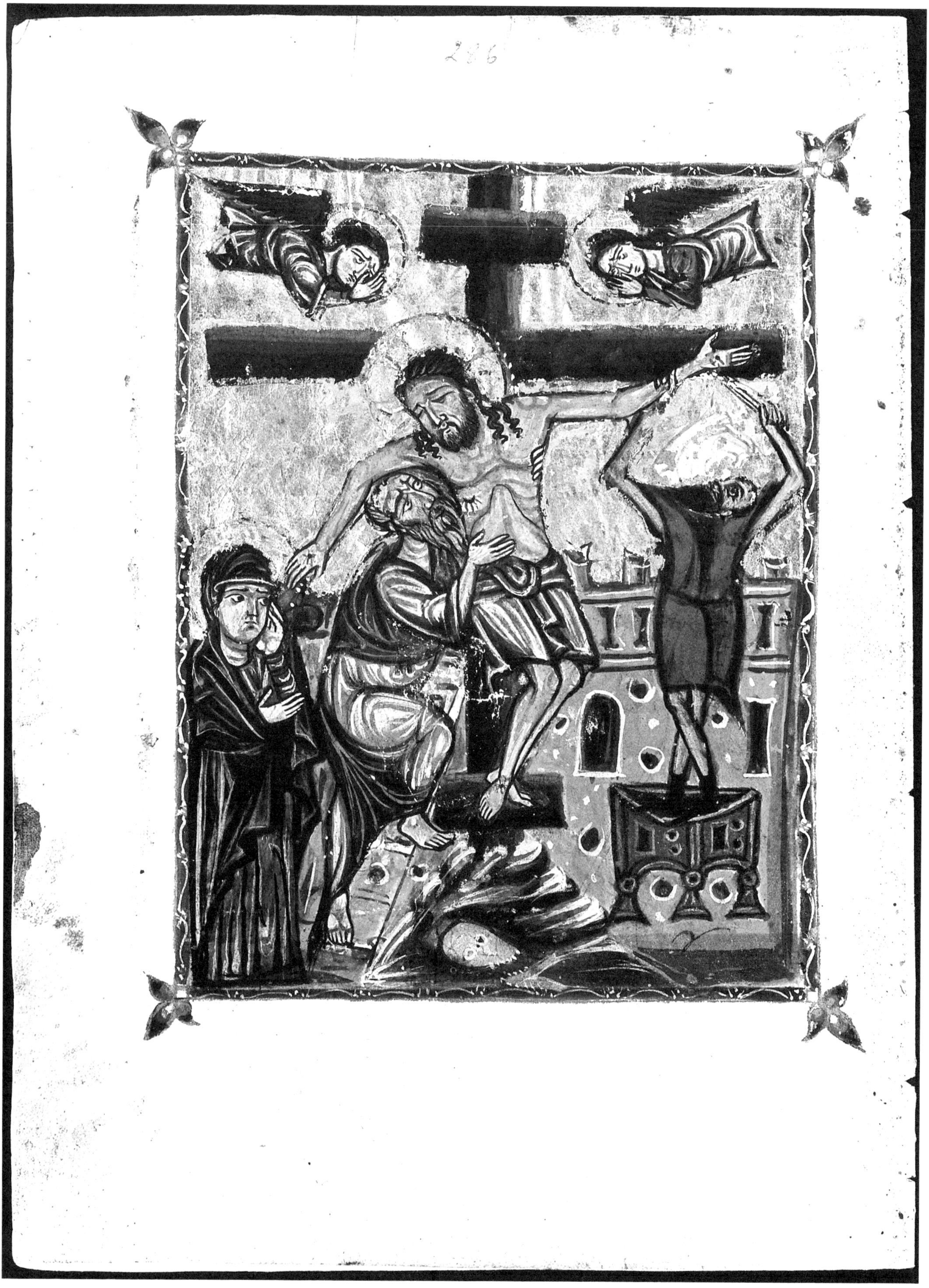

Page 286: Descent from the Cross. By Tʿoros Taronecʿi.

Page 298: Portrait of St. Luke. By the Second Painter.

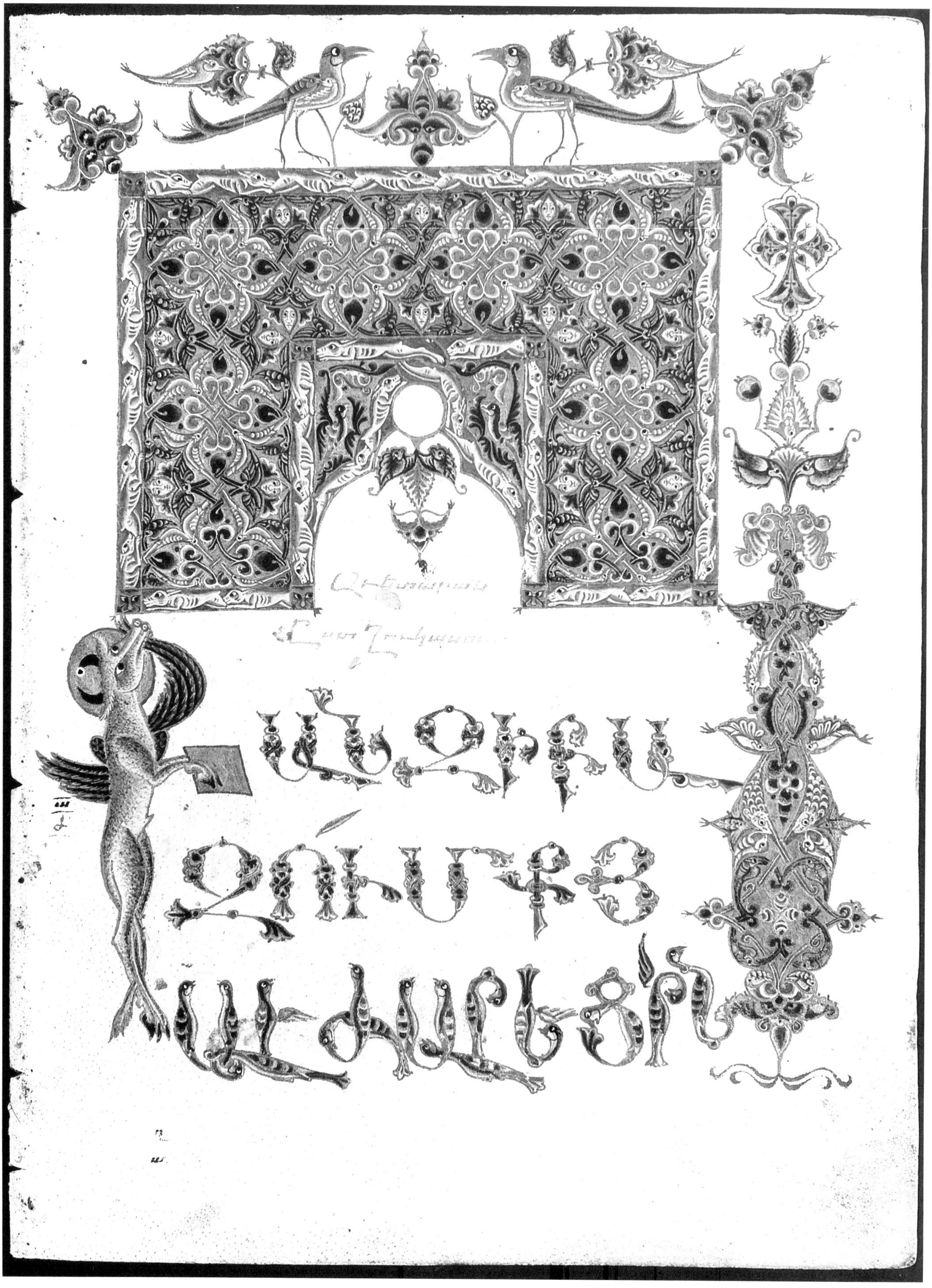

Page 299: Incipit to the Gospel of Luke. By the Second Painter.

Page 305: The Annunciation. By the Second Painter and T'oros Taronec'i.

Page 312: The Visitation. By T'oros Taronec'i.

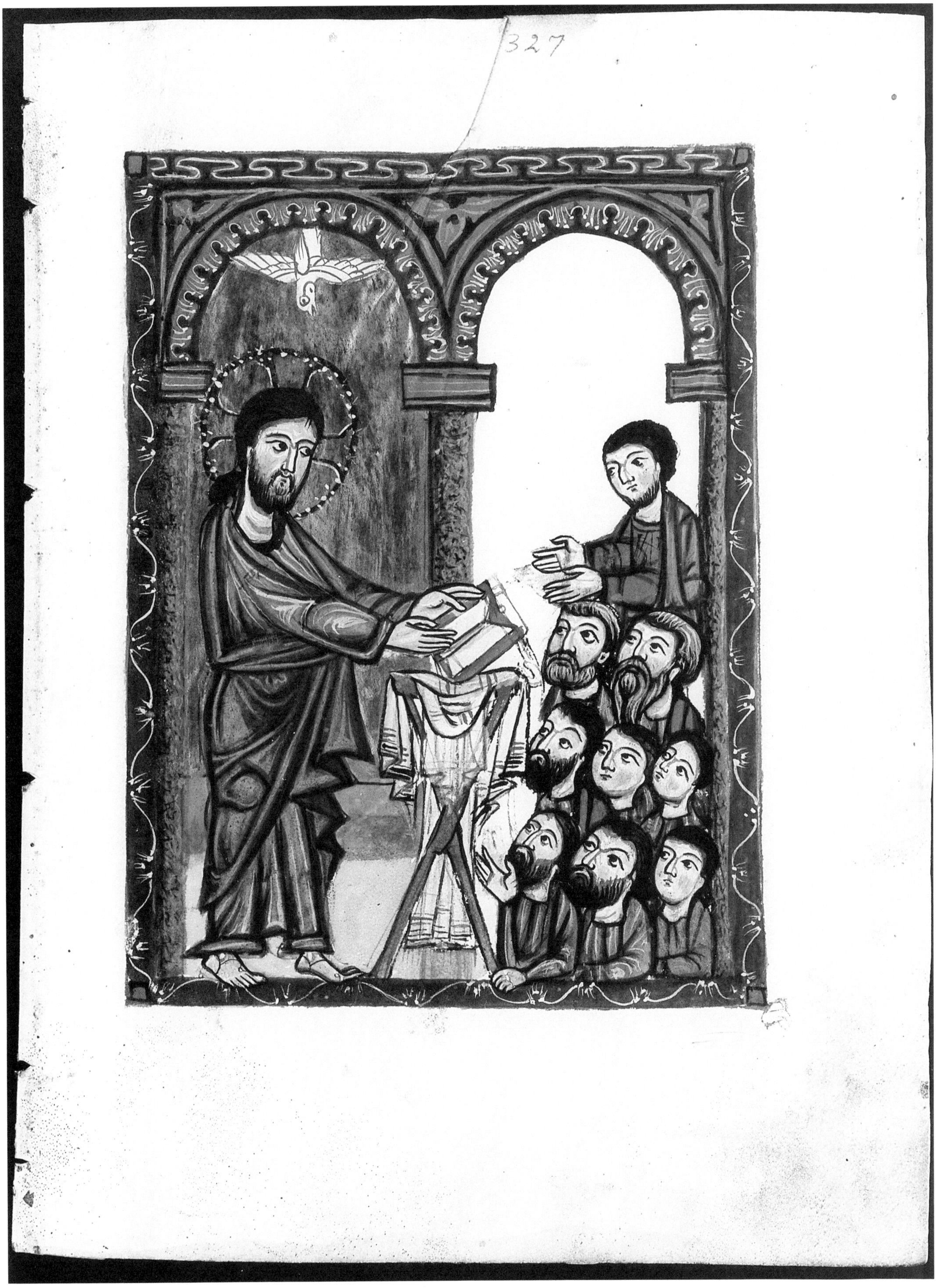

Page 327: Christ Reading in the Synagogue. By T'oros Taronec'i.

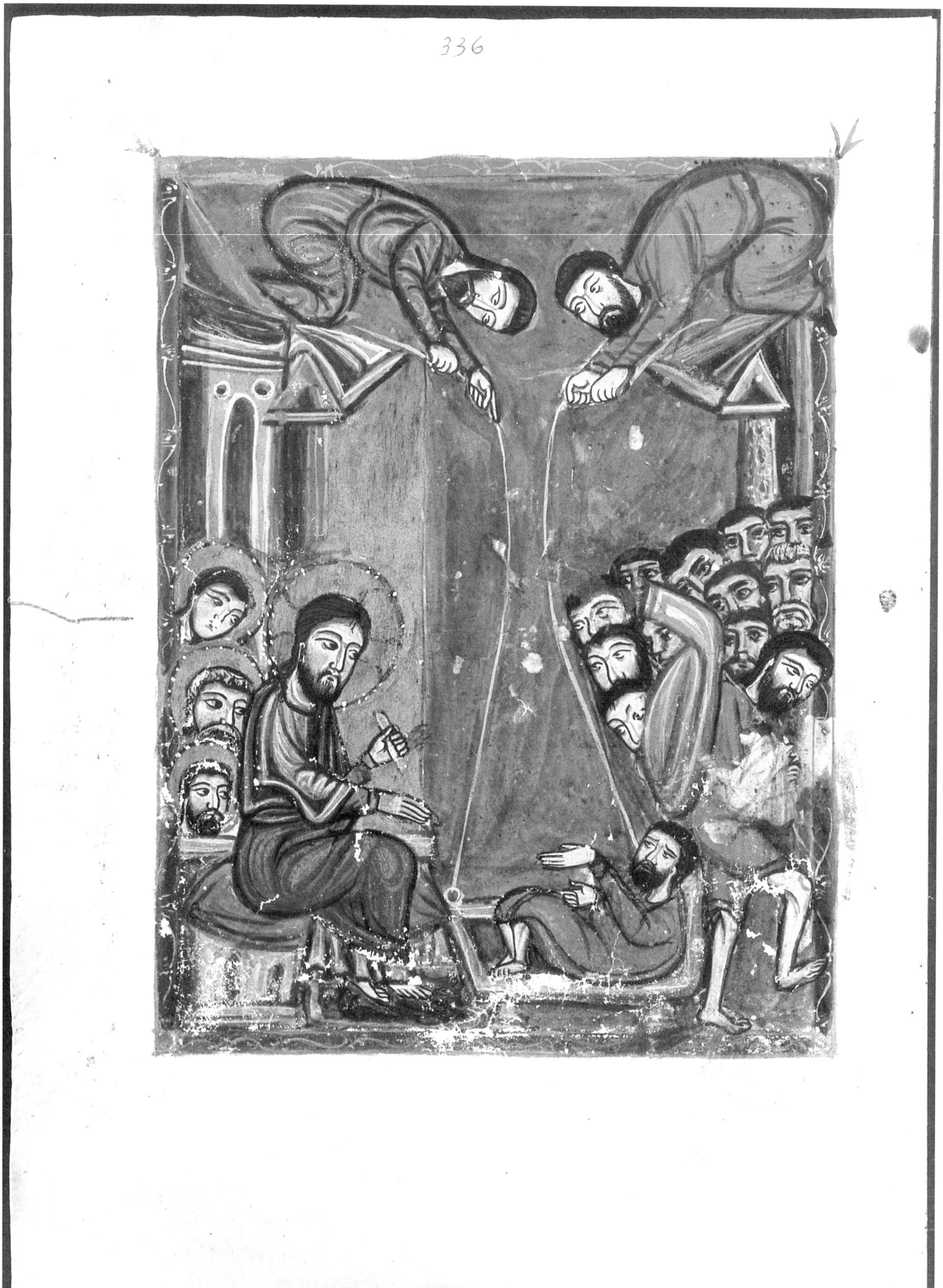

Page 336: The Cure of the Paralytic. By Tʻoros Taronecʻi.

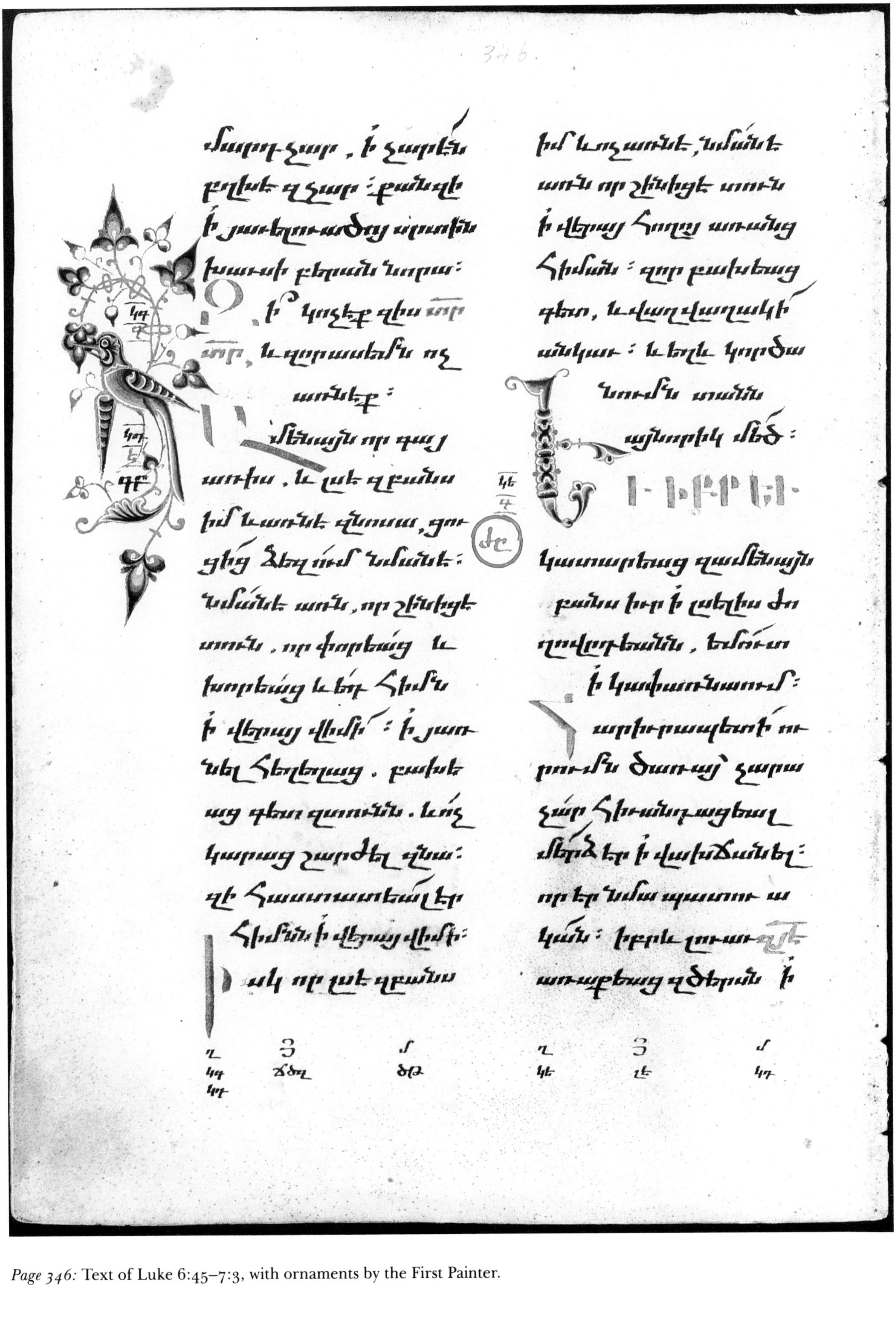

մարդ չար, ի չարէն
բղխէ զչար: Քանզի
ի յաւելորդաց սրտին
խօսի բերան նորա:
Զի՞ կոչէք զիս տէր
տէր, եւ զոր ասեմն ոչ
առնէք:
Ամենայն որ գայ
առ իս. եւ լսէ զբանս
իմ եւ առնէ զնոսա, ցու-
ցից ձեզ ում նման է:
Նման է առն, որ շինիցէ
տուն. որ փորեաց եւ
խորեաց եւ եդ հիմն
ի վերայ վիմի: Ի յառ-
նել հեղեղաց. բախե-
աց գետն զտունն. եւ ոչ
կարաց շարժել զնա:
զի հաստատեալ էր
հիմն ի վերայ վիմի:
Իսկ որ լսէ զբանս
իմ եւ ոչ առնէ, նման է
առն որ շինիցէ տուն
ի վերայ հողոյ առանց
հիման: զոր բախեաց
գետն, եւ վաղվաղակի
անկաւ: եւ եղեւ կործա-
նումն տանն
այնորիկ մեծ:
ԵՒ ԻԲՐԵՒ
կատարեաց զամենայն
բանս իւր ի լսելիս ժո-
ղովրդեանն, եմուտ
ի կափառնաում:
Հարիւրապետի ու-
րումն ծառայ չարա-
չար հիւանդացեալ
մերձ էր ի վախճանել:
որ էր նմա պատուա-
կան: Իբրեւ լուաւ զՅի-
սուսէ առաքեաց զծերս ի

Page 346: Text of Luke 6:45–7:3, with ornaments by the First Painter.

Page 351: The Anointing of Christ at Simon's House. By T'oros Taronec'i.

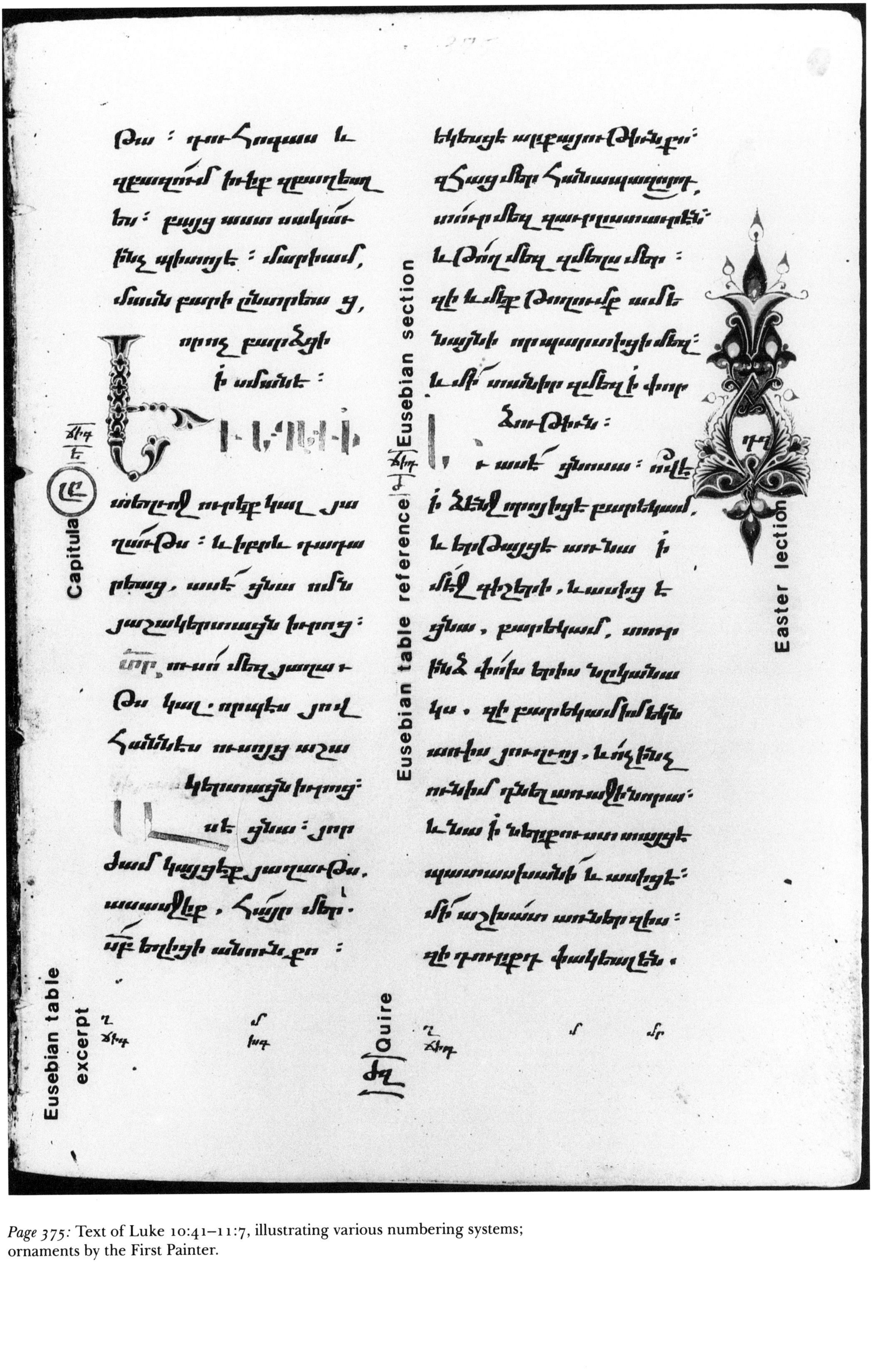

Page 375: Text of Luke 10:41–11:7, illustrating various numbering systems; ornaments by the First Painter.

Page 403: The Parable of the Cunning Steward. By Tʻoros Taronecʻi.

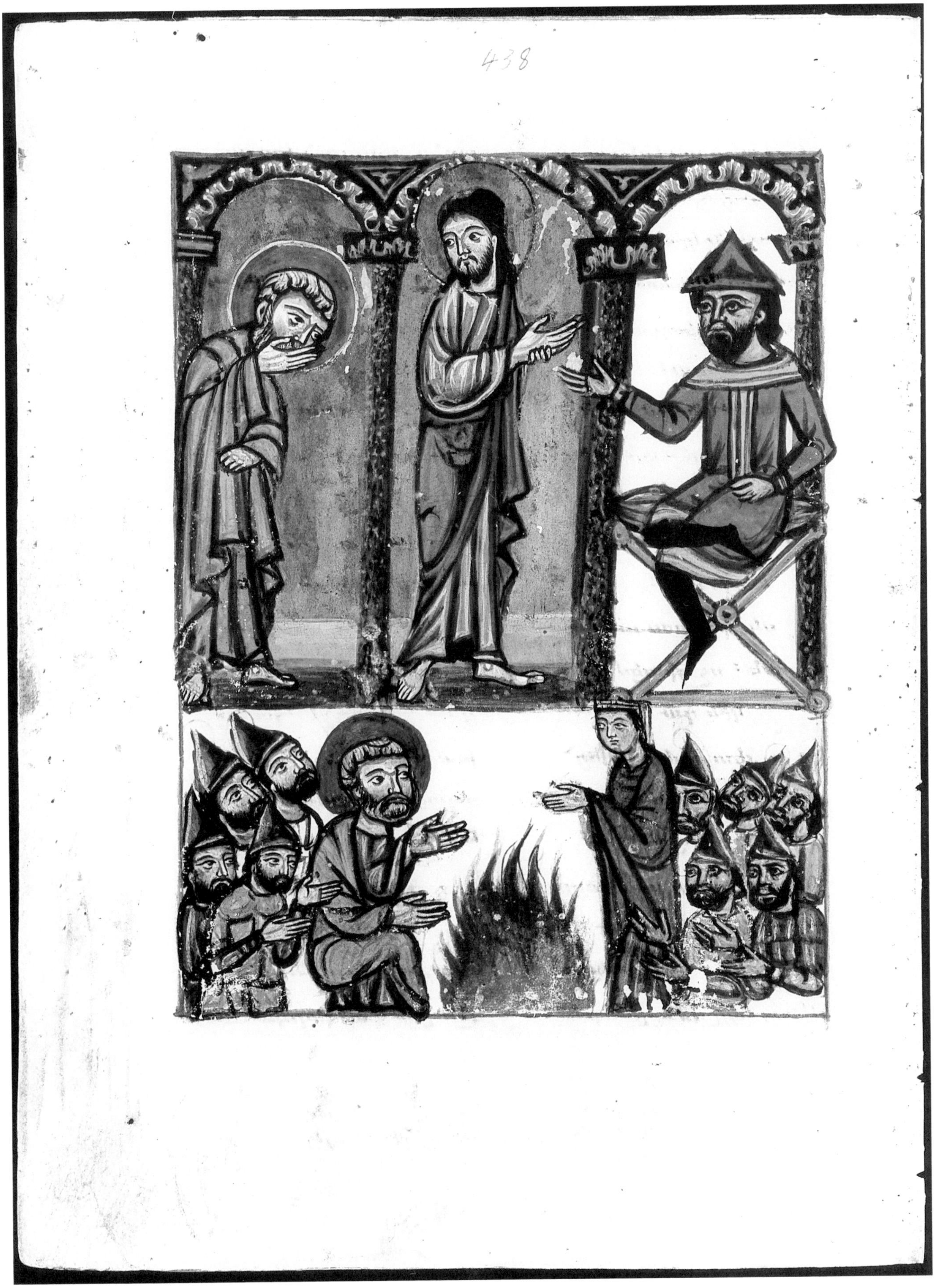

Page 438: Peter's Denial and Christ before Caiaphas. By T'oros Taronec'i.

Page 441: Christ before Herod. By T'oros Taronec'i.

Page 448: The Apparition on the Way to Emmaus. By T'oros Taronec'i.

Page 453: The Ascension. By T‘oros Taronec‘i.

Page 460: Portrait of St. John. By the Second Painter.

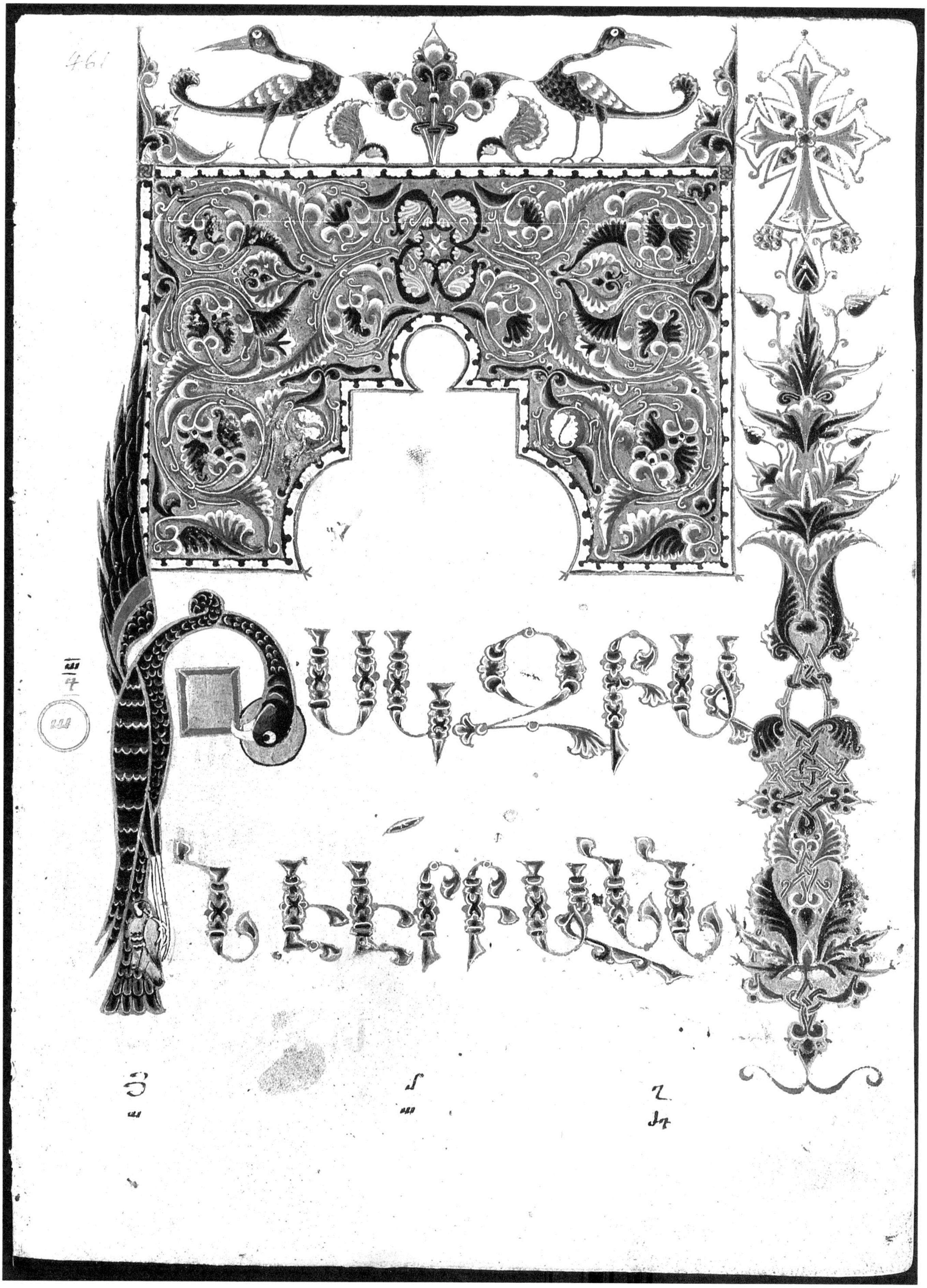

Page 461: Incipit to the Gospel of John. By the Second Painter.

Page 469: The Wedding Feast at Cana. By Tʿoros Taronecʿi.

Page 480: The Samaritan at the Well. By Tʿoros Taronecʿi.

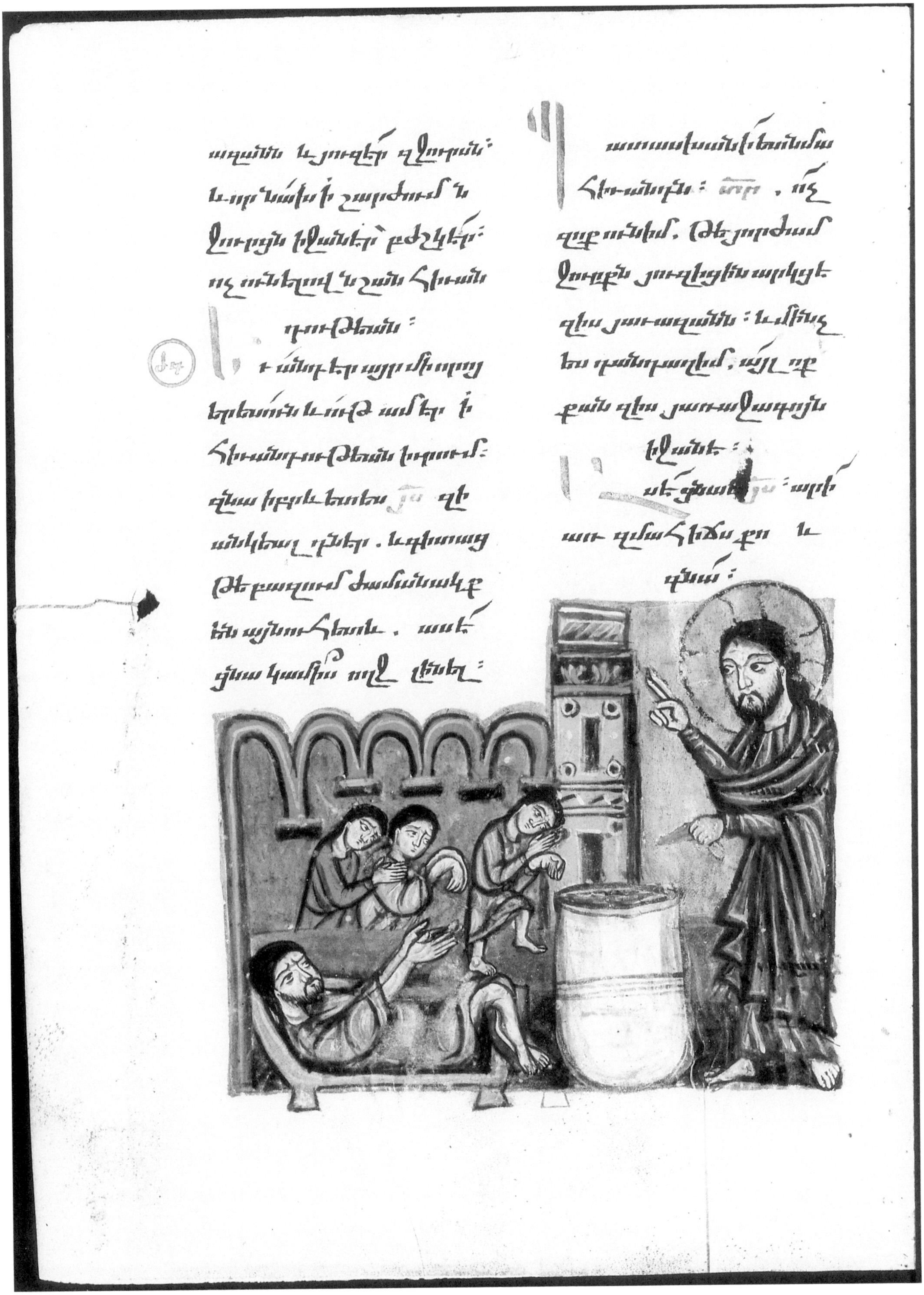

Page 484: The Cure of the Paralytic at the Pool. By Tʿoros Taronecʿi.

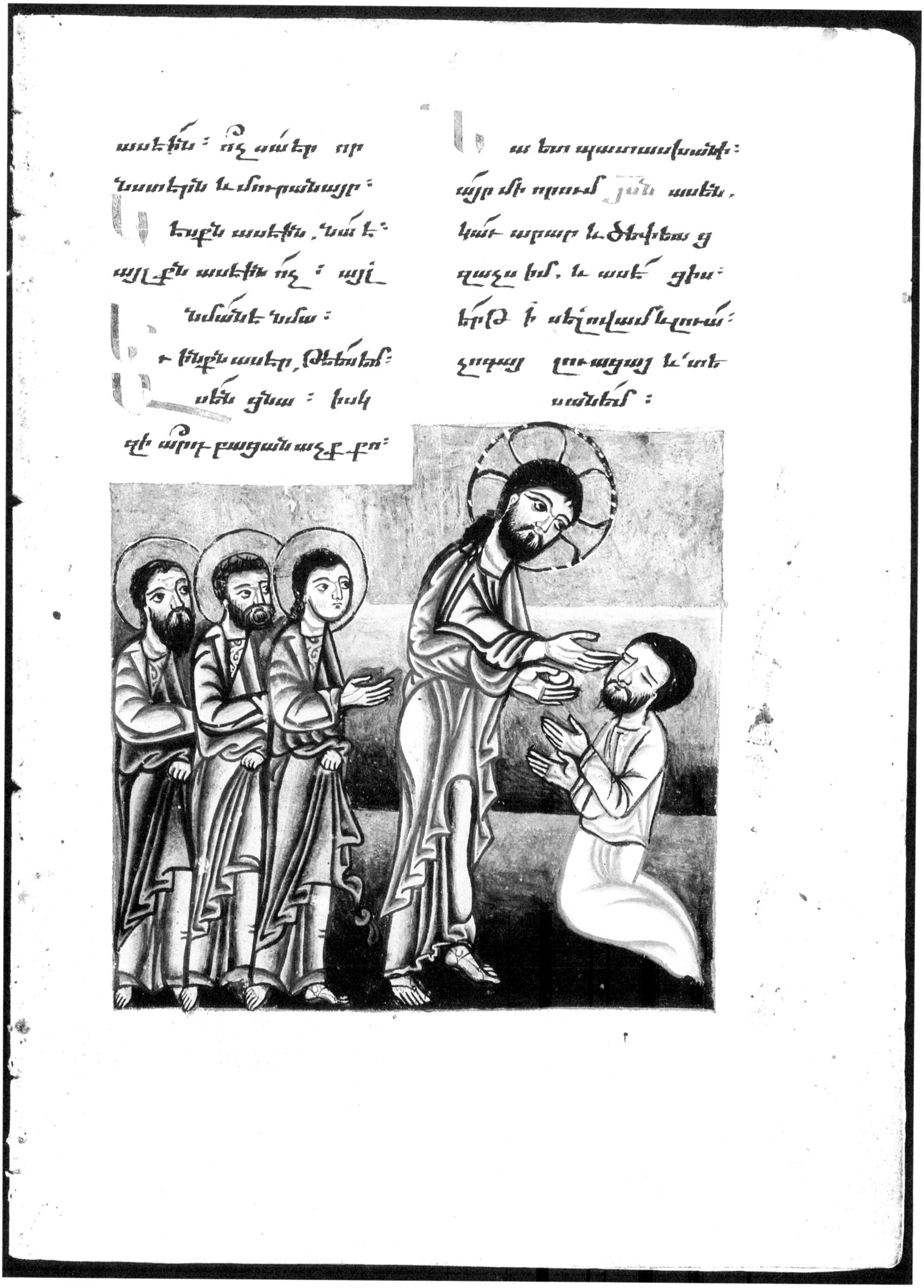

Page 509: The Cure of the Man Born Blind. By the Second Painter and T'oros Taronec'i.

Page 522: The Raising of Lazarus. By the Second Painter.

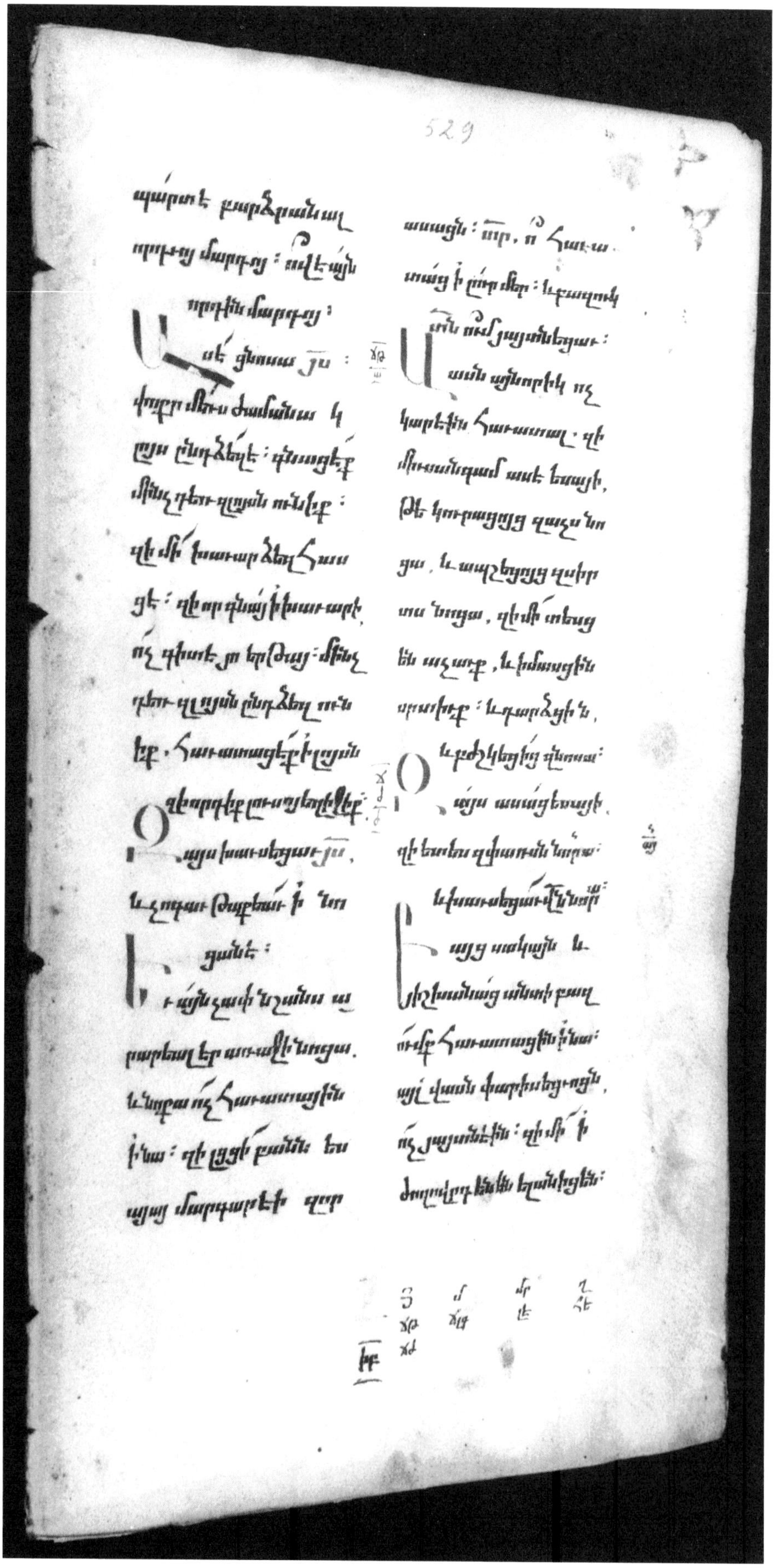

Page 529: The twenty-third quire, showing notches cut for stitching of binding.

Page 532: The Washing of the Feet. By the Second Painter and T'oros Taronec'i.

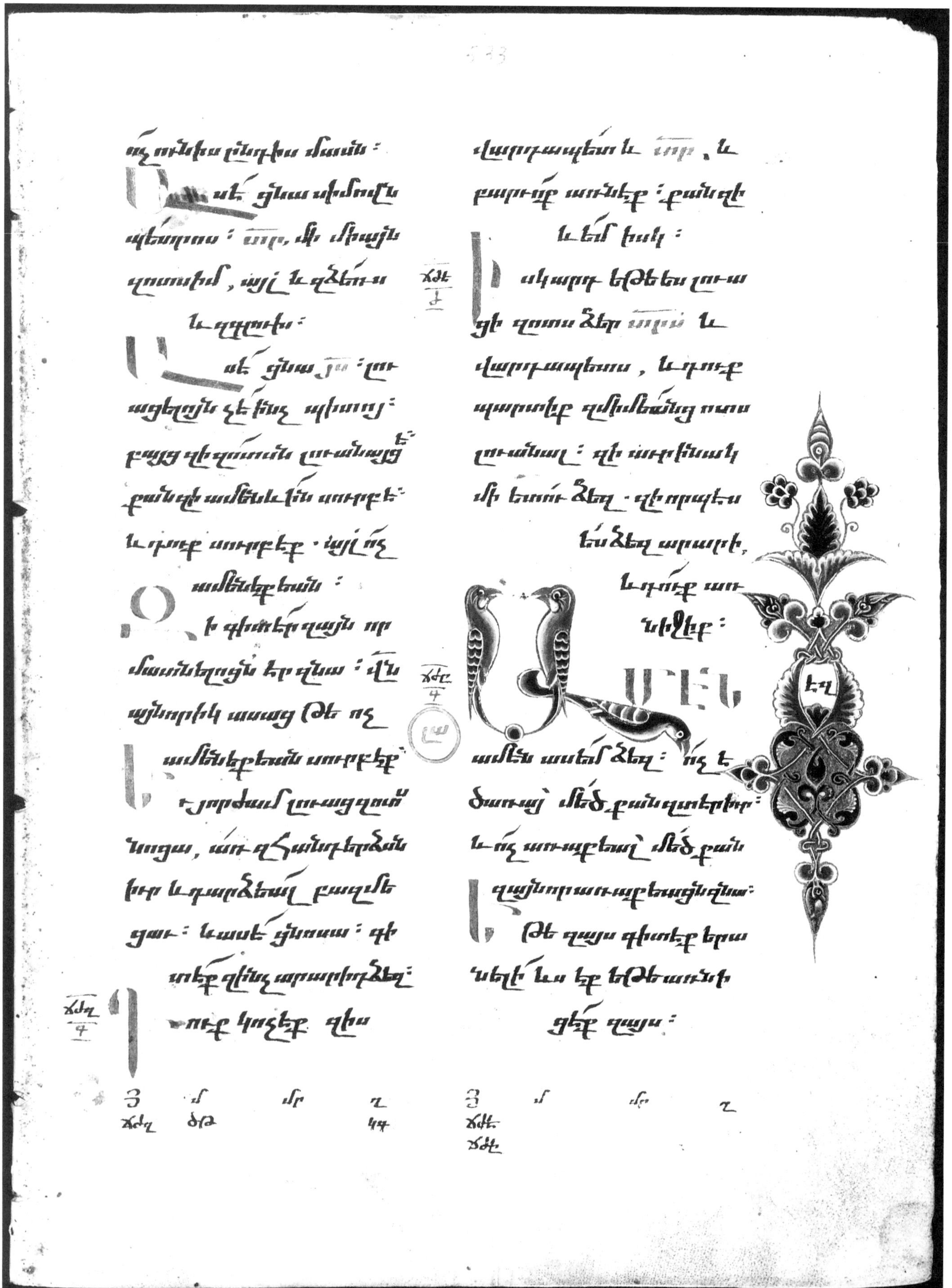

Page 533: Text of John 13:7–17, with ornaments by the Second Painter.

Page 538: The Promise of the Holy Spirit. By the Second Painter.

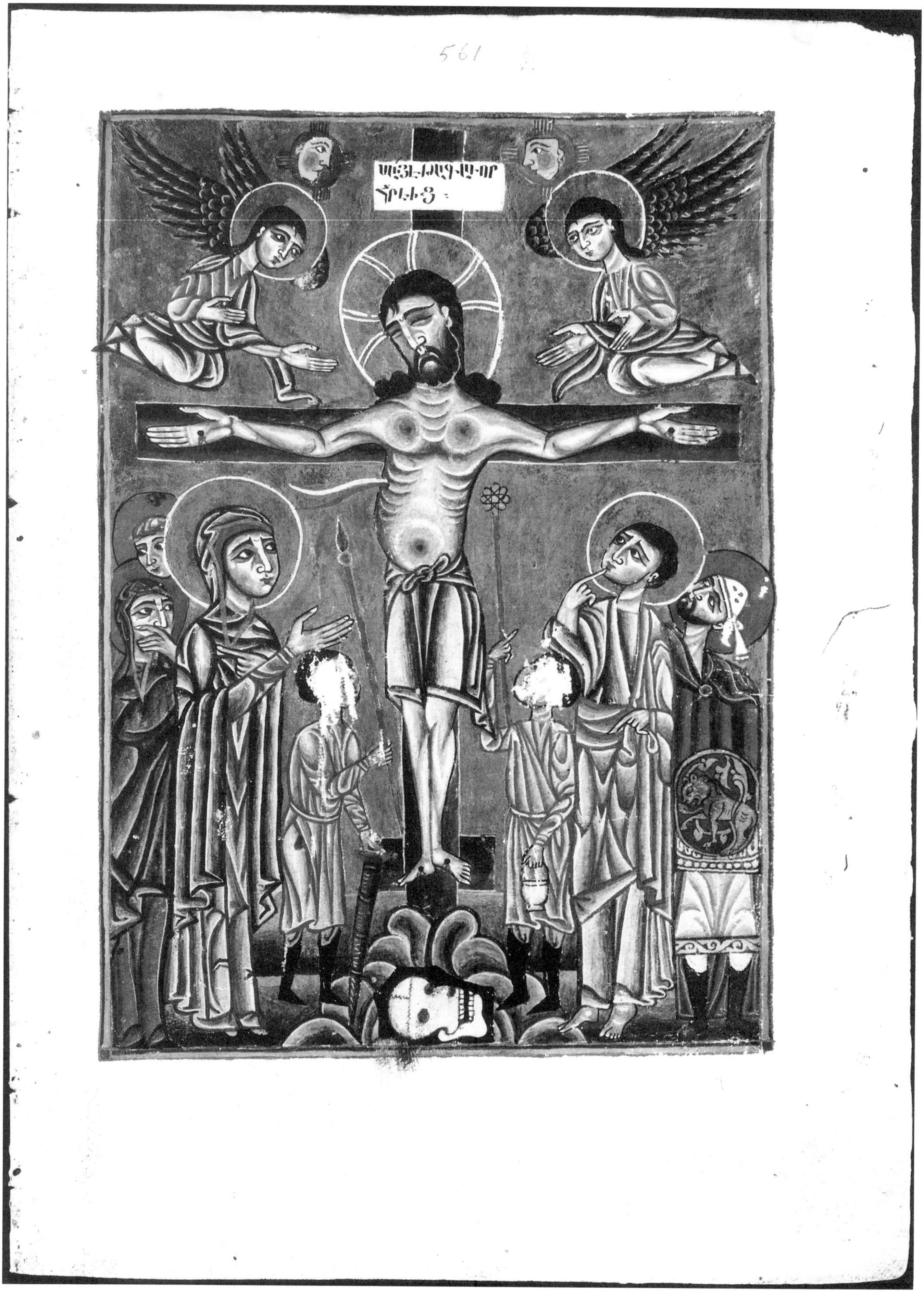

Page 561: The Crucifixion. By the Second Painter.

Page 570: Christ's Apparition at the Sea of Galilee. By Tʿoros Taronecʿi.

Back Doublure of the U.C.L.A. Gospel (1824–25).

Back Cover of the U.C.L.A. Gospel (1824–25).

Comparative Illustrations

Figure 21a: Canon Table Ten.
New Julfa, All-Savior 477, fol. 12 (1300).

Figure 21b: Canon Table Three.
Erevan, Matenadaran 10525, fol. 137v. By Sargis (1306).

Figure 21c: Canon Tables Six and Seven.
New Julfa, All-Savior 47, fol. 20 (1330).

Figure 27a. Incipit of Matthew.
New Julfa, All-Savior 477, fol. 16 (1300).

Figure 35a: The Genealogy of Christ (Abraham to Jechoniah). Baltimore, Walters 539, fol. 15. By T'oros Ṙoslin (1262).

Figure 35b: The Genealogy of Christ (Cainan to Adam, Luke 3:36–38). Erevan, Matenadaran 7651, fol. 142 (ca. 1270).

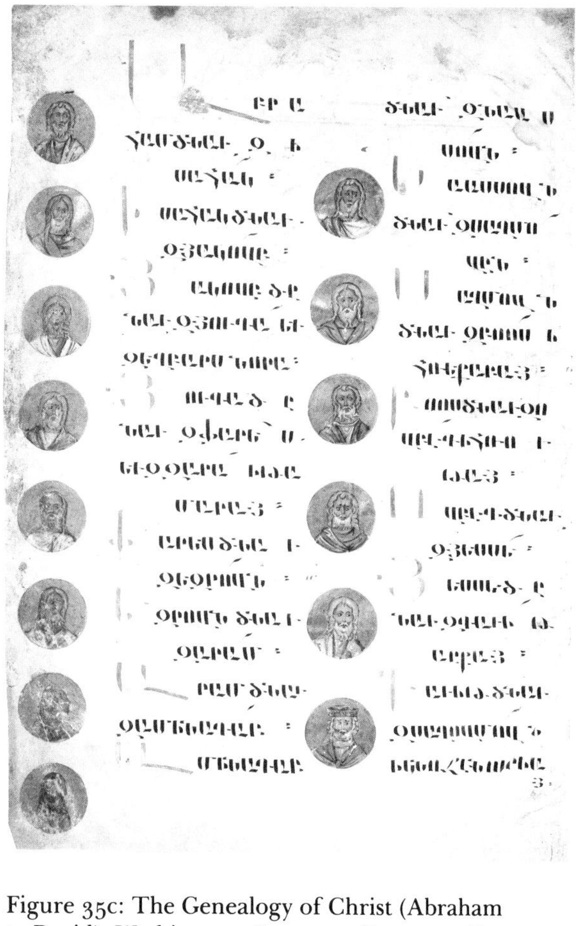

Figure 35c: The Genealogy of Christ (Abraham to David). Washington, Freer 32.18, page 2. By T'oros Ṙoslin (ca. 1270).

Figure 35d: Genealogy of Christ (Judah to Amminadab). Erevan, Matenadaran 212, fol. 17. By Awag (1340).

Figure 92a: The Beheading of John the Baptist. Erevan, Matenadaran 10780, fol. 37v (early eleventh century).

Figure 92b: The Beheading of John the Baptist. Baltimore, Walters 539, fol. 66. By Tʿoros Ṙoslin (1262).

Figure 92c: The Beheading of John the Baptist. Erevan, Matenadaran 7651, fol. 43. By Sargis Picak (1320).

Figure 99a: The Petition of the Canaanite. Erevan, Matenadaran 10780, fol. 40v (early eleventh century).

Figure 99b: The Petition of the Canaanite. Erevan, Matenadaran 7651, fol. 46v (ca. 1270).

Figure 99c: The Petition of the Canaanite. Erevan, Matenadaran 212, fol. 55. By Awag (1340).

Figure 103a: Peter Receives the Keys. Erevan, Matenadaran 10780, fol. 43 (early eleventh century).

Figure 103b: Peter Receives the Keys. Istanbul, Armenian Patriarchate, Zeytun Gospel, fol. 66v. By T'oros Ṙoslin (1256).

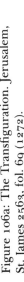

Figure 106a: The Transfiguration. Jerusalem,
St. James 2563, fol. 69 (1272).

Figure 106b: The Transfiguration.
Erevan, Matenadaran 4814, fol. 2v (1294).

Figure 106c: The Transfiguration.
Erevan, Matenadaran 6792, fol. 5v.
By Momik (1302).

Figure 106d: The Transfiguration.
Erevan, Matenadaran 7651, fol. 49. By Sargis Picak (1320).

Figure 106e: The Transfiguration. New Julfa, All-Savior 47, fol. 5v. By Kirakos (1330).

Figure 108a: The Cure of the Epileptic.
Erevan, Matenadaran 10780, fol. 45
(early eleventh century).

Figure 108b: The Cure of the Epileptic.
Erevan, Matenadaran 7651, fol. 50. By Sargis Picak (1320).

Figure 117a: The Blessing of the Children.
Erevan, Matenadaran 10780, fol. 49v (early eleventh century).

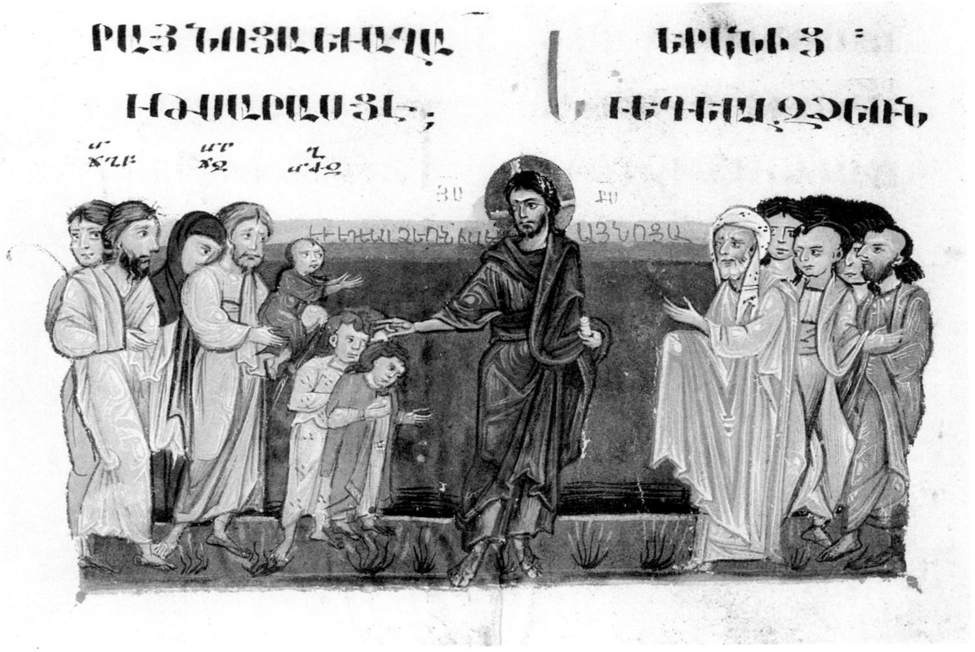

Figure 117b: The Blessing of the Children.
Baltimore, Walters 539, fol. 83v. By T'oros Roslin (1262).

Figure 117c: The Blessing of the Children.
Erevan, Matenadaran 7651, fol. 54. By Sargis Picak (1320).

Figure 122a: The Petition of the Mother of James and John. Erevan, Matenadaran 10780, fol. 52 (early eleventh century).

Figure 122b: The Petition of the Mother of James and John. Washington, Freer 32.18, page 124 (ca. 1270).

Figure 122c: The Petition of the Mother of James and John. Erevan, Matenadaran 7651, fol. 56v. By Sargis Picak (1320).

Figure 122d: The Petition of the Mother of James and John. Erevan, Matenadaran 212, fol. 67. By Awag (1340).

Figure 124a: The Cure of the Blind in Jericho. Erevan, Matenadaran 10780, fol. 53 (early eleventh century).

Figure 124b: The Cure of the Blind in Jericho. Washington, Freer 32.18, page 51. By T'oros Roslin (ca. 1270).

Figure 126a: The Entry into Jerusalem.
Ałtʿamar, wall painting (915–921).

Figure 126b: The Entry into Jerusalem.
Erevan, Matenadaran 10780, fol. 53v
(early eleventh century).

Figure 126c: The Entry into Jerusalem.
Erevan, Matenadaran 7729, fol. 325 (1202).

Figure 126d: The Entry into Jerusalem.
Erevan, Matenadaran 7651, fol. 57v (ca. 1270).

Figure 126e: The Entry into Jerusalem.
Erevan, Matenadaran 206, fol. 489.
By T'oros Taronec'i (1318).

Figure 126f: The Entry into Jerusalem.
Erevan, Matenadaran 6289, fol. 121.
By T'oros Taronec'i (1323).

Figure 126g: The Entry into Jerusalem.
Erevan, Matenadaran 6230, fol. 415v.
By Awag (1314).

Figure 156a: The Last Supper.
Jerusalem, St. James 2556, fol. 206v (1045–54).

Figure 156b: The Last Supper.
Erevan, Matenadaran 7736, fol. 18v
(eleventh century).

Figure 156c: The Last Supper.
Jerusalem, St. James 2563, fol. 166 (1272).

Figure 160a: The Agony in the Garden.
Erevan, Matenadaran 10780, fol. 70
(early eleventh century).

Figure 160b: The Agony in the Garden.
Jerusalem, St. James 2556, fol. 118 (1045–54).

Figure 160c: The Agony in the Garden.
Erevan, Matenadaran 7651, fol. 74v (ca. 1270).

Figure 162a: The Betrayal.
Erevan, Matenadaran 10780, fol. 71 (early eleventh century).

Figure 162b: The Betrayal.
Baltimore, Walters 539, fol. 116v. By T'oros Ṙoslin (1262).

Figure 166a: Peter's Denial.
Erevan, Matenadaran 10780, fol. 73
(early eleventh century).

Figure 169a: The Message from Pilate's Wife.
Erevan, Matenadaran 10780, fol. 74
(early eleventh century).

Figure 169b: The Message from Pilate's Wife. Washington,
Freer 32.18, page 183.
By T῾oros Ṙoslin (ca. 1270).

Figure 169c: The Message from Pilate's Wife.
Erevan, Matenadaran 212, fol. 90.
By Awag (1340).

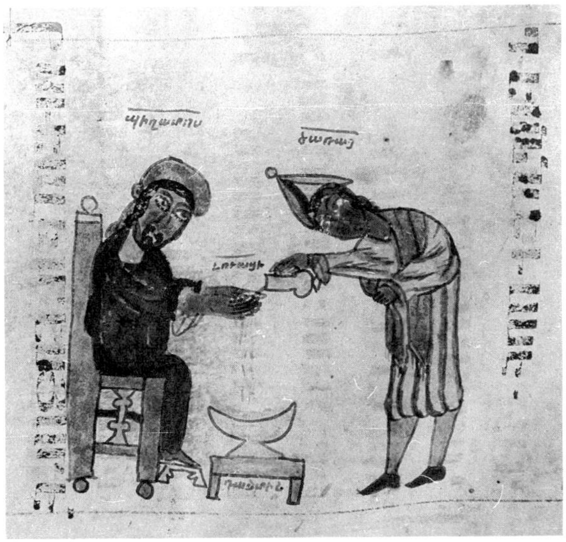

Figure 171a: Pilate Washes His Hands.
Erevan, Matenadaran 10780, fol. 74v
(early eleventh century).

Figure 171b: Pilate Washes His Hands.
Erevan, Matenadaran 7651, fol. 78v (ca. 1270).

Figure 171c: Pilate Washes His Hands.
London, British Library Or. 5304, fol. 23.
By Awag (ca. 1340).

Figure 171d: The Self-curse of the Jews.
London, British Library Or. 5304, fol. 23.
By Awag (ca. 1340).

Figure 171e: The Self-curse of the Jews.
Erevan, Matenadaran 212, fol. 91. By Awag (1340).

Figure 172a: The Mocking of Christ.
Erevan, Matenadaran 10780, fol. 75
(early eleventh century).

Figure 172b: The Mocking of Christ.
Baltimore, Walters 539, fol. 195.
By Tʿoros Ṙoslin (1262).

Figure 172c: The Mocking of Christ.
Erevan, Matenadaran 7651, fol. 79 (ca. 1270).

Figure 172d: The Mocking of Christ.
London, British Library Or. 5304, fol. 68.
By Awag (ca. 1340).

Figure 172e: The Mocking of Christ.
Erevan, Matenadaran 212, fol. 91. By Awag (1340).

Figure 173a: The Way of the Cross.
Erevan, Matenadaran 10780, fol. 75v
(early eleventh century).

Figure 173b: The Way of the Cross.
Erevan, Matenadaran 212, fol. 91v.
By Awag (1340).

Figure 179a: The Women at the Tomb.
Jerusalem, St. James 2556, fol. 132v (1045–54).

Figure 179b: The Women at the Tomb.
Erevan, Matenadaran 2743, fol. 114
(eleventh century).

Figure 179c: The Women at the Tomb.
Jerusalem, St. James 2563, fol. 176 (1272).

Figure 179d: The Women at the Tomb.
Erevan, Matenadaran 7651, fol. 81v (ca. 1270).

Figure 179e: The Women at the Tomb.
Erevan, Matenadaran 10525, fol. 351.
By Sargis (1306).

Figure 188a: Portrait of St. Mark. Vienna, Mekhitarist Library 460, fol. 99v (ca. 1313).

Figure 194a: The Call of James and John. Erevan, Matenadaran 10780, fol. 81 (early eleventh century).

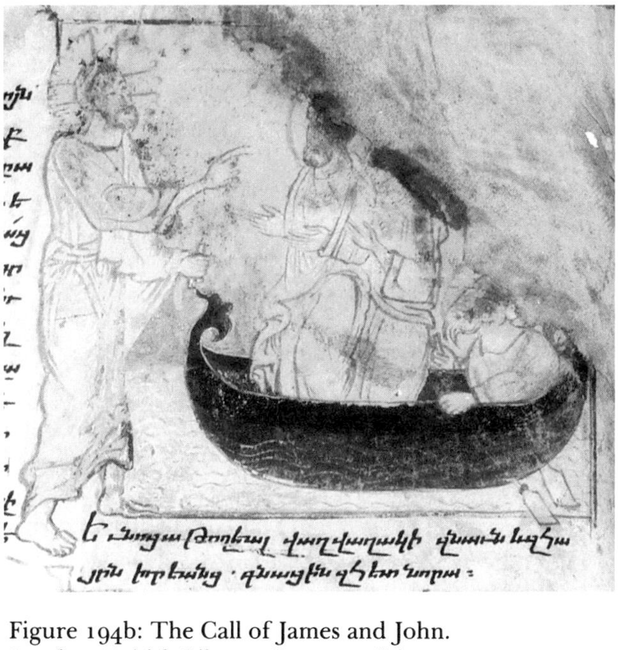

Figure 194b: The Call of James and John. London, British Library Or. 5304, fol. 10v. By Awag (1340).

Figure 197a: The Cure of the Leper.
Erevan, Matenadaran 10780, fol. 82v
(early eleventh century).

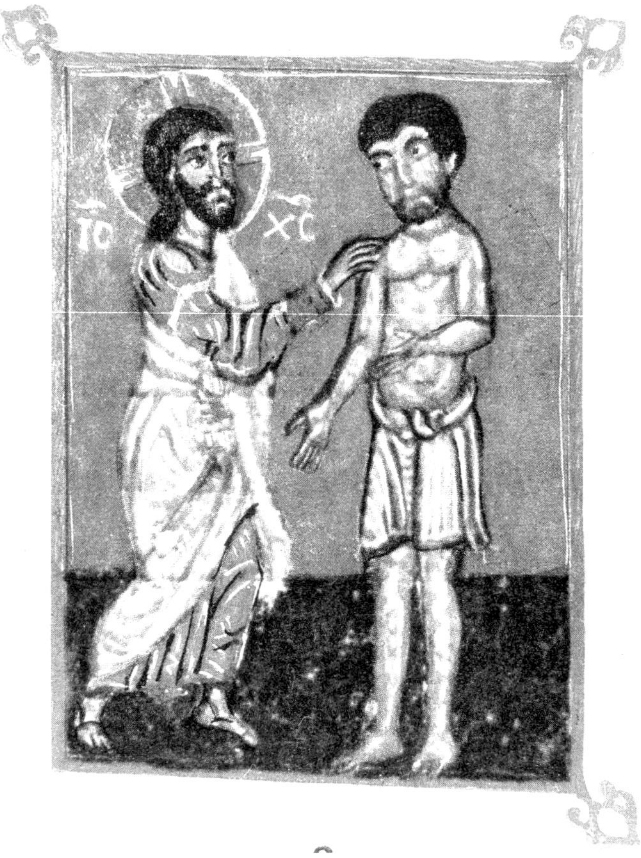

Figure 197b: The Cure of the Leper.
Venice, San Lazzaro 888/159, fol. 149
(twelfth century).

Figure 197c: The Cure of the Leper.
Erevan, Matenadaran 7651, fol. 87 (ca. 1270).

Figure 211a: First Storm at Sea.
Erevan, Matenadaran 10780, fol. 90
(early eleventh century).

Figure 211b: First Storm at Sea.
Washington, Freer 32.18, page 397.
By T'oros Ṙoslin (ca. 1270).

Figure 211c: First Storm at Sea.
Erevan, Matenadaran 7651, fol. 94 (ca. 1270).

Figure 216a: The Woman with Hemorrhage and the Petition of Jairus. Erevan, Matenadaran 10780, fol. 92 (early eleventh century).

Figure 216b: The Woman with Hemorrhage and the Petition of Jairus. Baltimore, Walters 539, fol. 148v. By Tʿoros Ṙoslin (1262).

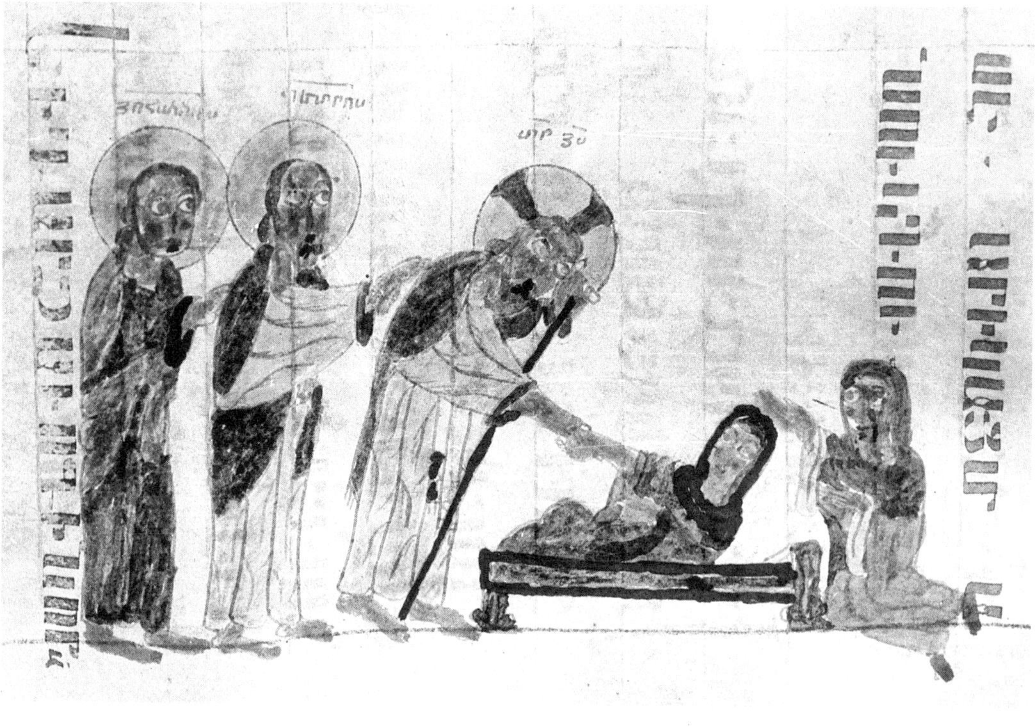

Figure 218a: The Raising of Jairus' Daughter. Erevan, Matenadaran 10780, fol. 158v (early eleventh century).

Figure 218b: The Raising of Jairus' Daughter.
Erevan, Matenadaran 7651, fol. 158 (ca. 1270).

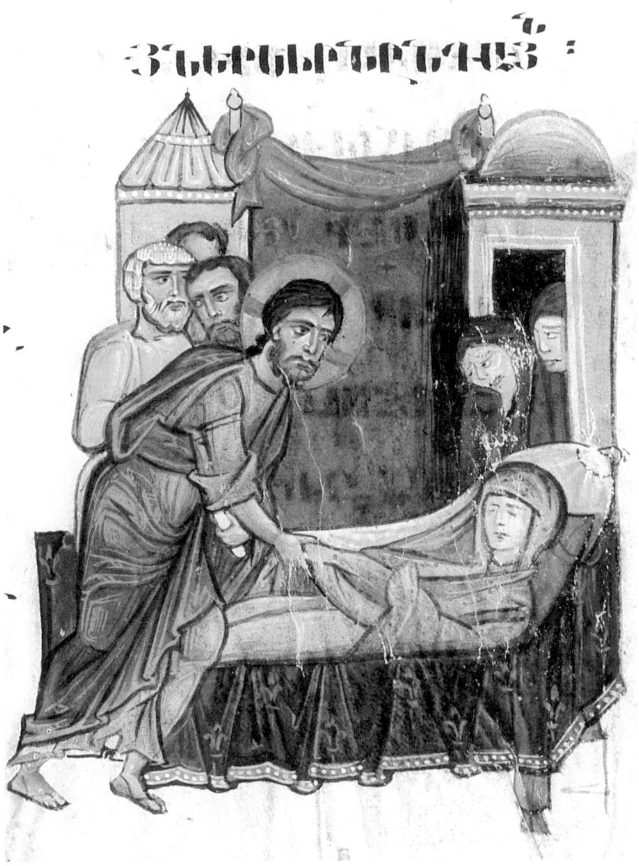

Figure 218c: The Raising of Jairus' Daughter.
Baltimore, Walters 539, fol. 44v.
By T'oros Roslin (1262).

Figure 227a: The Second Storm at Sea.
Erevan, Matenadaran 10780, fol. 96v (early eleventh century).

Figure 227b: The Second Storm at Sea.
Erevan, Matenadaran 7651, fol. 45. By Sargis Picak (1320).

Figure 227d: The Second Storm at Sea.
London, British Library Or. 5304, fol. 15v. By Awag (1340).

Figure 227c: The Second Storm at Sea.
Erevan, Matenadaran 7651, fol. 100v.
By Sargis Picak (1320).

Figure 235a: The Cure of the Blind Man at Bethsaida. Erevan, Matenadaran 7651, fol. 105 (ca. 1270).

Figure 235b: The Cure of the Blind Man at Bethsaida. Washington, Freer 32.18, page 255. By Tʿoros Ṙoslin (ca. 1270).

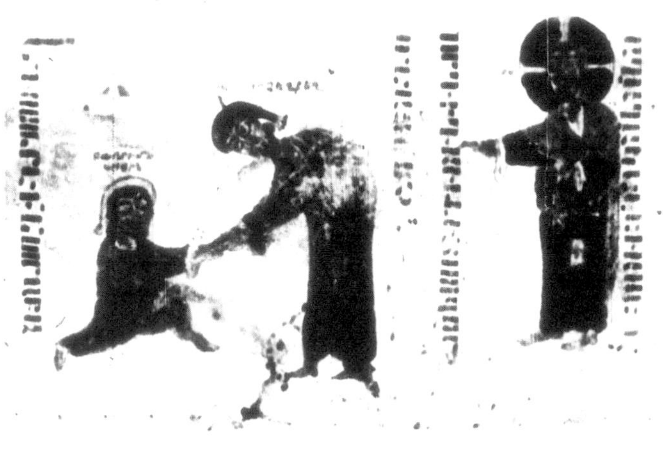

Figure 250a: The Cure of Blind Bartimaeus. Erevan, Matenadaran 10780, fol. 109v (early eleventh century).

Figure 250b: The Cure of Blind Bartimaeus. Erevan, Matenadaran 7651, fol. 113. By Sargis Picak (1320).

Figure 250c: The Cure of Blind Bartimaeus. Washington, Freer 32.18, page 278. By Tʿoros Ṙoslin (ca. 1270).

Figure 255a: The Lesson of the Withered Fig Tree. Erevan, Matenadaran 10780, fol. 111v (early eleventh century).

Figure 255b: The Lesson of the Withered Fig Tree. Erevan, Matenadaran 4806, fol. 8v. By Hovsian (1306).

Figure 255c: The Lesson of the Withered Fig Tree. Erevan, Matenadaran 7651, fol. 114v. By Sargis Picak (1320).

Figure 255d: The Fig Tree. Hartford, Case Memorial 3, fol. 69. By Tʿoros Taronecʿi (1331).

Figure 259a: The Question of Tribute to Caesar.
Erevan, Matenadaran 10780, fol. 113v (early eleventh century).

Figure 259b: The Question of Tribute to Caesar.
Erevan, Matenadaran 7651, fol. 117.
By Sargis Picak (ca. 1320).

Figure 259c: The Question of Tribute to Caesar.
Erevan, Matenadaran 212, fol. 133v.
By Awag (1340).

Figure 263a: The Widow's Mite.
Erevan, Matenadaran 7651, fol. 119. By Sargis Picak (1320).

Figure 263b: The Widow's Mite.
Washington, Freer 32.18, page 499.
By T'oros Roslin (ca. 1270).

Figure 269a: The Anointing of Christ at Bethany.
Erevan, Matenadaran 10780, fol. 119
(early eleventh century).

Figure 269b: The Anointing of Christ at Bethany.
Washington, Freer 32.18, page 167.
By T'oros Roslin (ca. 1270).

Figure 269c: The Anointing of Christ at Bethany.
Erevan, Matenadaran 7651, fol. 122.
By Sargis Picak (1320).

Figure 269d: The Anointing of Christ at Bethany.
London, British Library Or. 5304, fol. 33v.
By Awag (1340).

Figure 271a: The Preparation for Passover.
Erevan, Matenadaran 10780, fol. 119v
(early eleventh century).

Figure 271b: The Preparation for Passover.
Erevan, Matenadaran 7651, fol. 122v.
By Sargis Picak (1320).

Figure 271c: The Preparation for Passover.
Washington, Freer 32.18, page 303.
By T'oros Ṙoslin (ca. 1270).

Figure 271d: The Preparation for Passover.
Erevan, Matenadaran 212, fol. 140v.
By Awag (1340).

Figure 283a: Christ Ascending the Cross.
Erevan, Matenadaran 10780, fol. 125v
(early eleventh century).

Figure 283b: Christ Ascending the Cross.
Erevan, Matenadaran 212, fol. 146.
By Awag (1340).

Figure 286a: The Crucifixion and the Descent from the Cross. Jerusalem, St. James 3624, fol. 9v (1041).

Figure 286b: The Descent from the Cross.
Washington, Freer 32.18, page 323a.
By T'oros Ṙoslin (ca. 1270).

Figure 286c: The Descent from the Cross.
Baltimore, Walters 539, fol. 125.
By T'oros Roslin (1262).

Figure 286d: The Descent from the Cross.
Erevan, Matenadaran 979, fol. 193.

Figure 286e: The Descent from the Cross, with Fragments of the Portraits of St. John and Carpianos.
Erevan, Matenadaran 10525, fol. 352v. By Sargis (1306).

Figure 286f: The Descent from the Cross.
Erevan, Matenadaran 212, fol. 148. By Awag (1337–40).

Figure 298a: Portrait of St. Luke.
Erevan, Matenadaran 7737, fol. 334 (thirteenth century).

Figure 305a: The Annunciation.
Jerusalem, St. James 2563, fol. 184.
By Tʿoros Ṙoslin (1272).

Figure 305b: The Annunciation.
Venice, San Lazzaro 1917, fol. 153.
By Tʿoros Ṙoslin (1272).

Figure 305c: The Annunciation.
Erevan, Matenadaran 206, fol. 474v.
By Tʿoros Taronecʿi (1318).

Figure 305d: The Annunciation.
Jerusalem, St. James 2360, fol. 149.
By Tʿoros Taronecʿi (1321).

Figure 305e: The Annunciation.
Erevan, Matenadaran 6289, fol. 143.
By Tʿoros Taronecʿi (1323).

Figure 305f: The Annunciation.
New Julfa, All-Savior 47, fol. 1v. By Kirakos (1330).

Figure 312a: The Visitation and the Annunciation.
Jerusalem, St. James 3624, fol. 6 (1041).

Figure 312b: The Visitation and the Annunciation.
Erevan, Matenadaran 7736, fol. 11a (eleventh century).

Figure 327a: Christ Reading in the Synagogue. Erevan, Matenadaran 10780, fol. 141v (early eleventh century).

Figure 327b: Christ Reading in the Synagogue. Istanbul Patriarchate, Zeytun Gospel, fol. 211v. By T῾oros Ṙoslin (1256).

Figure 327c: Christ Reading in the Synagogue. Erevan, Matenadaran 7651, fol. 143 (ca. 1270).

Figure 327d: Christ Reading in the Synagogue. Erevan, Matenadaran 212, fol. 167. By Awag (1340).

Figure 336a: The Cure of the Paralytic.
Erevan, Matenadaran 10780, fol. 145 (early eleventh century).

Figure 336b: The Cure of the Paralytic.
Jerusalem, St. James 2556, fol. 143v (1045–54).

Figure 336c: The Cure of the Paralytic.
Erevan, Matenadaran 7651, fol. 146v (ca. 1270).

Figure 336d: The Cure of the Paralytic.
London, British Library Or. 5304, fol. 27. By Awag (1340).

Figure 351a: The Anointing of Christ at Simon's House. Erevan, Matenadaran 10780, fol. 153 (early eleventh century).

Figure 351b: The Anointing of Christ at Simon's House. Venice, San Lazzaro 888/159, fol. 158 (twelfth century).

Figure 351c: The Anointing of Christ at Simon's House. Baltimore, Walters 539, fol. 369. By T'oros Roslin (1262).

Figure 351d: The Anointing of Christ at Simon's House. Erevan, Matenadaran 7651, fol. 153v (ca. 1270).

Figure 403a: The Parable of the Cunning Steward, First Part. Erevan, Matenadaran 10780, fol. 183 (early eleventh century).

Figure 403b: The Parable of the Cunning Steward, Second Part. Erevan, Matenadaran 10780, fol. 183 (early eleventh century).

Figure 403c: The Parable of the Cunning Steward. Erevan, Matenadaran 7651, fol. 181. By Sargis Picak (1320).

Figure 438a: Peter's Denial and Christ before Caiaphas. Erevan, Matenadaran 10780, fol. 202v (early eleventh century).

Figure 438b: Peter's Denial and Christ before Caiaphas. Baltimore, Walters 539, fol. 305. By T'oros Ṙoslin (1262).

Figure 438c: Peter's Denial and Christ before Caiaphas. London, British Library Or. 5304, fol. 53. By Awag (1340).

Figure 441a: Christ before Herod.
Erevan, Matenadaran 10780, fol. 204
(early eleventh century).

Figure 441b: Christ before Herod.
Washington, Freer 32.18, page 520.
By T'oros Ṙoslin (ca. 1270).

Figure 441c: Christ before Herod.
Erevan, Matenadaran 212, fol. 230 (drawing).
By Awag (1337–40).

Figure 448a: The Apparition on the Way to Emmaus. Erevan, Matenadaran 10780, fol. 207v (early eleventh century).

Figure 448b: The Apparition on the Way to Emmaus. Jerusalem, St. James 2568, fol. 244 (1268–84).

Figure 448c: The Apparition on the Way to Emmaus. London, British Library Or. 5304, fol. 54v. By Awag (1340).

Figure 453a: The Ascension.
Baltimore, Walters 539, fol. 316v. By T'oros Ṙoslin (1262).

Figure 453b: The Ascension.
Erevan, Matenadaran 7651, fol. 207v (ca. 1270).

Figure 453c: The Ascension.
Venice, San Lazzaro 1917, fol. 230.
By T'oros Taronec'i (1307).

Figure 453d: The Ascension.
Erevan, Matenadaran 206, fol. 494v.
By T'oros Taronec'i (1318).

Figure 453e: The Ascension.
Jerusalem, St. James 1941, fol. 7v. By Awag (1334–36).

Figure 460a: Portrait of St. John.
Venice, San Lazzaro 1917, fol. 234v.
By T'oros Taronec'i (1307).

Figure 460b: Portrait of St. John.
Erevan, Matenadaran 353, fol. 548v.
By T'oros Taronec'i (1317).

Figure 460c: Portrait of St. John.
Erevan, Matenadaran 8936, fol. 12.
By T'oros Taronec'i (1317).

Figure 460d: Portrait of St. John.
London, British Library add. 15411, fol. 241v.
By T'oros Taronec'i (1321).

Figure 460e: Portrait of St. John.
Jerusalem, St. James 2360, fol. 222v.
By T'oros Taronec'i (1321).

Figure 460f: Portrait of St. John.
Erevan, Matenadaran 6289, fol. 225v.
By T'oros Taronec'i (1323).

Figure 460g: Portrait of St. John.
Hartford, Case Memorial 3, fol. 236v.
By T'oros Taronec'i (1331).

Figure 460h: Portrait of St. John.
Erevan, Matenadaran 3393, fol. 198v (1309).

Figure 460i: Portrait of St. John.
Formerly New York, Harutiun Hazarian Collection, fol. 170v (1628).

Figure 461a: Incipit of John (detail).
New York, Metropolitan Museum of Art 38.171.2 (ca. 1300).

Figure 461b: Incipit of John (detail).
New York, Pierpont Morgan Library M620, fol. 297
(seventeenth century).

Figure 469a: The Wedding Feast at Cana.
Erevan, Matenadaran 10780, fol. 214 (early eleventh century).

Figure 469b: The Wedding Feast at Cana. Washington, Freer 32.18, page 548.
By T'oros Roslin (ca. 1270).

Figure 469c: The Wedding Feast at Cana.
Erevan, Matenadaran 7651, fol. 212v (ca. 1270).

Figure 469d: The Wedding Feast at Cana.
Hartford, Case Memorial 3, fol. 240v.
By T'oros Taronec'i (1331).

Figure 480a: The Samaritan at the Well.
Erevan, Matenadaran 10780, fol. 220 (early eleventh century).

Figure 480b: The Samaritan at the Well.
Baltimore, Walters 539, fol. 331v. By Tʿoros Ṙoslin (1262).

Figure 480c: The Samaritan at the Well.
Erevan, Matenadaran 7651, fol. 216v (ca. 1270).

Figure 484a: The Cure of the Paralytic at the Pool. Erevan, Matenadaran 10780, fol. 222v.

Figure 484b: The Cure of the Paralytic at the Pool. Erevan, Matenadaran 7651, fol. 220 (ca. 1270).

Figure 509a: The Cure of the Man Born Blind. Erevan, Matenadaran 10780, fol. 236 (early eleventh century).

Figure 509b: The Cure of the Man Born Blind. Venice, San Lazzaro 16, fol. 341v. By Sargis (1331).

Figure 522a: The Raising of Lazarus.
Venice, San Lazzaro 141, fol. 232 (eleventh century).

Figure 522b: The Raising of Lazarus.
Erevan, Matenadaran 7644, fol. 345.
By Avedik (1260– 70).

Figure 522c: The Raising of Lazarus.
Jerusalem, St. James 2563, fol. 333. By T'oros Ṙoslin (1272).

Figure 522d: The Raising of Lazarus.
Erevan, Matenadaran 10525, fol. 138. By Sargis (1306).

Figure 532a: The Washing of the Feet.
Erevan, Matenadaran 10780, fol. 248 (early eleventh century).

Figure 532b: The Washing of the Feet.
New Julfa, All-Savior 36, fol. 7. By Ignatios of Ani (1236).

Figure 532c: The Washing of the Feet.
Jerusalem, St. James 2563, fol. 340v. By Tʿoros Ṙoslin (1272).

Figure 532d: The Washing of the Feet.
New Julfa, All-Savior 47, fol. 7v (1330).

Figure 538a: The Promise of the Holy Spirit.
Baltimore, Walters 539, fol. 379. By T'oros Ṙoslin (1262).

Figure 538b: The Promise of the Holy Spirit.
Venice, San Lazzaro 1917, fol. 274v. By T'oros Taronec'i (1307).

Figure 561a: The Crucifixion.
Erevan, Matenadaran 7736, fol. 19 (eleventh century).

Figure 561b: The Crucifixion.
New Julfa, All-Savior 36, fol. 8v. By Ignatios of Ani (1236).

Figure 561c: The Crucifixion.
Venice, San Lazzaro 1917, fol. 143v. By T῾oros Taronec῾i (1307).

Figure 561d: The Crucifixion.
Erevan, Matenadaran 206, fol. 509. By T῾oros Taronec῾i (1318).

Figure 561e: The Crucifixion.
Erevan, Matenadaran 7651, fol. 261v. By Sargis Picak (1320).

Figure 561f: The Crucifixion.
New Julfa, All-Savior 47, fol. 8. By Kirakos of Tabriz (1330).

Figure 570a: Christ's Apparition at the Sea of Galilee.
Erevan, Matenadaran 212, fol. 306v.
By Awag (1340).

Figure R1: Esayi Nčʿecʿi Teaching.
Jerusalem, St. James 365, page 2 (1301).

Figure R2: Headpiece of the Encyclical of Nersēs Šnorhali. Venice, San Lazzaro 1108/265, fol. 187 (1318).

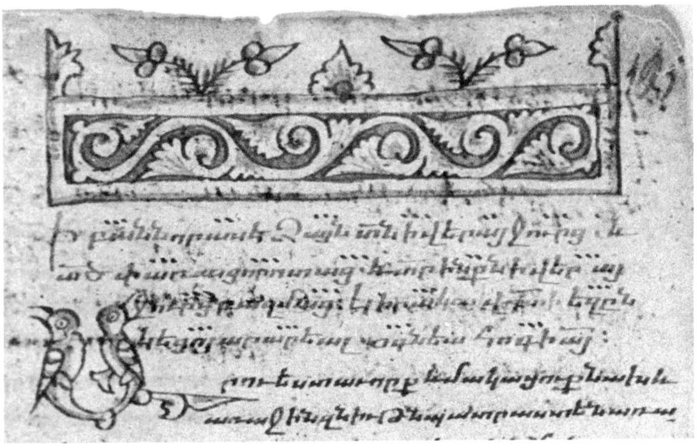

Figure R5: Chapter Heading. Erevan, Matenadaran 2187, fol. 105. By Tʿoros Taronecʿi (1346).

Figure R3: The Mother of God. Venice, San Lazzaro 1108/265, fol. 181v. By Yohanēs (1317–18).

Figure R4: Portrait of Grigoris and Mamaxatʿun. Venice, San Lazzaro 1108/265, fol. 182. By Yohanēs (1317–18).

Figure R6: Author Portrait of Dionysius Thrax.
Erevan, Matenadaran 6897, fol. 2.
By T'oros Taronec'i (1317).

Figure R7: Mother of God Eleousa, Chapter Head.
Erevan, Matenadaran 6897, fol. 86.
By T'oros Taronec'i (1317).

Figure R8: Mother of God Eleousa, Heading of Luke (detail). Hartford, Case Memorial 3, fol. 153. By T'oros Taronec'i (1331).

Figure R9: Carpianos, Heading of Eusebian Prologue (detail). Hartford, Case Memorial 3, fol. 3. By T'oros Taronec'i (1331).

Figure R10: Virgo Lactans, Heading of the Gospel of Mark. London, British Library add. 15411, fol. 92. By T'oros Taronec'i (1321).

Figure R11: Mother of God Hodegetria, Chapter Heading. Jerusalem, St. James 95, fol. 4. By T'oros of T'onrak (1331).

Figure R12: Presentation in the Temple.
Jerusalem, St. James 95, fol. 38v. By Tʿoros of Tʿonrak (1331).

Figure R13: The Heading of the Works of Chrysostom. Erevan, Matenadaran 1379, fol. 2.
By Tʿoros the Deacon (1334).

Figure R14: Portrait of Vardapet Kirakos.
Erevan, Matenadaran 1379, fol. 160v. By Manuēl (1334).

Figure R15: Heading of the Eusebian Prologue.
Venice, San Lazzaro 1007/12, fol. 356.
By an assistant to T'oros Taronec'i (1331–32).

Figure R16: Canon Table.
Venice, San Lazzaro 1007/12, fol. 357v. By an assistant to T'oros Taronec'i (1331–32).

	DATE DUE		